SWEDEN

FINLAND

Helsingfors

ESTHONIA

Stockholm

Novgorod

VOLGA R.

Nijni
Novgorod

MUSCOVITE

LAKE
PSKOV

DOMINIONS

GOT-
LAND

Moscow

Riga

Kalmar

TEUTONIC
ORDER

BALTIC SEA

Voronezh

KHANATE
OF THE
CRIMEA

POMERANIA

Vilna

Danzig

LITHUANIA

BRANDENBURG

Berlin

Thorn

Warsaw

Pinsk

Kiev

ONY

Dresden

Breslau

ODER R.

VISTULA R.

POLAND

DNIEPER R.

Prague

BOHEMIA

SILESIA

Cracow

Lemberg

GALICIA

UKRAINE

Presburg

MOLDAVIA

YEDISAN

Salzburg

Vienna

Buda

Jassy

DNIESTER R.

CRIMEA

AUSTRIA

HUNGARY

Balaklava

Agram

x Mohacs

TRAN-
SYLVANIA

VENETIAN
REPUBLIC

Zara

Belgrade

WALLACHIA

BLACK   SEA

PAPAL
STATES

BOSNIA

SERVIA

Bukharest

Sinope

Chieti

Cattaro

MONTE-
NEGRO

DANUBE R.

BULGARIA

Varna

ADRIATIC SEA

OTTOMAN

Nish

Gaeta

Benevento

Sofia

Adrianople

Angora

Naples

Taranto

Constantinople

NAPLES

CORFU
(TO VENICE)

Janina

RUMELIA

EMPIRE

Salonica

AEGEAN
SEA

Smyrna

Messina

Athens

CHIOS
(GEN)

Adalia

Palermo

SICILY
(SP)

MOREA

(VEN)

RHODES

CYPRUS
(VEN)

MALTA
(SP)

SEA

CRETE
(VEN)

TRM

The
Reformation
Era
1500–1650

# Harold J. Grimm

Ohio State University

# The
# Reformation
# Era 1500–1650

Second Edition

Macmillan Publishing Co., Inc.
New York

Collier Macmillan Publishers
London

Macmillan Publishing Co., Inc.
866 Third Avenue
New York, New York 10022

Collier-Macmillan Canada, Ltd.
Toronto, Ontario

Library of Congress catalog card number: 72–91167

Printing:          8 9      Year:

to
Thelma and Jane

# Preface

The favorable reception of the first edition of this book has encouraged The Macmillan Company to offer a new edition. The widespread interest of "the present generation" in religion, noted in 1954, has continued, although perhaps with a change of focus, and the ecumenical approach of the first edition has been vindicated by events of the last two decades. The similarity of the Reformation Era to our space age with its rapid and profound changes accompanied by its search for truth, meaning, relevance, and identity is sufficient justification for telling the story of the rise of Protestantism and the renewal of Catholicism in its complete setting.

To make the book more useful, I have made numerous changes that reflect recent Reformation scholarship, incorporated a gallery of portraits of prominent religious and political leaders, added an appendix of the chief rulers, and revised the bibliography completely.

It is impossible to acknowledge all those who in one way or another enabled me to write this narrative of the Reformation. Among the many colleagues to whom I am grateful for assistance, I must mention Gerhard Ritter, Conrad B. Gohdes, Wilbur H. Siebert, Walter L. Dorn, John T. McNeill, Ernest G. Schwiebert, Sydney N. Fisher, and especially Roland H. Bainton, who read the entire original manuscript and made many valuable suggestions. The errors and shortcomings that persist are my own.

I am particularly indebted to my students, whose intellectual curiosity and dedication to scholarship have provided constant inspiration. Among them I must single out George S. Robbert, my able and faithful research assistant. I also acknowledge my indebtedness to Hugh Sebastian, Harry H. Cloudman, and James J. Carroll, Jr., of The Macmillan Company for encouraging me to write the volume and to revise it in its present form. I am grateful to Dean N. Paul Hudson of the Graduate School of The Ohio State University for granting me finan-

# Preface

cial assistance for this project, to Director of Libraries Lewis C. Branscomb and his staff at the same university for their many services, and to Theodore R. Miller for going beyond the line of duty in making the maps. To my wife and daughter I owe a special debt of gratitude for their patience and understanding.

*Columbus, Ohio*                                                    H. J. G.

# Contents

# Contents

## Part Three
## Spread of Protestantism and Revival
## of Catholicism

# Maps

# Illustrations

# Introduction

The Reformation had its inception in the search for the answer to a typically medieval question, How can I be saved? The answer that Luther found after years of inner conflict, prayer, and study involved basic theological assumptions that threatened to undermine the well-integrated doctrinal system and the highly developed ecclesiastical hierarchy of the Church. The rapidity with which the doctrines of Luther and the other reformers spread throughout Europe is evidence of a general concern over the question of salvation and also of a strong dissatisfaction with the secularized church for not adequately serving the religious needs of the people.

This is not to say, however, that other interests did not immediately become involved. The entire structure of Western Christendom was by 1500 in such a state of delicate equilibrium that the interjection of any serious controversy might tip the scales and lead to widespread revolution. So many fundamental changes had taken place since the age of Innocent III, when the Church dominated virtually every aspect of life, that representatives of various interests felt themselves in disagreement with prevalent conditions and sought to alter existing institutions to fit their changing needs. Nearly every economic, social, political, and religious group had its reform program. It is for this reason that Luther, who courageously demanded a religious reformation, was at first looked upon as a hero by nearly all people who desired a change.

The Reformation Era was, accordingly, an upheaval in nearly every sphere of thought and action. The breakdown of medieval conceptions and institutions and the threat to

# Introduction

the unity of Western Christendom led thoughtful people to develop reform programs often in conflict with one another; far-reaching economic changes were accompanied by social maladjustments that frequently led to violence; the development of compact states by ambitious territorial rulers was opposed by various political elements who occasionally used religious dissatisfaction to further their political ends; and religious changes themselves were seldom made without disturbances and even bloodshed.

Nevertheless, the chief Protestant reformers refused to become involved in the many nonreligious schemes that accompanied every religious change. By reviving the evangelical character of the early Church and applying it to the circumstances of their own day, they infused Christianity with dynamic qualities that made it a continuing influence in western civilization. By reviving the best features of medieval Christianity, the Catholic reformers promoted piety and learning, thereby restoring a good measure of the glory and prestige of Catholicism.

As the Reformation Era neared its close, however, religious movements, both Protestant and Catholic, lost much of their dynamic character, and aggressive territorial rulers assumed the initiative in directing the thoughts and actions of the people. By the middle of the seventeenth century, most European states had become secularized, and religion, like other vital elements of society, was being used to further the interests of the state.

The victory of the secularized territorial state was accompanied by the gradual secularization of European society and culture as a whole. Religious standards, by which economic, social, and political behavior had previously been measured, were to a large degree replaced by secular standards, ascertained primarily by the observation of man's social behavior. The relegation of religious authorities and faith to the background in European life marks the end of the Reformation Era and the beginning of the Era of the Enlightenment.

In these pages the word *Reformation* is used in its conventional sense, that is, involving the rise of an evangelical Christianity, called Protestantism, that could not accommodate itself to the old theology and ecclesiastical institutions. Because the rise of Protestantism occurred outside the old church, the movement is often called the Protestant Revolt. This term, however, calls attention only to its negative aspects and is therefore not used here. All the reform movements that were contained within the old church, whether they were native to Catholicism or were prompted by Protestant successes, are grouped together under the term *Catholic Reformation*. The word *Counter Reformation* is used to designate only that phase of the Catholic Reformation which was concerned with stopping the growth of Protestantism and regaining people and lands for Catholicism. The term *Reformation Era* is used to refer to all the religious movements of the period in their total setting.

2

# Part One

## Europe on the Eve of the Reformation

# 1 The Changing Social Structure

Although the emergence of Protestantism was prompted solely by religious motives, the hopes and aspirations of the reformers were almost immediately translated into economic, social, political, and cultural terms. For this reason the history of this religious phenomenon cannot be understood apart from these other concerns of the Europeans.

About 1500 the aggressive leaders of all European classes were dissatisfied with the status quo and gave expression to their dissatisfaction through a powerful new medium, the printing press. Because more people were now literate than ever before, a larger number could be reached by those interested in reforms, and dissatisfaction could be marshaled to become a significant force.

## Economic Changes

Much of the dissatisfaction among Europeans at the beginning of the sixteenth century can be attributed to far-reaching economic changes. The relative self-sufficiency of the feudal manorial system of agricultural production and the monopolistic regulations of the merchant and craft guilds, which provided a considerable degree of security in the towns, were being replaced by new forms of production and distribution. And the medieval insistence upon "a just price" and "a fair living" for all could not be maintained in the face of the powerful urge for profits that accompanied these changes.

The high degree of economic prosperity that had been attained in Europe by the thirteenth century gave way to a prolonged period of economic depression during the late

# Part One: Europe on the Eve of the Reformation

Middle Ages, caused primarily by a large number of plagues and famines and wars on an unprecedented scale, that greatly decreased the population and hampered trade. Whereas the great majority of the people suffered from the depression, a few, like Jacques Coeur in France, the Medici in Italy, and the Fuggers in Germany, rationalized their businesses, developed new techniques, cooperated with the rising territorial rulers, and thereby amassed great fortunes.

But these merchant princes were the exceptions. Consequently, great enmity developed between the lower middle classes and the aristocratic patricians. Many were the reform programs that demanded the cessation of monopolies and a better distribution of wealth. The peasants, who had retrogressed rather than advanced in status since the thirteenth century, joined the malcontented groups whenever the opportunity to register protests presented itself.

## Expansion of Europe

By the end of the fifteenth century, however, the phenomenal discoveries of new lands and the subsequent expansion of Europe led to such a rapid increase in commercial activity that the period has been called the Commercial Revolution. This occurred after a long period during which Europe had been contracting as a consequence of the conquests of the Ottoman Turks. Now, within the span of a single life, such as that of Martin Luther (1483–1546), European seamen reached India and the Far East by sailing around Africa; discovered the two vast continents of North and South America and became familiar with their coasts from the Strait of Magellan to Labrador on the east and to Cape Mendocino on the west; circumnavigated the globe, proving that the earth was round; and established a direct trade with the natives of the Far East and the New World. The remarkable achievements not only fired ambitions, love of adventure, and desire for material gain but accentuated the stresses and strains in Latin Christendom.

Geographical location, a religious crusading zeal, and an early consolidation of royal institutions combined to make Portugal the first country to engage successfully in overseas activities. Having driven the Moors from their soil and having defeated them across the Strait of Gibraltar at Ceuta in 1415, the Portuguese carried their crusade farther into Africa. Supported by Prince Henry the Navigator, motivated by a desire to strike a final blow at the Moors from their rear, and encouraged by the prospects of establishing trading posts, the seamen pushed farther south along the western coast of Africa until finally, in 1487, Diaz succeeded in sailing around the cape that the Portuguese king named Good Hope. In 1497 and 1498, Vasco da Gama sailed up the eastern coast of Africa to Mambosa and across the Indian Ocean to Calicut in India. In 1500 Cabral, sailing southwesterly to take advantage of the trade winds, discovered the coast of Brazil, which became a part of the vast colonial empire of the Portuguese.

Before the Peace of Augsburg was concluded in 1555, the Portuguese had set up trading posts in Brazil, along the African coast, at Ormuz in the Persian Gulf, in India, and in the East Indies. And they had established trade routes that connected Lisbon with such far-flung places as Newfoundland, Brazil, New Guinea, and Japan.

Spain followed Portugal in building a colonial empire after her chief provinces of Castile and Aragon had been united by the marriage of Isabella and Ferdinand and the Moors had been driven out of Granada (1492). There, as in Portugal, a strong crusading fervor was combined with a spirit of adventure and a desire for profit to produce a national enthusiasm that helped make her the dominant European country in the sixteenth century.

The four voyages of Christopher Columbus, from 1492 to 1502, took him to most of the West Indies, along the coast of Honduras and Panama, and to Trinidad off the northern coast of South America. These voyages gave Spain a claim to much of the New World. They were followed by those of a large number of explorers and conquistadores, who, by the end of the reign of King Charles I (Emperor Charles V) in 1556, had carried the Spaniards to Yucatan, Mexico, Florida, and the lands along the Rio Grande and Colorado River in North America; to Central America; and to almost all the coast and much of the interior of South America, except Brazil. Magellan, in the service of Spain, had sailed through the strait bearing his name, into the Pacific, and to the Philippines.

Although the voyages of John Cabot in 1497 and 1498 established English claims to the eastern shores of North America, no attempts were made by England to send colonists to the New World or to seek direct trading routes with the Far East until after the middle of the sixteenth century. The merchants of England, like those of the Low Countries, France, and Germany, remained content to develop their European trade.

## Organization of Commerce

Under the impact of an increasing demand for goods, merchants improved not only methods of transportation and communication but also the organization of commerce and finance. Progressive rulers aided them by building roads and bridges, reducing highway robbery and piracy, and abolishing the tolls exacted by countless local authorities.

During the sixteenth century the private messenger system of the merchants was replaced by a number of collective messenger services,

7

maintained by groups of merchants, cities, and even states. The German imperial postal system was granted as a monopoly to the well-known Taxis family, who eventually made of it an international institution.

Transportation by sea was also improved. By 1500 Venetian and Hanseatic shipbuilders were constructing vessels with a capacity of as much as two thousand tons. The great majority, however, carried about five hundred tons. Seamen had mastered the art of tacking, that is, sailing close to or across the wind, and were using a compass with a dial and pivoted needle, an astrolabe for computing latitude, reliable astronomic tables, new maps, and sailing charts.

Merchant guilds often formed intercity leagues, or *hanses,* for greater protection and efficiency. Among the best known were the *hanses* of Flanders and northern France, comprising at one time as many as sixty towns; the Merchant Staplers of London, engaged in exporting wool to the Continent; and the Hanseatic League, which at its height numbered about ninety towns and dominated the trade of northern Germany, Scandinavia, the Baltic countries, and northern Russia.

The temporary partnerships developed in Italy gave way to permanent family partnerships and these in turn to the regulated and joint-stock companies of the sixteenth and seventeenth centuries. In the regulated companies, authorized by royal charters, the individual members conducted their own business but shared the expenses involved in providing transportation, warehouses, docking facilities, and protection. In the joint-stock companies, also authorized by royal charters, the members, not necessarily merchants, pooled their capital and received shares proportionate to their investments. They did not conduct their own business but selected officers to serve the company as a whole. Both forms of chartered companies were used not only for trading but also for colonizing and were often given such sovereign rights as settling on specific grants of land, governing colonists, maintaining armies and navies, legislating for colonists, and trying cases involving local disputes.

The increase in the activities of the merchants was accompanied by an improvement of business techniques. Although most merchants still engaged in both wholesale and retail trade, served as bankers, and supervised their own transportation, some differentiation in business activities appeared. With the establishment of permanent markets in Bruges and other commercial entrepôts, bourses, or places of exchange, were set up where one could buy merchandise by sample and transfer large amounts of goods with speed and efficiency. At Amsterdam, where the bourse occupied a separate building as early as 1531, large amounts of stock, money, and goods changed hands.

The growing insistence upon efficiency in business led to the systematic keeping of accounts. Bookkeeping ceased to be a haphazard affair. In 1494 there appeared in printed form one of the first important treatises on the subject of double-entry bookkeeping, written by Luca Pacioli. It offered sound advice on the keeping of journals and ledgers as well as easily remembered sayings to serve as guides to businessmen. The desire of the rising capitalists to reduce the making of money to a scientific abstraction and to rationalize their pursuits is shown by the fact that in the seventeenth century more than four hundred books on bookkeeping were published in Dutch alone.

Industrial production also increased rapidly after the middle of the fifteenth century. Those medieval craft guilds which continued to produce for local consumption persisted until the Industrial Revolution, but they became increasingly reactionary and monopolistic. Consequently it was more difficult than previously for journeymen to become masters. To improve their lot, they frequently organized guilds of their own. But these journeymen's guilds were invariably suppressed, and their members became day laborers. These constituted a restless and dissatisfied element throughout Europe in the sixteenth century.

The most significant changes occurred in those industries which produced goods for a growing market, over which the guilds could exercise little or no supervision. Consequently there appeared, particularly in the textile industries of the Low Countries and northern Italy, the entrepreneur, or middleman, who took the raw materials and partly finished goods from one group of workers to another, marketed the products, and took the profits and losses. In this home industry, or putting-out system, large numbers of workers became dependent upon conditions over which they had no control and frequently broke out in revolt.

Production in ever larger amounts also led to a greater need for capital investments. This was particularly true in the mining industry, stimulated by the need of money and the development of artillery for the incessant wars. The invention and development of machinery for the exploitation of veins of ore less accessible than previously attracted the surplus capital of such merchants as the German Fuggers and Welsers.

Agricultural production also felt the effects of the expansion of commerce and industry, the growth of cities, and the development of a money economy. There was a growing tendency among wealthy townsmen to invest in tenant farming or share farming. In some parts of Europe whole areas were converted to a single kind of cultivation, as in wool growing in England and Spain. Moreover, territorial rulers frequently imposed new taxes upon the peasants and attempted to regulate wages and conditions of labor to the advantage of the landowners. Although many peasants were now free, few of them owned the land that they cultivated, and many still owed their lords a multiplicity of vexatious feudal services and dues. Caught between decreased income and increased dues, they frequently became the prey of greedy moneylenders. The widespread unrest of the peasants led to revolts in many parts of Europe and reached a climax in Germany shortly after Luther's break with Rome.

## The Rise of Capitalism

The fundamental changes in commerce, industry, and agriculture were accompanied by a corresponding increase in the use of money, the development of new banking techniques, and the rise of a capitalist spirit. Even though the production of gold and silver coins was greatly increased, the demand greatly exceeded the supply. Consequently new means of exchange were developed, such as bills of exchange, drafts, and letters of credit. The use of such techniques in turn led to the establishment of clearing, by means of which the transfer of hard money was obviated by the setting off and canceling of debts by bankers. By 1500, banks of deposit had been established throughout much of Europe. There money was placed for safekeeping and transferred from one account to another by means of checks, still written in the presence of the banker.

The handling of papal revenues, gathered from all parts of Latin Christendom, was a highly lucrative business. The transfer of this business from the house of the Medici in Florence to that of the Fuggers of Augsburg late in the fifteenth century helped to make this German banking family the most powerful one during the Reformation. Having begun business as weavers, the Fuggers increased their fortunes by expanding into industry, mining, and finance until, by the time of the death of Jacob II (1459–1525), who was also called Jacob the Rich, they had a capital of approximately two million gold gulden. Like other banking firms, they loaned large sums of money to important religious and political leaders and gained, in return, monopolies and concessions as securities. But because they were still limited by their social status, they were often at the mercy of the rulers and remained politically conservative. The lesser merchants, on the other hand, usually challenged their monopolies and joined movements of reform.

With the decline of the medieval economy of scarcity and its many regulations designed to give people a "fair living" and goods sold at a "just price" and with the greater opportunities to make money, a new attitude toward economic matters manifested itself among businessmen that may be called the capitalist spirit. Because money was no longer loaned primarily to assist those who were in need but also for profit, biblical, canonical, and other restrictions upon usury were either circumvented by casuistry or completely ignored. This new spirit began to touch nearly every phase of European life. Feudal services and dues were commuted to money payments; agricultural production came to be looked upon as a means for making profit; merchants and even some nobles invested accumulated surpluses in commercial and industrial enterprises; entrepreneurs began to own raw materials, warehouses, and the means of production; labor was hired as a means of creating new wealth; territorial rulers sought to increase their power by tapping all available sources of income; and even church offices and means of grace were frequently viewed in terms of financial returns.

Although the capitalist spirit was not fully developed by 1500, it was strong enough to contribute to the general unrest of the times. The older chivalric virtues of honor and personal loyalty gave way in many places to the middle-class virtues of honesty, industry, and integrity, and the medieval sense of corporate responsibility yielded to an emphasis upon individual initiative.

## Social Adjustments

The emergence of a large class of townsmen threatened to disrupt that social stratification which medieval man had considered ordained by God for all eternity. The medieval conception of the clergy as constituting the head, the nobility the arms, and the peasants the feet of the corporate body could not long persist in the face of those economic and political changes which were disrupting the medieval way of life. There was no place in this conception for that class which accumulated money by profiting from commerce, industry, and finance and used its wealth to gain social status and political power.

Changes in population also had an important effect upon the social stratification in Europe. Although the number of nobles declined or remained stationary, increases occurred among peasants and townsmen. Some areas had not regained by 1500 the population that they had lost in the 1300s, but the population of western and central Europe as a whole had increased from about fifty-three million in 1300 to about seventy million in 1500. About a tenth of the population now lived in the cities. England and Wales now had a population of nearly four million, France sixteen, Germany twenty, Italy ten, and the Iberian Peninsula ten.

Although late-medieval European cities are not to be compared in population with those of today, expanding commerce and industry had increased the size and importance of many of them. In 1500 Florence, Milan, Venice, and Naples in Italy and Antwerp, Bruges, Ghent, and Brussels in the Low Countries each probably had approximately one hundred thousand inhabitants. Paris may have had eighty thousand and London forty thousand. Cologne, the largest city in Germany, had about sixty thousand, and Augsburg, Strassburg, Nürnberg, and Magdeburg each had more than thirty thousand. These figures, obviously, are only educated guesses, and fluctuations in population continued as in the past, caused by shifts in trade routes and by wars, famines, and plagues.

# Part One: Europe on the Eve of the Reformation

## The Townsmen

By 1500 most European cities had developed a high degree of autonomy in managing their own affairs. This was especially true of the eighty-five free imperial cities of the Holy Roman Empire. Almost everywhere there had appeared a small, hereditary class of patricians who served the "general welfare" of their cities as the representatives of all the classes. They and other wealthy merchants rigidly controlled the political and economic life of their communities, monopolizing commerce, speculating in raw materials, controlling production, and manipulating finance.

The power and opulence of these *nouveaux riches* were apparent in their luxurious way of life. They lived in imposing mansions and palaces that rivaled those of the nobles. In these, whether they were the open palaces along the Grand Canal in Venice, the fortified residences of Florence, or the impressive homes of the Hanseatic merchants with their brick, Gothic façades, were to be found products from the Far East and the New World, comfortable furniture made by the newly invented lathes, gold and silver plate, mirrors placed in beautiful frames, ornate candelabra holding large numbers of candles, shelves of books, and frequently works of art. They often bought landed estates and titles and provided themselves with the accouterments of the nobles. To display their wealth and influence, the men frequently wore broad, impressive hats, coats with expensive fur collars, and ornate rings. The rich fabrics and stylish dress, the elaborate hairdressing and high hats, and the beautiful jewelry of the women were usually objects of envy on the part of noblewomen; but they also elicited the bitter complaints of preachers of that day.

## The Craftsmen

By far the most numerous class of townsmen were the small urban proprietors, comprising largely traders, small shopkeepers, guild masters, journeymen, and officials. This class was as a rule a fairly contented, hard-working, stable element. But for political, even more than for economic reasons, this class occasionally revolted against the patricians. Where they succeeded they either shared the government with the patricians, as in Augsburg, Strassburg, and Zurich, or seized complete control, as in Speyer.

The most restless and dissatisfied inhabitants of the cities were the members of small guilds; inhabitants of the suburbs, who were a kind of second-class citizenry outside the walls; free laborers and mercenary soldiers, who constituted a colorful floating population; and journeymen who found it impossible to become guild masters. Usually living from hand to mouth and often objects of charity, these people had in common a strong distrust of those in power. It is to them that social-revolutionary and radical religious leaders appealed.

## The Peasants

Although there were great political, economic, and social differences among European peasants at the beginning of the sixteenth century, most of them shared a general dissatisfaction with the inherited establishment, which prevented them from obtaining a greater share of the benefits accruing to society because of their labor. Princes, feudal lords, ecclesiastical prelates, and wealthy townsmen profited from their labor and exercized judicial control over them. Matters were made worse because the prices of their products, such as grain, did not increase in relation to the cost of industrial products until near the middle of the sixteenth century, an economic condition that also adversely affected the feudal nobility.

Significant for the spread of the Reformation were the strong religious overtones in the grievances of the peasants, especially those in Germany, caused to a large extent by the Church's being an exceptionally wealthy landowner that demanded increasingly large tithes and services from the peasants. After the middle of the fifteenth century, the flag of numerous rebelling peasants carried not only the device of the *Bundschuh,* or peasant's shoe with ankle strings, but also the white cross and a picture of the Crucifixion. Numerous leaders pointed to the differences between the treatment that peasants were receiving under inherited institutions and under those prevailing among Christians in the New Testament. It is no wonder that the authorities occasionally equated unrest with the reading of the Bible.

To make matters worse, other classes almost universally despised the peasants. The frequent references in the literature of that day to the "dumb peasant" bear eloquent testimony to the fact that their toil and improved status had not gained respect for them. Most of them still lived in small huts with thatched roofs of straw, wooden chimneys covered with clay, dirt floors, and rude tables, benches, stools, and beds. Cattle, poultry, and peasants often occupied the same buildings. The clothing of the peasants was simple, consisting of woolen undergarments and linen and woolen outer dress. Usually isolated from the outside, their world was dreary, brightened only by Church festivals, local market days, and occasional traveling entertainers. Nevertheless, in many parts of Europe the peasants were becoming literate, were determined to improve their status, were conscious of their importance in society, and joined movements of reform.

## Feudalism

By 1500 feudalism had to a large extent already lost its reason for existence, for the kings and princes, with their mercenary and standing armies supported by territorial taxation, could more efficiently provide protection than the anachronistic feudal cavalry. Almost everywhere in fifteenth-century Europe the Swiss pikes, the English longbows, the Bohemian handguns, and the new cannon produced by the Bureau Brothers in France and by the foundries of Sweden defeated and dispersed the heavily armored knights.

Changing forms of economy also rendered the feudal lord dispensable. Many aspects of manorial economy persisted, but the emergence of a money economy, the manumission of serfs, the appearance of new forms of agricultural production, the growth of commerce and industry, and the increasing role played by territorial rulers in economic matters all tended to lessen the economic importance of the feudal lord.

Feudalism as a system of government had likewise declined. Baronial and manorial justice gave way to the superior justice of the national and territorial courts, and everywhere it became apparent that the nobles could not prevent the growth of highly centralized administrative and financial institutions whose trained personnel came from the lower classes and could be relied upon to serve the interests of a central government.

But the more feudalism declined, the more tenaciously the nobles clung to their rights, privileges, and social status. Although many served as officers in mercenary and standing armies, others moved to royal and princely courts to gain what favors and privileges they could. Still others stubbornly resisted the trend of events and became robber barons, plundering villages and exacting tribute from merchants along highways and rivers.

Chivalry, however, the social code of the feudal warriors, did not decline with feudalism but actually reached its height during the late Middle Ages. Although the virtues of personal fidelity, bravery, courtesy to equals, and respect for women were rapidly deteriorating, they were extolled in many ways. Determined to perpetuate their social status, the nobles worked out elaborate codes of heraldry and formed aristocratic orders of knighthood, such as the English Knights of the Garter, the French Knights of the Star, and the Burgundian Knights of the Golden Fleece.

Residing in castles with intricate systems of defense, many feudal lords managed to live much more comfortably than did their ancestors of the twelfth and thirteenth centuries. Like the patricians of the towns, wealthy nobles bought the luxuries of the East, upholstered furniture, rugs, tapestries, comfortable mattresses for their beds, and a great variety of clothing. Many of their castles now had running water, lead piping, bathtubs, and sanitary latrines.

### The Clergy

The social position of the clergy was also undergoing important changes at the opening of the sixteenth century. There was a greater differentiation than ever between the clergy and the laity. By means of a number of election decrees, the laity had been excluded from the administrative affairs of the Church, which consequently became in personnel, cult, and culture intrinsically a church of priests. Although both laymen and clergy had originally participated in the service of the Mass, it was later withdrawn into the confines of the choir, while the laymen merely looked on.

By reducing many of its services to what amounted to money payments, the church became increasingly wealthy. As administrators of this wealth, many of the clergy, particularly the great prelates, gave a disproportionately large share of their attention to secular matters. It is no wonder that many townsmen looked upon the clergy as hoarders of wealth who drained their cities and lands of gold and silver. The poorer classes also often resented this wealth, as well as the tremendous power that the clergy exercised over them "from the cradle to the grave."

The pope, as the absolute ruler over the clergy and all the Church lands, ranked among the highest monarchs of Christendom, and his magnificent court in Rome became the envy of the most powerful kings. The cardinals, the high officials in the papal *Curia,* the archbishops, bishops, and abbots, and all the higher clergy throughout Europe lived on a relatively high social plane. Usually men of noble birth who had obtained their positions through political influence or by the expenditure of large sums of money, they lived on a par with kings and princes. This was particularly true in western Germany, where, for example, the archbishops of Mainz, Trier, and Cologne were also electors in the Holy Roman Empire and ruled their territories like kings.

The lower secular clergy often fared little better economically than their poorest parishioners. Often so badly educated that they did not understand the Latin that they read in the services, they lost the respect of the people in many places. In others they joined and led forces of discontent.

Likewise, the general decline of interest in and support of monasticism was reflected in the deteriorating status of the regular clergy. Wealthy laymen became more inclined to spend their money for relics and pilgrimages than to give it to hospitals and chantries. Even the famous monastic and cathedral schools of the Middle Ages lost their ascendancy in education and culture to the towns, and an increasing number of laymen took the places of the clergy as poets, chroniclers, artists, and teachers.

The growing importance of the middle classes can be discerned also in religious matters. It is significant that the strong inclination toward mysticism in the late Middle Ages, which placed more emphasis upon Christian ethics and learning than upon the Church and the sacraments, found its origin and greatest support in the urban centers of the Rhine and the Low Countries. Eager to raise their social status, the townsmen as a rule supported their territorial rulers in weakening the power of the clergy as well as that of the nobility. Their opposition to the authority of the Church is clearly seen by the support that they gave to early reform programs.

## The Rise of Territorial States

Another significant aspect of late-medieval life was the emergence of the territorial state. Everywhere in Europe the spirit of universality, inherited from imperial Rome and fostered by the Roman Catholic Church and the Holy Roman Empire during the Middle Ages, gradually gave way to territorial particularism. There occurred a general transfer of allegiance in which the territorial state, whether a kingdom, a principality, or a city-state, profited at the expense of the feudal lords, towns, guilds, and clergy. It must not be assumed, however, either that national impulses had been absent in the Middle Ages or that they were as strong in the fifteenth and sixteenth as in the nineteenth and twentieth centuries. Aroused by fear or hate, by a desire for adventure or security, or by a hope for profit, national sentiment made itself felt at this early date and was frequently utilized by the territorial rulers to their own advantage.

The townsmen were particularly eager to cooperate with the rulers in ending the decentralization of medieval political life, for they especially suffered the evil effects of the private wars of the nobles, the plundering of robber barons, and the many duties, tolls, and other exactions of the lords. Most kings and princes saw the advantage of favoring the townsmen at the expense of the nobility. In return for aiding the towns in gaining their freedom from feudal control and for providing them with protection, the rulers received both taxes and services from the townsmen. They were not slow to realize that these townsmen—trained in Roman law, skilled in administrative matters, adept in developing new methods of warfare, and possessing no inherited titles and privileges— would serve them better in centralizing the functions of government than members of the nobility and clergy.

### Territorial Unification

It was the aim of the territorial ruler to gain the allegiance of his people with respect to every aspect of their lives: economic, social, political, cultural, and religious. His middle-class advisers, administrators, and lawyers accordingly developed the divine-right theory of government, insisting that for reasons of security the ruler should have complete authority in his territory and that he obtained this authority directly from God.

When the ruler was strong enough he compelled the feudal assemblies, to which townsmen had been added during the thirteenth century, to meet and grant him special, nonfeudal income and authority. For administrative matters he relied increasingly upon a small circle of advisors, the *Curia Regis,* or royal court, whose various legislative, executive, and judicial functions gradually became differentiated and were turned over to trained specialists. Royal and princely courts encroached upon the jurisdiction of baronial, manorial, communal, and ecclesiastical courts, each ruler striving to develop a law common to his entire territory.

Moreover, territorial mercenary armies had supplanted feudal levies by 1500. The development of gunpowder, guns, and cannon had increased the importance of the infantry and the artillery at the expense of the feudal cavalry. As territorial rulers gained control of the new methods of warfare, feudal lords were compelled to enter their service, often as captains who raised, trained, fed, and led the mercenaries under the general supervision of the rulers or their clerks. Royal navies, although not so well organized as the armies, had also made their appearance by 1500.

The maintenance of a growing administrative personnel and of large mercenary armies taxed the resources of the late-medieval rulers so that they found it necessary to tap all possible sources of income. Townsmen with their new forms of wealth, as well as clergy and nobility, were asked in their assemblies for special aids and taxes, both direct and indirect. Import and export duties were extended and increased so that they provided a large part of the royal income. This partially explains the growing concern of the rulers for the economic prosperity of their territories.

Finally, late-medieval rulers encouraged their people to look to them for leadership in cultural and religious matters. Although some of them attempted to master the art of writing, nearly all patronized literary men and artists, maintained court choirs and musicians, and assumed a large role in the conduct of religious affairs. They established new universities and attracted to them teachers who would bring glory to their countries. The construction of palaces and other public buildings also encouraged art and aroused a patriotic interest in cultural achievements.

### Western Europe

The most rapid development of territorial states occurred in western Europe, where people were compelled to look to their rulers for security and the realization of their ambitions. In the Iberian Peninsula, for example, the protracted crusades against the Moors called for strong, centralized leadership. This was at first provided by the rulers of small Christian states in the northern lands. As these rulers pushed the Moors southward, their states became consolidated into four kingdoms: Castile, Aragon, Portugal, and Navarre.

### Spain and Portugal

The most important step toward the consolidation of political power in the Iberian Peninsula was taken in 1469, when Prince Ferdinand of Aragon and Princess Isabella of Castile were married and brought these states together into a personal union. Isabella became queen of Castile in 1474 and Ferdinand king of Aragon in 1479. After that the two sovereigns ruled nearly four fifths of the peninsula, that part which became Spain.

Ferdinand and Isabella first concentrated on consolidating all authority in their hands. They began in Castile, where they suppressed the warlike nobility; brought the power and wealth of the three great military–religious orders under the control of the crown; curtailed the authority of the Cortes, or assemblies; increased royal revenues by encouraging, regulating, and taxing economic activity; and strengthened their authority in religious matters.

Believing that religious uniformity was important for the maintenace of law and order as well as for the good of their subjects' souls, the Catholic sovereigns, as they were called, sought to purge Spain of every tendency toward heresy. In 1480 they established the Spanish Inquisition, to be used especially against suspected heretics among the Christianized Jews (Marranos) and Moors (Moriscos). Combining both ecclesiastical and civil authority, the Inquisition became one of the most significant means of extending royal authority over the Church in Spain. In 1492 the rulers not only drove the Moors out of Granada but also issued a decree that required all Jews to be converted to Christianity or leave Spain. It is estimated that about fifty thousand Jews were baptized and about one hundred sixty-five thousand driven out of the country.

Although the lands south of the Pyrenees had played a negligible role in European affairs prior to the union of Castile and Aragon, the Catholic sovereigns now wished to make Spain the outstanding country of Europe. So crafty was Ferdinand in furthering Spanish interests that he was considered a prototype for duplicity in Machiavelli's *The Prince*. After having agreed, for example, to Charles VIII's invasion of Italy, he later joined the alliance against the French king and obtained possession of Naples. To increase their prestige further, the Spanish rulers gave their eldest daughter Joanna in marriage to Archduke Philip the Fair, son of Emperor Maximilian and Mary of Burgundy. Another daughter, Catherine of Aragon, was married to Henry VII's son Arthur, the Prince of Wales, and, when he died, to his younger son Henry, who became Henry VIII of England.

Isabella died in 1504, leaving the conduct of Spanish affairs in the hands of Ferdinand. Although, according to Isabella's will, her place on the Spanish throne was to be taken by Joanna, the latter became unfit to govern because of a mental illness, and her husband Philip was unable to make good his claims to her share of the rule. Ferdinand thus became the sole ruler of Spain. During the war of the Holy League (Spain, Venice, and the papacy) against France and the Empire, Ferdinand seized the lands of Navarre lying south of the Pyrenees (1512). When he died, in

1516, he passed on to his grandson Charles (Philip had died in 1506) control of all the Iberian Peninsula except Portugal.

Because of her long crusade against the Moors, her struggle to maintain her independence in the Iberian Peninsula, and her great achievements in maritime affairs, Portugal probably had a more highly developed sense of nationality than any other country on the eve of the sixteenth century. Cooperating with the townsmen, the kings exploited the overseas possessions to their mutual advantage, made Lisbon one of the busiest ports in Europe, suppressed the unruly nobility, maintained religious uniformity by means of the Inquisition, and appropriated all the functions once exercised by the Cortes.

### France

Like Spain and Portugal, France experienced a high degree of territorial unification, administrative centralization, and national sentiment during the late Middle Ages. Partly responsible for this was the fact that this country, comprising a bewildering congeries of feudal states, had relatively easily defined boundaries, within which French-speaking people predominated. The kingship of these lands, moreover, was in the hands of the Capetian family, which ruled in unbroken succession from 987 to 1328, through the collateral Valois line to 1498, and the Orleans and Angoulême branches to 1589. Thus there was seldom a question of succession to the throne, and there was invariably an heir who had been schooled in the royal traditions, aims, and methods. Finally, the royal domain, once consisting of only the Île de France, was expanded until under Charles VIII (1483–1498) it embraced nearly all the lands within the present boundaries of France.

By 1500 the central government of France was firmly controlled by the king. The functions of the old royal council had become differentiated and entrusted to specially trained personnel. It consisted of (1) the *conseil du roi,* or privy council; (2) the *chambre des comptes,* or treasury; (3) the *chancellerie,* or chancery; and (4) the *parlement de Paris,* or law court, which not only exercised jurisdiction over primary or appellate cases for about two thirds of France but also had the right to register or refuse to register royal edicts. Local government was in the hands of bourgeois domain officials appointed by and responsible to the king.

The estates-general had originally possessed the right to grant all extrafeudal rights and taxes. It surrendered this right in effect toward the end of the Hundred Years' War, when it gave Charles VII the right to create a standing army (1439) and granted him a special tax, the *taille,* to enable him to support it. This tax, which he did not relinquish at the close of the war, became the chief source of royal income. For this reason the French kings could afford to let the estates-general atrophy.

National sentiment was aroused by the Hundred Years' War and by the grandiose scheme of Charles VIII to make France the dominant country of Europe. Hoping to emulate the glorious deeds of Charlemagne, he crossed the Alps into Italy in 1494, took Naples, and planned to lead a crusade against the Ottoman Turks. His dreams were shattered when Ferdinand of Spain drove him back into France. Louis XII (1498–1515), his successor, continued the struggle with Spain, which did not end until the Treaty of Cateau-Cambrésis in 1559.

## England

England's insularity and her Norman type of feudalism enabled her kings to develop royal institutions relatively early. From the royal concil, whose functions had become specialized, there had sprung the three courts of common law: (1) the Exchequer, which supervised royal finances and tried fiscal cases; (2) the Common Pleas, which tried cases between private individuals; and (3) the King's Bench, which had jurisdiction over cases in which the king was a party.

The English king's power was, however, curtailed by certain privileges of Parliament. Unlike the Estates-General in France, Parliament had not relinquished its right to grant or withhold extrafeudal grants of money. Out of this right and the custom of bringing petitions developed its participation in legislation. It had also gained the right to choose the king from among the members of the royal family.

The Tudor rulers of England were especially adept at developing a strongly centralized monarchy. Henry Tudor, who had brought the turbulent Wars of the Roses to an end with his victory at Bosworth Field, became King Henry VII (1485–1509). He deprived unruly barons of their political power by replacing them with reliable persons in the royal council and taking from them many old feudal privileges. The most effective instrument that he used against them was the Court of the Star Chamber, which he had created especially for this purpose. To make himself as independent of Parliament as possible, he avoided involvement in foreign wars, developed sources of income already at his disposal, and practiced strict economy.

Henry's foreign policy reflected his domestic concerns. He negotiated a number of commercial treaties with other countries; made a treaty with France in which the French king recognized Henry's title to the English throne; and, in 1501, married his son Arthur to Catherine, daughter of Ferdinand and Isabella, thus obtaining the recognition of these rulers and a large dowry. In 1502 he gave his daughter Margaret in marriage to James IV of Scotland, thus lessening the tension between that country and England. At his death he handed down to his son Henry VIII (1509–1547) (Arthur had died in 1502) a secure title to the throne, a strongly centralized government, a relatively prosperous country, and a well-filled royal treasury.

## Central Europe

In central Europe ambitious princes, feuding nobles, powerful Church prelates, and wealthy city-states prevented the development of those royal institutions that were enabling western European monarchs to concentrate authority in their hands. Northern Italy was still nominally a part of the Holy Roman Empire; but after the defeat of the emperors by the papacy in the thirteenth century, no ruler was strong enough to prevent the development of a number of autonomous states. Among these, five played a dominant role at the close of the Middle Ages: the duchy of Milan, the republic of Florence, the republic of Venice, the Papal States, and the kingdom of Naples.

The duchy of Milan, which long played the role of the aggressor on the Italian Peninsula under its Visconti and then Sforza rulers, was thwarted in its ambitions by Florence, which carried the torch of liberty and finally developed a balance of power that maintained a precarious peace throughout much of the fifteenth century. It was Duke Ludovico Sforza who urged Charles VIII of France to take Naples, hoping thereby to retain his control of Milan. He lived to regret this move, for he died a prisoner in a French fortress after Louis XII had taken his duchy in 1499.

Florence, which retained her republican institutions into the sixteenth century, had experienced her golden age under Cosimo and Lorenzo de' Medici. But after the death of Lorenzo in 1492, she lacked the leadership to enable her to play a significant role in Italian affairs. Twice the members of the Medici family were expelled, and finally, in 1530, Emperor Charles V made a member of that family the hereditary ruler. In 1569 Florence became the grand duchy of Tuscany.

Venice, with her stable merchant oligarchy, retained her wealth and political power well into the sixteenth century. The shift of the center of trade from the Mediterranean Sea to the Atlantic Ocean then began to rob her of her predominance as a great commercial and maritime power.

Extending across the Italian Peninsula in the center were the Papal States, comprising such heterogeneous territories as the Papal Patrimony, the Romagna, the Campagna, the march of Ancona, and the duchy of Spoleto. The attempts of the popes to consolidate and centralize the administration of these lands explain to a large extent their involvement in the unsavory political affairs of the peninsula. By the time of the Reformation it was clear that the papacy had become firmly established on a territorial basis.

The kingdom of Naples was situated in the southern third of Italy. Until 1282, when the Sicilians threw off the yoke of the Angevin rulers, Sicily was part of the kingdom of Naples. From that time it was ruled by the king of Aragon. In 1435, however, it was again joined to Naples when Alphonso of Aragon became the Neapolitan king (1435–1458). When he died without legal heirs, Sicily went to his brother, and Naples was given to his illegitimate son Ferdinand I. Although conditions in Naples had long been unstable, they reached an acute stage during the baronial revolts under Ferdinand. It was this situation that invited the aggression of France and Spain.

Ferdinand the Catholic, a descendant of the legitimate branch of the house of Aragon, claimed Naples as his inheritance, and Charles VIII claimed the kingdom through the house of Anjou. Charles also advanced a claim to Milan, because the brother of his great-grandfather had married into the Visconti family. We have seen how these claims led to the French invasion of Italy in 1494 and the failure of Charles in the face of the formidable opposition supplied by the Holy League. When he died, his successor, Louis XII, continued the claims and took both Milan and Naples. After various changes in fortune, however, he was finally compelled to give up these possessions and return to France. The rivalry over the control of Italy between the successors of Louis XII and Ferdinand constitutes an important factor in the Hapsburg-Valois wars of the sixteenth century.

### Germany

In Germany, as in Italy, no territorial consolidation took place on a national scale. Instead, the Holy Roman Empire was being reduced in both size and importance. Although the emperors clung to the idea of a universal sovereignty, they failed to develop those royal institutions necessary for the creation of a strong territorial state. The country thus remained divided into more than three hundred virtually autonomous political units. Much of the land was ruled by archbishops, bishops, and abbots.

The German rulers were still elected during the late Middle Ages, but the right of election went by default to a small number of powerful princes. By the Golden Bull of 1356 the number of electors was fixed at seven: the archbishops of Mainz, Trier, and Cologne, the duke of Saxony, the margrave of Brandenburg, the count palatine of the Rhine, and the king of Bohemia. On the death of an emperor, the archbishop of Mainz, who was the imperial chancellor, was compelled to call a meeting of the electors at Frankfurt for the purpose of choosing a new ruler. This was done by a simple majority vote. The successful candidate was then permitted to assume the title of king of the Romans at the coronation at Aachen and the title of emperor. Theoretically the pope should have bestowed the latter title upon the incumbent in a separate coronation at Rome.

The particularism of the German princes was furthered by this electoral system, for the electors usually chose a man who would be too weak or not inclined to infringe upon their prerogatives. When elected, an emperor was not likely to strengthen the imperial position. Instead, he used every opportunity to increase the lands, power, and prestige of his own dynasty.

The desire to put an end to the feudal anarchy prevalent in Germany in the fifteenth century led to the creation of the imperial diet, or *Reichstag.* It consisted of three houses: (1) the house of electors, in which usually only six of the seven electors sat, for the king of Bohemia attended only the election of the emperor; (2) the house of princes; and (3) the house of free cities. The imperial knights, who like the free cities owed their allegiance directly to the emperor, were not represented in the diet. Because the three houses, or estates, of the diet were determined to prevent the emperor from exercising any real authority over them, he was invariably dependent upon the income and authority derived from his own family possessions.

It is no wonder that a ruler like the Hapsburg Frederick III (1440–1493) devoted what little interest he had in political matters to his Austrian territories and seldom visited the rest of the Empire. His do-nothing policy encouraged the rising demand for political reforms, called *gravamina,* which grew more vocal toward the end of the century; and conditions reached such a deplorable state that the German electors made Maximilian king of the Romans and practically retired Frederick in 1486. Although active, genial, and popular, Maximilian I (1493–1519) was too visionary to carry any of his imperial plans through to a successful conclusion.

Nonetheless, Maximilian left an indelible stamp upon Germany and the rest of Europe. He made good his claim to the lands of the Burgundian state, many of which had been alienated from the Empire, and engaged in a struggle with Louis XII of France on their behalf. As the "royal matchmaker," he married his son Philip to the Spanish Joanna and, by affiancing his granddaughter Mary to the nine-year-old Louis, who inherited the kingdoms of Hungary and Bohemia in 1516, he laid the basis for the later acquisition of these countries by the Austrian rulers. Finally, pressed by the need for support against the advancing Turks and the French invasion of Italy, he made concessions to the German reform party.

The imperial reforms during the reign of Maximilian were not designed to strengthen the emperor but rather to unify Germany for military reasons, arrest her territorial disintegration, and put an end to the internal feuds. At the diets of Worms in 1495 and Augsburg in 1500, the estates formally proclaimed the *ewiger Landfrieden,* or perpetual internal peace; created the *Reichskammergericht,* or imperial supreme court; imposed a general tax, *allgemeiner Pfennig,* upon all inhabitants more than fifteen years of age; and established a *Reichsregiment,* or im-

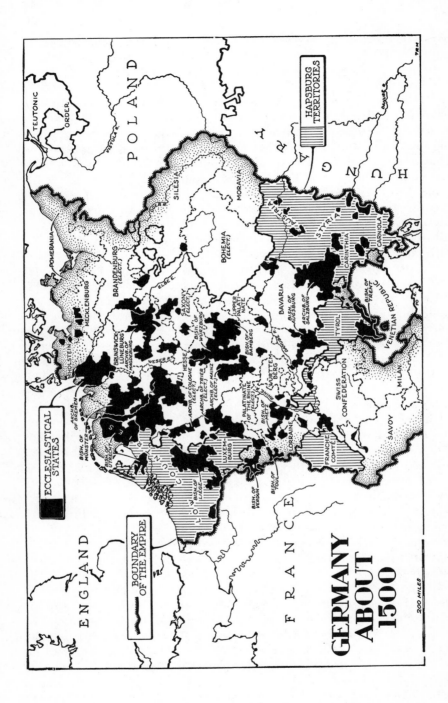

TEUTONIC
ORDER

POLAND

VISTULA R.

HAPSBURG
TERRITORIES

HUNGARY

DANUBE R.

POMERANIA

SILESIA

MORAVIA

MECKLENBURG

BRANDENBURG
(ELECT.)

ODER R.

BOHEMIA
(ELECT.)

AUSTRIA

STYRIA

CARINTHIA

CARNIOLA

HOLSTEIN

ARCH.
OF BREMEN

ELBE R.

BRUNSWICK
LUNEBURG
(ARCHB. OF
MAGDEBURG)

SAXONY
(ELECT.)

BISH. OF
WÜRZBURG

HESSE

UPPER
PALATI-
NATE

BAVARIA

BISH. OF
AUGSBURG

ARCHB. OF
SALZBURG

TYROL

BISH. OF
TRENT

BISH. OF
MÜNSTER

BISH. OF
UTRECHT

WESER R.

ARCHB. OF COLOGNE
(ELECT.)

ARCHB. OF TRIER
(ELECT.)

ARCHB. OF MAINZ
(ELECT.)

BISH. OF
BAMBERG

RHINE R.

WÜRTTEM-
BERG

DANUBE R.

VENETIAN REPUBLIC

ELECTORATE

PALATINATE
OF THE RHINE
(ELECT.)

BISH. OF
METZ

LUXEM-
BURG

BISH. OF
LIÈGE

LORRAINE

BISH. OF
VERDUN

BISH. OF
TOUL

FRANCHE
COMTÉ

SWISS
CONFEDERATION

MILAN

SAVOY

ENGLAND

FRANCE

ECCLESIASTICAL
STATES

BOUNDARY
OF THE EMPIRE

GERMANY
ABOUT
1500

200 MILES

T.R.M.

perial council of regency, for the purpose of cooperating with the emperor in selecting imperial officials and formulating and executing domestic and foreign policies.

At the Diet of Cologne in 1512, the territories actually under imperial control were divided into ten *Kreise,* or circles, for administrative and military purposes. They comprised Austria, Bavaria, Swabia, Franconia, Upper Rhine, Lower Rhine, Burgundy, Westphalia, Lower Saxony, and Upper Saxony. Not included were Bohemia, which paid no taxes to the Empire; the neighboring lands of Silesia, Lusatia, and Moravia; East Prussia, which had recognized the feudal overlordship of the Polish kings since 1466; the Swiss Confederation and the duchy of Savoy, which were virtually autonomous; and those Italian states that were still nominally a part of the Empire.

Although these reforms retarded it, they did not stop the disintegration of the amorphous Holy Roman Empire. To counteract the effectiveness of the newly created institutions, Maximilian created in 1502 his own *Hofrat* (aulic or privy council), to which gravitated most of the imperial administrative functions.

It is highly significant for the religious history of Germany that the failure of the imperial reforms was accompanied by the growth of the territorial principalities, each of which strove to develop compact sovereignties similar to the kingdoms of western Europe. Because the princes of these lands began to obtain control over the religious affairs within their principalities long before the Reformation, a greater diversity of religious doctrines and organizations was possible in Germany than in the centralized national states of western Europe.

In Bohemia religious and social demands were combined with the political to produce a strong national sentiment. Toward the close of the fourteenth century this sentiment culminated in the Hussite movement. John Hus (1369–1415), whose emphasis upon the supreme authority of the Bible and the denial of the primacy of the pope, together with his demand for far-reaching reforms, led to his excommunication and ultimate burning at the stake at Constance, had inspired a national consciousness among the Czechs that has survived to this day. The Hussite Wars (1420–1433), which followed his death, threatened to split the Empire. But internal civil wars between moderate and radical Hussites confined the hostilities largely to Bohemia. These continued after the Council of Basel in 1436 recognized the moderates as the true sons of the Church.

Bohemian unity was further impaired under King Vladislav (1471–1516). Because he was also king of Hungary and spent most of his time there, the Bohemian nobles continued to extend their authority and increased their wealth at the expense of both the crown and the Church.

Despite the strong influence of Germans upon Denmark, Norway, and Sweden during the Middle Ages, these countries never came under the control of the Holy Roman Empire. Instead, each country developed its own language, territorial loyalties, and institutions. For a while, however, they were brought together by Margaret of Denmark, regent of that country from 1376 to 1387 and elected queen of Denmark, Norway, and Sweden in subsequent years. Although this remarkable woman, called the lady king by the merchants of Lübeck, had her grandnephew Eric of Pomerania (1412–1449) elected as her successor and tried to make the union permanent, the draft of provisions for such a union, called the Union of Kalmar (1397), was never accepted by the respective councils of the three countries.

### Eastern Europe

Although the rulers of western Europe found it relatively simple to develop territorial loyalties on the basis of a relative racial and linguistic homogeneity, those of eastern Europe faced almost insuperable obstacles in this respect. In 1500 the population was predominantly Slavic, except in East Prussia, where it was mostly German; in the Hungarian Plains, where it was largely Magyar; and in southern Russia, where the Tartars were in the majority. Yet there existed in all these lands racial islands that have caused no end of difficulties throughout modern history.

There was also a great diversity in religious belief. In western Europe all the inhabitants were Roman Catholic, with the exception of a few Jews scattered throughout the entire area, a few Moslems still living in Spain, and an almost negligible number of heretics. In eastern Europe, on the other hand, there were, in addition to the Roman Catholics, converted by missionaries from western and southwestern Europe, many Greek Orthodox Christians, converted by way of Byzantium, and large numbers of pagans who resisted the missionary efforts of both Christian churches.

Cultural differences were also strong. The extended presence in this part of Europe of the Tartar conquerors and the proximity of Byzantium, whose culture, religion, and political institutions were adopted by many eastern rulers, tended to give parts of Slavic Europe cultural characteristics that differentiated it from western Europe.

The conflict between eastern and western ideas and institutions in the countries of eastern Europe led to the emergence of a strong Slavic nationalism toward the end of the Middle Ages. Although the Teutonic Knights, together with the Hanseatic merchants, had pushed eastward along the Baltic Sea to the Gulf of Finland, other Germans, merchants and nobles, had migrated to eastern Europe, bringing with them their business methods, manorial institutions, and culture, thus intensifying the confusion and arousing the antipathies of the indigenous populations.

# 1. The Changing Social Structure

## Poland

Poland had emerged as a separate state in the tenth century. Early in the thirteenth century, the ruler of Poland appealed to the Teutonic Knights to Christianize and subdue the Slavic Prussians north of his lands. Because he gave them the right to retain all the lands taken from the Prussians, the Germanization and Christianization of the areas was accompanied by the creation of a solid state under the firm hands of the grand masters of the order, a state that completely blocked the Poles from access to the Baltic Sea.

After the personal union of Poland and Lithuania under the Lithuanian Grand Duke Jagiello in 1386, and after the conversion of the Prussians and the Lithuanians to Christianity, the position of the Teutonic Knights became precarious. They not only lacked their original reason for existence but now stood in the way of a greatly enlarged and expanding Poland. The defeat of the Knights by the Poles and the Lithuanians at Tannenberg (Grünwald) in 1410 was followed the next year by the first Peace of Thorn, which provided that the Knights give up Samogitia and pay an indemnity. By the second Peace of Thorn of 1466, Prussia was divided into two parts. West Prussia, including Danzig and Thorn, was given to Poland, thus providing that country with an outlet to the sea. East Prussia, with Königsberg as its capital, was retained by the Knights, but as a fief of the Polish crown.

Although the Polish kings had by 1500 added important territories to their country, they had been unable to develop their royal authority. Unlike the townsmen of France, those of Poland, who consisted largely of Germans and Jews, were little inclined to support the growth of royal authority. Instead, the Polish gentry, or lesser nobility, gradually increased its political influence at the expense of the king, the magistrates, the townsmen, and the peasants. Although Poland thus had the appearance of being one of the important territorial states of Europe and experienced a golden age in culture, the economic and political bases for the construction of a great state were being undermined. The prosperity that the towns had achieved in the late Middle Ages now decreased, and the peasants were reduced to the status of serfs. The nobles, on the other hand, obtained complete control of the national diet, whose members were chosen by them in their provincial assemblies. They also retained their right to elect their kings, who became mere titular heads of the state.

## Russia

The history of eastern Europe became further complicated by the rise of another predominantly Slavic state, Russia. During the long period of Tartar domination, the princes of Moscow, one of the frontier principalities, rose to prominence. Ivan I (1325–1341) made himself the sole collector of Russian tribute for the khan. He and his successors used to the fullest this advantage over the other Russian princes and even over the khans not only to increase their wealth but to expand their possessions and consolidate their political power in imitation of the oriental despotism of their overlords.

When Constantinople, the capital of the Greek Orthodox Church and the "second Rome," fell to the Turks in 1453, the grand prince of Muscovy declared Moscow the new religious capital, the "third Rome." Soon afterward, Ivan III (1462–1505) took as his second wife the niece of the last emperor of Byzantium, claimed descent from the caesars, and adopted the double-headed eagle as well as the court ceremonial of the Byzantine emperor. Having increased his power at home, he took advantage of the internal disturbances and weaknesses among the Tartars and threw off their yoke (1480). Aware of the dynastic difficulties in Lithuania and Poland, he invaded the former and finally added Kiev, Smolensk, and Chernigov to Moscow, which became a European power of considerable importance.

### Hungary

The history of Hungary was closely tied to that of central and western Europe. Converted to Roman Catholicism by German missionaries in the tenth century, its rulers later cooperated with the papacy in its conflicts with the emperors and invited Roman ecclesiastics and Benedictine monks to educate the Hungarians, endowing them with large tracts of land in return. The wealthy bishops, however, soon constituted, together with the great feudal magnates, powerful, independent political figures.

Hungary became an important European state under King Matthias Corvinus (1458–1490), a popular border lord who had won acclaim as a military hero in wars against the Turks. With the support of the lesser nobles, he broke the power of the magnates, created a well-organized central administration, and greatly increased the royal revenues. Like a typical Renaissance despot, he maintained a lavish court, became a generous patron of culture, practiced the art of diplomacy with skill and cunning, and sought glory on the battlefield. If he had followed up his successes against the Turks instead of interfering in Bohemian affairs, he might have rendered Hungary and Europe a great service.

When Vladislav, the king of Bohemia, was elected the successor of Corvinus, the latter's work was quickly undone. Because he was more interested in courting the favor of the Hapsburgs than in strengthening royal authority in Hungary, he married his young son Louis to Mary, the granddaughter of Emperor Maximilian, and his daughter Anne to Mary's brother Ferdinand. The Hungarian nobles consequently soon formed a party of opposition, led by Stephen Zapolya, the prince of Transylvania.

This opposition was so effective that Vladislav was soon at the complete mercy of the nobles, and Hungary was unprepared to meet the formidable threat of the Ottoman Turks.

### The Ottoman Turks

The infiltration of the Ottoman Turks into Europe was the last of a long succession of invasions by Mongolian nomads from central Asia. The constant threat of a Turkish conquest throughout the fifteenth and sixteenth centuries greatly influenced the course of events in Europe, though it failed to consolidate Europe politically or to prevent the split of Roman Christianity.

Beginning in northeastern Asia Minor in the thirteenth century, the Ottoman Turks spread rapidly, conquering the lands of the Seljuk Turks and the Byzantine Empire with the utmost ease. In the middle of the fourteenth century they bypassed Constantinople and poured into the Balkan Peninsula. By the end of the century they had completed the conquest of the Balkan lands and defeated a formidable army of ten thousand Europeans led by Emperor Sigismund. In 1453 they finally took Constantinople after a siege of several months.

Constantinople, or Istanbul, became the capital of the Ottoman Empire, and its churches became Mohammedan mosques. The methodical Mohammed II (1451–1481) consolidated his conquests, laid siege to Rhodes, and fought an extended war with Venice. He not only took possession of a number of Venetian commercial posts but exacted from the "queen of the Adriatic" an annual tribute of ten thousand ducats in return for granting her the right to trade in the Black Sea region. By the end of the fifteenth century, the Turks were again in a position to threaten Hungary, Austria, Bohemia, and Poland.

## The Declining Influence of the Church

The important economic, social, and political changes of the late Middle Ages caused great stress and strain within the Church. In order to survive as an institution, it was compelled to adjust itself to the new economy with its new forms of wealth, the new social structure with its new interests, and the ambitious territorial rulers with their desire for increasing wealth and influence. Compromises, which were inevitable, led to a growing secularization and its attendant corruption and immorality. The demand for the reform of this secularized Church was not new, but it increased throughout the fifteenth century until reform was accepted as necessary by most conscientious Christians. So many people had a stake in the venality and corruption, however, that no renovation was possible until the demand for reform was led by persons who believed that they were carrying out the will of God and at the same time had the support of the new religious, cultural, and political forces.

## Papal Claims to Secular Authority

The evils of the secularization of the Church were most dramatically reflected in the history of the papacy. Under the leadership of such popes as Gregory VII, Innocent III, and Boniface VIII, there was developed the doctrine of *plenitudo potestatis,* or the fullness of power, according to which the pope had absolute authority over the Church. He was not only the supreme spiritual head, the vicar of Christ on earth, but also the supreme administrator, lawgiver, and judge. Not content, however, with the role ascribed to the papacy by the medieval doctrine of the "two swords," which had assigned to it supreme authority in spiritual matters, the popes and their canon lawyers eventually claimed for it also ultimate authority in secular matters.

The secular pretensions of the papacy were already hotly contested by the emperors in the Middle Ages. Although the popes emerged victorious over them by the middle of the thirteenth century, their victory was short-lived. Boniface VIII (1294–1303) denied Edward I of England and Philip IV of France the right to tax the clergy and issued the bull *Unam Sanctam* (1302), in which he declared that no human beings, including kings, could be saved unless they were subject to the pope; but he failed to intimidate the kings and died in humiliation. Clement V (1305–1314), a Frenchman, not only took up his residence at Avignon, where the papacy remained until 1377, but he pronounced Philip IV innocent of blame in the attack that had been made upon Boniface and admitted that kingdoms, like the papacy, were governed by divine right.

Illustrative of the declining political influence of the papacy and the growing importance of royal authority in France is the fact that the French nobles, clergy, and townsmen who met in the first estates-general in 1302 supported the king in his controversy with Boniface. His advisers, largely lawyers trained in Roman law, provided the theoretical justification for his claims. They maintained that the French king was "emperor in his own kingdom," argued that rights ascribed to the emperor by Roman law were equally the rights of their monarch, and suggested that the jurisdiction of all the ecclesiastical courts be given to the royal courts. They demanded that the Church be drastically reformed and that the pope transfer to the king all his territorial possessions in return for an annual pension, so that he might be relieved of all secular responsibilities.

The efforts of Pope John XXII (1316–1334) to intervene in the internal strife in Germany that accompanied the election of Louis IV (1314–1347) eventually ended in a further reduction of the actual influence of the popes in secular affairs. In the Declaration of Rense in 1338 the German electors asserted that a king elected by them needed no papal confirmation. The Golden Bull of 1356 omitted all reference to the role of the pope and denied him the right to rule the Empire during a vacancy of the imperial throne.

More important than the controversy between John XXII and Louis IV was the political theory that was developed in support of the latter. William of Ockham (d. 1349), an English Franciscan educated at Oxford, was primarily concerned with limiting the power of the pope in spiritual matters and therefore stressed the freedom of the entire body of Christian believers. But in support of Louis IV he revived the old distinction between secular and spiritual powers and maintained that the pope had no jurisdiction over the emperor. He also reflected the medieval dislike for arbitrary power in his contention that the emperor's power was derived from the electors, who represented all the Germans.

Much more systematic were the political theories developed by Marsilio of Padua (1270–1342), an Italian patriot and Aristotelian Averroist educated at Padua and Paris. In the *Defensor pacis,* or *Defender of the Peace,* which he wrote with the assistance of John of Jandun, one of his colleagues at the University of Paris, the arguments in support of the state as the sole defender of peace are derived from a rationalist observation of contemporary life based to a large extent upon Aristotle's *Politics.* Although revelation is not denied, it is not considered in this analysis of the functions of the state and the Church. Marsilio concludes that the Church, as only one element of society, is a part of the secular state with respect to temporal matters; that secular law, as distinct from divine law, is derived from the whole body of citizens, at least from the dominant citizens; and that the executive, preferably an elected monarch, must perform the functions of government for the good of the whole and according to the secular law.

The Church, according to Marsilio, must confine itself solely to spiritual functions. The ecclesiastical hierarchy, including the pope, derives its authority from the whole body of Christians, the *universitas fidelium.* There is no difference in rank among the clergy. It can not even be proved that the pope is the successor of Peter and that Peter was the chief of the Apostles. He reasoned further that the forgiveness of sins is more important than all the ceremonies of the Church, that God alone can forgive sins, that the Bible is the sole source of divine revelation and divine law, and that therefore the canon law and the traditions of the Church have no validity except insofar as they conform to the will of Christians as a whole. The ultimate authority in spiritual matters rests in the general Church council, in which laity as well as clergy are represented and which must be called by the secular rulers, for they are responsible for the welfare of the entire community of citizens.

Although Marsilio's ideas concerning the two great communities were still vague in many respects and could not have been carried out in practice in the fourteenth century, many of them reappeared in the teachings of Wycliffe and Hus and the reformers of the sixteenth century. They also reflected the tendency of the state to take precedence over the Church in the conduct of public affairs. The papacy continued to lose its influence over secular matters until, by the end of the Middle Ages, its secular functions were reduced to those of an Italian Renaissance prince.

### Spiritual Supremacy of the Popes

To understand the growing opposition to the papacy, it is necessary to examine its claims to spiritual supremacy. These were supported in medieval times by the ecumenical or general Church council, the only body that in the first centuries of Christianity had possessed ultimate authority over the entire Church. By the thirteenth century this body had come under the complete domination of the pope, for he summoned it, submitted its agenda, presided over its meetings, supervised the work of its important committees, confirmed its decisions, and approved its canons.

Inspired by the revived interest in Roman law, churchmen began to codify the canon law, which was based on the Bible, the canons of the general Church councils, and the papal decretals. This codification and the subsequent changes and additions came to be known as the *Corpus juris canonici*. The jurisdiction of this law extended not only to cases involving the members of the clergy and matters of faith and discipline but also to those involving the sacraments. Thus the courts could adjudicate such important secular matters as those related to marriage, contracts made under oath, and last wills and testaments.

Whereas the Church could not hold over those who broke its laws the threat of capital punishment, it could withhold its benefits. The most effective weapons at the disposal of the popes were excommunication, which could deprive the sinner of communion with the faithful, and the interdict, which could do the same for entire groups of individuals. These were powerful weapons; but the frequent use of them, even for political reasons, tended to blunt them and decrease the prestige of the popes.

In order to administer the increasing number of duties assumed by the popes, there was developed a highly efficient bureaucratic machinery centered in the papal *Curia*, or court. Although the chief advisers and officials were the cardinals, it became necessary to add many other officials, such as notaries, secretaries, and clerks. These gradually came to be grouped into the following departments: (1) the *rota Romana*, or consistory, which served as a supreme court; (2) the *cancellaria apostolica*, or chancery, which prepared papal documents and bulls; (3) the *poenitentiaria apostolica*, or penitentiary, which administered excommunications, interdicts, indulgences, and dispensations; and (4) the *camera apostolica*, or chamber, which managed papal finances.

# 1. The Changing Social Structure

Because of the gradual change from a manorial to a money economy and the growing expenses of the *Curia,* the papacy supplemented its old forms of income by new ones and developed an intricate system of taxation. Christendom was divided into collectorates from which taxes were brought by papal collectors to the *camera.* These taxes included the tithe, a part of the income of the clergy; the annates, a part or all of the first year's income of the holder of a benefice; the census, a tax paid by rulers who were vassals of the pope and by monastic or other religious groups who were directly under the supervision of the pope; vacancies, the income from vacant benefices; and procurations, payments for the entertainment of traveling popes or papal representatives. Among the forms of income paid directly to the papal chamberlain were the payments made by archbishops for the pallium, fees for the preparation of papal bulls and provisions, charges for papal indulgences and dispensations, and income from cases tried by the *Curia.*

The increased attention devoted to administrative and fiscal matters, the development of a luxurious court that attracted all kinds of hangers-on, and the natural search for preference and position in a system in which one man had so much power and wealth at his command led not only to a widespread secularization of the papacy and the Church at large but to corruption as well. Resentment against this state of affairs found expression in a persistent demand for reforms and also in the growth of heresy.

## The Growth of Heresy

Although heresy had appeared at various times during the Middle Ages, it now became associated with powerful political and social movements that made it a formidable threat to the unity of Christendom. Significantly, it was directed primarily against the increased authority of the papacy. It was greatly accentuated after the attempt to bring the papacy back to Rome had ended in the disgraceful papal schism (1378–1417), when there were two, and eventually three, rivals, each claiming to be the supreme head of the Church.

John Wycliffe (1320?–1384), a master at the University of Oxford, preached and wrote at a time when there was considerable social unrest in England, when his country was engaged in the Hundred Years' War with France, when Parliament was making strong protests against what it considered the tyranny of the popes at Avignon, and when liberal ideas similar to those of William of Ockham and Marsilio of Padua were being freely discussed at Oxford and other intellectual centers. In seeking a solution to the problem of the relation between reason and faith, Wycliffe turned to the basic ideas of St. Augustine and to the literal, rather than traditional, interpretation of the Bible.

By providing his countrymen with an English translation of the

Bible, Wycliffe enabled them to see for themselves the great differences between the simplicity of early Christianity and the power and wealth of the Church of the late Middle Ages. He attacked the luxury and venality of the popes and demanded that Church property be seized and managed by secular governments. Believing with Marsilio that the Church was originally a community of equals, he denied the authority of the pope over all Christendom and preached instead a religion of personal piety and the universal priesthood of believers, who were predestined to be saved by God's wisdom and standing in a direct relation to God.

On the basis of these revolutionary conceptions, Wycliffe attacked the monastic orders, which set one class of Christians apart from others, and the sacramental system, by means of which the clergy could bestow or withhold God's grace. He went so far as to deny the doctrine of transubstantiation, adopted by the Fourth Lateran Council in 1215, which maintained that the bread and wine in the sacrament of the Eucharist actually became the body and blood of Christ. Like other reformers, he attacked such external good works as the veneration of saints and their relics, the sale of indulgences, and the making of pilgrimages.

Although Wycliffe's demand for reforms proved abortive, and the Peasant's Revolt of 1381 helped to discredit his movement, the Lollards, as his followers were called, continued to spread his doctrines, even though on a limited scale. These doctrines were also carried to Bohemia, where they greatly influenced John Hus (1369–1415).

As the eloquent preacher in the Bethlehem Chapel in Prague and later as the rector of the nationalized University of Prague, Hus aroused his Czech countrymen to a high pitch of national enthusiasm and developed heretical ideas similar to those of Wycliffe, although he did not accept the latter's denial of the doctrine of transubstantiation. His attack upon the theory of indulgences, called forth by the preaching of a papal indulgence for a crusade against the Christian king of Naples, resulted in his excommunication by the pope. He found refuge outside Prague and devoted himself to study and writing. The chief product of his pen, *Concerning the Church,* developed the Wycliffite teachings concerning the universal priesthood of believers, stating in no uncertain terms that Christ was the sole head of the Church.

The career of Hus was cut short by the Council of Constance when it condemned him as a heretic and turned him over to the secular authorities to be burned at the stake in 1415, despite the fact that he had been given a letter of safe conduct by Emperor Sigismund. But neither the burning of Hus nor the preaching of a crusade against his followers could stamp out their heresy or their national enthusiasm.

The moderate followers of Hus were known as Utraquists, for they continued to believe in Communion in both kinds, *sub utraque specie,* or as Calixtines, for they demanded the cup, the *calix,* for the laity. They were brought together by a confessional statement known as the Four Articles of Prague (1420), which demanded (1) the free preaching of the Word of God, (2) Communion in both kinds, (3) confiscation of the property of the clergy, and (4) secular punishment for clergy living in mortal sin. While these Utraquists, comprising largely influential townsmen, were inclined to compromise with the Catholic Church, the radicals, called Taborites after the name of their chief stronghold, continued the struggle against the Church and the Empire until they were greatly reduced in numbers and influence.

Despite the continued efforts of the papacy to end the Bohemian heresy, there emerged in that country an independent church, that of the *Unitas Fratrum,* or New Unity of the Brotherhood, which was basically Protestant in doctrine and practice. It not only confiscated the property of the Church and the monasteries, but kept alive the heretical doctrines of Hus, which merged with those of Lutheranism and Calvinism in the sixteenth century.

## The Conciliar Movement

It is a strange coincidence that the tendency of Western Christendom to split into two or more camps under the schismatic popes came at the time when most Europeans desired unity. Even Wycliffe and Hus had no intention of destroying the *corpus christianum,* the medieval conception of religious and social solidarity that tied men together with one another and with God. This solidarity was particularly desirable in the face of the steady advance of the Ottoman Turks into Europe and the increasing demand for another crusade.

Because the schismatic popes did not provide the leadership needed to reform the Church and re-establish unity, a number of learned men suggested that only a general council of the Church could carry out the "reformation in head and members." Basing their conciliar theories on the ideas of Marsilio of Padua and William of Ockham, upon the widely accepted principles of natural law, and upon the early history of the Christian Church, outstanding scholars such as Pierre d'Ailly and Jean Gerson of France and Nicholas of Cusa of Germany argued that only a general Church council represented the will of the entire Church and could end the schism, reform the Church, and put an end to heresy. Moreover, because the popes and the rest of the ecclesiastical hierarchy were but the creatures and instruments of the will of the Church, they should be bound by the decisions of such a council. Because the popes would not call a council, certain teachers of canon law at Bologna suggested that the cardinals had the right and obligation to do so.

Accordingly a number of cardinals from each papal obedience, or rule, agreed to call a meeting of a council at Pisa in 1409. Although this body acted too rapidly and made matters worse by creating a third pope without compelling the other two to resign, the principle of a limited papacy had gained wide acceptance.

The Council of Constance (1414–1418), called at the insistence of Emperor Sigismund, proceeded more cautiously and finally succeeded in ending the papal schism. Although it failed to solve the problem of heresy by having Hus, Jerome of Prague, and the bones of Wycliffe burned and made little progress with reforms, it enunciated two revolutionary decrees. The first, called *Sacrosancta* (1415), stated that the general council had its authority directly from Christ and that therefore the entire Church was bound by its decisions. The second, called *Frequens* (1417), provided for regular meetings of the general council.

Because the nations represented at Constance could not agree on a common program of reforms, the council had to content itself with suggesting that the newly elected pope carry on negotiations for reform with the individual nations. In these circumstances it is easy to understand how the pope, desirous of first strengthening his control over the Papal States and regaining the influence lost during the period of the schism, gave little or no attention to reforms.

The Council of Basel (1431–1449), which again came to grips with the problems of heresy and reforms, failed largely because the rulers of western Europe and the pope settled their differences at the expense of the council. This relatively easy success lulled the papacy into a false sense of security so that it devoted much of its attention to political interests and cultural pursuits.

Meanwhile many of the French clergy, aware of their inability to reform the entire Church, urged Charles VII to call an assembly of his clergy at Bourges to carry out reforms in the French Church. In the Pragmatic Sanction of Bourges (1438), the French clergy reaffirmed the conciliar theory of the supremacy of a general council over the pope. But they also laid down the following basic rights, called Gallican Liberties: (1) the right of the French Church to elect its own clergy without papal interference; (2) the prohibition of the payment of annates to the papacy; and (3) the limitation of the number of appeals from the French courts to the Roman *Curia*. Thenceforth the French Church came increasingly under the control of the French kings.

In 1448 the pope concluded the Concordat of Vienna with Frederick III. This agreement provided for the abolition of provisions and reservations and confirmed a previous concordat that had given the emperor the right to nominate the incumbents of all the important ecclesiastical offices in the Hapsburg lands. But it completely defeated and demoralized the German reform party and gave the pope more control over the Church in Germany than in any other country. The German people, hopelessly divided politically, were at the mercy of the papal financial exactions, and consequently religious dissatisfaction readily spread among them.

The conciliar movement, which had begun auspiciously, failed in the face of papal intransigence and the determination of the territorial rulers to conduct all the affairs in their lands to their own advantage. Yet the high idealism and the demand for reforms persisted, even after men had lost confidence in the ability of a church council to solve their problems.

## The Clergy and the Reform Movement

The popes of the postconciliar period, apparently oblivious of the seriousness of the demand for reforms, devoted much of their attention to regaining their position in European affairs, developing the Papal States into a strong territorial government, and making the *Curia* the patron of the Italian Renaissance. They not only condemned the conciliar theories, as did Pius II in the bull *Execrabilis* (1460), but rendered them ineffective by concluding concordats with the European rulers.

Chosen by a cardinal college in which the leading princely families of Italy were represented, the Renaissance popes distributed the many lucrative offices at their disposal to their relatives and friends, often for monetary and political considerations. With the election of Tommaso Parentucelli, a humanist, as Pope Nicholas V (1447–1455), began the golden age of the papal patronage of Renaissance culture. He brought a large number of scholars, including Lorenzo Valla, the well-known critic of the papacy, to Rome to translate Greek manuscripts into Latin, founded the Vatican Library, and planned to rebuild the basilica of St. Peter's, the Vatican, and the entire city. Pius II (1458–1464), another humanist pope, continued to patronize the Renaissance. Yet his pontificate, like that of Nicholas V, was free from serious scandals.

The colorful [Francisco della Rovere,] who became Pope Sixtus IV (1471–1484), however, initiated an ambitious program designed to establish the political power and prestige of the papacy both at home and abroad. To do this, he resorted to shameless nepotism and stooped to political intrigue in his attempt to liquidate rival feudal families in the Papal States and enemies in the city-states. Among his positive contributions was the building of the Sistine Chapel.

Flagrantly immoral was Innocent VIII (1484–1492), father of sixteen children whom he openly recognized and whose weddings he celebrated in the Vatican. To increase his income, he received an annual subsidy of forty-five thousand ducats from the Turkish Sultan Bayazid II for keeping as prisoner the latter's brother, a contender for the throne.

Political corruption and immorality in the Vatican reached their height under Rodrigo Borgia, who became Alexander VI (1492–1503). He was grossly immoral, indiscriminate in the means used to combat his enemies, and obsessed with the desire to provide wealth and power for his children, especially the ambitious Cesare Borgia and the clever Lucrezia. He carried the secularization of the *Curia* to such extremes that even the highly sophisticated townsmen of Italy began to listen attentively to the preaching friars who were condemning the papacy and calling the clergy and laity to repentance.

Ignoring these symptoms of a mounting religious dissatisfaction, the popes continued to pursue their secular ambitions. Giuliano della Rovere, who followed Alexander as Pope Julius II (1503–1513), concentrated on creating a modern, strongly centralized government in the Papal States and on making his influence felt in European affairs as a warrior and a statesman. His patronage of Bramante, Raphael, and Michelangelo in the beautification of the Vatican and in the beginning of the construction of St. Peter's brought the magnificence of the *Curia* to a new height but also aroused still further ·the conscience of Christendom.

Giovanni de' Medici, son of Lorenzo the Magnificent, who became Pope Leo X (1513–1521), had been selected by the cardinals because they felt that his quiet, affable nature was needed as an antidote to the warlike propensities of his predecessor. He aptly characterized his pontificate by saying to the Venetian ambassador at Rome, "Let us enjoy the papacy, since God has given it to us." Although he preferred to indulge in refined social intercourse with his literary and artistic friends, he was compelled to concern himself with political affairs when Francis I (1515–1547) became king of France and sought fame by making conquests in Italy. The political problems raised by the French victory at Marignano (1515), added to Leo's other secular interests, resulted in a scandalous neglect of his spiritual activities and intensified the demand for reforms.

### Papal Indulgences

Among the papal practices that further increased religious dissatisfaction was the granting of indulgences. Originally the *indulgentia,* or permission, to relax or commute the satisfaction or penance of a penitent sinner rested with the congregation, which had imposed this outward sign of sorrow. When the system of private penance was substituted for public penance, and the priests, who had charge of Church discipline, tended to abuse the power of granting indulgences, this power was assumed by the bishops. Episcopal abuses in turn led the popes to reserve to themselves the right of granting indulgences.

The dangers in this practice greatly increased during the papal struggle for control over the entire Church, particularly during the thirteenth century, when theologians formulated the conception of a "treasury of merits." This was a storehouse of the good works of Christ, the saints, and all good Christians that the pope could distribute by means of in-

St. Peter's Basilica

*Alinari. Art Reference Bureau.*

dulgences to those who were not certain that they had rendered sufficient penance to take care of all the temporal punishment that they deserved. Although such indulgences were originally granted as rewards for virtuous deeds, they eventually came to be sold for money.

A second important theological change was the conversion of penance, with its four steps of *contritio cordis* (sorrow for sins), *confessio oris* (confession before the priest), *satisfactio operis* (manifestation of sorrow), and *absolutio* (pardon), into a sacrament in which the granting of absolution preceded the satisfaction. This had the effect of reminding the sinner that the absolution, although it removed both the guilt and the eternal punishment, did not free him completely from temporal punishment on earth or in purgatory. If the priests did not impose sufficient penance or if the sinner could not perform all the penance required, the temporal punishment would be continued in purgatory. This element of uncertainty led to a new conception of the indulgence. Its use as a relaxation of imposed penance was gradually replaced by its use as a means of transferring to the sinner good works from the "treasury of merits." Thus the indulgence granted remission of the penalties still left after the absolution.

A third change was made when a number of theologians drew a distinction between contrition and attrition. Still holding that contrition as sorrow prompted by love was taken into consideration by God in pardoning a sinner, they maintained that there was another kind of sorrow, attrition, which was prompted by less worthy motives, such as fear of punishment. Although it was believed that this less worthy sorrow was perfected by the absolution in the sacrament and that God would remit eternal punishment, there was less certainty with respect to the remission of temporal punishment. Therefore indifferent Christians were likely to resort to indulgences to ease their consciences.

Most uneducated people, who could not comprehend the subtle distinctions of theologians, naturally confused eternal and temporal punishment and believed that they could actually buy their salvation. The popes in their bulls promulgating indulgences drew the distinction between the guilt of sin and the penalties of sin, though many people believed that they could buy remission of both. It was at first the practical effect that the selling of indulgences had upon the morality of the people, rather than the theological explanations, that aroused strong opposition to them. They were attacked particularly after the remission of temporal punishments in purgatory was extended in the fifteenth century to include both the living and the dead.

Although indulgences were granted for a growing variety of purposes, the *Curia* used them chiefly as a source of revenue. For this reason the popes frequently employed bankers to manage the financial matters. After these bankers, the local bishops, the indulgence sellers, and the rulers—whose permission usually had to be obtained before the sales could be made in their territories—had all received their share, only about a third of the total receipts reached the papal treasury.

The sale of indulgences became a big business when the popes began to issue jubilee indulgences. Boniface VIII granted a plenary, or full, indulgence to all pilgrims who visited Rome for the jubilee of 1300. In 1400 and again in 1450 large numbers of Christians thronged to Rome and received indulgences for making the pilgrimage. In the following year papal legates took the indulgences to those who had been unable to visit the Holy City. Paul II shortened the time between jubilees to twenty-five years so that one could be celebrated in 1475 and another in 1500. Julius II announced a new indulgence in 1506, the proceeds of which were to be used for the construction of the new basilica of St. Peter's in Rome.

By 1500 the papacy had developed a financial system second to none and had large sums of money at its disposal. But the flowing of wealth to Rome tended to corrupt the *Curia*. Simony was practiced openly, and all kinds of office seekers sought their fortunes there. Scarcely any important office was obtained without the payment of fees. Pluralism, or the holding of more than one office, also became a common evil, with some papal favorites holding as many as five bishoprics. And with the evil of pluralism went the evil of absenteeism.

Even though relatively few people were familiar with the evil effects of the secularization of the Church at its center, they learned firsthand of the corruption in the dioceses and parishes. The bishops, recruited almost exclusively from the ranks of the nobility, saw their authority and influence greatly curtailed not only by the popes but also by the territorial rulers. As a consequence of this pressure from two sides, many bishops, especially in Germany, sought to retain their influence by secular means. The episcopal courts, like the Roman *Curia,* often became thoroughly secularized and reflected the worst abuses found in Rome.

Many parish priests and mendicant friars disapproved of the development of an ambitious oligarchy of prelates of noble blood. Living close to the people whom they served, they frequently became their spokesmen in their objection to the secularization of the Church and its attendant corruption.

# 2 Religious and Intellectual Life

Toward the close of the fifteenth century there were many conscientious and thoughtful persons who wished to reform the Church and society and restore the unity of Latin Christendom. Although their programs differed greatly in origin and character, it is possible to distinguish two main groups. One used the traditionally medieval approach of piety and mysticism, the other the methods and content of late-medieval learning.

## Late-Medieval Piety and Mysticism

Demands for reform were voiced particularly by the friars of the chief mendicant orders, the Franciscans, the Dominicans, and the Augustinians. Supported by some popes and territorial rulers, these friars went from place to place, assailing laxity and corruption throughout the Church and assisting conscientious prelates in re-establishing discipline in their convents and dioceses. The Franciscans, under capable leadership, set their houses in order and regained some of the influence that they had once had among the masses of the people. Because the two divisions of the order, the Observants, or Spiritual Franciscans, who rigidly interpreted the teachings of St. Francis, and the Conventuals, who deviated somewhat from them, continued to disagree, Leo X in 1517 finally recognized them as separate orders.

The Dominicans were also permeated by the spirit of reform. They again took seriously their original mission of educating the people in orthodox Christianity, helped organize many parishes so they would better serve the needs of the people, and became active in the Inquisition.

# Part One: Europe on the Eve of the Reformation

Most active in the reform movement of the latter half of the fifteenth century were the Augustinian Eremites. Originally hermits, the Augustinians were eventually brought under a conventual rule by the papacy. Devoted to the Virgin Mary and Augustine, both of whom were their patrons, they led abstemious lives, became serious students of theology, and practiced the art of preaching. Because of their sincerity and devotion, they were well received by the people, particularly in Germany. Their professors of theology taught in a number of German universities, and their preachers attracted large crowds in their convent chapels, located in most of the large cities.

Preaching to the laity in the vernacular became recognized as one of the most important functions of the priests as well as the friars. Large numbers of manuals on the art of sermonizing were written for the benefit of preachers. At least six editions of the *Postilla* of Nicholas de Lyra, a Franciscan, were published between 1471 and 1509. Luther considered it one of the best and most valuable manuals of that period.

Popular preachers like Johann Geiler of Kaisersberg (1445–1510), for whom a pulpit was endowed in the cathedral at Strassburg, admonished the masses to repent of their sins and vehemently attacked corruption among the clergy. Of particular interest is his denunciation of the luxury of the clergy, simony, the buying of indulgences, and relic worship.

Much of the preaching, to be sure, accomplished little in the way of reform but attempted to frighten the people into a proper morality. The constant emphasis upon sin and death, vividly portrayed in pictures as well as sermons, tended to make people look upon Christ as a stern judge. Consequently they turned to the Virgin Mary to intercede with Christ in their behalf. In this they were encouraged by the Franciscans, who were engaged in spreading the doctrine of the Immaculate Conception of Mary, and the Dominicans, who urged the use of the rosary in saying the Lord's Prayer and the Ave Maria. Many churches and shrines were dedicated to the Virgin, sculptors and painters portrayed her beauty and her motherly qualities, and hymns were composed to convey the depth of her sorrows.

Motherly intercession was carried a step further when, encouraged by the Franciscans, the Carmelites, and the Augustinians, Germans began, about the middle of the fifteenth century, to call upon Mary's mother Anne to intercede with the Virgin to plead with Jesus. St. Anne was also called upon to make barren women fertile and to assist women in childbirth. Attempts of cults to have her declared immaculately conceived ended in failure.

Other saints were similarly honored and promoted by cults. One of the best known of these was the cult of the Fourteen Helpers in Need, which had its origin in Germany. Among these fourteen saints were Bar-

bara, called upon for protection against lightning, Blaise against throat troubles, Christopher against sudden accidents, Denis against headaches, Vitus against epilepsy, and Margaret against insanity. Leonard, Nicholas, and Rochus were the particular patrons of the peasants. Various countries and regions also had their special saints.

The making of pilgrimages to view the relics of the saints in reliquaries and shrines was also encouraged. Whereas relatively few Europeans could make pilgrimages to the Holy Land, most of them had access to shrines. Next to Rome, the most frequented shrine was that of the Apostle St. James at Compostella in Spain, which was visited particularly by those wishing to be cured of illnesses. Of the many shrines in England, the most important were Our Lady of Walsingham and the tomb of St. Thomas Becket in Canterbury. St. Michel on the coast of Normandy attracted large numbers of Germans as well as Frenchmen, and especially children. The most famous shrines in Germany were those at Aachen, where holy relics attracted an estimated one hundred forty thousand pilgrims in one day in 1496; Cologne, where the bones of the Three Magi were preserved in a magnificent gold receptacle, ornately embellished with precious stones; and Trier, where was kept the holy garment of Christ, declared authentic by a papal bull in 1515. Among the collections of relics made by German princes was that of Elector Frederick the Wise, Luther's ruler. It contained about five thousand items, including a thumb of St. Anne, straw from the manger in which Christ was born, and a part of the cross on which Christ was crucified.

The reading of the Bible in the vernacular was also encouraged by some, particularly by the leaders of the small evangelical groups that existed in many parts of Europe. Translations appeared with increasing frequency, especially after the invention of printing by movable type. No fewer than twenty-five editions of the Gospels and Epistles, twenty-two editions of the Psalms, and eighteen editions of the entire Bible were published in the German dialects alone before 1517. All had been made from the Vulgate of St. Jerome.

There was as yet no official opinion concerning the Bible's place as the ultimate authority in matters of doctrine and ethics, for not until the Council of Trent did the Catholic Church officially give tradition a status of equality alongside the Bible. But the popes and other high Church officials as a rule disapproved of its translation into the vernacular, for they feared that laymen not trained in theology might misunderstand it and use it for revolutionary purposes. This was interpreted by many to mean that the Church was attempting to suppress the Word of God, the gospel. Eventually the words *gospel* and *evangelical liberty* became revolutionary slogans that implied political and social as well as religious programs of reform.

The imaginative minds of many late-medieval people were particularly attracted by the Book of Revelation and the apocalyptic ideas associated with it. These were frequently portrayed in books, religious plays, and art. Although churchmen often designated certain secular rulers as Antichrist, others used the term to denounce corrupt churchmen. Many people expected the coming of Christ and the Antichrist in the immediate future. The effect that prophecies had upon all classes of people is well illustrated by the astounding, if temporary, successes of Girolamo Savonarola (1452–1498) in the Renaissance city of Florence.

### Savonarola

Savonarola was born into an Italian family that was in close touch with the Renaissance culture of the brilliant court of the Este family at Ferrara. Deeply religious by inclination, however, he turned against the secular interests of the Renaissance and, in 1475, entered a Dominican convent. He was sent to the convent of San Marco in Florence in 1482 and became a preacher in the church of San Lorenzo, the church of the Medici family. Believing that God had given him the mission of calling people to repentance before the impending day of judgment, he preached powerful sermons that struck awe and terror into the hearts of the Florentines. His prophecies, which he believed were revealed directly to him by God, appeared to come true with miraculous accuracy. For example, he foretold the death of Innocent VIII, the coming of a foreign power with a large army as a scourge of God, and the collapse of the Medici rule in Florence.

The forcefulness of Savonarola's message made him the man of the hour among the Florentines. They accepted not only his program of religious reform but also his political views concerning a democratic theocracy. In December, 1495, a new constitution, much like that of the Venetian republic, was accepted. It provided for a Great Council, comprising about three thousand citizens, that is, persons thirty or more years of age whose fathers, grandfathers, or great-grandfathers had served the city as officials. This Great Council was a closed legislative and electoral body that chose the members of the Signory and other officials. It was this interference in political matters and the concomitant necessity of his joining a political party that eventually proved to be Savonarola's undoing.

For the time being, however, Pope Alexander VI, who was incensed at his political as well as his religious activities, attempted to destroy Savonarola's popularity. He demanded that Savonarola appear for a hearing in Rome, and forbade him to preach. But the reformer openly defied the pope, declared it man's duty to resist him when he was in error, and appealed to a general Church council against him. Popular enthusiasm for Savonarola's leadership meanwhile reached its climax in the carnival of 1497, in which the usual pomp and splendor were replaced by the burning of articles of luxury and "vanities" that had been gathered by his followers—false hair, playing cards, immodest books, pagan art, and trinkets of all kinds.

Excesses such as this, however, together with the reformer's open defiance of the pope, led many people to desert him. His political moves also became unpopular. Charles VIII of France, upon whom he was depending to enforce a reform of the Church, left Italy in 1495 and did not return to aid the cause. The masses began to waver in their loyalty, and the upper classes assumed the offensive against him.

In 1497 the pope excommunicated Savonarola and threatened to place an interdict upon Florence. The fact that the reformer continued to preach as an excommunicate alienated more followers and gave the rival Franciscans an opportunity to arouse greater hostility against him. Finally, to prove that their cause had divine support, Savonarola and some of his fellow Dominican friars agreed with the Franciscans to submit to the ordeal by fire. The Signory gave its permission, despite the disapproval of the pope. But because the Dominicans and the Franciscans could not agree on certain details, the ordeal was indefinitely postponed. The disappointed populace now turned against Savonarola, and the Signory, which had come into the hands of his enemies, arrested him.

Subjected to torture, Savonarola confessed that he had not received his prophecies directly from God. After he had been declared a heretic by the papal commissioners sent to try him, the hostile Signory accused him of treason and condemned him and two fellow friars to death. The following day the three were hanged and their bodies burned. Although no miracle occurred to save Savonarola, as some of his loyal followers had expected, they were greatly impressed by the faith and courage with which he had faced death and hailed him as a martyr and saint.

Savonarola's best-known work, *The Triumph of the Cross* (1497), was a defense of Christianity against the skeptical and pagan tendencies in the Italian Renaissance. Written in the best style of the humanists, it breathed the spirit of the late Middle Ages with its apocalyptic views and Neoplatonic mysticism. But in his unfinished exposition of Psalms 31 and 51, written in prison, he approached the position of the Protestant reformers by stressing justification by faith. Unlike the Protestant reformers, however, Savonarola had no quarrel with the dogmas or the organization of the Church.

## Mysticism

Of great importance in the reform of Christianity along medieval lines were the mystics, who sought religious satisfaction primarily by stressing pious living and proximity to God. This was a religious approach favored especially by townsmen, who found scholastic subtleties beyond them and preferred a simple, practical, and intuitive theology.

# Part One: Europe on the Eve of the Reformation

The movement was strongest along the Rhine River in Germany and in the Low Countries during the fourteenth and fifteenth centuries.

In Germany Master Johannes Eckhart (1260–1327), a Dominican scholar, developed his speculative, pantheistic theology concerning God as the one true being permeating all life, and man's ability to become one with God. Johann Tauler (1300?–1361), another Dominican and one of Eckhart's followers, developed a less abstract, more social Christian mysticism, which influenced, among others, both Luther and the Jesuit Canisius. Another product of the German mystics was the anonymously written book that Luther called *A German Theology* and published in 1516. It taught complete abandonment of oneself to the will of God until the soul became one with God through Christ.

In the Low Countries mysticism took a new form, called the *devotio moderna*. It was inspired by Gerard Groote (1340–1384), a well-educated lawyer who had become a Carthusian monk and, after leaving the monastery in 1369, devoted the rest of his life to reforming the clergy and teaching the young. His followers, called the Brethren of the Common Life, constituted a semimonastic order of laymen and clergy who took no irrevocable vows but sought to live lives of piety according to the ethics of the Sermon on the Mount. In seeking to carry their ideas into practice they cultivated the inner life, lived by the work of their own hands, cared for the poor, and educated the young.

Probably the best-known member of the Brethren of the Common Life was Thomas à Kempis (1380–1471), who spent more than seventy years of his long life at the convent of St. Agnes near Zwolle. It is to him that most scholars ascribe the writing of the great classic of these mystics, *The Imitation of Christ*. Thoroughly medieval in every respect, the author accepted traditional dogmas with childlike simplicity, urged the use of the sacraments, stressed the monastic virtues, and sought salvation by loving God and imitating Christ. In effect, however, it tended to personalize religion and to minimize the importance of formal Christianity. Its emphasis upon peace of soul, purity of thought, and simplicity of life made it one of the most widely read books of his day.

The mysticism of the Brethren could not, because of its abnegation of society and of reason, bring about the thoroughgoing reforms needed to restore the effectiveness of the Church. Its emphasis upon inner spirituality, however, greatly influenced the Christian humanists and some of the reformers. An excellent example of this influence is Johann Wessel of Gansfort (1419?–1489). Educated in the school of the Brethren at Zwolle and a close friend of Thomas à Kempis, he nonetheless deserted the medieval conservatism of his teachers and combined the piety of the New Devotion with the scholarship of the New Learning. His desire for the certainty of salvation led him directly to the study of the Bible. At Cologne, Paris, and Rome he learned to master Greek as well as Latin and studied Hebrew.

Gansfort's preoccupation with the Bible, which he placed above the authority of the popes and the Church councils, led him to some conclusions that Luther, in 1522, stated were remarkably like his own. God alone, Gansfort maintained, could forgive sins, and man was saved by his faith and his love of communion with God. Consequently he greatly minimized the importance of the Church and the priestly hierarchy, questioned the need of confession, and strongly criticized the granting of indulgences. He exerted a strong influence upon the humanists of his acquaintance, but he shunned arguments. His works were not published until after the beginning of the Reformation.

## Late-Medieval Scholarship

Dissatisfaction with late-medieval conditions in the Church and the demand for reforms were also prompted by rapid and far-reaching intellectual changes. Largely responsible for these changes was the growing importance of the townsmen with their strongly secular and practical interests that attracted them to the secular culture of the Romans and the Greeks and led them to participate in the great excitement over the gathering of ancient manuscripts. In their enthusiasm for learning they also embraced the literature of the Church fathers, the texts of the Bible, and the Hebrew learned tradition. The rapidity of these changes was made possible by the development of printing, which made available at relatively low cost and with few errors all the major classical authors. Learning was therefore no longer confined to the universities but was promoted wherever men took an interest in gathering libraries and pondered over the contents of their books.

### Scholasticism

Scholasticism, which had produced a remarkable synthesis of all learning during the high Middle Ages, had by 1500 resolved itself into vehement conflicts among the schoolmen in which ecclesiastical politics were frequently a determining factor. Differences and distinctions arose that had little meaning for the majority of the people of the late Middle Ages. Scholasticism did not again become a vital force until it had been synthesized with other learning by the humanists of the Platonic Academy and purged of its subtleties by leaders of the Catholic Reformation. The two most important tendencies of scholasticism in the latter half of the fifteenth century were called the *via moderna* and the *via antiqua*.

The *via moderna*, which became the dominant trend at the universities of Erfurt and Vienna, followed William of Ockham in his doctrine that universals have no reality outside man's mind and are merely names. This position was called nominalism (from *nomen,* Latin for "name"). Philosophical realists, who stressed the importance of particulars, accused Ockham and his followers of furthering skepticism with respect to theology by minimizing such doctrines as that of the Trinity. Because Ockham held that one could not base faith on reason but had to accept the authority of the Bible and the Church, his enemies accused him of holding a double theory of truth. His emphasis on God's omnipotence, according to which God predestined some men to salvation, seemed to contradict his views concerning man's freedom of will and ability to contribute toward salvation by good works. Although he explained this by stating that God could do anything whatsoever according to God's absolute power (*potentia absoluta*), God actually does only what God has chosen to do (*potentia ordinata*), thereby allowing man to contribute to his salvation. Ockhamism was revived and made highly effective by Gabriel Biel (d. 1495), a member of the Brethren of the Common Life, whose writings, particularly his explanation of the Mass, had a strong influence on Luther at Erfurt.

The semi-Pelagian position of the nominalists proved confusing and unacceptable to those scholastics who reacted in favor of philosophical realism, which maintained that universals were real and existed before particulars, and to those who believed scholasticism as a whole irrelevant and useless. The scholastic reaction against nominalism, called the *via antiqua,* developed at Paris and Louvain after 1473 and exerted a strong influence upon learning at the universities at Cologne and Leipzig. Its proponents stressed the importance of reason (dialectics) and a knowledge of nature for the understanding of theology and urged the study of the Bible and other early sources of Christianity. Some of these Thomists became well-known preachers of repentance and reform, thereby giving the movement renewed vitality. Cajetan, the able opponent of Luther, helped make it a powerful force in the Catholic Reformation.

### Italian Humanism

The Italian humanists of the fourteenth and the first half of the fifteenth centuries were nearly all hostile toward the scholastic method, although none of them denied the fundamental doctrines of the Church. They were so enthusiastic over the classics, manuscripts of which they and their patrons gathered in large libraries, that they placed them alongside the sources of Christianity as their authorities. Because they were eager to get at the content of the classics, their method was primarily rhetorical and philological. Interested primarily in applying the classics and Christianity to life, they were concerned with ethics rather than theology.

Because the Italian humanists were preoccupied with ascertaining the meaning of texts, it is not surprising that they eventually used their philological techniques in the examination of religious documents. Lorenzo Valla (1405–1457), for example, wrote a treatise, *On the Donation of Constantine,* in which he showed that the document that had been used to substantiate the temporal power of the papacy could not have been written at the time of Constantine but was a forgery of the eighth century. Although Nicholas of Cusa and Reginald Pecock had previously questioned its authenticity, Valla left no doubt that it was spurious.

More important still was the great stimulus that Valla gave to biblical scholarship by his *Annotations on the New Testament,* published for the first time by Erasmus in 1505. On the basis of his study of a number of Latin and Greek manuscripts, Valla came to the conclusion that the Vulgate translation contained a number of errors. His findings stimulated the studies of Erasmus, Jiménez, Reuchlin, and other biblical humanists of the sixteenth century.

The interest of the humanists in the environment in which the classics had been produced also aided them in gaining a new sense of historical perspective. The static medieval conception of the world was supplanted by a dynamic one, concerned with personal observation and comparison.

## The Platonic Academy

The rapid recovery of Greek manuscripts and contact with Greek scholars from Byzantium aroused a strong interest in Plato, an interest that had not completely died out in the Middle Ages, despite the great veneration for Aristotle. Humanists were intrigued especially by Plato's imaginative attempt to bring all things, material and spiritual, into one great unity of ideas culminating in God. Interest in Plato was cultivated particularly by the members of the Platonic Academy in Florence, patronized by both Cosimo and Lorenzo de' Medici.

Among the outstanding members of the Platonic Academy were Marsilio Ficino (1433–1499) and Giovanni Pico della Mirandola (1463–1494). Ficino translated all Plato's dialogues into Latin by 1468. Then he turned to the development of his own philosophy, in which Neoplatonism, the doctrines of Augustine, German mysticism, and even the scholasticism of Thomas Aquinas played an important part. In his formulation of the first distinctly Renaissance philosophy, he retained the traditional medieval conception of the hierarchic gradation of all creatures; but he included an optimistic faith in the acquisition of the one truth and the ultimate union of man with God. Man could achieve this by willing to do so and by using love, rather than reason, as the dynamic motivating force.

The search for a conception of unity was extended much further by the young Pico della Mirandola, who saw in all religions the same yearning of the soul to be reunited with God. Impressed with the idea of an all-embracing unity by his studies in scholasticism at the Sorbonne in Paris, he included in his philosophic system also the great body of Hebrew literature. In spite of the fact that there had been many Jewish settlements in Europe throughout the Middle Ages, Christians had ignored the contributions to learning made by Hebrew scholars. Now for the first time Pico and his contemporaries made a thorough study of the Talmud and the cabalistic writings. The latter contained a theosophy, probably influenced by Arabic works, that gave an attractive explanation of man's relation to God and suggested the importance of love, as opposed to reason and will, in achieving this union.

Although the Renaissance philosophy of the members of the Platonic Academy deviated little from the traditional theology, especially from the Augustinian and mystical tradition, Pico's orthodoxy was questioned. Of the nine hundred theses that he formulated to prove the validity of his theology, however, Innocent VIII and the *Curia* condemned as heretical only a few. The introduction that Pico had written for his theses, that which he called "Oration on the Dignity of Man," contains an excellent summary of his philosophy. In it he expresses his hope that man can purify Christianity by study. This optimism was carried by his students to countries outside Italy and became an important characteristic of Christian humanism.

## Christian Humanism in Western Europe

The humanists in northern and western Europe, indifferent to the predominantly secular spirit of the earlier Italian humanists and to the sentimental and occasionally erotic writings of the later ones, laid more emphasis upon Christian than classical sources. And they sought with greater determination to bring the results of their scholarship to bear upon the critical problems of their day. Although there were many differences among them, depending upon the degree to which individual humanists stressed either Christian or classical antiquity and were influenced by their indigenous culture, they can be classified as Christian humanists.

Despite their individual differences, all Christian humanists were motivated by an optimistic belief that they could reform society and restore the unity of Christendom by means of the New Learning, for they were convinced that a proper understanding of Christian and classical antiquity would lead to true piety and piety to reform. It is for this reason that they established and supported schools, disseminated the classics in printed form, and prepared new editions of the Bible and the writings of the Church fathers.

Christian humanists were not, however, revolutionaries. They exposed corruption and other evils in existing institutions, but they did not advocate their abolition. They were more concerned with proper conduct than with theology, with learning than with faith, and with nature than with grace. Yet they questioned no fundamental doctrines of the Church. To preserve the solidarity of the medieval Christian community, most of them refused to follow the Protestants in their separation from Catholicism.

## Spanish Humanism

In Spain, as in all European countries outside Italy, humanism was patronized by the rulers of the respective kingdoms and principalities. Francisco Jiménez de Cisneros (1436–1517), archbishop of Toledo, a cardinal, Queen Isabella's confessor, provincial of the Franciscan order, and grand inquisitor, had as one of his chief aims the use of humanism in the reform of the Church. He fostered the New Learning, particularly at the University of Alcalá, which he had founded in 1500. To raise the level of spirituality among the Spaniards, he had a large number of religious writings translated into their tongue, including *The Imitation of Christ* of the Brethren of the Common Life and *The Life of Christ* by Ludolf the Saxon, a German mystic.

The first printed Greek text of the New Testament was completed at the University of Alcalá in 1514, although it was not published until 1520. This was followed in 1522 by the publication of the famous Polyglot Bible, called the Complutensian Polyglot after the ancient Roman name of the city of Alcalá. This work, the first of its kind, was published in six volumes and contained the Hebrew, Greek, and Aramaic texts, the Targumim, the Septuagint, the Vulgate, and a Latin translation of the Septuagint and the Targumim. The tremendous cost involved was borne solely by Jiménez, for he was greatly concerned with correcting the errors in the Vulgate. He personally supervised the work and engaged the translators.

Best known among the Spanish humanists who participated in the translation of the Polyglot Bible was Elio Antonio de Nebrija (1442?–1522), who had been educated in Italy. Because he pointed to a number of errors in the Vulgate, he was prosecuted by the Inquisition. He was saved from punishment, however, by the influence of Jiménez.

Juan de Valdés (1500?–1541), well known as a master of Castilian prose, came under the influence of both mysticism and Erasmian humanism. Although he severely attacked abuses in both Church and state, he stoutly maintained that he was primarily interested in reforming man, not the Church. His great emphasis was upon a "return to Christ."

Most influential of the Spanish humanists was Juan Luis Vives (1492–1540), who spent most of his creative life in Louvain, Burges, and

England. Like Erasmus and More, his friends, he applied the philosophy of the New Learning to the reform of society and education. In his *On the Help of the Poor,* published in 1526, he advocated a system of government social service that included such proposals as making extensive case studies, public support of the worthy poor, public rearing of foundlings, free medical service for the indigent, and provision of work for the unemployed poor. In his *Causes of the Corruption of the Arts* he urged a complete, well-rounded education for young people, including girls.

Christian humanism influenced the court of Charles V to a considerable extent. A number of humanists, including Alfonso de Valdés (d. 1532), brother of Juan, were in the emperor's entourage and transmitted to him some of their religious ideas. These played no small part in making him critical of the Church under papal leadership. Spanish humanism, patronized by the rulers and shorn of its secular tendencies by the growing forces of the Catholic Reformation, adapted itself to this vigorous movement and to the character and interests of the Spanish people.

### French Humanism

Humanism did not gain a strong foothold in France until it received royal support during the last decade of the fifteenth century. Foremost among the French humanists was Guillaume Budé (1468–1540), who had studied in Italy and had brought home a scholarly interest in the classics and a superb skill in the use of both Latin and Greek. As the librarian of Francis I and in the interest of freeing learning from the influence of the scholastics, he urged the king to found and endow the royal college (1530), which later came to be known as the Collège de France.

Although Budé remained chiefly concerned with making the classics known to his countrymen and with harmonizing classical culture with a moderately reformed Catholicism, Jacques Lefèvre d'Étaples (Faber Stapulensis, 1455–1536) became deeply engrossed in religious matters and closely approximated the evangelical zeal of the Protestants. His long preoccupation with the revived Aristotelianism and Platonism of the Florentine humanists, medieval mysticism, the cabala, the natural philosophy of Raymond Lull (1225–1315), and the writings of the Church fathers culminated in a Christian humanism that found its greatest satisfaction in the study of the Bible. In 1509 he published his *Psalterium quintuplex* with its five different versions of the Latin psalms and a critical commentary. Three years later appeared his commentary on St. Paul's Epistles, in 1522 his commentary on the Gospels, and from 1523 to 1525 his French translations of the New Testament and the psalms, based on the Vulgate.

Like other Christian humanists, Lefèvre ignored the medieval commentaries on the Bible and turned to the study of the text itself, finding in its simplicity and humanity a satisfaction and joy that he imparted to many others, the common people as well as the scholars. His study of the Bible led him to the conclusion that man was not saved primarily by will, intelligence, and good works, but by mystical illumination, love, and faith in the grace of God. Luther used his commentaries in preparing his early university lectures.

Lefèvre's disciple, Guillaume Briçonnet (1470–1533), who became bishop of Meaux in 1516, further applied Christian humanism to the practical problems of his day. His mystical piety and interest in religious reforms had a profound effect upon the development of Protestantism in France. Among the Christian humanists whom he brought to Meaux were Gérard Roussel (d. 1550), Guillaume Farel (1489–1565), and Lefèvre. He appointed Lefèvre his vicar general to teach and establish discipline and piety among the clergy of his diocese. He also influenced his friend and disciple, Margaret d'Angoulême (1492–1549), sister of Francis I and wife of Duke Charles of Alençon and later of Henry d'Albret, king of Navarre. Despite her mystical and evangelical piety, as expressed in her *Mirror of a Sinful Soul,* and her support of Protestant refugees, she remained Catholic and was on good terms with the Catholic clergy. Although Lefèvre and Briçonnet were both eventually persecuted by the Sorbonne for their heretical inclinations, neither of them formally renounced Catholicism. The Sorbonne, the citadel of religious orthodoxy in France, recognized no distinction between Erasmian reforms and Lutheranism.

Among those French humanists who saw little value in attempting to reform the Church but made sport of it and of society as a whole, the best known was François Rabelais (1494–1553). In his coarse, satirical stories, written in French and eventually published under the title *The Inestimable Life of the Great Gargantua, Father of Pantagruel,* he gave free expression to his hatred of hypocrisy, traditions, and inherited institutions; his impatience with zealous Protestants as well as ascetic and indifferent Catholics; and his belief in the inherent goodness of man, freedom of thought, and man's ability to solve his problems by means of reason and common sense. He demonstrated his faith in science and medicine by devoting most of his time to them. His skeptical spirit remained alive in France throughout the religious wars of his century and came to full fruition in the Age of the Enlightenment.

## English Humanism

With the re-establishment of internal peace and security in England by Henry VII, Englishmen renewed their cultural contacts with Italy. William Grocyn (1446–1519) and Thomas Linacre (1460–1524), students at Oxford, visited Italy and studied the classics in the main centers of humanism. Upon their return they began to lecture at Oxford, where they aroused enthusiasm for the New Learning. Cambridge, where Erasmus lectured from 1510 to 1513, also came under the influence of the humanists and played its part in developing a new conception of life. William Caxton's printing press, set up at Westminster in 1477, played an important part in making the New Learning known to a broad reading public.

Christian humanism was best represented by John Colet (1467?–1519), who had attended the lectures of Grocyn and Linacre and had been attracted to the study of the Bible by Marsilio Ficino and Pico della Mirandola, with whom he had studied in Florence. He began his illustrious career as a teacher, lecturing on St. Paul's Epistles at Oxford. There he became the close friend of both More and Erasmus. In 1505 he became dean of St. Paul's Cathedral in London, where he gained considerable attention by explaining entire books of the Bible in his sermons. Like other Christian humanists, he always sought the direct meaning of the biblical texts; but he never questioned the authenticity of the Vulgate.

Upon the death of his father in 1510, Colet used all his considerable inheritance (his father had been the Lord Mayor of London) in refounding the famous school at St. Paul's. The school was attended by more than 150 boys, who were taught classical, biblical, and patristic literature. In a sermon at the opening of a convocation of English bishops in 1512, which was called to consider the extirpation of heresy, Colet insisted that a thorough reform of the Church and its clergy and a return to the purity of primitive Christianity should precede any attempt to enforce religious uniformity.

The most scintillating of the Oxford humanists was Sir Thomas More (1478–1535), also a disciple of Grocyn and Linacre and an intimate friend of Colet and Erasmus. Whereas he shared the enthusiasm of his friends for the New Learning and expressed interest in church reform, he devoted most of his thought and writing to political and social matters, with which he became familiar during an eventful legal and political career. Because he had served with distinction on foreign embassies and in Parliament, the king made him lord chancellor in 1529.

Drawing upon his own observations as well as upon classical and contemporary sources, More gave the intellectual world his conception of an ideal community by publishing his satire, the *Utopia* (1516). It was not translated into English until after his death. On the imaginary island of Utopia, which is described, all men lived in a state of political, economic, and social equality. They elected not only the representatives to their common assembly but also their king and local magistrates, whom they could remove if they threatened to become absolute. Believing that every citizen should be gainfully employed, he pictured a society in which the people worked for only six hours a day and devoted their leisure time to intellectual pursuits. The laws were administered equally and justly,

Sir Thomas More

*by Hans Holbein the Younger*

towns were planned to provide a beautiful and wholesome environment, education was open to all, and peace was maintained by means of a few simple treaties with the neighboring countries. The religion of the island, based on reason and nature, was deistic in its main features. A common public service was provided in which people of all shades of belief participated. As a matter of fact, religious differences were encouraged.

One must not conclude that the humanist religious ideas expressed in the *Utopia* reflected More's own deep convictions, for he remained a faithful Catholic with strong ascetic tendencies. Moreover, he defended Henry VIII in his quarrel with Luther over the Lord's Supper and as lord chancellor proceeded vigorously against the evangelical reformers. When the king broke with the papacy in 1532 and inaugurated his own reformation, More resigned. Because of his steadfast opposition to royal supremacy over the Church, he was finally beheaded in 1535. His *Utopia* was a literary product written for the humanists, not a revolutionary blueprint for the masses.

## Christian Humanism in Germany

The Germans were in touch with Italian humanism from its beginnings, largely because of their geographical proximity to Italy, their traditional political connections with that country, and their economic contacts with the great Italian commercial and industrial centers. The sons of wealthy German townsmen and the students of German universities were greatly impressed with the culture of the Italians and visited their centers of learning in growing numbers. The relative peace in Germany during the fifteenth century was conducive to the development of intellectual interests.

The German humanists became especially proficient in Greek and Hebrew, as well as in Latin. Many of them, influenced by the mysticism of the Rhenish region and the Low Countries, were attracted particularly to the Bible and became interested in re-establishing primitive Christianity. Because scholasticism had not permeated the German universities to the same extent as it had the University of Paris and other institutions of learning in western Europe, the humanists found less opposition there. Furthermore, the German humanists were sensitive to the criticism of the Italians, who had considered them crude barbarians, and were consequently inclined to examine their Germanic backgrounds for evidences of greatness. The *Annals* and *Germania* of Tacitus and the works of Caesar and Strabo gave them respectable classical sources for their romantic and nationalist utterances.

This feeling of incipient national loyalty was strengthened by a widespread demand for religious reform and the resentment of the Germans against the interference of the papacy in German affairs. Nonetheless,

German humanism still remained primarily concerned with its own intellectual interests, planned reforms by means of education only, and ultimately refused to identify itself with more popular movements.

Among the early humanists who were primarily concerned with spreading the gospel of the New Learning, the most typical was Rudolf Agricola (1444–1485), called the educator of Germany. Having received his early training at the famous school of the Brethren of the Common Life at Deventer, he continued his studies at Louvain and Paris. He then went to Italy, where he remained for a decade, gained an enviable reputation as a Greek scholar, and acquired an interest in the study of Hebrew. In 1482 he was called to lecture on rhetoric at the University of Heidelberg. He was partly responsible for making this university a prominent center of the New Learning.

A younger German humanist, Conrad Celtis (1459–1508), well illustrated the ambient character of the movement in its early stages. After studying at a number of universities in Germany and Italy, he devoted his life to winning converts to humanism. In 1487 he received the crown of poet laureate in Nürnberg. Then he went to the young University of Cracow in Poland, where he studied mathematics and astronomy and gathered about him young men of kindred spirit. He later taught at the University of Ingolstadt in Bavaria and finally settled down at the University of Vienna. There he established what was called the Danubian Sodality, a circle of humanists patterned after the Italian academies. He appealed to his many followers not only because of his literary ability, but also because of his intense patriotism. His *Germania Illustrata,* a historical description of Germany, was intended to arouse a sense of national loyalty among his countrymen. His *Noremberga* was a glowing account of the city of Nürnberg, one of the important German centers of humanism and art.

The best-known product of the school of the Brethren of the Common Life in Schlettstadt in Alsace was Jakob Wimpheling (1450–1528). Having completed his education in Heidelberg, he became a highly productive humanist reformer, historian, and pedagogue at the Latin school that he founded at Strassburg. He used his linguistic skill to arrive at a better understanding of the Bible and primitive Christianity. This in turn aroused in him a strong desire to reform the Church. As a historian he called the attention of the Germans to their past and struck a popular note in his objection to the flow of money from Germany to the papal *Curia.* As an educator he advocated a thorough classical training for all classes of people, an appreciation of the German language and traditions, and the practice of Christian virtues in the spirit of the *devotio moderna.* His writings, many of them printed in the form of pamphlets, circulated by the thousands throughout the German lands.

One of the most important centers of German humanism was the

University of Erfurt, where Luther studied as a young man. Its faculty had joined Cologne and Paris in demanding reforms during the conciliar period. Although Cologne later reverted to a strongly conservative position, Erfurt retained its interests in reform. Like other universities, it included in its curriculum lectures on "poetics," based on Aristotle. In these lectures students became familiar with the classical authors. There were also frequent references to them in the lectures on grammar and ethics. It is not strange, therefore, that the faculty was friendly to the wandering humanists who lectured and studied there. But when young radicals appeared who vigorously attacked scholasticism, the relations between the humanists and the theologians became strained. The outstanding leader of these radical humanists was Mutianus Rufus (Konrad Muth, 1471–1526), a canon at nearby Gotha.

Mutianus, or Mutian, became so engrossed in humanism after a sojourn in Italy that he embraced a mystical Platonic philosophy with strong heretical tendencies. Although he believed that historical Christianity was necessary for the masses, he felt that humanists should embrace his nobler conceptions. To this end he brought his followers at Gotha and Erfurt together into an esoteric circle, known as the *Mutianus ordo*. Veritable pilgrimages were made to Gotha and Erfurt, and a voluminous correspondence was carried on with humanists throughout Germany. In it was reflected the bitter hatred of this circle for scholasticism and the ecclesiastical hierarchy. Later in life Mutian seems to have repented of his radical humanism and devoted himself exclusively to the study of the Bible and the Church fathers.

## *Reuchlin*

Christian humanism in Germany was represented at its best in the life and work of Johannes Reuchlin (1455–1522). From the Brethren of the Common Life, under whom he had studied at Schlettstadt, he obtained his emphasis upon inner spirituality. At the University of Paris he embraced the current theological doctrines of the *via antiqua* with its emphasis upon a thorough acquaintance with the writings of Thomas Aquinas and the chief sources of Christianity, undergirded by an understanding of nature and society. At Paris, Freiburg, Basel, and Orleans he studied law, but also acquired such a thorough mastery of the Greek language that the Italians hailed him as the "transalpine Greek." As a lawyer, statesman, and educator at the court of the duke of Württemberg he became familiar with practical problems. And during his visits to Italy he absorbed the philosophy of the Platonic Academy.

Inspired by Marsilio Ficino and Pico della Mirandola, Reuchlin continued his study of Neoplatonism and became interested in the cabala. This interest, as well as his desire to read the books of the Old Testament in the original, led him to the study of Hebrew, of which he became the foremost Christian scholar in Europe.

It was Reuchlin's scholarly interest in the Hebrew writings that was responsible for his involvement in a bitter controversy that robbed him of the peace and quiet that he had hoped to enjoy after his retirement to private life in 1513. Conservative theologians were irritated by the fact that he and other laymen dared to criticize the conventional interpretation of Bible passages on the basis of a direct linguistic analysis. Furthermore, they objected to the heretical tendencies they found in the writings of many humanists. Added to this was a strong, persistent resentment of some Christians against the Jews as the people who had crucified Christ, as well as a widespread suspicion that scholars who had intellectual intercourse with Jews were tainted with heresy.

The conflict between the humanists and the conservative theologians became exceedingly bitter when Johannes Pfefferkorn, a Jew of Cologne who had renounced his Judaism for Christianity, published invidious pamphlets against the Jews. Apparently believing that they could easily be converted to Christianity if they were deprived of their Hebrew literature, desiring to gain the favor of the Church, and supported by the Dominicans at Cologne, he appealed to Emperor Maximilian in 1509 to have the Jews turn in all their books and to have these examined by Reuchlin, by Jakob von Hochstraten, prior of the Dominican Convent in Cologne and inquisitor general for the dioceses of Mainz, Trier, and Cologne, and by the universities of Mainz, Cologne, Heidelberg, and Erfurt. During the discussions that followed, Reuchlin, who disliked controversy, felt compelled to state forcefully that only openly blasphemous works, such as *The Generations of Jesus,* might be burned, and these only after they had been examined and condemned according to proper legal procedure. He vigorously defended the use of Jewish works on philosophy and science; the Talmud, which contained much of value to Christians; the cabala, which supported Christian theology; and biblical manuscripts, prayer books, and hymns in Hebrew.

Reuchlin's courage infuriated the conservatives. After the publication of venomous pamphlets on both sides, in which most of the educated people of Germany took a lively interest and several of them participated, Hochstraten cited Reuchlin to appear before his Court of the Inquisition to answer the charge of heresy. The latter refused and appealed to Pope Leo X, who remitted the case to a commission that met in Speyer in 1514, exonerated Reuchlin of heresy, and made Hochstraten pay the costs of the process.

Hochstraten, however, won to his side the influential papal confessor, Sylvester Prierias, who prevailed upon Leo to reopen the case. The pope, finally aware of the seriousness of the controversy, which had been intensified by Luther's attack on the sale of indulgences, in 1520 annulled the decision of the commission at Speyer, declared some of Reuchlin's views dangerous, compelled him to pay the costs of the trial, and condemned him to silence.

Reuchlin had meanwhile, in 1514, published the letters of some of his supporters under the title *Letters of Famous Men*. This title suggested to the members of Mutian's circle the title of one of the best-known satires of this period, the *Letters of Obscure Men*. The first edition, consisting of forty-one letters, appeared in 1515. Another series, containing sixty-two letters, appeared in 1517. The writers of these letters were supposedly the clerical opponents of Reuchlin, seeking advice and encouragement from a master at the University of Cologne. Writing in intentionally bad Latin and expressing themselves in inconceivably poor verse, and assuming such laugh-provoking names as Baldpate, Goose-preacher, and Manure-spreader, these alleged correspondents made the conservatives appear ignorant, pedantic, and vain. Throughout the letters appears the theme of the sanctimoniously immoral cleric who seeks advice in the most ludicrous situations. When it was reported that some of Hochstraten's followers believed these letters to be authentic, the laughter of the humanists knew no bounds. A stern papal bull forbidding the reading of the book only served to increase its popularity.

The authorship of the *Letters of Obscure Men* remained a secret and is still a controversial subject. It is generally agreed, however, that Crotus Rubeanus was responsible for most of the letters of the first edition and that Ulrich von Hutten (1488–1523) wrote most of the letters of the second.

## Ulrich von Hutten

Hutten deserves special mention because he was the most outspoken and forceful critic of the papacy, monasticism, and scholasticism among the German humanists and helped inflame the German spirit of nationality against the papacy at the beginning of the Reformation. As a member of a noble Franconian family belonging to the free imperial knights, he clung tenaciously to their love of freedom. Both his nationalism and love of freedom were accentuated by his study of humanism at Cologne, in the Erfurt Circle, Frankfurt on the Oder, and in Italy.

Driven by his wild passion to create a united Germany under the leadership of his emperor, and tortured by a frail body and the physical inflictions induced by syphilis, which was then spreading through Europe like a plague, Hutten lived an erratic existence. After obtaining a bachelor's degree at Frankfurt, he went to study law at Bologna but devoted his time partly to fighting in the armies of the emperor and partly to writing. In 1514 he returned to Erfurt. Then he engaged in a feud with the duke of Württemberg, which had begun over the murder of one of his cousins. This personal attack was later broadened to include a general literary attack upon the territorial princes, who were despised by most of the imperial knights as being responsible for their declining status. Meanwhile he returned to Italy, where he became proficient in Greek. In 1517 he was crowned poet laureate by Emperor Maximilian. Later he entered the service of Archbishop Albert of Mainz as a counselor, which position gave him an opportunity to study and write and become acquainted with many important literary and political personalities.

After Luther's defiant stand with respect to indulgences, Hutten came to the support of the Reformation, hoping to use this religious movement in support of his broader program of national reform. But he did not realize the basic differences between his humanism and Luther's theology and failed to enlist the services of the reformer. Later he joined forces with the imperial knights in their struggle against the territorial lords. When that conflict ended disastrously, he fled to Switzerland, where he died a miserable and lonely death.

The most important publications of Hutten are his edition of Lorenzo Valla's *Donation of Constantine* (1519), dedicated to Pope Leo X, and his bitter satires against the papacy, *The Roman Trinity* and *The Observers,* both of which appeared in 1520. *The Roman Trinity* is a dialogue in which the author summarizes by three's all his grievances against Rome. In *The Observers,* patterned after the satires of Lucian, he portrays two observers flying over Germany. They find conditions there greatly in need of reform and agree that the papacy is responsible for most of the evils.

Despite Hutten's many writings on the national theme, he never evolved a practical program of political or religious reform. His fearless and brilliant invective, like his life, served no visible positive ends. But his writings give us a clear conception of the dissatisfaction and conflicts, the vague dreams and aspirations, of the German people at the beginning of the sixteenth century.

## Erasmus of Rotterdam

Whereas Ulrich von Hutten reflected the romantic nationalism of northern humanism, Desiderius Erasmus of Rotterdam (1469?–1536) was in every respect a cosmopolitan, optimistically devoted to the restoration of the unity of Christendom. In his life and work the movement begun by the members of the Platonic Academy in Florence and continued by Reuchlin in Germany, Colet and More in England, and Lefèvre in France reached its highest stage of development. Based upon Stoic, Platonic, and Christian ethics, influenced by the mysticism of the Brethren of the Common Life, and strengthened by the writings of the Church fathers, the humanism of Erasmus laid particular emphasis upon the inwardness of religion, virtuous living, and moral social relationships.

Erasmus

*by Hans Holbein the Younger*

# 2. Religious and Intellectual Life

Erasmus was by general acclaim the prince of the humanists, who constituted, as it were, a large international literary sodality, or correspondence society. As the recognized leader of this fraternity, he exercised a strong influence upon virtually all the humanists, many of the reformers, and important political and religious leaders. No one was too proud to be delighted publicly with a letter from this literary colossus.

## *Early Life and Education*

Yet the beginnings of Erasmus were humble and obscure. We are not even certain of the date of his birth. In his earlier letters he indicated that he was born at Rotterdam in the province of Holland in 1469. But in later letters he tended to move the date back, even as far as 1466, the birth date of his older brother. He probably did this for the purpose of placing his illegitimate birth at a time prior to his father's ordination as a priest, thereby making it easier for him to obtain a papal dispensation legitimizing his birth.

The young Erasmus began his education in a private school at Gouda near Rotterdam, his father's parental home. But he was soon taken by his mother to the school of the Brethren of the Common Life at Deventer, where he remained about nine years. Although he was apparently not pleased with the kind of education that he received there, he obtained a thorough training in Latin. And toward the end of his schooling there his love for the great literary masterpieces of the ancient world was stimulated by an understanding humanist teacher and by a visit of Rudolf Agricola.

After the death of both his parents, Erasmus hoped to enter a university. But his guardians sent him to the seminary of the Brethren at Hertogenbosch, where he remained two years. Then, after the small estate of his father had been used up, he entered the monastery of the Augustinian Canons—not to be confused with the Augustinian Eremites—at Steyn, near Gouda. There he continued the reading of the classics and patristic literature. He was particularly impressed by Jerome because of his knowledge of the ancient literature and biblical languages and by Lorenzo Valla because of his intellectual attainments, critical attitude, and undogmatic Christianity. Meanwhile he also practiced the art of writing. He eventually developed a graceful, lucid, and flexible Latin style. Probably because his mother tongue, the Dutch, was not yet a literary vehicle, he was determined always to think, speak, and write in Latin.

Because of his literary ability and pleasing personality, Erasmus had little difficulty in obtaining the position of secretary to the bishop of Cambrai, in whose service he became acquainted with many leading personalities of his day. He was ordained a priest at Utrecht in 1492. Three years later the bishop permitted him to go to Paris to obtain the degree of bachelor of theology.

Erasmus matriculated at the university and took up his residence in Montaigu College, whose rule, patterned after that of the Brethren of the Common Life, was apparently too rigid and whose food was too meager for his delicate constitution. Consequently he lived for a while with some English students whom he was tutoring. Because his small income from the bishop did not suffice, he sought other patrons and students. Among these was William Blount, or Lord Mountjoy, who became the tutor of Prince Henry, later King Henry VIII of England.

Eager to obtain his degree, Erasmus devoted himself to the prescribed theological studies. The scholasticism taught at Paris at that time, however, was no longer concerned with the profound theological and metaphysical problems of the twelfth and thirteenth centuries but with those logical subtleties that had brought it into disrepute during the late Middle Ages. The discussions of such doctrines as the Immaculate Conception of Mary, popular in the Sorbonne at that time, made him contemptuous of the mental gymnastics of traditional theology. In his sermons and lectures, following his receipt of the degree in 1498, he emphasized personal piety rather than theology.

From the letters of Erasmus we learn that he experienced his first moments of unadulterated happiness on the first of his six or more visits to England. In 1499 he went there at the invitation of Lord Mountjoy, in whose country house at Greenwich he met young Thomas More and the children of Henry VII, including Prince Henry. In the autumn of that year he was at St. Mary's College at Oxford, where he met Colet. Colet urged him to stay at Oxford to lecture; but Erasmus, realizing his limitations, particularly in the use of Greek, decided to return to Paris for further study.

## Literary Works

When Erasmus was ready to resume his studies at Paris, he became ill and was advised by a physician to give up serious study for the time being. Therefore he turned to the pleasant task of reading widely in the Latin classics. While he was thus occupied, the thought occurred to him that he might render a valuable service to young scholars by culling from these authors their best quotations and publishing them, together with brief comments. Thus was born the first edition of his *Adages*, published in 1500. This book, which appeared in numerous editions to the year of his death, almost immediately established his fame. It was read and quoted by most of the educated people of the sixteenth century, including Luther. The many translations that were made into the vernacular languages of Europe made these bits of classical wisdom available to a broad reading public.

Erasmus further familiarized his contemporaries with the classics by publishing, in 1501, the first edition of Cicero's *De officiis.* But he also turned in earnest to the study of Greek and in 1506 published his translations of Euripides and Lucian. Most important, his determination to serve religion by dispelling ignorance, especially among laymen, led to the writing of his *Enchiridion,* or *Handbook of the Christian Knight,* published in 1503. This brief manual on Christian ethics gives expression to his basic theological orientation, his "philosophy of Jesus," as he called it. It is above all biblical, not scholastic, concentrating on God's plan of salvation and man's response to it. At the center is the crucified Christ, who draws man to God through the Holy Spirit. The Holy Spirit, given man at baptism, calls man to acts of piety and love. These, not traditions and forms, should determine man's conduct. Accordingly, the emphasis is on inner spirituality. There is no value in fasting, invoking the saints, going on pilgrimages, and buying indulgences. Piety and love are furthered by learning. Erasmus hated ignorance as much as Luther and Calvin hated sin.

In an abbey library near Louvain, Erasmus found a copy of Lorenzo Valla's *Annotationes ad Novum Testamentum,* which stimulated his interest in biblical studies and which he edited and published in 1505. When he returned to England that same year, John Colet encouraged him to make his first translation into Latin of the New Testament. During his third visit, while he was lecturing at Cambridge (1510–1513), he made a new translation, based upon four Greek manuscripts found in England, five found in Basel, and one loaned to him by Reuchlin. When his task was completed he went to Basel, where the printer Froben published this first edition of the *Novum Testamentum* in 1516. The second edition appeared in 1519 under the title *Novum instrumentum.* This included not only the Greek text, but Erasmus' Latin translation and notes. It was monumental evidence of his belief that the purification of the text of the Bible would greatly contribute to the purification of Christian life. Because the conservative theologians considered such a work a reflection upon the Vulgate of Jerome, however, Erasmus tactfully dedicated his volume to Pope Leo X, who, incidentally, commended it highly. It went through four further editions. Martin Luther used it in making his German translation of the New Testament.

During his third visit to England Erasmus wrote his *Praise of Folly,* his most widely read book. He wrote it in the home of Thomas More, while awaiting the arrival of his books from Italy and while suffering from a severe attack of lumbago. It was his intention to point out the evils and pet foibles of his day somewhat in the fashion of Lucian. Unlike the boisterous and crude authors of the *Letters of Obscure Men,* he hurled his shafts with a lightness and delicacy of touch, with a scintillating wit and kindly irony, that did not often miss the mark. Folly, the amiable woman who personified human weaknesses, should not be condemned but praised, he stated, for without her men would not marry and procreate, governments and other institutions would not survive, literature would not flourish, and the Church would lose its following. Drawing his illustrations from the classics, the pasquinades of the Italian humanists, and the satires of the Germans, and also from his own rich experience, he held them before his contemporaries as a mirror, inviting them to do away with outward formalities, to exercise moderation, and to live worthy Christian lives.

The *Praise of Folly* was followed by another, much shorter, satire, a dialogue called *Julius Excluded from Heaven,* written shortly after the death of Pope Julius II in 1513 and published anonymously in 1517. In it the "warrior pope" is pictured as swaggering before the gates of heaven but prevented from entering by his predecessor, St. Peter.

The success of this dialogue encouraged Erasmus to write others, published together under the title *Familiar Conversations*. He used as his framework for this remarkable collection the exercises written for his students in 1497. This manual of style was to be "useful not only for polishing a boy's speech but for building his character," as he stated on the title page. The dialogues, forty-eight in the final edition, constitute a mine of information concerning the life and times of Erasmus. Their style, dry humor, and brilliant thrust and parry still delight the reader.

By 1516 the writings of Erasmus had brought him to the pinnacle of his fame. Publishers eargerly sought his books and important persons sought his services. Money came from many sources, so that he no longer felt the pinch of poverty. Even Charles I, king of Spain and later emperor, recognized his talent, appointed him one of his counselors, and sent him to the University of Louvain to add to its reputation.

Erasmus wrote his *Education of a Christian Prince* (1516) for Charles and dedicated it to him. Unlike his well-known contemporary, Machiavelli, who in his *The Prince* and *Discourses* justified political expediency in the name of "state necessity," Erasmus followed Plato, Aristotle, and Thomas Aquinas in considering politics a branch of ethics and insisting that the prince should recognize his moral obligations to his people. His love for them, Erasmus maintained, should evince itself in the advancement of learning, the promotion of prosperity, and the preservation of peace.

In this practical guide for rulers, as in the *Julius Excluded from Heaven,* Erasmus gave forceful expression to his pacifism, in which he stood almost alone among his contemporaries. He agreed with Cicero that an unjust peace was preferable to a just war and that every attempt should be made to solve differences by arbitration. He repeated his views in a treatise called *The Complaint of Peace* (1517), translated into many vernacular languages and republished frequently to this day.

The hatred of Erasmus for all the pomp and ceremony of the princes at the expense of the people led him to make many attacks upon monarchy and to praise, upon occasion, the republican institutions of some of the European cities. In the *Beetle,* one of his adages, he castigated those rulers who rendered their people miserable by their haughty demeanor, ruthless ambitions, and disregard of justice. Yet he remained suspicious of the masses and agreed with Luther that the tyranny of the princes was a lesser evil than the anarchy of the mobs.

## Erasmus and Lutheranism

Erasmus was given an opportunity to defend his views in the conservative atmosphere of the University of Louvain in Brabant. He matriculated there as Master Erasmus, professor of sacred theology, in 1517, a few months before Europe was aroused by Luther's attack upon papal indulgences. His most serious encounter with the conservatives of the university arose in connection with the Lutheran movement. Almost at the outset Hochstraten identified him with the Wittenberg reformer, despite the fact that Erasmus remained tactfully neutral in the controversies between Luther and his enemies and repeatedly asserted that he had never read Luther's books. When the universities of Cologne and Louvain openly condemned Luther, Erasmus tried to save both the cause of learning and the life of Luther by urging upon both parties moderation and arbitration. He explained his wavering between the Scylla of Lutheranism and the Charybdis of Rome by admitting that he did not have the strength and courage required for martyrdom.

Because Erasmus was so constituted by nature and inclination that he could see the good and bad on both sides of an issue, even at a time when people were compelled to take sides in the religious controversies, he was condemned by influential persons in both camps. He continued to believe that truth could be attained only by the educated, whereas Luther taught that divine truth was imparted to the simplest believer by faith. The great humanist continued to respect tradition as the gradual unfolding of Divine Providence, whereas the great reformer believed that tradition had deviated from the truth and should be broken. The former placed his faith in human reason, the latter considered reason a stumbling block to faith.

Erasmus was infuriated by Ulrich von Hutten's attempt to activate the principles of humanism in which they both believed. He could not understand why Hutten, like Luther, would select one thing as the highest good and defy history and tradition to realize it. All tradition, religion, and learning, he believed, are part of a great whole, moving under the influence of God's will, and must therefore not be dealt with separately. Like the scholastics, he considered it disastrous to place reason and faith in juxtaposition.

# Part One: Europe on the Eve of the Reformation

When the papal nuncio Aleander was in the Low Countries, proceeding against the heretics there, he demanded in an interview with Erasmus that he recant the objectionable statements that he had made against the Church. Fearing that he would be apprehended as a heretic, Erasmus fled to Basel (1521). There he remained for nearly eight years, the longest period of time that he spent in one place.

## Last Years at Basel and Freiburg

In the more liberal atmosphere of Basel, Erasmus spent much of his time seeing his books through the presses of his intimate friends, the Frobens and Amerbachs. He gave particular attention at that time to the editing and translating of the writings of the Church fathers, of which thirty volumes appeared during his stay at Basel.

But the momentous events of the decade did not permit Erasmus to give his undivided attention to scholarly pursuits. He was immediately affected when the Zwinglian Reformation reached Basel. The reformers there, impatient with the conciliatory attitude of the city council, began a series of iconoclastic and other excesses. When they obtained complete control of the council, Erasmus feared that he would be identified with them. Consequently he moved to Freiburg in the Breisgau in 1529.

While continuing his altercations with the Lutherans, the Zwinglians, and the Catholics, he developed still further his own ideas of reform. True to his "philosophy of Jesus," he stressed the historical Jesus as opposed to the Jesus of the theologians; minimized, but did not deny, the veneration of the saints and the importance of the sacraments and other parts of the Church ritual; placed a strong emphasis upon Christian morality as opposed to formality; proposed and practiced scholarly and devout use of the Bible; and urged that all reforms be carried out by duly constituted secular authorities. Such a moderate program, however, pleased only a few and continued to irritate many on both sides. He was branded as a heretic at the Council of Trent, which convened nine years after his death, and some of his books were placed on the Index of Prohibited Books.

Although Erasmus was received with great honors at the University of Freiburg, was accorded every consideration by the inhabitants, and was honored by visits and letters from friends throughout Europe, his six years in this city were saddened by the constant threat of revolt and war and by the tragic fate that befell his friends More and Fisher in England: both of them had preferred death to submission to Henry VIII's religious policies. He worked as hard as ever, revising old books and writing new ones. Yet he preferred to return to Basel to spend his last days. He did so in the summer of 1535 and died in that city in June of the following year. The magnificent funeral given him was evidence of the esteem in which he was held by many of his contemporaries.

## Humanism and the Reformation

Although humanism was by no means identical with the Reformation and did not even lead directly to it, it did much to prepare the way. The most obvious contributions of the humanists were their philological techniques and experience, acquired in the study of the classics, and their interest in and publication of patristic literature and biblical texts. These in turn gave them a knowledge of primitive Christianity, which they readily contrasted with the Church of their own day. Many of them came to look upon the highly organized ecclesiastical hierarchy, the secular activities of the clergy, and the hair-splitting refinements of scholasticism as corruptions of Christianity. Thus they demanded reforms and urged that the Church return to the preaching of the simple gospel of Jesus and promote morality and peace.

Although Christian humanists continued to believe in a higher and a lower plane of morality, one for the clergy and one for the laity, they were aware of the gulf that separated the Christian and the natural man and sought to narrow it. They attempted to apply to the society of their day the ethics of the Sermon on the Mount, supplemented by the ethics of the Stoics. Their criticism of immorality among the clergy did much to intensify the dissatisfaction of Europeans with the Church.

Equally important was the emphasis of the Christian humanists upon the inwardness of religion, which led them to minimize such externals as images, liturgy, Church festivals, and even the sacraments. By emphasizing the importance of the study of Scripture, early Christian traditions, and the Church fathers, Erasmus anticipated basic emphases of Luther and Melanchthon. He exerted a considerable influence on Butzer, Capito, Zwingli, and some of the English reformers. But Erasmus himself declined to draw the consequences of his religious views, primarily because they would threaten the unity of Christendom. It was this concern, more than anything else, that separated him from the Protestant reformers.

Christian humanism as a predominantly intellectual movement could not present a common front or evoke a dynamic popular enthusiasm against the conservative and reactionary forces of that period of storm and stress. With but few exceptions, humanists remained aloof from the turmoil that accompanied the Reformation, preferred the contemplative life, and believed that they could best carry out their reforms within the framework of the traditional Church. Although there were strong religious elements in Italian as well as northern humanism, there was no one formula for binding together large numbers of people in a positive, dynamic religious movement.

Stressing the fundamental goodness of man and ignoring the Augustinian doctrine of original sin, the humanists remained fundamentally optimistic with respect to what could be accomplished by combining the study of the classics with that of Christianity. This attitude contrasted sharply with the Lutheran emphasis upon faith and the Calvinist emphasis upon predestination. Submerged throughout most of Europe by the tumult accompanying the Reformation, humanism appeared again in a new form in the movement of the Enlightenment, when the *philosophes,* basing their optimism to a large degree upon the scientific achievements of the sixteenth and seventeenth centuries, conjured up another "heavenly city."

# Part Two

# The Reformation in Germany

# 3

## Luther's Break with Rome

### Luther's Education and Early Religious Experiences

It was in Germany that the dissatisfaction and the unrest of the late Middle Ages reached such great heights that it led to a revolt against the papacy. This is not difficult to understand, for in the first place, the lack of political unity in Germany had enabled the papacy to exert a greater influence there than in other countries and to impose to a greater extent those financial exactions which aroused deep resentment among virtually all classes. In the second place, the search for religious satisfaction, for an answer to the common question "How can I be saved?" was stronger there than elsewhere and found expression in a serious criticism of the Church and its clergy for failing to provide that satisfaction. In the third place, there were in Germany large numbers of educated laymen, largely bourgeois in outlook, who became conscious of the restraints that inherited institutions, particularly those of the Church, placed upon them.

The resentments, and also the hopes, of the Germans were epitomized in the life and work of Martin Luther (1483–1546). Despite the apparently inexorable nature of the movements pointing toward the Reformation, it is difficult to imagine the German break with the papacy without the deep religious convictions and determined leadership of this man. When he took up the cause of religious reform, which had made little progress during the fifteenth century, the dissident elements in all classes looked upon him as their spokesman and hoped that he would help them solve all their problems: political, economic, and social, as well as religious. Not until a number of years had passed did it become clear to them that Luther's primary concern was a religious one and that he would reform society as a whole only by preaching the gospel and making man aware of his ethical responsibilities.

Despite the attempts of scholars to find explanations for Luther's role in history by examining his early life, they have disclosed nothing unusual except, perhaps, his constant preoccupation with religious matters. He was born in Eisleben, in the county of Mansfeld, November 10, 1483, the first child of a couple who had recently come to that town. He was baptized the next day, St. Martin's Day, and was named in honor of that saint. His mother, Margarethe, née Ziegler, came from a burgher family in Eisenach. His father, Hans, son of a Thuringian peasant of Möhra, became a miner. When it seemed that Eisleben would not offer sufficient opportunities to provide for his family, he moved to Mansfeld in 1484, where he became the successful lessee of several smelting furnaces and mining shafts. His importance in his community is shown by the fact that as early as 1491 he was chosen to represent his municipal quarter in the town council. By 1507 he was considered one of the outstanding citizens of Mansfeld. Far from being poor, as some biographers would have it, Hans Luther was able to provide Martin with an excellent education and buy him expensive books.

The religious education that Martin Luther received as a boy, both at home and in the Latin school of Mansfeld, contained nothing that could foreshadow his later activities as a reformer, for his parents and acquaintances were typical representatives of late-medieval Catholic piety. The available documents do not reveal that there was at Mansfeld any unusual criticism of the Church, such as was found in some other parts of Germany. Although Martin was taught that Christ was the judge who would weigh his deeds on Judgment Day, he had the characteristically medieval faith that his appeal to Mary, the apostles, and the saints as mediators would result in ultimate salvation. The current popular superstitions and beliefs in personal devils and witches must have stirred his youthful imagination and influenced him for many years; and he could not have been untouched by the then popular visits to religious shrines, even in his neighborhood.

Even though his parents employed the universally accepted pedagogical advice of Solomon not to spare the rod in rearing children, there is no indication that his early training by parents, clergymen, or teachers was exceptionally harsh for that day. His later criticisms of this training were made in the light of his new evangelical and humanist ideas concerning education.

The curriculum of studies at Mansfeld was like that of other late-me-

dieval schools. Martin was thus immediately introduced to the study of
Latin grammar and syntax, became familiar with the writings of a number of classical authors, especially the moralists, and was taught religion
and music to enable him to participate in the religious services of the
Church. However, because the schools of the smaller towns usually did
not offer instruction in composition (rhetoric) and logic, and because it
was customary for boys to complete their elementary education as wandering scholars, Luther was sent to Magdeburg in his fourteenth year,
undoubtedly to the cathedral school, where he was taught by members of
the Brethren of the Common Life.[1]

There is no reason to assume that Luther's teachers at Magdeburg
implanted any heretical notions in him during his year of study there. On
the contrary, the Brethren must have increased in him the Catholic piety
already instilled in him at Mansfeld, for they were known for their orthodoxy. They not only encouraged people to read devotional literature and
vernacular translations of the Bible but stressed the conscientious observance of all Church services. We know that the impressions made by the
elaborate processions and ceremonies of this city, the seat of an important
archbishopric, remained in Luther's memory the rest of his life. He was
particularly moved by the monastic piety and self-denial of Prince William of Anhalt-Zerbst, guardian of the Franciscan monastery, whom he
once saw trudging through the streets barefooted and carrying a heavy
burden on his back.

Luther completed his preparatory education in the beautiful Thuringian town of Eisenach, where he was sent in 1498. The fact that he had
numerous relatives and friends there must have weighed heavily among
the motives that prompted his father to select this town.

It is highly significant that Luther's environment in Eisenach was one
of traditional Catholic piety. In this town of about four thousand people,
nearly one out of every ten persons belonged to the clergy. The lad's fine
voice soon attracted the attention of Kuntz Cotta and his wife Ursula, a
highly respected and well-to-do burgher couple, who helped him in many
ways. Among his other benefactors were Heinrich Schalbe, with whom he
frequently had meals, and Johannes Braun, vicar of the church of St.
Mary, whose love for poetry and music represented broader cultural interests than Luther had previously experienced. Three years of pleasant
and stimulating life at Eisenach must have strengthened Luther's apparently natural inclinations toward religious interests. But he was also

[1] Luther stated in 1522 that he had gone to school with the *Nullbrüder*, the popular German designation for the members of the Brethren of the Common Life. Because the Brethren had no school in Magdeburg at that time, it is assumed that Luther attended the well-known cathedral school, at which some members of the
Brethren taught.

given a thorough medieval training in advanced grammar, rhetoric, and poetry, in which he excelled and which adequately prepared him for his studies at the university.

## Luther at Erfurt

Ambitious Hans Luther had accumulated enough of this world's goods to enable him to carry out his plan of sending his oldest son to the University of Erfurt in 1501 for the purpose of preparing him for a legal career. This university ranked highest in reputation among the German universities at the beginning of the sixteenth century, especially in the liberal arts and in law.[2] Virtually all of its students were required to live in closely supervised colleges (collegiae) or hostels (bursae). Luther lived in the college of St. George, where his activities were strictly regulated and where there prevailed a rigid monastic atmosphere. Because his father paid all his expenses, he did not find it necessary to accept charity or ecclesiastical benefices.

The city of Erfurt was the most important commercial center in Thuringia and, with its approximately twenty thousand inhabitants, ranked in size with such German cities as Lübeck, Strassburg, Danzig, and Nürnberg. Its aggressive burghers, who recognized the sovereignty of both the archbishop of Mainz and the Wettin dynasty of Saxony, not only had founded their own university but had demonstrated their piety by constructing so many churches and other religious edifices that the inhabitants called their city the little Rome. Almost every monastic order was represented. Such an environment apparently tended to increase Luther's medieval piety and respect for ecclesiastical institutions.

The curriculum of the university, likewise, was such that a young man with primarily religious leanings would be given every conceivable encouragement. But it is important to note that the faculty of philosophy was permeated with the nominalism of William of Ockham, the influential English Franciscan of the fourteenth century, and of his great disciple, Gabriel Biel (d. 1495). These "modern" theologians by no means denied Aristotle but merely opposed the followers of Thomas Aquinas, who emphasized the real existence of universal concepts outside the mind.

Luther called Ockham his "master" and accepted without question the scholastic teaching of his Erfurt professors. Thus he accepted the Aristotelian logic, metaphysics, ethics, and physics of his day and retained this cultural orientation even as a reformer, except where it conflicted

[2] The courses studied for the degree of bachelor of arts—usually obtained in eighteen months—included grammar, rhetoric, logic, physics, and philosophy. To obtain the master's degree, two more years of study were required. During this period the same subjects were taught on a higher level, and to them were added courses in mathematics—comprising the music, arithmetic, geometry, and astronomy of the quadrivium—metaphysics, and ethics.

Martin Luther

*by Lucas Cranach*

with his new theology. Like his fellow Ockhamists, he stressed the difference between reason and faith, insisting that the knowledge acquired by faith in revelation was not demonstrable by reason; but there is no indication that he went beyond this in his Erfurt days. He did not even take an interest in the antiecclesiastical attacks of Johann von Wesel (1400–1481), a former professor at Erfurt who was eventually condemned as a heretic, although Luther had read his nonheretical philosophical and theological works.

Because humanism did not take a firm hold in Erfurt until after Luther left the university and because, as he himself later stated, his heavy schedule did not allow him much time to hear the occasional special lectures on "the poets," one cannot assume that he became a devotee of the New Learning or was greatly influenced by it. To be sure, he enjoyed the classical authors, especially Virgil, Plautus, Cicero, and Livy, but as a student he seemed unaware of a conflict between the humanist and scholastic ideals.

Luther received the bachelor of arts degree at the beginning of the autumn term, 1502, ranking thirtieth in a class of fifty-seven. This degree entitled him to become a member of the teaching body at the university. While assisting in the teaching of grammar and logic, he continued his studies and at the end of the customary period passed the master's examination, ranking second in a group of seventeen candidates, in February, 1505. His proud father presented him with a copy of the *Corpus iuris civilis* and thereafter addressed him with the formal *you* (*Sie*), instead of the familiar *thou* (*Du*). Confident that his brilliant son would not be satisfied with remaining a poor *magister* but would follow a profitable legal career, he even planned a suitable marriage for him.

At the age of twenty-one, Luther seemed willing to accede to his father's wishes and, at the beginning of the summer semester, in May, 1505, registered as a student in the Faculty of Law. Apparently, however, he was unhappy with this choice; he must have wondered whether he should follow his religious inclinations, which had been furthered at every point in his education, or obey the wishes of his father. Whatever his reasoned solution to this problem might have been, it was an accident that led to his entrance into the monastery at Erfurt on July 17 of that year.

As Luther was returning to Erfurt from a visit to his home on July 2, 1505, he was thrown to the ground by a flash of lightning during a heavy thunderstorm near the village of Stotternheim, a few miles from Erfurt. Believing at that instant that he would die without the last sacrament, he called upon St. Anne and vowed that he would enter the monastery if he were spared from death. He immediately repented of this vow, but, certain that God had spoken to him in the storm, he was determined to bow to the divine will. Two weeks later he summoned his companions to a farewell dinner, on which occasion he announced his decision. The next day these friends accompanied him to the monastery and tearfully watched the gates close behind him. His father was infuriated when he learned of his son's decision and did not give his consent to the step until a plague had taken away two of his younger sons and a letter had reached him bearing the false report that Martin had also died.

## The Augustinian Eremites at Erfurt

The monastery that Luther had selected was the Augustinian order of Eremites. This order, founded in Italy in the thirteenth century, was particularly strong in Germany, where there were more than two hundred houses. About thirty of these, including the one at Erfurt, belonged to a separate branch or congregation called the Observantines, which followed the rigorous observance of the rule of the order as a consequence of a fifteenth-century reform movement. The vicar-general of the Observantines at the time of Luther's entry was Johann von Staupitz, a man of piety and understanding who tempered the rigid discipline of the order with kindness and thereby exerted a great influence upon the highly conscientious young Luther.

The Augustinian monastery at Erfurt was known throughout Germany not only for its exemplary life but for its emphasis upon learning. Its theological seminary—in which Luther was prepared for ordination as a priest and obtained the degrees of Bachelor of Theology, Master of the Sentences, and Licentiate—was connected with the University of Erfurt, where the Augustinian students heard a number of their lectures. Its scholasticism, like that of the university, was Ockhamistic, for both Staupitz, who visited the monastery frequently, and Johann Nathin of Neuenkirchen, professor of theology at the monastery, had studied under Gabriel Biel at the University of Tübingen. The writings of Biel, Pierre d'Ailly, and Ockham were diligently read by Luther until he could quote whole passages from them from memory.

Although the Augustinian Eremites bore the name of the great bishop of Hippo, they apparently knew little of his evangelical, experimental theology and followed the prevalent Neo-Pelagian tendencies [3] of the scholastics, stressing the necessity of man's working out his own salvation. Emphasis was placed upon God's sovereign will as well as man's freedom of will, which enables him to become good even without divine grace. The good work that man does merits divine grace by itself and thus earns him salvation. This philosophical bent in effect minimized the importance of Christ's suffering and death. In true nominalist fashion the Erfurt Augustinians also exalted faith above reason in arriving at reli-

[3] Pelagius, the well-known British monk and opponent of Augustine, maintained that man has complete freedom of the will to do good or evil. He also denied the presence of original sin and the doctrine of baptismal regeneration.

gious truth and accepted the absolute authority of the Church as the guardian of this truth. Whereas Luther ultimately rejected the nominalist doctrine of salvation after his study of Paul, he clung to its emphasis upon faith in opposition to the entire scholastic structure based on reason and eventually came to consider faith in the Bible sufficient for salvation.

Luther's professors and superiors also taught the usual scholastic respect for the Church, its sacraments, and its hierarchy. Although the early Christian conception of the Church as a mystic communion of believers, the "bride of Christ," through which the individual secured grace, was retained, the practical conception of the Church as a specific institution within which the priesthood dispensed grace in the sacraments gained the ascendancy. The pope alone, as the successor of Peter and the bishop of Rome, could grant authority to the rest of the hierarchy, thereby maintaining unity throughout the "body of Christ." Whereas Ockham and his followers of the fifteenth century questioned the absolute power of the pope, the Ockhamists at Erfurt during Luther's time seem to have been avowed papal supporters.

It was through the sacraments that the clergy maintained their spiritual authority over the people. By the middle of the fifteenth century the number of sacraments had been officially fixed at seven: baptism, confirmation, penance, the Eucharist (the conclusion of the ceremony of the Mass), extreme unction, marriage, and ordination (holy orders). Whereas Augustine and the early Church fathers defined the sacrament as an outward and visible sign of an inward and invisible grace, the sacramental rite eventually came to be looked upon as primarily an instrument for conveying spiritual grace, that is, for miraculously and intrinsically (*ex opere operato*) sanctifying the individual. The Ockhamist emphasis upon the spiritual character of the sacrament greatly influenced Luther's theological development.

Whether or not Luther was unusually concerned with the question of his own salvation when he entered the monastery, he soon made this concern the center of his studies and activities. This brilliant young master enthusiastically submitted himself to the training in humility prescribed for the novitiates and diligently read the "Bible with the red binding" that had been presented to him when he was taken into the monastery.

# Development of His Evangelical Theology

Despite the fact that Luther took his novitiate seriously, his concern over his salvation was not quieted by the "monastic baptism," that is, by his taking the vows in September, 1506, a step that was believed to carry with it the remission of both the guilt of and the punishment for sins. On the contrary, the more he thought about the enormity of his sins and the little that he could do to satisfy a righteous God, the less comfort he found in the traditional medieval scholasticism and the monastic methods for quieting a distressed conscience, and the more he was inclined to follow the advice of Staupitz to lay aside the theological commentaries and study the Bible. There he would find that God had promised to give God's righteousness to man in and through Christ Jesus, if only he would believe and trust in the promise.

In 1507 Luther was ordained a priest and on May 2 he celebrated his first Mass, an occasion that, according to his later utterances, caused him further distress. This distress was caused, first of all, by his strong sense of the importance of the rite and his feeling of complete unworthiness. In preparation for it he had studied Biel's *Canon of the Mass,* which had impressed him with the great responsibility of the priest who, if he correctly observed the details of the rite, miraculously created the body of Christ and gave the sinner God's forgiveness in remembrance of Christ's death on the cross. In the second place, he was greatly disturbed by his father's attitude toward his becoming a priest. Although his father had appeared at the meal given in honor of Luther's elevation to the priesthood and had presented the monastery with twenty gulden to defray the costs, he did not hesitate to state before the monastic dignitaries seated at the table that he did not believe that God had called Luther to enter the monastery. Furthermore, he pointed out that Scripture demanded that one should "honor one's father and mother." Luther firmly believed that he had followed God's will, but he never forgot his father's appeal to the Bible in opposition to the authority of the Church.

## His Inner Conflict

It was after his first celebration of the Mass that Luther began to have serious doubts concerning his own righteousness and the monastic life as the surest means for finding salvation. Endowed by nature with a sensitive conscience, intense emotions, an impetuous temper, a strong will, and a powerful intellect, he took his monastic life and studies much more seriously than the average monk. However, no matter how meticulously he observed the rigorous rule of his order and studied scholastic theology, he could find neither a "gracious God" nor absolute certainty with respect to his personal salvation by means of his "martyrdom," as he later called his experiences in the monastery.

Luther's difficulty did not lie in his failure to understand the teaching of the Church concerning the importance of faith, works, and grace, but in his inability to accept them and to believe with assurance that a righteous God would save him. When he examined his life, as he was required to do constantly as a monk, he found that he was not leading a perfect life of love for God; and when he pondered over this problem in terms of scholastic theology, he could not bow without question to the authority of the Church.

The crux of Luther's "martyrdom" was his conception of sin and the tendency to sin (concupiscence) as measured in the light of the perfection or righteousness of God. Despite his faithful use of the sacrament of penance, he was aware of his natural proclivities toward imperfect spiritual attitudes, such as pride and anger, and could not be certain that God as his stern judge would find enough merits, either his own or those of Christ and the saints, to save him from eternal damnation. Thus he came to fear and despise the words *law, justice,* and *righteousness.* Because of the emphasis of his day upon the performance of good works and the rendering of satisfaction in the sacrament of penance, he did not interpret God's righteousness as making him righteous through Christ Jesus, but rather as a standard for judging his own righteousness. This attitude of fear and uncertainty was accentuated by the Ockhamistic doctrine of predestination, which emphasized the omnipotence of God, and by the familiar picture of Christ sitting as a judge on a rainbow, with a lily protruding from one ear and a sword from the other.

Luther received temporary comfort in the monastery from his confessor, who explained to him that God commanded man to hope for salvation; from the mystic, evangelical works of St. Bernard and Gerson, which emphasized turning to God for help; and from the considerate Staupitz, who confessed his own failure to live a perfect life and urged him to think of Christ's death on the cross as an evidence of God's love toward a sinner. However, Luther was searching for absolute certainty that a righteous God would accept him, and this certainty he could not find until he had discarded the doctrine of merits and developed the emphasis of Paul upon God's righteousness as justifying man by faith. Meanwhile he devoted himself wholeheartedly to the increasingly numerous duties placed upon him.

## His First Lectures

In the autumn of 1508 Luther was sent to the Augustinian monastery at Wittenberg to continue his studies in theology and to lecture on Aristotle's *Ethics* in the newly founded university. Frederick the Wise, the elector of Ernestine Saxony, had, in 1502, obtained from Emperor Maximilian I a charter to found a university in his chief residential city, then numbering about three thousand inhabitants.[4] The relations between the Augustinian monastery and the university of Wittenberg were similar to those between the Augustinian monastery and the university at Erfurt. The Augustinian monks held the professorship of the Bible as well as the

---

[4] The university at Wittenberg was a territorial university, founded as a rival to that of Albertine Saxony at Leipzig.

lectureship in Aristotle's *Ethics;* and Staupitz, the vicar-general of the Augustinian Observantines, was the first dean of the faculty of theology. Luther, however, was much more interested in theology, "the queen of the sciences," than in philosophy and was gratified to receive the degree of bachelor of the Bible (*Baccalaureus biblicus*) in the spring of 1509, for this degree entitled him to lecture also on the Bible.

In the autumn, after a fruitful year of close contacts with Staupitz, Luther was transferred to Erfurt, where the theological faculty gave him the degree of *Sententiarius* and where he delivered lectures on theology for about two years. In preparation for these lectures he studied thoroughly not only the *Sentences* of Peter Lombard, but the works of William of Ockham, Gabriel Biel, Pierre d'Ailly, Duns Scotus, Hugo of St. Victor, St. Bernard, and the Church fathers, but especially the Bible. His marginal notes in some of these books reveal his critical attitude toward his sources, his Ockhamist emphasis upon faith as opposed to reason, and his leaning toward Augustine, although he had not yet accepted the latter's doctrine of "irresistible grace." Man, Luther still maintained, was free to choose between good and evil, and original sin was for him the absence of righteousness. Original sin involved (1) guilt (*culpa*), which was removed in baptism, and (2) lust (concupiscence), which remained as punishment.

Luther's faith in man's ability to merit salvation was further weakened by the shock that he received when he saw at first hand how secularized the papal *Curia* at Rome had become. He was sent, in the autumn of 1510, on a mission to the general of the Augustinian order at the Holy City as a representative of that group of Observantines which opposed a union of their section with the Conventuals, a step favored by Staupitz. Although the mission failed, Staupitz later gave up his plan and apparently held no grudge against Luther for having opposed him. The real significance of his brief sojourn in Rome lay in the fact that the future reformer visited the city, then consisting of about forty thousand inhabitants, when it was the center of the Italian Renaissance movement and when Julius II, its generous patron, was pope. He frequently referred to his search for religious satisfaction as a zealous pilgrim and his disappointment at finding secularism, formalism, and religious indifference everywhere. It is apparent that he did not find in Rome the certainty of salvation, the lack of which lay at the bottom of his religious anxieties.

After his return to Erfurt in the spring of 1511, he found the differences between him and the majority of the monks on the matter of union such that he was happy when Staupitz again sent him to Wittenberg. There he became subprior of the Augustinian monastery, preached to the monks in the chapel at the Black Cloister, and prepared himself for the degree of doctor of theology, which he received October 18, 1512. He then took the place of Staupitz on the theological faculty, lecturing on biblical literature.

## Discovery of Justification by Faith Alone

As an Ockhamist, Luther concentrated on the study of the Bible as the divinely inspired word of God, which he considered more important than all theological works. But he was bound by his doctoral oath to interpret it according to the authority and tradition of the Church. He lectured on the psalms from 1513 to 1515; on the Epistle to the Romans from 1515 to 1516; on Paul's letters to the Galatians, Hebrews, and Titus from 1516 to 1519; and again on the psalms in 1519. An examination of these lectures reveals that he was changing his method of exposition of the Bible. He gradually discarded the traditional fourfold interpretation of the scholastics—the literal, allegorical, tropological, and anagogical—for the newer grammatical-historical interpretation.

It was during the period in which he was giving these lectures that Luther clarified his views concerning the question of justification and began to develop the new evangelical theology that eventually brought him into conflict with the Church. He later stated that it was in the tower of the monastery at Wittenberg that he arrived at his illuminating interpretation of Romans 1:17: "For therein is the righteousness of God revealed from faith to faith: as it is written, The just shall live by faith." He clarified this passage in his exposition of Romans 3:24: "Being justified freely by his grace through the redemption that is in Christ Jesus." This highly significant discovery, which grew out of his own religious experience and theological study and which he found substantiated in the writings of St. Augustine, marked the turning point of his career. He called the discovery his entry into the "gates of paradise."

Like Paul, Luther conceived of God as the ultimate, absolute perfection and righteousness, and man, because of original sin, as imperfection and unrighteousness. Therefore he could not feel certain of salvation as long as he measured his merits by the standards of a righteous God and an exacting divine law. Unlike the scholastics, who interpreted righteousness or justice only in a legal, active sense, as God judging a sinner, Luther now interpreted it in an evangelical, passive sense, as God imputing righteousness to a believing sinner, that is, making man acceptable by constantly giving him the attributes of God. This, he maintained, was done by God's grace and mercy.

Luther, therefore, developed a new conception of grace that, he believed, did not operate magically and mechanically through the sacraments, but directly, as a constant, dynamic, ethical force in the individual, enabling him to combat sin—which is always present until death—and to fulfill the law, which requires righteousness. God had made this possible by sacrificing Christ on the cross.

# 3. Luther's Break with Rome

Luther's emphasis upon the omnipotence of God and the impotence of man is reflected in his doctrine that God draws man into fellowship freely, even giving him the power to believe. Thus he discarded the nominalist doctrine that God considers the works or merits of man acceptable and on the basis of these imputes righteousness to him through grace. Not even faith should be considered a merit. Luther thus accepted the doctrine of predestination but stated that the very fact that a man became concerned over his election was an indication that he had been elected.

The assurance that God would save the sinner, Luther now held, could be obtained by any Christian who in humility and resignation recognized that he was a sinner and believed in the unequivocal promise of the gospel. Living in a close fellowship with God, the believer would grow in faith and trust, regenerated by God's grace, so that he could fulfill the law and perform acts of love toward his fellow men.

It is interesting to observe how Luther gradually came to interpret the entire Bible in the sense of his Pauline conception of justification and how he found support for his views in the works of Augustine and Dionysius and the medieval mystics, St. Bernard, Master Eckhart, Tauler, and Gerson. He was particularly influenced by a book of an unknown author of the fourteenth-century circle of mystics in western Germany called *Friends of God*. He published a small part of this book in 1516 under the title *A Noble Spiritual Book,* and the entire work in 1518 under the title *A German Theology*. Both this book and the sermons of Tauler, a Dominican preacher who belonged to the same circle of mystics, contained a personal, experimental, evangelical element that appealed to Luther and to which he referred in showing the scholastic theologians that his doctrines were not new and revolutionary. Leaning heavily upon the letters of Paul and the Gospel of John, these mystics had opposed the intellectualism of the scholastics and stressed the impotence of man because of original sin, man's inability to merit forgiveness, and the necessity of believing and trusting in salvation in Christ. But they had not developed the Pauline doctrine of justification.

There is also evidence to indicate that Luther became acquainted with the writings of the Unity of the Czech Brethren, especially the widely known and controversial *Apologia* of their leader, Brother Lucas, printed in Nürnberg in 1511. Although Luther was impressed with the biblicism of this branch of the spiritual descendants of John Hus, he long retained the Saxon distrust of all things Czech and seems to have confused these Brethren with the Hussite Utraquists. Nonetheless, his views were similar enough to those of the Brethren that his opponents accused him of Hussite doctrines immediately after the publication of his Ninety-five Theses in 1517.

Luther also showed considerable interest in the New Learning. He

# Part Two: The Reformation in Germany

made use of the biblical scholarship of Valla, Pico, Lefèvre d'Étaples, Reuchlin, and Erasmus; joined the humanists of his day in their assaults upon scholasticism, sympathizing openly with Reuchlin in his conflict with the theologians of Cologne; shared their demands for reform; and enjoyed their support during the first critical years of his activities as a reformer. They even hailed him as "Eleutherius," the free man. He numbered among his close friends the Augustinian humanist Johann Lang, who became the prior of the monastery at Erfurt and later a professor at Wittenberg; Georg Spalatin, the chaplain, librarian, and private secretary of Frederick the Wise, as well as the tutor of his nephews; and Christoph Scheurl, professor of canon law at Wittenberg and later jurisconsult at Nürnberg. Despite these close associations with the humanists, he remained primarily a theologian and did not hesitate to break with them if they did not accept his new theology.

It is highly significant that Luther did not develop his conception of justification by faith alone solely in the quiet seclusion of his monastic cell but in an active life as a professor, a monastic vicar, and a city preacher. As a professor at the university at Wittenberg he fired his students with enthusiasm for those teachings which were beginning to attract increasing numbers to the new seat of learning. In their academic disputations, candidates for degrees brought these teachings out into the open and tested them in debates with those who clung to the traditional doctrines.

The chief attacks of Luther were directed against what he considered the obfuscation of theological truth by the scholastic use of Aristotle's philosophy, dialectics, and ethics. But he also attacked the nominalist doctrine concerning freedom of the will, which conflicted with his religious experience. Such attacks not only involved him in bitter disputes but gained for him close friends and supporters. Because his well-known colleagues on the faculty—Johann Lang (1488–1548), his tutor in Greek; Andreas von Carlstadt (c. 1480–1541), originally the head of the Thomist group; and Nicholas von Amsdorf (1483–1565), leader of the Wittenberg Scotists—soon gave him their approval and cooperation, his religious views made themselves felt throughout the university. Biblical-humanist studies were furthered, and courses connected with scholastic studies were dropped for lack of students.

Luther had an opportunity to carry his religious ideas into practice as an administrator in the Augustinian order. As subprior of the monastery at Wittenberg under the prior Wenceslaus Link, he shared administrative responsibilities, instructed the young monks with the assistance of Lang, and preached in the monastery chapel. In May, 1515, the order elected him district vicar, placing him in charge of the ten, later eleven, monasteries in Thuringia and Meissen. His heavy correspondence relative to monastic matters and his sermons to the monks breathe the spirit of the reformer who still respected all the inherited institutions and doctrines, but who demanded evidences of sincere religious life among the monks. He brought the monastery at Wittenberg such a good reputation that it had many more applicants for admission than it could accommodate, despite the fact that monastic life was in general losing its attraction for young men.

Luther's contacts with the world about him were greatly increased when, in 1515, the town council invited him to preach at the City Church as a substitute for the regular pastor, who was ill. In this position, which he retained for the rest of his life, he carried his religious ideas directly to the laity as he developed them, preaching sermons in which he brought the most difficult theological problems down to earth in a language that all could understand and thundered forth his demands for a reform in Christian life. It was especially in the confessional that he noted the evil effects of indulgences, the abuses of which he had for a number of years attacked in his sermons and disputations.

## The Indulgence Controversy

Nothing more clearly shows the concatenation of political and economic with religious affairs than the events leading to the indulgence controversy. The particular indulgence that aroused Luther's wrath was the plenary Jubilee Indulgence, inaugurated by Pope Julius II (1503–1513) to obtain funds for rebuilding the basilica of St. Peter's in Rome and, after considerable hesitation, revived by Leo X (1513–1521). By a special arrangement between the pope and the North-German princes, this indulgence had not been sold in their territories; but when Albert of Hohenzollern, the youngest brother of Elector Joachim of Brandenburg, needed money for procuring the archbishoprics of Mainz and Magdeburg and the bishopric of Halberstadt, an exception was made in these three ecclesiastical areas and in Brandenburg.

At the beginning of the sixteenth century the rivalry between the rulers of Brandenburg and electoral Saxony centered in Magdeburg, a well-fortified commercial city on the Elbe River. This archbishopric, which included the bishopric of Halberstadt, was the richest principality between the two electorates.

When, in the autumn of 1513, the archbishop of Magdeburg, brother of the elector of Saxony, died, the cathedral chapter of that archdiocese chose as the new incumbent Albert, then only twenty-three years of age. About the same time the chapter at Halberstadt made him acting bishop. The union of the two benefices in the person of Albert, not yet old enough to hold such offices, required a papal dispensation. This was obtained in Rome by the representatives of the interested parties, but at considerable expense.

The next year, when the archbishop of Mainz died, the chapter of that archdiocese was compelled to fill this vacancy for the third time in ten years. Because huge payments had been made to Rome in the first two instances, and because the chapter was already heavily in debt, it finally elected Albert, who was considered able to meet the financial costs involved in obtaining the office and who had promised personally to assume the expenditures involved in certain political exigencies.

The dispensation, the pallium, and the other expenditures involved in obtaining these ecclesiastical offices cost Albert a total of thirty-four thousand ducats, which amount was paid by the Fuggers. Pope Leo X agreed that only half of the income from the sale of indulgences should go into the papal treasury for rebuilding St. Peter's and that the other half should be retained by Albert and the Fuggers. Albert was made the chief commissary of the sales, with the right to appoint his subcommissaries. The official chosen for Magdeburg and Halberstadt was Johann Tetzel (d. 1519), prior of the Dominican monastery at Leipzig. He himself assumed the role of indulgence preacher, accompanied by Fugger agents and armed with the right to prohibit all religious functions that might interfere with his business.

Luther did not know about the details of the bargaining at Rome, but he was amazed at the secular tone of the papal bull and the instructions of Archbishop Albert. The purchase of indulgences, regulated by a scale according to the ability of the recipient to pay, would, it was made clear, (1) give plenary remission of sin as well as punishment of sin in purgatory, after absolution by a confessor of the sinner's own choice; (2) assure the purchasers and their departed relatives eternal participation in the merits of the saints of the Church without confession; and (3) obtain for the dead in purgatory plenary remission of all sins without confession or contrition, the usual provisions of the sacrament of penance. Although the official doctrines of the Church were repeated by Tetzel and other indulgence preachers as a matter of form, their enthusiasm led ignorant people to look upon the procedure as primarily a financial transaction. The mercenary character of these sermons was severely attacked by many conscientious Christians, including Tetzel's fellow Dominicans.

Luther, solicitous for the spiritual welfare of those under his care, noticed the bad effects of the indulgence traffic when Tetzel began to preach at Jüterbog and Zerbst, near Wittenberg and the boundary of Saxony. When he demanded of some of his parishioners that they mend their sinful ways, they confronted him with Tetzel's indulgences. Some even threatened to report him to the subcommissary, who had the right to cite for excommunication any person who refused to recognize Tetzel's indulgences.

# 3. Luther's Break with Rome

## *The Ninety-five Theses*

After thoughtful deliberation, Luther felt impelled to make an issue of the abuse of indulgences. For this reason he prepared his Ninety-five Theses, which he offered for academic discussion and debate. On October 31, 1517, the eve of All Saints' Day, when many pilgrims were gathering in Wittenberg to view Frederick the Wise's collection of relics [5] and to receive indulgences for so doing, Luther nailed these theses on the door of the Castle Church, the official bulletin board of the university. That it was his intention to offer them only for theological discussion and to warn churchmen of the dangers of the sale of indulgences, and not to arouse the public, can be gathered not only from his own statements but from the fact that he wrote the theses in Latin, not in German.

The Ninety-five Theses show Luther's respect for the sacraments, institutions, and offices of the Church. He came to the defense of the pope, whose authority he believed threatened by the exaggerated pretensions and huckstering attitude of the indulgence preachers, and sent copies of the theses to Archbishop Albert and Bishop Jerome of Brandenburg with letters explaining his action. For the most part he used a calm, academic style in attacking the worst features of the traffic. He stated in his first thesis that when Jesus Christ demanded that men repent (Matt. 4:17) "he willed the entire life of believers to be one of repentance." He restricted the significance and value of indulgences to symbolizing the Church's remission of ecclesiastical penalties and maintained that such remission of penalties could apply only to the living. There was, he stated, no such thing as a treasury of merits; the only true treasure consisted of the "holy gospel of the glory and grace of God." The climax of the theses was his vigorous criticism of the pope for not granting indulgences gratis, if he really had the power; for extracting money from the poor for rebuilding St. Peter's instead of using his own immense wealth.

Although Luther's theses did not constitute an unequivocal statement of his new theology, they reflected his own religious experience to a considerable extent. He drew a distinction between repentance (the attitude of a contrite sinner) and penance (the formal, sacramental act); and he affirmed that a truly penitent sinner did not attempt to escape punishment by indulgence but accepted it in humility and faith. Contrition, which he considered the most important part of the sacrament, resulted in forgiveness without indulgence. Therefore the sale of indulgences was leading people into a false security with respect to salvation, for it had to do only with the least important part of the sacrament of penance and therefore tended to weaken not only Christianity but papal and ecclesiastical authority.

[5] The collection comprised enough holy relics to provide indulgences for a total of 127,799 years and 116 days in purgatory.

Pope Leo X and Cardinals

*by Raphael*

If Luther expected the indulgence issue to remain on an academic level, he was greatly mistaken. Johann von Wesel (1400?–1481) had previously been condemned as a heretic for preaching against indulgences; and there was no reason why Luther should be permitted to make with impunity a similar attack, even though the indulgence theory had not yet hardened into a theological dogma. The Ninety-five Theses were soon translated into German, printed, and distributed widely, for the reading public liked their spirit as well as their contents. Luther was soon embroiled in a controversy that would permit no appeasement. Archbishop Albert immediately reported him to Rome, demanding for him a *processus inhibitorius*. But Leo X, considering the controversy merely a monastic quarrel between the Augustinians and the Dominicans, refused to intervene. Tetzel, however, won the support of the Saxon chapter of his order, which, in January, 1518, sent a formal denunciation of Luther to the papal *Curia* and won to its side influential persons close to the pope.

Meanwhile Luther's enemies did not hesitate to brand him as a heretic. Dr. Johann von Eck (1486–1543), professor of theology and chancellor at the Bavarian university at Ingolstadt, and onetime friend of Luther, called him a Bohemian, referring to the similarity of his views with those of John Hus. Sylvester Cardinal Prierias (Silvestro Mazzolini), the Dominican theological adviser of Leo X and censor of books, who had played a leading role in the trial of Reuchlin, likewise accused him of heresy. Luther answered these accusations by publishing his carefully prepared *Resolutions Concerning the Virtue of Indulgences* (1518), an explanation of the Ninety-five Theses that he dedicated to the pope, for he still believed that Tetzel's abuses were perpetrated without the approval of the Roman *Curia*. Although he stated that he held no views contrary to the Bible, the fathers, and the Church, he intimated that popes and even church councils could err and laid greater stress than before on the gospel as the Christian's greatest treasure.

When the sale of indulgences virtually ceased, Leo X felt impelled to act. He first sought to exert pressure upon Luther through the Augustinian order. Luther was accordingly called before the council of the general chapter of the Saxon province at Heidelberg. The Heidelberg Disputation of April 26, 1518, gave him an opportunity to make a spirited defense of his new theology, to attack the doctrine of the freedom of the will and Aristotle's reign in theology, and to express a defiant refusal to recant his views. His courageous stand won him many friends among those who had come to hear him, including Martin Bucer, who later played a conspicuous role as a reformer.

Convinced of the correctness of his position and still hopeful that the pope and other high officials of the Church would grasp the significance of his religious views as applied particularly to the indulgences, Luther sent Leo a copy of his *Resolutions*, together with a letter in which he denied the accusations of his enemies, appealed to his right as a professor of theology freely to discuss religious matters, and reaffirmed his obedience to the Church and the pope as the "minister and servant of the keys." Meanwhile, however, the Dominicans had succeeded in inducing the pope to demand his appearance in Rome within sixty days as a suspect of heresy. On August 7, 1518, Luther received the summons, with a copy of "A Dialogue Against the Presumptuous Conclusions of Martin Luther," written by Prierias. The cardinal accused Luther of heresy in injudicious and haughty words and stated that, because of the absolute and infallible power of the pope, it was not necessary to reason with a heretic.

The next day Luther requested that Elector Frederick the Wise intervene, thereby recognizing that the indulgence controversy had become so complicated politically and ecclesiastically that he was in need of expert secular assistance. It was immaterial to him what happened to his own person—though he did not seek martyrdom—but he was determined to save the cause whose champion he had become. That it was not fear that prompted him to take this step can be inferred from his firm answer to Prierias and the bold stand that he took in his *Sermon on the Validity of Excommunication,* delivered in May and published in August. In this sermon he argued that true Christians are spiritually bound together by faith, hope, and love as well as externally in the sacraments and other rites of the Church; that a Christian is excommunicated spiritually only by God because of sin; and that excommunication by the Church deprives him only of external communion and may be just or unjust. If the Christian is excommunicated unjustly for a righteous cause, he must suffer the injustice in the hope that God will save him.

## Hearings Before Cajetan

Knowing that a hearing in Rome would lead to death or life imprisonment, Luther wished to be heard on German soil. Frederick, who would have preferred to have his popular professor compromise with the ecclesiastical authorities, nonetheless acceded to his request and made arrangements at the imperial diet assembled at Augsburg to have the papal legate Cajetan give him a hearing in that city.

Cardinal Cajetan (Thomas de Vio), the general of the Dominican order, was the most learned theologian at the Roman *Curia* and probably realized that Luther's doctrine on the indulgences was not in a strict sense heretical. For this reason he seemed to treat Luther's case primarily as a matter of discipline and with an eye to the delicate political situation confronting the papacy in Germany. Emperor Maximilian was feeble and ill. People with political interests at stake were consequently concerned about the problem of a successor. Therefore, even though the papal prosecution of the "notorious heretic and schismatic" had begun in earnest and three papal writs were on the way to Cajetan, Frederick the

Wise, and the provincial head of the Augustinian order in Saxony, demanding that the "son of perdition" be immediately seized, Cajetan agreed to receive Luther and to attempt to gain a retraction.

The Elector Frederick had obtained this concession from Cajetan because the latter realized that even though Emperor Maximilian had voiced the Dominican condemnation of Luther, the territorial princes at the Diet of Augsburg, which had closed September 23, 1518, were in no mood to follow his commands unquestioningly. He had also sensed the antipapal spirit of the representatives who had once more disapproved of the heavy flow of German money into the papal treasury. Moreover, all but Frederick the Wise and the elector of Trier had agreed to choose Maximilian's grandson, Charles I of Spain, as his successor. If Charles should become emperor, the balance of power in Italy, as well as in Europe, would be upset and the pope's political influence greatly weakened. Therefore Cajetan was disposed to winning over Frederick, first in the matter of putting down the heresy and then in the matter of the imperial election.

Luther was totally unaware of the complicated political maneuvers or of the disposition of Cajetan to be conciliatory. He therefore expected to be tried for heresy and burned at the stake. He arrived at Augsburg on foot October 7; but he did not appear before Cajetan until the 12th, a day after he had been given a letter of safe conduct by the emperor. As at Heidelberg, he was here looked upon as a hero by many prominent persons. Conrad Peutinger, an influential patrician and humanist, entertained him with a dinner.

Thus encouraged, Luther attended three hearings before Cajetan from October 12 to 14. The cardinal tried to disarm him with friendliness and to induce him to revoke without discussion his doctrines concerning the sacrament of penance and the treasury of merits as expressed in his seventh and fifty-eighth theses, respectively. But Luther, no matter how humbly he appeared before the great churchman and how willing he was to be taught by the great scholar, would not retract without being shown by reason on the authority of Scripture, the Church fathers, and papal decrees that he was in error. Therefore he could not accept the Thomistic doctrine of penance, even though it was affirmed by Leo X.

Cajetan could not, as the representative of papal absolutism and a staunch defender of the *via antiqua,* make any concessions to Luther, even if he had so desired, and Luther could not budge one step from his doctrine of justification by faith alone and was greatly disappointed that Cajetan with all his learning failed to understand those deep religious questions that had originally led him to his new theological views. The exchange of diametrically opposite views ultimately led to heated words and an impasse that no further discussion could resolve. Luther went so far as to assert that the Council of Basel had been correct in maintaining that the pope could err and that he could not accept Pope Clement VI's bull *Unigenitus* of 1343 with its definition of the treasury of merits because it was contrary to Scripture.

Luther, after the third hearing, made another attempt to have his case tried by an impartial court in his appellation, "From the Pope Badly Informed to the Pope to Be Better Informed," repeating that he was willing to bow to well-reasoned arguments drawn from the Bible. On the night of October 20–21 he slipped out of the city on a horse provided him by a canon of the cathedral.

In Nürnberg, on his way home, Luther first saw a copy of the papal brief of August 23, 1518, in which the pope had declared him a notorious heretic and had instructed Cajetan how to deal with him. Although he could not believe that the brief had been written by Leo, he no longer felt that the pope would be an impartial judge. Consequently, after his return to Wittenberg on the first anniversary of his nailing of the theses on the door of the Castle Church, he began to prepare for publication his *Acta Augustana,* or the proceedings of his hearings at Augsburg. Then he wrote his daring appeal, requesting that a general Church council hear his case. He completed this appeal on November 28. It was published December 11, without Luther's consent and against the wishes of the elector, who still believed that he could arrange a fair hearing by other means. Although such an appeal had been condemned as heretical by Pius II in his bull *Execrabilis* of 1460, Luther based his use of it upon the conciliar theories developed in the fifteenth century and still supported by several theologians at the University of Paris. Expecting excommunication and forceful arrest at any time, and not willing to involve his elector in a difficult dilemma, Luther seriously considered fleeing to France and placing himself under the protection of Francis I and the University of Paris.

Frederick, however, had no intention of withdrawing his protection from Luther, even though the pope had published for circulation throughout Germany Cajetan's statement concerning indulgences as an official condemnation of Luther's doctrines and even though the cardinal had written the elector a letter warning him of the dire consequences of his support of Luther. In his answer to Cajetan, on December 8, he absolutely refused to deliver Luther to the pope, stating that if the professor had been proved guilty of heresy by an impartial judge or council, he himself would have proceeded against him. Luther was overjoyed at the elector's outspoken support of his cause and decided to remain in Wittenberg, at least until the pope had excommunicated him.

## The Mission of Miltitz

Frederick's belief that Luther's case might be solved without the latter's departure from Wittenberg was well justified by subsequent events. The pope, having learned that Emperor Maximilian I lay seriously ill, probably on his deathbed, dispatched Karl von Miltitz, a Saxon noble-man active in the Roman *Curia* as papal chamberlain and secretary, to Frederick the Wise to gain the latter's good will by presenting him, through Cardinal Legate Cajetan, with the golden rose [6] and papal bulls pertaining to the enlargement of his collection of relics. But the overly ambitious Miltitz exceeded his commission, which was merely to report to Cajetan and the pope on the possibility of inducing Luther to retract or the elector to surrender him to Rome. Having learned from the elector at Altenburg that it would be futile to proceed along these lines, Miltitz arranged to deal directly with Luther.

Luther thoroughly understood the man with whom he had the inter-views in Spalatin's home below the castle in Altenburg from January 4 to 6, 1519. Yet he treated him respectfully and eventually promised that he would refrain from further attacks upon his adversaries, if they would do likewise; write humbly to the pope, stating that he had not wished to harm the Church; urge the people publicly to remain loyal to the Church; and submit his case to the archbishop of Salzburg. However, Luther's letter of submission to the pope contained such strong statements in defense of his actions that the nuncio submitted to the pope in its stead a highly distorted account of the interviews. The pope, having been led to believe that Luther was sorry for his heretical statements and could be induced to retract, was happy to believe the best and to welcome back into the arms of the Church his "beloved son," the erstwhile "son of perdition." What would have happened to Miltitz if his trickery had become known will remain a mystery. This and all other problems related to the indulgence controversy were suddenly overshadowed by the death of Emperor Maximilian on January 12, 1519.

## The Election of Charles V and His Dynastic Politics

Maximilian died before the electors could assemble at Frankfurt and choose his grandson Charles his successor, as five of the seven had agreed to do at the Diet of Augsburg the previous year. Therefore the question of succession was again open. Although such an election had been of relatively little European significance in the fifteenth century, it aroused the interest of everyone in 1519, for Germany, like Italy, had become an important factor in the rivalry among the rising territorial states of Europe and the papacy.

It is highly significant evidence of the change in international affairs that the three young rulers who as contemporaries dominated the Euro-

[6] The golden rose, blessed by the pope on the fourth Sunday in Lent, was a highly prized possession, for it was given to but one ruler annually for outstanding service to the Church.

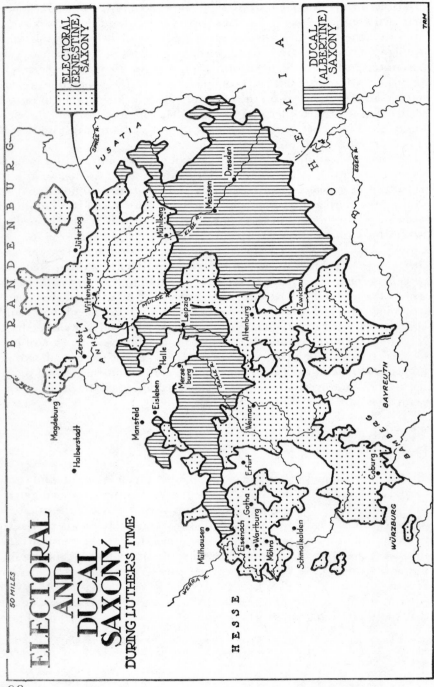

ELECTORAL AND DUCAL SAXONY
DURING LUTHER'S TIME

50 MILES

ELECTORAL (ERNESTINE) SAXONY

DUCAL (ALBERTINE) SAXONY

BRANDENBURG

LUSATIA

SPREE R.

BOHEMIA

EGER R.

Jüterbog

Zerbst

ANHALT

Magdeburg

Halberstadt

Mansfeld

Eisleben

Wittenberg

Mühlberg

ELBE R.

Meissen

Dresden

MULDE R.

Leipzig

Altenburg

Zwickau

Halle

Merseburg

SAALE R.

Weimar

BAYREUTH

BAMBERG

Coburg

Erfurt

Gotha

Eisenach

Wartburg

Möhra

Schmalkalden

Mühlhausen

WERRA R.

HESSE

WÜRZBURG

TRM

98

pean political scene during the first half of the sixteenth century—
Charles I of Spain (1516–1556), Francis I of France (1515–1547), and
Henry VIII of England (1509–1547)—were candidates for the imperial
crown. The crown of itself had little more to offer than prestige, but the
possession of it might be instrumental in determining which ruling house
should dominate Europe.

Although both the Empire and the papacy had long receded to the
background in the European political scene, the two heads of medieval
Christendom might still play significant roles. The pope was concerned
not only with the problem of a threatening Lutheran heresy, which
might weaken or destroy his religious authority, but with his political autonomy and security in Italy. Although Henry VIII's candidacy was not
taken seriously, the rivalry between Charles I and Francis I became intense, for both had strong support. Therefore the pope was compelled either to choose between the Spanish king, who was also the king of Naples, or the French king, who was also the ruler of Milan, or to support a
third candidate. As we have seen, he long supported the candidacy of
Francis after the battle of Marignano. But he began to fear the growing
power of Francis and consequently switched his support to Frederick the
Wise, to whom he suggested that he could make "any personal friend" a
cardinal and endow him with an archbishopric. Although Frederick realized that a strong German prince could as emperor make Germany a
powerful political force, he realized his limitations and refused to be a
candidate.

The electors thus had to choose between Francis and Charles. Few of
them seemed seriously concerned with the fate of Germany as a whole.
Their chief interest was to maintain their "liberties" as individual territorial lords. Therefore they took personal advantage of the huge bribes
offered them by the two rivals,[7] and finally decided against Francis. On
June 28, 1519, they unanimously elected Charles. They felt that the
grandson of Maximilian had enough German blood to satisfy the romantic national sentiment aroused during the latter's reign and would guar-
antee their cherished privileges. As a matter of fact, they compelled
Charles to restore both the imperial supreme court (*Reichskammergericht*) and the imperial council of regency (*Reichsregiment*), both
of which had been created by Maximilian but had been discontinued; to
use German and Latin as the official languages of the Empire; to hold all
meetings of the imperial diet in Germany; to give imperial positions only
to Germans; to permit the diet to determine whether or not foreign
troops were to be used in the imperial army; and to place the imperial

[7] The election costs amounted to nearly 900,000 gold guldens, of which approximately a half went to the electors and their assistants in the form of bribes. The fact
that the Fuggers and the Welsers loaned Charles more than 500,000 guldens for
bribes had much to do with his election.

government in the hands of the council of regency during the emperor's absence. The humanists and the romantic German patriots expected much from Charles, the "noble blood from the house of Austria."

With the unanimous election of Charles—he was crowned king at Aachen in 1520 and emperor in Bologna in 1530—the balance of power of Europe was tilted in favor of the Hapsburgs, and the French were encircled and placed on the defensive. Moreover, the papacy, as an ecclesiastical and Italian power, was compelled to come to terms with an emperor who could act independently. But Charles, obsessed with the desire of creating a great universal dynastic empire strongly supported by Catholic Christianity, used up his energies and resources in his opposition to the rise of Protestantism and in his pursuit of territorial ambitions, mingling as a typical Hapsburg the chivalric spirit of the Middle Ages with the shrewd statecraft of his century.

It is not surprising that Charles was motivated by dynastic ambitions, for Maximilian, the "royal matchmaker," had been eminently successful in bringing the Hapsburgs into control of much of Europe and, eventually, of the New World. Maximilian himself had married Mary, daughter of Charles the Bold of Burgundy. Their son Philip had inherited the Hapsburg possessions as well as the Burgundian lands. His marriage to Joanna of Castile, daughter of Ferdinand and Isabella, was blessed with six gifted children, all of whom became important figures in European politics: Eleanore, queen of Portugal and later queen of France; Charles, archduke of Austria, duke of Burgundy, king of Spain, and emperor; Isabella, queen of Denmark; Ferdinand, archduke of Austria, king of Germany, and finally emperor; Mary, queen of Hungary and later regent of the Low Countries; and Catherine, queen of Portugal.

Charles, the older son, was born in Ghent in 1500 and spent his youth in the Low Countries, where he not only learned French as his "mother tongue" but absorbed the brilliant culture of the Burgundian court and acquired training in the Burgundian diplomacy, which was at that time concerned with maintaining peaceful relations with both England and France. He was raised by his aunt Margaret, regent of Burgundy after his father's death; Chièvres, later his chief minister; and Adrian of Utrecht, later Pope Adrian VI.

## Charles as Ruler

Elected emperor at the age of nineteen, Charles approached his multitudinous tasks with youthful vigor, dogged persistence, and exceptional ability, and developed his plan for establishing a dynastic empire that would make him not only the guardian of the peace of all Europe but the political champion of a universal church reformed along Erasmian lines. But the obligations placed upon him in what amounted to a personal government were so great and the problems of a rapidly changing

60898

political world were so complex that he failed to carry to a successful conclusion his grandiose plans. Although he dominated the political scene through much of the first half of the sixteenth century, he eventually recognized his failure, abdicated in 1556, and withdrew to his imperial villa near the monastery of San Yuste in Spain.

As duke of Burgundy,[8] he originally attempted to make this wealthy region with its population of approximately three million the center of his dynastic empire. Although he consolidated his control over the provincial assemblies and autonomous communes by strengthening the federal institutions and retained his capable aunt Margaret as regent, or stadholder (1507–1530),[9] the Low Countries pursued a relatively autonomous course and refused to be used for imperial ends against their own interests.

Greater success attended Charles' efforts in Spain, even though the Spaniards at first considered him a foreigner and resented the fact that he did not speak their tongue and brought with him, in 1517, the year after his election as king, his Flemish advisers. Realizing that he would need Spanish support for his dynastic politics, he increased the royal control over the various parts of the country by a firm but tactful policy. He showed his affection for the people by learning their language and devoting much of his time to the development of their government. He even followed their wishes in marrying Isabella, the sister of the king of Portugal. Under his rule the Spanish army became the best in its day, the Spanish colonial empire was organized to produce considerable wealth, cordial relations were maintained with the Church, and general internal peace and security prevailed.

Charles gave little personal attention to the Hapsburg possessions. These comprised Austria, Styria, Carinthia, and Carniola. He placed the administration of these lands in the hands of his brother Ferdinand in 1521. When King Louis II of Bohemia and Hungary died in 1526, Ferdinand gained control of these lands with his sister Mary as the widowed queen and assumed the most pressing obligation as the ruler of these eastern countries, namely, stemming the advance of the Ottoman Turks into Europe. Because the estates of these lands provided little revenue for imperial purposes, Ferdinand was constantly compelled to seek money and other assistance from Charles to enable him to fulfill his functions as archduke of Austria.

The Ottoman Turks, who had consolidated their control over Constantinople and the Balkan provinces and had added Syria, Arabia, and

[8] The Burgundian lands comprised the Free County of Burgundy (Franche-Comté), Luxemburg, Flanders, Brabant, Holland, and smaller provinces. By adding Friesland and other territories he rounded out his Burgundian possessions to consist of seventeen provinces.

[9] Margaret was replaced at her death by Charles' sister Mary, the widowed queen of Hungary, who remained regent to 1555.

*101*

Egypt to their empire by the end of the fifteenth century, were brought to the height of their power by Suleiman the Magnificent (1520–1566), who had become sultan the same year that Charles was crowned king at Aachen. By his seizure of Belgrade, the gateway to Hungary and the Hapsburg lands, in 1521, and of the Island of Rhodes, in 1522, Suleiman came into conflict with Charles both along the Danube and in the Mediterranean. The Turkish victory at Mohács over King Louis II of Hungary, who was drowned while fleeing from the battle, was followed by the siege of Vienna in 1529. When the siege failed, Suleiman gave up his plan to penetrate the heart of Europe and devoted himself to subjugating Hungary. This proved troublesome and costly, for Ferdinand, with the support of several Magyar nobles, continued to dispute his control of that land.

Charles was also involved in the complicated politics of Italy. As Spanish king he was the ruler of Naples, Sicily, and Sardinia, and as emperor he inherited the claim to the duchy of Milan, a fief of the Empire, lost to France at the battle of Marignano in 1515.

### The Hapsburg-Valois Rivalry

The chief political concern of Charles was the determination of Francis I to prevent the encirclement of France by the Hapsburgs and to establish the hegemony of the Valois dynasty in Europe. This Hapsburg-Valois rivalry persisted throughout the reign of these two monarchs and was not concluded until the Peace of Cateau-Cambrésis in 1559. The first phase of this rivalry kept Charles out of Germany for about a decade.

The chief lands in dispute between the two dynasties were Navarre, which Francis claimed, but part of which had been seized by Ferdinand of Spain; Cerdagne and Roussillon on the border of Aragon, which Charles wanted to incorporate in his kingdom; Flanders and Artois, to which Francis laid feudal claim; the duchy of Burgundy, which had been taken from Mary of Burgundy by Louis XI and which Charles wished to regain; the kingdom of Naples, which Francis claimed as heir to the house of Anjou; and Milan, which Charles desired to secure the connections between Spain, Italy, and Germany.

Hostilities broke out when a French army invaded Navarre and took Pamplona in 1521, only to be driven back into France. The next year Pope Adrian VI (1522–1523), the former tutor of Charles, joined with Venice and the imperial army to retake Milan. Finally the French were decisively defeated at Pavia in 1525. Francis was taken prisoner and sent to Madrid, where he was kept prisoner until he signed the Treaty of Madrid (1526), by which he agreed to give up Burgundy, Flanders, Artois, and Tournai and to marry Charles' sister Eleanore.

Once back in France, the French king repudiated the treaty, even though his sons had been left in Madrid as hostages, and resumed the war. Fearing the ambitions of the successful Charles, Pope Clement VII (1523–1534), the city-states of Venice and Florence, and the duke of Milan, whom Charles had given the duchy as an imperial fief, joined France in the defensive League of Cognac. Charles sent Frundsberg and Bourbon at the head of imperial forces into northern Italy. But the soldiers, who had long waited in vain for their pay, mutinied and compelled their leaders to perpetrate the sack of Rome in 1527. Clement VII was imprisoned in the castle of Sant' Angelo until the autumn of 1528. The war dragged on until both sides agreed to the "women's peace," the Peace of Cambrai of 1529, negotiated by Louise of Savoy, the mother of Francis, and Margaret, the aunt of Charles. Francis gave up his claims to Flanders, Artois, and Italy, and Charles renounced his claim to Burgundy and gave up the sons of Francis held as hostages since 1526. Charles made his first appearance in Italy in that year, and in 1530 he was crowned emperor by the pope at Bologna.

It is only against the background of the complicated political problems confronting Charles V that one can understand the postponement of the important religious questions raised by the indulgence controversy. Even though the emperor considered religious uniformity essential to the development of his dynastic empire, every time he prepared to come to grips with the Lutheran movement he found himself confronted with a more immediate political crisis.

## The Leipzig Debate, June 27 to July 16, 1519

On June 27, 1519, the day before the election of Charles V, began the fateful Leipzig Debate, which not only was the first climax of the indulgence controversy but marked the beginning of Luther's realization that an almost unbridgeable gulf existed between him and the authorities of the Church. The first actors in this drama were Carlstadt, Luther's colleague at the University of Wittenberg, and Johann Eck, of the University of Ingolstadt. These two theologians had for months exchanged theses concerning the authority of Scripture, freedom of the will, and other related questions after Luther had promised Miltitz to keep silent on condition that his enemies do likewise. Considering himself attacked in this exchange of theses, Luther had again entered the fray by publishing theses of his own against Eck. In the last of these he had defiantly expressed the doubt whether the power of the pope could be justified historically. After a careful study of the canon law and the history of the Church, he had concluded that the primacy of the bishop of Rome rested solely upon the papal decrees of the preceding four centuries and was contradicted by the first eleven centuries of the history of the Church, the Council of Nicaea, and the Bible.

Although the debates were begun by Carlstadt and Eck on the subjects of free will and divine grace, Luther was soon drawn into the conflict. From the fourth to the fourteenth of July he tested his skill with that of the capable, well-educated, and self-assured Eck. Although Eck proved to be the more learned student of scholastic theology, canon law, and the reform councils, Luther was better informed on the Bible and early Church history.

In the debates between these two men, which shifted from a rather harmless metaphysical speculation to the more dangerous questions concerning ecclesiastical authority, especially the papal primacy, Luther ventured to assert that (1) the pope exercised his authority by human, not by divine, right and was therefore not infallible, although he should be obeyed in order to prevent schism; (2) the Church of Rome was not supreme over the other churches; (3) the Church councils could and did err because they were composed of erring men and did not exist by divine right; and (4) Scripture was the ultimate, divine authority in all matters pertaining to religion.

When Eck sought to arouse the old national prejudices against Luther by calling him a Bohemian and classifying him with Marsilio of Padua, John Wycliffe, and John Hus, Luther at first brushed aside this allegation as irrelevant. But he later pointed out that the Council of Constance had not condemned all the articles of Hus as heretical. When Duke George of Saxony, who was present at the debate, heard the reference to the Hussites, with whom he had had no little difficulty, he openly showed his hostility to Luther.

The rest of the debate, concerned with purgatory, indulgences, and penance, was an anticlimax, for it brought forth few differences of opinion. Luther concluded his part by a caustic reference to Eck's traditional interpretation of scriptural texts, and Eck closed with an equally sarcastic remark about Luther's preference of the authority of Scripture to that of the Church fathers.

As a consequence of his experiences with Eck, his former friend, Luther turned more than before to the Bible as his authority and asserted his beliefs with increasing certainty. Instead of merely offering theses for academic discussion, he now presented theses that he affirmed as personal, immovable convictions, even though some of these were branded as heretical by his enemies. Most despised by those who were concerned with the maintenance of the status quo were his basic convictions, which had been clarified during the Leipzig Debate: (1) that the Bible should be the sole norm in matters of faith and doctrine (*sola scriptura*); (2) that Christ's Church, both militant and triumphant, was a spiritual communion of saints; and (3) that the papacy, the entire hierarchy, and the Church councils were human institutions that were to be obeyed only for the sake of peace and unity.

The official outcome of the debate, that is, the decision with respect to the winner, was overshadowed by other events of much greater immediate importance. It was agreed that the arguments, which had been recorded by four secretaries, should be submitted to the universities of Paris and Erfurt for a decision. Duke George supported Eck in demanding that only the professors of theology and canon law be included as judges. Erfurt, however, refused to give its opinion, and Paris long remained silent. Meanwhile, following the publication by Froben of Basel of all Luther's writings in two widely circulated editions (1518 and 1519), the universities of Louvain and Cologne drew up articles condemning a number of Luther's doctrines. When the Sorbonne at Paris finally responded, in April, 1521, it made no reference to the Leipzig Debate and the question of papal primacy but condemned many of Luther's doctrines as heretical, associated him with earlier heretics, and demanded that his books be burned and he be compelled publicly to retract his heresies. Eck felt that he had been cheated of the fruits of his victory, and Luther and his supporters immediately published answers to the above attacks.

Thoroughly disappointed with the debate as a whole and disillusioned with respect to his ability to have the convictions growing out of his own personal experience and study discussed calmly, Luther returned to Wittenberg determined to discover the truth by further study of the Bible and church history. He never completely surrendered his hope that his "mother Church" could be reformed and its unity maintained; yet he never wavered in his stand upon the fundamental doctrine of justification by faith alone, which he had discovered in the monastery. This was to him not something subjective but an objective truth that, he firmly believed, could be understood and recognized by every Christian if only he listened to the gospel without hardening his heart against it. Luther felt that this gospel was God's gospel and that he had been given the divine call to defend it against all those who attempted to pervert it. This stand partially explains those characteristics for which he has been most widely criticized: his unyielding attitude on all matters in dispute, his belief that all those who opposed him were agents of the devil, and his tendency to use violent language in attacking his enemies.

The significance of his new theological orientation became apparent in the many works that he wrote in the year following the Leipzig Debate, the publication of which kept several printers busy: his exegetical works on Galatians and the psalms, polemical writings in which he developed points raised at the Leipzig Debate, and many devotional works and sermons. Most significant in these works was the development of his views concerning the sacraments. These, he held, do not work mechanically (*ex opere operato*) but through faith in the promises of Christ, which they signify.

Luther doubted whether there were more than three sacraments, namely, baptism, the Lord's Supper, and penance, for he at that time defined a sacrament as a rite having an outward sign, such as bread and wine, and a divine promise of salvation to those who received it in faith. Baptism, he now maintained, did not magically remove sin but symbolized the drowning of sin and the spiritual rebirth through God's mercy and grace that takes place throughout the life of the Christian because of his faith.

The Lord's Supper was for Luther a divine sign of the communion of all believers with one another and Christ. By 1520 he had definitely denied the Catholic doctrine of transubstantiation, that the substance of the bread and wine were transformed into the body and blood of Christ; but he continued to believe in the real presence of Christ in the sacrament. Moreover, he insisted that faith was absolutely necessary for making the sacrament effective. He preferred communion in both kinds, that is, giving the communicant both the bread and the wine, but he did not insist upon it and suggested that the matter be determined by a Church council.

In the sacrament of penance, he believed, sins were forgiven solely because of faith in God's promise, not because of repentance, good works, or the authority of the clergy. He pointed to the danger of relying upon such expedients as making pilgrimages, praying to saints, fasting, confessing, and giving alms when the sinner could be saved alone by faith—not faith in the Church, the chief characteristic of medieval piety, but faith in God. Repentance, which should be positive and constant, would be followed by absolution without the aid of the priest. Faith, growing out of love for the gospel, would produce good works, or satisfaction, as evidence of spiritual freedom. Thus penance became for him a positive expression of faith, the confessional an expression of the personal relationship of the sinner with God, and the office of the keys a brotherly service.

### New Supporters

Luther was disheartened by the fact that the faculty of Erfurt had declined to judge the outcome of the Leipzig Debate and that the churchmen would not take seriously his demand for a reformation that would more nearly conform with the vigorous spirituality that had existed at the time of Paul. On the other hand, he was encouraged by the many individuals and groups who for various reasons were dissatisfied with the present state of affairs and came to his support—often, however, without understanding the basic reasons for his bold protest.

Among the most vocal and influential friends of the reformer were the humanists, who believed that he stood for their freedom of intellectual activity and hailed his support of Reuchlin in the latter's struggle with the conservative scholastics. Luther himself felt a close attachment to them at this time. The cautious Erasmus wrote him that many persons in the Low Countries and England were interested in his work, but he warned Luther not to become too controversial and made it clear that he himself was not desirous of becoming involved in the theological debates that were inflaming people on both sides. Ulrich von Hutten, whose publication of Valla's *Donation of Constantine* had had a strong influence upon Luther's attitude toward the papacy, wished to make the reformer his ally in a national revolutionary movement against Rome. In the fall of 1519 Crotus Rubeanus wrote his widely read defense of these two men, the *Oratio pro Hutteno et Luthero.*

Among the many other humanists who encouraged Luther during these critical years was Philip Melanchthon (1497–1560), the precocious grandnephew of Reuchlin who had come to Wittenberg to teach Greek in 1518. Later the faithful co-worker of Luther, he made his greatest contributions to the Reformation by helping to systematize the Lutheran theology, devoting much attention to teaching the new doctrines as the *praeceptor Germaniae,* and making Luther's teachings part of the culture and learning of his day.

Important humanist circles in the German cities, the episcopal courts, and the universities also furthered Luther's cause. At Nürnberg Albrecht Dürer, Willibald Pirkheimer, and Lazarus Spengler were members of a circle of intellectuals who supported the reformer. Spengler, secretary of the city council of Nürnberg, was the first prominent member of the laity to assume an active role as a leader of the Reformation. We have already seen that Peutinger and his friends in Augsburg were interested in Luther. Religious discontent in that city centered chiefly in the Carmelite monastery, the prior of which, Johann Frosch, entertained Luther during the hearings with Cajetan. At Basel the printer Johann Froben began publishing Luther's works, especially for sale abroad.

The fact that Eck had tried to identify Luther with the Hussites at the Leipzig Debate aroused the interest of a number of Bohemians in his reform program. Jan Poduska (d. 1520), pastor of the important Teynkirche in Prague, and Wenzel Rozdalovsky, his vicar, sent Luther a copy of Hus' *Concerning the Church.* Luther did not find time to read this work immediately, but it eventually made a strong impression upon him.

Largely through the work of Hutten, the imperial knights came in increasing numbers to the support of Luther. Their unique position in the Empire, as directly responsible only to the emperor, was being threatened by the territorial princes who were developing centralized states within the Empire. Believing that any powerful movements of national proportions would serve their cause, they tended to sympathize with Luther. In 1520, for example, when it seemed as though force would be used against the reformer, Silvester von Schaumburg offered him one hundred knights for protection. Franz von Sickingen, the well-known protector of the humanists, offered to give him an asylum at his castle, the Ebernburg. But Luther, grateful as he was for such manifestations of interest in his cause, preferred to rely upon the protection of his elector and never deviated from his religious program, despite the attractive allurements of other groups.

## The Crises of 1520 and 1521

Although the pope had failed to prevent the election of Charles V, he did not immediately resume the prosecution of Luther. On the contrary, as we have seen, he still seemed to hope that the elector would do his best to silence Luther or send him to Rome for trial. At the Roman *Curia*, however, there was no disposition to drop the case. Even those who agreed with many of Luther's arguments with respect to papal authority would not admit this openly for fear of their effect upon church discipline. Moreover, to agree to the reformer's demand to call a general council would, according to the papal advisers, tend to loose the pent-up hostilities of the various groups that had long demanded reforms.

Not until Eck appeared in Rome in the spring of 1520 did the third commission appointed by the pope to examine Luther's doctrines—it included Eck and Cajetan—finally draw up a draft of a bull of condemnation, listing forty-one errors ascribed to Luther. This draft was finally accepted by the papal consistory and officially signed on June 15. The bull, known as *Exsurge domine,* or *Arise, O Lord,* condemned Luther for heresy for holding doctrines contrary to the Bible as interpreted by the Church fathers, the councils, and the popes, and demanded that he retract his heresies within sixty days, on pain of excommunication. It also warned all Christians to reject these heresies and to burn the writings of Luther. Because the bull gave Luther an opportunity to retract his heresies, the actual excommunication did not take place until a supplementary bull, the *Decet pontificem romanum,* or *It Is Fitting That the Pope,* issued January 3, 1521, was published the next October, four years after the outbreak of the indulgence controversy.

If the *Exsurge domine* was designed to convey to the German people the idea that the pope was desirous of silencing Luther out of purely religious motives, it widely missed its mark. If the pope believed that he could silence Luther without giving him the hearing that the latter had demanded and that he could quiet the people who were seething with discontent without doing a thing about reforming the abuses in the Church, he was greatly mistaken. The many people who had come to look upon the Wittenberg reformer as their spokesman in political, economic, and social, as well as religious, matters would not meekly accept the condemnation of Luther solely on papal and curial authority. Frederick the Wise, conscious of his influence as the outstanding prince of the Empire, was determined to protect his popular professor. Eck soon became aware of the temper of the people when he appeared in Germany late in the summer to publish the bull. At Leipzig, Erfurt, Vienna, and even Ingolstadt, copies of the bull that had been posted in public places were smeared with filth and torn to pieces. In other places princes and bishops forbade its publication because they feared a popular tumult.

In all the excitement that followed, Luther remained belligerent, violent, and self-confident, for he was certain that the growing support coming to him from all sides was an evidence of God's will that he should continue the struggle against the pope. He now considered the pope the Antichrist of the Apocalypse, who ruled a church that had become the "most lawless den of robbers, the most shameless of all brothels, the very kingdom of sin, death, and hell." Luther publicly announced his reaction to the papal attack, especially to the public burning of his books at Cologne, Mainz, and Louvain, before a gathering of university students and professors on the morning of December 10, 1520, the end of the sixty-day period of grace given him in the bull. Just outside the eastern gate of the city, at the city dump, a large bonfire was started, into which Luther ceremoniously threw a number of books that supported the authority of the papacy and the Catholic hierarchy. The list included Gratian's *Decretals,* Clavisio's *Summa* on penance, a number of books written by Emser and Eck, and, most significant of all, a copy of the canon law. Finally, probably acting on a sudden impulse, he consigned to the flames also a copy of the *Exsurge domine.* For him the die was cast.

## Pamphlets of 1520

Meanwhile, exasperated by the arguments that the supporters of the papacy had advanced on behalf of papal absolutism and informed of the fact that Leo X was taking steps officially to condemn his doctrines, Luther published his three significant pamphlets of 1520. These served not only to nullify all attempts of the peacemakers on both sides but to arouse the German people to a defiant stand against the papacy. Circulated among the people in the form of printed pamphlets, they no longer reflected the spirit of a humble monk seeking enlightenment on doctrinal matters but that of a bold leader of the people demanding a revolutionary break with Rome. A widely read tract of this period pictured him as a German Hercules.

The first of these pamphlets, the *Address to the Christian Nobility of the German Nation,* that is, to the emperor and the estates of the Empire, the duly constituted political authorities, was written in German, probably with the assistance of the Saxon court advisers and Luther's colleagues at Wittenberg. It was primarily concerned with ecclesiastical politics. The four thousand copies of the first edition were sold within three weeks, and many other editions followed. Drawing upon his own studies of the Bible and Church history as well as upon contemporary sources, such as the grievances presented at the Diet of Augsburg in 1518 and the national sentiments of the humanists best reflected in Hutten's *Vadiscus,* Luther called upon the Germans to reform the Church and all society. Because the papacy and the general Church councils had failed to take the lead, he now turned to the secular state, which he considered divinely ordained to maintain order among all people, clergy as well as laity.

After summarizing the many evils recognized by most of his contemporaries, Luther demanded in violent and uncompromising terms that German rulers radically reform the papacy and the entire ecclesiastical hierarchy, whose inviolate character he denied. The pope was not, he maintained, the sole interpreter of Scripture, had no legal or divine authority in secular matters, and did not have the sole right to call Church councils. Therefore the government should not only put an end to such evils as the financial exploitation of the German people and the trafficking in religious matters but deprive the pope of all political rights. Many of the ecclesiastical functions should be taken over by a German primate, exercising his authority through a German national assembly representing the German Church. He also favored the repression of the mendicant orders because of their interference with Christian liberty, the suppression of enforced celibacy of the clergy, and the abolition of punishment for heresy. The heretic should be overcome with arguments, not fire.

Luther also demanded that the German rulers give their attention to educational, legal, and social reforms. He urged them to follow the example of the University of Wittenberg, which had dethroned Aristotle, had substituted the study of the Bible for that of Lombard's *Sentences,* and had turned its attention to the study of languages, mathematics, and history in place of scholasticism. Furthermore, he opposed the medieval conception of the two laws, canon and civil, denying the validity of the former as a mere reflection of the arbitrary wishes of the papacy and giving precedence to the latter. Without striking at the roots of the social evils in Germany, he at least saw the need for curbing the luxury, unfair business practices, and general low morality of his day.

The second of the revolutionary pamphlets, which Luther called *The Babylonian Captivity of the Church,* was largely theological in nature and was intended for theologians and scholars. Therefore it was written in Latin. In it he summarized his new theology, drawing the conclusions of his justification by faith alone, particularly with respect to the sacraments. He condemned the papacy for holding the Church in captivity by distorting the original meaning and purpose of the sacraments and reserving for the clerical hierarchy the rights that belonged to all Christians as members of the universal priesthood of believers, in short, of depriving individual Christians of their freedom to approach God directly and personally through faith. Because all Christians were priests, they should freely select those of their number who were qualified to preach the gospel and administer the sacraments.

Luther now maintained that there were only two sacraments, baptism and the Lord's Supper, or at the most three, for he still saw some sacramental values in penance. In reality, he stated, there was only one sacrament, namely, the forgiveness of sins, which comes alone from the individual's free, direct contact with God. Because he could find no mention in the Bible of confirmation, matrimony, holy orders, or extreme unction as conveying divine grace, he rejected them as sacraments.

With respect to the Lord's Supper, or the Eucharist, Luther insisted that the pope had for centuries held Christians captive by withholding the cup from them; teaching the doctrine of transubstantiation, made a dogma of the Church by the Fourth Lateran Council in 1215; holding that the sacrament was of itself a good work; and considering it a sacrifice by means of which the priest magically offered up Christ. Although Luther denied the doctrine of transubstantiation, he accepted the words of institution literally, believing in the real presence of Christ in the elements after consecration. But he placed the greatest emphasis upon its significance as the new testament, or covenant, between Christ and man, established at the institution of the Lord's Supper. It was for Luther a visible sign of God's forgiveness of sins through faith in Christ.

Likewise, the sacrament of baptism involved for Luther not merely a promise of forgiveness of sins through faith but also a regeneration of man. It was not a single sacramental act that magically wiped out original sin, as the scholastics maintained, but a process that continued throughout life.

Luther made his sharpest attack upon papal interference with Christian liberty in his treatment of penance. He stated that the tyranny consisted of distorting the simple biblical teachings of contrition, confession, and satisfaction. The popes had made a merit of contrition, had made confession a monopoly of the clergy, and had hindered the regeneration of man by burdening satisfaction with all sorts of meritorious works, even granting absolution before demanding satisfaction.

This treatise was soon translated into German and, contrary to Luther's wishes, widely circulated. It aroused a great storm of protest from the conservative theologians, even drawing a stern rebuke from the pen of Henry VIII of England, whom the pope rewarded with the title, "Defender of the Faith," a title still carried by the British rulers.

Luther wrote the third important pamphlet, *The Freedom of the Christian Man,* in Latin for the pope in October, 1520. It was published in a German translation in November. Not polemical in nature, it was written as the reformer's last attempt to seek peace with the Church. He took this occasion to summarize for both the pope and the people the doctrines developed on the basis of his own personal experience. It was thus a confession of his own faith, of his conception of the evangelical, Pauline way of life. Though conciliatory in tone, it contained no retraction of any of his doctrines.

The freedom of a true Christian, Luther states, consists of his emancipation from a reliance upon works, castigation of self, withdrawal from the world, and institutional formalism, but also of his living an active life in the joyous confidence that man is justified by faith alone. This freedom must not, however, be interpreted as license, for it imposes upon a Christian the obligation to discipline himself and serve others, to make his outward life conform to his inner spirit and faith. In one of the finest passages on Christian service in religious literature, Luther shows that Christians, conscious of their freedom from the law of the Old Testament, live lives of service because they are bound to do so by faith and love.

## The Diet of Worms

That the newly crowned emperor would not be influenced by Luther's pamphlet to take the lead in a vigorous reform movement was made evident by the fact that he followed the advice of the papal nuncio Aleander to publish an edict demanding the burning of Luther's books in the Low Countries. Although Charles was not averse to reform as such, or even to the curtailment of papal power, he soon made it clear that he would live up to his coronation oath to maintain the orthodox faith and defend the Church. It was inconceivable to him that a simple monk should be permitted to question the authority of the Church. Rebellion against the Church, moreover, might lead to rebellion against the state; and the unity of the Church appeared to him an indispensable aid in holding together the scattered lands of his dynastic empire. It would have appeared absurd for him to espouse the cause of a German national church in the light of his main interests.

However, Charles could not ignore the aroused temper of the German people or the legal rights of the electors who were demanding certain reforms. Therefore he seemed to waver between following the advice of Aleander, one of the two papal nuncios at the diet, and that of Frederick the Wise. Aleander suggested that he publish in Germany an edict against Luther similar to the one he had published in the Low Countries and carry out the papal bull *Exsurge domine*. Frederick the Wise and his supporters urged that Luther be given a hearing at the emperor's first diet, which he had summoned to meet at Worms on January 6, 1521.

Even though the position of Aleander was strengthened by the promulgation of the papal bull of excommunication against Luther January 3—it reached Aleander February 10—Charles finally, on March 6, agreed to the demand of the electors that Luther be cited to Worms for a hearing with respect to the doctrines contained in his published books but without the right to argue on behalf of their contents. The emperor also gave Luther a letter of safe conduct both to and from Worms, to which Frederick the Wise added a similar letter of his own. Despite the fact that Aleander published in Worms a modified edict against Luther's books under the emperor's name, this edict did not prevent the reformer from going to the hearing that he had long requested. He was accompanied by Sturm, the congenial imperial herald; Amsdorf, his colleague at the university; Petzensteiner, a fellow monk; and Suaven, a student. The party was later joined by Justus Jonas, a canon at Erfurt.

Needless to state, neither the papal bulls nor the emperor's request that he cease writing against the papacy deterred Luther from preaching the gospel. Like Leo X, Charles V and his advisers seemed completely to misunderstand the profound nature of the search for religious truth and satisfaction evinced by the German people and epitomized in their leader Luther. For the reformer the issue was now clear: it was the Word of God that was being threatened by the forces of the devil, led by the pope as Antichrist. With this conviction, he cared nothing for his own security or any political consideration. Therefore he refused the military assistance offered him by Hutten and the other imperial knights, believing that Antichrist could be conquered only by the preaching of the gospel. The hearing at Worms would give him the opportunity to testify before the great on behalf of the gospel.

As the carriage, drawn by three horses and bearing Luther and his small party, proceeded to Worms, increasingly large groups of people gathered to see the man who had dared to defy both pope and emperor. The churches in which he preached were filled to capacity. When Spalatin wrote him of the dangers facing him at Worms, he answered that he would enter Worms despite the "gates of hell and the powers of darkness." Spalatin later wrote that Luther had said that he would go to Worms even if there were "as many devils in it as there were tiles on the roofs of the houses." When the party entered Worms on April 16, after a fortnight of travel, their arrival was announced by a trumpet blast from the tower of the cathedral, and they were met by a great crowd of people who accompanied them to Luther's lodgings in the Hospital of the Knights of St. John.

Because Luther was summoned to appear before the diet the next day, much of his time was devoted to seeing the advisers of Frederick the Wise at the Hospital. These sought to outmaneuver Aleander, who had drawn up the questions to be asked Luther in such a way as to obtain a partial or complete recantation at the first hearing. Therefore the advisers urged Luther to counter such tactics by avoiding a direct answer and requesting time for a careful consideration of the questions.

Encouraged by friends on all sides, Luther entered the presence of the emperor and the estates with complete composure and obvious interest in the spectacle. He was asked whether he was the author of a number of books that had been placed on a table in front of him and whether he would recant any part of them. To the first question he replied in the affirmative, adding that the list was not complete. To the second, he stated that he wished for time to consider such an important matter so that he might answer "without detriment to the Word of God and danger to my salvation." The emperor and the estates were surprised that he was not ready to answer the second question, but they gave him twenty-four hours to consider his reply.

Luther appeared before the emperor and estates the following day in a larger, but crowded auditorium. Although he had been kept waiting two hours, he appeared in a confident mood. When the presiding officer asked him whether he would defend all the books that he recognized as his, or whether he would retract any of his published statements, he answered in a loud and firm voice, stating in both Latin and German that it would be impossible to give a simple answer. One classification of his books dealt solely with practical religious matters in such a manner that even his opponents recognized their value. If he condemned these he would be denying the truth. A second classification dealt with papal tyranny and other ecclesiastical abuses. If he recanted these he would be guilty of encouraging tyranny. The third classification comprised books that he had written against individuals in defense of the gospel, and therefore he could not retract them. If he had written more harshly than became his profession, he did so as a human; and if he erred, which was human, he wished the emperor, the estates, and any one else to correct him on the basis of the Word of God. If they would convince him of error, he would recant and himself throw the books into the fire.

When, after further deliberation by the emperor and the estates, Luther was told that the doctrines of the Church were not to be argued and was asked to give in a clear, simple statement his answer, whether he would retract the heresies in his books, he defended his personal conviction in the well-known, fateful words: "Unless I am convinced of error by the testimony of Scripture or by clear reason, . . . I cannot and will not recant anything, for it is neither safe nor honest to act against one's conscience. God help me. Amen." During the confusion that followed this statement, Luther was warned that his conscience would not be considered when an infallible Church council would examine his errors. To this he responded that he could prove that general councils had erred. The emperor, arising from his seat, protested that he had had enough of arguments against the councils and left the assembly in anger. Luther, happy that he had withstood the ordeal and defended the truth, withdrew to his quarters, where he received the felicitations of his friends.

Luther's courageous act at Worms has rightly been regarded as an important step in the history of the development of religious liberty. He steadfastly maintained that the authorities of both the Church and the Empire were bound to convince him, an individual, of his errors before condemning him. On the other hand, this was still a far step from complete religious individualism and the denial of authority. This position, supported by the subsequent history of the reformer, shows that he firmly believed that by his personal religious experience and study he had arrived at the absolute religious truth, which did not permit any individual interpretation. It was his duty to show the authorities this truth, and it was their obligation to defend it. If the papacy would not do so, he would turn to the government. If the emperor refused to do so, he would turn to the territorial lords.

Although Emperor Charles had made up his mind that, after the expiration of the period of the safe-conduct, he would proceed against this monk who had dared to believe that the Church had erred for a thousand years, the majority of the members of the diet wanted more time for deliberation. This attitude reflected the strong antipapal sentiment at the diet and the revolutionary temper of the people. One of the committees was in fact busy composing another long list of grievances against the papacy. The estates finally induced the emperor to permit the establishment of a commission to examine Luther's writings with the purpose of pointing out his errors and gaining a recantation, for they did not want him to be condemned without a hearing. Charles again promised that if Luther recanted, he would intercede with the papacy on his behalf.

Neither the hearing before this commission, headed by the archbishop of Trier, nor subsequent negotiations with the archbishop at his dinner table resulted in a retraction. Luther would submit his writings to the judgment of the appropriate political or ecclesiastical authorities, but only with the provision that they would be tried on the basis of the Word of God as found in Scripture or by clear reason. He believed that he had the right to defy the wishes of the emperor and the estates, for the Bible compelled him to obey God rather than man in spiritual matters.

When it became obvious that no compromise was possible, Luther, on April 25, asked the archbishop of Trier for permission to leave for Wittenberg on the following day. The elector obtained this permission from the emperor, but Luther was not to preach on the journey. Although he refused to promise that he would not preach, he set out the next morning. By a previously made secret arrangement, however, the party in which he was traveling was intercepted by trusted friends in the Thuringian Forest that evening, and Luther was spirited off to the Wartburg Castle, overlooking Eisenach, where he remained disguised as "Knight George" for nearly a year.

Meanwhile Charles V had Aleander prepare an edict against Luther. But because the emperor was eager to obtain the military and financial support of the estates for his war against Francis I, he did not submit the edict to them until after they had formally granted him the desired aid on May 23 and after he had officially closed the diet two days later. Then he submitted the edict to what amounted to a small number of picked men in a special session. On May 26, 1521, the emperor affixed his signature to the edict and its copy in a German translation. However, the document bore the date May 8.

The Edict of Worms accused Luther of both heresy and disobedience to established political authority. It stated that because the emperor had failed to secure a retraction from him, he was compelled, "with the unanimous consent and will of the estates," to enforce the papal bulls against Luther. Luther was accordingly placed under the imperial ban. All subjects were forbidden to assist or even communicate with him, on pain of being arrested and having their property confiscated. All his books were condemned as heretical and were ordered to be burned. No books or pamphlets were to be published that criticized the papacy, the hierarchy, the institutions of the Church, or the official dogmas.

The imperial edict completed Luther's break with the past. Excommunicated by the Church and outlawed by the Empire, he was compelled by his own conscience, religious conviction, and faith to defy both church and state, despite his great respect for both institutions. Some critics have accused him of unwarranted stubbornness and uncompromising dogmatism in insisting that the authorities try his case on the basis of Scripture, and others have pointed to the intransigency of the pope and his predominantly Dominican advisers, who refused to do anything about the reforms demanded by Luther. The papacy might have deprived Luther of much popular support by making a serious attempt to allay the widespread dissatisfaction among the people. But it is doubtful whether in 1521 the two diametrically opposite points of view could have been resolved by compromise. Be that as it may, it was natural that Luther, deprived of help from both of the great medieval authorities, should rely upon his electoral prince and appeal directly to the people. By so doing, he became a leader of a religious movement that had in effect become a revolution.

The emperor had come to this, his first, diet, determined to settle all the important German problems, of which the heresy of Luther was on the surface the least important, so that he could get on with his war against Francis I. To obtain the support of the estates, he had restored the council of regency and reconstituted the imperial supreme court. He had also attempted to solve the problem of the succession to the Hapsburg lands by giving to his brother Ferdinand the Austrian lands and the claims to Bohemia and Hungary, while retaining Franche-Comté and the Low Countries for himself. But he had not consolidated his position sufficiently to enable him to enforce the edict against Luther. The reformer, undaunted by the show of authority and supported by the skillful diplomacy of his elector, continued his religious activities without interruption.

# 4 The Growth of Lutheranism

The fear of popular unrest, expressed by religious and secular authorities during the first years of the Reformation, had been well founded. It seemed as though every German with grievances looked to Luther for redress, especially after the publication of his revolutionary pamphlets of 1520. Luther's own religious program, which he expressed in a forcible idiomatic German as well as in Latin, became the program of the masses, and such words as *gospel* and *liberty* became the watchwords of a movement that tended to become much broader than the purely religious reforms envisioned by Luther.

## Luther at the Wartburg and the Radicals at Wittenberg

At the Wartburg Luther had an opportunity to consider those events that had driven him inexorably from the position of a monk, professor, and preacher demanding reforms in conformity with his new theology to the position of a leader of a widespread national movement against Rome. Frequently he was troubled by doubts whether he, one person among many thousands, was able to oppose the entire medieval Church supported by the Empire. But he eventually dispelled such doubts by doing hard work of a constructive nature. By gradually building an evangelical church separated from Rome, he carried into practice, as far as circumstances would permit. his new theology and demonstrated his innate conservatism.

Luther's inner conflict during his stay of almost ten months at the Wartburg was accentuated by his physical inactivity, by lack of contact with his friends, and by disturbing news from the outside. This conflict found characteristic expression in his many references to the devil. He was quick to see in every opponent and obstacle the work of Satan. This tendency is an indication of the religious dualism that became so pronounced in his theology. Although God's grace was for him a dynamic force for good, struggling for the soul of man and his regeneration, he picturesquely conceived of evil, engineered by the devil, as a dynamic force working for the destruction of the soul. By faith in God the individual permitted the forces of good to operate successfully against the forces of evil; but because evil was not vanquished in this life, the struggle continued until the soul was released from the body. One's own ability and the use of force were of no avail, for only the preaching of the gospel would provide victory.

This certainty that God would combat the forces of evil without man's efforts was reflected in all Luther's letters and sermons sent to his friends from the Wartburg. The many rumors and the popular excitement that followed his disappearance after the Diet of Worms were soon allayed when he established contact with his friends, without divulging the exact location of his "island of Patmos," or "region of the birds." By his voluminous correspondence he attempted to keep the Reformation in line with his own doctrines and to prevent the uncertainty and violence that, he felt, would destroy all that had thus far been achieved. He urged Melanchthon and others to preach the evangelical message in the vernacular, made suggestions for reorganizing the University of Wittenberg, gave encouragement to those who feared the future, and answered the polemical tracts of his enemies.

Meanwhile Luther applied still further his new doctrines to Christian life and practice. In a pamphlet, *Concerning Confession, Whether the Pope Has Power to Order It,* he adduced Bible passages to show that the Christian had the right to confess his sins to God alone; that priestly confession and absolution, though not denied by the Bible, were inventions designed to enslave Christians; and that the power of forgiving sins was given by Christ to the entire Church, not only to the clergy. Even more significant was his opposition to what he considered the distorted views concerning the role of the clergy in the Church. Arguing that the Bible and the early Church sanctioned the marriage of priests and that the Western Church had imposed celibacy as a further means for suppressing freedom, Luther came to the defense of one of his students, a priest, who had taken a wife and whom his ecclesiastical superior had accused of an infraction of the canon law.

Luther's attack upon the unique position of the clergy was extended to the monks in his work *On Monastic Vows,* also written at the Wartburg. He maintained that because virtually all monks took the monastic vows in the hope of earning merits on a higher plane than ordinary

The Wartburg Castle

# Part Two: The Reformation in Germany

Christians—contrary to the "New Testament reign of liberty and faith"—these vows were not binding, despite ecclesiastical authority to the contrary. Moreover, the chastity that they vowed was contrary to human nature and reason. The vow of poverty, he insisted, was in most instances a sham, for the monks did not seek out those monasteries that rigidly practiced that virtue but used monasticism to obtain a false religious security and live lives of ease. Obedience was generally looked upon as mere obedience to a prior, whereas the true Christian was obedient to God above all; and God demanded an active life of service to others, not withdrawal from the community. Although he stated his case against monastic vows with dogmatic certainty, he cautioned his friends at Wittenberg to permit monks and nuns to exercise complete freedom in determining whether or not they should revoke their vows. Yet when he returned to Wittenberg, only the prior had remained in the Augustinian monastery.

Luther was also compelled to give his attention to the practical question of the celebration of the Mass and Communion in both kinds when Carlstadt, his colleague at the university, and Gabriel Zwilling, a forceful preacher of the Augustinian order, attempted to enforce changes in Wittenberg. In order to clarify still further the doctrines that he had expressed in *The Babylonian Captivity*, he wrote his pamphlet *On the Abrogation of Private Mass*. Like the priestly hierarchy of the Middle Ages, he maintained, the Mass as a sacrifice had no sanction in the New Testament, which refers only to a memorial of Christ's sacrifice.

The news that Luther received concerning the overzealous activities of some of his followers in carrying out his reforms filled him with forebodings of serious social as well as religious disturbances. Although he wrote Spalatin and Elector Frederick, criticizing them for withholding from publication some of his polemical writings, and demanded of the archbishop of Mainz that he cease encouraging superstitious practices by permitting the sale of indulgences, he consistently refrained from inciting revolt and urged his followers to carry on reforms through duly constituted political authorities.

In defiance of the Edict of Worms and contrary to the wishes of his elector, Luther traveled incognito to Wittenberg to learn firsthand how serious the disturbances had become. Upon his return to the Wartburg he once more made clear his views with respect to the importance of obeying the political authorities in his *Faithful Exhortation to All Christians to Guard Against Revolt and Tumult*. Although he can justly be criticized for not realizing that a revolt against ecclesiastical authority might lead to a revolt against the political and social order, he cannot be accused of inconsistency. His entire concern centered in a religious problem and excluded political, economic, and social considerations, except insofar as these could be improved by praying, hearing the gospel, and requesting reforms of the established authorities.

*120*

In further preparation for the preaching of the gospel of Christ, which he considered his chief mission, Luther continued the study of Hebrew and Greek. As an aid to those preachers who could not write their own sermons, he prepared his first collection of short sermons, called *postils* or *homilies,* in which he expounded his evangelical doctrines in simple, homely language, free of all scholastic subtleties. As the father of the modern evangelical sermon, he demonstrated how the Bible could be made a lively, dynamic force. For him the entire Bible was primarily a testimony of Christ that he, like Paul, felt compelled to bring to all people.

Undoubtedly the greatest product of the Wartburg days was Luther's translation into German of the New Testament, achieved in the unbelievably short period of eleven weeks. Numerous translations of the New Testament and the Bible as a whole had previously been made; but this was the first one not based on the Vulgate translation of Jerome. Luther used the second edition of Erasmus' New Testament, published in 1519. By using the official German of the Saxon chancery, not his own colloquial Saxon dialect, he helped create a standard German for all Germany. The first edition of this translation was published in September, 1522, for which reason it became known as the September Testament. It is estimated that five thousand copies were sold in two months, two hundred thousand in twelve years. Luther did not begin the translation of the Old Testament until he had returned to Wittenberg and could avail himself of the knowledge of Hebrew of his colleagues.

## The Wittenberg Disturbances and Luther's Return

Meanwhile, difficulties were encountered in putting Luther's evangelical doctrines into practice in Wittenberg. Although Melanchthon and Amsdorf wished to proceed slowly, Carlstadt and Zwilling were impatient about getting on with the reforms. The elector, characteristically cautious and diplomatic, seemed unwilling to antagonize the emperor, the estates, and especially the council of regency, which had condemned the marriage of the clergy and the celebration of Communion in both kinds. Consequently all the old forces of dissatisfaction and unrest again appeared and made difficult the transition from the period of criticism of the old state of affairs to the construction of a new, evangelical order. The situation at Wittenberg called for Luther's vigorous leadership.

Carlstadt, who had a large following at the university and was influential in the Church of All Saints as archdeacon, made repeated attacks upon clerical celibacy, the Mass, and ceremonies. In his enthusiasm he tended to emphasize the significance of continuing revelation, thereby minimizing the importance of theological learning. On Christmas Day, 1521, he celebrated Communion in All Saints Church in both kinds without priestly vestments. In reading the service he omitted the passages referring to the sacrifice and did not elevate the host; and he extended the bread and the cup to the communicants, though previously only priests had handled them. Moreover, having gone so far as to state that the clergy should be compelled to marry, he set an example by taking a wife on January 19, 1522. He was followed in this respect by Justus Jonas, provost of All Saints Church, and many other clergymen.

Gabriel Zwilling made similar revolutionary innovations in the Augustinian monastery. He preached fiery sermons against the traditional conception of the Mass and dispensed the Lord's Supper in both kinds in a nearby parish. Incited by his sermons, reckless enthusiasts resorted to acts of violence against the conservative clergy and in the churches. Zwilling urged that monasteries be dissolved and that monks and nuns be insulted in public. On the day after the dissolution of the Augustinian chapter at Wittenberg, January 11, Zwilling led the Augustinians in removing the altars in the monastery chapel, burning saints' pictures, and destroying other images as "emblems of idolatry."

Although most of these changes were accepted by the inhabitants of Wittenberg, the intervention of the elector led to great differences of opinion. This intervention was precipitated by the appearance of three "prophets" of Zwickau. Their actual influence on the reform movement in Wittenberg was not great, but their presence tended to discredit the other reformers, particularly Carlstadt and Zwilling, who were already disliked by the elector. One of these radicals was Markus Stübner, formerly a student of the University of Wittenberg. He was accompanied by Nicholas Storch and another companion whose name is not known, both of whom were illiterate weavers. Melanchthon was at first impressed by their knowledge of the Bible, their belief that they were directly inspired by God, and their claim that they could prophesy by means of visions; yet he was disturbed by their opposition to infant baptism, which, they insisted, was supported by Luther's doctrine that faith was necessary to make the sacrament effective.

The introduction of revolutionary innovations without the authority of the elector led the town council to enter into negotiations with a committee of the university to draw up an ordinance regulating the religious life of the community in harmony with the new evangelical doctrines. This document, adopted on January 24, contained the following provisions: (1) that the Lord's Supper be celebrated as instituted by Christ and as reintroduced by Carlstadt; (2) that the number of altars in the churches be gradually reduced to three; (3) that a "common purse," or fund, be set up to administer the church revenues on behalf of the poor; (4) that the religious and social fraternities be abolished and their assets be turned over to the common fund; and (5) that begging and prostitution be abolished.

Whereas the elector believed that the city council had proceeded too far, Carlstadt and Zwilling continued with their iconoclastic program, believing firmly that they were carrying Luther's doctrines to their logical conclusions. Further incidents of violence and confusion, however, were followed by Carlstadt's conversion to a more moderate course and Zwilling's departure from Wittenberg. The elector, apparently ill and no longer equal to the demands of the situation, sent an uncompromising order to the council on February 17, demanding that the old order be restored until a general decision could be reached for all Germany. Because the reformers were at a loss how to get out of this difficulty, they asked Luther to return to Wittenberg immediately.

## Luther's Return to Wittenberg

Despite the fact that Luther had been pleased with the early changes made at Wittenberg and had mentioned that he might bring Carlstadt a wedding gift, the series of incidents that had led to the elector's order of February 17 apparently caused him to believe that the devil had intervened, as seen in the activities of Carlstadt and his enthusiastic associates. He also wrote the elector in no uncertain terms that he should show faith in the Lord in supporting the gospel, chided him for his interest in holy relics, taunted him for relying on a cautious diplomacy, and stated that he, not Luther, was in need of protection. He would return to Wittenberg despite the council of regency and Duke George; if it were necessary, he would even go to Leipzig, "though it rained Duke Georges for nine days." Nor did he fear the emperor. If Charles could not comprehend God's will and would try to dispose of Luther and stop the preaching of the gospel, Frederick should not intervene.

Despite the fact that the elector officially forbade Luther to return, the resolute reformer left the Wartburg and arrived at Wittenberg on March 6. Two days later he began to preach in the City Church the series of eight sermons by means of which he quickly gained control of the situation. He praised the reformers for their knowledge of the Bible and their acts of faith; but he scolded them for neglecting Christian love, which considers the weakness of others and does not become impatient or cause offense. If he had been approached in the matter of innovations, as he should have been, he would have warned the leaders against the use of force and the neglect of Christian freedom. In religious matters, he maintained, one must use only persuasion. Preaching the gospel would change the hearts of men and accomplish wonders, as it had done in his case while he "slept and drank a glass of Wittenberg beer with Philip and Amsdorf." Furthermore, no changes should be made in such ceremonies or rites as did not jeopardize faith, and decisions concerning nonessentials, such as marriage of the clergy, monasticism, fasting, and the proper use of pictures and images, should be left entirely to the individual conscience. Finally, nothing should be done without the consent of the government, God's instrument for the maintenance of order.

The changes that followed were in accord with Luther's program of conservative reforms. The Mass was restored to its original form, except that the passages dealing with the sacrifice were omitted; confession was restored; and pictures and images were again permitted in places of worship. By such means the reformers put an end to the disturbances. All the enthusiastic innovators became reconciled to the more expedient reforms except Carlstadt and the "prophets." Carlstadt vigorously asserted his right to carry out his conception of the scriptural commands and never became completely reconciled to Luther. Three of the "prophets" came to Luther to convert him to their conception of revelation. The interview ended in an attitude of mutual hostility that augured ill for the future.

## Luther's Polemics

Meanwhile Luther was compelled to answer the increasing number of attacks by his Catholic enemies. These, however, seemed to lack an understanding of the real character of the new evangelical movement and were on the whole content with accusing Luther and his followers of previously condemned heresies, to base their accusations upon scholastic and canonical authorities, and to resort to personal abuse. The positive movement of the Catholic Reformation, which later marshaled its own dynamic scholastic, mystical, and evangelical forces, had not yet gained sufficient momentum to stop the spread of Lutheranism. The polemics of Luther and his followers, on the other hand, frequently lacked the vigor and originality of the first years of the Reformation and were often characterized by vilification and personal abuse. Dogmatic and defiant, they denied the validity of the medieval additions to and interpretations of the teachings of the primitive Church and spoke of their interpretations as God's own. They made generalizations concerning both the secular and the regular clergy that showed a lack of Christian restraint. But they wrote these works in the heat of battle and with a holy zeal to crush a powerful and equally bellicose opponent.

Eck continued to be the most active opponent of Luther, who, in turn, gave back every blow in kind. Eck's most widely read polemic was his *Manual of Common Doctrines Against Luther and Other Enemies of the Church,* which was circulated in forty-six editions. Many of his forceful sermons against Lutheranism were also circulated in published form.

Probably the most interesting of the Catholic polemical writings was *The Defense of the Seven Sacraments Against Martin Luther,* penned in 1521 by Henry VIII of England as an answer to the reformer's *The Babylonian Captivity.* It was dedicated to Pope Leo X, who, in gratitude, conferred upon the king the title of Defender of the Faith. The polemic, however, hardly deserved the papal praise accorded it, for it contained only the well-known arguments against Luther's theology, presented in a contemptuous and vituperative manner. Luther, whom Henry called the "worst wolf of hell" who "belches forth" filthy, evil words against the pope, the "chief pastor" of the Church, answered this effusion after a German translation by Emser had appeared in 1522. In his *German Answer to King Henry's Book* of that year, Luther countered the charges of inconsistency by stating that his views on faith and good works had remained the same, as could be seen in his books, but that his views concerning the papacy had changed during the bitter controversies of the last few years. He further restated his position on the Lord's Supper with skill and conviction. But he did not miss the opportunity to return abuse for abuse, thereby harming the cause of Lutheranism in England. Sir Thomas More and Bishop John Fisher of that country, as well as Hieronymus Emser of Leipzig, Johann Cochlaeus, and Duke George of Saxony, answered Luther's attack upon the king.

Cochlaeus, a humanist who had at first been friendly to Luther but had become a supporter of Aleander at the Diet of Worms, elicited the especial wrath of Luther by challenging him to renounce his safe-conduct and engage in a disputation with him. This the reformer refused to do. The bitter controversy, in which both men resorted to unedifying vilification, was not concluded until Cochlaeus published a biography of the reformer in 1549, three years after the latter's death. It contained many vicious misrepresentations of fact, which have been used by enemies of Luther to this day.

Much has been written concerning Luther's use of violent and frequently uncouth language. Although this was characteristic of the age in which he lived, he himself recognized his tendency to be excessively violent; and he explained that his strong emphasis upon sex in his polemics concerning celibacy and marriage was necessary to illustrate God's law of nature, which cannot be overruled by force without detriment to the individual, society, and the Church. Although he lacked the more delicate taste of Calvin in such matters, he cannot be accused of being intentionally coarse. Taken as a whole, Luther's polemics tended to clarify the issues at stake and to consolidate his following.

## Organization and Spread of Lutheranism

As soon as order had been established at Wittenberg, Luther and his friends took up the task of constructing an evangelical church along conservative lines. Although urging the leaders to follow moderation and toleration toward those who had not yet comprehended the significance of the gospel, Luther insisted that those who had should be firm in their opposition to the forces of evil.

# Part Two: The Reformation in Germany

Contrary to Luther's expectations, the simple preaching of the gospel did not solve all difficulties and differences of opinion. Consequently he resorted upon occasion to vigorous practical measures for the maintenance of order. He went on numerous missions to those centers where serious controversies had developed and wrote many letters and pamphlets urging vigorous action in abolishing the Mass, relic worship, and other nonevangelical usages. He also persisted in his demands that his elector put an end to the old practices in All Saints Church in Wittenberg until the latter finally agreed to do so in 1524. Like Carlstadt during the Wittenberg disturbances, Luther now argued that in matters of conscience a Christian should obey God rather than man.

Meanwhile Luther also reformed the order of service in the parish church at Wittenberg, substituting for the defunct daily Masses a short daily worship, in which the chief emphasis was placed upon reading and expounding the Bible. In the Sunday service, in which the Lord's Supper was celebrated, the preaching of the gospel in the vernacular likewise received the chief emphasis, although Luther retained most of the medieval liturgy, including the Gloria, the Hallelujah, the Nicene Creed, the Sanctus, and the Agnus Dei. With the assistance of two able musicians he adapted the Gregorian music to the German translation with happy artistic results. Communion in both kinds followed the sermon. But Luther did not insist that congregations elsewhere follow the service at Wittenberg in every detail, for he maintained that freedom should be practiced in all externals, such as the use of vestments, candles, and music. Although the private Mass was abolished, individual confession before Communion was permitted. The great concern in making changes in the service was to make it intelligible to the participants; therefore the vernacular was used both in the liturgy and in the singing of hymns.

The baptismal service was also translated into German, for Luther wished to make the parents of those baptized aware of the importance of this sacrament, by means of which the infant became regenerated, was "delivered from the devil, sin, and death," and was made a member of the Christian communion of saints. Although he wished to simplify the rite, he retained it in its traditional form, for he did not want to offend weak Christians.

Luther's emphasis upon the preaching of the gospel and the participation of the members of the congregation in the religious services was reflected also in his plans for the administration of the church. In his significant work *On Secular Government,* he distinguished between the spiritual realm, which consisted of preaching the gospel and in which no force should be used, and the secular realm, which was divinely ordained to maintain order and which the Christian must obey in secular matters. The ideal society, according to Luther, would be the one in which the Christian government would protect all divinely created classes in their respective callings and maintain order in the preaching of the gospel. Thus preaching and governing were, according to him, complementary callings, the former operating in the sphere of religion and ethics, the latter in matters pertaining to order.

In his attempts to approximate the conditions of the primitive Christian Church, Luther replaced the ecclesiastical hierarchy of the medieval Church with the spiritual democracy of the New Testament. He insisted that the congregation had the right not only to decide doctrinal matters and call pastors and teachers but to appropriate and administer ecclesiastical revenues for the good of the whole community. Accordingly a common treasury received money from the entire community, and from it the congregations paid their preachers and teachers, maintained schools, and cared for the poor. The wishes of the congregation were usually executed by both the city council as the chief administrative body and the chief pastor as a superintendent, or bishop.

## Visitations

If Luther could have carried out his conception of the Church as a spiritual communion (*corpus mysticum*) of believers—invisible and visible at the same time—there would have been no state control of the church in Saxony or the other Lutheran lands. Each independent congregation would have cooperated with every other congregation because of the faith and love common to all, without legal coercion of any kind and with the assistance of the state only in secular matters. However, the influence of the territorial prince in religious matters had become so strong in Europe by the sixteenth century that Luther could not effectively oppose his assumption of functions that were purely spiritual. Furthermore, the many theological and administrative differences and difficulties became so great that Luther himself felt the need of the strong arm of the state to maintain the peace and order demanded by Paul. Finally, the Diet of Speyer of 1526 decided that each estate should act in carrying out the Edict of Worms as it would if it had to answer only to God and the emperor, giving virtual recognition to the growth of the territorial churches.

Urged by Luther and other reformers to exercise his authority as the foremost member of the church in correcting the abominable religious and moral conditions and establishing order in Saxony, Elector John (1525–1532) appointed a committee of visitation to examine the affairs of the four districts into which the electorate was divided. This committee, consisting of two electoral councilors (Hans Metzsch and Benedikt Pauli) and two theologians (Martin Luther and Justus Jonas), was given the right not only to examine the spiritual needs of the people but to exercise secular and spiritual functions. Although Luther insisted that the committees chosen for the visitation of all Saxony were only temporary expedients—that is, that the elector served in the capacity of a bishop only until the organization of the church had been completed—this marked the beginning of the state control of the Lutheran Church.

That Elector John looked upon the visitation as an instrument of the state that he should control can be gathered from "The Instruction," which he gave his committee in June, 1527. Although he stated that he would not compel people to believe as he did, he charged the committee with the task of depriving of their positions those clergymen who did not conform. Furthermore, he requested the committee to take an inventory of all the income and possessions of the church and to see to it that the salaries of the clergy and teachers were paid and the poor were given adequate provisions. Finally, he requested it to appoint superintendents to supervise the doctrines, administration, and private morals of the clergy.

The first extensive visitation revealed a deplorable state of affairs among the congregations, prompting the elector to request Melanchthon to draw up the *Instruction of the Visitors to the Pastors* (1528). This ordinance summarized the evangelical doctrines in a simplified form, providing for their enforcement by means of excommunication; outlined a general order of public worship and discipline; defined the supervision of the clergy of each of the four Saxon districts by a superintendent who was empowered to inform the elector of cases of recalcitrance; and demanded a better system of education for both the laity and the clergy. In the preface that Luther wrote for this ordinance, he explained that the visitation had become necessary because of the indolence of the bishops and the inability of the pastors. But he repeated his emphasis upon the fact that this was a temporary expedient and that the prince was expected to interfere only to prevent anarchy. The spiritual functions, he insisted, belonged only to the church.

The Saxon method of organizing the church was adopted, with certain modifications, by other German princes who had embraced Lutheranism. The grand master of the Teutonic Knights, Albert of Brandenburg (1490–1568), became Lutheran in 1525, reconstituted his lands as a secular duchy under the feudal suzerainty of the king of Poland, and, upon Luther's recommendation, introduced the visitation the next year. By 1528 Brandenburg, Brunswick-Lüneburg, Schleswig-Holstein, Mansfeld, and Silesia had become Lutheran and had begun to use the visitation for carrying out practical reforms.

In Hesse, Landgrave Philip had convened a synod of clergy and laymen at Homberg in 1526 for the purpose of adopting Lutheranism. The church ordinance that was prepared by Francis Lambert, a former Franciscan from Avignon, provided for a democratic organization in which the congregations elected their own pastors, elders, and deacons and sent their pastors and elected representatives to an annual territorial synod or assembly. This synod was charged with the responsibility of caring for the church as a whole and providing each district with a superintendent. The landgrave was permitted only to take part in the deliberations and to vote. When Philip showed the constitution to Luther, the latter warned that it was not suited to the needs of Hesse and induced the Hessians to adopt the visitation in its stead.

The practical organization of the Reformation in the cities was in some respects patterned after the organization at Wittenberg. Usually the city council designated one of the city clergy as superintendent and made him responsible for the religious life of the entire city. The property and income of the monasteries and endowments for Masses were now used for educational purposes and for the care of the poor, and courts were set up for maintaining church discipline and trying cases, particularly those arising out of matrimonial problems. In some respects the cities of southern Germany, such as Strassburg and Augsburg, maintained considerable autonomy in religious and ecclesiastical matters and for a while provided protection and help for religious refugees of various shades of Protestantism. The cities of northern Germany were provided constitutions by Johann Bugenhagen, the city pastor at Wittenberg after 1523. Brunswick introduced the Reformation in 1528, Hamburg the following year, and Lübeck in 1531, the constitution of each of these serving as the model for many other cities and towns.

### Means Used to Spread the Gospel

Meanwhile the doctrines of the Reformation were spread more rapidly than ever. Both the pope and the emperor appeared helpless in their efforts to stem the tide. Preachers proclaimed the evangelical message from pulpits, on the streets, and even in taverns, and printed pamphlets in countless numbers brought the gospel to people of all classes. The fine arts, too, were used in the service of the Reformation.

The chief centers of the movement were Saxony and Thuringia, where devoted followers were found in Zwickau, Magdeburg, Erfurt, and Weimar; at Heidelberg and along the Rhine, where Luther had gained a considerable following early in his conflict with the papacy; in such cities of southern Germany as Nürnberg, Augsburg, and Strassburg, where the way had been prepared by humanists and other educated middle-class leaders; and in the Low Countries, where mysticism and humanism tended to make the people receptive and where Augustinian monks eagerly spread Luther's doctrines. In these lands, ruled by Charles V, the Edict of Worms was strictly enforced from the beginning; and there two monks, Hendrik Vos and Jan van der Eschen, became the first martyrs to the evangelical movement on July 1, 1523.

The leaders of the Reformation were regularly ordained priests, former humanists and monks, and often people with little learning or experience in religious matters. One of the most influential preachers and leaders was the learned Martin Butzer, Latinized as Bucer (1491–1551), a Dominican monk who became chaplain of the imperial knight Franz von Sickingen, preached in the important city of Strassburg from 1523 to 1549, and finally accepted the invitation of the English reformers to visit their country. He became a professor in Cambridge, where he died in 1551. One of the most learned reformers was Wolfgang Capito (1478–1541), a humanist trained in law and theology, who had served as a preacher and professor in Basel and as a preacher and counselor of the archbishop of Mainz before assuming the duties of a preacher and a professor of theology in Strassburg in 1523.

Among the reformers who developed in Luther's environment were Justus Jonas (1493–1555), Johann Bugenhagen (1485–1558), and Johann Agricola (1499–1566). Jonas, a humanist who had studied at Erfurt and Wittenberg, became a professor at Erfurt (1518), where he introduced his humanist and religious reforms, taught law and theology at Wittenberg after 1521, and in 1541 went as superintendent to Halle. Bugenhagen, a schoolmaster in a Premonstratensian monastery in Pomerania, was won to Luther's cause after having read the latter's *The Babylonian Captivity*. While he was preacher in the City Church in Wittenberg, he performed a great service for Lutheranism by preparing church constitutions for the cities and territories of northern Germany. Agricola, who gained great popularity because of his collection of proverbs, served as a court preacher in Berlin after 1540.

Of the many colleagues and friends of Luther at Wittenberg who aided him in his gigantic task of organizing and spreading the evangelical movement, the most helpful was Philip Melanchthon (1497–1560). He was a brilliant humanist, a grandnephew of Reuchlin, who had come to Wittenberg in 1518 after Luther had convinced the elector that Greek and Hebrew should be taught at the University. Luther learned much of both these languages from Melanchthon, and urged him to continue his classical studies. But Melanchthon was overpowered by the personality and the religious convictions of Luther and consequently turned his attention principally to the study of the New Testament. Through him many young humanists were attracted to Luther's cause. As a teacher, standing faithfully beside the prophet, he made Lutheranism a part of the culture and learning of northern Germany. Moreover, he devoted his talents to systematizing Luther's doctrines, often developed in the heat of bitter conflicts, in his *Loci communes (Main Concepts)*, published first in Latin in 1521 and later in a German translation by Spalatin.

The importance of printing in the spread of the Reformation can scarcely be exaggerated. And the Reformation also furthered the development of printing. The most popular form of Reformation literature was the pamphlet, published in small, quarto size and usually provided with

1526

VIVENTIS·POTVIT·DVRERIVS·ORA·PHILIPPI
MENTEM·NON·POTVIT·PINGERE·DOCTA
MANVS

Philip Melanchthon

by *Albrecht Dürer*

woodcut illustrations. Dealing with a great variety of subjects, they were written in the form of prose, verse, dialogues, and letters and bore such captivating titles as *Karsthans, a Happy New Year* and *I Wonder Why There Is No Money in the Land*. Although some pamphlets were published anonymously, others carried the names of important religious and lay leaders, including women such as Ursula Weydin and Argula von Staufen.

The most popular forms of art used in the service of the Reformation were the woodcuts, developed to a high degree by the Nürnberg master Albrecht Dürer (1471–1528), who sympathized with Luther but did not directly further his cause. His students, especially Hans Sebald Behaim, made use of a new illustrative technique, the religious and political cartoon. Developed largely in connection with the portrayal of Antichrist, it tended to become exceedingly crude and often obscene. Some of the best of these were provided by Lucas Cranach the Elder (1472–1553), who painted in Wittenberg after 1504. His illustrations for the September Testament, which show the influence of Dürer, make use of new, primarily Reformation themes, such as Jesus and the children and Jesus and the adulteress. He was surpassed in the portrayal of such scenes by Hans Holbein the Younger (1497–1543), who produced his pictures of New Testament themes between 1523 and 1531.

The painting of portraits, which had become popular among the great Italian artists by 1500, was used to preserve the likenesses of the leaders of the Reformation. The best portraits that we have of Luther are those by Cranach the Elder. However, these do not compare artistically with those of Erasmus and More by Holbein the Younger or with the copper etching of Melanchthon by Dürer.

Peter Vischer (d. 1529), the well-known producer of bronze figures as well as paintings, also brought the artistry of the Renaissance into the service of the Reformation. In his drawing of an allegory of Luther's work (1524) now in Goethe House in Weimar, he portrayed Luther as an untheological Greek hero and god who, with a shield strapped to his back, leads the free conscience and the German people to the resurrected Christ. Behind lies the destroyed edifice of the papacy, with pride, greed, and love of luxury in ignominious flight. Before him stand three beautiful girls who represent faith, hope, and love, while a fourth removes the blindfold from justice.

The singing of hymns, as we have seen, was widespread during the late Middle Ages. To Luther, however, goes the credit of making congregational singing a part of the church service, symbolizing his emphasis upon the believer's direct access to God. The "Wittenberg Nightingale," as he was called by the Nürnberg meistersinger Hans Sachs (1494–1576), not only had a well-trained tenor voice and showed an exceptional understanding of the polyphonic music of his day, but played musical instruments with skill and composed beautiful popular melodies. The best secular and sacred music of his day was performed in the informal musicales after dinner in his home. His favorite composer was Josquin Després, whom he considered a musical genius.

Melanchthon and other friends of Luther supported him in making music a means for teaching the gospel in church, school, and home. The medieval and contemporary music of the Catholic Church was appreciated and adapted to Protestant needs, but a distinctly Protestant music did not develop until the end of the sixteenth century. The importance of music in the schools can be seen by the fact that the cantor ranked next to the rector, or school head. This importance was largely responsible for the development of a middle-class music in Protestant Germany, which came to differ fundamentally from the music of the Catholic chapel choirs. Moreover, people were urged to sing doctrinal and other religious hymns at their work and play.

The best-known hymn writers of Luther's day were Hans Sachs, who wrote "O Gentle Jesus" to replace the Catholic "O Gentle Mary"; Lazarus Spengler, who gave us "Through Adam's Fall We Sinnéd All"; Paul Speratus, the composer of beautiful doctrinal hymns; and Johann Walther, Luther's cantor, who helped to organize the music in the evangelical church and to select the Germanized Latin chorales for use in the new service. Luther, like the other hymn writers of his day, produced original hymns and also adapted many of the popular medieval hymns to his needs and translated a large number from the Latin. The best-known original hymn by Luther is "A Mighty Fortress Is Our God," based on Psalm 46 and called by the poet Heine the "Marseillaise of the Reformation." It has been translated into more languages than any other hymn. He adapted from among the pre-Reformation hymns "May God Be Prais'd Henceforth." One of the hymns that he translated from a Latin hymn of the eighth century begins with these words:

> Creator, Spirit, Holy Dove,
> Visit Thy people from above,
> Fill them with graces and restore
> Thy creatures as they were before.

Although Luther avoided the use of secular folk tunes, these became an important source of German chorales. At first the melody was sung in unison. Then the congregation sang the melody, which was in the tenor voice, while the choir carried the other parts. The melodic and choral forms of the stately hymns as we know them today did not develop until the eighteenth century. In Luther's time the scale and the harmonic system of the chorale were still those of the Gregorian chant, with its great freedom and variety of rhythm. Gradually, however, the composers introduced a simpler form of harmony by placing the melody in the upper voice and the accompanying parts below, a form of harmonic progression of chords with which we are familiar today. When the choir and the congregational singers were separated, about 1600, contrapuntal music was continued in the motet, and the simple chord progression was retained for the congregation. The latter was then accompanied by an organ.

Collections of evangelical hymns soon appeared in increasing numbers. In 1524 there were published the so-called *Achtliederbuch* (*Book of Eight Hymns*); the *Enchiridion* of Erfurt, containing twenty-six hymns, eighteen of which had been composed by Luther; and the *Gesangbüchlein* (*Little Book of Songs*) of thirty-two hymns, published by Walther, which Luther provided with an introduction and Lucas Cranach the Elder with woodcuts. So effective were these hymns of "the singing church" in spreading the Reformation that Luther's enemies often feared them more than his sermons.

Religious drama was also used to bring Luther's teachings to the people. In a carnival play of 1522, for example, written by Niklaus Manuel of Bern, Christ and the apostles meet an elaborate papal procession. In the first climax Peter, upon seeing the pope, asks who he is. When told that the pope is his successor, he peers through his eyeglass and remarks that the man has no feet. When assured that he has feet, Peter asks why he is being carried. In the final scene, Christ, accompanied by the poor, the sick, and the needy, meets the pope in all his splendor. Peasants, armed with the Bible, lead Christ away. Joachim Greff, one of the poets in Luther's circle, wrote a play based on the story of Lazarus, for which Luther wrote a four-part musical composition similar to the motet.

Although catechisms existed long before the time of Luther, they were now revised to reflect the new evangelical spirit, and their use was systematized so that both the clergy and the laity could learn at least the fundamentals of Christian faith and doctrine. From 1516, when Luther began to preach in the pulpit of Simon Heinz at Wittenberg as a supply preacher, he used the sermon to bring down to the level of the people the doctrines that he had developed on a high intellectual plane. Sermons explaining the Ten Commandments, the Apostles' Creed, and the Lord's Prayer were published in pamphlet form, and as early as 1520 such sermons were collected and published in the form of confessional "mirrors," the forerunners of the Small Catechism.

During the following decade about thirty catechetical works appeared. Prepared for daily use in home and school, these were usually printed on charts or placards that were hung on the walls, where they could be frequently seen. In some of them, the dialogue form with questions and answers, familiar in the Middle Ages and popular among the humanists, was used. During this time the word *catechism* was first used in reference to a book as well as to oral instruction in general. The words of institution of baptism and the Lord's Supper were added to the three original parts—the Ten Commandments, the Apostles' Creed, and the Lord's Prayer—and an understanding of all five was made a condition for admission to communion.

Luther's catechetical charts of 1529 contained three additional parts: the *Benedicite* and the *Gratias,* taken from the well-known *Breviarum romanum;* the Morning and Evening Prayers, based in part upon catechetical works of the fifteenth century; and the Table of Duties. Such charts were published in Low German in Hamburg by Bugenhagen in 1529. In later editions in High German they were given the name Small Catechism.

Luther himself published a more extensive volume in 1529 that he called the German Catechism but that eventually came to be known as the Large Catechism. In its final form this volume contained not only the texts of the Ten Commandments, the Creed, and the Lord's Prayer, and the words of institution of baptism and the Lord's Supper, but a detailed exposition of the texts, a confessional exhortation, and a lengthy preface explaining the use of the catechism.

## Defections from Lutheranism

Despite the vigorous leadership of Luther and his followers, the preaching of the gospel did not lead to the expected Reformation of the entire Church or prevent a division among those who had originally supported the Lutheran movement. Luther did not seem to realize that the Bible might be interpreted differently by different people, that the denial of the authority of the Church might lead to a great variety of interpretations. Furthermore, because various dissatisfied groups had joined the movement of protest against the abuses and doctrines of the medieval Church, it was natural that they should eventually make known their respective positions.

Although Luther clung tenaciously to the doctrines that he had developed and built up a Church with a definite body of doctrine, many intellectuals and social revolutionaries parted company with him. But he did not want the Church to split into factions and to the end of his life believed that the unity of the Church could be restored.

### The Humanists

Probably the most serious defection from the ranks of the early reformers was that of those humanists who had originally hailed Luther's bold stand against papal authority and ecclesiastical abuses but who were gradually alienated by his dogmatic stand on religious questions. Such a parting of the ways should cause no surprise, however, for the differences between Luther and the humanists were fundamental. Whereas Luther, with his overwhelming sense of sin, stressed the absolute corruption of human nature and the complete dependence of man upon the grace of God, the humanists emphasized the goodness and dignity of man. Furthermore, whereas Luther appealed to the common people in their mother tongue, the humanists wrote for the cultured elite in polished Latin and feared the consequences of arousing the passions of the masses.

Luther was at no time inclined to compromise with the humanists or any other group in order to obtain support for his cause. Believing that God would see to it that the gospel triumphed, he let the chips fall where they might. Within the Catholic Church, however, there was still a considerable element of toleration, so that the humanists, who sought intellectual freedom only for themselves, could remain unmolested, provided they showed tact. Thus, although a large number of them became Protestants, many others remained Catholics. But later in the century, when the Council of Trent provided Catholicism with an official, definite body of doctrine and sought to prevent deviations by means of the Index and the extension of the Inquisition, when much of Europe became involved in bitter religious strife, humanism virtually ceased to be a strong intellectual force.

Although Reuchlin, the Hebrew scholar, had waged a vigorous war against the conservative theologians of the Church, he did not join the Lutheran movement. He even disowned his grandnephew Melanchthon for having done so. Mutian, Pirkheimer, Crotus Rubeanus, and other humanists who had originally hailed Luther as a hero resented his attack upon the institution of the Church and his violent break with the papacy.

### Luther and Erasmus

Particularly significant was the attitude of Erasmus, the "prince of the humanists," to whom most enlightened Europeans looked for leadership in solving the religious crisis. Even though he was at first cautious and noncommittal with respect to Luther's early reforms, he frequently showed his sympathy, for the two had much in common. As a matter of fact, the followers of Erasmus believed that he had "laid the egg that Luther hatched," for he had opposed the obscurantism of the scholastics, had appealed to the Bible as the ultimate authority in religious matters, had minimized the importance of the sacraments, had emphasized inner spirituality, had objected to the excessive ecclesiastical regulation of men's lives, and had attacked the evils in monasticism. But he had never denied the authority of ecclesiastical tradition. Moreover, he was by nature averse to assuming responsibility for the widespread unrest that followed his critical attacks and advised both sides to refrain from violence. When that did not succeed, he turned against Luther.

The open break between Luther and Erasmus came in 1523, precipitated by the bitter attack of Ulrich von Hutten upon the latter for refusing to support the Lutheran cause, by certain letters of Luther in which he asserted that Erasmus lacked the fortitude of a Christian leader, and by the insistence of Henry VIII of England and others that the prince of the humanists take up his pen against Luther. In that year Erasmus began to plan his *Diatribe on Free Will,* which appeared in print in Basel in August, 1524. In it he came to grips with the cardinal difference between Luther and the humanists—belief in the impotence of man's will as opposed to the freedom of the will in religious matters. Ignoring, and probably not understanding, the personal religious motives that had compelled Luther to take a firm stand, Erasmus approached the problem as an intellectual and presented his arguments as a critical scholar, not as a dogmatic thinker and believer. Although he sympathized with much of Luther's evangelical teaching, he concluded that the power of the will, derived from reason, was not destroyed with Adam's fall.

Erasmus failed to take into account Luther's distinction between justification and sanctification, between the "natural man" before conversion (whose will was impotent) and the converted man (whose will was freed by the grace of God). Therefore he considered the denial of the freedom of the will a dangerous doctrine, for it might relieve man of moral responsibility. The traditional doctrine of the Church seemed to him much more reasonable and practical. While weighing both sides of the question, however, Erasmus did not commit himself definitely on one side or the other, for he admitted the bondage of the will because of the fall of man, though he assumed man's capacity to do good by virtue of a "restricted freedom."

Luther replied by publishing, in 1525, his *Bondage of the Will,* in which he criticized Erasmus for his skepticism and restated his theological position that man was saved solely by faith, irrespective of merit. This doctrine was for him the essence of Christianity, not merely a matter of erudite speculation. Unlike Erasmus, he did not approach the question from the point of view of man but from that of the revealed God, virtually unknown to natural man, who was divinely righteous, omniscient, omnipotent, and omnipresent. He believed that the divine will was immutable and that therefore it foresaw, determined, and affected everything. Unlike Calvin, however, Luther did not concern himself much with the problem of predestination. He accused Erasmus of confusing the law, which makes man aware of his sin, with the gospel, which alone saves, and concluded by showing how he had experienced the depths of despair by attempting to earn his own salvation and had found peace of soul by believing in God's grace and bowing to the divine will.

Despite the relatively moderate and impersonal tone of the *Bondage of the Will,* Erasmus considered it an attack upon his own person as well as upon humanism. Consequently he bitterly impugned Luther and his movement in his *Heavy-Armed Soldier,* published in two parts in 1526 and 1527. With this attack the break was completed between the scholar and the prophet.

## Social Revolutionaries

Because of Luther's fundamentally conservative point of view with respect to political, economic, and social matters, it was obvious that he would sooner or later come into conflict with the social revolutionaries. As long as their preaching and writing were peaceful, he was inclined to tolerate them, for he believed that many of their demands were justified and that the spreading of the Word of God would eventually right all wrongs. But after the Diet of Worms he consistently warned all his supporters against the use of force. Therefore he vigorously opposed all who advocated violence or took up arms to bring about religious or social changes. As the conservative nature of Luther's Reformation became more and more obvious, the great mass of the lower classes, especially of those peasants and townsmen who were not faring well during the great political, economic, and social changes of the period, became increasingly radical in their views and demands until much of Germany was involved in a revolution.

For more than half a century before the outbreak of the Peasants' Revolt, the peasants had voiced opposition to the tendency of the princes and the landowners to ignore the peasants' rights as embodied in customary law and to introduce the principles of the Roman law that generally favored the landholders. Although the peasants were not poverty-stricken in most parts of Germany, but self-confident and even belligerent, many of them were dissatisfied with their status and demanded important changes. Old payments and services had lost their justification. Many landlords, to meet their financial needs, revived old rights at the expense of the peasants. Added to this provocation were the new taxes imposed by the territorial estates, especially after 1500. Moreover, many people, especially the masses in the towns, felt the pinch of rising prices and came to detest the increasing number of monopolies during this period of the commercial revolution.

For many years the lower classes had looked for a savior in the form of a "resurrected" Frederick Barbarossa who would free them from oppression. A number of pamphlets containing programs for reform made their appearance. One of the best known was called the *Reformation of Emperor Sigismund,* written in 1438 by a clergyman of Augsburg and published for the first time in 1476. When Sigismund failed them, the lower classes turned in vain to Frederick III and, finally, to his son Maximilian. The *Reformation of the Emperor Frederick III,* published in 1523, demanded among other things reform of the clergy, the confiscation of ecclesiastical property, the abolition of tithes and taxes, the nullification of imperial laws, and the limitation of the incomes of merchants.

## 4. The Growth of Lutheranism

As it became apparent that the emperor would not or could not liberate them, the lower classes, led by enthusiastic if not always capable preachers and reformers, gained a greater confidence in themselves and determined to take the matter of reforms into their own hands. This was particularly true in southwestern Germany, where the feudal holdings were especially small and could hardly support the increasing demands made upon them by the ambitious landholders and princes. It was there, after 1493, that the peasants first formed organizations to obtain justice by direct action. Their emblem, which consisted of a shoe with a long string attached to it, was called the *Bundschuh*. Frequently joined by townsmen and the lower clergy, they staged uprisings that were brutally suppressed by the authorities.

As time went on, the *Bundschuh* programs began to incorporate religious ideas and doctrines, probably influenced by the Christian egalitarianism and socialism of the followers of Hus, aimed particularly at the papacy and ecclesiastical property but also at the emperor. One of these followers, Hans Böhm, a bagpiper of Nicklashausen, claimed that the Virgin Mary had told him of the coming of the kingdom of God and, in 1476, while sitting naked in a stream, preached to the peasants of Würzburg concerning the state of nature until the crowd was dispersed by the bishop. He was ultimately burned as a heretic. Throughout the peasant uprisings, religious and political motives were found alongside the economic and social. Wandering priests, monks, students, and artisans, filled with vague ideas concerning humanist utopias, astrological notions with respect to impending catastrophes, and apocalyptic visions, harangued the multitudes in the language of the people, quoting Scripture to suit their particular notions.

Although sporadic outbreaks among the peasants occurred in several regions in southern Germany before the appearance of Luther, it cannot be denied that the evangelical movement tended to hasten the crisis that broke out in all its fury in 1524. To the well-known medieval demands for "divine justice" they now added the cry for "gospel justice." When Luther preached his religious doctrine of justification by faith alone, which minimized the role of the highly developed organization of the Church; when he taught the universal priesthood of believers who are all equal before God and do not need the mediation of priests and saints; when he spoke of the freedom of the Christian that comes to those who believe in the gospel, the oppressed translated these doctrines into political, economic, and social terms and looked to him as their leader. They were further encouraged by the democratic implications of his practical attacks upon greedy princes who ignored the just grievances of the common man and whom he warned in 1523 of the impending judgment of God that would descend upon them because of their obstinacy. The peasants were also impressed by his attacks upon the avarice of the merchants, whose monopolistic and usurious practices were impoverishing honest people, and the greed of higher clergy who robbed them of their money and deprived them of the liberty promised in the gospel. But the peasants and their leaders did not see that political, economic, and social grievances lay on the periphery of Luther's thinking, that he wished to bring about all such changes through the free preaching of the gospel and regularly established, constitutional channels.

## The Peasants' Revolt (1524–1525)

The Peasants' Revolt broke out without unified leadership or program at Stühlingen in the southwestern part of the Black Forest in June, 1524, when the countess of Lüpfen demanded that the peasants gather strawberries and snail shells for a banquet. The articles of grievance that they drew up expressed opposition to the seizure of common lands by the lords, the excessive burdens in taxes and forced labor, the unfair administration of justice, and the preservation of game for the lords. Led by Hans Müller, a former *Landsknecht,* the peasants marched to Waldshut, a town that was already in revolt against Austria. The revolt quickly spread to all the districts about Lake Constance and then to Swabia and Württemberg. The attempts of Georg Truchsess, the general of the Swabian League, to negotiate with the insurgents or suppress them were of no avail, primarily because most of the military forces of the League were engaged in the wars in Italy.

Despite the rapid spread of the revolt to about a third of Germany, it had not yet become violent by the early months of 1525, for the princes were still negotiating with the leaders. The most widely accepted plans for obtaining the "divine justice" demanded by the peasants were embodied in the Twelve Articles, which began to circulate at Memmingen in February, 1525. The first article demanded the right of each community to choose its own pastor; the second agreed to pay the great tithe on grain but protested against the minor tithes; the third denounced serfdom as contrary to the gospel and Christian freedom; the fourth and fifth demanded the right to fish, hunt, and cut wood in the common forests; the sixth, seventh, and eighth insisted on relief from excessive feudal dues, forced labor, and rents; the ninth protested against the making of new laws and demanded impartial justice and a return to "the old written law"; the tenth opposed the seizure of common lands without fair payment for them; the eleventh called for the abolition of the heriot, or inheritance tax, which unjustly oppressed widows and orphans; and the twelfth stated the willingness of the peasants to withdraw any articles contrary to the Word of God.

In the Twelve Articles, as in a number of similar manifestoes, the peasants assumed that they were acting according to the gospel proclaimed by Luther, and they promised not to use force to achieve their ends except as a last resort. Accordingly, the leaders of the Swabian peasants submitted their articles for arbitration to a commission of four, comprising Frederick the Wise, Luther, Melanchthon or Bugenhagen, and an imperial representative.

But not all peasant demands were so moderate, and the farther the movement spread, the more revolutionary and violent it became. In Franconia it began in the ecclesiastical territories of Bamberg and Würzburg and eventually reached the imperial city of Rothenburg, where a number of nobles, including Götz von Berlichingen—immortalized in one of Goethe's dramas—were compelled to join the movement as "brothers." In the Austrian lands, especially in Tyrol, Salzburg, and Styria, the masses were inflamed by such leaders as Michael Gaismair, who demanded the acceptance of a constitution that provided for a popular government directly under the Archduke Ferdinand, confiscation of Church property, common ownership of all property, government by men versed in the Bible, and state control of trade, industry, and mining. But before establishing his kingdom of God on earth, Gaismair said that it would be necessary to kill all godless people. In Alsace and Lorraine the peasants were determined to seize all common lands without negotiating with the owners and to recognize no government that was not in harmony with the will of the people.

In Saxony and Thuringia the chief events were associated with the name of Thomas Müntzer, a radical mystic who had settled at Mühlhausen in 1524 and had attempted to set up a theocratic state in that Thuringian town. Müntzer was one of the ablest and best-educated leaders of the lower classes. He had studied at the universities at Leipzig and Frankfurt and had been recommended by Luther for the position of pastor at Zwickau. There he developed his doctrines concerning the inner light—that is, the direct and continued revelation of the Holy Ghost—gleaned primarily from the writings of the medieval mystics. When he taught that the unlearned could gain this inner light by means of dreams and ecstatic visions and that his followers were the elect children of God who could exclude unbelievers by force, the town council of Zwickau, in the spring of 1521, started proceedings against him. To forestall such action he fled to Prague, where a similar fate awaited him.

For more than a year, from the spring of 1523 to the summer of 1524, Müntzer was a preacher at Alstedt, near Eisleben, where he further developed his mystic theology of the cross and his ideas concerning the elect community of saints. Finally, when he preached a violent sermon calling upon the elector of Saxony, who was in his audience, to use force to establish an apocalyptic kingdom on earth and denouncing Luther and his followers for being slavishly bound to the Bible, he was summoned to Weimar for a hearing. He then fled to Mühlhausen, where a revolutionary crusade was already under way. The town council expelled him, but he returned early in 1525, when the revolutionary movement in Thuringia was at white heat, goaded in part by his exhortation of 1524: "heed not the cries of the godless. . . . On while the fire is hot. Let not the blood cool on your swords"! But his communist theocracy at Mühlhausen was short-lived, for it was soon suppressed by the victorious princes.

Meanwhile the revolt seemed to carry everything before it. More than forty monasteries and castles were destroyed in central Germany alone. The movement, however, lacked organization and leadership. When the princes recovered from the first shocks of the revolt, and when the German soldiers began to return from Italy after the battle of Pavia (February 24, 1525), the uprising quickly collapsed. Elector John of Saxony (successor to Frederick the Wise, who had died during the revolt), Landgrave Philip of Hesse, and Duke Henry of Brunswick joined forces and defeated Müntzer in May. Although Müntzer was beheaded after a speedy trial, John, Philip, and Henry showed moderation in punishing the peasants. But little clemency was shown elsewhere. The army of the Swabian League under Truchsess ruthlessly suppressed the rising in Swabia and Franconia, and the duke of Lorraine crushed the movement in western Germany.

Throughout about a third of Germany the princes pursued the hapless peasants with such brutality and vengeance that thousands of them were killed. On the other hand, their social status was not altered to any appreciable extent, for few princes and landholders dared to increase the obligations of the peasants. Probably the greatest loss suffered by the peasants was political. Deprived of weapons and the means of protecting themselves, they lost the right to participate in important social movements and thus their ability to improve their status among the estates. The lesser nobility, many of whose castles had been destroyed, tended to settle in the cities and to accept service in the courts of the territorial princes. The princes alone seemed to be the victors.

### Luther and the Peasants

Luther's prestige as a leader of the people suffered because of the role that he played in the Peasants' Revolt, even though he was thoroughly consistent and impartial throughout. He sympathized with the demands of the peasants and, in his *Admonition to Peace in Response to the Twelve Articles* (April, 1525), severely criticized the princes whom he held responsible for causing the revolt by suppressing the preaching of the gospel. He even called the peasants "dear brethren" and "friends." But in the same pamphlet he accused them of confusing the gospel and human rights. The Christian, he maintained, had no right to appeal to natural right and take justice into his own hands but must suffer injustice. Although he agreed with the first and the last of the twelve articles, he insisted that the others must be taken up with the proper authorities.

His *Admonition to Peace* came too late to have any influence upon the revolt, for the peasants had already begun hostilities before its publication.

Luther showed his great concern over the resort to violence when he risked his life by going to Thuringia in an attempt to stop hostilities. There he urged the peasants to negotiate with Frederick the Wise, who was willing to listen to their demands. He continued his preaching in the revolutionary centers, despite the insults of the masses, until he had word that the dying elector wished to see him. When he returned to Wittenberg, the elector had died.

In the heat of his conflict with Müntzer and the other Thuringian leaders, all of whom he lumped together as murderous rebels, and when the revolt threatened Wittenberg itself, Luther wrote his deplorably virulent *Against the Murdering Hordes of Peasants,* in which he exhorted the princes to be "both judge and executioner," to "knock down, strangle, and stab . . . and think nothing so venomous, pernicious, or Satanic as an insurgent. . . . Such wonderful times are these that a prince can merit heaven better with bloodshed than another with prayer." He insisted that it was the prince's duty, as "God's sword on earth," to suppress all revolt. The prince should first try to treat with the peasants, but if they should prove obstinate, then he should use the sword, for it was necessary to protect the innocent peasants by severely punishing the rebellious leaders.

Despite the extenuating circumstances that explain Luther's fury, he would better have served his cause by not publishing the pamphlet. Many of his contemporaries, who were accustomed to cries for blood, criticized him for his severity. After the suppression of the revolt he wrote *The Terrible Story and Judgment of God Concerning Thomas Müntzer,* in which he admonished the princes to be lenient with the peasants, and his *Circular Letter Concerning the Severe Booklet Against the Peasants,* in which he explained his severity and condemned the tyrants who continued to harass them.

Because Luther believed that the peasants had misinterpreted and betrayed the gospel, he subsequently displayed a strong distrust of them. And he turned increasingly to established authority to maintain the peace and order that he considered necessary for the spread of the gospel. Generally conservative in political and social matters, he accepted the divine-right theory of the Pauline epistles and consistently believed that any person who urged the violent overthrow of the political and social order of his day was an instrument of the devil.

It is no wonder that the Lutheran movement lost some of its popular appeal. Although the princes, who had put down the revolt without help from the weak imperial council or the absent emperor, and Lutheranism, which had denied medieval theories supporting opposition to tyrants, drew closer together, the period of strong popular support of Lutheranism came to a close. Many disillusioned peasants and townsmen now turned to the Anabaptists, who promised to bring the kingdom of heaven down to earth.

## Luther's Marriage

It was in the midst of the storm and stress of the Peasants' Revolt that Luther announced his decision to marry Catherine von Bora, a significant step both for him and for the evangelical cause. He had taught that the clergy should marry, but he had considered the state of marital bliss out of the question for himself, particularly because he was constantly expecting to be put to death as a heretic.

Luther's change of mind came unexpectedly as a consequence of practical considerations. Catherine was one of twelve nuns who had been spirited away from the cloister Nimtzsch near Grimma on the eve before Easter, 1523, by Leonhard Kopp, a respected city councilor of Torgau. Luther had not only encouraged this but had helped gather contributions for the support of the nuns. Three of them went to their families. The remaining nine were taken to Wittenberg, where the reformers saw to it that they were married or placed in suitable homes.

After two years all the former nuns had been satisfactorily provided for except Catherine. She apparently was not beautiful, but she came from an old noble family, was healthy, and had a cheerful disposition. Her mother had died when Catherine was still a child, and her father had married a second time, which accounts for the fact that she did not return home and never received money from her father. When a match between her and a young student from Nürnberg failed to materialize, Luther picked for her a minister, one Dr. Glatz, whom she promptly rejected. Probably because her case seemed hopeless (she was already twenty-six!), she made what seemed like a ridiculous suggestion to Dr. Amsdorf of Magdeburg: she would be willing to marry him or Luther. Luther was then forty-one.

What followed does not read like a campus romance. Luther decided to marry Catherine to please his father, to spite his enemies, and to give expression to his faith before his expected martyrdom. To the surprise of his friends and the chagrin of Melanchthon, Luther and Catherine were married June 13, 1525, in the company of a few friends. Two weeks later there followed the public declaration and a wedding banquet in the Black Cloister. It was attended by Luther's parents and by friends from far and near. The banquet was followed by a dance at the town hall. The couple then moved into the Black Cloister, which had been renovated for them.

This marriage proved to be a blessing for Luther and did much to further the traditions of a new institution, the Protestant parsonage. Luther did more than any other person to hallow the Christian home in

Germany. He was affectionate with Catherine, whom he often jokingly called "My Rib," "Lord Katie," or, punning on the word "Katie," "*Kette,*" the German word for chain. His efficient wife cared for him during his many illnesses, so that later her doctor-son called her half a doctor, and she managed the affairs of this household so well that Luther was a moderately well-to-do man at his death. Saving was particularly difficult, for Luther was overly generous and constantly entertained colleagues, students, friends, and strangers at his table. The *Table Talks,* notes jotted down by a number of these guests and later published by them, attest to the happiness of this household, despite its many cares.

The marriage was blessed with six children. Hans was born in 1526, Elizabeth in 1527, Magdalene in 1529, Martin in 1531, Paul in 1533, and Margaret in 1534. Luther's letters to his friends contain many allusions to these children, to both the joys and the sorrows that go with raising a family. They were well brought up and provided for. Hans studied law and became a counselor in the court at Weimar. Martin studied theology but did not become a preacher. Paul became a distinguished physician who served in a number of German courts. It was through him that the male line of the Luther family was continued until 1759. There are still descendants of Luther through Margaret, who married a member of a wealthy Prussian noble family.

## The Rise of Zwinglianism

Lutheranism was retarded in its growth not only by the defection of the humanists, the Peasants' Revolt, and the rise of various left-wing reform movements, but also by the appearance of another form of state-church Protestantism, Zwinglianism. The emergence of this branch of Protestantism, though resting to a great extent upon the work of Luther, caused a serious rift in the evangelical movement precisely at the time when it was threatened by vigorous action on the part of the emperor and the Catholic princes of Germany.

The explanation for the chief differences between Lutheranism and Zwinglianism is to be found, in the first place, in the political conditions existing in the Swiss Confederation and its relations with the other European powers; in the second place, in the cultural milieu of Switzerland and southern Germany; and in the third place, in the unique position that the Swiss cantons had played in the conciliar movement. Decisive, too, were the differences in the personalities and training of the respective reformers.

Switzerland was nominally still a part of the Holy Roman Empire. Actually it was a loose confederation of thirteen virtually autonomous cantons, lying outside the administrative circles of the Empire and held together by several defensive treaties. These cantons were represented in

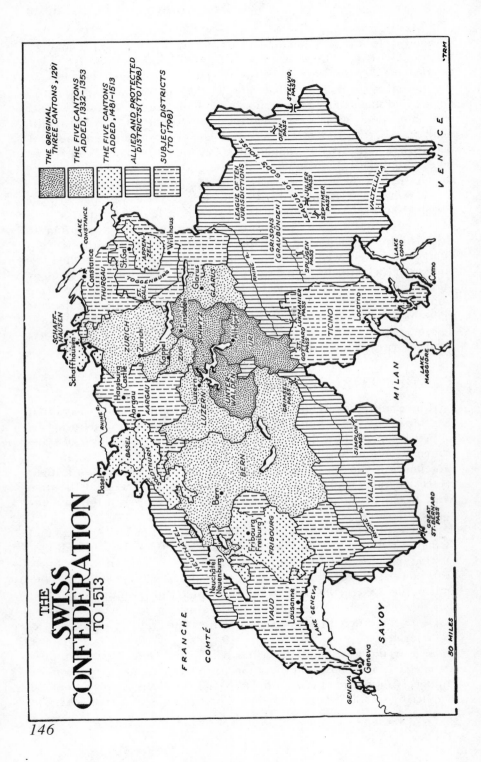

THE
SWISS
CONFEDERATION
TO 1513

THE ORIGINAL
THREE CANTONS, 1291
THE FIVE CANTONS
ADDED, 1332-1353
THE FIVE CANTONS
ADDED, 1481-1513
ALLIED AND PROTECTED
DISTRICTS (TO 1798)
SUBJECT DISTRICTS
(TO 1798)

STELVIO.
PASS

VENICE

OFEN
PASS

LEAGUE OF TEN
JURISDICTIONS

LEAGUE OF THE
GOD'S HOUSE

LAKE
COMO

LAKE
CONSTANCE

APPEN-
ZELL

GRISONS
(GRAUBÜNDEN)

LEAGUE JULIER
PASS
SEPTIMER
PASS

St.Gall

Wildhaus

Constance

THURGAU

ST.
GALL

TOGGENBURG

Como

SCHAFF-
HAUSEN

Schaffhausen

SPLÜGEN
PASS

VALTELLINA

Glarus

GLARUS

Einsiedeln

SCHWYZ

RHINE R.

ST. LUKMANIER
PASS

ZURICH

Zurich

ZUG

URI

ST.
GOTTHARD
PASS

TICINO

Locarno

LAKE
MAGGIORE

Kappel

Luzern

UNTER-
WALDEN

MILAN

RHINE R.

Hapsburg
Castle

Aargau

AARGAU

LUZERN

GRIMSEL
PASS

BASEL

Basel

SOLOTHURN

BERN

SIMPLON
PASS

VALAIS

RHONE R.

GREAT
ST. BERNARD
PASS

NEUCHÂTEL

Neuchâtel
(Neuenburg)

Bern

Fribourg
Freiburg

FRIBOURG

VAUD

Lausanne

FRANCHE

COMTÉ

LAKE GENEVA

SAVOY

GENEVA

Geneva

50 MILES

TRM

146

a weak diet that met in Zurich, Lucerne, or some other city to conduct whatever business they had in common. After the last futile attempt of the Hapsburg emperor to subdue the Swiss in the Swabian War in 1499, the Swiss Confederation was to all intents and purposes an autonomous state within the Empire until it received complete independence in 1648.

The Confederation originally consisted of the three forest cantons of Uri, Schwyz, and Unterwalden, which had formed a political union in 1291. They were later joined by Lucerne (1332), Glarus (1351), Zurich (1351), Zug (1352), Bern (1353), Solothurn (1481), Fribourg (1481), Basel (1501), Schaffhausen (1501), and Appenzell (1513). During the Italian wars, following the invasion of Italy by Charles VIII of France, they were joined as "allies" by the cantons of Valais and Grisons (Graubünden), the abbey of St. Gall, the counties of Neuenburg and Toggenburg, and the cities of Biel, St. Gall, Rottweil, and Mühlhausen, later also Geneva. These "allies" enjoyed the protection of the Confederation and were obligated to give it their military support. But most of Switzerland consisted of subject territories, ruled by the individual cities and lands within the cantons. In addition to these political units, there were the common bailiwicks, or condominiums, such as Aargau, Thurgau, and the Tessin lands, which had been taken over by the Confederation and were ruled in common as subject provinces.

Although the Swiss cantons could present a united front in the presence of outside danger, they were often badly divided at other times. In their successful battles against the Hapsburgs and other enemies, their infantrymen had gained the reputation of being the best soldiers in Europe. This led to the unfortunate rivalry for the services of these troops as mercenaries among the great powers, whose rulers gave pensions to many influential persons in Switzerland. This was an evil that led to much corruption and internal strife. However, because of the increasing emphasis being placed upon cavalry and artillery by the beginning of the sixteenth century, the Swiss infantry no longer constituted sufficient military strength to enable the diet to participate successfully in such power-political struggles as the Hapsburg-Valois rivalry. The humiliating defeat of the Swiss soldiers at Marignano in 1515 was followed by a peace in which the victorious French attempted to make the Confederation a permanent dependency in return for an annual subsidy. The attempts of the papacy to draw the Swiss out of the French orbit led to a bitter rivalry and further internal divisions.

The internal political situation was complicated still further by the many conflicts involving ambitious cities, powerful bishoprics, and important old monasteries. To an exceptional degree, the evangelical sermons of the reformers became programs of economic and political reforms.

In addition to these political stresses and strains, there were those of an economic nature. The basis of the economic life of the Swiss was agricultural, with the most emphasis placed upon the raising of cattle and the making of cheese. Although most of the peasants had been freed from the worst abuses of serfdom, they still were compelled to give their secular and spiritual lords many kinds of services, tithes, and ground rents. Like the peasants of Germany, they sought to be relieved of these and to improve their economic position.

The industries, concentrated in a number of growing cities, suffered not only from the antiquated methods imposed by the guilds but also from the disturbances caused by the Italian wars. Notable exceptions were the linen industry of St. Gall and the book industry of Basel.

Despite the vicissitudes of war and a general decline in industrial production, commerce continued to flourish. The merchants were supported in every possible way by the diet. Furthermore, they had access to the important region of Lombardy as far as Milan and, after the conclusion of the Treaty of Fribourg in 1516, had many trading concessions in France. In exchange for grains, salt, wool, and iron, they exported primarily linen, cattle, and cheese.

Both Christian humanism and mysticism were found throughout Switzerland and southern Germany, where they aroused the interests of the educated people, particularly the laity, in the Bible. After the break with Rome, this interest found expression in a general disposition to look upon the Bible as a guide in political and social, as well as religious, matters. This explains in part the early rise and rapid spread of Anabaptism in these parts.

Because of their intense loyalty to their local governments and the Confederation, the Swiss were disinclined to accept the domination of the papacy in religious matters. Moreover, the great Church councils held in the Swiss cities of Constance (1414–1418) and Basel (1431–1449), with their strong antipapal sentiment and demands for reform, were still fresh in their minds. Moved by the humanist and mystical tendencies already referred to and proud of their independent cultural achievements, the Swiss evinced not only a critical attitude toward the outward observances of the Church but a renewed search for religious satisfaction. When, for example, Leo X requested twelve thousand soldiers from the Swiss in 1518 for a war against the Turks, the diet promised only ten thousand, adding that it would gladly send two thousand priests to make up the requested number. In 1520 the diet threatened to seize any simoniac, or dealer in ecclesiastical benefices, who dared to come into Switzerland, to sew him into a sack, and to drown him in the nearest river. The diet also took firm action against abuses connected with the sale of indulgences. The cantons, like the territorial states of Germany, were taking measures not only to carry on reforms for the public welfare but to strengthen their own political authority.

## Zwingli (1484–1531)

Opposition to the various recognized evils found its best expression in the life and work of Huldreych (Ulrich) Zwingli, who was born on January 1, 1484, only seven weeks after Luther's birth. His birthplace was Wildhaus, the highest village in the Toggenburg Valley, which was under the sovereignty of the abbot of St. Gall. Coming from a locally prominent family, he was given a good education, first by an uncle, a priest and dean at Wesen, then at schools in Basel and Bern. He began his university studies at Vienna (1500–1502), where he became interested in humanism. He completed them at Basel, where he obtained the degree of bachelor of arts in 1504 and the degree of master of liberal arts in 1506. Unlike Luther, he never became a doctor of divinity. Although he was as a student chiefly interested in the study of the classics, and in music, in which he displayed considerable skill, he was also greatly influenced by Thomas Wyttenbach of Basel. This exponent of Erasmian humanism imparted to him a strong interest in biblical theology and a critical attitude toward abuses in the Church.

Zwingli began his priesthood at Glarus in 1506. There he devoted much of his leisure time to the study of Latin and Greek as well as to the writings of the humanists. The writings of Pico della Mirandola and Erasmus seem to have exerted the greatest influence upon him. There he also published his first literary efforts. One was a fable (1510), in which the lion as the emperor, the leopard as the king of France, and the fox as Venice attempt to drive the ox as Switzerland out of his pasture; but they are prevented from doing so by the shepherd, the pope. The other, called *The Labyrinth* (1515–1516), likewise assailed corruption in Switzerland, particularly the pension system, which made his country a slave of France and other foreign powers. As chaplain for the Swiss troops who, in the service of the papacy, participated in the battles of Novara (1513) and Marignano (1515), he had become acquainted with the moral and political evils growing out of the traffic in Swiss soldiers, and he now stubbornly opposed the renewal of the alliance with France, which had expired in 1515.

Having aroused the animosity of influential people in French pay by writing and preaching against these abuses, he was compelled to leave Glarus in 1516. He went to Einsiedeln. There a famous shrine, containing the black image of the Virgin Mary, was the goal of many pilgrims. He continued his studies there and gained a good reputation as a humanist and a patriotic preacher, sharply criticizing the "Judaizing ceremonies" of the Church and pointing to Christ as the sole mediator between God and man. He was strengthened in his Christian humanism by his personal contact with Erasmus, whom he visited at Basel and whose writings he studied with great interest. That he was still in the good

OCCVBVIT ANNO ÆTATIS XLVII·
1531

Kunstmuseum Winterthur. Photo Swiss Institute for Art Research, Zurich.

Ulrich Zwingli

*by Hans Asper*

graces of the pope is shown by the fact that he requested and obtained the position of a papal acolyte with its accompanying papal pension.

On the first day of January, 1519, Zwingli became a parish priest in the Great Minster of Zurich, a position that he had eagerly sought. Although his first sermons there indicate that he was still a good Catholic, they show his exceptional ability to explain the Bible in a direct manner, without recourse to scholastic explanations and legendary examples. They also show his unabated interest in uncovering ecclesiastical abuses. It was largely through his preaching that the selling of indulgences was prohibited in Zurich.

But Zwingli also continued to attack political and social abuses, particularly the giving of pensions and the sale of mercenaries. As a consequence, Zurich was the only canton that did not accept the treaty that in 1521 placed the Confederation as a whole under French pay. The majority of the populace supported his demands for reform. Although the canton shortly afterward supplied the papacy with troops, despite the opposition of Zwingli, pensions and mercenary service were soon prevented by heavy penalties. Because he carried his reform program to other cantons, he aroused the opposition of many influential countrymen who were making huge profits by selling "blood for gold."

Meanwhile Luther's attack upon indulgences and his break with Rome had won him a large following in Switzerland. Many of his writings were printed in Basel and sold throughout the Swiss cantons. Among his most interested followers was Zwingli, who embraced evangelical doctrines in the latter half of 1519, after he had barely escaped death during a plague that took the lives of nearly a third of the population of Zurich.

Despite considerable opposition to his reform program, Zwingli preached against fasting, private confession, the Mass, monasticism, the celibacy of the clergy, and the use of pictures and music in the church services. In the spring of 1521 he was made a canon of the Great Minster, with an increase in salary. The city council of Zurich, in which there were many supporters of Zwingli, especially among the leaders of the craft guilds, was at first mainly concerned with maintaining order and therefore intervened in religious matters only to the extent of demanding that the priests of the city confine themselves to preaching the gospel and refrain from introducing "human inventions."

Disturbances could not be avoided, however. When Zwingli preached against fasting during Lent, in 1522, and several prominent persons openly broke the fast, the bishop of Constance prevailed upon the Zurich council to prohibit such violations and demanded that it safeguard the ordinances of the Church. Zwingli replied in his *Beginning and End,* a strongly worded defense of the authority of the Bible as opposed to that of ecclesiastical tradition. Soon after, with ten other priests, he sent petitions to the bishop and the Swiss diet, requesting the free preaching of the gospel and permission for marriage of the clergy. Although the petition was denied, Zwingli secretly married a widow, Anna Reinhart Meyer. But he did not make this step public until the spring of 1524. Others married openly.

When these and other acts of defiance led to much unrest and confusion, the diet of the Confederation supported the bishop of Constance in his attempt to suppress evangelical preaching. Thereupon the Zurich council accepted Zwingli's suggestion that all the issues at stake be clarified and settled at a formal disputation. Assuming the offensive, Zwingli prepared his Sixty-seven Conclusions for this occasion. In them he emphasized his belief that the Word of God was the sole rule of faith; that one could be saved only through faith in Jesus Christ; that those who lived in Christ comprised the true Church, the communion of saints; that the Mass was but a commemoration of the one and only sacrifice on the cross and a seal of redemption through Christ; that Christ was the only mediator between God and man; that man could not be saved by works alone; that ecclesiastical, hierarchical power was not based on the Bible, as was the secular power of the state; and that all Christians owed obedience to the secular government unless it acted contrary to the Word of God.

Among the approximately six hundred people present at this first Zurich Disputation, which met on January 29, 1523, were learned men from far and wide, as well as the official representatives of the bishop of Constance, headed by Johann Faber, formerly a friend and supporter of Zwingli. Although Faber maintained that this body did not have the right to decide religious questions, the city council, taking over the ecclesiastical authority of the bishop, decided on the same day to give Zwingli the right to preach the gospel and initiate evangelical reforms.

As in parts of Germany, official sanction of the evangelical teachings was followed by violence and revolutionary action, particularly in connection with the abolition of the Mass and the use of images. Because Zwingli desired to avoid disturbances of all kinds and wished to bring about changes by means of education and governmental sanction, a second disputation was called to meet on October 26, 1523, to deal primarily with questions concerning the Mass and images. It convened in the City Hall and was attended by members of the council, 350 clergymen, 10 doctors of theology, and others, a total of probably 900. It lasted three days. Although Zwingli and his colleague Leo Jud, or Judae (d. 1542), ably presented the Protestant cause and urged vigorous action, Martin Steinli of Schaffhausen defended the Mass and the cause of moderation with equal ability. The council, not yet willing to abolish the Mass and images, banished several iconoclasts and appointed a commission, including Zwingli and Jud, that it charged with the task of educating the people with respect to the evangelical doctrines. For this purpose Zwingli wrote, in November, 1523, his *Short Christian Introduction,* which the council distributed among all the clergymen of the canton.

Despite the opposition of the bishop of Constance and the Swiss diet, the canton of Zurich carried out religious reforms in a vigorous fashion. During the year 1524, pictures, statues, crucifixes, candles, and other ornaments were removed from the churches and destroyed, decorated walls were whitewashed, the bones of the local saints were buried, altars were replaced by tables, organs were dismantled, and the singing by choirs was abolished. The congregational singing of hymns was not introduced until late in that century. Little remained but bare, cold edifices that would hardly detract the attention of the worshipers from the hearing of the simple, unadorned Word of God. Pilgrimages and processions naturally ceased, and the church year was reduced to four festivals: Christmas, Good Friday, Easter, and Pentecost. Monasteries were dissolved and their properties were taken over by the state to be used for the care of the unfortunates and the education of the young.

During Holy Week in April, 1525, communion was celebrated according to the Zwinglian usage for the first time. Following as closely as possible the observance of the primitive Christian Church, Zwingli took his place at the head of a simple table that was covered with a white linen cloth and on which were placed Communion cups and plates of wood. After praying and reading in German the words of institution and pertinent Scripture passages, Zwingli and his assistants partook of the bread and wine and then distributed these sacred symbols among the people, going from pew to pew. Those parts of the liturgy that were retained from the Mass, that is, the Introit, the Gloria in Excelsis, the Creed, and a number of responses, were read in the Swiss vernacular by the people, the men alternating with the women. The same year Zwingli provided his followers with a simplified baptismal service in the vernacular, from which he had deleted the formula of exorcism and other parts that he had not found warranted by the New Testament.

Like Luther, Zwingli laid great emphasis upon providing the people with the Bible in their native tongue. The New Testament was printed as early as 1524. Under the able leadership of Leo Jud and with the assistance of Konrad Pellikan and Theodor Bibliander, the entire Bible was translated and published in Zurich by Froschauer in 1530, thus antedating the publication of Luther's completed Bible by four years. Jud also wrote three catechisms, one in Latin and two in German, published a translation of the *Imitation of Christ,* wrote the first Helvetic Confession, and produced an excellent Latin edition of the Old Testament, completed after his death by Pellikan and Bibliander.

A unique innovation in the administration of the church of Zurich was the special court concerned with marital and moral cases. Under

Zwingli's influence all questions concerning matrimony, previously considered a purely ecclesiastical concern, were turned over to a special civil court consisting of representatives of both the state and the church. Gradually all matters concerning private morals were referred to this court. As in Lutheran lands, the Zurich government obtained control of all ecclesiastical matters and cooperated with the reformers in maintaining doctrinal uniformity.

To provide evangelical preachers, the endowed chapter of the Great Minster was reorganized as a theological school, called the Carolinum, in June, 1525. The candidates were first thoroughly grounded in the Hebrew, Greek, and Latin languages, philosophy, and mathematics, and then given a course in "prophesying," or expounding the Scripture. In his *Lehrbüchlein,* or treatise on education, Zwingli explained his course of studies in terms of Old Testament practices. Pellikan and Bibliander were among the first professors of this school. It became a university in 1883.

## Spread of Zwinglianism

The Zwinglian Reformation gained most of its followers in the large and wealthy cantons and the free imperial cities. Wherever the demands for reform became acute, the cantonal government assumed the functions of the bishop and cooperated with the clergy in introducing doctrinal as well as administrative changes. Although the local congregations were given control over all local matters, the legislation and administration of religious matters of common concern were assumed by an annual synod of clergymen. A general superintendent, called the *antistes,* was placed over all the ministers.

The largest and most aristocratic canton of Switzerland, Bern, was among the first to follow the lead taken by Zurich. There the chief reformers were Berchthold Haller (d. 1536), a friend of Melanchthon, who became a teacher in Bern in 1518 and a pastor at the cathedral there in 1519; and the well-known layman Niklaus Manuel (d. 1530), a gifted poet and statesman, who spread evangelical ideas by his satirical religious plays and used his influence in winning over the city council. The Reformation Edict of the council was issued in February, 1528, following the success of the evangelical leaders at the public disputation that had been held in the city January 6 to 26. Zwingli, Oecolampadius, Capito, and Bucer had participated on the side of the reformers.

The wealthy and cultured episcopal city of Basel soon followed the example of Bern. The way had been prepared by Wyttenbach, Erasmus, Capito, and Froben. The actual leadership, however, was in the hands of Johannes Oecolampadius (1482–1531), a brilliant classical and Hebrew scholar who had studied law in Bologna and theology in Heidelberg and Tübingen, a warm friend of both Melanchthon and Zwingli. In 1522 he became the pastor of St. Martin's Church in Basel and later began his professorship at the university. In these positions he gradually initiated evangelical reforms with the consent of the conservative council and the help of Zwingli. After the Disputation of Bern, in which he had taken a part, a large number of citizens compelled the council to break completely with Rome (February, 1529). Thereupon Oecolampadius became the *antistes* of Basel and completed the reformation of the city and the canton. After the death of his mother and at the age of forty-five, he married Wilibrandis Rosenblatt, the comely widow of Keller. She later married Capito, and finally Bucer, whom she also survived.

In St. Gall it was Vadian (Joachim von Watt, 1485–1551), a humanist, physician, and statesman, who was chiefly responsible for introducing the Zwinglian reforms. He was assisted by Johannes Kessler (1502–1574), a saddler by trade, who also taught in the Latin school, preached evangelical sermons, and eventually became the *antistes* of that canton. A reformed order of service was introduced as early as 1527. Two years later the famous monastery of St. Gall, founded by an Irish missionary of that name in the eighth century, was dissolved, and its possessions were confiscated. However, it was re-established a few years later, and its new abbot, Diethelm Blaurer, became a prominent leader in the Catholic Reformation. Schaffhausen introduced the Reformation in 1529.

At Glarus, where Zwingli had labored for ten years, Aegidius Tschudi (1505–1572), the Catholic author of a well-known history of Switzerland, attempted to conciliate the friends and enemies of the Zurich reformer, while his Protestant cousin, Valentin Tschudi, Zwingli's successor at Glarus, preached to both Catholics and Protestants. This was probably the first example of the broadminded religious approach called latitudinarianism. Most of the congregations of the canton, however, became Zwinglian.

In Grisons, Zwinglianism made gains among all three of the ethnic groups, the German, the Romansh, and the Italian. Because about a third of the citizens remained Catholic, however, religious freedom was permitted from the outset. Each congregation was given the right to choose its confession by a majority vote.

The story of the Reformation in the Italian valleys of Grisons is of particular interest because it involved hundreds of Protestant refugees from the Italian Inquisition who settled there about the middle of the sixteenth century. Among them was Pietro Paolo Vergerio (1498?–1564), a Venetian lawyer, a prominent papal official, and a bishop, who had long been active in persecuting the Protestants. He became converted in 1548, fled to Grisons, where he preached Reformation doctrines from 1550 to 1553, and finally went to Tübingen, where he became a counselor of the duke of Württemberg, a position that he held the remaining years of his life. His many published works and extended correspondence reflect his bitter antipathy toward the papacy and also his vacillation in doctrinal matters, probably a consequence of his ambition to become the conciliator between Lutheranism and Zwinglianism.

Zwinglianism also spread to Germany, where a number of humanists and Landgrave Philip of Hesse became friends and supporters of the Zurich reformer. When the diet of Augsburg of 1530 requested a statement of the Zwinglian theology, the four German cities of Strassburg, Constance, Lindau, and Memmingen submitted the first confession of the Reformed Church, the *Confessio tetrapolitana,* prepared by the Strassburg reformers Bucer and Hedio. It retained its significance as the authoritative statement of the German Reformed Church until the appearance of the Heidelberg Catechism of 1563.

## The Sacramentarian Controversy

Zwingli published the first systematic exposition of his theology in his *Commentary on the True and False Religion* in March, 1528. It was dedicated to Francis I and had considerable influence upon the growth of Protestantism in France. In this statement the essential differences between Zwingli and the other reformers were made apparent. Drawing largely upon the New Testament and Christian humanism, he developed doctrines that were less logical than those of Calvin and less empirical than those of Luther, but more practical and less bound to traditions than either of these two, although he accepted the ecumenical creeds and considered the Bible the inspired word of God.

Concerned above all with a practical plan of salvation, rationally conceived, Zwingli looked upon the Bible as the infallible, divinely inspired word of God, the sole, immutable, objective divine law that should regulate Christian faith and practice. Luther, on the other hand, drawing upon his doctrine of justification by faith, made a sharp distinction between the law and the gospel. Both reformers, however, believed that Christ was the only source of divine grace.

Zwingli's conception of God as the omnipotent cause and ruler of all things was influenced by both the Scotist emphasis upon the majesty of God and the Platonic pantheism of the humanists. Beginning with his conception of the absolute sovereignty of God and the identity of divine foreknowledge and foreordination, he developed his conception of predestination. God elects freely and "gives faith to those who are elected and ordained to eternal life," so that they may believe in Christ, who has expiated for original sin. Thus Zwingli believed that unbaptized children, and even non-Christians, might be elected to salvation. God foreordained for damnation only those who heard and rejected the gospel. However, this doctrine did not lull the Zwinglians into complacency or lead them to fatalism. On the contrary, feeling certain that they belonged to the elect because they believed the gospel, they strove hard to demonstrate their faith by their actions, and their strong convictions gave them the courage to face insuperable difficulties.

It was particularly Zwingli's doctrine of the sacraments that brought him into conflict with the followers of Luther. Like the latter, Zwingli believed in the authority of a state church, or people's church, and opposed religious subjectivism, but he differed from Luther in maintaining that the sacraments were mere signs and seals of divine grace already given, not the means of giving grace. Thus he taught that baptism did not regenerate the individual and that the Lord's Supper did not of itself provide grace through the corporal presence of Christ. In other words, he interpreted both sacraments in a rational and spiritual sense.

Because the city council of Zurich authorized the Zwinglian innovations from the outset, the relation between church and state was closer there than in Lutheran Saxony. Zwingli himself was dependent for his position upon the council, which had assumed the administrative functions of the bishop. Although Zwingli believed that the Church consisted of the elect only, he maintained that the test of election was simply faith. But he considered the entire Protestant population of Zurich, even those who were compelled to attend church, the true body of the elect. Baptism and the Lord's Supper were, in effect, the signs that indicated membership in this new Israel.

Zwingli's conservatism with respect to Church ordinances early became apparent in his conflict with the Anabaptists of Zurich, called Swiss Brethren. Despite the fact that these left-wing reformers did not support the Peasants' Revolt but generally lived quiet lives of piety and devotion, stressing inner, spiritual regeneration and sanctification, they were soon persecuted by Zwingli and the government of Zurich. After attempts to convince the leaders of their errors, three public disputations were held during the year 1525. The government declared that their doctrines had been refuted and demanded that all parents have their infants baptized. When the Brethren refused to do so, they were exiled or imprisoned. Some were executed.

In his conflict with the Anabaptists, Zwingli developed still further his distinctive conception of the sacraments. He now argued that infant baptism was supported by the fact that circumcision of infants had been demanded in the Old Testament; insisted that this sacrament, like the Lord's Supper, was merely a sign—similar to the white cross on a field of red, known to all the Swiss—of the means of grace, demanded by Christ; and emphasized more strongly than ever his conviction that salvation depended upon divine predestination rather than faith and baptism. Luther, during the same period, strengthened the Pauline bases of his theology, stressing the role of faith and the doctrine that the sacraments were the means whereby God freely imparted grace.

# Part Two: The Reformation in Germany

It was because of these fundamental differences between Luther and Zwingli that they became involved in a bitter controversy over the Lord's Supper. Both had originally expressed themselves in similar terms as opposed to transubstantiation and the conception of the Mass as a sacrifice. Both had expressed belief in the words of promise, the communion of believers, the real presence of Christ, and the importance of the sacrament as a sign to strengthen faith in the promises of Christ. But Zwingli had long been inclined to follow Erasmus, who had emphasized the commemorative, symbolic side of the Lord's Supper, that is, the spiritual communion of the believer with Christ, who was really present in the bread and wine.

Zwingli was strengthened in his symbolical interpretation by the views of Cornelisz Hoen, or Honius (d. 1524), a Christian humanist of the Low Countries. From the writings of Johann Wessel of Gansfort and others, Hoen had evolved a symbolical conception of the Lord's Supper that he explained by stating that the words, "This is my body," actually mean, "This signifies my body," pointing out that Christ used such analogies in other biblical passages. Hoen had written Luther to the same effect in 1522, but the latter had answered that he felt bound to accept the exact words of institution in their clear meaning, even though he was by nature prone to accept the symbolical view. Thus Zwingli considered the sacrament a memorial, a means for increasing faith, and a thanksgiving for grace already received, at which Christ was present only according to his divine nature and to those contemplating him in faith. Luther, on the other hand, declared that it was both a sign and a vehicle of grace and that Christ really was present in the elements, the bread and the wine, explaining this by means of his doctrine of the ubiquity of Christ's resurrected body.

The Sacramentarian Controversy at first centered in Strassburg, to which Carlstadt had fled after he had developed sharp differences with Luther over the Lord's Supper. Whereas the city council of Strassburg expelled Carlstadt and Zurich refused to welcome him, the Strassburg theologians leaned toward his spiritual interpretation of the Lord's Supper and advanced the argument that Christ's body could not be present in the Lord's Supper because it was "at the right hand of God." Oecolampadius, the Strassburg theologians, Bugenhagen, and others immediately joined in the controversy, but Luther and Zwingli did not attack each other openly until 1527.

Zwingli began his attack by publishing his *Friendly Exposition,* in which he criticized the views expressed by Luther in his *Sermon on the Sacrament of the Body and Blood of Christ Against the Radicals,* published in 1526. Thereupon Luther answered Zwingli directly in his informative but vehement polemic, *That These Words, "This Is My Body," Still Stand Against the Radicals* (1527). Zwingli's caustic answer, *That These Words . . . Retain Their Original Meaning* (1527), was followed by Luther's *Confession Concerning the Lord's Supper* (1528), in which he attempted to set "the heretics" right by using the words of Paul. The literary phase of the controversy was concluded with an answer to this booklet by Oecolampadius and Zwingli.

Martin Bucer, the Strassburg theologian, was greatly impressed by Luther's last tract, for he saw that when Luther used the term *real presence* he did not refer to the outward, physical presence of Christ, but to a sacramental union. As a consequence he made a long and determined effort to harmonize the positions of the Lutherans and Zwinglians.

The controversy between Luther and Zwingli centered largely on the questions of the omnipresence of the body of Christ and the relation of Christ's divine and human natures. Zwingli argued that the words of institution referred only to the divine nature. In support of this interpretation, he used a figure of speech called *alloiosis,* or rhetorical exchange; that is, he stated that when the Bible speaks of one nature of Christ, it uses the terms that belong to the other. Luther, emphasizing the union of the two natures of Christ, insisted that the bodily nature could also be present in the Lord's Supper. But although Zwingli was willing to agree to differ in this particular instance for the sake of maintaining unity in what he considered the essentials, Luther charged him and his followers with a perversion of the entire Bible and would have no fellowship with them.

### The Marburg Colloquy

The climax of the Sacramentarian Controversy was reached at the religious discussion at Marburg (October 1 to 3, 1529). Philip of Hesse had requested this colloquy for the purpose of presenting a united political front against the Catholic princes. Although Zwingli had welcomed the suggestion, for both religious and political reasons, Luther had opposed it as he had all political alliances for religious reasons, for he did not believe that force should be used in matters of faith. Melanchthon had hesitated to unite with what he considered the radical religious groups for fear of offending the Catholics, with whom he still hoped to come to an agreement. But in deference to the wishes of the landgrave and their own prince, Luther and Melanchthon, accompanied by Jonas, Brenz, Menius, Cruciger, Rörer, Myconius, Agricola, and Osiander, met at Marburg to discuss religious doctrines with Zwingli, Oecolampadius, Bucer, Capito, and Sturm. Landgrave Philip of Hesse and Duke Ulrich of Württemberg were also present.

Despite Luther's statement at the first meeting that the two parties were "of a different spirit," they came to a general, though not unreserved, agreement on fourteen articles dealing with such matters as the Trinity, the person of Christ, faith, and baptism. There was even much agreement on the fifteenth article, concerning the Lord's Supper. Both sides denied the sacrificial character of the Mass and the Capernaitic eat-

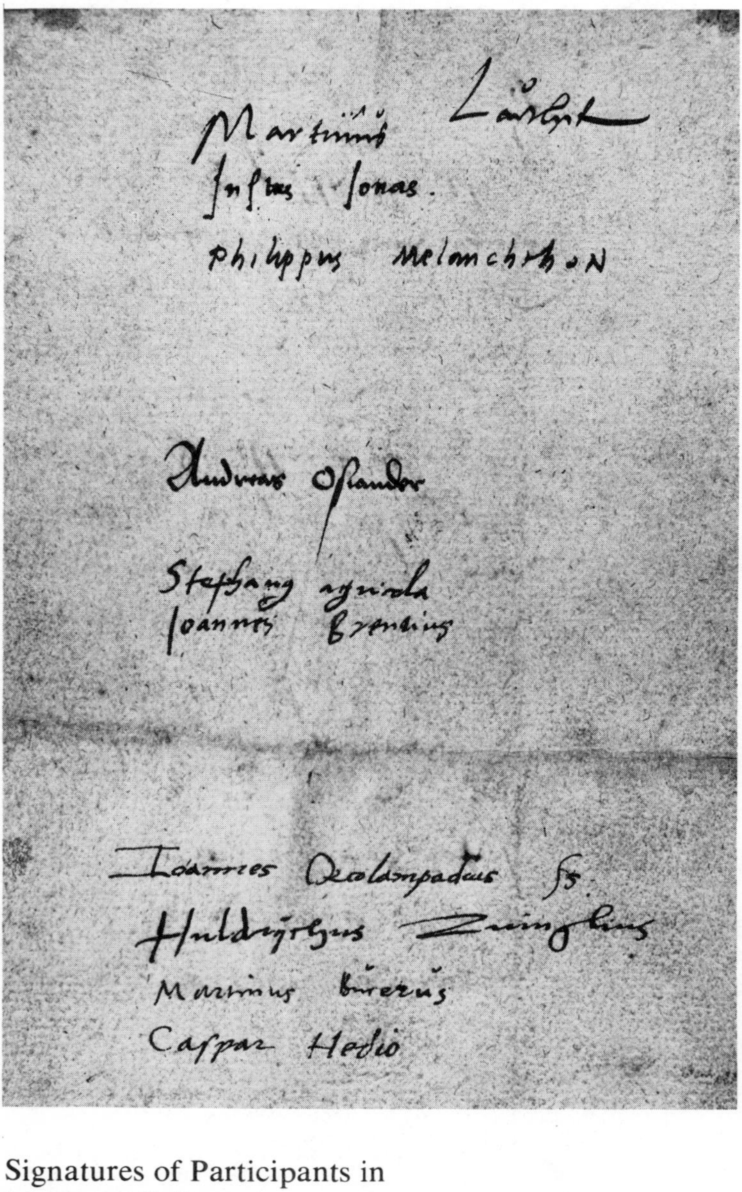


*Foto Marburg. Art Reference Bureau.*

Signatures of Participants in
Marburg Colloquy

ing of the actual body of Christ. They also agreed that both bread and wine should be given the communicant, that the Lord's Supper was a "sacrament of the true body and blood of Jesus Christ," and that the spiritual partaking of the body and blood was necessary to every Christian. They differed only with respect to the bodily presence of Christ. But they agreed to refrain from further polemical writing and to study this problem in Christian love.

After the formal meeting had ended, Luther drew up a formula in which he described Christ's body as being present "essentially and substantively," but not "qualitatively, quantitatively, or locally." Bucer was at first willing to accept this formula, but Zwingli refused, for he could believe in only a clearly spiritual presence and feared that the common people would look upon this concession as the beginning of a return to the Roman interpretation. The break between Zwingli and Luther was therefore final. Luther's formula, however, became the basis for the agreement between him and the theologians of southern Germany in the Württemberg Concord of 1534 and the Wittenberg Concord of 1536.

In his controversies with the Catholics, Luther had denied the scholastic explanation of the Lord's Supper, which differentiated between the substance and the accidents, that is, held that the bread and wine could be the body and blood of Christ and still have the accidents of bread and wine (color, taste, smell, and so on); and he had denied the inherent grace in the sacrament as such, insisting that faith was essential to render it effective. In his controversies with those who believed in the spiritual presence of Christ, however, he seemed to revert to the medieval position that the sacrament itself embodied grace because of the bodily presence of Christ, although he still held that faith was essential on the part of the recipient, that the sacrament did not operate mechanically.

It is easy to see why Luther and Zwingli remained adamant in their respective positions. Luther not only believed that Zwingli's theology had much in common with that of the left-wing reformers but also suspected the Zurich reformer of sympathizing with the leaders of the Peasants' Revolt. Zwingli, on the other hand, was highly suspicious of anything that looked like a Catholic reaction. Moreover, he did not believe that the sacraments or any of the "ceremonies" of the Church were of great importance. Luther's inability to recognize the Swiss as his brethren and Zwingli's fear of a Catholic reaction further narrowed the course of the Reformation, which had seemed about to engulf all Europe.

## Political Developments, 1521–1531

The political circumstances of the decade following the proclamation of the Edict of Worms were such that Lutheranism spread with little centralized resistance. The edict could not be enforced by Charles, primarily because he was engaged in the first of the series of wars growing out of the Hapsburg-Valois rivalry. Although his forces defeated the French and took Francis I prisoner in the Battle of Pavia in 1525, and although Connétable Charles of Bourbon turned against the French king, the emperor could not gain all his political objectives and bring the rivalry to a final conclusion.

In the Peace of Madrid of 1526, which Francis I was compelled to sign, he gave up his claims to Milan, Genoa, and Naples, as well as Flanders, Artois, and Tournai; and he permitted Charles to add the duchy of Burgundy to his possessions. Francis gave his knightly oath that he would carry out the terms of the treaty. As additional securities he married Eleanor, the sister of Charles, and left his sons in Madrid as hostages. Once back in France, however, he repudiated the treaty and resumed the war.

Meanwhile the Turks under Suleiman I, the Magnificent (1520–1566), captured Belgrade (1521) and the Island of Rhodes (1522). In 1526, when it appeared that Charles might be able to devote his attention to the Lutheran movement, the Turks defeated and killed King Louis of Hungary, brother-in-law of Charles, in the Battle of Mohács. While much of Hungary was overrun by the Turks, matters were complicated by the disputed succession and bitter rivalry between John Zapolya, who was elected king by the Magyar nobles and was supported by his overlord Suleiman, and Ferdinand of Hapsburg, who was elected king at Pressburg and secured his control over much of western Hungary.

In 1529 the Turks besieged Vienna for the first time. After several attacks had failed to daunt the defenders, among whom were many Lutherans, the Turks withdrew. A few years later, in 1533, after Suleiman had left Hungary to meet a new threat from the shah of Persia, he made a peace with Ferdinand by the terms of which the latter was permitted to retain the lands that he had held against the Turks and Zapolya was given the rest. Both rulers, however, were compelled to pay tribute to the Turks. Although this peace remained in force until Zapolya's death seven years later, the war against the Hapsburgs continued in the Mediterranean.

The political situation in Europe became further complicated by the death of Leo X in December, 1521. The conclave of cardinals, divided by a rivalry between the supporters of Cajetan and those of the Medici, surprised everyone by choosing as Leo's successor the bishop of Tortosa, Adrian VI (1522–1523), the last non-Italian pope. Adrian was a Netherlander by birth, a former professor of theology at Louvain, once a tutor of Charles V, and finally Charles' regent in Spain. Adrian was motivated by a sincere desire to establish peace and order in Christendom. Mistrusted and despised by the secularized college of cardinals, however, he experienced only misfortunes. He failed to bring about peace between Charles

V and Francis I, to stop the Lutheran movement, and to carry out reforms in the Roman *Curia*. When he lost his life during a plague in Rome, he was followed by Giulio de' Medici, who assumed the name Clement VII (1523–1534). Although Clement was honest and industrious, he lacked strength of character and knowledge of the European political affairs in which he attempted to play a leading role. His conspiracy against Charles led to disastrous consequences for the papacy.

In Germany the imperial council of regency attempted in vain to quell the increasing number of disturbances appearing throughout Germany and to enforce the Edict of Worms. Although Frederick the Wise was the only elector openly to defend Luther, this body hesitated to take action for fear of a revolt on the part of the people. Furthermore, many of the imperial agents and advisers sympathized with Luther, and the Catholic princes hesitated to take action that might strengthen the power of the emperor at their expense. Because the council's deliberations failed to produce results, Charles ignored it and in 1523 made Ferdinand his viceroy in the Empire.

The reluctance of the princes to strengthen the power of the emperor accounts also for the failure of the three diets held at Nürnberg, 1522–1524. In the first of these, which convened in March, 1522, the estates were concerned almost solely with providing aid for a war against the Turks. In the diet that met in the winter of 1522–1523, the estates warned the emperor that the enforcement of the Edict of Worms would lead to widespread popular revolts and insisted that the Lutheran problem be settled at a free general church council consisting of laity as well as clergy and meeting on German soil within a year. The diet also attempted to regulate economic matters in the interest of the Empire as a whole. It passed a law against monopolies, limiting the amount of capital that might be held by a company, and, to provide the government with much-needed income, imposed a customs duty of 4 per cent on trade. The German cities, however, prevailed upon Charles to veto both laws.

The third Diet of Nürnberg, which met in January, 1524, abolished the impotent council of regency and postponed still further the religious question, despite the fact that Campeggio, the papal legate, had insisted that Charles and Ferdinand enforce the Edict of Worms. Once more the estates asked that the religious matters be referred to a Church council. However, because they saw the futility of requesting a general council, they demanded the calling of a German council, to meet in Speyer before the end of the year.

## The Knights' War

The urgency for political action to prevent the further disintegration of the Empire under the impact of Lutheranism was demonstrated by the Knights' War of 1522–1523, also called the Sickingen Feud. The imperial knights, whose status had been reduced almost to that of captains of mercenary soldiers by the decline of feudalism and the rise of territorial states, hoped to regain their political influence by strengthening the authority of the emperor at the expense of the princes. Their outstanding leaders, Franz von Sickingen, who had made his castle, the Ebernburg, a place of refuge for humanists and reformers, and Ulrich von Hutten, the humanist knight, hoped to use the Lutheran movement to serve their political purposes. Luther, who knew nothing of their intentions, would have opposed such political action.

In August, 1522, Sickingen, hoping that the Lutherans would rally to his cause, made his ill-fated attack upon Trier, the seat of the elector and archbishop of an ancient ecclesiastical principality. The forces of the archbishop withstood the siege. The next year a league composed of Trier, the Palatinate, and Hesse decisively defeated the knights at Sickingen's castle at Landstuhl. Sickingen was mortally wounded in the battle and Hutten fled to Switzerland. It is significant that the council of regency could prevent neither the revolutionary action of the knights nor the retaliatory action of the princes. Although the knights were no longer a political force in Germany, their attempt to identify the Lutheran movement with their revolt enabled Catholic princes to point to the political dangers inherent in religious heterodoxy.

To provide the papacy with political support in its efforts to enforce the Edict of Worms and check the spread of unrest, Campeggio, in June, 1524, formed the Regensburg Union, consisting of Archduke Ferdinand, the two dukes of Bavaria, the cardinal-archbishop of Salzburg, and a number of bishops of southern Germany. The league proceeded to stamp out heresy and inaugurate a moderate reform program. The next year a similar league was formed in northern Germany, called the League of Dessau. Its leading members were Duke George of Saxony, Archbishop Albert of Mainz, the elector of Brandenburg, and the two dukes of Brunswick. The same year the Lutheran princes formed a union of their own under the leadership of Elector John of Saxony and Landgrave Philip of Hesse. This union, called the League of Torgau, grew rapidly, especially after the Peace of Madrid, when it was believed that Charles V would be able to devote attention to the Lutheran problem.

## The Diets of Speyer

The emperor decided to enforce the Edict of Worms at the Diet of Speyer in the summer of 1526. But he was unable to attend, and the Lutheran princes of northern Germany stood together so firmly and were supported by so many Catholic princes who did not wish to be deprived of their "liberties" that the edict could not be enforced. Instead, a number of reforms were carried out, and it was again decided to postpone the Lutheran problem until it could be taken up by a Church council. Most significant was the recess, or act, that provided that each state should conduct its religious affairs in accord with its obligations to God and the emperor. This recess further strengthened the principle of territorial control of religion, which was expressed by the phrase, *cuius regio, eius religio,* and was ultimately accepted in the Peace of Augsburg in 1555.

Charles and Ferdinand were compelled to make concessions to the German princes because of two events that occurred in the year in which the diet met. One was the Battle of Mohács, the other the formation of the League of Cognac. When, however, the vicissitudes of battle again favored him, Charles sent a demand to the diet, once more assembled in Speyer in 1529, that it revoke the recess of 1526 and proceed against Lutheranism. The majority of the estates complied with the wishes of the emperor. They repealed the recess of the preceding diet, ordered the Catholic estates to carry out the Edict of Worms, commanded the Lutheran estates to prevent no one in their lands from hearing the Catholic Mass and to cease making further changes, and demanded the suppression of Zwinglianism and Anabaptism.

Thereupon the Lutheran estates, consisting of the elector of Saxony, the dukes of Brunswick, the margrave of Brandenburg, the landgrave of Hesse, the prince of Anhalt, and fourteen free imperial cities, drew up a strong protest to the emperor on April 19. This protest stated that the recess of 1526, having constituted a treaty between the Catholic and Lutheran estates, could not be repealed without the consent of both parties and that the Lutherans could not be compelled to act contrary to their faith or conscience. In any case, they believed that they must obey God rather than man. Because of this action they were called the Protesting Estates. Eventually all those who left the Catholic Church were called Protestants. Charles, free for the time being to give his attention to German affairs, ignored the protest and prepared to attend the diet that was to meet at Augsburg the next year.

Because of the impending imperial action, efforts were made to bring all the Protestants together into a strong political union. This desire for union had been intensified by the strained relations precipitated by one Otto von Pack, an official of the duke of Saxony, who in 1528 had told Landgrave Philip of Hesse that he had discovered a treaty made by the Catholic princes in which they had agreed to exterminate the Lutherans. Although the letter that purported to substantiate this treaty was found to be a forgery, the relations between the Catholic and Lutheran princes had been strained to the breaking point. It is generally believed that Luther wrote "A Mighty Fortress Is Our God" during this critical period.

Philip of Hesse immediately started negotiations with Francis I, Zapolya, and the South-German cities that, under the influence of Zwingli, were also interested in a political union. After the protest at Speyer he succeeded in forming a secret defensive alliance with Electoral Saxony,

Strassburg, Nürnberg, and Ulm and wrote to Zwingli, asking him to participate in the religious discussion at Marburg already described, preliminary to the formation of a general Protestant union.

Meanwhile, under the leadership of Margrave George of Brandenburg, Elector John of Saxony, and the city of Nürnberg, a number of meetings were held by princes and theologians for the purpose of finding a theological basis for a political union. The results of these deliberations were embodied in seventeen articles announced at Schwabach on October 16, 1529, and known as the Schwabach Articles. But because these articles reflected the anti-Zwinglian views expressed by Luther in his *Confession Concerning the Lord's Supper* of 1528, Strassburg, Ulm, and other South-German cities refused to sign them and gravitated toward Zurich, politically as well as doctrinally. Even Electoral Saxony and Hesse came to disagree over the right of resistance to the emperor, the former denying the right, the latter affirming it.

### The Diet of Augsburg, 1530

While the Protestants were divided among themselves, Charles V was preparing to come to Germany—for the first time since 1521—to preside at the Diet of Augsburg (1530) with the hope of solving the religious problem, creating a united front against the Turks, and having his brother Ferdinand crowned king of the Romans. Charles had repulsed the Turks at Vienna, had concluded the second period of the Hapsburg-Valois rivalry, had solved his differences with Clement VII at Bologna, and had been crowned emperor by the pope in that city in February, 1530. He was, incidentally, the last emperor to receive his crown from the papacy.

Elector John of Saxony, one of the first to arrive at Augsburg, attempted to gain the good will of the emperor by sending him a copy of the Schwabach Articles and assuring him of the loyal intentions of the Lutherans. But this move was counteracted by the demands for vigorous action on the part of Campeggio, who accompanied Charles. Campeggio demanded the enforcement of the Edict of Worms and the cessation of Protestant preaching in Augsburg while the diet was in session. Eck, furthermore, published a pamphlet that listed more than four hundred heretical statements that had been made by the Protestants. Despite this unfavorable atmosphere, Elector John obtained the support of many Protestant estates for the confession that had been prepared by Melanchthon and had this read publicly in the German language by the Saxon Chancellor Beyer on June 25.

Elector John's vigorous action stood in marked contrast to that of Melanchthon, who had written and continued to revise the confession in such a manner as to be least offensive to the Catholic theologians. In his conversations with Alfonso de Valdés, an imperial secretary, Melanchthon even expressed his willingness to accept the withholding of the cup from the laity, clerical celibacy, and the reintroduction of certain Catholic ceremonies.

Although the original German and Latin copies of this Augsburg Confession (*Confessio Augustana*) are lost,[1] the printed edition of 1531 indicates Melanchthon's concessions to Catholicism. It consisted of two parts. The first contained the chief articles of faith, based on the Schwabach Articles. The second part explained the Lutheran position with respect to such reforms as giving the cup to the laity, denial of the sacrificial character of the Lord's Supper, opposition to the celibacy of the clergy, and the abrogation of monastic vows. This position had already been stated in the Torgau Articles, formulated by the Wittenberg theologians in the preceding March. The Introduction to the Augsburg Confession was written by Chancellor Brück.

The attempts to appease the Catholic theologians and to show that the Lutherans disagreed fundamentally with the Anabaptists and Zwinglians were made obvious by the omission from the confession of such topics as purgatory, the veneration of the saints, transubstantiation, and the universal priesthood of believers. Luther could not attend the diet because of the Edict of Worms. He stayed at the nearby Castle Coburg, where he kept in constant contact with the events transpiring at Augsburg. His letters of this period show his resentment at the dissimulation of those who would compromise with the Catholics.

Despite the concessions, the Catholics could not accept the Augsburg Confession. They were even more severe with the *Tetrapolitana,* the confession of the four South-German cities of Strassburg, Constance, Lindau, and Memmingen that had been presented on July 9. This confession, prepared by Capito and Bucer, contained a sharper attack on ceremonies and a greater emphasis upon the authority of the Bible than the *Augustana.*

On the suggestion of the Catholic estates, Charles had Campeggio, with the assistance of Eck, Faber, Cochlaeus, and others, draw up a *Confutatio,* or *Refutation,* that was read on August 3. Thereupon the emperor, who maintained that he was God's instrument for preserving the true faith, declared the Protestant position untenable and threatened to use force as the protector of the Church. But the fact that he had not yet obtained the support of the estates against the Turkish danger led to further negotiations, in which both Melanchthon and Eck showed some willingness to compromise, but which were interrupted by Luther's firmness and the energetic action of the Protestant princes, particularly Elector John of Saxony, supported by his counselor Spalatin.

---

[1] The German copy was deposited in the imperial chancery, where it disappeared. The Latin copy was taken to Brussels and eventually to Spain, where it was destroyed by Philip II.

# Part Two: The Reformation in Germany

As a protest against the emperor's assertion that the Lutheran confession had been refuted, and in answer to the *Confutatio,* Melanchthon write his *Apology,* which was later revised and printed in Latin (1531) and eventually made a part of the Lutheran credo. Although Charles [2] seemed for a while to vacillate between a conciliatory and an adamant position, he finally expressed his determination to enforce the Edict of Worms, reconstituted the imperial supreme court so that it would be less favorable to the Protestants in cases involving the secularization of ecclesiastical property, promised to call a general council of the Church to settle the religious questions, and demanded that the Lutherans return to the Catholic Church by April 15, 1531.

The vigorous action threatened by Charles V was followed by a greater solidarity among the Protestants. The South-German cities, irritated by the political tactics of Charles V, were drawn closer to the Lutheran princes. Moreover, to meet the imperial threat, the Protestant estates formed the Schmalkaldic League in February, 1531.

## Zwingli's Political Maneuvers

Meanwhile Zwingli, thoroughly convinced that he was God's prophet for spreading the faith, was preparing to use political means for carrying out the divine will in Zurich and all Switzerland. He soon obtained control of the city council of Zurich and directed its internal and foreign affairs in a theocratic fashion. But some cantons, especially Bern, which had to defend itself against the ambitions of the duke of Savoy, could not give Zwingli their wholehearted support. Because of his political ambitions, Zwingli did not stop with planning alliances with Philip of Hesse and Francis I of France, to the latter of whom he dedicated two important works, *Concerning the True and False Religion* and *An Exposition of the Christian Faith,* but threatened to destroy the traditional relationship among the Swiss cantons.

For the purpose of defending the new faith and increasing its influence in the confederation, as well as adding to the territorial possessions of Zurich, Zwingli made a number of treaties (*Burgrechte,* or Christian Civic Alliances) with other states. Beginning in 1527, he allied Zurich with the reformed imperial city of Constance, an alliance that appeared to the Catholic cantons to be a step in the direction of absorbing the important common territory (*Vogtei*) of Thurgau. This action was soon followed by a treaty between Constance and Bern. By the spring of 1529 the cities of St. Gall, Biel, Mühlhausen, and Basel, and a little later, Schaffhausen, joined this Christian Civic Alliance, a confederation within a confederation.

As a counterstroke, the five "forest cantons" of Uri, Schwyz, Unter-

---

[2] By making some concessions, Charles had succeeded in winning support for the election of Ferdinand as king of the Romans at this diet. He was crowned at Cologne on January 5, 1531.

walden, Lucerne, and Zug bound themselves together (1524) for the purpose of suppressing heresy. Joined by Fribourg and Wallis, these cantons formed, in April, 1529, an alliance with Ferdinand of Austria, the traditional enemy of the Swiss Confederation. This alliance was designed to check the growth of heresy; but it also provided for the acquisition of lands from the Protestant cantons.

Violence accompanied this formation of alliances. One Jacob Kaiser, an evangelical preacher, was burned alive in the spring of 1527. This and similar incidents led Zwingli to make far-reaching plans to take the initiative against the Catholic cantons. Despite the reluctance of Bern to begin the war and send aid to Zurich, and without obtaining the consent of his other allies, Zwingli completed his plans for war.

### Civil War in Switzerland

In June, 1529, the main body of the Zurich troops, about four thousand strong, marched to Kappel on the border of the canton of Zurich, where it was met by a larger number of Catholic soldiers. But Zwingli, who had accompanied the Protestant army, decided to await developments elsewhere before beginning the attack. While the two armies faced each other on the border—the common soldiers, unmoved by the policies of their leaders, exchanged food and pleasantries—Bern let it be known that it would support Zurich only if its army were attacked. Thus Zwingli was compelled to listen to those who preferred to arbitrate.

An armistice was declared, and a peace, called the First Peace of Kappel, was drawn up on June 26, 1529. It permitted the forest cantons to retain their Catholicism but compelled them to sever their alliance with Ferdinand of Austria and to allow the Zwinglian congregations to continue unmolested in the common bailiwicks. Nothing was done about the abolition of foreign pensions and the sale of mercenaries.

Zwingli returned to Zurich in a belligerent mood. Apparently oblivious of the possible effects of his actions upon the future of the Swiss Confederation, he made plans for a formidable anti-Hapsburg league that would include the German princes and cities, France, Venice, Denmark, England, Bohemia, Hungary, and even the Turks. The outcome of the Marburg Colloquy, however, and the reluctance of Bern to admit Philip of Hesse into the alliance of evangelical cantons, prevented Zwingli from making even a small beginning. France and Venice showed no interest, and Charles V ignored the Zwinglian confession, the *Fidei Ratio,* which Zwingli had sent to Augsburg in 1530. The Lutherans also remained indifferent to Zwingli's plans. Consequently Zwingli had to be content with a much more modest alliance system. By January, 1530, Zurich, Bern, and Basel had made a treaty of alliance with Strassburg, and in the summer of that same year Zurich and Basel made a separate treaty with Philip of Hesse.

Disappointed, but still undaunted, Zwingli and his followers assumed the offensive in the common bailiwicks, contrary to the provisions of the peace of 1529. Believing that Austria, with whom the forest cantons had retained their alliance, would strike at the earliest opportunity, Thurgau and Rheintal were forcibly reformed and the lands of the abbot of St. Gall were seized and given to the Protestant city of St. Gall.

When the leaders of the forest cantons saw that not only their faith but their legal position within the confederation was threatened by the political actions of Zurich, they declared at the diet of January, 1531, that they could no longer live peacefully with the Protestant cantons. Bitter feelings on both sides led to acts of violence. A feud in Grisons, begun by an Italian adventurer, was erroneously interpreted by Zwingli as the beginning of a concerted Catholic attack and caused him to strike immediately.

Zwingli prepared for an offensive war, but Bern again refused to supply him with military aid, not only because it was involved in political difficulties in western Switzerland but also because it resented the growing influence of Zurich in eastern Switzerland. Zwingli nevertheless succeeded in establishing a blockade against the central cantons that deprived them of grain, wine, salt, steel, and iron. When he met with stout resistance in his own city council, he brought it into line by threatening to resign.

The Catholic cantons, threatened by the blockade, prepared for a war of desperation toward which the common people could no longer remain indifferent. Without awaiting help from Austria, their eight thousand troops crossed the boundary of Zurich at Kappel on October 11, 1531. There they met the less determined and poorly prepared troops of Zurich, numbering only about two thousand, and quickly defeated them, killing many prominent religious and civic leaders of Zurich. The armed Zwingli was found wounded on the battlefield by his enemies. He was unceremoniously killed, his body was quartered by the hangman and burned, and his ashes were scattered to the winds. Yet this battle was not decisive, for the Protestants had available many thousands of men who had not yet tasted battle. The will to fight, however, was gone, especially after a body of four thousand Zwinglian troops had been surprised and routed by six hundred Catholics in another battle the night of October 24.

Although the Catholic leaders were certain that such victories were given them by the Lord of Hosts, they were still suffering from the effects of the economic war and did not receive the expected aid from Austria. Therefore they were as willing as the Zwinglians to conclude hostilities.

The treaty, called the Second Peace of Kappel, was signed in Zug on November 20, 1531, between Zurich and the five forest cantons. A few days later it was confirmed by Bern, Glarus, Fribourg, and Appenzell. Its chief provisions were the following: (1) The five forest cantons were permitted to retain their "true, undoubted, Christian faith." Zurich was likewise permitted to retain its Protestantism, although it was implied that this involved serious deviations from the true faith. (2) Existing beliefs in the common bailiwicks were to remain as they were, and the Catholic minorities were given legal protection against the Protestants. (3) Both sides were compelled to give up their alliances with foreign powers. (4) The Protestant cantons were compelled to annul their Christian Civic Alliances and pay indemnities, and Zurich and the city of St. Gall were forced to restore the abbey of St. Gall and its lands.

With the death of Zwingli and the signing of the Second Peace of Kappel, Swiss Protestantism lost its belligerency. Under the leadership of Heinrich Bullinger (1504–1575), Zwingli's son-in-law and successor, it concentrated on its spiritual work. But Zurich, thoroughly defeated and bankrupt, could neither maintain unity among the Swiss Protestants nor stem the spread of a rejuvenated Catholicism. Bern and Geneva gradually emerged as the new leaders of Swiss Protestantism.

Although the settlement of the religious conflict on a cantonal basis [3] further weakened the unity of the Swiss Confederation, it prevented either side from dominating the other by force and kept the country from interfering in the subsequent religious wars in France and Germany. In a sense, therefore, it was in large part instrumental in developing the policy of neutrality that has characterized the modern history of Switzerland.

[3] The cantons that remained Catholic were Uri, Schwyz, Unterwalden, Lucerne, Zug, Fribourg, and Solothurn. Zurich, Bern, Basel, and Schaffhausen remained Protestant. In Glarus, St. Gall, Appenzell, Thurgau, and Aargau both faiths were represented. Most of the subject territories and towns remained Catholic. The French cantons of Geneva, Neuchâtel, and the Vaud became completely Calvinist.

# 5 Consolidation of Lutheranism (1530-1555)

## Protestant Politics, 1530–1547

Despite Luther's insistence upon the separate and distinct functions of the spiritual and secular "kingdoms" and his determination to prevent the encroachment of the princes as well as the emperor upon the Church's freedom in religious matters, Protestantism like Catholicism became so much a part of the political history of the German estates that it cannot be understood apart from that history. His emphasis upon justification by faith, the freedom of the Christian man, and the universal priesthood of believers continued to exert a powerful influence upon his contemporaries, in some areas leading to the achievement of considerable political freedom. But the tendency toward territorial control of Christianity, both ecclesiastical and doctrinal, was too strong everywhere in Europe to permit Protestantism or Catholicism to develop without political interference.

Charles V seemed as determined as ever in 1530 to become the protector and arbiter of Christianity. He had succeeded in pronouncing upon religious matters at Worms in 1521 and Augsburg in 1530. But he was so involved in the complicated Hapsburg-Valois rivalry that he could not prevent the German estates, whether Protestant or Catholic, from gaining control of religious matters. In the struggles that followed the Diet of Augsburg of 1530, however, the Protestant estates could not have succeeded in consolidating Lutheranism without the direct and indirect aid of the Catholic estates.

Although the great majority of the estates at the Diet of

# Part Two: The Reformation in Germany

Augsburg supported Charles in his decision to stamp out Lutheranism, only Elector Joachim of Brandenburg and Duke George of Saxony were willing to risk a civil war to attain this end. Charles himself had few troops and little money at his disposal for carrying on the struggle alone. This partially explains his hesitancy at the very moment when the Protestants, expecting vigorous action, met in the small town of Schmalkalden on the southwestern border of Electoral Saxony, where, in February, 1531, they formed the defensive alliance known as the Schmalkaldic League. It accepted the Augsburg Confession as its official doctrinal statement.

## The Schmalkaldic League

The Schmalkaldic League, virtually an *imperium in imperio,* became to all intents a strong anti-Hapsburg European power that carried on diplomatic negotiations with other powers. It originally comprised seven princes of northern Germany—the elector of Saxony, the landgrave of Hesse, the two dukes of Brunswick-Lüneburg, the prince of Anhalt, and the two counts of Mansfeld—and the cities Magdeburg and Bremen. Many estates at first hesitated to join the League because they could not accept the revolutionary theory that the emperor's powers were limited by the electors who chose him and that a minority in the diet was not bound by the majority.

Martin Bucer greatly strengthened the Schmalkaldic League by his various attempts to bring the Protestant groups together. He not only succeeded at the Coburg in putting Luther into a conciliatory frame of mind toward the Strassburg theologians but eventually brought a number of the South-German cities into the League. His attempts to win over the Zwinglians, however, failed, for it was now the Zurich reformer who was not in a mood to compromise.

The Swiss disaster at Kappel seemed to Ferdinand a propitious time for beginning a widespread attack upon Protestantism. But Charles again hesitated, for he feared another attack by Francis I, who was already planning an alliance with Clement VII. Clement, furthermore, opposed the calling of a general Church council demanded by Charles. To make matters worse, the Turks were preparing for another attack upon the Austrian lands. To prevent this, Charles was again compelled to seek the support of all the German estates.

Meanwhile the dreaded day of April 15, 1531, had passed quietly, without the attack in force that the Protestants had been led to expect. And when the diet met in Regensburg in the summer of 1532, the Schmalkaldic League was so powerful that Charles was forced to make further concessions to the Lutherans. A truce, called the Peace of Nürnberg because it resulted from negotiations in that city, postponed the religious settlement, ordered the processes against the Protestants in the im-

# 5. Consolidation of Lutheranism (1530–1555)

perial supreme court thrown out, and stipulated that no attacks were to be made against the Lutheran estates before the meeting of a general Church council. Although this Peace of Nürnberg was not published, the Protestants agreed to take the emperor at his word and patriotically supported him in his war against the Turks.

Suleiman, who had begun to march on Vienna in April, 1532, was surprised by the appearance of the emperor with eighty thousand troops. After meeting determined resistance in Austrian Hungary, the sultan gave up his plans and in September withdrew to the south. But Charles refused to continue the campaign, for threats to the Hapsburg dynasty appeared elsewhere.

Pope Clement VII, eager to retain his political influence in Italy and irritated by the demands of Charles for a Church council that, it was rumored, might take from him the Papal States, made an alliance with Francis I in the autumn of 1533. According to its terms, the French king agreed to oppose the calling of a council in return for the papal support of the reacquisition of Milan and Genoa and the creation of a strong state in northern Italy for Henry, the king's second son, who was to marry Catherine de' Medici, Clement's niece. Thus it was now the pope who prevented Charles from attacking the Lutherans and the Turks.

The failure of Charles to act decisively against the Protestants during the years 1530 to 1532 permitted the Protestant estates to consolidate the churches in their territories. When his next opportunity to intervene came, fifteen years later, the Protestants were so thoroughly established that force could achieve little or nothing. His postponement of the issues in 1532 must not, however, be interpreted as a recognition of the principles of Protestantism. He still wished to reform the Church within the traditional framework, but he believed that it was possible to bring the Protestants back into the Catholic fold, especially after the more activist Zwinglians had been defeated.

During the turbulent decade following the Peace of Nürnberg, the fiery and headstrong Philip of Hesse (1504–1567) emerged as the leader of the Schmalkaldic League, overshadowing and often in conflict with the new elector of Saxony, the cautious and pious John Frederick (1532–1547; d. 1554). Under Philip's dynamic leadership, the first large territory of southern Germany was won over to Lutheranism, namely Württemberg. This territory, which had been acquired by the Hapsburgs in 1520, had long been the scene of bitter anti-Protestant action, while its deposed Lutheran Duke Ulrich and his Catholic son Christoper were plotting to regain the land. Francis I was induced to send French troops to aid Philip in restoring Ulrich to the throne, while the dukes of Bavaria persuaded the Swabian League, which had long supported the Hapsburg cause in southern Germany, to remain neutral. In May, 1534, the Hapsburg troops were decisively defeated and the following month

Ferdinand signed a treaty that recognized Ulrich as the duke of Württemberg, although the territory was to be held as a fief of Austria. Duke Ulrich was permitted to establish Lutheranism in the duchy, and Ferdinand agreed to stop the proceedings in the imperial supreme court against members of the Schmalkaldic League. Thereupon the elector of Saxony finally agreed to recognize Ferdinand as king of the Romans.

The addition of Württemberg to the list of Protestant territories was considered one of the master strokes of Philip of Hesse. Meanwhile the Schmalkaldic League was strengthened by the introduction of Lutheranism in a number of northern cities and states. Goslar and Brunswick became Lutheran in 1528, Göttingen in 1530, Lüneburg in 1531, Bremen in 1532, and Hanover in 1534. The duchy of Mecklenburg embraced Lutheranism in 1533, Anhalt and Pomerania in 1534.

Probably the greatest blow to Catholicism came in 1539, when Duke George of Saxony, the staunchest and most sincere Catholic prince of Germany, died and was succeeded by his brother Henry, who immediately made his important duchy Lutheran. This was also a great triumph for Luther, who accepted the invitation to attend this occasion and preached in the same hall in the Pleissenburg in which he had debated with Eck twenty years before. Even the three ecclesiastical electors of Mainz, Trier, and Cologne were seriously considering becoming Lutherans.

Furthermore, the cities of southern Germany again became interested in reaching an understanding in religious matters with the Lutherans. Accordingly Bucer, Capito, and others visited Luther in his home in May, 1536, to discuss their differences. Lengthy discussions disclosed their ·substantial agreement on the Lord's Supper and other doctrines formerly in dispute. The results of these discussions were embodied in a document prepared by Melanchthon and called the Wittenberg Concord. Although this step did not bring the Lutherans and the South-German Protestants into an organic union, it ended their bitter conflicts. On the other hand, it drove a wedge between the latter and those Zwinglians who continued to insist upon the symbolical interpretation of the Lord's Supper. Although the Swiss could not accept the Wittenberg Concord, they expressed their desire to live on cordial terms with the Lutherans. Luther, on his part, maintained friendly relations with Bullinger, Zwingli's successor.

Charles, meanwhile, was compelled to turn his attention to the western Mediterranean, where the Barbary corsairs of Algeria and Tunisia were harassing the coastal cities of Spain and ruining Spanish commerce under Kheireddin Barbarossa, a renegade Christian who had acknowledged Suleiman as his suzerain and had been given command of the Turkish fleet. In 1535 Charles attacked the Moorish city of Tunis, which had previously been seized by Barbarossa. He took the city as well as Barbarossa's eighty-two galleys, but the pirate leader himself escaped to Algiers.

## Third Hapsburg-Valois War

Francis I chose this opportunity to begin his third war with Charles (1535–1538). The "most Christian king" shocked a rather callous Europe by not only assisting Barbarossa but, in 1535, concluding a treaty with Suleiman that gave the French certain extraterritorial rights in his lands, called capitulations, and the right to trade within the Ottoman Empire. Thus allied with the foe of Christendom, Francis overran Savoy on his way to Italy. There the death of Francesco Sforza of Milan provided him with an excuse for reviving the French claims to that duchy. But the appearance of Charles in Provence compelled Francis to give up his Italian campaign. This inconclusive war was brought to an end by the equally inconclusive Treaty of Nice (June, 1538), which reaffirmed the provisions of the Treaty of Cambrai and left Francis in control of about two thirds of Piedmont. Francis agreed to break his alliance with Suleiman.

The political and religious situation of Europe had meanwhile been greatly changed by the election of a new pope, the Farnese Paul III (1534–1549), a much better diplomat than his predecessor and the first pope to be convinced of the necessity of a thorough-going reformation of the Church. Although he was guilty of nepotism, he attracted capable and sincere advisers to the Roman *Curia* and planned to call a general Church council as soon as peace could be restored between the two great Catholic powers. However, he alienated a number of Catholic princes in Germany, who began to take seriously the suggestion that a German national church council might create a German Church similar to the Anglican Church.

Charles V, irritated by the pope's anti-Hapsburg policies, involved in the third war with Francis, and greatly concerned over the advance of Lutheranism in Germany and the Austrian lands, adopted a conciliatory attitude toward the Lutheran princes and considered calling a German national Church council in defiance of the pope. Accordingly he sent Held, his vice-chancellor, to Germany in October, 1536. But Held, an ardent Catholic and former member of the imperial supreme court, acted contrary to the broad instructions given him by Charles. Supported by Ferdinand, he announced that the cases against the Protestant princes that were pending in the imperial court would not be quashed, as promised in the Peace of Nürnberg of 1532; and finally, in June, 1538, he formed a league of Catholic princes at Nürnberg to enforce this decision.

The summoning by Paul III of a general Church council to meet at Mantua in 1537 prompted the members of the Schmalkaldic League, who feared that this council would plan an attack upon them and who detested the bellicose Held, to meet in a congress at Schmalkalden in February, 1537. Although the Lutherans had hitherto consistently considered themselves a part of the Catholic Church and had demanded that either a general or national Church council should settle the issues raised by the Reformation, they now made it clear that they would accept the invitation to the council only if (1) the council were free of papal control, (2) all the estates were represented on equal terms, (3) the Bible were made the sole basis of judgment, and (4) the council met on German soil. These demands were tantamount to declining the invitation.

Instead of presenting their grievances at a general council, which, incidentally, did not meet until 1545, the Protestant princes had Luther draw up a new statement of faith. The reformer gladly complied, for he was not pleased with the concessions made to Catholicism in the Augsburg Confession and the Apology. Furthermore, because he felt that death was approaching, he wished to present a final statement of his doctrines and faith. The articles that he prepared came to be known as the Schmalkaldic Articles. Published for the first time in 1538, they were soon considered authoritative. Although they were not formally adopted by the princes at Schmalkalden, they were approved by most of the theologians present and constituted a virtual Lutheran declaration of independence from Rome. They demanded (1) the acceptance of the doctrine of justification by faith alone, (2) the abolition of the Mass as a sacrifice, (3) the use of monastic and other foundations for Protestant churches and schools, and (4) the denial of the divine right of the pope to rule the Church.

When Held's measures threatened to lead to civil war, Charles replaced him with the archbishop of Lund, who quieted the members of the Schmalkaldic League by agreeing to quash the ecclesiastical suits in the imperial court for six months and to submit the religious differences to an assembly of theologians and laymen that should meet in 1539. The Treaty of Frankfurt of April, 1539, which provided for another truce between the emperor and the League, was followed by conferences between Protestant and Catholic theologians and laymen at Hagenau, Worms, and Regensburg in 1540–1541. Although the two sides came closer together than ever before, especially in the *Book of Regensburg,* which lightly passed over basic differences, it became clear that no sincere compromise was possible, even though the papal legate Contarini, for example, was willing to make some doctrinal concessions that were later repudiated by the pope.

## Bigamy of Philip of Hesse

Despite the fact that Charles failed to bring about a compromise between the Protestants and the Catholics to serve his political purposes, he succeeded in weakening the offensive power of the Schmalkaldic

# 5. Consolidation of Lutheranism (1530–1555)

League and prevented its cooperation with the formidable array of enemies opposing him. Partly responsible for the weakness of the League was the rift created among its members by the bigamy of Philip of Hesse. Philip was married at the age of nineteen to a daughter of Duke George of Saxony. As he grew older he was inclined to bemoan the fact that he could not maintain normal conjugal relations with her. Instead, he led a grossly immoral life, for which he felt little remorse until he came under the influence of Luther. His interest in solving his personal problem by a bigamous marriage was aroused by the assertions of some Anabaptists that this was permissible to Christians and by Luther's statement in *The Babylonian Captivity* that bigamy was not as serious an offense as divorce. Moreover, Pope Clement VII, on the advice of Cajetan, had wanted Henry VIII to use this way out of his personal predicament.

Philip finally obtained the consent of Luther, Melanchthon, and Bucer for his marriage to Margaret von der Saal, which took place early in 1540. Luther's argument, specious as it may seem, was based upon his conviction that marriage was a matter involving primarily the individuals and God. Because Abraham and others had broken the divine law with impunity, and because the gospel did not of itself regulate man's external actions, a pastor might make an exception to the law, which was in this case also an imperial law, and permit bigamy in order to correct a greater evil and prevent something much worse. He insisted that God would in this case consider the second marriage the real one, even though it was not sanctioned by law. In addition, Luther as Philip's confessor demanded that, for the good of the social order and the Church, such an arrangement should be kept in the strictest secrecy; that Philip should even "tell a good strong lie for the sake and good of the Christian Church." Such a dispensation—Luther never condemned dispensations as such—would become invalid once it was made public. But Philip, hoping to obtain the sanction of Charles V, did not keep the bigamy a secret. Consequently he not only embarrassed the Protestant reformers and gained the animosity of other Protestant rulers, but he became a tool in the hands of the emperor.

This state of affairs was clearly demonstrated by the case of the duchy of Cleves on the lower Rhine. When its Duke John died in 1539, his son William inherited not only this duchy but, through his mother, Jülich and Berg. At the same time the estates of the duchy of Gelderland, which had never been absorbed by the Burgundian rulers and whose duke had died without heirs in 1538, recognized William as their ruler, despite a treaty that had recognized Charles V's claim to the land. Thus this ambitious duke inherited a powerful state east of the emperor's possessions in the Low Countries.

Although a number of his cities had become Lutheran, William leaned toward the Erasmian conception of Christianity. Like Henry VIII of England, William made few basic changes in his Church but usurped many functions of the pope. The marriage of one of his sisters, Sibylla, to Elector John Frederick of Saxony in 1527 had been followed by close co-operation with the Schmalkaldic League. The marriage of another sister, Anne, to Henry VIII of England and William's negotiations with Francis I of France for a political alliance made it clear to Charles that he could not ignore this ambitious anti-Hapsburg prince.

In 1541 Charles won from Philip of Hesse a promise that he would do his utmost to prevent the duke of Cleves from joining the Schmalkaldic League, in return for which the landgrave was promised protection against personal attacks and advancement in the service of the emperor. His son-in-law Maurice (1541–1553), who succeeded his father as duke of Albertine Saxony that same year, was made a party to this arrangement. Joachim II of Brandenburg, who had gained a control over his Church comparable to that of Henry VIII, was confirmed in this control in return for his promise to support the emperor's plan. Thus the Schmalkaldic League was split into two parties, and Charles was in a position to substitute a policy of repression for the former policy of conciliation. But all that he could accomplish against the Protestants at this time was the defeat of Duke William of Cleves and the seizure of Gelderland in 1543, for he once more became involved in a war with Francis.

### Fourth Hapsburg-Valois War

The fourth war with Francis (1542–1544), like the third one, was begun by the French king after Charles had made an attack upon the Barbary corsairs. But this time the emperor's fleet, which appeared before Algiers in October, 1541, was destroyed by a storm.

Charles also suffered reverses in Hungary. John Zapolya, the rival ruler of Archduke Ferdinand, had died in 1540. But Ferdinand did not obtain his throne, which had been promised him by a previous treaty. Instead the Hungarian nobles crowned Zapolya's infant son, John Sigismund, king and called upon Suleiman for aid. The Turks, determined to bring Hungary under their direct control, seized Buda in 1541 and once more threatened Austria. Again Charles was compelled to call upon Lutherans as well as Catholics in his struggle against the Turks and the "most Christian king" of France, who had supported Suleiman. But the imperial army, led by the incompetent Joachim II of Brandenburg, failed to retake Buda in the autumn of 1542 and returned to Germany in disgrace.

In western Europe the Hapsburg cause seemed in an equally bad plight, for Francis had created a formidable anti-imperialist league that included France, Turkey, Cleves, Sweden, Denmark, and Scotland, and the pope was hostile to both Charles and Ferdinand. Meanwhile the Lutheran princes were making notable gains. Duke Henry of Brunswick—whose brutal treatment of his wife was almost as scandalous as the big-

# 5. Consolidation of Lutheranism (1530–1555)

amy of Philip of Hesse—was one of the most important Catholic princes in Germany. He unadvisedly seized the towns of Brunswick and Goslar, against which cases pending in the imperial court had been suspended by Charles. Landgrave Philip and Elector John Frederick, arguing that they were supporting the emperor, seized the duke's lands in 1542, which were then reformed by Bugenhagen. Albert of Mainz permitted the spread of the Protestant Reformation to Magdeburg and Halberstadt in return for a special grant of taxes in 1541. Hermann von Wied, archbishop and elector of Cologne, invited Bucer and Melanchthon to introduce Protestantism into his lands the following year. His neighbor, Francis of Waldeck, bishop of Münster, Minden, and Osnabrück, followed his example in 1543. The city of Hildesheim became Lutheran and forced much of the bishopric of Hildesheim to do likewise.

When it looked as though all Germany might become Protestant, Charles, already strengthened by his alliance with Henry VIII, succeeded in isolating Duke William of Cleves. In the summer of 1543, he seized Zutphen as well as Gelderland, detached them from the Empire, and added them to his lands. He also compelled William to repudiate his Protestantism and to marry Mary, the daughter of Ferdinand.

The members of the Schmalkaldic League, however, whose help was still needed against France and the Turks, gained from the emperor the promise, at the Diet of Speyer in February, 1544, that the religious questions would be solved by a national Church council. John Frederick, who received the assurance that he would obtain Cleves if William died without heirs, now led the Germans in establishing friendly relations with the Hapsburgs. The kings of Sweden and Denmark also dropped their alliance with Francis. The French king, with only the pope and the sultan to aid him, was no match for Charles and Henry VIII. When the emperor appeared within sight of Paris, Francis agreed to make a peace that completely ignored Charles' surprised ally Henry VIII. The Peace of Crépy of September, 1544, provided that Francis should give up his claims to Naples and his overlordship to Flanders and Artois. He further promised that he would help Charles against both the Turks and the German Protestants.

The Peace of Crépy and an armistice concluded with the Turks at Adrianople the next year gave Charles an opportunity to turn his attention to Germany. The general Church council was finally called by Pope Paul III to meet at Trent on March 15, 1545, with the obvious purpose of forestalling the attempts of Charles to solve the religious issues in Germany by calling a national Church council. But the emperor informed the pope through the papal legate Farnese that he was merely bargaining with the Protestant princes to gain time. Paul therefore gave him both money and troops for a war against the Protestants. Whether or not Charles was serious, he arranged for another fruitless religious colloquy at Regensburg, for which Melanchthon wrote *The Wittenberg Reformation* and at which Bucer and the Spaniard Malvenda were the outstanding spokesmen of the two sides. When the Protestant estates withdrew their representatives from this colloquy, it was clear to all that war was inevitable. Charles was now convinced that he could solve the religious problem only by force.

At the Diet of Regensburg, which met in June, 1546, but was not attended by the members of the Schmalkaldic League, Charles refused to renew the Peace of Nürnberg and made continued efforts to divide the Protestants. He concluded an offensive treaty with Pope Paul III, who, in return for promising aid against the enemies of Charles, obtained Parma and Piacenza for members of his family. At the same time Charles signed a treaty with Bavaria, which, however, continued to negotiate in secret with the Protestants.

Probably the greatest diplomatic gain made by Charles was winning the support of Maurice of ducal Saxony, one of the most enigmatic figures of this period. Invited to come to Regensburg to treat with the emperor, the young duke was determined to make the most of his advantage and, although he was a Lutheran by conviction, seized the opportunity to settle an old score with John Frederick of electoral Saxony. In return for his support of the imperial cause, Maurice was promised the electoral title, the administration of the sees of Magdeburg and Halberstadt, and immunity for himself and his people from whatever decrees the Council of Trent should pass against the Protestants. It was a bitter pill for Charles to swallow to be compelled to make such concessions to Maurice and to have so many Protestants in his camp when it was his basic religious policy to re-establish Christian unity.

## Lutheranism to the Death of Luther, 1546

Because the Lutheran princes had been made responsible for the religious affairs of their territories by the Diet of Speyer of 1526, and because the Peasants' Revolt and the disturbances caused by religious radicals had caused Luther to think less of the ability of man to exercise his religious liberty with restraint, the Lutheran movement tended to become increasingly authoritarian. This became apparent not only in the more frequent use made of the articles of faith, which, as we have seen, had been drawn up for political as well as religious reasons, but in the organization of the Church within the various territories.

Luther persistently maintained that his elector exercised the ecclesiastical functions of a bishop only as a temporary measure and continued to hope that the preaching of the gospel would make Christians worthy of their liberty and capable of conducting their own religious affairs. The prince as God's sword on earth should merely maintain order.

# 5. Consolidation of Lutheranism (1530–1555)

Because, according to Luther, Christians were members of a universal priesthood of believers, all the powers of the priesthood were vested in them. The medieval distinction between the spiritual and secular estates (*Stände*) was unscriptural. All belonged to the same estate, although they filled different offices (*Ämter*). Only because society demanded a proper division of labor did the Christian community select certain of its members to preach, administer the sacraments, and exercise ecclesiastical discipline. In other words, baptism, not ordination, made Christians priests. Therefore all that was necessary for the assumption of an ecclesiastical office was the divine *vocatio,* or call, given to the incumbent by the members of the Christian community. Ordination, according to Luther, thus involved only the entrusting of the office to a person called by a Christian congregation and adequately prepared to preach and administer the sacraments. Although a short ceremony with the laying on of hands was soon introduced, Luther did not consider this necessary.

To ensure the appointment of capable pastors, the elector decreed in 1535 that the theological faculty at Wittenberg formally examine candidates for the ministry and that the town pastor and his assistants ordain them. Because the need for clergymen was great, many emergency preachers without any formal training were ordained. Some of these had merely served as understudies to older pastors.

According to Luther's doctrine of the universal priesthood of believers, the Roman hierarchy of the clergy was discarded. The congregation became an autonomous, self-governing body that called a pastor as its spiritual head who was responsible to it and retained his right to preach and administer the sacraments only as long as he held his office. In a large congregation the pastor might have a number of assistants, such as deacons, chaplains, and preachers.

## Consistories

Despite Luther's differentiation between spiritual and secular functions, the German princes and cities invariably assumed control of those ecclesiastical functions that had previously belonged to the bishops. Thus the visitation, which began in electoral Saxony as a temporary expedient, became a permanent feature of government of this and other German territories. As a consequence of the thorough Saxon visitation of 1532, changes were made that laid the basis for the Lutheran consistorial court. This civil court was patterned after the consistorial court of the medieval bishop. It consisted of theologians and lawyers appointed by the elector. Like the episcopal court, it had complete control of all matters involving ecclesiastical discipline, particularly the trying of matrimonial cases. In practice the old canon law, revised to conform with Lutheran doctrines and practices, served as the basis of decisions. Luther believed that the jurisdiction over disciplinary cases had been usurped by the bishops and rightly belonged to the civil courts.

# Part Two: The Reformation in Germany

The first consistorial court, which acted under electoral authority and whose decisions had legal validity, was established by Elector John Frederick at Wittenberg in 1539 and was given permanent form three years later, when two other consistories were established, one at Zeitz and one at Zwickau. These consistories, each comprising four commissioners, two of whom were theologians and two lawyers, and a number of minor officials, had final jurisdiction over the clergy, tried cases involving gross immorality among the people, were charged with maintaining uniformity of worship, were expected to make annual visitations in their respective districts, and were given the right of excommunication. They were also empowered to call synods to deliberate on ecclesiastical matters. The general synod was attended by the superintendents of the various districts, the district synod by the superintendent and all the clergy of the district.

Despite the fact that Luther approved of the creation of these courts as necessary evils, he vigorously opposed their tendency to take over cases involving grave offenses against morality, which he believed belonged to the ordinary civil courts; to regulate the religious life of the people; to apply civil penalties for purely ecclesiastical offenses; and to establish religious uniformity. In actual practice, the members of the consistories, though appointed by and responsible to the elector, deferred to the theological members and ultimately to Luther in spiritual matters. Thus the state did not exercise authority in the spiritual realm during Luther's lifetime, although the elector maintained that it was his right to do so. In time, however, the consistory became an instrument in the hands of the rulers of Saxony and other Lutheran territories for the strengthening of their control over the religion of their subjects. Consequently Lutheranism lost much of the dynamic character that it had had when it emphasized the religious freedom of the Christian and the congregation.

Luther himself steadfastly refused to identify his invisible church of believers with the territorial church and never wanted his followers to be called Lutherans. It was Melanchthon who for the first time, in the 1543 edition of his *Loci communes,* identified Luther's followers with the "true visible church on earth."

## Education

One of the important reasons behind Luther's support of the visitation and the establishment of the consistorial courts was his recognition of the need for educating young people for service in the church, the state, and society as a whole. By insisting that the state, as well as the parents, had a sacred obligation to educate children, he won the reputation of being one of the first advocates of compulsory primary education for all. People, he maintained, did not have the right to leave their children ignorant, for God commanded them to provide the church with good Christians and intelligent pastors and teachers and the state with good

# 5. Consolidation of Lutheranism (1530–1555)

citizens and capable administrators and jurists. All these, he believed, served God better than people of high birth. Leadership in both the spiritual and the secular realms, he maintained, rested with the educated middle-class and common people.

Luther was particularly interested in the study of history, which, he stated, revealed many evidences of God's providence not found in the Bible. He also appreciated the educational value of Aesop's *Fables,* which he placed next to the Bible for its spiritual values and made compulsory reading in the schools. He prepared a small edition of the *Fables* in the German language that is highly regarded for its fine prose. He also encouraged the study of music and singing in the primary schools, the Latin grammar schools, and the universities, for he believed that music ranked next to theology with respect to spiritual values. He also stressed the value of studying the great works of the classical authors, especially those of Cicero, Vergil, Plautus, Terence, Horace, and Ovid. Although he appreciated the literary and moral contributions of the pagan authors, he severely criticized the reading of obscene works written by them and their Renaissance imitators.

By seeing to it that educated teachers were appointed and given regular salaries from established endowments and other ecclesiastical incomes taken over by the secular governments, Luther did much to improve education in the German schools. He and his colleagues also reformed the curriculum and the teaching in the University of Wittenberg and encouraged the founding of new universities. Much emphasis was placed upon the dignity of the academic degrees and the value of scholarly disputations. Important dignitaries of the state and the church took part in university functions. The many appeals for educated young men for service in church and state attracted many fine minds to these new universities. The fact that the connections between the universities and the papacy had been severed in the Protestant lands and that they were now territorial institutions explains the many other changes that took place as a consequence of the Reformation.

Melanchthon, called the *praeceptor Germaniae,* or teacher of Germany, rendered invaluable service to German education by writing new textbooks in grammar, rhetoric, logic, physics, and ethics. These embodied the best of the new humanist pedagogical principles. His Latin grammar, which was published in about fifty editions, was the standard grammar for more than a hundred years. His *Loci communes,* as we have seen, was the first systematic textbook of Lutheran theology. After conducting the first thorough survey of the German schools, he drew up his *School Plan for Electoral Saxony* (1528), in which he enunciated his new educational principles and provided for a more practical division of children into three classes, or divisions, for instruction. The children were to be taught fewer subjects and these more thoroughly; and they were to be well grounded not only in practical subjects but in classical Latin as well. In some of the schools, especially those of northern Germany, Greek and Hebrew were taught in the highest division.

Under Melanchthon's influence, many monasteries were transformed into territorial schools that gained enviable reputations. The newly established higher schools of learning at Nürnberg and Magdeburg and the new universities of Marburg and Königsberg felt the intellectual stimulus of the humanist content and method furthered by Melanchthon and Luther. Among the best-known city grammar schools was the one organized by Johann Sturm in Strassburg in 1535. His influential pedagogical work, *The Correct Exposition of Letters in the Schools* (1537), consisted primarily of the application of Melanchthon's principles with respect to the division of classes. Eight classes, however, were established in place of Melanchthon's three. Because of his success as a teacher, Melanchthon's advice was sought by teachers and rectors throughout Germany.

## Luther as a Church Authority

The growth of an authoritative Lutheranism was evident not only in the organization of religion and education by means of visitations and consistories but by the unique position that Luther came to occupy during the last fifteen years of his life, both as the dean of the theological faculty at Wittenberg and the final arbiter of questions of a doctrinal or ecclesiastical nature. So great was his influence and so certain was he of the objective truth of his faith that he was frequently called the Protestant pope by his enemies.

Luther's amazing creative ability and tireless attention to the many detailed problems of the Lutheran congregations are shown by his voluminous correspondence, and the interest of his followers in all his utterances is seen in the copious notes that his table companions preserved for us in the *Table Talks*. Although these notes are not uniformly reliable, they provide a useful source of information concerning the reformer's views on all kinds of subjects. Because of his great generosity, his table was always graced by the presence of many guests, ranging from poor students to important officials of church and state.

Because of Luther's dependence upon the Bible as the sole and unequivocal source of his faith and his eagerness to give it in its entirety to the people in their mother tongue, he worked tirelessly with Melanchthon, Bugenhagen, and Aurogallus in preparing a translation of the Old Testament to accompany his translation of the New Testament. This tremendous task was completed by 1534, when Hans Lufft, a Wittenberg printer, published the first edition of the entire Bible. Great care was taken to make this Bible attractive as well as useful. In addition to the illuminated initials, it contained 124 woodcuts, some of which covered an entire page and were done in color. Revisions were made until the end of

# 5. Consolidation of Lutheranism (1530–1555)

Luther's life, for he and his colleagues never tired of trying to make this a masterpiece of eloquence and poetry. So excellent was this German Bible that it is still used by most German Protestants.

As an expositor of the Bible, Luther clung consistently to his conviction concerning its unity. For him the God of the entire Bible was the father of Jesus Christ and Jesus Christ was the eternal word of God proclaimed in both the Old and the New Testaments. For this reason he was critical of the Old Testament book of Esther and referred to the New Testament books of Hebrews, James, Jude, and Revelation as being of less value than the others. The Bible was for him the living word of Christ, as active today as in the past. He never tired of insisting that preachers faithfully proclaim this word, both the law and the gospel, for the salvation of all.

The Augsburg Confession was also referred to increasingly as an authoritative statement of the Lutheran faith. It is not clear exactly when the adherence to this confession was first made a part of the doctoral oath of theologians or of the ordination of the clergy in electoral Saxony. We know that it was required there by 1546, and in Pomerania as early as 1535. The reasons for such a requirement are to be found in the continued presence in Lutheran lands of radical evangelicals who refused to conform to the doctrines and practices of the territorial churches.

Like the reformers of other established Protestant churches, Luther associated the radical evangelicals with insurrection and consequently saw in their activities the work of the devil who was threatening to destroy the gospel. Confronted with those who would carry his evangelical doctrines much further than he, he emphasized more than ever the objective nature of the gospel truth and the sacraments of baptism and the Lord's Supper as divinely established means of obtaining divine grace. His consistency in this matter is to be seen in his basic belief that only the Word of God could save the sinner. He insisted that because the Bible demanded that all persons be baptized, infants should not be excluded, for they could believe, even if they could not understand. Whether or not this was reasonable made no difference to him.

As late as 1528 Luther strongly opposed the brutal persecution of religious radicals, insisting that everyone should be allowed to believe according to his conscience; that the most that might be done to a "false teacher" was to banish him. But after that time, and when it appeared as though the various sectaries might destroy his own work in Saxony, he appealed to the generally accepted law and custom that force could be used in opposing blasphemy and sedition. In a letter that he called "Concerning the Sneaks and Hedge-Preachers," written in 1532, he condemned the surreptitious activities of those unordained persons who carried their apocalyptic and other notions to the uneducated common people in the fields and forests, thus breeding unrest and revolt. Such persons who preached without a regular call should be driven out of the land. After the violence at Münster in 1535, he reluctantly joined Melanchthon in agreeing that in extreme cases of blasphemy and treason, the death penalty might be imposed by the civil government. In January, 1536, the government of electoral Saxony found three rustics guilty of blasphemy and sedition and executed them.

Luther also became involved in a bitter controversy with Johann Agricola (1499–1566), a product of Wittenberg and the director of the new Latin school at Eisleben until 1537. In that year he returned to Wittenberg as a theologian and a preacher. At first an ardent supporter of Luther, he gradually developed strong antinomian doctrines; that is, he opposed the necessity of preaching the law. Luther had taught that both the Mosaic and the moral law had, after New Testament times, only the negative value of preparing the sinner for grace by making him aware of his sins. Agricola denied even this value of the law, believing that repentance should be instilled only by the preaching of the gospel.

The antinomian controversy lasted intermittently from 1537 to 1540, while Agricola remained in Wittenberg. Although Luther had never ignored the role of law in Christian life, he now emphasized more than ever the need for disciplining Christians, almost in a Calvinist sense. He could not agree with Agricola that the church on earth consisted of congregations of saints, for he held that it consisted of both earnest and hypocritical persons. The Christian must continue to fight sin as long as he lives, even though God's righteousness is imputed to him. The preaching of the law incites him to continue the struggle. The controversy became so bitter that the elector, at Luther's request, began proceedings against Agricola as a heretic. But before the trial could take place, the latter fled to Berlin, where he accepted the position of court preacher.

Although Agricola had deserved Luther's hostility because of his inane methods of attack, his views were probably not as extreme as Luther believed. By lumping him and all antinomians together with the evangelical radicals as perverters of law and gospel and Christian morality, Luther displayed his growing impatience with those who differed from him. In the winter of 1543–1544 he also made bitter attacks upon the Zwinglians and the mild-mannered Schwenkfeld, thereby reviving for a short time the Sacramentarian Controversy. Even Melanchthon and Bucer felt his sharp shafts when he upbraided them for being too compromising in their views concerning the Lord's Supper. His *Short Confession of the Holy Sacrament* of 1544, written in defense of his views concerning the real presence, shows the irascibility of his later years at its worst. Yet we must never overlook the fact that he remained the staunch friend of Melanchthon until the end, despite their fundamentally different approaches to theology and culture.

Luther's growing irritability was also evident in his attitude toward the Jews. In his earlier years he had pleaded for mutual tolerance and brotherly love between Christians and Jews. He had hoped that, because the worst abuses in the church had been eliminated by the Reformation, many Jews would be won over to Christianity. As he grew older, he became exceedingly impatient with those rabbis of his acquaintance who would not accept his belief that the Old Testament pointed unmistakably not only to the coming of Jesus but to the virgin birth, and who could not see that the destruction of Jerusalem and the fifteen hundred years of wandering of the Jews without a kingdom was God's punishment for their unbelief. Added to the refusal of the rabbis to be convinced by his arguments were rumors of the introduction of certain Hebraic rites, such as circumcision and the celebration of the Jewish sabbath, in Bohemia and elsewhere. In 1543, Luther published his two vitriolic blasts, *The Jews and Their Lies* and *Schem Hamphoras,* and his *Last Words of David,* written in a much calmer and more scholarly fashion. It must be noted, however, that his enmity had been provoked for religious, not racial, reasons, for he still hoped that some Jews at least would be convinced by the gospel.

Much of Luther's impatience with those who differed with him was the consequence of a recurring illness that followed an almost fatal gallstone attack early in 1537 and of the increased burdens placed upon a weakened body. Although buoyed up by a firm religious faith and a strong sense of humor, he became increasingly pessimistic and depressed. The death of his daughter Magdalene at the age of thirteen years made matters much worse. Furthermore, he became so disturbed by the worldly preoccupations of the people of Wittenberg that he threatened to leave them in 1544; and in 1545, while on a visit to Zeitz, he decided not to return home. Only the promise of the town council to attempt to improve the morals of the citizens brought him back.

Death came to Luther on February 18, 1546, at Eisleben. He had gone to the place of his birth to arbitrate a quarrel between the two counts of Mansfeld over some inconsequential disputes concerning the division of their lands. Successful in this mission, he breathed his last in the presence of Count Albert and the countess, his own sons Martin and Paul, Justus Jonas, Aurifaber, Coelius, his servant Ambrosius, and the physicians. He was asked by Jonas, "Will you stand firm in Christ and the doctrine which you have preached?" To this he answered "Yes," his last word. On February 22 he was buried in the Castle Church at Wittenberg, where his remains lie today.

## Lutheranism in the Scandinavian Countries

Although Luther's influence was felt in all European countries, outside Germany his particular forms of doctrine and church polity found their best expression in the Scandinavian countries. There the Reformation was at the outset closely associated with political, economic, and social conditions. To be sure, the religious ideas of Luther were first spread by young men who had studied at Wittenberg or had come under the spell of Luther's writings and by those Germans who had settled in the large commercial centers in the Scandinavian lands. But the religious movement was generally led by the rulers themselves to further their own dynastic interests.

The Union of Kalmar of 1397, by means of which the nobles of the three Scandinavian countries had agreed to unite under the Danish ruler, never became more than a dynastic union. Because each of the countries retained its own laws and customs, the Danish kings had the utmost difficulty in establishing orderly government. Sweden, especially, was almost constantly in a rebellious state. The Danish kings could rule this country only through Swedish administrators.

While the rulers of most other European countries were increasing their royal authority, the Danish king was losing his to both the nobles and the higher clergy. Because neither Denmark nor Sweden had a law of succession, every ruler had to make concessions to the nobles and the clergy in order to be elected; and the kings frequently gave large appanages to their sons in order to strengthen their dynasties. Thus the royal domain dwindled in size, while the nobles and clergy increased in power and wealth. Furthermore, the medieval assemblies of free peasants were gradually supplanted by a council of state, consisting of nobles and higher clergy. The king's court, meanwhile, became filled with Germans, which further weakened his influence at home.

The higher clergy, usually trained abroad, were inclined to be foreign in outlook, which alienated them from the people. They also vied with the nobles in acquiring large fiefs. By the time of the Reformation they had acquired more than half of the land in Denmark.

The economic and political condition of the once proud and powerful free peasants had deteriorated with that of the king so that by 1500 they were virtually landless peasants and serfs, at the mercy of the great landlords. Because of the domination of the commerce and trade of the Scandinavian countries by the Hanseatic League, no strong middle class emerged that might have supported the king against the nobles and the higher clergy.

Christian II (1513–1523), a typically Renaissance king, planned to construct a strong territorial state similar to those in other parts of Europe. He was well educated, had a vigorous personality, and was ruthless in his methods. Reared in the household of a townsman, he gained a clear conception of the importance of economic factors in government, became sympathetic to the cause of the common man, and grew determined to weaken the strangle hold that the nobles and the higher clergy had on the throne.

# 5. Consolidation of Lutheranism (1530–1555)

Among the king's bourgeois advisers was Sigbrit Willems, a native of Amsterdam and the mother of his mistress Duiveke (Dutch for "Little Dove"). Mother Sigbrit had become an innkeeper in Bergen, Norway, the country that Christian had ruled as regent before becoming king. Thoroughly at home among the prosperous townsmen of the Low Countries and endowed with great natural ability, she became the king's chief counselor, particularly in commercial and fiscal matters. She retained her influence even after Christian, in 1515, married Isabella, sister of the future Emperor Charles V, and after the murder of her daughter in 1517. When a jury of peasants accused a nobleman of poisoning the mistress and imposed upon him the death penalty, the struggle between the king and the nobles became more bitter than ever.

## Christian and Sweden

The first test of Christian's ability as a ruler came when he set out to force Sweden, which had become virtually autonomous, to submit to his authority. He was favored by a serious division among the Swedes that culminated in a civil war. The one party, led by Gustavus Trolle (d. 1535), the archbishop of Uppsala, supported the regularly appointed administrator of Sweden, who favored cooperation with the king. The popular party, led by Hemming Gad, bishop of Linkoeping, had set up Sten Sture as its administrator. During the civil war that followed, Trolle appealed to Christian and Pope Leo X for help. The Swedes deposed Trolle in 1517, and Leo excommunicated Sture. In January, 1520, Sten Sture was defeated and mortally wounded by Christian's forces. His widow, Christina, continued the valiant defense of Stockholm until the king persuaded her to give up in return for a general amnesty.

Christian was crowned king of Sweden in Stockholm November 4, 1520. But a few days later, during the coronation festivities, he broke his solemn promise of amnesty by having those nobles and magistrates who had led the opposition to him tried by a court of twelve churchmen. On the same day on which they were tried and condemned as rebels, they were beheaded in the market place. Among the more than eighty who were executed in this notorious "bath of blood" was the father of Gustavus Eriksson, the future king of Sweden.

## Christian and Denmark

Christian's policies in Denmark bore more lasting fruits. He promptly ignored the promises he had made to the nobles and clergy before his elevation to the throne. Supported by the townsmen and the peasants, he ignored the royal council, imposed taxes upon the nobles, made illegal financial demands upon the clergy, and, as a climax, promulgated his revolutionary Secular and Ecclesiastical Code (1521–1522), by means of which he attempted to establish a state church. According to its provisions, a new royal supreme court was given ultimate jurisdiction in ecclesiastical and civil cases, with no appeals permitted to the Roman *Curia;* ecclesiastical courts were denied the right to try cases concerning property; nonresidence of the clergy was forbidden; the clergy could not acquire landed property or inheritances unless they agreed to marry; and no person could be ordained unless he had studied at a university and could teach and preach in the Danish language.

In order to weaken the nobility and strengthen the peasants and the townsmen, the king deprived the former of the feudal right to ship-wrecked property, abolished serfdom, reformed municipal governments, encouraged commerce in a variety of ways, gave Danish merchants preference over Hanseatic merchants, improved roads, and introduced Flemish horticulture.

To further learning, Christian made Paul Eliae (Povul Helgsen), a Carmelite friar who had become an admirer of Erasmus and Luther, the chief lecturer at the University of Copenhagen and appealed to his uncle, Elector Frederick the Wise, to send him an outstanding Lutheran theologian to teach at the Danish university. But Martin Reinhard, who came to Copenhagen in 1520, knew no Danish and proved most ineffective. The next year Carlstadt appeared; but after the Edict of Worms, Christian lost interest in Lutheranism, for he did not wish to offend Charles V, his brother-in-law. Carlstadt left Denmark in disgust.

Involved in bitter struggles with his enemies in Sweden, in difficulties with the pope, in a war with the city of Lübeck, and in a controversy with Duke Frederick of Schleswig and Holstein, who was his uncle, Christian became too discouraged to put down a rebellion of some of his nobles late in 1522. Even though the peasants and the townsmen loyally supported him, he offered no serious resistance when, in 1523, the Danish nobility and clergy deposed him and made Duke Frederick their king. Instead, Christian fled to Flanders. In 1531 he was thrown into a dungeon, where he remained in virtual solitary confinement for seventeen years. The remaining eleven years of his life were spent in somewhat less restricted confinement.

## The Reformation in Denmark

Although the nobles had compelled the new king, Frederick I (1523–1533), to promise that he would respect their privileges and prevent the preaching of heresy, they could not completely undo the work begun by Christian II. As a matter of fact, the new king soon drove a wedge between the nobles and the clergy, to the great detriment of the latter. Influenced by Lutheranism before his accession to the throne, he made use of it to attain his political ends by permitting and encouraging Lutheran preachers to spread the Reformation.

One of the most important of these preachers was Hans Tausen

# 5. Consolidation of Lutheranism (1530–1555)

(1494–1561), a member of a Johannite priory who had been sent by his superior to study at Rostock, Cologne, Louvain, and finally Wittenberg. Recalled in 1524 because of his attraction to Luther, he broke openly with Catholicism and began preaching Lutheran sermons, supported by the king's general, Johann von Rantzau, who had come to know Luther at the Diet of Worms in 1521. Soon others followed Tausen's footsteps. In 1524 appeared the first Danish version of the New Testament, followed five years later by the much better edition of Christian Petersen (d. 1554), called the father of Danish literature.

Encouraged by the spread of Lutheranism in Denmark and supported by those nobles who had enriched themselves by seizing church lands, Frederick, in 1526, repudiated the papal nominee to the archbishopric of Lund and, with the consent of the royal council, confirmed another candidate and retained the confirmation fees instead of sending them to the pope. These actions were tantamount to assuming the position of the pope in his own country and establishing a national church.

Frederick was further encouraged in his defiance of the bishops and the papacy when Albert of Hohenzollern, the grand master of the Teutonic Knights who had adopted Lutheranism and secularized his lands in 1525–1526, asked him for the hand of his daughter Dorothea. The marriage was solemnized in June, 1526. Frederick's Lutheran inclinations were strengthened by the example of his son Christian, who began to introduce a new Lutheran church order in his duchies of Schleswig and Holstein in 1526. This task was completed by Bugenhagen in 1541. Frederick appointed Tausen and others as his court chaplains, thereby freeing them from all episcopal control. When the bishops sought, at the Diet of Odense in 1527, to prevent the king from continuing to further the Lutheran cause, they secured some minor concessions but failed in their main objectives. Thereafter the Reformation spread rapidly throughout Denmark.

At the Diet of Copenhagen in 1530, the bishops hoped to emulate the apparent success of Charles V at Augsburg by summoning the Lutheran preachers to appear before them, the king, and the nobles. But to their surprise, Tausen presented his Forty-three Articles, which he and twenty of his fellow preachers defended publicly with popular acclaim. Matters were not improved when the bishops presented their Twenty-seven Articles condemning the preachers and the latter answered with their Apology. The efforts of the bishops were repaid only by further Lutheran gains.

Frederick was not destined to complete the Reformation of his country, however, for his attention was diverted to other matters. When Christian II made an attempt to regain the throne with the aid of Charles V and the discontented parties in Denmark, Frederick joined the Schmalkaldic League. But he died soon after, in 1533, and his country was plunged into a civil war that lasted for three years. The bishops succeeded in undoing much that had been accomplished by the Lutherans. But the most serious division occurred over the selection of a new king.

Whereas the Lutherans and most of the nobles supported Christian of Schleswig and Holstein, the bishops for a while backed his half-brother Hans, who was still a child. The democratic townsmen and peasants joined the democratic city of Lübeck in an attempt to put the imprisoned Christian II on the throne. When Copenhagen was seized by the forces supporting Christian and it looked as though all Denmark would join the capital in recognizing him, the nobles made an alliance with King Gustavus of Sweden and the tide turned. Lübeck, which had actually sought to seize Denmark for itself, was defeated; Christian II again displayed his inability to lead in a crisis; and the Lutherans and nobles triumphantly entered Copenhagen and proclaimed Duke Christian their king.

The new king, Christian III (1536–1559), supported by the nobles, immediately seized the bishops, who were accused of causing the civil war, and released only those who agreed to give up all their former property and privileges. At a national assembly held in Copenhagen the same year, Lutheranism was introduced as the state religion. Monasteries were secularized and all Church property not already appropriated by the nobles was given to the crown.

In 1537 Bugenhagen crowned the king and queen—previously the prerogative of the archbishop of Lund—and began the reorganization of the Danish Church. Seven superintendents were nominated by the king and ordained by Bugenhagen, merely a priest. Later the superintendents were again called bishops. At the same time a new Church Ordinance, approved by Luther and adopted by the National Assembly of Odense in 1539, became the basic law of the Danish Church. It provided for the election by the people of the local clergy, who, in turn, elected delegates. These chose the provosts and deans who served under the bishops. The king was the *episcopus supremus,* or head of the church. Church property was supervised by special officials of the bishop, and with him they cared for the finances of the churches, the schools, and the hospitals. Eventually the Augsburg Confession was adopted, a new liturgy was provided, and a new Danish translation of the Bible was begun.

## The Reformation in Norway and Iceland

Virtually no preparation had been made for the adoption of Lutheranism in Norway. The first leaders seemed more inclined to despoil the wealthy churches and monasteries in and around Bergen than to preach their convictions and reform abuses. So strong was the antipathy of the Norwegians to Frederick I and Duke Christian of Schleswig and Holstein that they willingly followed their Archbishop Olaf Engelbrektsson of

# 5. Consolidation of Lutheranism (1530–1555)

Trondhjem (Trondheim), head of the Norwegian council, in his support of the exiled King Christian II; and after Frederick I's death, they participated in the Danish civil war on the side of Lübeck. Thus Christian III's victory in Denmark was followed by his compelling Norway to surrender its autonomy and to accept him as its king without a regular election and with complete control over the country.

The submission of Norway was followed by the introduction of Lutheranism from above, the first steps involving the appointment of superintendents to replace the Catholic bishops. Because of the lack of Lutheran teachers and preachers and the difficulty of the Danes in making themselves understood among the common people, little was done to extend the new faith. Priests were left in most of the parishes until they died, and their positions were often left vacant for many years. Attempts to impose the new church upon the country led not only to a strong resentment on the part of the Norwegians but also to frequent unrest and disruption of their economic and social life.

Iceland, which had belonged to Norway, now became a Danish province. There the Reformation was introduced by Oddur Gottskálkson (d. 1556), who had studied in Germany and returned a Lutheran in 1533. As a secretary of the bishop of Skálholt, the southern see of the country, he gained a strong secret following. He made an Icelandic translation of the New Testament, which was published in 1540. That same year Gissur Einarsson (d. 1548), another Lutheran who had been educated in Germany, became bishop of Skálholt. But when Christian III attempted to introduce the Danish ecclesiastical system, a powerful reaction took form under the leadership of the bishop of the northern see. Long after the latter's execution for treason in 1550 and the introduction of Lutheranism by royal decree in 1554, conservative Icelanders continued to detest the new state church, until the Lutheran Gudbrandur Thorláksson, bishop of Hólar from 1571 to 1627, began to win them over. He not only had the entire Bible published in the Icelandic language but encouraged the writing of Lutheran hymns.

## The Swedish Revolt and Reformation

The adoption of Lutheranism in Sweden was intimately connected with its achievement of independence and the foundation of the modern Swedish state by Gustavus Eriksson, later known as Gustavus Vasa (1523–1560), *vasa* being the sheaf on the family coat of arms. This young noble, who had studied for several years at Uppsala, was a fugitive in southern Sweden when the Stockholm massacre took place. Early in 1521 he gathered a force of local peasants and began driving out the Danes. He was chosen king by a Swedish diet at Strengnäs on June 7, 1523. A few days later he entered Stockholm in triumph.

The new king faced almost insuperable obstacles, especially financial difficulties, for the country was virtually bankrupt after years of disturbance and war. The Church, which owned about one fifth of the land, and the nobles, who had become virtually autonomous rulers, claimed exemption from taxation. What little trade remained was in the hands of Hanseatic and Danish merchants. The peasants, who had supported Gustavus, refused to accept any further taxation. And the city of Lübeck, from which Gustavus had borrowed heavily to finance his revolution, insistently pressed for repayment.

In these circumstances Gustavus was eager to obtain what he could from the Church. In this he was supported by a strong national resentment against the papacy for its having interfered on the side of the Danes during the revolt and by a rising Lutheran movement. Leo X had supported Gustavus Trolle, who had been deposed by a national diet as the "Swedish Judas Iscariot" in 1517, and had placed under the ban Sten Sture, who had defeated Christian II. Adrian VI, in 1522, sent Johan Magnusson, a Swede and a former student of his at Louvain, to Sweden as his legate to establish better relations with Gustavus. Although Magnusson was chosen archbishop by the canons of Uppsala, Adrian insisted that the deposed Trolle be restored. Clement VII made the same demand and defied the wishes of the Swedes by appointing an Italian to the see of Skara. But when Gustavus obtained a forced loan from his monasteries and churches, refused to restore Trolle, and made it clear that he would have no foreigners serve in the Swedish Church, Clement, early in 1524, appointed Magnusson to serve as archbishop until a decision could be made with respect to Trolle. The pope, however, would not remit papal levies. With this impasse negotiations ceased.

Meanwhile the king, who had a personal predilection for Lutheranism, did everything to encourage its spread. Many people had already been converted by two sons of a Swedish blacksmith, Olaf (Olavus) and Lars (Laurentius) Petersson (Petri). Olaf (1493–1552), who had studied at Wittenberg and had returned to Sweden in 1519, became a master and dean at the cathedral school at Strengnäs, where he greatly influenced the archdeacon Lars Andersson (1482–1552), a well-educated theologian who had long opposed the secularization and corruption of the Church.

Although Olaf was accused of heresy by Bishop Brask, the king did not take action against him. Instead, he brought him to Stockholm as a city clerk in 1524 and sent his brother Lars (1499–1573) to be professor of theology at Uppsala; and he made Lars Andersson archdeacon of Uppsala and royal chancellor. Early in 1525 Olaf defied the Church by openly taking a wife. The same year the king ordered Archbishop-elect Magnusson to get under way a Swedish translation of the Bible. The translation of the New Testament, begun by Lars Andersson but largely the work of Olaf Petersson, appeared in 1526. A translation of the entire Bible, much of it based on Luther's German version, was published in 1540–1541.

# 5. Consolidation of Lutheranism (1530–1555)

The Swedish people readily accepted Lutheran doctrines and generally supported attacks of the king upon churchmen and their possessions. Gustavus not only seized much of the property of the wealthy Bishop Brask but finally banished Archbishop Johan Magnusson.

Still unable to solve his financial difficulties, Gustavus took the decisive step with respect to his relation with the papacy and his own clergy at the Diet of Vesterås in 1527. When the chancellor presented the financial needs of the king and showed that the ecclesiastical property was the chief source of new income, the bishops answered that they would follow the advice of the pope and defend their property rights. Then the king stated that he would resign, demanded reimbursement for the money he had spent in their service, and stalked out of the assembly. After three days of heated discussion the members of the diet agreed to conform to his wishes in what was known as the Vesterås Recess. It provided that all property not absolutely needed by the Church should be given the king —and he was to decide whether it was needed; that the nobles were to regain all the tax-exempt lands that they had given the Church since 1454; that all taxable land be surrendered; and that preachers were to preach the "pure Word of God" until the diet could decide upon all pending religious matters following a disputation.

Without awaiting the disputation, the diet passed the Ordinances of Vesterås, which provided for the confiscation of most of the Church property, for the teaching of the gospel in the schools, and for royal confirmation of the higher clergy. The lower clergy were to be appointed by the bishops. Compulsory confession was abolished. Although nothing was stipulated with respect to doctrine, Lutheranism spread rapidly under royal protection. In 1528 three bishops-elect were consecrated by the bishop of Vesterås without papal confirmation. Many monasteries, deprived of property and income, closed their doors.

In Sweden, as in the other Scandinavian countries, Lutheranism was introduced gradually under the leadership of the ruler. Consequently much emphasis was subsequently placed upon the education of the people in the doctrinal and ecclesiastical changes. In 1529 the first Swedish book of services was published, followed the next year by the first book of hymns and in 1531 by the Swedish *Mass Book*. The episcopal system was retained, but the bishops lost their former legal rights and economic privileges. Lars Petersson became the first Lutheran archbishop of Uppsala in 1531. Because he was ordained by Bishop Peter Magnus of Vesterås, who had been consecrated in Rome in 1524, the apostolic succession was maintained in Sweden. In 1539, Gustavus, desirous of depriving his church of all vestiges of power, had Lars Andersson and Olaf Petersson convicted of treason and thereafter ruled the church through a superintendent directly responsible to him.

Eric XIV (1560–1568), the son of Gustavus, leaned toward Calvinism and accordingly abolished some of the traditional rites and fast days. When he became involved in a foreign and domestic war and permitted the churches to deteriorate, he was dethroned by his scholarly brothers, John and Charles. The former, as John III (1568–1592), leaned toward Catholicism, the religion of his wife Catherine, daughter of King Sigismund II of Poland. Although he restored the election of bishops to the clergy and the choice of ministers to the people, subject to episcopal confirmation, he was unable to unite the church with Rome.

John was succeeded by his son Sigismund (1592–1599), a convinced Roman Catholic who was already king of Poland (1587–1632). To forestall the reintroduction of Catholicism, Sigismund's uncle Charles called a national synod, attended by lay as well as ecclesiastical representatives. This synod, which met at Uppsala in 1593, reaffirmed the Lutheran position that the Bible was the sole source of doctrine, adopted the Augsburg Confession as its doctrinal standard, again made Luther's catechism the basic text for instruction, and re-established the Church Ordinance of Lars Petersson as authoritative in matters of worship. This important step secured Sweden for conservative Lutheranism and placed it on the side of the Protestant powers during the religious struggles of the seventeenth century. Sweden adopted the Lutheran Formula of Concord in 1686.

Finland, which was a possession of Sweden, shared its religious history. The first preacher of Lutheranism was Peter Särkilahti, who had studied in Germany and who began his evangelical preaching in 1524. Among those who carried on his work was Michael Agricola (1508–1557), who became a master at Wittenberg in 1539. He published a Finnish translation of the New Testament in 1548 and of the Psalms and some of the Prophets in 1551. This work earned him the reputation of being the father of Finnish literature. The administration of the church was under the archbishop of Uppsala, with eventually two bishops in Finland, one at Åbo and another at Viborg.

## Lutheranism in Eastern Europe

The history of the Reformation in eastern Europe differs from that in the west and the north primarily insofar as there were no strong territorial rulers there who could canalize that powerful movement and use it to their own advantage. Instead, Protestantism, brought east by merchants and young men who had studied at western European universities, was usually supported by virtually autonomous nobles. Thus no one form of Protestantism gained precedence in any of the larger political units. All attempts to bring the various Protestant groups together failed, and a revived Catholicism, under Jesuit leadership, was consequently enabled to regain many areas that had become predominantly Protestant.

The only exception to this general observation was East Prussia, held

# 5. Consolidation of Lutheranism (1530–1555)

by the Teutonic Knights as a fief of the Polish crown. Albert of Hohenzollern, the grand master of the Teutonic Knights, became a secret adherent of Lutheranism at the Diets of Nürnberg in 1522 and 1523. In 1525 he secularized his lands, assumed the title of duke under the suzerainty of the king of Poland, and began the religious reorganization of East Prussia along Lutheran lines.

The lands of the Livonian Brethren of the Sword, comprising the Baltic regions of Kurland, Livonia, and Estonia, and associated with the Teutonic Knights since 1237, also felt the impact of Lutheranism at an early date. There, as in East Prussia, important commercial communities of Germans had maintained their cultural connections with western Europe and welcomed the new ideas coming from Wittenberg. William of Hohenzollern, youngest brother of Duke Albert of East Prussia, became archbishop of Riga in 1539 and continued to spread the Reformation in Livonia. In 1554 the Diet of Womar proclaimed the entire country Lutheran. But William was unable to imitate his brother by establishing a secular state there because of the differences among the Livonian estates.

In 1557 the Muscovites began their invasions. The Swedes seized Estonia, and Denmark part of Kurland. In 1561 Poland annexed Livonia and made the greater part of Kurland a duchy under the Polish crown. In 1563 Muscovy in turn took part of Livonia from Poland. Despite the partition of the lands, the upper classes have retained their German Lutheranism and culture to the present day and have brought the Reformation to the non-Germans in their Estonian and Latvian tongues.

## The Reformation in Poland

The history of the Reformation in Poland is much more complicated than that of any country considered thus far. Although this kingdom, extending from the Baltic Sea almost to the Black Sea, was one of the largest states in Europe at the beginning of the sixteenth century; although its prosperous cities profited from the large amount of trade flowing north and south, east and west, and its agricultural land supplied wheat for much of Europe; and although Polish scholars made many important contributions to the culture of their day, the king was unable to develop a strong monarchy and to control the religious life of his people to the advantage of the entire country.

Chiefly responsible for the weakness of the Polish monarchy were (1) the heterogeneity of the population, (2) the economic decline of the cities after the turn of the century, and (3) the entrenched power of the nobles (*szlachta*). The Lithuanians constituted the largest ethnic group. They differed from the Poles in historical background and culture, but, like them, they had been converted to Roman Catholicism. The Ruthenians, or Little Russians, on the other hand, were members of the Greek Orthodox Church. Many Germans lived in western Poland, especially in the cities, where they, together with the Jews, controlled much of the economic life of the country; but they had no vital interest in supporting the crown.

Dissatisfaction among all classes became acute after the effects of the Turkish conquests in the Balkans and the discovery of new trade routes to the Far East were felt in the Polish cities. Both secular and ecclesiastical magnates took advantage of the social unrest to seize control of a number of cities and, through their diets, to weaken the others. Thus the king became more dependent than ever upon the many unruly nobles, who not only retained the right to elect their king but, in the national diet of 1505, passed a statute that stipulated that no new business should be considered without the unanimous consent of the three estates, that is, the king, the senators, and the representatives of the local diets of nobles; that the king should have no standing army; and that nobles should not be permitted to engage in commerce.

The peasants, who had lost their earlier rights to the ambitious nobles and were becoming serfs while feudalism was dying out in western Europe, were in general illiterate and helpless and were usually served by priests who knew little more than they. The majority of them remained loyal to Rome, despite the venality and corruption of many of the upper clergy.

The chief opposition to the upper clergy came from the nobles and the townsmen. The nobles disliked them primarily because they belonged to the higher class of magnates and usually obtained their lucrative positions from the king. Many of the sons of nobles studied at the western European universities and at their own renowned University of Cracow and thus became familiar not only with Erasmian humanism but with Protestantism. The townsmen, predominantly German, had always maintained their contact with the cultural and religious currents in western Europe and now welcomed the Protestant preachers who began to appear among them.

When Protestantism spread to such West-Prussian urban centers as Danzig, Elbing, and Thorn from East Prussia and Livonia, King Sigismund I (1508–1548), fearing that this area might be joined to the duchy of East Prussia, tried in vain to stamp out Lutheranism. Even more futile were his attempts to crush heresy in Lithuania and Greater Poland, which included Gnesen and Posen. One of the first influential Polish reformers was the former Dominican Andrew Samuel, a preacher at the cathedral of Posen. Threatened with persecution in 1542, he fled to Leipzig and later to a parish in Masuria, then ruled by his protector, Duke Albert of Prussia. Jan Seklucyan, another evangelical reformer at Posen, fled to Königsberg, where he published a Polish translation of parts of the New Testament, catechisms, hymn books, and numerous theological works.

# 5. Consolidation of Lutheranism (1530–1555)

Both political and religious developments reached a critical stage during the reign of Sigismund II Augustus (1548–1572), who lacked the ability to give Poland capable leadership. He carried on a losing struggle with Ivan IV (1533–1584) of Muscovy and permitted the hereditary union of East Prussia and Brandenburg under Elector Joachim. The diet of nobles passed legislation that further weakened the Polish cities and, by means of a law called Execution, gained control of executive and legislative functions. Moreover, by the Union of Lublin of 1569, the nobles of Poland and Lithuania brought the two countries into a closer union, to be ruled by one king and one diet.

The Polish nobles, who now were in control of the country, could determine the religious policies of their own lands. This accounts for the fact that various forms of Protestantism eventually found support in Poland. The spread of Lutheranism was accompanied by the growth of Anabaptism and the influx of the Bohemian Brethren. Calvinism also eventually found many adherents, especially among the humanistically inclined nobles of Lesser Poland—in Cracow, Lublin, and Sandomir.

Anti-Trinitarianism, brought to Poland in 1551 by Lelio Sozzini, among others, was further developed by his nephew Fausto Sozzini (1539–1604), a jurist who had left the court of the Medici at Florence, had turned to the study of theology, and had developed Unitarian views while at Basel. The chief center of Unitarianism was Racow, where the Socinians, or Polish Brethren, as they also were called, had their own church, school, and printing press.

The chief doctrinal statement of the Socinians is found in the Racow Catechism, prepared by Fausto Sozzini and published in the Polish language in 1605. Socinianism is a form of rational supernaturalism that recognizes the Bible as the sole source of religious truth, which can be ascertained only by the criteria of reasonableness and moral usefulness. God's absolute power and will are made known through revelation. Christ, though not divine, teaches man God's will by means of his miracles, resurrection, and ascension. Man is by nature free of sin and endowed with freedom of the will. The sacraments are mere symbols. The church, organized in presbyteries and synods, is primarily an institution of learning about God.

The Protestant nobles became so numerous that they dominated the diets from 1552 to 1565. In 1555 they induced the diet to suspend the jurisdiction of the ecclesiastical courts, thereby in effect giving legal recognition to Protestantism. About the same time, Jan à Lasco (d. 1560), a Pole of noble birth who had studied at Wittenberg and later had become a Calvinist, made unsuccessful attempts to achieve religious unity among the Protestants. If Sigismund, who officially supported the Catholic Church but permitted the growth of Protestantism, could have placed himself at the head of Protestantism, he might have regained much of his royal authority. Instead, he encouraged Stanislav Hosius (d. 1579), the bishop of Ermland, in his successful policy of playing one Protestant group against another, accepted the decrees of the Council of Trent, and invited the Jesuits to help regain Poland for Catholicism.

When Sigismund, the last member of the Jagellon dynasty, died without an heir, the national diet passed the Compact of Warsaw (1573), which affirmed its principle of religious liberty for all religious groups. After much debate, Henry of Valois (1573–1574) was chosen king, after having agreed to religious liberty for the noble adherents of all faiths— the subjects were to follow their lords. But when he learned that his brother, King Charles IX of France, had died, he abandoned the throne of Poland to assume that of his mother country. After another interregnum, in which Poland was almost plunged into civil war, Stephen Báthory (1576–1586), prince of Transylvania, became king. Although he continued to permit religious freedom, he favored and supported the Jesuits.

## The Reformation in Bohemia

At the beginning of Luther's work as a reformer, no country outside Germany seemed more likely to accept his doctrines than Bohemia, which was still loosely associated with the Holy Roman Empire. Its national sentiment, fostered during the Hussite wars, did not make Archduke Ferdinand, its king since 1526, a popular figure. Real political authority lay in the diet, or national assembly, which reflected various shades of religious opinion. All three religious groups of the country welcomed Luther's teachings: the Catholic German nobles and townsmen; the Utraquists, or moderate Hussites who had made peace with Catholicism; and the Bohemian Brethren of the Unity (*Unitas fratrum*), who, after the suppression of the Taborites in 1453, had continued many of the evangelical and social views of the early Hussites.

The best-known Lutheran reformer who worked among the Germans of Bohemia was Johannes Mathesius (d. 1565), whose sermons on the life of Luther have had a wide circulation. He served a congregation in Joachimstal, aided by Nikolaus Hermann (d. 1561), a cantor who wrote several popular Lutheran hymns.

Lutheranism was brought to the Utraquists by Gallus Cahera, who had studied in Wittenberg in 1523 and had called Luther's attention to the religious conditions in Bohemia. That same year Luther dedicated his book on *The Institution of the Ministry* to the city council of Prague and urged that body to break completely with Rome. But the conservative wing of the Utraquists eventually gained the upper hand and prevented a union with the Lutherans.

The Bohemian Brethren were also willing to establish connections with Wittenberg. It was for them that Luther wrote his *Adoration of the*

# 5. Consolidation of Lutheranism (1530–1555)

*Sacrament* in 1523. Although they did not agree entirely with Luther's conception of the Lord's Supper, and although Luther disliked their tendency to withdraw from the world, negotiations for unity began in earnest in 1532, when Jan Augusta became the leader of the Brethren. It was Augusta's hope to make his group assume the lead in developing a large evangelical party without doctrinal differences. This ambition attracted several Bohemian nobles to the Brethren and led to protracted negotiations with Luther, Bucer, and Calvin, but without lasting success.

The years of persecution of the Bohemian Brethren from 1548 to 1552 caused many of them to flee to Poland and Prussia. In 1564, Augusta tried to unite with the Utraquists and establish a national evangelical church. When this failed, Jan Blahoslav (1523–1571), who had been one of the elected bishops of the group in exile, succeeded in strengthening the spiritual life of the Brethren by translating the New Testament into the Czech language (1568). The Brethren maintained their separate existence until 1575, when they joined the evangelical estates in signing the Bohemian Confession.

Lutheranism also spread to Moravia, especially to such mining centers as Iglau, where Paul Speratus (1484–1551), a former humanist, preached to both Germans and Slovaks. In this small country the Utraquists, the Bohemian Brethren, and the Anabaptists joined the Lutherans and gained a sense of religious toleration for one another exceptional for that day.

## Lutheranism in Hungary and the Austrian Lands

Hungary, like other eastern European countries, had large settlements of Germans among whom Lutheranism found staunch adherents. Many native sons—Magyar nobles—studied humanism and theology in German universities and adopted Lutheranism. Although persecutions took place under Louis II for both national and religious reasons, the political division and confusion following the disaster at Mohács in 1526 made possible a greater religious freedom. Although Zapolya was not friendly to the Germans, his excommunication by the pope forced him to treat them with deference; and Ferdinand, who relied upon the Germans in his part of Hungary, could ill afford to attack them openly for religious reasons.

One of the best-known Hungarian reformers was Matthew Dévay (1500–1545), a former humanist who had studied at Cracow, had become a priest, and had adopted Lutheranism while studying at Wittenberg. Upon his return to Hungary in 1531, he began an active evangelical ministry that resulted in repeated imprisonment under Zapolya and Ferdinand. But he gained the protection of a powerful nobleman, on whose lands a prosperous Protestant school was established (at Sárvâr) by Silvester Erdösy (d. 1560). Erdösy, who had studied at Wittenberg, translated the New Testament into the Magyar language. He and Dévay, by the publication of their religious works and Magyar grammars, became the fathers of Hungarian literature.

Although most of the Magyar nobles became Protestant, the reformers could not create a strong church organization. Only after Ferdinand had threatened to take severe measures against them did five Hungarian cities unite in a common confession (*Confessio pentapolitana*) based on the Augsburg Confession. But national sentiment made cooperation with the German Lutherans difficult. Furthermore, many Hungarians, educated in humanism, found the Zwinglian and Calvinist interpretations of the Lord's Supper more satisfactory than those of Luther. Eventually, therefore, the Magyar Protestants formally accepted the Calvinist confession and the Heidelberg Catechism of 1563, whereas the Germans and some Slovaks continued to adhere to the Augsburg Confession. Those who supported the Hapsburgs generally remained Catholic.

In Transylvania the Germans, whose ancestors had come from western Germany in the twelfth century at the invitation of the Hungarian king, almost immediately adopted Lutheranism. Their leader was Johann Honter (d. 1549), a former humanist who had studied at the universities of Vienna, Cracow, and Basel. After 1533, as a scholar, teacher, pastor, and publisher in his native city of Kronstadt, he extended the Reformation first among the Germans and then all Transylvania. His chief works were the *Reformation Formula* of 1543 and *The Reformation of the Saxon Churches in Transylvania* of 1547. After his death the representatives of the Lutheran churches elected a bishop to head the national church, which recognized the Augsburg Confession as its doctrinal authority. The Magyar nobles, even the family of Zapolya, became Lutheran. Only the Rumanians and the indigenous Transylvanians remained Greek Orthodox. In 1554 the national assembly granted religious freedom to adherents of all faiths.

Conditions in the Austrian lands were also of such a nature that it was difficult for Archduke Ferdinand to suppress Lutheranism. Each of the divisions—Lower Austria, Upper Austria, Styria, Carinthia, and Carniola—retained its own assemblies and other feudal institutions. Despite the stringent edicts of the archduke against heresy and the execution of a number of Protestant leaders, Lutheranism was adopted and encouraged by a number of important nobles in all these Austrian lands. Many of the sons of the nobles were sent to the universities of Wittenberg, Tübingen, and later Geneva. Several cities, such as Graz and Klagenfurt, joined the nobles in using Lutheranism as a form of protest against the Hapsburg policies.

The spread of Lutheranism in Carniola and Carinthia owed much to the services of the nobleman Johannes Ungnad von Sonnegk (1493–1564). He was compelled to flee to Württemberg, where he set up a printing press for the purpose of providing his countrymen with Lutheran literature. He was ably assisted by Primus Truber (1508–1586), another exile. Together they translated the Bible into the Slovene tongue, thereby laying the basis for modern Slovene literature. Ungnad employed several croatian exiles in his printing establishment and published the Bible and many other works in the Croatian language. Italian books also were published by this remarkable press.

## The Religious Wars to the Peace of Augsburg (1546–1555)

The religious war that Luther had anticipated with dread did not break out until after his death. Charles V, as we have seen, was by 1546 finally ready to solve the religious problem in Germany by force of arms. Because he had so many Protestants in his camp, however, he pretended that he was not preparing to attack the Schmalkaldic League for religious reasons, insisting that he was acting only against those estates that had opposed him. Accordingly he proclaimed the imperial ban against John Frederick of electoral Saxony and Philip of Hesse for having harmed imperial interests in the Pack Conspiracy of 1528, having attacked Württemberg in 1534, and having seized Brunswick in 1545.

Nevertheless, Charles was apparently aware of the fact that the medieval Empire and the medieval Catholic Church were locked in a death struggle with territorialism and nationalism on the one hand and Lutheranism on the other. He not only received the blessings of Pope Paul III for going to war against the "enemies of God," who had refused to attend the Council of Trent, but wrote his sister Mary and his son Philip that his real reason for attacking the Schmalkaldic League was to protect the Catholic Church.

Meanwhile the members of the League, particularly electoral Saxony, Hesse, Württemberg, and most of the imperial cities, were preparing to meet the attack. Although the League had a superior military force and possessed an outstanding commander in the person of Schärtlin of Burtenbach, it was handicapped by a lack of decision, for every military question had to be decided by a council of war that lacked unity and vigorous leaders. Thus when Charles took a relatively small military force to the Danube River in the autumn of 1546 and Schärtlin planned to block the Tyrolese passes to prevent additional troops from Italy from joining him, the council recalled him for fear of offending Bavaria and Ferdinand. Although Schärtlin, John Frederick, and Philip at one time had a force of fifty-seven thousand men, as compared with six thousand under Charles, they permitted the emperor to increase his army by the addition of troops from Italy and the Low Countries and withdrew from southern Germany. Their reasons were that they did not have sufficient money

**Emperor Charles V**

*by Titian*

to pay their troops and that Duke Maurice had treacherously invaded electoral Saxony.

John Frederick was so successful against both Maurice and Ferdinand that Charles V, who had formally transferred the electoral title to Maurice in October, 1546, hurried north to the Elbe River. John Frederick, with only a third of his army with him, was overwhelmed by Charles at Mühlberg in April, 1547, and taken prisoner. In the capitulation of Wittenberg in May, John Frederick was forced to give up to Maurice the electoral title and much of his land. Philip of Hesse was induced by the promises of good treatment by his son-in-law Maurice and the elector of Brandenberg to give himself up to Charles. The emperor, nevertheless, made him a prisoner. Both Philip and John Frederick were taken to the Diet at Augsburg and then to the Low Countries.

Charles was now apparently master of the Empire. The Schmalkaldic League had been defeated, its leaders had been imprisoned, all the Protestant cities of southern Germany except Constance had come to terms with him, Cologne had been forcibly returned to Catholicism, and most of northern Germany, with the notable exceptions of Magdeburg and Bremen, had bowed to his authority.

However, Charles was still far from accomplishing his fundamental objectives of restoring religious unity and establishing a firm dynastic authority in the Empire. The pope could not view the emperor's military successes without alarm, for he was determined to use the Council of Trent for the purpose of condemning Protestantism and strengthening papal control. Charles, on whose side were several Protestant princes, was equally determined to reform the papacy and solve the German religious difficulties, by means of a German church council, if necessary.

The differences between Charles and the pope were accentuated by the Tridentine decree of January, 1547, concerning justification by faith, and by Charles' obvious attempts to control the council. Therefore the conciliar representatives, with the exception of the emperor's clergy, adjourned to Bologna in March of that year. Paul III made overtures to the French king and even withdrew his troops from the Schmalkaldic War. To make matters worse, Paul's son Pier Luigi Farnese, who ruled a principality not yet recognized by Charles, was murdered, and the emperor was suspected of having had a hand in the act. Charles in turn threatened a second sack of Rome, and in January, 1548, declared all future decrees of the council in session at Bologna null and void and formally demanded that the council reconvene at Trent.

In these circumstances Charles sought to solve the religious cleavages in Germany without papal sanction at the Diet of Augsburg, which had met in September, 1547. His first step was to attempt to strengthen his position by the formation of a new league, similar to the old Swabian League, that should embrace all Germany and lie outside the authority of the diet. When the territorial princes killed this proposal by simply doing nothing about it, he dropped the matter. But he succeeded in assuming the authority of nominating the judges of the imperial supreme court and reserving to his own aulic court (*Hofgericht*) jurisdiction over questions of Church property and other episcopal matters.

## The Augsburg Interim

Charles aroused even greater opposition by means of a curious document drawn up by theologians of various religious groups and known as the Augsburg Interim (June, 1548). Although the basic Catholic doctrines were retained, a few weak concessions to the Protestants were made, such as permission for clerical marriages with papal dispensation, Communion in both kinds, a slight restatement of the doctrine of justification by faith, reference to the pope as supreme bishop, and recognition of the need for reforms. Because the impression was given that this Interim would apply to Catholics as well as Protestants until a national Church council should finally solve the entire religious problem, the Protestant princes were maneuvered into accepting it, and it was proclaimed an imperial law in May, 1548. But it was another matter to enforce the Interim's acceptance. Paul III was particularly incensed over the provisions for reform, and the Germans were in no mood to have it forced upon them with the aid of Spanish troops.

In attempting to impose his religious policy upon the German people, Charles showed how little he understood them. In southern and central Germany, where he demonstrated his power with the presence of Spanish troops, there was at the outset a formal acceptance of the Interim. Duke Ulrich of Württemberg conformed because of his expectation of receiving certain imperial favors, Philip of Hesse in the hope of obtaining better conditions of imprisonment, and the rulers of the electoral Palatinate and Brandenburg-Ansbach because of their desire for union. For this reason religious leaders like Brenz and Bucer, who refused to comply, were forced into exile. But even in these regions formal acceptance meant little, for the people simply stayed away from Mass, and governmental authorities themselves provided means of circumvention.

In northern Germany those princes who had submitted to the emperor also formally accepted the Interim. Elector Maurice, who was now the ruler of strongly Lutheran lands, including Wittenberg, was compelled to make further concessions. Accordingly the conciliatory Bishop Pflug of Naumburg and Melanchthon helped Maurice work out a compromise known as the Leipzig Interim in 1548, which was substituted for the Augsburg interim. It was essentially Lutheran but contained such Catholic features as the use of the Latin language in the services, the observance of Catholic fast and feast days, and the recognition of the seven

# 5. Consolidation of Lutheranism (1530–1555)

sacraments of Catholicism. This Saxon compromise was also adopted by the estates of electoral Brandenburg. In both territories, however, the majority of the clergy continued to teach and preach as before.

Popular resistance to the Augsburg Interim was centered principally in those areas of northern Germany not touched by the Schmalkaldic War. Magdeburg, which had successfully defended itself against the imperial troops, became the most important asylum for the exiles. Strong attacks against those who had become traitors to the Lutheran cause issued from its presses and aroused opposition throughout Germany. Important cities like Hamburg, Bremen, Lübeck, Hildesheim, and Göttingen openly defied the Interim, and Duke Henry of Brunswick could not force his estates to accept it.

Charles was so deceived by the formal acceptance of the Interim in many areas that he believed that he could extend it to the Scandinavian countries, England, and even Russia. He became even more optimistic when Paul III, shortly before his death, recognized the Interim and dissolved the council meeting at Bologna, and when his successor, Julius III (1550–1555), came to an agreement with Charles and reopened the Council of Trent in May, 1551. But no real compromise with the Lutherans was possible, and the papal and imperial points of view remained as contradictory as ever.

The Germans were further alienated from Charles because of his dynastic policies. They disliked his high-handed treatment of the diet, the indignities he inflicted upon John Frederick and Philip, and especially his attempts to force upon them the election of his son Philip to the imperial throne. This last step even led to a quarrel between Charles and his brother Ferdinand, for the latter believed that the emperor was attempting to exclude him from the imperial succession. Not until 1551 did the brothers agree to a succession that provided that Philip should follow Ferdinand, and that Maximilian, Ferdinand's son, should follow Philip in the succession. But the electors ignored this scheme.

The foreign policy of Charles was equally unpopular among the Germans. Henry II (1547–1559) of France had succeeded in concluding a peace with England. His zeal in persecuting the Protestants in his country was accompanied by a rapprochement with the pope and antipathy toward the emperor. England, under Edward VI (1547–1553), became an asylum for many German exiles and a center of opposition to Charles, especially because Princess Mary was seeking the emperor's help against the strongly Protestant innovations of Parliament and the royal council. In the Mediterranean Charles lost Tripoli in 1551, and in Hungary the Turks once more made preparations for an attack upon Ferdinand.

When it looked as though Charles would be forced into another war with France and the Turks, his German supporters began to desert him. One of the first to do so was Margrave Hans of Küstrin, who had fought on the imperial side in the Schmalkaldic War. Having aroused the emperor's ire by not accepting the Interim, he formed, in February, 1550, a defensive league with John Albert of Mecklenburg and Duke Albert of Prussia. This league watched with suspicion the movements of Maurice, who was conducting the siege of Magdeburg for the emperor. But Maurice, having achieved his original goals through cooperation with Charles, was already prepared to desert him and join the Protestant princes, for he was angered by the imprisonment of his father-in-law Philip, did not like to continue to play the role of Judas among his fellow Lutheran princes, and strongly opposed the emperor's plans.

Taking full advantage of the national antipathy of the Germans to the "Spanish servitude" and their hatred of the Interim, Maurice skillfully gained control of the League, to which were added also Duke George of Mecklenburg, the young Landgrave William of Hesse, and Duke Albert of Prussia. Early in 1552 these princes concluded with Henry II of France a treaty that illustrates how much more they were concerned with their territorial particularism than with German unity. In return for financial assistance against Charles they agreed to give Henry, as "imperial vicar," the three strategically located bishoprics of Metz, Toul, and Verdun. The only prince to oppose this first of many steps of sacrificing imperial lands on the altar of territorial particularism was Hans of Küstrin, who left the League in protest.

### The "War of Liberation"

In the so-called War of Liberation that followed, Henry II revived those claims upon Flanders, Milan, and Naples that had been dropped in the Peace of Crépy and sent thirty-five thousand troops to Lorraine. At the same time Elector Maurice, Landgrave William of Hesse, and Margrave Albert Alcibiades gathered an equal number of men in Franconia. Charles, overwhelmed by such large forces and not certain of the loyalty of his own brother, fled to Carinthia. The Council of Trent, fearing a military solution of the religious issues, broke up in April without definite plans for the future.

Maurice began negotiations with Ferdinand, representing the emperor, at Linz and later at Passau. But the Protestant position was being weakened by the desertion of Margrave Albert Alcibiades, who was pillaging Franconia, where he hoped to create for himself a duchy out of the bishoprics of Bamberg and Würzburg; by the strong resistance of Strassburg to Henry II's attack; and by the support given Charles by such imperial cities as Nürnberg and Ulm, which feared the princes more than the emperor. Therefore Maurice was forced to accept the decision of Charles that the religious question could be solved only by a religious council. The tentative settlement known as the Peace of Passau (August, 1552) provided that Landgrave Philip be released from captivity—John

# 5. Consolidation of Lutheranism (1530–1555)

Frederick had already been liberated—and guaranteed the Lutherans religious freedom until the next meeting of the diet.

The emperor made one more attempt to defeat the French. He concluded an unsavory alliance with Albert Alcibiades and tried vainly to take Metz.[1] When this failed, Charles left Germany and the next year gave his brother Ferdinand complete authority to settle German affairs. Albert, however, continued his wild career of plunder in Franconia until Maurice, who had fought in Hungary against the Turks with Ferdinand after the Peace of Passau, returned to restore order. With the support of Ferdinand and the League of Heidelberg, which had been formed to enforce peace, he attacked and defeated Albert at Sievershausen in July, 1553. But he had to pay for the victory with his life at the age of thirty-two years. He was succeeded by his conciliatory brother August. His cousin John Frederick, who did not regain his electoral title, died early the next year. Order was not established, however, until Albert had been decisively defeated in 1554 and had fled to France.

## The Peace of Augsburg

The diet that was given the task of providing peace finally met in Augsburg from February to September, 1555. It is significant that the peace was made without the presence or the direct influence of the emperor and without able papal representation. Pope Julius III died in March, 1555. His successor, Marcellus II, who was chosen in April, died the next month. The summer was gone before Paul IV (1555–1559) could formulate a definite program of action with respect to Germany. Moreover, the German electors and most of the princes were conspicuous by their absence. Although the Catholic princes, or their representatives, were in the majority, the Protestants probably represented the larger population. Both groups were compelled to agree to disagree in religious matters, for their prior concern was the maintenance of their privileges as territorial rulers. Of the three bodies that carried on the work of the diet—the council of electors, the council of princes, and the cities—the council of princes or their representatives assumed the initiative.

After lengthy negotiations and many compromises, the terms of the Peace of Augsburg were made known in the recess published by Ferdinand in September, 1555. The chief provisions were the following: (1) The Lutheran princes, the imperial knights, and the imperial cities were guaranteed security equal to that of the Catholic estates, and both were obligated to maintain "eternal, unconditional peace." (2) Each estate was given the right to choose between Catholicism and Lutheranism, according to the principle *cuius regio, eius religio*, although this term was not

[1] It was at this siege that Paré became famous for his skillful surgical work among the wounded soldiers of Charles.

used in the Peace. But the Lutherans obtained the verbal assurance, the secret Declaration of Ferdinand, that the adherents of the Augsburg Confession would be tolerated in the Catholic ecclesiastical territories. It was not clear whether or not the Calvinists were included. (3) All Church lands seized by the Lutheran estates prior to the Peace of Passau of 1552 were to be retained by them. (4) According to the "ecclesiastical reservation," every ecclesiastical prince—archbishop, bishop, or abbot—who became Protestant would forfeit his title, lands, and privileges. Although the Lutherans vigorously opposed this provision, they accepted the recess that included it.

Evidence of the weakness of the Empire and the growing strength of the princes is to be found in the provisions made for the enforcement of the peace. The estates were unwilling to give the emperor the power, for they feared that he would use it to further his dynastic interests and involve the Empire in foreign wars. Consequently they gave the elector of Mainz the authority to call an imperial deputation when peace was threatened. With its help he was to decide upon appropriate measures.

In most respects the Peace of Augsburg merely recognized a *fait accompli* in the Empire, namely, the emergence of territorialism, which not only prevented the evolution of a national state similar to that of France, for example, but gradually brought the economic, cultural, religious, and political activities of the German people under the influence of the particularistic princes. The monarchy gradually receded into the background and imperial authority became a mere shadow of its former self. Consequently Germany ceased to play a dominant role in international affairs until the days of Frederick the Great of Prussia. What is worse, it became the battleground of nations, which it remained until well into the nineteenth century.

Although it would be historically unjust to expect of the German princes that which no other territorial ruler of that day did, that is, to grant religious toleration to their subjects, they can be criticized for not having recognized at least the Calvinists, if not the Anabaptists and Socinians. Their failure to do so not only prevented the more activist groups from invigorating Protestantism in Germany but was in part responsible for the outbreak of the Thirty Years' War in the next century. Another serious mistake was their failure to clarify the "ecclesiastical reservation" and the questions involving the recognition of Lutherans in Catholic ecclesiastical lands. It was relatively easy to maintain peace in the large states of northern Germany; but in southern Germany, where Catholics and Protestants in many instances lived side by side, serious difficulties presented themselves. The Protestants as a rule attempted to enforce religious freedom for their co-religionists in Catholic lands; but they were not willing to tolerate Catholicism in their territories.

The legal recognition of Lutheranism tended to make the Lutheran princes self-satisfied and complacent, while the Catholic princes, fearing further losses, banded together not only to retain what they still had but, with the aid of the forces of the Catholic Reformation, to regain what they had lost. Meanwhile both Catholic and Lutheran religious leaders devoted more thought to a definition of their respective theologies than to the basic religious forces that had been released by the Reformation at its beginning. The destruction of medieval Christian unity during the first half of the sixteenth century was recognized by the Peace of Augsburg. That this was a great loss can be seen by the strong ecumenical movements of the twentieth century. But one cannot lay the blame for this loss upon the princes at Augsburg, for the break had become so complete by 1555 that it is difficult to conceive of any force strong enough to restore unity.

One must not overlook the positive contributions of the Peace of Augsburg. Above all, Germany was given a much-needed respite from religious war. For the Protestants "related to the Augsburg Confession," this was the first indisputable legal recognition of their territorial churches. Most territorial princes took seriously their new responsibilities as heads of their respective churches. Moreover, the estates at Augsburg had been willing to discuss the question of religious toleration and now permitted a certain amount of toleration in those imperial cities in which Catholics and Protestants had lived together for many years. Finally, by making provision for the free movement of Christians from one territory to another because of religious conviction, the estates recognized one important aspect of the principle of religious freedom. For better or worse, the use of force by the Church had been greatly weakened. There remained the final step of freeing the individual Christian from the religious authority of the ruler.

Charles V, fully aware of the failure of his grandiose dream of establishing religious unity under the protection of a strong Hapsburg empire, had already given his brother Ferdinand the authority to conclude peace at the Diet of Augsburg. He abdicated formally in 1556. Ferdinand succeeded him as emperor, and Philip became the ruler of Spain, the Low Countries, and the Spanish possessions in Italy. Charles withdrew to a villa near the monastery of San Yuste in Estremadura in Spain, where he died in September, 1558.

# Part Three

## Spread of Protestantism and Revival of Catholicism

# 6 New Forms of Protestantism

## The Anabaptists and Other Evangelical Radicals

The tendency of Protestantism to proliferate became apparent from the beginning of the movement, especially among the radical reformers. Luther's doctrines concerning the *sola scriptura,* justification by faith alone, and the universal priesthood of believers struck a ready response among people of all classes. But many of these were not content to move as slowly as he, and fundamental differences soon appeared. Some sought to substantiate social, political, and economic views by reference to Scripture. Others, like Thomas Müntzer and the "Zwickau prophets," believing in a continuing revelation and evincing spiritualistic tendencies, hoped to establish a true kingdom of God on earth by either peaceful or forceful measures. Still others, strongly biblical in their approach, sought a complete separation of church and state, striving to set up free, confessional church bodies, living in accord with biblical commands. Still others questioned fundamental doctrines that both Catholics and Protestants held in common.

It is difficult to classify the various movements of the radical reformers, especially because they seemed to spring up almost simultaneously wherever conditions permitted, and their leaders, persecuted in one place, would appear at another. Most historians, finding among them at least one common denominator, namely opposition to infant baptism, have attempted to lump them together under the term *Anabaptism,* derived from the Greek word for "baptizing again." But opposition to infant baptism was not synony-

*217*

mous with belief in adult baptism. Despite the many attacks upon infant baptism, the first known case of an adult baptism was that administered by Conrad Grebel (1498–1526) when he baptized George Blaurock (1480?–1529) in the house of Felix Manz (d. 1527) in Zurich in January, 1525.

Because the main tenets and practices of evangelical Anabaptism were established by Conrad Grebel, the leader of the Swiss Brethren, he may be considered the founder of the movement that spread to the northwest and was eventually organized by Menno Simons in the body known today as Mennonites. There are today more than four hundred thousand baptized members of this church in Switzerland, France, Germany, North and South America, and Russia.

Grebel, a member of a prominent patrician family and a humanist, became interested in the evangelical movement as a member of the Zwinglian circle of friends in Zurich. It was from Zwingli that he learned the basic Reformation doctrines. But he and other similarly inclined men broke with Zwingli when the latter refused to accept their strict biblicism, their opposition to infant baptism, their distrust of civil government, and their doctrine of a free, confessional church.

It was Grebel's conception of a free church, consisting of freely committed and practicing believers, as opposed to the *Volkskirche,* or inclusive state church of the Catholics and most Protestants, that formed the basic doctrine of the Anabaptists. In other words, one was not, according to Grebel, born into the church but was accepted on profession of faith and the promise to lead a holy life. Practically, this took place at the time of baptism, as explained in the Schleitheim Articles of 1527, the first attempt to bring all the Anabaptists together into one body. Because the church was to be a true, visible communion of believers leading lives of holiness—Anabaptists did not accept Augustine's doctrine concerning the invisible church—unbelievers were to be excluded and the unfaithful banned. Although the Anabaptists were not perfectionists, they expected the brethren to obey the commands of God and lead lives of holiness.

The church service was to be very simple, to contain nothing not found in the primitive Church. Baptism signified for the instructed, penitent, and believing person—thus only the adult—that he had been reborn and must live a new life. It was both an act of confession and a promise to act according to God's commands. The Lord's Supper was also merely a remembrance, a meal of fellowship, signifying a union with Christ and the brethren. It should not be celebrated in a church, for fear of encouraging "false devotion," but in private homes and in the evening, according to Christ's example.

The pastor, or shepherd, of the Anabaptists was to be chosen by the congregation and supported by it, for it was considered unscriptural to live by rents and tithes. The duties of the pastor were to read the Scripture, admonishing the brethren according to its laws; lead the services, consisting essentially of prayers and the breaking of bread; and care for the spiritual welfare of the brethren, administering discipline and banning the unfaithful.

The doctrine concerning the separation of the faithful from the world, the conception of the church as a suffering church, led most Anabaptists to embrace the practice of nonresistance during persecution and oppression. They would neither take up the sword in defense of the state nor, as members of a church that was holy and thus truthful, give an oath. Many felt that they could not serve the state, or the world, in any capacity. Although Grebel's views concerning the Christian's attitude toward the world grew out of his conception of the suffering church, many of his followers attempted to carry out in detail the precepts of the Sermon on the Mount.

It is apparent that the Anabaptists were less interested in theology than in the practical application of biblical teachings to the affairs of this world. Despite the fact that Grebel had been a humanist and was skilled in the use of Latin, Greek, and Hebrew, his teachings were not based on any of the intellectual currents of his day but solely on the early Reformation doctrines of Zwingli and his own independent study of Scripture. His ultimate aim was, like that of most evangelical radicals, the restitution of primitive Christianity. Many of the Anabaptists, like Grebel, came from the upper middle classes; but this form of evangelicalism appealed particularly to the lower classes. The political, economic, and social teachings of the Anabaptists, ranging from opposition to tithes and the taking of interest to Christian communism, reflected lower-class interests.

Whereas Zwingli had at one time expressed serious doubts concerning the scriptural basis of infant baptism, he eventually made denial of it tantamount to heresy and defiance of political authority. Like Luther and the later exponents of the inclusive church, he felt that Anabaptism meant disorder and confusion and opposed it with vigor. In this he and the other reformers were supported by the Roman law, for the Justinian Code provided the death penalty for the repetition of baptism. The term *Anabaptizer,* which meant "rebaptizer," as we have seen, was invented for the purpose of condemning those who believed in adult baptism, even though they believed in only one baptism and preferred to be called simply *Baptists.* Thus the Anabaptists were severely persecuted by the civil authorities as well as by the Catholic and Protestant churches. In the sixteenth century *Anabaptism* was thus synonymous with distortion of truth, opposition to God, blasphemy, and danger to the established order. Accordingly both the Catholic and the Protestant estates agreed to suppress the Anabaptists at the Diets of Speyer, in 1529, and Augsburg, in 1530.

# Part Three: Spread of Protestantism

The persecution of the Swiss Brethren began, as we have seen, after the religious disputation of January 17, 1525, when Zwingli and the city council of Zurich determined that the Anabaptists should conform or go into exile. Grebel and Manz left the city to spread their views and encourage the Brethren elsewhere. In May of that year, Eberli Bolt of Canton Appenzell was arrested in Catholic Schwyz and became the first martyr of the Swiss Brethren. Later in the summer, Grebel, Manz, and Blaurock were arrested in Grüningen. After another disputation in Zurich and two trials, the three were condemned to life imprisonment, charged with rebellion against political authority. The three escaped, however. Manz was arrested again late in 1526 and on January 25, 1527, was killed by drowning. Grebel had died of the plague while in exile in the summer of 1526. Blaurock fled to the Tyrol, where he ministered to the Brethren and was burned at the stake in 1529.

As the Swiss Brethren fled from the persecution of the Zwinglians, they carried their ideas to southern Germany, Upper Austria, Moravia, Hungary, the Low Countries, and elsewhere. There they came into contact with left-wing ideas that were in some instances at variance with those developed by Grebel and summarized by Michael Sattler and others in the Schleitheim Articles.

Perhaps the most successful leader of the Anabaptists was Jakob Hutter, or Huter, who organized communistic congregations in Nikolsburg, Moravia, that became thriving economic and spiritual communities. Although he was burned at the stake in Innsbruck in 1536, congregations of his followers, called Hutterite Brethren, remained in Moravia until 1622, in Hungary and Transylvania into the eighteenth century, and in the Ukraine, Canada, and South Dakota, to the present time.

Another well-known organizer of Anabaptists was Balthasar Hubmaier (1485–1528). As an evangelical preacher at Waldshut in Austria he announced in January, 1525, that God had given him the command to repudiate infant baptism. He was accordingly rebaptized by Wilhelm Reublin on Easter of that year, together with most of his congregation, and then began baptizing other adults. His book on *The Christian Baptism of Believers* (1525) won him many followers. In the following winter, however, he was arrested in Zurich and was compelled to retract his Anabaptist views. He then went to Constance, Augsburg, Regensburg, and finally to Nikolsburg in Moravia, where he converted the Lutheran congregation there to Anabaptism and gained a large following on the estates of the rulers of Liechtenstein. By his preaching and writing he attracted persecuted people from many parts of Germany and Switzerland. But he was soon seized by the Austrian authorities and burned at the stake in Vienna in March, 1528. His courageous wife was drowned in the Danube River. The congregaton at Nikolsburg, however, remained an important center of Anabaptism, whence its doctrines were spread to other parts of Europe.

Anabaptist leaders were also for a while active in Nürnberg. Among these was the spiritualist Hans Denk (d. 1527), a well-educated humanist and rector of the school of St. Sebald. On January 21, 1525, the same day that Grebel baptized Manz in Zurich, he and "three godless painters" were driven out of the city. At Augsburg he met Hubmaier and joined the Anabaptists. Drawing heavily upon German mysticism and Christian Platonism, he wrote many influential booklets in which he called for the construction of true Christian communities governed by God's laws. Dissatisfied with the agitational methods of the Anabaptists of Augsburg, however, he withdrew from the movement shortly before his death.

At Augsburg a strong congregation of Anabaptists was organized by Hubmaier. Among the most active leaders there was Hans Hut, a follower of Müntzer who had been baptized by Hans Denk in 1526. Hut, however, soon came into a conflict with his colleagues because of his radical views concerning the end of the world and the coming of the kingdom of God. His views were opposed by the so-called Synod of Martyrs, which met in Augsburg in August, 1527, under the leadership of Hans Denk. Virtually all the "evangelists" sent to various parts of Germany, Switzerland, and Austrian lands suffered martyrdom. Soon after the meeting of this group, the city council vigorously persecuted the remaining participants and within a year stamped out Anabaptism.

Strassburg became the next chief center of Anabaptism in southern Germany. There an active congregation flourished for about five years, largely because Capito, Zell, and Bucer prevented the city council from using force to suppress the movement, urging instead that the people be instructed by means of religious discussions, several of which were held. At the well-attended Strassburg Synod of 1533 occurred an open debate between Bucer and Melchior Hofmann. The latter, an uneducated Swabian furrier's apprentice who had become Lutheran and had been active as a preacher in Livonia, Sweden, Denmark, and northern Germany, had got into difficulties with authorities everywhere because of his bitter polemics, iconoclastic tendencies, and differences with Luther concerning the Lord's Supper. In his edition of *The Revelation of John* he had called Luther the Apostle of the Beginning of the third and last stage of history, who had, alas, become a Judas; and himself the Apostle of the Last Days, which he had stated would come in 1533.

After his debate with Bucer, Hofmann was compelled to leave Strassburg. He then went to the Low Countries, where he gained many followers. These came to be called Melchiorites. They combined the views of the Sacramentarians—those who believed in the symbolical interpretation of the Lord's Supper—with Hofmann's apocalyptic Anabaptism. In

1533, the year in which he believed the end of the world would come, he returned as the Prophet Elias to Strassburg, the "New Jerusalem." He was soon thrown into prison, where he remained until his death in 1543.

The Anabaptists exerted their greatest influence in the Low Countries, where the long period of persecutions under Charles V had served to strengthen rather than weaken the movement. One of the most active leaders there was David Joris (1501–1556), an artist and poet from Delft who embraced radical mystical ideas and dreamed of the coming of the millenium, of which he considered himself the leading prophet. His strange mystical and chiliastic doctrines were published in his *Book of Wonders* in 1542.

Faith was for Joris not assent to a creed but spiritual experience, for God saves man solely by implanting the Word in his heart. Those who argue over religious matters and persecute others do not, he maintained, have the true faith. The true church, therefore, never persecutes. On the contrary, it is a suffering, persecuted church, which, on the positive side, demonstrates Christian love by being meek, gentle, and lowly.

Many of Joris' followers, including his mother, suffered martyrdom; but he miraculously escaped the persecutions and finally fled to Basel, where he lived under the assumed name of Jan van Brugge for many years, supported by money that he had collected from his Dutch followers. Keeping his religious views to himself, he was accepted as a respectable, conforming burgher, while secretly writing his followers letters in which he urged them to prepare for the millenium. Not until after his death was his identity disclosed, whereupon he was declared a heretic. His remains were exhumed and burned, together with his writings and a portrait of him.

Although most of the Melchiorites remained quietistic, the baker Jan Matthys of Haarlem, the tailor Jan Beukelsz of Leyden, and their apostles sent out a call to arms against all unbelievers, thereby combining the extravagent eschatology of Hofmann with a propaganda of action. They concentrated their activities in the episcopal city of Münster in Westphalia, near the Dutch border, where political, social, and religious conflicts had divided the townsmen into three groups: a small number of Catholics, who supported the bishop; the conservative Lutherans, who were strongly represented in the city council; and the Melchiorites, who had the backing of the guilds and the common people.

Philip of Hesse was called upon to mediate among these groups, but before he could do so, Beukelsz and other Melchiorites called upon the guilds, in February, 1534, to arise in arms against the bishop and the council and to create a democratic government. While the bishop and the conservative elements fled from the city, Matthys arrived and began to establish his "heavenly Jerusalem," his primitive communist society, by driving out the godless and burning all books save the Bible. The common ownership of all things was taught on the basis of biblical texts and introduced immediately.

After the death of Matthys in April, Beukelsz took his place as an ambitious dictator. He assumed the title of king under the name Jan van Leyden. Especially attractive to women and prey to the weakness of his own flesh, he caused much dissatisfaction by his introduction of polygamy and the enforcement of his will by unbridled brutality. Not until June 25, 1535, did Philip of Hesse and the bishop succeed in taking the city, after a long siege. The leaders of the commune were tortured to death and their bodies were placed in iron baskets, which hung in the tower of Lambert Church until 1881. After this brutal reprisal, Catholicism was restored in Münster and vigorous action was taken against the Anabaptists everywhere in Europe.

It was particularly under the able leadership of Menno Simons (1496–1561) that Anabaptism was purged of its radical elements and gained widespread respectability. He was a native of Friesland who had become a priest and then had been converted to Protestantism by Luther's writings. When he learned that his brother was among three hundred insurgent Anabaptists killed after the fall of Münster, he decided to devote his life to the service of those Christians who had hoped to established the kingdom of God on earth by means of the sword.

Menno Simons attempted to establish congregations of "reborn" Christians, patterned after the church of the Apostles. His chief doctrines, published in his *Book of Fundamentals* in 1539, were the following: True faith causes man to walk in the ways of Christ. Baptism does not confer grace. It is a divine ordinance that marks the spiritual rebirth of a Christian. The Lord's Supper is merely a memorial of the death of Christ and reflects the believer's faith. Only believers who walk in the ways of Christ constitute the true church. This free church has the right to excommunicate sinners. Service in the state, warfare, and the giving of oaths are contrary to Scripture, yet Christians must obey the government in all things not forbidden in the Bible. Although Menno Simons was orthodox in his teachings concerning the natures of Christ, he avoided the use of such terms as *Trinity* that were not used in the Bible.

The first congregation of the followers of Menno Simons, called Mennonites, was formed in East Friesland. From there they spread throughout the Low Countries and into northern Germany, where they absorbed remnants of other Anabaptist movements. They were governed by a central council of elders, to which members were elected. Doctrinal differences, particularly with respect to the use of the ban, led to an increasing number of divisions, especially after the death of Menno Simons. The rule of the elders declined and the various congregations became virtually autonomous. It was not until toward the close of the century that these congregations again began to cooperate. Through them, Anabaptism became a powerful, constructive religious force. The Independents, the Quakers, and the Baptists of a later day obtained many of their beliefs from the Mennonites.

Among the large number of evangelical radicals who are difficult to classify because they did not identify themselves with any one sect but who may be called evangelical spiritualists are Sebastian Frank (1499–1543) and Kaspar von Schwenckfeld (1489–1561). Sebastian Frank, a priest in Donauwörth in southern Germany, gave up his priesthood in 1528 and moved to Nürnberg, later to Strassburg, and then Ulm. He combined late-medieval German mysticism with rational humanism and emerged as a lone prophet who refused to have anything to do with the established churches or even with the organized congregations of Anabaptists. The entire church, he taught, had been ruined by Antichrist. Consequently it was God's will that it should be destroyed, in its Protestant as well as its Catholic forms. The only true church was the invisible, spiritual body of believers. Christians should follow only the inner revelation given them by the Holy Spirit. He exercised his greatest influence through such printed works as his *Chronica* (1531), one of the first Protestant biblical histories; his *Paradoxa* (1534), a collection of two hundred and eighty mystic statements designed to make the reader think for himself, published two years after he had been exiled from Strassburg at the instigation of Erasmus; and a collection of proverbs (1534). In him we find the beginnings of those pantheistic and antiecclesiastical attitudes that became common in the Age of the Enlightenment.

Kaspar von Schwenckfeld was a Silesian nobleman who early came under the influence of German mysticism and Luther's evangelical doctrines. Dissatisfied with Luther's lack of emphasis on ethics, he broke with him in 1525 and then took the side of Zwingli in the Sacramentarian Controversy. But he went further than Zwingli in his development of a completely spiritual conception of the Lord's Supper. He stressed particularly the inner experience and the rebirth of the Christian rather than his justification. After he gave up his position as counselor of a German duke, he wandered from place to place, preaching. His ideas were furthered by small groups of persons, most of them patronized by noblemen in Silesia and Württemberg. About 1720 a number of his followers, called Schwenckfeldians, migrated to the American colonies, where small congregations were established in Pennsylvania and Connecticut, some of which still exist.

In addition to the Anabaptists and the evangelical spiritualists, there was a third group of religious radicals, the evangelical rationalists. These were well-educated men who minimized the importance of the church and had anti-Trinitarian views. The best known representative of this group was Michael Servetus, who will be discussed later.

# Evangelical Movements in the Romance Countries

Lutheranism did not obtain a firm hold in the Romance countries, Spain, Italy, and France. In Spain and France a much greater degree of territorial control of religion had been achieved by 1500 than in Italy, and in all three the relations of the people and their rulers to the papacy were much stronger than in the rest of Europe. Moreover, the Neoplatonism of the humanists had been combined with mystical elements into a synthesis that was at first receptive to Luther's views but that either felt more at home in Catholicism or took the more radical form of anti-Trinitarianism.

## Spain

By the time Charles became the first Hapsburg ruler of Spain in 1516, the "Catholic sovereigns" had already removed many of the worst abuses in the Church under the capable leadership of Cardinal Jiménez, had obtained control of the selection of the important ecclesiastical officials, and, in their attacks upon the Moors and Jews, had developed the techniques of the Spanish Inquisition, created in 1480, for ferreting out heresy. Nevertheless, Italian humanism early gained a strong foothold among the educated classes of Spain; and after the advent of Charles and his Burgundian advisers, the Christian humanism of Erasmus found many devotees.

Luther's works, several of which had been translated into the Spanish tongue, were brought into Spain by merchants, soldiers, and royal officials stationed in Germany. Even though the reading of his works was specifically forbidden as early as 1521, there developed a movement called Lutheran, which combined the ideas of the reformer with humanist criticism and Spanish quietism and which from the outset met with vigorous opposition.

Among the first to reflect these new currents were the scholarly Castilian brothers, Alfonso and Juan de Valdés. Alfonso (d. 1532) was an Erasmian humanist and a secretary of Charles V. He is best known for his *Dialogue Between Lactantio and an Archdeacon,* in which he placed the blame for the sack of Rome (1527) upon the secularized papacy. Juan (d. 1541) was much more influenced by mysticism than his brother. Without ever denying the authority of the Catholic Church, he exerted a strong evangelical influence through his emphasis upon the value of biblical study and the importance of the individual conscience, not only among the Spaniards but particularly among the Italians, for he spent most of the last decade of his life on an island near Naples. By his emphasis upon the importance of a strong spiritual relation between the individual and

God and his denial that God need be placated by the sacrificial death of Christ, he in effect repudiated the doctrine of the vicarious atonement. His novel religious views are best expressed in his *Hundred and Ten Considerations.*

One of the centers of Spanish "Lutheranism" was Valladolid, where a small evangelical circle familiar with the writings of Juan de Valdés and the Protestant reformers lived a dangerous existence. Another circle, at Seville, consisted of more than a hundred members who met in small groups for reasons of security. They were led by Constantino Ponce de la Fuente, who exerted a strong influence by both preaching and writing, and by Juan Perez de Pireda, who later fled to Geneva, where he published a Spanish translation of the New Testament.

Two of the most prominent Spanish Protestants were the brothers Jaime and Francisco de Encinas, who had come into contact with the new religious ideas as students in the Low Countries. Jaime (d. 1547), who drew up a confession of faith in the Spanish language, was burned at the stake in Rome. Francisco (d. 1552?) went to Wittenberg in 1541, translated the New Testament into Spanish, associated with the Protestant reformers in Germany and Switzerland, taught Greek at the University of Cambridge, and died as a professor at the University of Strassburg.

Probably the best known among the Spanish evangelical rationalists was Michael Servetus (1511–1553), a native of Villanova who began to take an interest in theology while studying law at Toulouse. In 1530 he met Oecolampadius in Basel, to whom he explained his anti-Trinitarian views. These appeared in his *Concerning the Errors of the Trinity.* When this and others of his books aroused a storm of indignation among the Protestant reformers, Servetus went to Lyon, where he worked as a corrector of proof and editor, and then to Paris, where, under the pseudonym Villeneuve, he studied medicine. There, incidentally, he discovered the pulmonary circulation of the blood, for he showed that it was carried from the heart to the lungs, where it was aerated and changed color. Having got into difficulty with the medical faculty for lecturing on astrology, he left Paris in 1538, set up a private medical practice near Lyon, and, in 1544, became the friend and personal physician of the archbishop of Vienne, still under his assumed name. But he retained his interest in theology, and in 1553 he secretly published his *Restitution of Christianity,* a manuscript copy of which he had sent to Calvin in 1546. In it he gave expression to his speculations concerning the essence of primitive Christianity.

Servetus had been led to the study of the doctrine of the Trinity by his concern over the stubborn refusal of the Jews and the Moors in his native Spain to be converted to Christianity. The Christian conception of God as of one substance, but differentiated in three persons (God the Father, God the Son, and God the Holy Spirit), was construed by these as tritheism, or the belief in three Gods. Amazed by the fact that the word *Trinity* was not used in the Bible, and unfamiliar with the historical development of the doctrine and its terminology, he developed his own doctrines, which were clearly heretical. Although he did not deny that Christ, or the word, was coeternal with God the Father, he denied this attribute to the Son, who, he maintained, came into existence when the word was united with the man Jesus. He denied outright that the Holy Spirit was a person.

Whereas Servetus' doctrine of God offended virtually all Christians, his doctrine of man was particularly odious to Calvin. Building upon the Renaissance conception of man and the Neoplatonic conception of the unity of all created things, held together by the active principle, God, Servetus evolved the doctrine that man could participate in the divinity through the Son of God. This, he said, man actually did when he fed upon Christ, the "light of the world," in the sacrament of the Lord's Supper.

From the Anabaptists Servetus obtained the conception of the church as a free communion of true believers, the belief in the imminent return of Christ to judge the world, and opposition to infant baptism. Whereas these and his doctrines of God and man were considered heretical, his doctrines on the Trinity and rebaptism were also contrary to the Justinian Code, the law of the Empire.

When it became known that Servetus had written the *Restitution,* he was denounced as a heretic before the court of the Inquisition at Vienne. He was subsequently arrested, but he escaped from prison and fled. On his way to Italy he unwisely stopped at Geneva and visited the church in which Calvin was preaching. He was recognized, arrested, thrown into prison, and, after a long trial, burned at the stake in October, 1553.

## Italy

Although Lutheranism and other Protestant doctrines penetrated Italy, they were not embraced by large segments of the population. Like Germany, Italy was divided into many political units. But these could not be brought together into strong territorial states, particularly as long as the papacy, which was looked upon as a national institution, could control the political situation in its own interests. From an economic point of view, the importance of Rome as a center of Christendom was too great to permit the townsmen to take seriously any thoughts of reducing the power and wealth of that institution. Furthermore, the educated classes were strongly influenced by humanism, which could be highly critical of the Church and its hierarchy but did not deny its basic doctrines or the authority of the pope. Impressed with the dignity of man and his creative ability, the humanists could hardly be moved by the Protestant emphasis upon the total depravity of man and his justification by faith alone. The lower classes seemed to lack initiative, leadership, and the desire to change their social status or their religious doctrines.

Nevertheless, Protestantism gained a foothold in several centers, and a number of Italian reformers played important roles in developing and spreading its doctrines. Lutheranism was brought to Venice at an early date, for this city maintained strong commercial connections with the German cities. During the first years of the Schmalkaldic League the government of Venice protected Protestantism in the city, and its printing presses published many translations of Lutheran and Zwinglian works as well as Antonio Bruccioli's Italian Bible (1532). Even Anabaptism found its adherents, especially after the outbreak of the Schmalkaldic War.

The Italian anti-Trinitarians, as we have seen, developed the most extreme religious views. Like Servetus, they combined humanist, Neoplatonic ideas with elements of pre-Nicene theology to arrive at doctrines that were hostile to both Catholicism and territorially organized Protestanism. They held that Christ, born of Joseph and Mary, was not divine but human, although Christ had certain divine characteristics. He died solely to show God's righteousness, mercy, and promise. One of the early leaders of this group was Giorgio Biandrata (1515–1590), who became the leader of a group of anti-Trinitarians in and near Geneva, went to Poland in 1558—where he worked with Ochino—and five years later to Transylvania. There he became court physician to King John Sigismund and won over the Calvinist superintendent Francis David (d. 1579) to Unitarian views. In 1568 a Unitarian Church was established with David as its bishop. But because of differences among the leaders, the church split into several relatively small factions.

Lelio Sozzini (1525–1562), a jurist from Siena who had become interested in Lutheran and Anabaptist doctrines on a visit to Venice and Protestant centers north of the Alps, became particularly attracted to anti-Trinitarian views after the execution of Servetus. He lived for a while at Zurich, where the Calvinists grew suspicious of his theological speculations. His visit to Poland in 1551 does not seem to have had a great influence upon Protestantism in that country. But it is believed that he helped shape the views of his nephew Fausto Sozzini (1539–1604) through his writings, which he willed to Fausto. Fausto, as we have seen, was active in Poland after 1579, when he assumed the leadership of the anti-Trinitarians at Racow and implanted the stamp of his theology upon the movement called Socinianism. When, under Jesuit influence, the Polish Diet of 1638 put an end to the Socinian center at Racow, most of the Socinians fled to Holland.

From Venice Protestantism spread to other cities in northern Italy. Noteworthy was the circle of heretics at Padua, where many young Germans and Swiss went to study law. There Francisco Spiera renounced his Catholicism in 1548. But he suffered terrible pangs of conscience for fear of having committed the unforgivable sin against the Holy Ghost. It was at Francisco's deathbed that the bishop of Capo d'Istria, Pietro Paolo Vergerio (d. 1564), papal nuncio to Germany in 1535, believed that he received God's command that he become a Protestant. Vergerio, as we have seen, fled from Italy in 1549 and entered the service of the duke of Württemberg.

The University of Ferrara, like that of Padua, was well attended by Protestant students from Germany and Switzerland and became a strong Protestant center, supported for a while by the humanistically inclined Duchess Renée, a daughter of King Louis XII of France. Her countryman Calvin visited her in 1536, hoping to interest her in making Ferrara an asylum for persecuted Frenchmen. But the political dependence of Duke Ercole II (1534–1559), her husband, upon the papacy and the effectiveness of the Italian Inquisition soon put an end to Protestantism in Ferrara.

The most important evangelical center in Italy was Naples, where Juan de Valdés brought together an influential circle of devoted followers. Desirous of leading people "back to Jesus," he centered his attention upon the reading of the Bible and urged the cultivation of inward piety. He translated for his followers the Psalms and Paul's Epistle to the Romans and First Epistle to the Corinthians, adding his commentaries. He seemed to appeal particularly to members of the nobility and government officials who had been educated as humanists. Among the educated women of his group was the brilliant, beautiful, widowed, and childless Giulia Gonzaga, duchess of Fondi, for whom he wrote his *Christian Alphabet*.

Another Italian woman with evangelical tendencies was Vittoria Colonna (1490–1547), a writer of religious verse and a close friend of Michelangelo. One of the noblest women of her day, she did much to further simple piety and devotion to Christianity.

Among the highly influential members of the Neapolitan circle was Bernardino Ochino (1487–1565), a native of Siena who had sought religious satisfaction among the Franciscan Observants and then among the Capuchins, whose vicar-general he was from 1538 to 1541. Like Savonarola, whom he resembled in a number of ways, he preached sermons of repentance with such sincerity and beauty of speech that he attracted huge throngs wherever he went. From Juan de Valdés he learned to minimize more than ever outward observance and to stress inwardness of religion. But he also came under the influence of Protestant tracts that the pope had permitted him to read for the purpose of refuting them. He became greatly disturbed over the question whether he should openly adhere to Lutheranism, whose Christocentric theology he had privately embraced, or remain in the Church and attempt to draw together Rome and Wittenberg. This question was solved for him when he was summoned to

Rome in 1543 to answer for his attack upon Venice for imprisoning a preacher who had publicly expounded the Augustinian doctrine of grace.

Ochino, suspecting that he might be burned at the stake if he appeared in Rome, went into exile at the age of fifty-six. He first settled in Geneva, where he was cordially received by Calvin and was given charge of the church of Italian refugees. When marriage and the arrival of a daughter brought financial difficulties, he left Geneva and subsequently preached with much success at Basel, Augsburg, London, and Zurich. Exiled from Zurich in 1563 because he had uttered statements and published views not in complete harmony with the Reformed doctrines and because the Italians in the city were disliked on account of their business competition with the citizens, he fled to Poland and then to Moravia, where he died at the age of seventy-eight.

Much more successful was the career in exile of Pietro Martire Vermigli (Peter Martyr the Younger, 1500–1562), the brilliant son of a wealthy nobleman. At sixteen he entered the Augustinian monastery, then studied at Padua, and in 1533 was made prior of a monastery in Naples, where he joined the circle of Juan de Valdés. In 1541 he obtained permission of Pope Paul III to leave Naples, where he was being suspected of holding heretical views, and to preach at Lucca. The next year he met his friend Ochino in Florence. Both decided to leave Italy.

Vermigli joined the Italian "Diaspora" in Switzerland in 1542, first at Basel and later at Zurich, and then obtained a professorship in Old Testament theology at Strassburg. In 1547 he accepted an invitation by Cranmer to lecture in the University of Cambridge, where he remained until the persecution during Mary's reign forced him to return to the Continent in 1553. After lecturing again at Strassburg, he accepted a similar position in Zurich, where he spent his last years.

How close the Protestant influence of the Naples circle touched important Roman families is seen in the case of Galeazzo Caraccioli (1517–1586), a nobleman at the Neapolitan court and a nephew of Caraffa, who became Pope Paul IV. Converted by Juan de Valdés and Vermigli, Galeazzo endured many hardships for his faith. In 1551 he left his family and fled to Geneva, where he lived the rest of his life as the respected "Mr. Marchese."

Probably the most significant work published by an Italian reformer was *The Benefit of Christ,* written in Italian by Benedetto of Mantua and revised and published by Mercantonio Flaminio in 1540. Subsequently published in many editions, it was finally condemned by the Italian Inquisition. The first copy to come to light in recent times was discovered in Cambridge, England, in 1853. All similar literature suffered a like fate, and Italians with the slightest tendencies toward Protestantism either were martyred or joined their countrymen in exile.

## France

The reception of, Lutheranism in France was conditioned by three significant factors: (1) the influence of the king over ecclesiastical matters; (2) the unique social conditions in France; and (3) the growth of Christian humanism. The Pragmatic Sanction of Bourges, arranged with the papacy in 1438, had given the king considerable control over the collection of papal taxes and the appointment of important church officials. The Concordat of Bologna (1516) permitted the papal collection of annates but gave the French king the right to nominate the candidates to all vacant archbishoprics, bishoprics, and abbacies, although subject to papal confirmation. Because the popes invariably accepted the royal nominees, the ten archbishops, eighty-two bishops, and more than five hundred abbots, priors, and canons who owed their appointments to the king usually reflected his wishes as well as those of the Church. Accordingly, they cooperated with the king in correcting some abuses resented by Frenchmen but did little or nothing to correct the evils growing out of royal patronage and the worldly character of the upper clergy. The lower clergy, usually of the lower classes and underpaid, joined the large numbers of dissatisfied elements in voicing strong disapproval of the secularization of the Church, especially the corruption of the upper clergy.

Social discontent was strong among all classes. Although the worst features of serfdom had disappeared, the holdings of the great majority of the peasants were so small that it was difficult to wrest a living from them. All the sons of French nobles inherited noble titles, but by the principle of primogeniture all the lands went to the first-born. The younger sons thus constituted another restless element, and most of the nobles resented the loss of many of their feudal privileges to the French crown. The upper bourgeoisie, who had experienced much prosperity since the close of the Hundred Years' War, were more or less satisfied with the status quo, although they vied with the nobles for royal favor. The less fortunate craftsmen, however, as well as the landless laborers in the country, were particularly susceptible to ideas of a revolutionary nature. Possessing little more than their tools, they constituted a restless element that readily fled from persecution and spread social and religious dissatisfaction from place to place.

Christian humanism, as we have seen, received royal support for a considerable time, especially when Francis I, who was a typical Renaissance ruler, became king. Under the leadership of Guillaume Briçonnet, the bishopric of Meaux became an important center of Bible study, spiritual revival, and clerical reform. Although Briçonnet supported men who became Protestants, he himself remained loyal to Catholicism and, under royal pressure, issued a synodal decree in 1523 forbidding the possession and reading of Lutheran pamphlets, and another decree ordering the cessation of preaching against the saying of prayers for the dead and the invocation of the saints.

However, Luther's writings could not be kept from the dissatisfied elements in France. Issuing from the printing presses of neighboring cities in increasing numbers, these pamphlets influenced many Frenchmen. But because no popular Protestant leader emerged for many years, it was relatively easy to suppress outcroppings of religious dissent.

The conservative theological faculty of the Sorbonne soon became the center of opposition to all forms of religious reform, which it lumped together under the term *Lutheran*. As early as April, 1521, it condemned as heretical more than a hundred theses that it had culled from Luther's works. That same year it induced the Parlement of Paris to proclaim that persons having any of Luther's books in their possession should give them up or be subject to a heavy fine or imprisonment. Accordingly one Louis de Berquin of Picardy, who had become interested in Luther's theology, was seized and punished as a heretic in June, 1523. But he was not executed until 1529.

The reformers at Meaux continued to enjoy royal protection uninterruptedly until 1525, the year of Francis I's defeat at Pavia. In March of that year occurred an incident that tended to inflame the conservative opposition to reforms and led to the dispersal of the reformers of Meaux. Jean Leclerc, a wool carder who opposed the sale of indulgences, tore down Clement VII's bull concerning the papal jubilee that had been posted at Meaux and put up in its place a placard in which he referred to the pope as Antichrist. He was caught, branded, and later, when he desecrated religious images at Metz, burned at the stake. Louise of Savoy, the queen mother, eager to obtain the support of the pope against Charles, who was holding Francis I prisoner, induced the Parlement of Paris to institute proceedings against all heretics. The theologians of the Sorbonne, who declared that the reading of the French translations of the Bible fostered heresy, ordered them burned. Many persons suspected of heresy were imprisoned and a few were burned. Not even Margaret, the king's sister, who had long protected the reformers of Meaux, could save them now. As a consequence of these persecutions, the group dispersed. Lefèvre and Roussel fled to Strassburg, where they lived for a while with Capito. Farel had already fled to Basel in 1523.

When Francis returned from Madrid in March, 1526, he compelled the Parlement to suspend the persecutions and recalled the Meaux reformers. Lefèvre became the tutor of one of the king's sons and royal librarian at Blois. Later he joined Margaret d'Angoulême, who had married the king of Navarre.

Francis continued to protect the reformers until, late in 1527, he was compelled to call an assembly of notables to raise money for ransoming his sons, still retained by Charles V according to the provisions of the

King Francis I of France

*by Clouet*

233

Treaty of Madrid. Although the notables granted the request, the ecclesiastical members added the condition that he suppress all Lutheranism in France. Early the next year occurred a desecration of an image of the Virgin Mary in Paris. This aroused such strong popular indignation against the blasphemer that expiatory processions were made in which Francis himself took part. In April, 1529, Berquin, as we have seen, was burned at the stake.

Needless to state, the general suppression of heresy, organized by synods at Paris, Bourges, and Lyon, only served to give martyrs to people with Protestant leanings and led to the formation of determined groups of resistance throughout France. They were given a respite, however, when the king, in one of his unpredictable shifts of policy, sought a rapprochement with both the Turks and the Schmalkaldic League after it had become apparent that the Peace of Cambrai of 1529 had not brought the Hapsburg-Valois wars to a definite conclusion. At the same time he made the moderate reformer Jean du Bellay bishop of Paris and permitted Gérard Roussel to preach to large groups in the Louvre during Lent, 1533.

This policy of toleration was abandoned when the king desired to win Pope Clement VII's political support in the autumn of 1533. As his part of the bargain, Francis agreed once more to suppress heresy and received a papal bull for that purpose. The opportunity to enforce the bull came in November of that year, when the new rector of the University of Paris, Nicholas Cop, dared to elucidate in his inaugural address evangelical ideas that the Sorbonne considered heretical. When the king learned of this he ordered the Parlement to suppress the "Lutheran sect."

But the persecutions had barely begun when Francis made a treaty with the German Lutheran princes, aided Duke Ulrich of Württemberg in regaining his lands from the Hapsburgs, permitted evangelical reformers to preach in the Louvre, and even sent Bishop Bellay's brother William to Germany to attempt a reconciliation with the Lutheran theologians. Melanchthon's theological propositions were brought back to Paris in August, 1534. But they arrived too late, for once more a policy of conciliation had been replaced by one of suppression, induced by the famous affair of the placards.

On the morning of October 18, 1534, there appeared on the streets of Paris and other cities placards written in violent language by radical French reformers and printed in Switzerland with the title of *True Articles Concerning the Horrible Abuse of the Papal Mass.* One copy was even found attached to the door of the king's bedchamber at Amboise, where he was residing at the time. Such was the popular resentment and the royal displeasure that, by the end of the year, hundreds of persons had been imprisoned and eight executed. Francis, eager to win the good will of the new pope, Paul III (1534–1549), joined the expiatory processions in Paris and, early the next year, issued a royal decree ordering the complete suppression of heresy. Many Protestants left France at that time.

Political considerations, however, once more caused Francis to pursue a moderate course. At the death of the conservative chancellor Cardinal Duprat, he appointed in his place Antoine du Bourg, who favored the reformers. In his Edict of Coucy of July, 1535, the king ordered the cessation of persecution and promised that returning fugitives would be unmolested if they abjured their heresy. The Edict of Lyon of May, 1536, extended amnesty also to the Sacramentarians. But few of the reformers returned. Although the most able leaders remained in exile, the more timid and the moderates, alienated by the excesses of the radicals, made their peace with the Church. That same year there appeared in Basel Calvin's *Institutes of the Christian Religion,* which, as we shall see, gave the French Protestants a concise statement of doctrines and led them to look to this countryman as their leader.

The king, almost isolated in his third war with Charles, decided to uphold Catholicism. Accordingly he finally issued the severe Edict of Fontainebleau in June, 1540, which definitely placed him on the side of repression of all forms of Protestantism. The edict provided an efficient legal procedure for trying heretics, headed by an inquisitor-general. Two years later the Sorbonne published its Twenty-six Articles in answer to the French edition of the *Institutes,* and in 1544 published its *Index expurgatorius.* But the systematic persecution that followed served only to weed out the timid Protestants and to cause the faithful to organize their movement with utmost caution and secrecy.

Unfortunately this royal policy of suppression led to the brutal massacre of the peaceful Waldensians of the Durance Valley, separating the Dauphiné and Provence, who had been highly respected by their Catholic neighbors. Guillaume Farel, a native of the Dauphiné, had begun an evangelical movement among these simple followers of Peter Waldo and had induced them in 1530 to send two representatives to the Lutheran reformers in search of doctrinal enlightenment and agreement. On the basis of suggestions made by Bucer and Oecolampadius, they drew up a confession of faith in 1532 that contained some Lutheran features. They also provided money for a French translation of the Bible, later completed by Olivétan.

When the inquisitor of Provence learned of these Protestant activities of the Waldensians, he began to persecute them. They in turn appealed for protection to the king, who defended them on numerous occasions until 1545. In that year, Baron d'Oppède, the president of the Parlement of Aix who desired their fertile lands and prosperous towns, sent Francis the false statement that they were rebelling against the king. Without checking the reliability of this dispatch, the king decreed that all persons guilty of the Waldensian heresy should be executed. Thereupon Oppède marched without previous warning into the region, burned twenty-two villages, and murdered about three thousand Waldensian men, women, and children.

The next year occurred the execution of "The Fourteen of Meaux" by regular judicial process. These reformers had organized a Protestant church under Pierre Leclerc, brother of the wool carder who had been executed at Metz in 1526. Of the sixty persons who were suddenly arrested and accused of celebrating the Lord's Supper in the Protestant form, fourteen were sentenced to be tortured and burned at the stake. Eight of them refused the last rites of the Church and had to suffer the usual additional torture of having their tongues cut out for refusing to repent. Among the five reformers who were burned at Paris in the same year was the scholar and printer Etienne Dolet, who was condemned for having printed books written by Erasmus, Lefèvre, and Marot. Such repressive measures drove the Protestant movement underground and spread it so that it easily withstood the more persistent suppression of Henry II (1547–1559).

## England's Break with Rome

The beginnings of the Reformation in England in many respects parallel those in the Scandinavian countries. In both one must differentiate between the religious changes that took place among the people and the dynastic politics of rulers who took the initiative in breaking with Rome. And both of these considerations must be examined against the economic and social changes that drew these countries out of the relatively insignificant roles that they had played in European affairs in medieval times and that enabled them to assume positions of importance among the great powers of the sixteenth and seventeenth centuries.

Because Henry VII (1485–1509), the first of the Tudor monarchs in England, realized the necessity of broadening the support of his new dynasty to prevent it from being replaced by another, he encouraged the growth of towns and the rise of the townsmen by stimulating manufacturing, making commercial treaties with foreign powers, and maintaining peace. By carefully husbanding his income, he also minimized the necessity of frequently asking Parliament for money, thereby weakening its influence over him. At the same time he made a frontal attack upon those barons who had constituted a threat to royal authority.

Alongside the townsmen there appeared another important class with increasing economic and political influence, the sheep-raising landlords. Both classes cooperated in making the production of wool and woolen goods a most profitable enterprise, for the king as well as for themselves, for the revenues from these sources constituted an important part of royal income.

The barons, the townsmen, and the sheep-raising landlords all resented the great wealth of the Church and the secularization of its clergy. About one fifth of the national wealth was in the hands of the Church. The masses of the people, adversely affected by the enclosure of lands, the replacement of craft guilds by the domestic system, and the rise in prices, were also greatly dissatisfied with conditions in general. Their antipathies might readily be aroused against any institution that they might consider responsible for their adverse circumstances.

Opposition to the papacy was nothing new in England. National resentment against the authority of the pope had been expressed in the popular support of the Statute of Provisors and the Statute of Praemunire, enacted by Parliament in 1351 and 1353, respectively. William of Ockham (d. 1349), educated in Oxford, had served the emperor on the Continent and had developed political theories that were hostile to the papacy. Although kings had later cooperated with the popes in maintaining ecclesiastical control over the English people, the critical spirit aroused by John Wycliffe (1320?–1384) and continued by the Lollards had not been completely obliterated, especially not among the lower classes.

### Humanism and Lutheranism

The humanists in England, as elsewhere, were highly critical of abuses in the Church, although most of them remained loyal to the ancient institution. Nevertheless, the younger devotees at Oxford and Cambridge took an increasing interest in the large number of Lutheran tracts that began to enter the country as early as 1519. At Cambridge a group of young men, including John Frith, Robert Barnes, Hugh Latimer, and William Tyndale, met regularly in the White Horse Inn to discuss Lutheran doctrines and were dubbed "Germans."

Probably the most influential in spreading Protestant doctrines was William Tyndale (d. 1536), a student first at Oxford and then at Cambridge. Like Luther, he assumed the task of giving the ploughboy as well as the ecclesiastic the Bible in the vernacular. He began translating the New Testament on the basis of Erasmus' Greek text; but when he could not obtain the support of the bishop of London for his task, he accepted the financial assistance of a London merchant and, in 1524, went to the Continent to continue his work.

After an extended visit in Germany, which included Wittenberg, he completed the translation of the New Testament and published the first edition of six thousand copies at Worms in 1526. Many copies were smuggled into England. Although some of them were bought up by the bishop of London and burned in St. Paul's churchyard, the demand for them increased. Seven additional editions were printed in the following decade. Thus encouraged, Tyndale translated a few books of the Old Testament directly from the Hebrew and published these, along with other tracts, until 1536, when he was executed as a heretic in the Low Countries.

On the whole, however, few Englishmen publicly proclaimed Protestant ideas before the separation from Rome. Among the exceptions were Elizabeth Sampson of London and James Brewster and William Sweeting of Smithfield, all of whom expressed heretical views concerning the Lord's Supper. The first abjured her heresy, but the latter two were burned at the stake. Thomas Bilney and John Frith, who had been in Germany for a while, also suffered martyrdom. The policy of suppression under a powerful monarchy served to keep heretical views under cover. Cuthbert Tunstall (bishop of London), Cardinal Wolsey (chief minister of the king), and Thomas More (the famous Oxford humanist) were united in their opposition to Lutheranism.

It was probably Thomas More who induced Henry VIII (1509–1547) to answer Luther's *The Babylonian Captivity* with his *The Defense of the Seven Sacraments*. The controversy caused by this attack upon Lutheranism served to bring the views of both sides before the English people, who began to evaluate the issues for themselves in the light of their own interests. But it is doubtful whether the separation from Rome would have occurred if it had not been for the dynastic interests of the king.

Henry VIII had aroused much hope for an enlightened regime among the humanists, for he had as a prince supported them and displayed some talents in literature, languages, music, mathematics, and scholastic theology, although much that passed as his work, such as his attack upon Luther, was the work of his secretaries. He no sooner became king than he began to disclose his true character as an unscrupulous monarch who stopped at nothing in his drive to enhance his prestige and that of his dynasty.

Henry's reign began with the execution of his father's commissioners, who had gained great unpopularity because of their zealous collection of taxes due the crown. He created more good will by pardoning most of the debtors and offenders against the crown. Unlike his miserly father, the new king made his court the center of pageants and tournaments, which helped deplete the surplus in the treasury but also made Henry beloved by his people.

## Political Aims of Henry VIII

To make his reign more glorious, the young king turned to foreign affairs to emulate his martial predecessors, Edward III and Henry V. With no more worthy aim than the seizure of lands in France, he joined

Warwick Castle. Ewing Galloway, New York.

King Henry VIII of England

*by Hans Holbein the Younger*

239

the Holy League, formed in 1511 by Pope Julius II for the purpose of driving France out of Italy. Henry, like a babe in the woods, permitted his crafty father-in-law Ferdinand to use the English army to cover up Spanish operations in Navarre. With nothing to do, Henry's restless army returned home without orders from him. Thus humiliated, Henry led an army into France the next year, 1513, and won the brilliant but insignificant Battle of the Spurs at Guinegate. The Scots, meanwhile, invaded England but were decisively defeated on Flodden Field, where King James IV (1488–1513) lost his life.

King Ferdinand and Emperor Maximilian left Henry in the lurch by making a truce with Francis. Henry, who could only follow suit, arranged a treaty of his own with France in August, 1514. It provided that the English receive an annual subsidy from the French and that Mary, Henry's younger sister, be married to Louis XII.

The little that Henry gained from this war was primarily the work of the sagacious Thomas Wolsey (1475?–1530), the son of a poor butcher, educated at Oxford for a career in the Church. He had entered the royal service in 1506 and had been admitted to the royal council five years later. His successful management of the military expedition to France and his negotiation of the treaty with France led to even more rapid advancement. In 1514 Henry made him archbishop of York. The next year he became a cardinal and lord chancellor, and in 1518 a papal legate. With these honors came wealth, and with both an arrogance that made him one of the most detested men in England. Hampton Court Palace, which he built, gave evidence of both his position and his wealth. The king, realizing his ability, for a long time permitted him to conduct all domestic and foreign affairs with little interference. But Henry did not lose touch with what was going on, took credit for all successes, and permitted the criticism of his failures to fall upon Wolsey. As a churchman, the cardinal's life reflected many of the abuses to which his countrymen objected, for he was a pluralist, seldom visited his dioceses, rarely performed the spiritual functions of his various offices, and led a scandalous life.

In the field of diplomacy Wolsey attempted to play the role of mediator and seemed to sense the value of the theory of the balance of power. He involved England in the Hapsburg-Valois conflict when both Francis and Charles sought Henry's support in 1519. England was inclined to favor Charles, for England's Queen Catherine was his aunt. Moreover, Charles ruled the Low Countries, the chief market for English wool. And as emperor he could exert considerable influence in papal elections. Wolsey had hopes of obtaining the highest post in Christendom, not only to satisfy his personal ambitions but to be in a position to advance the interests of his king in Europe.

Henry invited Charles to visit him in England in 1520; but he also arranged to meet Francis soon after this in the famous "Field of the Cloth of Gold" near Calais, one of the last lavish displays of feudal splendor. Despite mutual expressions of the desire to maintain peace between the two countries, the fact that Francis threw Henry in a wrestling match made the latter jealous and further inclined him toward Charles, with whom he concluded an offensive alliance that was in effect when the first Hapsburg-Valois war broke out in 1521. Relations were immediately strained between England and Spain, however, when Leo X died and Charles supported the election of his former tutor Adrian as pope rather than Wolsey. Furthermore, the English expeditions of 1522–1523 against France accomplished virtually nothing and the war became exceedingly unpopular in England.

In order to support this costly war, Henry was compelled to call the Parliament of 1523, the first to meet in eight years. When Wolsey appeared in person to demand high subsidies, Parliament flatly refused. At a second visit of Wolsey, Sir Thomas More, who was speaker of the House of Commons, refused to debate the issue in the cardinal's presence. When Wolsey left, the king was voted about half the requested sum. Although Wolsey received the blame for the war and the consequent request for further taxes, Henry realized that he himself could easily lose his popularity.

When Adrian died, Charles again ignored Wolsey and supported the election of Giulio de' Medici, who became Clement VII. And when, in 1525, Charles defeated Francis at Pavia, he appeared to be a greater menace to peace than the French king. Henry at first wished to join Charles in sharing the spoils of victory. Because this would require more money, Wolsey tried to raise what was euphemistically called the amicable loan but was in fact a heavy tax without parliamentary consent. This tax aroused such opposition—even rebellion in Suffolk—that it had to be abandoned. Wolsey became even more unpopular than before, and Henry had to give up his plans for the moment. Charles accordingly ignored him and consolidated his victory. The sack of Rome by his soldiers in 1527 and the virtual imprisonment of the pope in the Castle of Sant' Angelo occurred at the very time when Henry was seeking the annulment of his marriage with Catherine. This question, discreetly called the king's business, now overshadowed every other issue, even the treaty that Wolsey had negotiated with France.

## The Annulment Proceedings

Henry had gradually lost interest in Catherine for a variety of reasons. In the first place, she had interfered with his European plans as early as 1514 by supporting the interests of her father, Ferdinand. In the second place, Henry desired a male heir to assure the continuation of his dynasty in England. Of all the children born to Catherine and him, only a puny daughter, Mary, had remained alive; and he feared that her reign would be disputed as that of Matilda, daughter of Henry I, had been. Not realizing that his marriage was blighted as a consequence of syphilis, he believed that God was punishing him for having married his brother's widow, contrary to biblical and canon law (Leviticus 18:16). Catherine had been married at the age of sixteen to Henry's older, fourteen-year-old brother, Arthur, who had died shortly thereafter. The following year, 1503, Pope Julius II had granted a dispensation to permit Henry to marry her. The marriage, consummated in 1509, caused considerable discussion, as did the papal dispensation. In the third place, in 1527 Henry fell deeply in love with Anne Boleyn, one of the queen's ladies in waiting.

Henry had a right to expect that Clement VII would not deny him the annulment, for he had rendered the papacy a great service by attacking Luther. Furthermore, he believed that the pope would see that the divine displeasure with this marriage had been carried out as threatened in Leviticus 20:21: "And if a man shall take his brother's wife, it is an unclean thing: he hath uncovered his brother's nakedness; they shall be childless." His first plan was to have Wolsey try the case in his legatine court and later obtain the approval of the pope. But it soon became evident that Catherine would not meekly submit to this disgrace and that the pope might reverse the decision upon appeal from her. Therefore Wolsey tried to obtain the prior sanction of the pope. Clement, however, realizing that a reversal of the papal dispensation would harm papal prestige, and being a virtual prisoner of Catherine's nephew Charles, was determined not to grant the annulment. He accordingly attempted to postpone taking definite action until he was in a more favorable position to act without political pressure.

To gain time, Clement first ordered Wolsey and Cardinal Campeggio to try the case in England as his legates, but he instructed the latter to try to induce Henry to drop the matter or Catherine to enter a monastery. Only after Henry threatened to join the Lutherans did the court finally open, in May, 1529. Late in July, after long, fruitless hearings, the court was adjourned to meet in Rome in October. Henry, realizing that there was now no chance of receiving a favorable decision, especially because Charles remained in political control of Italy, decided to try the case in his own courts, regardless of the consequences. But he could not do this without sacrificing his faithful chancellor, Wolsey, who had advised the appeal to the pope. The dismissal in disgrace of this able man and the confiscation of his property were met with rejoicing by most Englishmen. His death the next year was mourned by few.

Henry now placed himself at the head of the antipapal and anticlerical forces in England, which had previously been held in check. Although he made Sir Thomas More his new lord chancellor, he depended upon two other advisers who had recently gained his favor, Thomas Cranmer (1489–1556) and Thomas Cromwell (1485?–1540). The former, a Cambridge scholar with Lutheran leanings, had gained the good will of the king by suggesting that the question of annulment be submitted to scholars at the leading European universities and that, if they returned an unsatisfactory judgment, it be tried in the king's courts. Cromwell, a merchant of middle-class origins, had been Wolsey's secretary and had remained faithful to him to his death. This layman was retained in royal service, eventually becoming a member of the royal council, the king's chief secretary, and vice-regent in ecclesiastical matters. It was he who advised the king to declare himself the head of the English Church and settle the annulment case in his own courts.

Henry increased his popularity and at the same time took advantage of a rising national sentiment by posing as a victim of papal policy and by ostensibly placing the issue before the Parliament that he called in 1529. Because this body, during its life of seven years, consummated the separation from Rome, it has been called the Reformation Parliament. By his firm leadership and respect for this body's historical prestige, Henry, a skilled parliamentarian, succeeded in drawing its members and the English people with him in his break with Rome, thereby giving legal and popular sanction to every important step.

In its first session in 1529, this Parliament attacked a number of clerical abuses, including pluralities and nonresidence, but especially evils in the administration of the ecclesiastical courts. Henry hoped thereby to intimidate the clergy and to compel the pope to accede to his personal wishes. When this maneuver failed, he referred the annulment to the universities, although he could not take seriously the favorable response given by the majority of them. Thereupon he threatened the entire English clergy with the punishment of praemunire for having submitted to Wolsey's legatine court. In return for withholding legal action, however, he obtained from the clergy in Convocation, meeting in January, 1531, a huge grant of money and acknowledgment as the supreme head of the Church in England "as far as the law of Christ allows."

The next year the House of Commons sent the king a petition, probably drafted by Cromwell, seeking a remedy for other abuses in the church courts and curtailment of the power of Convocation to make ecclesiastical ordinances without royal consent. Henry used the petition to wrest from Convocation the so-called Submission of the Clergy, whereby they agreed that existing ecclesiastical laws should be referred for revision to a committee of clergy and laity chosen by the king and that no new ecclesiastical laws should be made without the king's consent. Although More immediately resigned the chancellorship in protest, Henry went much further by obtaining from Parliament the Act in Conditional Restraint of Annates, prohibiting the payment to the pope of the customary

Sir Thomas Cromwell

*by Hans Holbein the Younger*

annates, provided the king saw fit to use the act. But this club, held over the head of the pope, failed to intimidate him, with the consequence that Henry now decided to end all papal authority in England.

Henry married Anne, who was already pregnant, in January, 1533. The next month Parliament passed the Act for the Restraint of Appeals, which virtually abolished papal authority in England. Because the act was made retroactive, Catherine's appeal to Rome and Henry's suit, which had been referred to Rome, were both declared invalid. In March the king appointed Cranmer archbishop of Canterbury, thus placing him at the head of the highest ecclesiastical court in England. Cranmer had recently married a niece of Andreas Osiander, a Lutheran pastor at Nürnberg. Henry obtained the papal bulls recognizing this appointment by threatening to withhold all annates. Convocation, with Cranmer attending, then declared the marriage of Catherine contrary to divine law, but by a small majority. In May Cranmer announced the decision of his court that Catherine was no longer queen and that Henry's marriage to Anne was valid. Anne was crowned at Westminster in June, and a few days later the pope pronounced the sentence of excommunication on Henry, although the king was given more than two months to take back Catherine. The bull was later dated 1535.

## The Break with Rome

Parliament then proceeded to legalize the break with Rome. In two memorable sessions in 1534 it stopped all payments of the English clergy to the papacy, gave the king the power to confirm ecclesiastical appointments, forbade the payment of Peter's Pence to the papal *Curia,* passed an Act of Succession in favor of the heirs of Anne, and by the Act of Supremacy made Henry the "only supreme head in earth of the Church of England," but only as a layman, for he could not consecrate the clergy. Thus the Reformation Parliament greatly enhanced the power of the king and placed the Church under the complete control of the state. Like Cranmer, Parliament maintained that the king would be more likely than Convocation to carry out a thorough reformation of the Church. To enable Henry to enforce his authority, Parliament passed a severe Treasons Act, which made calling the king a "heretic, schismatic, tyrant, infidel, or usurper" punishable by death.

The Act of Succession carried the stipulation that all subjects should take an oath to support it. Among the few who refused to do so were Sir Thomas More and Bishop Fisher of Rochester. Although they did not deny the king's right to settle the succession upon Elizabeth, born to Anne in September, 1533, they refused to take the oath because doing so would commit them to declaring that Mary was illegitimate and imply the repudiation of papal authority. For this reason they were sent to the Tower. But they were not executed until the summer of 1535, after the oath had been given statutory form and a new Treason Act had made it high treason to deny that the king was the supreme head of the church. This act made impossible further negotiations with the pope.

To increase his wealth and at the same time draw the merchant and agricultural classes closer to him, Henry, with parliamentary sanction, dissolved the monasteries, thereby dispossessing those who had given him the most opposition. Cromwell, now the king's vice-regent in ecclesiastical affairs, had probably urged Henry to take this step. In the summer of 1535 Cromwell sent greedy and unscrupulous visitors to examine conditions in the monastic establishments. The archbishops and bishops were legally powerless to intervene. Although the findings of corruption were greatly exaggerated and were used as a mere pretext for seizing their property, which comprised about a tenth of the national wealth, it is true that many of the monasteries, especially the smaller ones, had failed to adjust themselves to new circumstances during the late Middle Ages. They no longer served as outstanding examples of piety, their educational methods were antiquated, they had lost their leadership in agricultural and other economic affairs, and they were unable to solve the problems of poverty that plagued England. In only a few areas in the north had they retained popular support.

On the basis of the relatively scanty findings of Cromwell's visitors, Parliament, in 1536, passed the first Act for the Dissolution, which suppressed every monastery with an income of less than £200 annually—376 in all—and turned the property over to the king. Such suppression of monasteries was not a new thing, however, for Wolsey had dissolved a few with the aid of Cromwell before the break with Rome. In 1539 a new Parliament passed an act that dissolved the rest of the monasteries and also vested their possessions in the crown. Such acts of suppression were usually accompanied by the spoliation of monastic shrines, including the wealthy one of St. Thomas Becket at Canterbury. Only a few monastic churches were spared and became cathedrals of newly created bishoprics.

Although Henry retained some of the confiscated monastic property, used some to provide pensions for dispossessed monks, and appropriated a pitifully inadequate amount for educational purposes, much of this property was given or sold at low cost to favored barons, gentry, and townsmen. These beneficiaries of the royal generosity were thus bound to both the Tudor dynasty and the new ecclesiastical order. The dropping from the House of Lords of twenty-eight abbots, representing a strong antiroyal element, further weakened opposition in that body.

The dissolution of the monasteries, about six hundred in all, greatly accentuated the economic and social discontent of the lower classes. Probably two thousand monks and nuns and eight thousand laborers attached to the monasteries were directly affected. The accumulation of discontent was particularly severe in Lincolnshire and Yorkshire in the north, where it led to a rebellion of noblemen, gentry, abbots, and priests, called the Pilgrimage of Grace (1536). Although this uprising was suppressed by the execution of forty-six of its leaders, Henry sought to put down and prevent subsequent disorders by establishing the extralegal Council of the North, consisting of royal appointees and given wide powers for enforcing the royal will.

## Doctrinal Changes

Despite the fact that Henry did not wish to make any more ecclesiastical and doctrinal innovations than necessary, the pressure for such changes became increasingly great, particularly among the middle classes and the divines at Cambridge and Oxford. Protestant ideas continued to spread and, with Tyndale's proscribed translation of the Bible in their hands, many Englishmen began to question traditional practices and doctrines. In 1537 there appeared the so-called Matthew's Bible, probably edited by John Rogers, a disciple of Tyndale. It included Tyndale's translation of the New Testament and parts of the Old Testament as well as the translations of the rest of the books by Miles Coverdale, a friend of Cromwell. Although the king at first permitted this translation to be used, he later forbade it because of its controversial marginal notes and the strongly Lutheran introduction to the Epistle to the Romans. A revision of this Matthew's Bible by Miles Coverdale, called the Great Bible, was accepted, and in May, 1541, Henry proclaimed that a copy of it should be made accessible in every parish church. Because Cranmer supplied the introduction for this edition of 1540 and five subsequent editions, the Great Bible was also named after him. Parliament, in 1543, forbade women and ignorant persons to read the Bible, even in their homes.

Cranmer's responsibility for introducing the English Bible to the people was his greatest achievement. Next to this was his preparation of an English service book, the *Book of Common Prayer*. He began during Henry's reign by preparing for use in all parish churches an English litany, or liturgical form of prayer with supplications and responses, to be sung or spoken. This litany was later incorporated in the *Book of Common Prayer*. In preparing the latter, he drew upon the Sarum Processional, the Roman Breviary, a Latin translation of Chrysostom's liturgy, and Luther's Latin litany.

Because many Englishmen were following Cranmer and Bishop Latimer of Worcester in adhering to strongly Protestant views, while a number of Catholics ventured to criticize the break with Rome, Henry forced Convocation to draw up the Ten Articles (1536), which he imposed upon the entire country. Although these articles were in general a reaffirmation of the Catholic faith, they omitted the word *transubstantiation;* approached the Lutheran doctrine of justification by faith, though retaining the emphasis upon good works; declared the Bible and the three historic creeds to constitute the sum of the Christian faith; reduced the number of sacraments from seven to three; denied that the Roman Catholic Church could release souls from purgatory; and forbade the superstititious use of relics and images.

The tendency of many persons to go much further in the direction of Protestantism, however, prompted Henry to have Parliament pass the reactionary Six Articles Act of 1539, which reaffirmed six basic Catholic doctrines: (1) transubstantiation, (2) withholding the cup from the laity, (3) celibacy of the clergy, (4) the inviolability of monastic vows, (5) the saying of private Masses, and (6) the importance of oral confession. Denial of the first article was punishable with death. The penalty for the first denial of the others was imprisonment and forfeiture of property, for the second denial, death. Henry used this "Whip with the Six Strings" to force England into a conservative position. Yet the number of persons executed was not as high as in most other European countries. One cannot admire the king's despotic measures, but it must be admitted that they prevented internal confusion and civil war at a critical time in England's history.

Henry was less successful in producing a large, healthy progeny. The unfortunate Catherine was released from her disgrace by death in 1536. Not long thereafter, Anne Boleyn, who had not given the king a son, was accused of incest and adultery and was sent to the block. On the day of her death, Cranmer gave Henry a dispensation that permitted him to marry Jane Seymour, and soon afterwards Parliament declared Anne's daughter, Elizabeth, illegitimate. Jane gave birth to a son, the future Edward VI, but she died soon after the baptismal service.

Because of the threat of war, Henry remained single for more than two years, using the possibility of a marriage alliance to gain his diplomatic ends. Upon the advice of Cromwell he finally sought an alliance with the Protestant princes and agreed to marry Anne, the daughter of the duke of Cleves. Relying upon a flattering portrait made of Anne by the artist Hans Holbein the Younger, he signed a marriage alliance in October, 1539. When Anne arrived in England, the king, completely disillusioned with her looks and personality, reluctantly went through with the marriage ceremonies. But when the alliance failed to produce the desired results and all danger of a war with Charles V seemed remote, he had Convocation declare the marriage null and void and sent Cromwell to the block, charged with having treasonably favored the Protestant cause. He then married Catherine Howard, who was beautiful enough for Henry but lacked a sense of morality. When, after little more than a year, he learned that she had committed adultery, he had her beheaded. His sixth and last wife was Catherine Parr, whom he married in 1543. She not only survived Henry, her third husband, but lived to marry a fourth.

Henry's prior concern with his internal affairs was reflected in his foreign policy. He retained the alliance made with France in 1529 in the hope that Francis would obtain for him the papal annulment of his marriage with Catherine. Even though the annulment did not materialize, he continued the alliance until the renewed outbreak of the Hapsburg-Valois wars in 1536. For a number of years he negotiated with the Protestant princes but remained neutral until Francis, fearing an alliance between Henry and Charles, urged the Scots to attack England in 1542. Henry, who had long sought an opportunity to extend his rule to Scotland, allied himself with Charles and sent one army across the Channel and another across his northern border. His troops took Boulogne, but when Charles made peace with Francis, Henry had to do likewise (1546) and had to be satisfied with an indemnity and control of Boulogne. Although his army under the duke of Norfolk defeated the Scots at Solway Moss in 1542 and although a treaty was arranged to have the infant Scottish heiress Mary and the child Edward married after they had come of age, Henry could not carry out his plans. In Scotland, as in Ireland, he failed to conciliate opposition to his ambitions and bequeathed serious problems to his successors.

## Protestantism under Edward VI and in Scotland

When Henry died in 1547, England was in need of a strong ruler, for the treasury was empty and the Catholic forces on the Continent seemed poised to strike a vigorous blow against Protestantism. Moreover, the religious and social forces released by the separation from Rome were straining to break through the restrictions placed upon them by royal authority. But the new ruler, Edward VI (1547–1553), was a frail lad of ten years on his accession to the throne. The Council of Regency of sixteen nobles, chosen by Henry in his will to represent equally the old faith and the new, was at the outset dominated by King Edward's uncle, Edward Seymour, earl of Hertford, who was in 1547 made both lord protector and duke of Somerset. The Council of Regency was then reconstituted as a royal council of twenty-six members, with Somerset at its head. The lord protector, who retained complete control of the government for three years, did his utmost to unite Scotland with England, extend the Protestant Reformation, and alleviate the distress of the common people, who were being adversely affected by the enclosure of lands and gradually rising prices.

Although Somerset alienated the Scots by using force to achieve his ends and created social conflicts at home by trying to aid the poorer classes, Protestantism made noteworthy gains under his moderate and conciliatory leadership. Parliament abolished the worst features of the Treasons Act, repealed the Act of the Six Articles, legalized Communion in

King Edward VI of England

*by Hans Holbein the Younger*

Thomas Cranmer

*by G. Flicke*

251

both kinds and marriage of the clergy, and enforced the law of 1545 that had required the dissolution of chantries, or endowments for chanting Masses for the dead. Again, little of the wealth thus acquired was used for education. Most of it went to the crown. A *Book of Homilies* in English was adopted for reading in the churches, many ceremonies were abolished, and the use of English in the church services was required.

In 1549 Parliament passed the first Act of Uniformity, which imposed upon all churches the form of service outlined in Cranmer's *Book of Common Prayer*. It is difficult to assess the strong imprint that this notable work by Cranmer has made upon the religious development of the English people. His attempt to avoid the bitter continental conflict concerning the Lord's Supper is evinced in his occasionally ambiguous references to this sacrament. He seemed to deny transubstantiation in one place by referring to the Lord's Supper as a pious memorial, but he left the interpretation of the sacrament to the readers. Although clergymen deviating from this service were to be heavily punished, laymen were free to accept or reject it.

The *Book of Common Prayer* was soon set to music; but no great chorales were composed, such as had become popular in Lutheran Germany. True, a Psalter of thirty-seven psalms "in common metre" appeared in Edward's reign and was completed during that of Elizabeth; but it lacked beauty and religious fervor.

When the peasants whom Somerset had tried to help broke out in a revolt in Norfolk in what was known as Robert Kett's Rebellion, the lord protector was compelled to use force against them. Consequently the social reactionaries in his council, led by John Dudley, now made earl of Warwick, held him responsible for the disturbances, had Parliament depose him, and, in January, 1552, had him executed for treason. Warwick, who had himself created duke of Northumberland, became the president of the council but did not make himself lord protector. Much less liberal and tolerant than Somerset, he reversed the policy of the Tudors by supporting the enclosure of lands and carried out a much more radical Protestant program, while at the same time furthering his own interests and satisfying his greed for Church properties. Reformers from the Continent, among them Martin Bucer, Pietro Vermigli, Bernardino Ochino, and Jan à Lasco, came to England at the invitation of Cranmer, in part to help him formulate a confession common to all the Protestants. Among those who could not accept the invitation was Melanchthon, who had gained a reputation abroad for his conciliatory attitude. Martin Bucer taught at Cambridge, Pietro Vermigli at Oxford. Congregations of refugees were established in London that were for a while led by Lasco.

A second Act of Uniformity (1552) made compulsory the use of a revised edition of the *Book of Common Prayer*. This edition shows the influence of Martin Bucer, who shortly before his death had submitted to

# 6. New Forms of Protestantism

Cranmer, at the latter's request, a detailed criticism of the first edition. In the new edition priests were referred to as ministers, altars as tables, and the Lord's Supper as a remembrance of Christ's sacrificial death. But Cranmer never accepted the view that the sacrament was a mere sign, for he believed that it conveyed to the believer what it signified. Punishment for using other services was now meted out upon laymen as well as the clergy, and all were compelled to attend the authorized Sunday services.

Cranmer's moderate Forty-two Articles defining faith were sanctioned by the royal council. Influenced by both Lutheranism and Calvinism, yet showing great originality, they contained such distinctly Protestant doctrines as justification by faith, emphasized the sole authority of the Bible, denied transubstantiation while still affirming Christ's real, spiritual presence, and accepted only two of the seven sacraments of Catholicism.

The attempts of Northumberland to suppress all heterodox opinion and also his use of confiscated Church wealth for himself and his friends led to much opposition and prepared the way for the Catholic reaction under Mary Tudor. His political ambitions reached their most daring form in his plot to exclude Mary from the throne and to crown in her stead Lady Jane Grey, who had married his eldest son Guilford Dudley. This plot failed and all three eventually were executed in face of the loyalty of the great majority of Englishmen to Mary.

## The Reformation in Scotland

In Scotland, as in England, the way for the penetration of Protestantism had been prepared by the Lollards and the humanists, though to a lesser degree. During the reign of James V (1513–1542), Lutheran tenets gained such a strong hold that they were not entirely superseded by those of Calvin in the latter half of the sixteenth century. Dissatisfaction with the Church was particularly strong in Scotland, for it owned about a half of the country's wealth and enforced the payment of tithes. The wealth was enjoyed by the higher clergy and some favored nobles, and the tithes were paid primarily by the lower clergy and the people. Moreover, the higher clergy generally supported the crown in its conflicts with the barons, with the consequence that the barons turned to Protestantism when Mary of Lorraine, widow of James V and mother of the infant Mary, became regent of Scotland and sought to bring the country under the influence of France and her brothers, the Guises.

The fact that the Scottish Parliament passed an act in 1525 forbidding the importation of Luther's books shows how early the German reformer's doctrines had spread to Scotland. Tyndale's translation of the New Testament also gained a wide circulation soon after its publication.

Propagandists of the new faith made their appearance in Scotland at an early date. Among them was a Frenchman, M. de la Tour, who accompanied the Scottish regent to Scotland in 1523 and who was burned at the stake in Paris in 1527 for spreading Lutheranism. Much more in-fluential was Patrick Hamilton, a Scottish humanist of noble blood, closely related to the king. He had studied at Paris, at Louvain, and in Germany prior to becoming a teacher at the University of St. Andrews in 1523. He openly propagated Lutheran doctrines until 1526, when he was cited for heresy by James Beaton, archbishop of St. Andrews, and fled to Germany. There he visited Wittenberg and attended the opening of the new University of Marburg in Hesse. After his return to St. Andrews early in 1528, he was tried and burned for heresy.

The persecutions during the reign of James V, though relatively few in number, merely served to drive Lutheranism underground and to pro-duce a large number of fearless leaders. These came out into the open after the death of the king in 1542. One of the most courageous Protes-tant leaders was George Wishart, who probably had visited both Ger-many and Switzerland. He accepted the Zwinglian interpretation of the Lord's Supper and published an English translation of the First Helvetic Confession. Upon his return to Scotland in 1543 or 1544, he spread his Protestant views in the northern and western parts of the country and gained many faithful supporters, best known of whom was John Knox (1505–1572), a former Catholic priest, notary, and private tutor.

But a reaction had meanwhile set in under the leadership of David Cardinal Beaton. He had Wishart tried and burned for heresy in 1546. This pro-Catholic and pro-French movement was instrumental in nullify-ing the marriage treaty that the pro-Protestant and pro-English groups had arranged with Henry VIII in July, 1543. It also led to a renewal of the struggle between Scotland and England, as we have seen, and to acts of violence at home.

In May, 1546, some of Wishart's friends of noble birth, who had sworn to avenge his death, entered Cardinal Beaton's castle at St. An-drews, murdered him in his chamber, and hung his body over the castle wall—with the knowledge and support of Henry VIII. They then called John Knox to be their preacher and held the castle in the name of the English until July, 1547, when French ships came to the aid of the regent and took the defenders, including Knox, to France and forced them to serve on the French galleys. The next year the Scottish Parliament, now controlled by the Catholics, accepted the French proposal that the infant Mary, Queen of the Scots, marry the French dauphin Francis, later King Francis II. To keep her out of danger, she was sent to Brittany, where she spent a happy childhood.

After nineteen months on the French galleys, Knox went to England, where he became one of the favored preachers of Edward VI's reign. But he left England with the Marian exiles in 1554 and went to Geneva and later to Frankfurt. After a bitter dispute with English divines at Frank-furt over the *Book of Common Prayer,* he returned to Geneva.

Meanwhile Mary of Lorraine had become the leader of the Catholic opposition to England during the war that was concluded in 1550. Capable as she was, however, she made the mistake of planning with the Guises and the French king to bring the country completely under French influence. When, in 1554, she brought in a number of French soldiers and advisers, resentment against her spread rapidly, especially among the barons. After the marriage of Mary and Francis in 1558, a large number of barons joined the forces of nationalism and Calvinism in defiance of the regent and the queen. But this story must be told in connection with the introduction of Calvinism into Scotland.

## Calvin to 1536

Whereas Lutheranism was confined largely to Germany and the Scandinavian countries, where it lost much of its earlier dynamic character, Calvinism, developed in France and Geneva, became an aggressive force that penetrated much of western Europe and even parts of Germany. The growth commenced during the last decade of Luther's life and continued with increasing vigor during the latter half of the sixteenth century, during which period it was embraced principally by the vigorous bourgeois elements engaged in political, economic, and social struggles with the old order. So strong was this connection that Max Weber and others have concluded that Calvinism exerted a powerful influence upon the growth of capitalism. Be that as it may, Calvinism became a dynamic international force that threatened to supersede Catholicism during the latter half of the century as Lutheranism had during the first.

John Calvin (Jean Cauvin—John early adopted the name Calvin, the Latinized form of Cauvin), who gave his name to this powerful religious movement, was born in the episcopal town of Noyon in Picardy, about sixty miles northeast of Paris, July 10, 1509. His ambitious father, Gérard Cauvin, had moved to Noyon from Port l'Evêque on the Oise River in 1481, had deserted manual labor for the profession of law and administration, had acquired the rights of the bourgeoisie, and had obtained a number of important offices in the town: he was one of the registrars of the town government, solicitor to the bishop and the cathedral chapter, secretary of the bishopric, attorney for the clergy, and fiscal agent for the county. He had increased his influence by marrying Jeanne Le Franc, the pious daughter of a well-to-do, retired innkeeper from Cambrai. He also had become a friend of the prominent noble family of Hangest, which gave two bishops to the diocese of Noyon during Gérard's lifetime.

Because Gérard was ambitious for his three sons, Charles, John, and Antoine, he sent them to an endowed school, where John displayed unusual proficiency in his studies and an interest in religion. In 1521, when John was only twelve years old but was preparing for the priesthood, his father obtained for him a benefice, or living, from the cathedral chapter. He received a second benefice six years later.

In 1523, at the age of fourteen, John was sent to the University of Paris with three sons of the Hangest family, accompanied by their tutor. He went to live with his uncle, Richard Cauvin, and then entered, with his young friends, the Collège de la Marche. There he had the good fortune of being instructed by Mathurin Cordier, one of the outstanding Latinists of his day. He soon transferred to the Collège de Montaigu, where Rabelais and Erasmus had studied and to which Ignatius Loyola came about the time that Calvin left.

John finished the customary arts curriculum and then studied at the Sorbonne, the citadel of religious orthodoxy. He followed the usual theological course along scholastic lines, attending lectures on the Bible and Peter Lombard's *Sentences*. That he was not the asocial being that his detractors have attempted to make of him is shown by the fact that he retained the friendship of the Hangest boys and became intimately acquainted with the family of the Swiss Guillaume Cop, member of the faculty of medicine and first physician of the French king. One of the sons of Guillaume, Nicholas, later became associated with Calvin in his first attack upon reactionary scholasticism, and another, Michel, later became a pastor at Geneva. John likewise associated with a fellow townsman and older relative, Pierre Robert, nicknamed Olivétan because he burned midnight oil studying. Already strongly influenced by Lutheran doctrines, Olivétan left Paris for Orléans soon after and later settled in Strassburg.

Calvin's studies in Paris were interrupted by his father's decision that he should give up theology for law. It seems as though this decision was prompted by Gérard's difficulties over fiscal matters with the cathedral chapter, which was at that time at odds with the new bishop, to whom Gérard gave his loyal support. In any event, John readily complied with his father's wishes and in 1528 went to Orléans, which had a much better faculty of law than Paris. Although there is nothing to indicate that he as yet had embraced Protestant opinions, he must have been influenced by the love for humanism and the spirit of inquiry that prevailed among the teachers and students at Orléans. Both Erasmus and Reuchlin had taught there. Calvin made use of his opportunities for studying, even to the point of injuring his health.

In 1529 Calvin went to Bourges to attend the lectures of a reputedly brilliant professor of law who employed humanist methods in his teaching. Although Calvin did not remain there long, his stay was important, for there he became the friend of the German Greek scholar Melchior Volmar (Wolmar), a man with Lutheran leanings whom he had met at Orléans and from whom he now learned Greek and probably also Hebrew. At Volmar's home he must have met a young lad of ten years,

Theodore Beza (de Bèze), whose parents had placed him under the care of this renowned teacher. Beza was destined to become Calvin's close friend, his successor in Geneva, and his biographer.

Calvin returned to Paris early in 1531 to see through the press a defense of one of the law professors of Orléans for which he had written a preface. While there he learned of the serious illness of his father. He therefore went to Noyon, where Gérard died soon after. The fact that the father had not bowed to the wishes of the cathedral chapter in the conflict over fiscal matters but had dared to accept excommunication by it undoubtedly had some influence upon John's attitude toward the Church, even though his brother Charles succeeded in having the ban lifted so that the father could be buried in consecrated ground.

The death of Calvin's father relieved him of his obligation to continue the study of law, although he must have completed the required work, for he received the degree of licentiate in law in Orléans the next year. Consequently he turned his attention almost completely to the more congenial pursuit of humanism, then flourishing in Paris under the encouragement of Francis I; continued the study of Greek and Hebrew; and published at his own expense his *Commentary on Seneca's Treatise on Clemency* (1532), a moral treatise written by the Roman Stoic philosopher and statesman for his former pupil, Emperor Nero. Although the commentary deals with ethical matters, there is no evidence of Protestant leanings in it. On the contrary, it is a typical product of Erasmian humanism. Calvin's quotations are drawn almost exclusively from Latin and Greek sources, only three from the Vulgate translation of the Bible. Like many other young humanists, Calvin sought by means of this first publication to obtain a position as a teacher.

As far as we know, Calvin showed no strong leanings toward Protestantism before 1533. It was in that year that he became intimately associated with Gérard Roussel, whom Francis I had permitted to preach his evangelical views to large crowds at the Louvre, and continued his friendship with Nicholas Cop, a professor of philosophy who was made rector of the University of Paris in October of that year. Encouraged by the friendly attitude of the king toward the humanist reformers, the extremists determined to make public their religious views as well as their hostility toward the scholastic theologians of the Sorbonne, who had recently suppressed the devotional *Mirror of a Sinful Soul*, written by the king's sister Margaret. This extremist statement was made in Cop's inaugural address, in which he emphasized the importance of God's grace in obtaining salvation, minimized the role of good works, and attacked the intolerance of the Sorbonne theologians. Although much of the address was drawn from an All Saints' Day sermon of Luther, as well as from Erasmus' preface to the third edition of his New Testament, it was not an open statement of Protestantism. Yet the theologians accused Cop of heresy and induced officers of the Parlement to initiate proceedings against him. Consequently he fled, ultimately arriving at Basel.

When the officers of the Parlement went to arrest Calvin, whom they accused of having been involved in the writing of the address, he also fled. Although befriended by Margaret, he decided to remain for a while at Saintonge near Angoulême under the pseudonym of Charles d'Espeville. At Saintonge, where he remained for about half of 1534, he was the guest of an influential student friend, Louis du Tillet, and had access to the large personal library of his companion's father, in which it is supposed that he wrote his first draft of the *Institutes*. While at Saintonge he also had an opportunity to visit Jacques Lefèvre, the aged humanist reformer, who was living his last days at Nérac, the capital of French Navarre, under the protection of Margaret of Angoulême. There also Calvin decided to resign his ecclesiastical benefices rather than take orders in the Church, which he would have been compelled to do if he had kept the benefices beyond the age of twenty-five. It is now generally accepted that it was at this time that he experienced what he later called his sudden conversion, for he was working on the *Institutes,* returned to Noyon to give up his benefices, and, after his release from a short imprisonment in his native town, began his period of wandering, accompanied by Tillet.

At Poitiers and Orléans Calvin found many evangelical-minded people, to whom he preached and for whom he administered the Lord's Supper in a simple, Protestant form. At the same time he wrote his first theological treatise, the *Psychopannychia (Vigil of the Soul)*, in which he attacked those evangelical radicals who held that between death and the final judgment the soul remained in an unconscious state. In this work he showed his complete reliance upon the Bible as his religious authority but evinced his dislike of heresy and strife. It was not, however, an attack upon Catholicism.

When, after the affair of the placards in the autumn of 1534, the French Protestants were severely persecuted, Calvin and Tillet fled via Metz to Strassburg, where they visited with Bucer, and finally to Basel, where they arrived early the next year. In this city, which had become Protestant in 1529, Calvin came into contact with such important Protestants as Wolfgang Capito, a humanist professor and evangelical preacher; Simon Grynaeus, a teacher of Hebrew; Oswald Myconius, the chief pastor of the city; Heinrich Bullinger, Zwingli's successor at Zurich; and Pierre Viret, who later became Calvin's colleague in Switzerland. Following his natural inclination to live in scholarly seclusion, he devoted himself to the study of Hebrew, assisted Olivétan in preparing his French Bible for publication for the Waldensians, and published the first edition of his *Institutes of the Christian Religion* (March, 1536).

The *Institutes,* a masterful, scholarly synthesis of Protestant thought, was originally written, as Calvin stated in the prefatory letter to Francis

I, to provide those interested in religion with the simple rudiments of religious knowledge; but it was now published for the purpose of defending his French Protestant brethren from the calumnies and persecutions that had threatened to wipe them out after the affair of the placards. In bold and fearless language Calvin stated that it was the duty of the French king to read this defense with an open mind and warned him that if he persisted in the persecution of the faithful, God would deliver the despised and punish the persecutors.

Although this first edition of the *Institutes* was published when Calvin was but twenty-six years of age and although it was much smaller than subsequent editions, it contained all the essential doctrines of the Calvinist theological system. Following the traditional scheme of the catechisms of his day, Calvin presented his exposition of the Ten Commandments, the Apostles' Creed, the Lord's Prayer, and the Sacraments in four chapters; but he added two more, one on the "false sacraments" and another on Christian liberty, ecclesiastical government, and civil administration.

The doctrines here set forth constitute a logical synthesis of the teachings of Augustine and other Church fathers, the scholastic theologians, the Christian humanists, Luther, and the Rhenish Protestants, for Calvin was a logical thinker and organizer rather than a primarily creative theologian like Luther. He followed Duns Scotus in his emphasis upon the majesty and absolute sovereignty of God and God's almighty, inscrutable will. From this he drew the conclusion that man was utterly worthless in the sight of God, that he could be saved only by the grace of God through the redemptive death of Christ on the cross. His distinctive emphasis upon divine predestination, or election, as a doctrine to give assurance and confidence to those who lived Christian lives was developed at a later date. The law, he maintained, was given to man not as a rule of salvation but as a mirror to show him his utter helplessness because of original sin, to serve as a warning to obstinate sinners, and to constitute a discipline for faithful believers.

Calvin explained, in the second chapter, that faith, given to the elect by the Holy Spirit through the word of God, was not a mere recognition of biblical truths but the placing of all hope and confidence in God and Christ's atoning death. Prayer, he stated in the third chapter, was the only way in which the Christian could approach God, for his own works could not save him.

The second half of the book seems to have been based to some degree upon Luther's *The Babylonian Captivity*. In the fourth chapter Calvin defined the sacraments as external signs that confirmed God's promises to the believers. Baptism, which should be administered to infants as well as adults, served to strengthen faith in the forgiveness of sins and provided an opportunity to confess God before men. The Lord's Supper was an exercise of faith. Whereas he rejected the medieval conception of the Mass as a sacrifice, he believed with Luther that Christ was "truly and efficaciously" present at the Lord's Supper, though in a spiritual, not a physical, sense.

Much more vigorous were Calvin's attacks upon Catholicism in his last two chapters. In the fifth he denied the sacramental character of the five remaining sacraments of Catholicism and attacked the medieval conception of orders, arguing that the Bible recognized only preachers and governors of the church called bishops, presbyters, or pastors, who were called with the consent of the congregations.

Calvin insisted that Christian liberty, treated in the concluding chapter, placed Christians above the law, although they freely submitted to it as a rule of life. This, however, did not preclude the proper enjoyment of the gifts of God such as property, food, wine, and the fine arts. Like Luther, he believed that God had instituted two governments for man, one spiritual and the other temporal. The former was to be ruled by ministers according to the Word of God alone, the latter by magistrates according to such civil and criminal laws as were necessary to maintain peace and an ordered society. The maintenance of peace and order, as in medieval times, involved punishment for "idolatry, sacrilege against the name of God, blasphemies against His truth, or other public offences against religion." Moreover, the Christian owed absolute obedience to this government except when it acted contrary to the Word of God. Unlike many of the other reformers, Calvin agreed with the general view of the medieval churchmen that the church was independent of the state. As we shall see, his struggle with the government of Geneva was primarily over this issue.

Much of Calvin's time, to within five years of his death, was devoted to the elaboration, clarification, and enlargement of this important and influential treatment of theology. A second edition, enlarged to seventeen chapters and intended as a doctrinal introduction to the study of the Bible, was published in Latin in Strassburg in 1539. Still dissatisfied, he made five additional revisions before publishing the final, definitive edition of 1559. This last edition was five times the size of the original and was given an entirely new arrangement. The materials were now divided into four books treating respectively of the Father, the Son, the Holy Ghost, and the Holy Catholic Church, each book containing from seventeen to twenty-five chapters, which in turn were divided into sections.

The first French translation of the *Institutes* was made by Calvin himself from the Latin edition of 1539 and was published in 1541. All subsequent Latin editions were followed by French translations. The final French edition, begun by Calvin as an entirely new translation, was published in 1560, but because it is not the equal of the edition of 1541 in clarity and style, it is generally assumed that it was dictated by Calvin, though not edited by him before publication. The French editions played an important role not only in the popularization of religious thought in French-speaking lands but in the development of the French vernacular as a literary vehicle.

Despite the fact that Calvin hoped to devote himself solely to his religious studies, the publication of the *Institutes* with its prefatory letter to Francis I forced him out of this seclusion, for it demonstrated to the French Protestants, who had hitherto been leaderless, that here was a man who not only had the ability to express himself clearly but could speak fearlessly for them. Yet it appears that before the book was off the press, Calvin had set out for Italy with Tillet, in all likelihood to visit Renée, wife of the duke of Ferrara and daughter of Louis XII of France, to seek her aid on behalf of his French brethren. Although she could do little for him at the time because of the opposition of her husband, she became his devoted follower and faithfully corresponded with him to the time of his death. After her husband's death she went to France and openly joined the Huguenots during the religious wars.

Calvin left Ferrara probably in April, 1536, and went by way of Basel to Paris, where there was a temporary lull in the persecution of the Protestants, to take care of some family business. In June he was once more on his way out of France, taking with him his younger brother, Antoine, and their sister, Marie. It seems as though Calvin was headed for Strassburg, where he hoped to settle down to a scholarly life, far removed from persecution and religious strife. But because the imperial troops were stationed along his way, preparatory to attacking the French in the third of the Hapsburg-Valois wars (1536–1538), he was forced to make a long detour through Geneva, where he arrived in the latter half of July, 1536.

Although Calvin intended to remain in Geneva only for the night, Farel, who was having great difficulties organizing the church in the newly reformed city, asked him to remain. When he pleaded that he was not the person for the task, Farel countered with the statement that God would curse him if he followed his own scholarly pursuits rather than Christ. Calvin yielded to this "dreadful adjuration" and, with the exception of a short exile, devoted the rest of his life and his remarkable talents for organization to molding the church of Geneva into a new form, patterned after his conception of the Word of God. So insistent was Farel that Calvin begin his new task immediately that he gave him only a few days for the purpose of straightening out his affairs in Basel.

# 7 The Emergence of Calvinism

## The Genevan Revolt

Because of the fortuitous circumstances that had combined to bring Calvin to Geneva, it is no wonder that he looked upon his work there as a direct commission from God. For this reason he remained firm in his determination to construct in this city a Christian community based upon the Word of God in the face of every kind of opposition. Geneva was destined to become the new center of Protestantism from which dynamic religious and political forces permeated all Europe. Whereas Lutheranism was being used by the German princes and cities to further their own political purposes, Calvinism, as developed in Geneva, exercised a profound influence upon the political development of much of western Europe. Whereas German pastors propounded the "pure doctrine" to their parishioners, leaving the state to develop a Christian police force and political ethics, Calvin and his followers left the strong imprint of their ethics upon the economic and social as well as the political ethics of Western civilization.

To show why Geneva became the center of Calvinism requires considerable explanation. As we have seen, most of the German cantons of Switzerland had accepted Zwinglian Protestantism by the time of Zwingli's death. Although most of these Protestant cantons had lost much of their reforming zeal, Bern, situated on the Protestant frontier, carried the Reformation into the adjacent French cantons of Valais, Geneva, and Neuchâtel.

One of the leading reformers supported by Bern was the fiery French Protestant, Guillaume Farel (1489–1565), who, as we have seen, had developed evangelical views while at Meaux and had fled to Basel in 1523. Driven in turn from Basel because of his vigorous opposition to Erasmus, he went to Montbeliard, Strassburg, and finally Bern. Late in 1526 he settled for a while at Aigle in Bernese territory, where he won many converts to Protestantism and helped make Bern itself a Protestant canton in 1528. Then, for about three years, he was an itinerant Protestant missionary in those parts of the Vaud that were administered jointly by Bern and Catholic Fribourg. Assisted by Pierre Viret (1511–1571), a Swiss native of Orbe, and Antoine Froment (1508–1581), like Farel a native of Dauphiné, he made Orbe, Grandson, and Morat important centers of expanding Protestantism. Neuchâtel became Protestant in 1530, Orbe and Grandson the following year. The next goal of these preachers was Geneva, which also figured prominently in the political ambitions of the city council of Bern.

## Political Conflicts

The episcopal city of Geneva, with a population of about seventeen thousand and situated on the southwestern tip of beautiful Lake Geneva (Leman), was an important gateway between the Alps and the Jura Mountains and was therefore coveted by both France and Savoy. It was long ruled by its own counts and bishops under the overlordship of the emperor, but the bishops succeeded in destroying the authority of the local counts by cooperating with the ambitious counts of Savoy (made a duchy by the emperor in 1417). The bishops, in turn, were forced to yield to the counts of Savoy the appointment of the episcopal deputy in Geneva.

Although the episcopal deputy was responsible for defending the city, jailing and executing prisoners, and trying certain civil and criminal cases, the bishop, still holding the city theoretically as a fief of the emperor, retained the rights to wage war, coin money, and hear appeals from the other civil and ecclesiastical courts. The townsmen, in 1387, obtained constitutional recognition of their custom of meeting in a general assembly for the purpose of selecting their officials, proclaiming laws, and concluding alliances. The officials, called syndics, and their counselors eventually constituted a Little Council of twenty-five, an executive body. By 1500 there were two other councils, the Council of Two Hundred and the Council of Sixty. The syndics assumed the right to maintain order and try important criminal cases. Thus, at the beginning of the Reformation, the government of Geneva was shared by the bishop, the episcopal deputy, and the townsmen.

The opposition of the townsmen to the house of Savoy was accentuated when, in the middle of the fifteenth century, the bishopric fell into the hands of Duke Amadeus VIII, elected pope at the Council of Basel. Although Amadeus was compelled to resign the papacy in favor of

Nicholas V, he retained the bishopric of Geneva, which office he had appropriated in 1444. After his death in 1451, the bishops were with but one exception incompetent creatures of the duke of Savoy.

When Bishop John (1513–1522), the notoriously immoral "Bastard of Savoy," oppressed the citizens beyond endurance, a revolutionary group of townsmen formed a party that they called *Eiguenots* (*Eidgenossen,* or confederates, from which the word *Huguenots* may have been derived) in opposition to those Genevans who favored Savoyard rule and were dubbed Mamelouks. To strengthen their position, the former made an alliance with Catholic Fribourg in February, 1519. But the short struggle that followed ended in an ignominious defeat for the *Eiguenots.* The duke compelled them to abandon their alliance with Fribourg and restored the authority of the bishop. But when, in 1525, the bishop left the city because he feared that the emperor might seize his lands after the emperor's victory at Pavia, the revolutionary party took this opportunity to conclude another alliance with Fribourg and one with Bern (1526); to force upon the bishop the acceptance of a Council of Two Hundred, patterned after a similar body in Bern and chosen by the Little Council; and later to abolish the authority of the episcopal deputy.

In 1530 the bishop, who had joined the forces of the duke, let loose upon the city a band of brigands. Bern, fearing that Geneva would be completely absorbed by Savoy, came to the aid of the city and drove out the brigands. But the Bernese did not want to see Geneva become independent. Therefore they restored both the episcopal deputy and the bishop. Nevertheless, the presence in Geneva of Protestant soldiers and the determination of Bern to spread evangelical doctrines there tended to intensify the revolutionary movement, for now religious motives were added to the political.

## Beginnings of Protestantism

Although the city government of Geneva preferred to retain Catholicism, it could not entirely ignore the wishes of its powerful Protestant ally, Bern. In October, 1533, Farel, accompanied by Olivétan and Antoine Saunier, came to Geneva with letters of recommendation to the council. However, when Farel was summoned by the episcopal deputy to appear before the episcopal court, he and his companions fled from the city, protected from the aroused people by the syndics. A month later he sent his young friend Antoine Froment to Geneva to propagandize the faith under the guise of teaching French. Froment gained such a large following that in January, 1534, he ventured to preach in a public square. Although the meeting was broken up and Froment was forced to flee, the nucleus of a Protestant congregation had been formed that included a number of prominent men.

In May, 1534, a riot occurred in Geneva in which a leader on the

Catholic side was killed. During the ensuing conflict between the two parties, the incompetent bishop of Geneva fled and the government was besieged by delegations from both Protestant Bern and Catholic Fribourg, urging it to settle the religious issue according to their respective wishes. Meanwhile Farel returned and, with the aid of his followers, seized the Franciscan monastery of Rive and began using its chapel as a Protestant church. When the government felt compelled to side with the stronger of its allies, Bern, Fribourg broke its alliance with Geneva. And when the bishop, having induced many of the inhabitants to leave Geneva, attacked the city with a strong military force and excommunicated the remaining citizens, the councils prepared for war and declared the bishop's office vacant. Although the majority of the remaining inhabitants were still Catholic, the awkward position of the councils gave Farel and Viret an opportunity to advance their cause, particularly by supporting the councils against the bishop, thereby linking Protestantism with the struggle for communal independence.

The tension was further increased in March, 1535, when a woman, supposedly instigated by the Catholic clergy, attempted to poison the Protestant leaders. In the circumstances Farel was able to persuade the syndics to authorize a public disputation between the Catholic clergy and the Protestant leaders that lasted throughout most of June, 1535. Because the bishop had forbidden the clergy to participate, only two clergymen with uncertain religious views ventured to present the Catholic side. Farel and Viret easily convinced the council of the superiority of the Protestant position. Thus encouraged, they seized a number of churches for their services. In August of that year they even took over the Cathedral of St. Pierre. In each case the mobs pillaged and broke images. On August 10 the Council of Two Hundred suspended the Catholic Mass. The confirmation of this action in November marks the definite break of Geneva with Rome. As a consequence, most of the Catholic clergy left the city.

## Success of Revolt

Meanwhile the political position of Geneva was becoming most critical. Although the bishop, with the aid of the duke of Savoy, was plundering the environs of the city and almost completely shutting off its contact with the outside world, Bern refused to send assistance, apparently in the expectation that Geneva's desperation would eventually lead its councils to come under Bernese jurisdiction in return for aid. But an unexpected change in diplomatic affairs made the Bernese alter their tactics. When Charles V, in preparation for his third war with Francis I, won Savoy to his side, the French king offered to aid the Genevans. Bern, fearing that much of the war would now be fought in western Swiss lands and that Geneva would eventually be absorbed by the French, declared war on

Savoy in January, 1536. It easily defeated the Savoyard troops, entered Geneva in February, and in March completed the seizure of the Vaud.

Although Bern demanded the rights over Geneva formerly held by Savoy, the protracted negotiations ended in freedom for Geneva, which even obtained the twenty-eight villages that had belonged to the episcopal see. In the elections of February, 1536, all the syndics chosen were supporters of Farel. Under their leadership the government assumed all the functions of the bishop, passed a number of edicts regulating the morals of the city, and ordered the citizens to attend sermons under penalty of fines—ample evidence that the strict regulation of conduct in Geneva did not originate with Calvin.

Despite the fact that the government of Geneva was to all intents autocratic, the general assembly continued not only to elect its syndics and treasurer—after 1529 also the five judges of the lower civil and criminal court—but also to give its assent to important matters touching the entire community. Therefore the question of becoming Protestant was laid before the citizens—heads of families—at a meeting of the general assembly in the Cathedral of St. Pierre on Sunday, May 21, 1536. On that occasion the people unanimously agreed "to live in this holy evangelical law and word of God" and to abandon "all Masses and other papal ceremonies and abuses, images and idols."

The unanimous action of the general assembly must not be construed as a unanimous support of Protestantism but rather as an expression of approval of the successful revolt against the bishop and Savoy. Moreover, the break with Rome occurred without adequate plans having been made for administering the church. In view of the previous experience of the councils in dealing with ecclesiastical matters, it appeared as though Geneva might develop a state church similar to those of Zurich, Bern, and other Swiss cities. But the lack of a creed and separate church discipline, as well as the relatively low state of popular morals, accentuated by years of living under secularized bishops, made the task of the Protestant leaders an extremely difficult one. Farel showed not only his Christian humility but also knowledge of human nature when he realized that he was unable to cope with the difficult problems and insisted that the young Calvin help him carry the responsibilities.

## Calvin at Geneva and Strassburg (1536–1541)

When Calvin returned to Geneva about the middle of August, 1536, after a short visit to Basel, he was given the position of "reader in Holy Scripture in the church of Geneva" and began lecturing on St. Paul's Epistle to the Romans. He was not an ordained minister and was not made a regular preacher until nearly a year later. The Genevan city government knew so little about him that its secretary referred to him in the

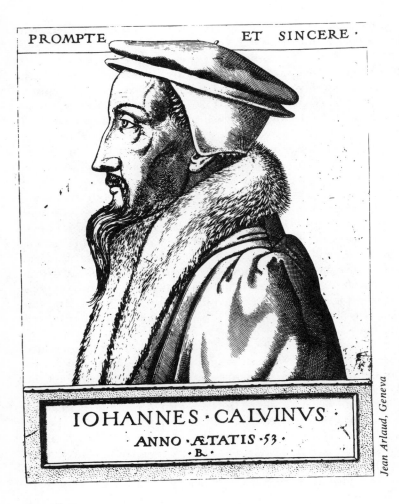

PROMPTE · ET SINCERE ·

IOHANNES · CALVINVS ·
ANNO · ÆTATIS · 53 ·
· B ·

Jean Arlaud, Geneva

John Calvin

*by René Boyvin*

268

register as "that Frenchman." He was given no income until February of the following year.

It was not long, however, before the city councils and the people of Geneva recognized the dynamic force and determination of their new religious leader. Bern, which had seized the Vaud from Savoy, had demanded that a religious disputation be held in its principal city, Lausanne, to determine whether Protestantism should be introduced there. The disputation opened October 1. Whereas the Catholic representatives were feebly led by an enthusiastic but not well-educated layman, the chief Protestant protagonists were Farel, Viret, and Calvin. Although Calvin went to Lausanne in a minor role and did not participate in the debate for several days, he soon distinguished himself by his forceful, extempore attack upon the corporal presence of Christ in the Lord's Supper and the brilliant display of his knowledge of the writings of the Church fathers. The Protestants were declared the victors and a Protestant church was established under the patronage of Bern. Despite the fact that Viret had been the chief pastor in the district, Pierre Caroli, a native of northern France who declared that he had been converted by Farel's arguments in the disputation in Geneva, was given the position by Bern.

Calvin gained a greater reputation among the Swiss Protestant leaders at a synod that met in Bern October 16 to 18 to consider the adoption of the Wittenberg Formula of Concord. Martin Bucer had proposed this step in order to unite all the Protestants; but the discussions did not lead to that end.

## Organization of Protestantism in Geneva

The first important task confronting Calvin and Farel in Geneva was the drawing up of the Articles Concerning the Government of the Church, which were adopted by the Little Council and the Council of Two Hundred and promulgated as law on January 16, 1537. Written by Calvin and based on the principles enunciated in the *Institutes,* these Articles proposed a systematic discipline among all the citizens; a confession of faith on the part of all, because only "worthy members" of the church could participate in the Lord's Supper; a thorough instruction in the fundamentals of faith to prepare the young for the confession and for a useful Christian citizenship; the singing of Psalms as an embellishment of the divine service; and the establishment of a civil commission to judge matrimonial questions according to the word of God.

For the maintenance of discipline, the government was to appoint lay officials in each of the twenty-six wards, or districts, of Geneva to watch over the conduct of the people and to report those guilty of misconduct to the ministers, who in turn had the right to excommunicate recalcitrant sinners. If a culprit was rash enough to make sport of the excommunication, the government was to take appropriate measures to stop such con-

# Part Three: Spread of Protestantism

tempt and mockery. By demanding that all the citizens publicly confess their faith, the reformers hoped to differentiate between those who "preferred to belong to the kingdom of the pope rather than the kingdom of Christ."

The Articles also laid great stress upon the education of the young, who should be taught the "outline" of the Christian faith and be examined by the ministers at stated intervals during the year. Calvin therefore wrote in Latin the first Genevan Catechism, on the basis of which another reformer, probably Farel, wrote a confession of faith in twenty-one articles. Both were published in February, 1537, in a French translation under the title, *Instruction and Confession of Faith, as Used in the Genevan Church.*

When the Little Council promulgated the Articles with but few alterations, it was apparently unaware of their significant implications. The provision for the maintenance of ecclesiastical discipline by means of a consistory in which laymen as well as clergymen exercised functions of the church was a consequence of Calvin's determination to re-establish the original self-government of the church as it had existed in apostolic times. He believed that pastors should not only preach but watch over the lives of their flocks.

However, the Articles were not enforced, for Calvin and Farel were immediately compelled to defend themselves against serious opposition. The first attack came from Pierre Caroli, who had been preaching the efficacy of saying prayers for the dead despite the vigorous protests of Viret. Calvin went to Lausanne to aid Viret in the ensuing conflict. In February, 1537, the question in dispute was submitted to two commissioners of the city of Bern. Moving immediately from a defensive to an offensive position, Caroli accused Calvin and Farel of the denial of the doctrine of the Trinity, a most serious charge at that time, particularly because of the storm of protest that had been aroused by the publication of Servetus' views earlier in that decade. In the heated debate that followed, Calvin referred Caroli to the newly published Catechism and Confession of Faith. But when Caroli stated that these did not conform to the Nicene and Athanasian creeds, Calvin haplessly stated that Farel and he believed in God, not in Athanasius. For this reason the commissioners adjourned the hearing. Calvin and Farel then appealed for another hearing at a general synod.

Such a synod, however, did not convene until May 14. Meanwhile damaging rumors were spread concerning the Genevan reformers. When they finally appeared before a synod of more than a hundred French-speaking Protestant ministers at Lausanne, Calvin defended his position and attacked that of Caroli with such skill—and personal abuse—that he and Farel were pronounced orthodox and Caroli was dismissed. This action was confirmed by a synod of German-speaking ministers at Bern at the end of the same month. Thereupon the city council of Bern exonerated Calvin and Farel and forbade Caroli to preach anywhere in Bernese lands. The brilliant but unstable Caroli returned to France and the Catholic fold, once more became Protestant, and again returned to Catholicism. Despite the fact that Calvin and Farel were vindicated, the council of Bern reprimanded them sharply, and they were for a while looked upon with suspicion by many of the outstanding German and Swiss reformers.

Another attack came from within Geneva. Two Anabaptists from the Low Countries who had begun working in Geneva challenged Calvin and Farel to a disputation. Although the city councils ordered them to submit their religious views in writing, Farel, who disliked this procedure, obtained permission to hold a meeting with them. The discussions are not known to us, but we know that the councils suddenly put an end to them. Calvin and Farel then induced the councils to suppress those Genevans who had been converted to Anabaptism.

The danger of internal split from this source was thus averted, but a much more serious one appeared. As we have seen, the Council of Two Hundred and the Little Council, which had approved the Articles, were aristocratic and almost self-perpetuating bodies, for the former chose sixteen members of the latter, and the latter chose the members of the former. However, the general assembly chose the four syndics and the treasurer, who generally acted in an executive capacity. When Calvin and Farel attempted to enforce the provisions of the Articles, a number of the old Genevan families, who did not wish to submit to the authority of the ministers and had supported the Reformation chiefly for political reasons, formed a powerful opposition party whose chief leader was Jean Philippe.

The opposition party gained a considerable following when the Council of Two Hundred ordered the civil officials to bring the people of their respective districts to the Cathedral of St. Pierre to confess their faith. A large number of persons refused and were not intimidated by threats of banishment. During the bitter struggle that followed, Jean Philippe proposed the examination of the faith of the citizens by a civil commission. But Calvin and Farel, still supported by the councils, remained intransigent and decided to exclude the opponents of the confession from Communion in the following January. The government, however, was reluctant to go that far.

The annual election of February, 1538, brought the malcontents to power. Jean Philippe and three other opponents of the ministers were made syndics and ten new members were elected to the Little Council. Instead of trying to cooperate with the new syndics, who were still inclined to be reasonable, the ministers denounced their opponents from the pulpit in unrestrained language. Moreover, patriotic opposition to

Calvin and Farel, the "foreigners," was fanned to white heat when it was learned that a Frenchman had tried, although in vain, to induce two members of Calvin's party to support Francis I's proposal of an alliance between Geneva and France.

The crisis came when the Council of Two Hundred voted to accept the "ceremonies of Bern," that is, the use of the font in baptism and unleavened bread in the Lord's Supper, as well as the observance of Christmas, Easter, Ascension Day, and Pentecost, ceremonies and rites to which Calvin and Farel had voiced no strong objection although they had discontinued them in Geneva. Hoping to establish religious uniformity throughout its newly acquired French-speaking Swiss lands, the council of Bern wished to obtain the approval of these ceremonies at a synod to be convened at Lausanne March 31, 1538, and asked Geneva to accept the ceremonies and to send Calvin and Farel to the synod. Because virtually all the pastors of these French-speaking lands were supporters of Calvin and Farel, the situation required the utmost tact and patience. Nonetheless, the Council of Two Hundred not only did not ask advice of the ministers before reaching its decision but peremptorily ordered them to attend the synod.

Calvin and Farel dutifully went to Lausanne, but we have no record of what role they played there. The council of Bern informed the councils of Geneva that the synod had unanimously approved the ceremonies and asked the ministers to introduce them immediately in Geneva, even though the council of Bern had planned to submit the same question for further discussion to a synod of German-speaking Swiss pastors to be held in Zurich. When the Little Council summoned Calvin and Farel to appear and state whether or not they would observe the ceremonies, they asked for permission to withhold their decision, pending the outcome of the synod at Zurich, especially because Communion was to be celebrated on the next Sunday, Easter Day. Although they were dismissed for the time being, the council imprisoned one of their colleagues for having made derogatory remarks concerning the government and on Saturday evening sent a messenger to ask them whether they would use unleavened bread the next day. Farel was not located and Calvin gave no answer. Consequently they were both forbidden to preach.

## Expulsion of Calvin and Farel

On Easter morning, April 21, to the utter astonishment of all, Calvin preached at St. Pierre and Farel at St. Gervais; yet they both refused to administer the Lord's Supper, explaining that they did not consider the use of unleavened bread wrong but that administering the sacrament amid such disturbances would tend to desecrate it. Swords were drawn, and so great was the commotion that the ministers barely escaped with their lives. The Little Council immediately summoned the Two

Hundred to meet on Easter Monday. The larger council gave Calvin and Farel three days in which to leave Geneva and in turn summoned the general assembly to meet on Tuesday. This popular body upheld the decision of the councils by a majority vote. Calvin and Farel, however, did not await its decision but left immediately for Bern, where they easily convinced the council of that city that they had been harshly treated and had never opposed the ceremonies of Bern.

The exiles next appeared at the synod of Zurich and presented their *Articles of Zurich,* explaining their conception of the role of the church in matters of discipline and organization. Although the synod accepted the Articles and urged Bern to seek the reinstatement of the ministers, it advised Calvin and Farel to be patient in trying to carry out their reforms. But Geneva would not permit their return. Therefore, early in June, they journeyed to Basel. There the two men separated. Farel went to Neuchâtel, where he had previously preached, and Calvin yielded to the persistent urging of Bucer to become one of the ministers at Strassburg. Once again the young reformer was prevented from withdrawing into scholarly seclusion and was faced with the difficult, practical problems of a minister. This decision was followed by the permanent rupture of his friendship with Tillet, who had agreed with Calvin on many of his religious ideas but preferred to remain within the Catholic Church.

## Calvin at Strassburg

Few cities could have given Calvin a better example of steady and harmonious progress in the reform of the Church than Strassburg, a busy commercial and industrial center. Situated in the Rhine Valley between Germany and France and connected by water with Switzerland and the Low Countries, it was the great entrepôt of both material goods and religious ideas. Although the Reformation had been introduced there as early as 1523, the city council permitted Catholic worship to continue. Led by the exceptionally tolerant Matthias Zell, Wolfgang Capito, Caspar Hedio, and Martin Bucer, the Lutheran clergy welcomed religious fugitives from many parts of Europe, including the Anabaptists. In 1538 the Catholic bishop suggested to the Protestant council that it call the illustrious Lutheran educator Johann Sturm to establish the famous gymnasium of Strassburg.

The religious leadership in Strassburg eventually gravitated into the hands of Bucer. In 1530, as we have seen, this reformer began in earnest his attempts to find some theological formula that would bring unity to divided Protestantism. With his predilection toward concord he combined a practical bent, evinced, for example, in his refusal to consort with extremists. This made him a valuable guide and teacher for Calvin.

Bucer succeeded in having Calvin made pastor of the congregation of approximately four hundred French exiles in Strassburg. Provided with an income that barely kept body and soul together, he nevertheless enjoyed the difficult tasks connected with his new position and his associations with the Strassburg scholars and the city council. Consequently he purchased citizenship there in 1539, a step that he did not take in Geneva until eighteen years after his return to that city.

Among Calvin's important contributions in Strassburg was his translation and adaptation of the Protestant liturgy developed largely by Bucer. It provided for the following order of worship: invocation, prayer, confession, absolution, singing of the Table of the Law, Scripture reading, sermon, singing of a psalm or hymn, and benediction. He published it in 1542 under the title *Prayer Book for French Churches, According to the Word of God,* which became the model for later Calvinist forms of worship. In 1539 he compiled a book of eighteen psalms, versified in French by Clément Marot and himself and accompanied by musical notation. Much as he valued the use of song in the church service, he felt that the organ would detract from the simplicity of the worship and the importance of the sermon, and therefore opposed its use. Because his congregation consisted of exiles, he was relatively free to put into practice his ideas with respect to both church service and church discipline. He compelled the members of his congregation to come to him for examination in the faith before taking Communion and exercised the right to ban those whom he considered unworthy.

Calvin also found time to lecture on theology in the school established by Sturm, expounding first the Gospel of John and later St. Paul's Epistles to the Corinthians. These lectures were well attended, attracting eager young men from not only France but other parts of Europe. He also found time to publish some of his theological works. In 1539 appeared the first revised edition of the *Institutes,* followed by the first of his many scholarly commentaries, the one on St. Paul's Epistle to the Romans. Mention must also be made of his *Small Treatise on the Holy Supper,* written in Strassburg but published in Geneva in 1541. In this, as in the revised *Institutes,* he reflected Bucer's interpretation of that sacrament. At the suggestion of Bucer, he also prepared anew his *Psychopannychia* (1542), first written in 1534. In 1540, at the invitation of the city councils of Geneva, he wrote his famous *Reply to Sadoleto.* The scholarly and devout Jacopo Sadoleto (1477–1547) had written the Genevans a letter, admonishing them to return to the Catholic fold. Calvin's answer was a brilliant defense of Protestant principles, highly commended by Luther.

Calvin's three years at Strassburg were on the whole peaceful as well as productive. They were marred by only one significant personal conflict. Caroli, who had returned to Switzerland and Protestantism and had been welcomed with open arms by Farel, came to Strassburg. Bucer, wishing to reconcile Calvin and Caroli, had them both appear at a conference of Strassburg preachers and teachers, but separately, for Calvin would not meet Caroli face to face. When Caroli brought up the refusal of Calvin and Farel to sign the ancient creeds in 1537, Calvin flew into a rage that he later regretted. The incident illustrated Calvin's propensity to give way to nervous excitement and wrath, which frequently obscured his fine personal qualities and irenic spirit. Yet his judgment of Caroli's character and religious uncertainty was correct, for the latter was unable to get along with the clergy at Strassburg or later those at Metz.

A strong, personal influence was exercised by Calvin upon those young theological students to whom he gave room and board in order to augment his pitifully inadequate income. Most of these men became fervent preachers of the gospel.

Calvin's overwork and austere existence so weakened his health that he finally agreed to follow the advice and example of Bucer and others to marry someone who was "modest, decent, plain, thrifty, patient, and able to take care of my health." Negotiations were begun with the family of a girl of noble birth and considerable money but were ended by her refusal to learn French. A happy, though at first unromantic, match was finally made in August, 1540, with Idelette of Buren in Gelderland, the widow of an Anabaptist from Liége whom Calvin had converted to the theology of the *Institutes*. The marriage was a happy one, marked by mutual respect, companionship, and love. In July, 1542, Idelette gave premature birth to a son, Jacques, who lived only a few days. Idelette, her health seriously impaired, died in March, 1549.

Calvin's stay of three years at Strassburg coincided with the attempts made by Charles V to solve the religious problem in the Empire by means of conferences of theologians. Calvin's attendance at these conferences brought him into touch with the important leaders and significant issues of his day. In February, 1539, he went in an unofficial capacity to a conference at Frankfurt to gain help for the French Protestants. There he met Melanchthon, with whom he established a long friendship despite their theological differences. He also gained much value from his attendance at the colloquies at Hagenau (1540–1541), where he displayed exceptional ability in evaluating both men and issues. The city council of Strassburg, accepting the advice of Melanchthon, sent Calvin to the important but also unsuccessful colloquy at Regensburg in 1541, where he took no leading rule but observed the negotiations conducted by such well-known persons as the moderate Catholic Cardinal Contarini, the intransigent Eck, and the conciliatory Melanchthon.

Despite the fact that Calvin had found for himself an important niche in Strassburg, he could not forget Geneva, to which he felt that God had called him. After a serious inner struggle and protracted delay, he accepted the invitation of the city councils, now dominated by his former supporters. Although his basic views had changed little, he had learned much about methods and techniques at Strassburg. He had also developed his ideas concerning predestination, church organization, and universal Protestantism under the direct influence of his foremost teacher, Martin Bucer. Yet, whatever he had learned at Strassburg he made his own with independence, fearlessness, and penetrating logic.

## Church and State in Geneva (1541–1553)

Calvin's absence from Geneva had been felt almost from the outset, for the ministers who had been left in control of the church lacked his qualities of leadership, and the members of the various cliques that dominated the city councils lacked the vision and understanding required to create a Protestant church directed by the state. Moreover, factional political conflicts so greatly undermined the authority of the government that there was a complete reversal of position with respect to the exiled reformers.

The political ineptitude of the party in control was demonstrated in 1539 in the negotiations with Bern concerning a new treaty that was to compose difficulties arising out of the original treaty of 1536. The Genevan representatives strangely accepted the twenty-one articles of the treaty, unfavorable to Geneva in almost every respect. But a copy was not placed before the Little Council until about three months later. Although this body refused to accept the treaty, it did not notify the council of Bern until five more months had passed. When the provisions of the treaty became known to the inhabitants of Geneva, they nicknamed the negotiators, and then also the party in power, the Articulants, or Artichauds, because of the articles.

Obviously this turn of events gave the opposition party, called Guillermins because they supported Guillaume Farel, their opportunity. In the election of February, 1540, two of their number were chosen syndics. When Bern tactlessly tried to compel Geneva to accept the treaty, the three negotiators of the treaty were compelled to flee the wrath of the populace, and their places on the Little Council were filled by Guillermins, which gave that party a majority. When, in June of that year, the negotiators were condemned to death, the excitement was reflected in a street brawl in which the hotheaded Jean Philippe, leader of the Artichauds, became involved and two persons were killed. Philippe was arrested, compelled by torture to admit that he had killed one of the victims, and beheaded. A second of the four syndics who had exiled Calvin and Farel died from injuries received when he was trying to escape from Geneva, and the other two were in prison, sentenced to death.

In these circumstances, it is not strange that the religious situation became critical and that public morality steadily declined. Consequently a number of Genevans began to demand the recall of Calvin. The church council, which the exiles had expected would exonerate them, was never convened. But the chief pastor of Bern, upon the request of Farel, called a meeting of the ministers of French Switzerland, including the Genevan ministers, in March, 1539, at which time Calvin and Farel were pronounced faithful in their service. Their successors recognized their mistake in not having consulted the exiles before assuming their posts in Geneva, and unity was restored among the French-speaking Protestant ministers. Subsequently Calvin wrote his most zealous partisans, urging them to support his successors, and, as we have seen, acceded to the request of the councils by answering Sadoleto's appeal to the Genevans to return to Catholicism.

After the Guillermins were in control of the government, their leaders, hoping to secure their victory by establishing internal order, induced the Little Council to make every attempt to bring Calvin back to Geneva. In October, 1540, the Two Hundred and the general assembly formally invited him to return. Calvin's friends were informed about the intentions of the councils and began to urge him to accept the invitation. Chief of these was Farel, who, although he had a right to resent the fact that he himself had not been asked to return, finally succeeded in convincing Calvin that it was God's will that he resume his work in Geneva. He even threatened to break off his friendship with Calvin if he refused to follow the divine will.

On September 13, 1541, Calvin, at the age of thirty-two, entered the city that was to be his residence for the rest of his life. In a confident and businesslike manner he immediately appeared before the city councils, took an oath that he would "be forever the servant of Geneva," and asked for a committee that would help him draw up a constitution for the church. The councils made his return easy by treating him with deference, providing him with a handsome home and garden overlooking the lake, and voting him a salary and allowances that finally ended his years of poverty. Calvin on his part made no melodramatic mention of his years in exile but promptly resumed the work that had been interrupted in 1538.

## The Genevan Church

Determined that he would proceed on his own terms, he immediately began to draft the Ecclesiastical Ordinances, the constitution of the church of Geneva, with the assistance of a committee of six members appointed by the Little Council. This task was completed in three weeks, and the proposals were then submitted to the Little Council, which examined them, made certain changes, and in turn submitted them to the Two Hundred, which passed them with minor alterations. They were approved by the general assembly November 20, 1541.

Although this ecclesiastical constitution did not grant Calvin all that he had desired, it permitted the church of Geneva a greater degree of freedom than that obtained for their churches by Luther, Zwingli, Bucer, and other reformers. The basic principles were those of the Articles of 1537 as modified by Calvin's experiences with the administrative system in Strassburg, adjusted to the situation in Geneva, and justified by appeal to the primitive Christian church as described in St. Paul's Epistles (Ephesians 4:11; I Corinthians 12:28; Romans 12:7). He thereby obtained divine sanction for the constitution, which placed the administration of discipline in the hands of the church, supported by the state. To carry out this provision, he was compelled to struggle with the city government the rest of his life.

The central and novel feature of the Ordinances was the recognition of the four divinely sanctioned offices of pastors, teachers, elders, and deacons, a division foreshadowed in the Strassburg church order of 1534 and in Bucer's church order for Hesse, published in 1539. The pastors, five in number in 1541, with three assistants, constituted the venerable company and were charged with preaching the gospel, administering the sacraments, and admonishing the members. They met in what they called a congregation every Friday to study the Bible and discuss theology. Four times a year they discussed their own qualifications as ministers. If they could not agree in important matters, they had to submit them for decision to the elders and, as a final recourse, to the city government, which served as a supreme court.

New ministers were to be elected by the venerable company after approval of the candidates by the government. The provision that the people had the right of "common consent" to the election meant little in practice. Contrary to Calvin's wishes, the "laying on of hands" at induction to office was not practiced. The incumbent gave a twofold oath: to be faithful to God in spiritual matters and to the state in secular matters.

To facilitate the administration of the church, the city was divided into three parishes. Services were frequent, as measured by our standards. Sermons were preached at two of the churches at daybreak on Sundays and at all of them at nine. Catechism classes were held at noon for the youth to the age of sixteen—when they made their profession of faith— followed by sermons in all the churches again at three o'clock. There was preaching in all the churches on Mondays, Wednesdays, and Fridays, and by 1560 on every day of the week. Although Calvin wanted to have the Lord's Supper celebrated at least once a month, he had to be content with its celebration four times a year. His request for permission to use the baptismal font was denied.

Calvin considered the teachers, or doctors, who were to instruct the young in "sound doctrine," part of the clergy and wished to have them appointed exclusively by the venerable company. But he was compelled by the Little Council to present the prospective teachers for examination to a committee of two members. The school, provided by the Ordinances, was to be served by a "teacher-in-chief," or principal, two "readers," and "bachelors" who taught the lowest age groups.

The elders, or presbyters, like their counterparts in Strassburg, were laymen who were responsible for the maintenance of discipline among the members of the congregation. The constitution provided that the Little Council choose twelve elders, corresponding to the number of apostles, with the advice of the ministers and subject to the approval of the Two Hundred. Two were to be members of the Little Council, four of the Council of Sixty, and six of the Two Hundred. Each elder had supervision of one of the twelve districts into which the city was divided. He was expected to visit each family in his district at least once a year.

The deacons, who were chosen in the same manner as the elders, assisted the pastors by supervising poor relief, visiting needy and sick members, and administering the city hospital, which cared for not only the sick but the widows and orphans. As in many other cities, the townsmen of Geneva were opposed to begging and sought to care for the poor and unfortunate in an orderly manner.

The heart of Calvin's administrative system was the consistory, made up of the twelve elders and the ministers, five in number at first. It met every Thursday, presided over by one of the syndics of the city government. Although Calvin did not preside, except occasionally as vice-president, he dominated the body from the beginning and through it successfully carried out his struggle with the government over the right of the church to independence in disciplinary as well as doctrinal matters.

Significant is the fact that the laymen in the consistory outnumbered the clergy and were considered officers of the church as well as the state. Citizens guilty of opposition to the accepted doctrine, or absence from church services, and of conduct unbecoming Christians were summoned to appear before that body for admonition, reprimand, and correction. In serious cases involving civil jurisdiction and penalties, the accused were turned over to the councils for judgment and punishment. In other cases the consistory could not only admonish and reprimand but excommunicate, although Calvin had been forced to accept the Little Council's interpretation that the civil authority was in no way impaired with respect to the right to excommunicate. It was over this issue that Calvin fought a bitter struggle with the councils until 1553, when he finally achieved independence of action for the consistory.

On the other hand, Calvin had no intention of invading the particular spheres of activity traditionally reserved for the civil authority. He followed Luther in maintaining that the secular government, like the church, was divinely established and that each had its own sphere of responsibilities. But Calvin, like Bucer, went further than Luther in asserting that the state was obligated to protect the church, establish the "true faith," safeguard private property, promote morality, and regulate the lives of its inhabitants according to the "word of God," or moral law. Thus religion became a law.

The form of government did not seem to concern Calvin much, for he believed that monarchy, aristocracy, and democracy were all supported by Scripture. However, he became increasingly distrustful of monarchy, which tended to detract from the majesty of God and endanger liberty, and of democracy, which tended to become anarchy. He personally preferred an aristocracy resting upon popular election, that is, a combination of aristocracy and democracy, a republican form of government.

In his discussion of law, Calvin stressed the importance of the Old Testament in the regulation of man's conduct. Of the moral, ceremonial, and judicial laws of Moses, however, only the moral had validity at all times and must not be neglected by the state. The moral law, he explained, demanded that men worship God in faith and piety and serve one another in love. All other laws must conform to the law of love. He seems to have identified natural law, which is "inborn in the minds of men" and which is reflected in the Mosaic code, with equity, which he interpreted in the popular sense of justice.

Calvin repeatedly emphasized the Christian's duty to obey the government, even when it is tyrannical, for he believed that God would punish corrupt rulers in due time. On the other hand, he insisted that rulers are under the authority of God and that Christians should "obey God rather than men." Moreover, in harmony with medieval political thought, he pointed out in the last chapter of the *Institutes* that lesser magistrates who are by the constitution of the state obligated to protect the people can and must resist cruel rulers. In this he did not differ from Bucer, who had given much thought to this question, and Luther, who eventually came to the conclusion that the princes had the right to resist the emperor by force if the latter ruled as a tyrant.

## Calvin's Struggle for Control

Despite the fact that the people of Geneva, like townsmen elsewhere in that day, were accustomed to minute regulations of conduct, they greatly resented the fact that the consistory, an ecclesiastical institution, did the regulating. Unlike the city councils, it could make no sharp distinction between serious offenses against society and simple unchristian conduct. But the citizens had agreed to live according to the "word of God," and the consistory had obtained constitutional status. Therefore Calvin's indomitable will prevailed throughout the ensuing conflicts until the condemnation and death of Servetus in 1553, when his increased prestige virtually put an end to all opposition.

The consistory went at its tasks with enthusiasm, if not with tact and forbearance. It even invaded the privacy of the family, occasionally questioning children of suspected parents. People were brought before it to answer for the slightest deviations from the extremely straight and narrow path. Absence from sermons, family quarrels, criticism of the ministers, attendance at theaters—especially because women with "brazen effrontery" were beginning to take women's roles—singing obscene songs, dancing, playing cards, and many smaller infractions fill the pages of the consistory's records. As in the rest of Europe, the more serious crimes and heresies—some of which were dealt with directly by the city government —were punished with great severity, and torture was freely used to extort confessions. We know that from 1542 to 1546 seventy-six persons were banished from Geneva and fifty-eight executed for heresy, adultery, blasphemy, and witchcraft, which were capital crimes in most of Europe.

During the first five years after his return, Calvin got along relatively well with the Genevan government, for each seemed to be testing the other's strength, and Ami Perrin, one of the influential leaders of the party in power, was under the spell of the reformer's strong personality. Calvin even employed his legal training in assisting the government in recodifying the city's laws and revising the constitution along conservative, aristocratic lines. He was also appointed a member of a committee that, in February, 1544, finally settled the political differences between Geneva and Bern. His advice was sought in such matters as the supervision of building construction, the military defense of the city, fire protection, taxes, commerce, and industry. Thus his legal training, vigorous action, and strong will made him one of the leading political figures in Geneva, although he never held an official political position.

However, as we have seen, Calvin's position of leadership was challenged after 1545, when he had succeeded in surrounding himself with like-minded ministers and the consistory had begun to carry out its tasks in earnest. Interestingly enough, cases involving breaches of chastity caused the most objection, for citizens guilty of this offense and punished by the council did not wish to be further humiliated by being forced to appear before the consistory for admonition. Others resented being deprived of the many amusements that had given Geneva an unsavory reputation. Still others, among them many representatives of old Genevan families, viewed the ministers as foreign intruders who were depriving them of the liberties gained in their struggles against Savoy and Bern. Although some exiled Artichauds, whom Calvin had permitted to return to Geneva, attempted to lead the opposition, they never constituted a political party. Calvin called them Libertines.

The first major issue between Calvin and the opposition developed in January, 1546, when Pierre Ameaux, a manufacturer of playing cards and a member of the Little Council who saw his business being ruined, called Calvin a Picard, a false preacher, and an evil person. The reformer, who maintained that the "honor of Christ" was involved, compelled the Little Council, the Sixty, and the Two Hundred to revoke a mild sentence imposed upon Ameaux and in its place compel him to march through the streets in humiliation and disgrace. This punishment only inflamed the gathering opposition.

In June of the same year a placard condemning the preachers and threatening them with revenge was found on the pulpit of St. Pierre's. The councils interpreted such a daring sacrilege as an evidence of widespread opposition. Furthermore, the general belief that such an act would be followed by divine punishment caused great unrest and led the councils to take immediate action. Consequently a suspect, one Jacques Gruet, an irreverent and indecent freethinker, was arrested that same day. Because certain private papers critical of Calvin and his supporters and opposing the moral discipline of Geneva were found in his home, he was charged by the government with blasphemy and sedition, neither of which was proved but which he was compelled to confess under torture and for which he was finally beheaded.

About the same time, Calvin became involved in a much more serious conflict with one of the oldest families of Geneva, the Favres, and with Ami Perrin, the influential syndic and erstwhile supporter of the reformers. François, the head of the Favre family, was called before the consistory to answer for immoral conduct and was excommunicated. His son was also in constant trouble because of his irreverence and immorality. His daughter, a veritable vixen and the wife of Ami Perrin, defied the consistory with even greater daring and got her husband into trouble by dragging him off to a forbidden dance. She was finally exiled and remained for a while at one of her father's estates. Calvin personally persuaded Perrin to express his regret, but the rift between the two grew larger as time went on.

Sent on a mission to France to congratulate Henry II upon his accession to the throne, Perrin became involved in negotiations leading to a French offer of an alliance with Geneva, which he did not report to the government upon his return. When the news leaked out, not only the Genevans but the Bernese became highly incensed. Since Charles V had succeeded in defeating the German Protestants in 1547, it looked as though he might attack the Swiss. Moreover, the presence of many French refugees in this "asylum for the members of Christ," especially following the fierce persecutions of Henry II, greatly intensified the patriotic feelings against the French preachers. Charges and countercharges, involving Calvin himself, gave the reformer no rest.

In 1553 Calvin's unpopularity was demonstrated by the election of an overwhelming majority of the opposition. Perrin, again made a syndic, attempted to put an end to the consistory's right to excommunicate. When Philibert Berthelier, the son of a patriot and martyr of 1519 and a popular leader of the opposition, was excommunicated, he appealed from the consistory to the councils for the right to commune. The councils gave him the permission, thereby calling into question the action of the consistory. Calvin opposed the councils and was prepared to refuse the sacrament to Berthelier, even though this defiance might mean exile. But Berthelier did not appear at the Lord's Supper, and meanwhile the case of Servetus was making a hero of Calvin. So he carried the day and compelled the councils to uphold the constitution.

It was thus in the defense of the "true faith" that Calvin increased his prestige both at home and abroad and finally won over the vacillating spirits and gained for the consistory unquestioned authority in religious matters. The councils became even more "Calvinist" than Calvin. Because his entire hold upon the Genevan community rested upon the faithful exercise of his duties as preacher and teacher, he was particularly zealous in maintaining the "pure doctrine" and countering any accusations of "false teachings" by persecuting persons suspected of heresy.

The first major case of doctrinal discipline involved the humanist Sébastien Castellio (1515–1563), a native of Savoy, with whom Calvin had become acquainted in Strassburg and whom he had called to head the school at Geneva. He did his work well, but when, in 1543, he applied for the position of regular minister, Calvin objected because he had denied the inspiration of the Old Testament book the Song of Solomon and the official Genevan interpretation of the article in the Apostles' Creed that referred to Christ's descent into hell. In support of the Protestant emphasis upon the absolute authority of the entire Bible, Calvin induced the Little Council to let Castellio go, but he gave him a certificate of recommendation, fairly stating the reasons for this action. Castellio settled in Basel, where he published an edition of Xenophon and his translation of the Bible into Latin and French. He also taught Greek at the university, where he continued his struggle for freedom of conscience in religious matters.

A more serious doctrinal dispute centered in Calvin's teaching concerning predestination. Jerome Bolsec (d. 1584), a former Carmelite monk of Paris, became Protestant and settled as a physician to a Protestant nobleman at Veigny, near Geneva, about 1550. Because of his continued interest in theology, he frequently attended the weekly meetings of the Genevan ministers, where he argued that in his doctrine of predestination Calvin inferred that God was the cause of all sin, a doctrine that was not only absurd but false. Calvin, who could not permit such an accusation to stand, branded Bolsec an accomplice of Satan and had him thrown into prison and tried by the Little Council. The case dragged on, for the council sought the views of the clergy at Basel, Bern, and Zurich, which, when they arrived, seemed evasive. Because, however, the acquittal of Bolsec would have forced Calvin to resign, the council banished the former in December, 1551. Bolsec eventually returned to France, renounced his Protestantism, and gained revenge against Calvin by publishing his *Life of Calvin* (1577), a scurrilous, falsified biography that was long used as a reliable source by the enemies of the Genevan reformer.

Although Calvin had won another victory, this affair had served to accentuate one of the least-liked doctrines that had found expression in the *Institutes* but that had hardly been mentioned in his sermons. Thereafter he was compelled to defend it on a number of occasions and thereby to emphasize its importance in his theological system.

Popular opposition to Calvin found yet another spokesman in the person of Jean Trolliet, a former monk, whom Calvin would not accept as a pastor. Trolliet also attacked Calvin's doctrine of predestination and appealed to the writings of Melanchthon in support of his views. Because Trolliet had many supporters in the government, Calvin made little headway against him until, by threatening to resign, he compelled the councils, in August, 1552, to declare that the *Institutes* contained "the pure doctrine" and should not be criticized. Trolliet acquiesced, but Calvin's troubles were by no means over.

### Calvin and Servetus

When, in 1553, Calvin's program for Geneva seemed to hang in the balance, the notorious case of Michael Servetus saved the day. Servetus had published his widely denounced *Concerning the Errors of the Trinity* in 1531 and his *Restitution of Christianity* in 1553. He had corresponded with Calvin on the doctrines of baptism, regeneration, and the nature of Christ, and Calvin had made it clear that his ideas were "the ravings of a heretic." To Calvin the historical doctrine of the Trinity was the only hope for fallen mankind.

In these circumstances, it is not clear why Servetus dared to stop at Geneva on his way to Naples after his escape from prison at Vienne, where he was being tried for heresy by the Catholic authorities. While staying in the city the night of August 13, 1553, he came to hear Calvin preach. He was recognized and arrested and placed on trial two days later. Calvin himself prepared the thirty-eight counts alleged against Servetus, but he did not appear at the trial in person until August 17. When the theological discussion of the nature of Christ bewildered the councils, they turned the trial over to the public prosecutor and shifted the accent from heresy to subversion of religion and the general welfare. The trial dragged on while the views of the other Swiss Protestants were awaited, for the councils did not want to act hastily in such an important matter. The fact that Bullinger and other Protestants had no doubts concerning the heretical nature of Servetus' teachings and supported the accusations of Calvin greatly discomfited the opposition. Finally, on October 25, the councils pronounced Servetus guilty on fourteen counts and condemned him to death by fire, contrary to the provisions of the Ordinances, which limited punishment to banishment. Calvin sought a milder form of death but to no avail. Servetus died at the stake the next day, after having cried out, "Jesus, Thou Son of the eternal God," thus steadfastly refusing to use the words, "eternal Son of God."

A few voices were raised against this use of force in religious matters, notably that of Castellio. For this reason Calvin wrote his apology, *A Defense of the Orthodox Faith.* In it he made little mention of the heresy of Servetus but stressed his blasphemy, despite the fact that the councils had made it clear that he had been condemned for his "false and completely heretical doctrine." Castellio presented his views in an anthology of opinions against persecution, called *Concerning Heretics, Whether They Are to Be Persecuted,* published under the pseudonym of Martin Bellius. In it he and the men whom he quotes argue that the meaning of the Bible is not unequivocally clear on all points, notably on the most controversial points; that the Trinity, predestination, and the future life are nonessentials to salvation and must be differentiated from essentials; that doctrinal systems merely approximate the truth; and that the burning of heretics is contrary to the teachings of a merciful God and a compassionate Christ. Most Protestant leaders, however, supported Calvin and breathed a sigh of relief when Servetus was gone. This new evidence of Calvin's prestige was not overlooked by his opponents in Geneva, who had compromised themselves by taking the side of Servetus.

## The Christian Commonwealth (1553–1564)

With the execution of Servetus, opposition to Calvin declined. Not only were the Genevans becoming weary of the schemes of Perrin and others to secure political power for themselves and their friends, but they were beginning to see the material advantages of the influx of refugees of high character and ability. Coming from France, Italy, Poland, Hungary, Scotland, and England, they brought their industrial and other skills with them and stimulated commerce. Calvin induced the government to subsidize the manufacture of textiles. The book business increased by leaps and bounds. The manufacture of watches, which made Geneva famous in modern times, was begun late in the century.

After the elections of 1555 all four of the syndics were Calvinists with strong support in the councils. Whereas the Calvinists moved to increase their support by granting citizenship to refugees—170 were so favored by 1556—the Perrinists tried in vain to deprive them of the right to carry arms and to vote for ten years. Popular excitement developed over the issue. During one particular demonstration, Perrin attempted to seize the baton of one of the syndics who had come to disperse the opposition. This incident was used by Calvin to induce the Little Council to sentence Perrin, Berthelier, and other leaders of the opposition to death for inciting riot. Perrin and Berthelier had escaped before the sentence, but four of the leaders were beheaded and quartered. This severe action marked the end of the Perrinist party in Geneva.

Another stroke of good fortune enabled Calvin to strengthen the hold of his party on the Genevan government. Bern, many of whose pastors were hostile to Calvin, gave refuge to the Perrinists and took a more antagonistic attitude toward Geneva. The treaty that it offered the Genevans to replace the one that was to expire in 1556 was so humiliating that the latter refused to accept it, thereby leaving the small state without an ally. However, the brilliant victory of the Spaniards over the French at Saint-Quentin in 1557, won under the leadership of the duke of Savoy, exposed both Swiss cities to danger. Consequently a treaty, called "the perpetual alliance," was signed in 1558. This treaty finally placed Geneva on a basis of equality with her powerful neighbor. The Perrinists thus saw disappear their last chance of using Bern to regain their power. When, however, Viret attempted to introduce Calvinist discipline in Bernese Vaud, virtually all the Calvinist preachers were driven out of Bernese lands (1559) and settled in Geneva.

## The Genevan Academy

Despite Calvin's years of conflict, the death of his wife in 1549, and his ill health, he was able to accomplish much of a constructive nature. Of great importance for the spread of Calvinism was the founding of the Genevan Academy in June, 1559. The school provided by the Ordinances had never prospered, and when the Little Council finally decided to create a "college," or "academy," in 1558, it lacked the teachers. But the Bernese expulsion of the Calvinist preachers and teachers from the Vaud brought to Geneva Viret and many of his companions, most important of whom was Theodore Beza (1519–1605), the humanist who as a lad had studied at Volmar's home in Bourges during Calvin's stay there. After a number of years in search of pleasure at Paris, Beza had turned to religion, had visited Geneva in 1548, and then had joined Viret as professor of Greek at the flourishing academy at Lausanne.

Beza and the other brilliant teachers from Lausanne became the instructors of Calvin's new academy. Beza was made the rector. This institution—the original building, completed in 1564, still stands—was under ecclesiastical control. According to its elaborate constitution, based to a large extent upon that of Johann Sturm's famous school at Strassburg, the institution was divided into two distinct parts, the primary *schola privata,* or gymnasium, headed by a principal and divided into seven classes, each supervised by a regent, and the secondary *schola publica,* which corresponded to the modern European university. In the former the young people were taught French, Latin, and Greek grammar and literature, as well as the elements of logic. In the latter the "public professors" taught Greek, Hebrew, philosophy, and theology. In both, instruction was gratis. Unlike the usual practice, the student received only a certificate of attendance, not a degree, upon his completion of the prescribed courses.

The Genevan Academy—called University today—immediately began to fulfill Calvin's ambition to train the young in the fundamentals of Christianity so that they could give an intelligent accounting of their faith and to prepare ministers to spread the gospel. At the time of his death the "private school" numbered twelve hundred students, the "public school" three hundred. Most of the students in the latter came from foreign countries and carried back with them not only Calvin's theology but his determination to create Christian commonwealths, no matter what the cost. Of great significance also were the political ideas developed by François Hotman and others in the law faculty.

## Cooperation of Council and Consistory

With the disappearance of opposition to Calvin, the consistory and the city government worked hand in hand in carrying out his ideas. Many of the leading members of the hostile parties had left Geneva, and those who remained became impressed with the growing prestige of the reformer. Consequently, in December, 1559, the council honored Calvin by finally granting him citizenship—the rights of *bourgeoisie*—without payment of the customary costs.

Calvin's participation in the practical affairs of Geneva and the consequent impact of Calvinism upon the economic, social, and political development of western Europe have been subjects of much debate among the historians of our century. Whatever one's views concerning these matters, it is obvious that Calvin, like Luther, had no intention of changing the medieval order and stressed the importance of the Christian's service to God *in* his particular calling; but he went further than Luther in his encouragement of the Christian to participate in the affairs of this world so as to serve God *through* his calling, thus honoring God by outward conformity to the divine moral law.

As a consequence of Calvin's example and teaching, Calvinism became much more aggressive than Lutheranism. This aggressiveness, rather than any definitely formed theories concerning society, explains the parallels one finds in Calvinism and capitalism. The Calvinists followed their leader's example of participating in those political, economic, and social activities that were changing the character of Western civilization during the sixteenth century. Success in business came to be looked upon as evidence of self-denial and hard work to the glory of God. On the other hand, it cannot be denied that this success in business was accompanied by a growing materialism and secularism that eventually tended to relegate religion to a secondary role. Nor must we forget that although Calvin participated in the public affairs of Geneva and his example might have encouraged middle-class virtues, he constantly preached the Christian virtues of self-sacrifice, humility, and joy in the salvation that God gives devout Christians. For Calvin, as for Luther, political, economic, and social matters lay on the periphery of his thinking.

Much has been made of Calvin's statements concerning usury, or the taking of interest. Contrary to widely held views, Calvin did not initiate the passing of a law that permitted the taking of interest. He merely agreed with the spirit of a statute already in force at Geneva that protected the poor from exorbitant interest rates on loans (that is, more than 5 per cent). As a matter of fact, Luther and Zwingli held similar views. When Calvin was asked his opinion, he denied the Aristotelian theory of the sterility of money and stated that the taking of interest was not contrary to Scripture; but he insisted that the borrower should profit as much as the one who loaned the money, and that the general welfare should not be harmed by the transaction. Such points of view illustrate that his primary concern was a religious and moral one and that he can in no way be held responsible for encouraging or discouraging the rise of capitalism.

The collaboration between the consistory and the councils was apparent in the tightening of ecclesiastical discipline, in which the councils often seemed more Calvinist than Calvin. Because the luxuries and foreign customs of some of the immigrants were eagerly imitated by some of the Genevans, they were the object of attack of much legislation. Particularly numerous and severe were the laws against adultery. The great development of the machinery of discipline and the increase in the number of penalties have led many historians to question whether the morals in Geneva had improved to any great extent. Yet John Knox, the Lutheran Johann Valentin Andreae, and the German Pietist Philipp Jakob Spener were greatly impressed with the exemplary conduct in the city.

Heresy, too, was attacked with sustained vigor after the Servetus affair. A number of persons were excommunicated by the consistory and whipped out of the city by the Little Council. Further executions also took place. But the insistence upon complete religious uniformity was not peculiar to the Genevans of the sixteenth century. Although Calvin had a high regard for the Italian congregation in Geneva, led by the able and devout Galeazzo di Carraccioli, nephew of Pope Paul IV, he had his greatest doctrinal difficulties, particularly over the Trinity, with some of the Italian immigrants.

## Calvin's Theology

As a matter of fact, the clarification of theology remained Calvin's chief concern during all the time-consuming struggles with his opponents. The chief product of this troublesome period was his definitive revision of the *Institutes,* completed in 1559. It appeared in both French and Dutch translations in the following year, in English in 1561, in German in 1572, and in Spanish in 1597. Because the Bible was for him the indisputable Word of God, he worked up to the time of his death on the improvement of Olivétan's French translation until it was virtually a new translation.

Most important among the other theological writings of Calvin were his *Treatise on Relics* (1543), one of the most forceful works of the Reformation on this subject; his *Antidote* (1547), an attack upon the Council of Trent; and his commentaries on all the books of the Old Testament and most of the New Testament. His mastery of philology, his knowledge of the history of the Church, his practical and logical approach, and his direct, grammatical interpretation of each Scripture passage help explain the wide use of his commentaries and his reputation as one of the outstanding theologians of his day.

By 1559, when the final edition of the *Institutes* appeared, Calvin's theological system had been completed, and predestination, which was implicit in his conception of the sovereignty of God's will, had become its central doctrine. Virtually all the Protestant reformers had emphasized St. Augustine's doctrine of predestination in opposition to the semi-Pelagian tendencies of the nominalists and Franciscans of the late Middle Ages. But whereas Luther, among others, had placed the loving and forgiving God of the New Testament in the foreground and, with his aversion to speculative theology, had been satisfied with dwelling upon the question of how man was saved, Calvin followed Bucer in stressing the autocratic God of the Old Testament and became increasingly absorbed with the question of why man was saved.

The basis of Calvin's theological system was, as we have seen, his doctrine of the absolute authority of God as eternal lawgiver and judge whose will is law. Man, on the other hand, he considered completely worthless because of sin, which he inherited from Adam. Therefore, he concluded, man can be saved only by direct divine intervention. This can occur only if man knows God. He knows God vaguely by nature, for this knowledge is implanted in all minds at birth; but this natural theology only makes him aware of his sin. Complete knowledge can come only from Scripture, the writers of which were merely the "amanuenses of the Holy Spirit." What they recorded thus constitutes the law of God, which must regulate the life of the Christian.

Faith, according to Calvin, is induced by the Holy Spirit through the Word of God at God's pleasure, for man can neither accept nor reject it. When man believes, he fears the penalty for his sins. Fear, in turn, leads him to repent, to look to Christ's redemptive death on the cross, and then, on the basis of the New Testament promises, to be assured that he is elected to salvation.

Luther, following Augustine, gave little consideration to the question concerning those who were not elected. Calvin drove logically to the ultimate conclusion that God sealed the fate of all persons in eternity, although he frequently asserted that the damned suffer because of their own sins. He even maintained that God decreed in eternity that there would be the fall of man in Adam and that he would then elect some of the damned for salvation.

This *decretum quidem horribile,* or terrible decree, as Calvin himself called it, did not, however, lead to fatalism, for the Calvinist who believed in the redemptive work of Christ was confident that God had elected him. Moreover, he was certain that his election must be demonstrated by conformity with the law of God. The divine decrees that, in his estimation, had compelled many to undergo severe hardships must also be obeyed in the constant struggle against the forces of evil. Thus predestination served as a powerful dynamic in the great struggles of the Calvinists against what they considered political and religious tyranny.

Like Bucer and other South-German reformers, Calvin became interested in drawing all Protestant bodies together. For this reason he made a determined effort to formulate his doctrines of the sacraments in such a way as to gain the acceptance of his views by both Lutherans and Zwinglians. Baptism, he insisted, was not only a symbol, but a divine seal by means of which man receives the promise of God's grace; but this promise is given only to the elect.

Calvin followed the Roman Catholics and the Lutherans in maintaining that the living Christ was present in the Lord's Supper and that the believer's "soul feasted on Him for a blessed immortality," for he considered Zwingli's symbolical interpretation too profane. On the other hand, he considered Luther's insistence upon the presence of Christ's human body and blood too close to the doctrine of transubstantiation and refused to accept the notion of the "ubiquity" of this body. Calvin insisted that the sacrament had no value without the Holy Spirit and the Word, and for this reason demanded that it always be celebrated with the words of institution. He believed that the body and blood of Christ are really and miraculously present in the Lord's Supper, but in a spiritual sense, and are consumed spiritually, by faith, through the mysterious intervention of the Holy Spirit. Insofar as he conceived of the sacrament as a means of grace and emphasized the real presence of Christ and the eating of Christ's body and the drinking of Christ's blood for one's salvation, he stood closer to Luther than to Zwingli.

Although Luther at first accepted Calvin's attempts to mediate in the controversies over the real presence, he remained suspicious of the sincerity of the Swiss theologians, so that no complete doctrinal agreement could be reached. Luther made a renewed attack upon the Zwinglians in 1544, two years before his death.

Calvin was much more successful in working out an understanding with the Zwinglians than with the Lutherans. Despite the fact that Bullinger and he had differed sharply since the formulation of The First Helvetic Confession of 1536, that Basel had seemed to favor the Lutheran doctrines, and that Bern had tended toward Lutheranism under some ministers and toward Zwinglianism under others, Calvin did not give up his attempts to draw at least the Swiss churches together.

Finally, in 1549, Calvin and Farel visited Bullinger at Zurich and formulated a draft of the Zurich Consensus, in which they announced their agreement on the interpretation of the Lord's Supper. The other Protestant churches, even that of Bern, eventually accepted this statement of doctrine, so that Zwinglianism and Calvinism became one body, called Reformed after 1580. Although Melanchthon had long held views concerning the Lord's Supper similar to those expressed in the Consensus, Calvin could not induce him to come out openly in support of it.

Even more important in drawing the Zwinglians and the Calvinists together doctrinally was the The Second Helvetic Confession of 1566, for the Zurich Consensus and the subsequent Geneva Consensus of 1552 had brought agreement with respect to only the doctrines of the Lord's Supper and of predestination. This new confession, published two years after Calvin's death, was eventually accepted not only by the Swiss congregations but by the Reformed churches in the Palatinate, France, Hungary, Poland, Austria, and Bohemia and was highly regarded by the Protestants in the Low Countries, Scotland, and England.

Like Zwingli, Calvin conceived of the church as a Christian commonwealth composed of the elect and encompassing the entire community. This commonwealth, however, was not to be ruled by the clergy or even in harmony with the letter of the Bible but by the church and the state each administering its own functions to the glory of God. This meant that the community must be made free of nonbelievers. This, in turn, involved setting up tests for determining who were the elect.

According to Calvin, the elect were those who (1) publicly professed their faith and their covenant with God, (2) walked in the ways of God, and (3) participated in the sacraments as a means of spiritually communing with God. It was the clarity of these criteria that to a large degree explains the activism of Calvinism and the Reformed churches. Certainty of election was accompanied by confidence in the future and the hope of building a kingdom of God here on earth. Moreover, the doctrine of predestination freed the Calvinists from concern about salvation and permitted them to devote their energies to what Calvin considered the chief end of life, namely, to honor God. Man, depraved in intellect and will, can do good because the majestic and inscrutable God performs good through him.

Only in Scotland and New England did the Calvinists succeed in approximating such Christian commonwealths on a large scale. In those countries where they were in the minority, they constituted a dynamic spiritual elite that heroically attempted to create the kingdom of God despite all obstacles.

# Early Spread of Calvinism

## The Palatinate

A doctrinal statement of great influence resulted from the spread of Calvinism to the Lutheran territory of the Palatinate. Elector Frederick III (1559–1576), disturbed by the bitter controversy over the Lord's Supper in his lands in the year of his accession, himself turned to the study of the sacrament. Convinced that the Calvinist interpretation was to be preferred to the Lutheran, he thereafter called Calvinist professors to his University of Heidelberg. Two of these, Caspar Olevianus (1536–1587) and Zacharias Ursinus (1534–1583), drafted the Heidelberg Catechism in 1563 with Elector Frederick's active participation.

This modified statement of Calvinist doctrines, in which the controversial issues concerning the Lord's Supper were avoided and the Calvinist view of predestination was stated in a milder form, became the doctrinal norm not only for the elector and his territory and for other Reformed churches in Germany but for the Philippists, or followers of Melanchthon. But unlike Calvin's church of Geneva, that of the Palatinate remained under the control of the state, for the elector maintained his authority by means of a consistory comprising three ministers and three laymen. Thomas Erastus (d. 1583), the personal physician of the elector and professor of medicine at Heidelberg, was outspoken in his opposition to the Genevan constitution, preferring instead a strong governmental control of doctrines and discipline. In England and Scotland, Calvinist tendencies toward a state church were called Erastian after him.

## France

From the outset of Calvin's reforming activities in Geneva, he was deeply concerned with the progress of the Reformation in France. To his great disappointment, a number of his followers there believed that it was possible to reform Catholicism from within by infusing it with new Protestant doctrines. He indignantly called these cautious harmonizers Nicodemites because of their refusal openly to profess Christ. Yet many French Protestants, including wealthy townsmen and intellectuals as well as artisans, followed Calvin's leadership. Those who could not flee to Switzerland or Germany formed small, compact groups that met in secret, worshiped in accordance with Protestant doctrines, and studied the

Bible as well as the increasing amount of Calvinist literature that was being brought to them. As these congregations grew in size, they were sent fearless ministers trained in Geneva who preached to the faithful bands in private homes, open fields, woods, and all sorts of out-of-the-way places.

Despite the fact that Francis I (1515–1547) and Henry II (1547–1559) persecuted the Protestants from time to time and that Queen Catherine de' Medici, a niece of Pope Clement VII, detested them, the French rulers were primarily concerned with the Hapsburg-Valois rivalry. Moreover, they seemed to know little about the state of mind of their people, being satisfied if the people obeyed their royal commands and supported their political ambitions with taxes. Not until toward the end of his reign did Henry II seem to realize that his country was rapidly going to ruin and that religious defection was widespread. And not until 1559 did he conclude the Treaty of Cateau-Cambrésis with Philip II of Spain, which finally enabled both monarchs to devote their attention to stamping out heresy in their lands. But Henry's accidental death at a tournament later that same year prevented the execution of his plans and led, as we shall see, to a long and bitter religious conflict.

In these circumstances Protestantism spread rapidly, despite Henry's creation, in 1548, of a special court in the Parlement of Paris, called by the people the *Chambre ardent* ("Court of Fire"), to try heretics, and despite the Edict of Châteaubriand of 1551, which codified the laws for dealing with Protestants, set up lower courts to expedite trials, and provided for special sessions of the law courts for the discussion of religion and the apprehension of judges suspected of heresy. Especially severe was the provision concerning the reading of Protestant books, particularly those printed in Geneva. Henry would have gone so far as to establish the Inquisition in France if the Parlement of Paris had given its consent.

Many were the victims of this repression, as recorded in Jean Crespin's *Acts and Monuments,* one of the most widely read martyrologies of this period. On the other hand, so many judges sympathized with the Calvinists that the king issued the Edict of Compiègne (1557), which forbade them to show leniency in any way.

Although the first converts to Protestantism were predominately townsmen, not a small number of nobles and even members of the royal family became Protestant. Margaret d'Angoulême, sister of Francis I and queen of Navarre, as we have seen, continued her correspondence with Calvin; her daughter, Jeanne d'Albret, mother of the future Henry IV, was a convinced Calvinist; Jeanne's husband, Duke Anthony of Bourbon and king of Navarre, likewise became Protestant in 1548, as did his brother, the prince of Condé. This imposing group of Protestants of royal blood and their followers, called Huguenots after 1552, was later joined by Gaspard de Coligny (1519–1572), nephew of the powerful

King Henry II of France

## 7. The Emergence of Calvinism

Connétable Ann de Montmorency, admiral of France, and commander of the French infantry, one of the noblest of all the French Calvinists.

Opposed to the Huguenots were the members of the Guise family, especially the three ambitious sons of Duke Claude of Guise (d. 1550): Charles, archibishop of Reims and later cardinal of Lorraine; Louis, later cardinal of Guise; and Francis, who succeeded his father as duke. The eldest daughter, called Mary of Lorraine by the Scots, was married to James V of Scotland and became the mother of Mary Stuart, "Queen of the Scots," who in turn was married to Henry II's son and dauphin, who became King Francis II (1559–1560) of France. The Guises, as we shall see, were not only bitter opponents of Protestantism but sought to gain control over the French monarchy and to establish a powerful dynasty.

The fruits of Calvin's labors became apparent when there was established in Paris, in 1555, the first French Calvinist church with a formal church service, regular preaching and administration of the sacraments, and a consistory of elders. During the next four years similar congregations sprang up throughout France to which, it is estimated, nearly half a million members belonged at the outbreak of the civil wars.

In 1559, when it looked as though Henry II would make a special effort to stamp out Protestantism, a number of French congregations sent their pastors and elders to meet in the first national synod in Paris, which lasted four days. At this synod a confession of faith, the *Confessio Gallicana,* was drawn up, a revision of a confession written by Calvin; and a system of discipline, the *Discipline ecclésiastique,* was accepted. The congregations, placed on a basis of equality and served by pastors who were all of the same rank, were to have their own consistories and to send representatives to local assemblies to determine doctrinal matters and manage administrative matters. These local assemblies, in turn, were to be grouped into provincial assemblies, which should convene annually. The ultimate authority in matters of doctrine and discipline affecting the entire church was to be the national synod. By 1561 this body represented more than two thousand congregations.

In a relatively short time the French Protestants felt impelled by the force of circumstances to take up arms against the Guise faction, which stood for a rigid Roman Catholicism and the principles of absolute monarchy. The leaders of the Huguenots were now virtually all men whose motives were strongly political. To his death in 1564, however, Calvin consistently refused to sanction the use of arms against the state, even though the Huguenots maintained that they were fighting to protect the king against those who would corrupt the monarchy. He especially disapproved of the efforts of the fanatically activist François Hotman to bring the German Protestants into the struggle on the side of the Huguenots.

Calvin also opposed the Conspiracy of Amboise of 1560, in which

Condé plotted to seize the weak King Francis II and destroy the growing influence of the Guises in the government. Calvin made it known in no uncertain terms that he would not countenance the use of violence except in accordance with definitely established constitutional principles. Accordingly he did his best to win over King Anthony of Navarre to the open support of the Protestants, but to no avail. As a matter of fact, Anthony went to the royal court at Paris and again embraced Catholicism.

Calvin sent Beza to Paris after the death of Francis II to discuss doctrinal matters in a religious colloquy supported by Catherine de' Medici, who had become regent for her minor son Charles IX (1560–1574) and was attempting to avoid bloodshed by conciliating the Protestants. Although this Colloquy of Poissy failed to bring religious agreement, the Huguenots had an opportunity to influence the queen mother. By the Edict of January, 1562, issued upon the advice of the conciliatory chancellor Michel de l'Hôpital, the Huguenots were permitted to worship outside the towns and organize in consistories. But although many Huguenots perpetrated fanatical acts of violence, this act of toleration drove the Roman Catholic faction into action. The duke of Guise stirred up the masses against the Huguenots by promising them a part of the confiscated property of the heretics. The slaying of a group of Protestants worshiping in a barn at Vassy on March 1, 1562, was the signal for similar violent attacks in Orléans, Toulouse, and other cities. Soon after, Condé left Paris and seized Orléans, while the duke of Guise went to Paris with Catherine, Charles IX, and Anthony. This action precipitated the French wars of religion, which Calvin could in no way prevent. But after the wars had begun, he supported his coreligionists.

## The Low Countries

Calvinism was brought to the Low Countries by Protestants fleeing from persecution in France and England and also by ministers coming directly from Geneva and Lausanne. The growth of the first Protestant movements had been greatly retarded by Charles V's introduction of the Inquisition. Despite the execution of hundreds of victims, mostly Anabaptists, heresy had persisted as a mixture of Lutheranism, humanism, and Anabaptism. The Netherlanders as a whole had accepted this religious repressive policy of Charles, for he had been born in the Low Countries and had appeared to further their interests. He had greatly expanded the Low Countries until in 1543 they comprised seventeen provinces, had provided these provinces with good government and military defense, had organized them into the Circle of Burgundy, which was virtually independent of the Empire (1548), and had brought them prosperity.

Opposition increased rapidly, however, after the abdication of Charles V and the accession of his son Philip II (1555–1598), who resided in the Low Countries from 1555 to 1559. The Netherlanders considered this Spanish-speaking ruler a foreigner and did not hesitate to defend their "liberties" against his policy of strengthening his royal authority. Thus religious and political motives combined to prepare for the revolt against Spain, which broke out during his reign.

The penetration of Calvinism into the Low Countries began in earnest after Philip's accession, for the Netherlanders were attracted particularly to its logical, dogmatic system, its emphasis upon the Bible as the law of God, and the representative character of its church organization. Congregations patterned after those of Geneva and Paris were formed and accepted the Heidelberg Catechism as their handbook of theology. In 1561, Guy de Brès, a French-speaking minister who had been trained in Geneva, drafted a Calvinist confession of faith in the French language. This Belgic Confession was accepted by a synod at Antwerp in 1566. Thus all the Calvinist congregations of the Low Countries were bound together by one confession only two years after Calvin's death. Because the native tongue of the inhabitants of the southern provinces was French, Calvinism spread there first. Later, as we shall see, it spread north, and the southern provinces returned to Catholicism.

### England

Continental Protestants and their doctrines were given a warm reception in England during the reign of Edward VI (1547–1553). Although Cranmer's leanings were at first Lutheran, he became particularly friendly toward Martin Bucer, Pietro Martire Vermigli, Bernardino Ochino, and Jan à Lasco, all of whom came to England during the years 1547 to 1549. Cranmer also invited Calvin to attend a "synod" of prominent Protestant theologians in England, which the latter could not do. Calvin's correspondence with Cranmer, Somerset, and the young king seems to have had slight influence upon developments in England, although his views were represented in the congregation of refugees organized by Lasco in London in 1550.

Calvin exerted a much greater influence upon the growth of English Protestantism during the reign of Mary (1553–1558), when many Englishmen sought refuge on the Continent. Some had already been in exile in Zurich after Henry VIII's Act of the Six Articles. For this reason, and because the Lutherans were generally unfriendly to them, some of them now went to Zurich, others to Strassburg and Frankfurt. Because of a split between the conservative and the more radical Englishmen at Frankfurt, the latter, headed by John Knox, went to Geneva. There they were in a congenial environment and further developed those doctrines and disciplinary methods that greatly influenced the subsequent growth of Protestantism in English-speaking countries.

The exiles returned to England after Elizabeth I (1558–1603) became queen. The Elizabethan Settlement ignored the church polity of Geneva, for the queen was determined that the crown should retain control of the church. But the influence of the Swiss Protestants, particularly those of Zurich, continued. In the controversy over the wearing of Anglican vestments, which took place during the first years of Elizabeth's reign and was called the Vestiarian Controversy, Thomas Sampson, dean of Christ Church, Oxford, and Lawrence Humphrey, president of Magdalen, Oxford, both of whom had been in exile in Zurich, strongly opposed the Anglican position. This opposition has been called the beginning of Puritanism.

Because Bullinger eventually went to the support of the queen in the Vestiarian Controversy, she came to rely upon him for advice rather than upon the Genevans, who generally sympathized with Sampson and Humphrey. Nor did it help matters that Knox had published at Geneva his *First Blast Against the Monstrous Regiment of Women* (1556), aimed at Mary of Lorraine and Mary Tudor. Calvin tried to make amends by dedicating his *Commentary on Isaiah* to Elizabeth in 1559 and two years later called the British ambassador's attention to a book defaming Anne Boleyn, Elizabeth's mother. Nevertheless, the theology of the Reformed Church, in the development of which Calvin had played a leading role, came to occupy a prominent place in the Thirty-nine Articles, and his more advanced doctrines concerning discipline were generally accepted by the Nonconformists.

### Scotland

Much greater was Calvin's influence in Scotland through the person of John Knox (1505?–1572), the son of Lowland peasants and a theologian after Calvin's own heart. Encouraged by Knox and fearing that Mary Stuart might become queen of France, the leaders of the Protestant party in Scotland, called the Lords of the Congregation, formed the Scottish Covenant (1557) for the purpose of establishing a Scottish congregation and defending the word of God. This was the beginning of the Scottish civil war, in which Calvinism and nationalism opposed Catholicism and the alliance with France. Knox supported the movement from his pulpit at Perth after his return in 1559, the same year in which Mary Stuart became queen of France. Scottish nationalism was aroused to white heat when the Guises urged Mary of Lorraine to stamp out Protestantism in Scotland and when many French troops were sent to the country to put down the rebellion. In desperation the Lords of the Congregation turned to Elizabeth, who sent them both money and ships. Although Elizabeth and Knox disliked each other, they proved mutually helpful during the Scottish revolt.

When Mary of Lorraine died in 1560, the Guises chose not to continue the struggle. By the Treaty of Edinburgh of that same year, most of the French troops were withdrawn from Scotland, Frenchmen were excluded from holding offices, and England was promised freedom from French attacks.

The Scottish Parliament that convened in 1560 rejected papal authority, withdrew the temporal and spiritual jurisdiction of the church prelates, abolished the Mass, and accepted the confession drawn up by Knox in the spirit of Calvin. This *Confessio Scoticana* thus became the law of the land. *The Book of Discipline* of 1561 provided for the reorganization of the new "Kirk" of Scotland. The local congregations, with their ministers, presbyters, and deacons, were represented by the kirk session. The local bodies constituted a presbytery, and over them were the provincial synods and the general assembly. The exact nature and functions of these bodies, however, remained nebulous. The observance of Sunday as a day of rest was rigidly maintained, but the other church festivals were abolished. Discipline was maintained in the districts by superintendents, who retained many of the functions that they or their predecessors had exercised as bishops. Church lands and endowments were not appropriated by the state. Many of them were kept by the nobles who had seized them during the revolt against Mary of Lorraine.

Mary Stuart returned from France in 1561, and the Scottish religious development was arrested by its involvement in the complicated political events of the latter half of the century. Many of the questions concerning the relation of church and state thus had to be postponed to a later date.

### Germany and Eastern Europe

Calvinism penetrated parts of Germany other than the Palatinate, despite the fact that Calvin made no attempts to interfere with the Lutherans, for whom he always showed great admiration. But congregations of refugees from France, England, and the Low Countries helped to spread Calvin's doctrines and ideas of discipline. Bucer and other Strassburg divines and also the Philippists likewise kept some of his doctrines alive in Germany. The congregation of French refugees at Strassburg, which Calvin had served, did not retain its identity for long. Under the encouragement of Philip of Hesse, John à Lasco established a congregation of refugees from various countries at Frankfurt that lasted until 1596. Other even more influential refugee churches sprang up in East Friesland and the lower Rhine Valley. Lasco organized one at Emden in 1544 and there published a catechism. Another congregation prospered at Wesel. These congregations became centers of strong Calvinist resistance during the attempts made to re-Catholicize these regions after the Schmalkaldic War.

Calvin had many followers among the nobles in Poland and closely followed the vicissitudes of the Protestants in that country. But the attempts of Lasco, who had returned to his native country in 1556, to create a unified Calvinist church there ended in failure. When the Catholic

Part Three: Spread of Protestantism

Counter Reformation began in Poland, the Calvinists could offer no more resistance than the Lutherans.

In Hungary a number of synods produced confessions containing strongly Calvinist doctrines, but under the capable leadership of two students of Melanchthon, the more moderate Reformed doctrines of the Heidelberg Cathechism gained the ascendancy. Here the churches gained sufficient strength to withstand the Counter Reformation. In the year of Calvin's death the Protestants of Transylvania split into two groups, the Calvinists of Klausenburg and the Lutherans of Hermannstadt. Calvinism also exerted considerable influence among the Bohemian Brethren, especially after the beginning of the seventeenth century.

Thus, when Calvin died at the age of fifty-five, after years of suffering from a number of painful ailments, his influence had been felt throughout much of Europe. It was even greater after his death, for Calvinism had become a strong, international movement, though Beza, Calvin's successor, was not as forceful a leader and gradually permitted the city councils to free themselves from the overwhelming influence of the consistory. Wherever Calvinism made itself felt, it was distinguished by its strong emphasis upon the Bible as a law, which found expression in blue laws as well as in strong iconoclastic tendencies—and also in a heroic certainty evinced in the wars of religion. Great emphasis was also placed upon high ethical standards and moral seriousness, which were greatly needed in the sixteenth and seventeenth centuries. Furthermore, the Calvinists did not fear to oppose governments that they believed were acting contrary to the Word of God nor hesitate to apply Calvin's ideas on church government as developed in Geneva to political situations elsewhere. Finally, Calvin had demonstrated his earnest desire to draw all Protestants together during the controversies concerning the Lord's Supper and thereby undoubtedly encouraged tendencies toward toleration that were frequently found among later Calvinists.

# 8 The Catholic Reformation

## Backgrounds

To the casual observer living in Europe about the middle of the sixteenth century, it must have seemed as though Roman Catholicism would eventually succumb to Protestantism, for it still remained on the defensive and showed few signs of spiritual vigor. However, by that time, powerful constructive forces were already taking shape within the venerable institution that, when directed by a reformed and consecrated papacy, not only regained much that had been lost to Protestantism but made new conquests among non-Christians and once more became a positive force in Western civilization.

This amazing revival of Roman Catholicism has been variously called Counter Reformation, Catholic Reaction, Catholic Reform, and Catholic Reformation. Because all four elements were present, the use of the term *Catholic Reformation* seems preferable, for it can be used to include the other three.

Among the positive forces that found expression in the Catholic Reformation were (1) the persistence of a strong medieval piety, strengthened by a new mysticism and reverence for the traditions of the Church; (2) Christian humanism, which generally remained loyal to Catholicism, despite its emphasis upon the value of pagan culture and philosophy; and (3) a revived scholasticism, purged of its late-medieval formalism and sharpened during controversies with the Protestants. These forces found expression in the reform of old and the rise of new religious orders, dedicated to the revival of spiritual life and service to others; a reformed papacy that could command the respect of Catholics and assume absolute authority in the affairs of the Church; and a Church council that met the challenge of Protestantism by planning reforms and reaffirming the validity of the medieval doctrines and traditions of the Church.

In less than half a century the strong religious dissatisfaction that had culminated in the Protestant Reformation had subsided, many of the abuses that had prompted the attacks against the Church had been eliminated, and in those countries that had broken with Rome there was little evidence that the perfect "kingdom of God" had been established on earth. Luther himself, during his last years, frequently uttered his keen disappointment over the fact that the preaching of the gospel had not made his Wittenbergers a real congregation of believers. Beza in Geneva and Bullinger in Zurich could not carry on with the same success as had their predecessors.

That is not to say that the Protestant Reformation did not foster widespread spirituality in its attempts to revive the fervor and faith of the primitive Christian Church. But where the movements did not combine with political, economic, and social currents, as in France and the Low Countries, the broad masses evinced their conservatism and piety in Protestant as well as Catholic countries. This was particularly true in Spain and Italy, where the masses looked upon the Protestant Reformation as an esoteric movement.

The most dynamic Protestant force of the latter half of the century was Calvinism, for it carried the brunt of the attack made by a revived Catholicism. Although it lost ground in France and much of eastern Europe, it helped Protestantism survive in England and Scotland and gained much ground in the Low Countries. Both Protestantism and Catholicism, however, became so deeply involved in the political affairs of Europe that one can hardly speak of a strong religious movement after the close of the sixteenth century. The rapidly growing secularized state was everywhere creating state churches that served political ends, though not without recognizing in varying degrees their Christian obligations. Not until the twentieth century did European states appear that dared to deny the validity of Christianity and openly act contrary to its basic ethical standards.

The exceptions to these general tendencies must not be overlooked. The Anabaptists and other left-wing Protestants failed to gain control of any European state or territory. But they continued, under the constant threat of persecution, to preach the gospel according to their respective convictions and to demand those rights of freedom of faith and worship that are generally accepted by Protestantism today.

It is noteworthy that militant Calvinism and Catholicism both had their origins in Romance countries. Although Catholicism had lost much of its constructive character in Germany and eastern Europe, the beginnings of a basically medieval Catholic Reformation are to be found in Spain and Italy.

## Spain

It was particularly in the Iberian Peninsula, where the crusades against Islam had continued throughout the late Middle Ages, that medieval piety first combined with a new quietistic mysticism and a renovated scholasticism to become a powerful religious force. Already, before the sixteenth century, Cardinal Jiménez de Cisneros (1436–1517) had led in the reform of the Spanish clergy with the cooperation of the Catholic rulers Ferdinand and Isabella; and the Spanish Inquisition, established in 1480 as a national institution, had been an effective instrument for preventing the spread of heresy. The few islands of Lutheran ideas, supported largely by the upper classes, were completely wiped out after the autos-da-fé of 1559–1560, when no persons were exempted from the jurisdiction of the Inquisition.

In distinctly medieval manner, the renewed spiritual life of Spain found expression in a revival of asceticism and monasticism. By the end of the seventeenth century there were reputedly more than nine thousand monasteries. The clergy constituted about a fourth of the entire population, and about half of all the land was owned by the Church. The ascetic movement displayed many characteristics of the Oriental religions but clearly received its strongest impetus from the German and Dutch mystics, especially the Brethren of the Common Life. The *Imitatio Christi* was one of the most widely read religious books in Spain.

As elsewhere, the ascetic mysticism in Spain tended to minimize the importance of the sacraments and of priestly mediation. This was particularly true of the *Alumbrados,* or Illuminati. But under such spiritual leaders as Garcia de Cisneros (d. 1510), a nephew of Cardinal Jiménez and abbot of the Benedictine monastery of Montserrat near Barcelona, Spanish mysticism was made highly practical and was used in the service of the Church. Garcia's mysticism was highly eclectic, for it combined features of the various mystic movements from that of St. Bernard of Clairvaux to the *Devotio moderna.*

The greatest and most typical of the Spanish mystics was St. Teresa of Jesus (1515–1582), born of a noble family in Ávila in Old Castile. She was canonized in 1622. She was the founder of the neo-Catholic quietistic mysticism, for she and her influential follower, St. John of the Cross (1542–1591), developed its terminology and spread its spiritual exercises. While still a child, she contemplated martyrdom among the Moors, whom her family had fought for generations. Then she indulged in reading romances of chivalry, which she later considered a serious lapse into worldliness. In 1535 she entered the Carmelite convent at Ávila, where she took her vows as a nun. Then for nearly twenty years she enjoyed those speculations, ecstacies, and visions that ultimately led to the rapture of intimate union with God.

It was a Franciscan mystic who finally induced Teresa to turn her attention to practical activities. After a special vision in which Christ commanded her to do so, she founded the Carmelite Monastery of St. Joseph at Ávila and wrote for it her *Constitutions,* eventually extended to all the foundations of the order. Later she founded a house of barefooted Carmelites, in which the rule was exceptionally severe; but in this as in all her foundations she provided time for meditation, examination of conscience, and prayer.

Like her predecessors among the Spanish mystics, Teresa developed definite steps for the attainment of perfect and lasting peace of mind. According to her experiences, the soul ascends the mystical ladder on the rungs of prayer of recollection, attained by concentration; the prayer of quietude, in which the half-asleep soul "touches the supernatural"; the prayer of union, in which the soul is overcome by love for the divine; and the prayer of ecstasy, or "spiritual marriage" of the soul with Christ, which conveys to it knowledge unobtainable in any other way. Such ecstatic experiences, which went far beyond the religious experiences of the Protestants, served to arouse that religious phantasy of the Spaniards that was so artistically portrayed in the paintings of El Greco, Ribera, and Murillo and in the literature of Cervantes, Lope de Vega, and Calderon. But in both literature and art, Spanish idealism is portrayed alongside strong materialism, the penchant for dreaming alongside love for action, emotional ecstasy alongside practical service.

The quietistic mysticism of the Spaniards, however, which in some instances found expression in Protestant leanings, was too powerful a force to be ignored by those who were eager to maintain orthodoxy. Even St. Teresa was for a while threatened by the Inquisition. To counteract such dangers, a renovated scholasticism made its appearance, stimulated by the reforms of Jiménez, who used the skills of the humanists in furthering his religious ends. Erasmian humanism, especially, gained considerable influence among the educated in Spain, which it retained until the middle of the sixteenth century, when the writings of Erasmus were condemned by the Inquisition.

The chief representative of this new scholastic movement was Melchior Cano (d. 1560), whose *Loci theologici* appeared posthumously in 1562. He and other prominent theologians purged scholasticism of its highly speculative characteristics and in elegant linguistic style considered the practical religious doctrines associated with the problem of salvation. By replacing arid dialectic methods with a thorough study of the Church fathers, they developed a new dogmatic and moral theology that placed the Catholics in a much better position than formerly to come to grips with the Protestant theologians. The Thomistic system, revived and revitalized, gained canonical status in the Church, and the University of Salamanca, the chief center of this neo-Thomism, spread its influence throughout Europe far into the seventeenth century.

### Italy

Although the upper classes in Italy had become more highly paganized than elsewhere, and although the lower classes had been little influenced by the intellectual and religious developments of the Italian Renaissance, strong currents of reform became evident early in the sixteenth century. Humanism itself, as it ran its course, became increasingly absorbed in religious affairs. The religious interests of such centers as the Platonic Academy in Florence had already in the fifteenth century exerted a strong influence upon the growth of Christian humanism north of the Alps. Thus one must not look upon the Italian reform movement as one having originated in Spain, even though the Spanish influences were strong. The main obstacle to reform in Italy was the paucity of effective leaders, until the sack of Rome in 1527 and the increasing spread of Protestantism greatly alarmed the papacy and its supporters and turned the attention of many intellectuals from material to religious interests.

In 1517, the same year in which Luther nailed his theses on the door of the Castle Church in Wittenberg, there was formed in Rome the Oratory of Divine Love, a society of about fifty clergymen and laymen devoted to the cause of reform. The first society of this kind had been formed in Genoa in 1497. It members, highly restricted in number, wished to revive spirituality by prayer, preaching and listening to sermons, frequent use of the sacraments, and the performance of acts of love. In the various Oratories in Italy, persons with highly diverse religious convictions—liberal humanists as well as reactionary theologians—worked side by side, united in their desire to maintain traditional Catholicism under the leadership of the papacy. However, in their development of a strong, personal religious consciousness, concerned with the practical problem of salvation, tendencies appeared that led some members close to the Lutheran emphasis of justification by faith alone.

As religious conditions in Italy reached a crisis, a growing number of members of the Oratories realized that mere personal devotion and religious activity would not save the Church or the Italian people. They became especially concerned with the progressive deterioration of morality, the appalling ignorance of the masses, the lack of sincerity on the part of many of the clergy, the strong paganization of religious and cultural life, and the widespread misery of the people, which could no longer be hidden by the beautiful façade of Renaissance culture. When the climax of confusion and ruin was reached in the sack of Rome in 1527, the Oratory of Divine Love in Rome disbanded. A number of its members then sought other means for furthering the reform of the Church and Italian society.

Among these reformers were several bishops who believed that they should begin with a policy of self-reform in their respective dioceses. They accordingly set about training their clergy to assume their religious responsibilities, establishing schools for the education of the young, providing care for the poor, and carrying on a vigorous campaign against venereal disease. Jacopo Sadoleto (1477–1547), bishop of Carpentras; Gian Matteo Giberti (1495–1543), bishop of Verona; and Gian Pietro Caraffa (1476–1559), bishop of Chieti, were particularly successful in reforming their respective dioceses. Sadoleto extended his influence outside his diocese and, as we have seen, sought to bring the Genevans back into Catholicism. Giberti not only introduced a rigid discipline among his clergy but, as a Christian humanist, maintained orthodox theology by furthering the study of the Bible. Caraffa, who later became Pope Paul IV, was a man of vigorous intellect, strong will, and austere morality who consistently and successfully fought for a reformation along medieval lines.

In many ways unlike Caraffa was Gasparo Contarini (1483–1542), a Christian humanist born of a patrician family in Venice and experienced in the political affairs of this city. He early became interested in the renovation of the Church, hoping to reconcile Protestantism and Catholicism by introducing a number of Protestant reforms. We have already had occasion to refer to his failure at conciliation at Regensburg in 1541. As bishop of Belluno after 1536, he carried on a successful program of reform. Like Eck, Campeggio, and Cajetan, who had all come into contact with the Protestant reformers, he felt that the Church could be saved only by a thorough cleansing of the Augean stables.

Scholasticism also underwent modifications in Italy, thereby becoming a strong instrument of Catholic reform. This was largely the work of Cardinal Cajetan (1469–1534), the Dominican with whom Luther had had a hearing in Augsburg in 1518 and who withdrew to his bishopric of Gaeta in 1527. In the interest of retaining complete unity of faith, he, Caraffa, and others cleansed scholasticism of its late-medieval accretions and used it in the service of the Catholic Reformation. Cajetan's commentary on the *Summa* of Thomas Aquinas became the standard interpretation of Thomism; but his exegetical works, strongly influenced by Erasmian humanism, aroused considerable opposition among Catholic theologians.

## Germany

The Catholic Reformation made its appearance in southern and western Germany soon after the rise of Lutheranism. But it lacked the vitality evinced in Spain and Italy. Berthold Pürstinger, bishop of Chiemsee, not only preached forceful sermons of repentance but published influential theological books. His *German Theology* of 1528 outlined the basic doctrines of the Catholic faith, drawn especially from Augustine. He, like other German bishops, made good use of visitations to compel the clergy to perform their duties and did much to improve the administration of their dioceses. In some areas, the singing of hymns was also encouraged at this time.

Many German humanists, some of whom had become Protestant but had returned to Catholicism, followed the lead of Erasmus in coming to the aid of the old faith. Johann Gropper (1503–1559) of Soest, for example, had, as chancellor of Cologne, supported Archbishop Hermann von Wied in his abortive reform program. But when the latter contemplated breaking with Rome, Gropper left his service. Gropper's *Manual of Christian Doctrine* (1538) contained the most detailed statement of Catholic dogma that appeared prior to the Council of Trent. But because of its vague position with respect to the doctrine of justification, it was placed on the Index of Prohibited Books toward the end of the century.

To counteract the influence of Luther's translation of the Bible, Catholic translations were also made, based on the Vulgate of St. Jerome and following the German translations of the Middle Ages. That of Hieronymus Emser (d. 1527), a theologian of Leipzig, imitated Luther's style but did not gain wide circulation. Much more successful was the translation by Johann Dietenberger (d. 1537), professor at Mainz, which was published in fifty-eight editions.

On the whole, German Catholic scholarship showed little improvement during Luther's lifetime. The chief polemical writers were Johann Eck (d. 1543) and Johann Cochlaeus (d. 1552), who remained content with accusing the reformers of holding doctrines previously declared heretical. That this kind of polemical writing was nonetheless popular is indicated by the fact that Eck's *Manual of Common Doctrines Against Luther and Other Enemies of the Church* appeared in forty-six editions.

## The Reforming Orders

The strongly medieval features of the Catholic Reformation are apparent also in the revival of monasticism. It was in the reforming orders that the movement found its most vigorous and characteristic expression. Both the older orders and those created especially to renovate the Church became aware of the crying religious and social needs of their day and assumed their responsibilities with a revived courage and devotion that must have surprised the Protestants.

Among the first of the new orders were the Theatines, founded in 1524 by Gaetano de Thiene (1480–1547). The name of the order was derived from *Theate,* the Latin for Chieti, Caraffa's former bishopric, which he had given up to become the first superior of the order. Gaetano, a member of the Oratory of Divine Love, wished to inculcate the ideals of that society among the secular clergy, for whose benefit he founded this new, exclusive, and aristocratic order. Living severely ascetic lives of poverty—its members were not permitted to retain their benefices or even to beg—the Theatines devoted themselves to preaching and administering the sacraments to the end that they might become models for a devoted secular clergy and check the spread of heresy. But they also supported the establishment of orphanages and hospitals at a time when the ravages of war, the plague, and famine created widespread misery in northern Italy.

Among the many eminent men who supported the Theatines were Contarini, the conciliatory Catholic reformer; Gregorio Cortese (d. 1548), a Benedictine reformer; and Reginald Pole (1500–1558), a cardinal related to the English royal family. In 1527 the order was transferred to Venice, and six years later a branch was established in Naples. Because, however, it was the purpose of Gaetano to concentrate on the development of outstanding leaders, the number of members in the order was kept small. Although there were only twenty-one Theatines in 1533, their influence was great. When Caraffa was made a cardinal in 1537, for example, he brought Theatine ideas and methods with him to the Roman *Curia*.

Caraffa was also instrumental in having two other new orders of regular clergy recognized: the Sommaschi, founded in 1528 by a once dissolute officer of a noble Venetian family, and the Barnabites, founded in 1530 by a former medical student of Verona. In both these orders conscientious, ascetically inclined persons organized groups for the purpose of disciplining themselves, spreading the faith, and caring for the unfortunate. They founded hospitals and orphanages, rescued fallen girls, of whom there were unbelievably large numbers in Italy at that time, and in other ways carried out the program initiated by the Theatines.

Unlike the Theatines, the Barnabites were eager to expand. They founded houses not only throughout Italy, but in Germany, Bohemia, and France. To assist them in working among the women, a female auxiliary was founded in 1535, called the Congregation of the Holy Angels, or Angelice.

Even more effective in caring for the physical and spiritual needs of the common people were the Capuchins. Unlike the members of the orders already described, many of whom were of noble birth, these came from the common people and understood their problems. They were an offshoot of a branch of the Franciscans, the Observants, who themselves had separated from the laxer majority, the Conventuals, during the late Middle Ages. The founder of the Capuchins, Matteo da Bascio (1495–1552), was a son of Umbrian peasants. He believed that the rule of St. Francis should be revived in all its severity. He and his followers even wished to wear the exact dress of the founder, including the four-cornered hood, called *cappuccio,* which led the people to call its wearer a *cappuccino,* or "little hooded man," a term of both affection and derision. Hence the name Capuchin.

Because the Conventuals placed many obstacles in the way of the Capuchins, the latter obtained from the pope in 1528 the right to have their own superior, although they still remained under the protection of the Conventuals. Their popular preaching and care of the sick and poor, especially during epidemics, endeared them to the common people; but they got into difficulties after Ochino, their vice-general, became Protestant in 1542.

Other older orders were reformed to meet the new needs and circumstances. The Dominican order, many of whose members had strong Protestant leanings, was not finally purged of its heretical preachers until Paul III conducted visitations among them in the 1540s. The success of Caraffa's sister in reforming the Dominican nuns at Naples was imitated elsewhere. Although the Augustinian Eremites were led by reforming generals, it took many years to make the order an effective instrument of Catholic reform.

Highly successful in spreading Catholic reform were the Ursulines, founded in 1535 by Angela Merici (1470–1540) and devoted to the education of girls of all classes. In 1572 the members of the society were bound to the three monastic vows and came to constitute an order. Ursuline convents soon spread to France, where their schools, which had much in common with those of the Jesuits, played an important role in strengthening Catholicism after the religious wars. Elegance and refinement of manners were inculcated alongside piety and devotion.

Likewise interested in education and the cultural refinement of religious observance were the Oratorians, whose founder and leading spirit was Philip Neri (1515–1595), a member of an old Florentine family who gave up a life of pleasure and cheerfully devoted himself to personal missionary work in the city of Rome. He eventually took priest's orders in 1552 and began his active career as a confessor and leader of regular afternoon exercises in prayer that came to be called Oratories. Following no set forms, this congregation of secular priests, established by Gregory XIII in 1575, read religious, mostly mystical, literature and frequently performed motets. The singing of canticles developed into the oratorio of the next century. Among the followers of the Oratorians were Palestrina (d. 1594), the reformer of Catholic church music, and Cardinal Baronius (1538–1607), the author of *Ecclesiastical Annals* and other Catholic historical literature.

## The Jesuits

Whereas the majority of the reforming orders hoped to strengthen Catholicism primarily by means of prayer and self-mortification, the Jesuits were much more practical in their approach. With their highly developed discipline and organization, they became the chief instrument of the Catholic Reformation.

The founder of the Jesuits was Ignatius Loyola (1491?–1556), the adventurous knight Don Iñigo de Onaz y de Loyola, born in the Basque province of Guipuzcoa. As an officer in the army of the vice-regent of Navarre, he dreamed of the adventures pictured in the late-medieval romantic literature and at the same time learned to master his will by means of military discipline. But his military career was cut short when he was wounded—multiple fractures in one of his legs—at the siege of Pamplona in 1521, during the first of the Hapsburg-Valois wars.

Because his leg had to be reset, he lived through the extreme tortures inflicted in the name of bone care and surgery. To while away the dreary and painful days, he turned to reading. Because no knightly romances were at hand, he read with increasing interest the lives of saints and a *Life of Christ* by Ludolf of Saxony. Realizing that he would be crippled for life and that he would have to give up his knightly ambitions, he decided to take up the sword on behalf of the Virgin Mary and as soon as possible to set out on a pilgrimage to the cave of Manresa at Montserrat near Barcelona.

Ignatius arrived at Montserrat in the spring of 1522, his leg not yet healed and suffering from an illness that nearly took his life. There, as a humble penitent, he stood watch before an image of the Virgin Mary; and in a general confession lasting three days he formally closed the previous chapters of his life. Then he intended to set out on a pilgrimage to Jerusalem. An outbreak of the plague, however, compelled him to remain at Manresa for nearly half a year. During these months he, like Luther, was beset with struggles of conscience. But he did not overcome them by a theological approach through justification by faith. Instead, he decided by an act of the will to rid himself of these inner conflicts as satanic in origin and to pursue a rigid course designed to focus his attention upon the benevolent divine influence in his soul. Thus his inner experiences led him to embrace a new religious technique, not a new theology.

The inner experiences by means of which Loyola found peace of soul were set down in Spanish in his *Spiritual Exercises*. Although this book leaves much to be desired with respect to literary form, it shows exceptional insight into religious psychology. It is divided into four parts, each one to be followed for a week. The first part is intended to make one aware of the damnable nature of sin, the second of the significance of the life of Christ, the third of the Passion story, and the fourth of the Resurrection and Ascension. Thus, by means of ordered meditation, Loyola dramatized the traditional account of salvation and made it a part of his own personal experience. In other words, he provided a discipline whereby he and his followers could by a series of progressive resolutions

St. Ignatius Loyola

(*Seville, University Church*)

compel themselves to detest sin, join the ranks of God and God's servants, and finally have this decision tested and confirmed.

By strengthening his will, the Jesuit would proceed from meditation to action; by completely mastering himself, he would steer a middle course, avoiding all extremes; by always having in view his ultimate religious purpose of serving God and saving souls, he would adapt himself to circumstances, thereby subordinating the means to the end. Thus excessive self-mortification was avoided and religious exercises were adapted to the needs and physical capacities of the individual as well as to what was feasible and practical. On the other hand, the discipline of the will in the Stoic sense, which is not harmful, must be practiced constantly to the end that the person could renounce his own will in complete humility and merge it with the will of God. Thus Loyola, although accepting without question the authority of the Catholic Church, combined the Renaissance conception of personality and the late-medieval aims of the mystics, thereby creating a new conception of holiness that found its fullest ex-expression in a practical activity on behalf of God.

The *Spiritual Exercises,* then, was not a book of devotion, like the *Imitation of Christ,* which Loyola prized highly, but a severe, semimilitary, spiritual discipline. By means of it the personality was not merged in a mystic union with God but was developed by the force of a determined, hardened will, a rigidly calculated self-control, and a religious idealism of heroic proportions. Every religious emotion, every sinful thought or inclination, every emotional response to the reading of the Mass was recorded in diaries and tablets and analyzed by the individual and his confessor.

Fortified by his experiences and resolutions at Manresa, Loyola set out for Jerusalem early in 1523 to convert the Mohammedans, but with no thought of founding a new religious order. There he came to the realization that he could accomplish nothing without a good education, particularly in theology. Although already thirty years of age, he decided to correct this deficiency. This required nearly a decade of great effort.

Loyola began by enrolling with young boys in a preparatory school in Barcelona. At the University of Alcalá he gathered about him the first small circle of like-minded students and inhabitants of the city. Suspected of being a member of the *Alumbrados,* he was twice imprisoned by the Spanish Inquisition but finally acquitted of heresy. After a short sojourn at Salamanca, he went to Paris in 1528, where he continued his philosophical and theological studies at the Collège de Montaigu. With his winning personality and an uncanny understanding of human nature, he gathered about him a number of faithful and able students as followers: Pierre Le Fèvre (Peter Faber), the son of peasants of Savoy, who became active in the Counter Reformation in Germany; Francis Xavier, a Basque nobleman who became well known as a missionary to the Far East;

Diego Lainez, of an old Castilian Jewish family and Loyola's successor as general of the Jesuits; and the Spaniards Alfonso Salmerón and Nicholas Bobadilla and the Portuguese Simon Rodriguez, who later distinguished themselves as scholars.

The Society of Jesus had its inception, at least potentially, when, on August 15, 1534, Loyola and his six companions met in the chapel of St. Denis at Montmartre to dedicate themselves to a life of service to God. After Le Fèvre, the only priest among them, had read Mass, the seven took the vows of poverty and chastity and bound themselves to go to the Holy Land to do missionary work after the completion of their studies. If that mission should not prove feasible, they would place themselves completely at the disposal of the pope.

In 1537 Loyola and his companions, now ten in number, met in Venice, were consecrated as priests, and prepared to set out for Jerusalem. Because, however, no ships were sailing because of a war between Venice and the Turks, they decided to "seek their Jerusalem in Rome," probably at the suggestion of Caraffa, who met Loyola in Venice and tried to induce him and his followers to become Theatines. It was at this time that this small band assumed the name of Society of Jesus.

## Nature and Work of the Society of Jesus

Loyola and two companions went to Rome to offer their services to Pope Paul III. The others became active in northern Italy, particularly in university centers. Because the services that they rendered the Church were similar to those of the Theatines and because they were occasionally suspected of heresy, they had difficulty gaining the recognition of the pope. But when Contarini, who had joined Loyola in his "exercises," and King John III of Portugal, who needed missionaries for his East Indian colonies, lent their support, the pope constituted the company an order in the bull *Regimini militantis ecclesiae,* in September, 1540.

By this time the main purposes of the order were being clarified. The members continued their practical work among the unfortunates, establishing poorhouses, workhouses, and houses for reclaiming prostitutes; but it soon became clear that they were particularly suited to operate in three areas in which they established an ever-increasing reputation: (1) educating the young, (2) leading the masses back to Catholicism, and (3) promoting a high religious earnestness among individuals by means of the confession and the "exercises."

The greatest emphasis was placed on education. Loyola and his learned followers made use of the methods of the humanists but introduced a military discipline into their schools that permeated every phase of learning. Preparatory schools were founded as separate institutions or in connection with universities. Jesuits became professors at all the Catholic universities and gained control of the curricula of several of them.

# Part Three: Spread of Protestantism

Their chief emphasis was not upon the development of intellectual independence and individuality but upon a refined, humanist facility of expression and a strong devotion to the authority of the Church. They developed a uniform educational system, divided the pupils and students into definite classes, used regular examinations for promotions, and improved the textbooks. Because of these effective pedagogical methods, large numbers of influential persons sent their boys to Jesuit schools.

To counteract heresy, the Jesuit fathers preached simple, popular sermons in which they avoided polemics and dogmas and stressed morality and practical Christianity. Such popular instruction was supplemented by catechetical instruction, in which the people were grounded in the fundamentals of Catholicism, and by the confessional. The fathers gained access to the important courts of Europe. By becoming the confessors of influential persons, they exerted a great influence upon politics. Everywhere they revived inner spirituality, confidence, and certainty, thereby providing a welcome relief from the storm and stress of the religious disturbances that had threatened the stability of the old order. Thus the Society of Jesus became the most important instrument of the Counter Reformation. Loyola was particularly eager to win Protestants back to Catholicism, and his followers were highly effective in inducing secular rulers to use their political authority in suppressing Protestantism.

Loyola set down his views concerning the organization of his order in the *Constitutions,* accepted in its main features by the fathers in 1550 and formally approved by the general congregation of the professed fathers in 1558. Unlike the constitutions of other orders, it provided for an extremely strict education and supervision of its members. During the novitiate of two years, every tendency toward individual self-expression was crushed and there was inculcated an absolute obedience toward one's superiors and the papacy. Moreover, the supreme authority lay not in the general chapter but in the office of the general, chosen by a congregation of all the fathers.

The military character of the organization, the severe discipline, and the absolute identification of the individual will with that of the superior became apparent in the provisions made for the training of young men for admission into the order. Applicants were carefully screened according to high standards of intellect, character, physical well-being, and social adaptability. During the novitiate, these young men were placed in houses of probation where the master constantly subjected them to spiritual exercises, humiliating tasks, and trials of all kinds, reminding them always that they must in the end forsake everything—their individual rights and inclinations, their own judgment, even their former friends and relatives, of whom they were allowed to speak only in the past tense.

Those novices who withstood the severe tests in the houses of probation took the three monastic vows of poverty, chastity, and obedience and were carefully divided according to their abilities. Some were assigned to simple manual tasks as secular coadjutors. Others, designated as approved scholastics, entered a Jesuit college, took the usual arts course, became teachers, then studied theology, and, after another year of trial, were made priests and were called spiritual coadjutors. A relatively small number of these were permitted to study two more years. After passing a rigid examination they were permitted to take the fourth vow of absolute obedience to the papacy and to enter the ranks of the professed fathers, the core of the order. Thus the ultimate purpose of this thorough training was to develop spiritual soldiers of unquestioning obedience with respect to their actions, will, and even thoughts.

For the purpose of maintaining rigid military discipline in this rapidly expanding order, Loyola provided a highly centralized form of administration. The various houses were grouped together into provinces and these into five large "assistancies," those of Italy, Spain, France, Germany, and the English-speaking countries. The assistancies were placed under assistants who, with the general and his admonitor, or confessor, resided in Rome and comprised the central staff of the order. The general, the assistants, the heads of the provinces, and the rectors of the houses were chosen by the general congregation of the order, although the general, chosen by a majority vote, invariably chose the lesser superiors. The general congregation, consisting of the general and the deputies of the provinces, had no parliamentary functions but was called only in case of necessity, usually to elect a general. The general was given six assistants who were to see to it that he did not abuse his authority or in any way deviate from the oft-repeated injunction to serve the "greater glory of God." The lesser superiors were likewise provided with assistants.

The rigid discipline of the Jesuits was not the only feature that differentiated it from other orders. Women were excluded and special habits were dispensed with. Moreover, absolute independence of the order was sought by the forbidding of donors or others to exercise any kind of an influence. Finally, the Jesuits were not bound to the usual monastic duties, such as choir services. For this reason they were frequently opposed by other orders. In 1558 Pope Paul IV, who disliked the Jesuits, compelled the general congregation to introduce the recitation of the Church offices in the choir and to reduce the terms of office of the general from life to three years. But after his death the next year, the order continued as before.

Loyola was unanimously elected the first general of the order in 1541 by the original ten members, four of whom were not in Rome but sent their votes in writing. When he died, in 1556, the order had about a thousand members and about a hundred houses grouped into twelve provinces. It had established such famous institutions as the Roman College (1551) and the German College (1552), which were given annual subsidies by the pope.

Lainez, Loyola's successor, was not chosen general until 1558, and then by a vote of thirteen out of twenty, indicating the strong opposition to him. Under him there was a tendency for the general to become the absolute master of the order. Increased bureaucratic administration was necessitated by the order's rapid growth. At its height, in 1624, it had more than sixteen thousand members. Faithful to the commands of the papacy, the Jesuits constituted the shock troops of the Catholic Reformation.

## Successes of the Jesuits

The first successful conquests by the Jesuits were made in such Italian centers of heresy as Venice, Naples, and Ferrara, where they established important houses. Although the order was openly mistrusted by Charles V and opposed by the Dominicans and the higher clergy in Spain, it eventually gained a firm foothold there. But it was more successful in Portugal, where Francis Xavier and Simon Rodriguez gained both royal and popular support. This country became the first separate province of the order in 1546. Because of the hostile attitude of the Sorbonne and the Parlement of Paris, the Jesuits were unable to establish their order in France until 1555, when they gained a foothold in the Auvergne. Lainez opened the way in Paris by the wisdom and tact that he displayed at the Colloquy of Poissy in 1561.

It was in Germany that Ignatius planned to concentrate the chief efforts of the order. Pierre Le Fèvre made his appearance there as early as 1540, when he attended the religious colloquies at Worms and Regensburg. Two years later he and two other Jesuits accompanied the papal nuncio on a tour of the Protestant territories.

The chief leader of the Catholic Reformation in Germany, however, was Peter Canisius (Peter Kanis de Hondt, 1521–1597), a native of Gelderland who had studied in the gymnasium at Cologne. Upon the completion of his university studies, he met Pierre Le Fèvre at Mainz and performed the Jesuit exercises with him. He made it his ambition to win the Germans back to Catholicism, not by polemics but by moderation, kindness, and religious edification. He began to carry out his plans soon after joining the order in 1543, encouraged by the success of Jesuits who had obtained the support of a number of German bishops and of the Wittelsbach and Hapsburg families. After the death of Eck in 1543, the University of Ingolstadt in Bavaria was supplied with Jesuit professors, including Canisius. Two years later the first German Jesuit college was established at Vienna. Canisius became its head in 1552. Within seven years the number of students enrolled there reached a total of five hundred. Similar Jesuit colleges were founded at Cologne and Prague in

1555, Ingolstadt in 1556, Munich in 1559, and Mainz, Trier, Würzburg, and Speyer in 1567.

The activities of Canisius were not confined to teaching, for he was made provincial of the order for Upper Germany in 1556, went on important preaching missions to the larger cities of these lands, and served Emperor Ferdinand as adviser and ambassador. Not the least of his services to the Catholic Reformation was the publication in both Latin and German of his Large Catechism in 1556 (designed to counteract the success of Luther's Large Catechism) and his Small Catechism (intended to replace Luther's Small Catechism). These catechisms were so well conceived and so positive in their approach that they were published in hundreds of editions throughout Europe and even in Asia and Africa.

Canisius spent his last years in Fribourg, Switzerland, where he continued the reforms initiated by Borromeo, whose district of Milan reached into Switzerland and whose Helvetian College trained missionaries for work in the Swiss cantons. For his singular devotion to the Catholic Reformation, Canisius was canonized in 1925. In Fribourg, as elsewhere, the Catholic cause was also furthered by the rapidly expanding activities of the Capuchins. In the French-speaking lands Francis de Sales brought many people back to the old faith. In 1597 he even attempted to reconvert the aged Beza.

The foreign-missionary activities of the Jesuits began during the lifetime of Loyola. Probably the greatest of their missionaries was Francis Xavier (1506–1552). He landed at the Portuguese settlement of Goa in India in 1542, attacked the immorality, corruption, and brutality of the colonists there and, after a few months, began his long and fruitful journeys. He first traveled through southern India, Malaya, and the Moluccas, teaching and baptizing large numbers of natives and reconverting lapsed Christians. After his return to Goa in 1548 he set out for Japan, where he labored for two years. He died of a fever on an island near Canton in December, 1552, after having reputedly won hundreds of thousands of Orientals to the Christian faith. Only in China and Japan were the missions established by him stamped out in the seventeenth century. In China the Jesuit successes were nullified by a bitter quarrel with the Dominicans, who attacked the former for carrying their policy of adaptation so far as to include such a Chinese rite as ancestor worship, although the Jesuits did not intend to permit the giving of divine honor to the ancestors.

In the western hemisphere the Jesuit fathers were most successful during the sixteenth century in Brazil, for there they also had the support of the Portuguese king. In that country they rendered a valuable service by opposing the enslaving of the natives and by assuming the task of civilizing them. Much of their success stemmed from the ability and tact of Father José d'Anchieta (1533–1597), who induced the natives to settle in villages, worked patiently among the wildest tribes in the most formidable regions, and patiently set out to educate them. He wrote a grammar and a dictionary in the native tongue and became rector of the college of San Vicente. In 1578 he was made provincial of the order in Brazil. His labors firmly established the Jesuit missions in Brazil and prepared the way for subsequent successes in the rest of South America.

## The Reform of the Papacy

After the failure of the fifteenth-century Church councils to reform the Church "in head and members," it became increasingly clear that such an ambitious program could be realized only with the active leadership of the papacy. Proponents of the conciliar theories gradually gave up their emphasis upon the necessity of a reformation from below and recognized the absolute authority of the papacy in religious matters. When a general council finally met, in 1545, the popes retained control of it and were given the duty of executing its decrees.

The need for strong papal leadership was recognized during the twelve sessions of the Fifth Lateran Council at Rome, lasting from 1512 to 1517. It agreed that the chief obstacles to a vigorous spiritual leadership of the pope grew out of his temporal responsibilities. Instead of attacking the problem of reforms with vigor, however, the Lateran Council made a number of timid recommendations with respect to religious, administrative, and fiscal matters that aroused so much antagonism among those with a personal stake in the corruption that the recommendations could not be carried out. Yet this Lateran Council approved the concordat of Leo X (1513–1521) with Francis I of France, which enabled the French king to introduce a number of salutary reforms in his country.

The confusion in high places in the Catholic Church reflected the great divisions among its people as a whole. Whereas the leaders of the mendicant orders were primarily concerned with the reform of gross abuses, the Christian humanists demanded, at least for themselves, a freer interpretation of theology, which would amount to a synthesis of the traditional theology with humanism. Most of the theologians, however, demanded a revival of Thomistic scholasticism as the *sine qua non* of any reformation of the Church. When large segments of Christendom began to separate from Rome, there were many advisers close to the papacy who, influenced by both humanism and the revival of Augustinian doctrines, advised conciliation. Others refused to deviate in any way from the Thomistic theology and the accepted traditions of Catholicism. The story of the reform of the papacy is the story of the success of the latter over the former.

A further difficulty facing the popes was the complicated political situation in Europe, which required their constant attention as rulers of the Papal States. They frequently failed to gauge not only the dynastic and national ambitions of the chief political leaders of Europe but also the religious motives of the followers of Luther, Zwingli, and Calvin. Leo X, for example, was baffled by the uproar created over what he had considered a quarrel among monks and played a predominately political role during the events leading to the election of Charles V. This position greatly weakened Leo X's position as arbiter in the religious conflicts. Although much of his attention was devoted to political and cultural interests, he recognized the need for reforms in the *Curia*. Accordingly, he replaced self-seeking cardinals with devout and scholarly men, including Cajetan, general of the Dominicans, and Egidio Canisio (Giles of Viterbo), general of the Augustinian Eremites.

Adrian VI (1522–1523), Leo's successor, was conscientiously devoted to the cause of reform, but he soon alienated most of the Roman clergy by his reform proposals. As a devoted follower of Thomism, he was unappreciative of the Renaissance culture, which a large number of churchmen had embraced. His attempts to wipe out corruption in the papal bureaucracy, especially that associated with the sale of offices, threatened the prosperity of Rome, which largely rested on these abuses. In the face of strong opposition he accomplished little or nothing. It seems as though the Roman clergy needed to be shocked into action by a great catastrophe before they would accept a leader dedicated to reforms.

Clement VII (1523–1534), a cousin of Leo X, could accomplish little more than Adrian, despite his sincerity, personal integrity, and good intentions. Beset by political difficulties of the first magnitude, he was poorly informed concerning conditions outside Italy, conducted an ineffective and wavering diplomacy, and experienced a series of crises that culminated in the sack of Rome and his imprisonment in the castle of Sant' Angelo. Meanwhile his failure to meet the religious issues of his times with a vigorous spiritual program resulted in the break from Rome of England, Sweden, and several German territories.

The only solution now seemed to lie in the calling of a general church council, although most German princes demanded the calling of a national council, at least a "free Christian council on German soil." Charles V, who was consistent in his desire for a general council, threatened to support the Germans in their demand for a national council whenever it suited his political purposes. Clement, on the other hand, feared a general council and accordingly postponed taking the only action that might have stopped the spread of Protestantism. Worse still, he subordinated the reform program to family interests, so that finally friends as well as foes considered him unreliable.

Apparently unaware of the fact that the resources of the papacy were insufficient to enable him to play an effective political role on behalf of the Medici family, Clement steered a fatally devious course that was determined in the last analysis by the ambitions and successes of the two dominant political figures of Europe, Charles V and Francis I. Although

Charles was motivated by a strong dynastic consciousness and wished to serve Christendom by eliminating heresy and cleansing the Church of abuses, he nevertheless followed the advice of his astute chancellor Gattinara in using the demand for a Church council to gain his political ends.

Francis I, unlike Charles V, did not seem to take his religion seriously but tended to follow Machiavellian precepts with little compunction of conscience. Thoroughly egoistic and devoted to his pleasures, he was inclined to accept the leadership of strong advisers, such as his mother and Montmorency. Yet he was persistent in serving his own purposes and determined to maintain the Valois glory and power against his chief enemy, Charles.

The main centers of conflict were the duchy of Milan, the possession of which gave Francis hegemony in Italy, and the Low Countries, the "pearl of the Burgundian lands." Generally supported by his own people and uninhibited by religious scruples, the "most Christian king" of France joined hands with the enemies of Charles—the Turks, the Barbary Corsairs, and the Protestant princes—when such alliances served his purposes. Thus Francis adumbrated the modern principles of the balance of power, whereas Charles still thought in terms of medieval universalism. For this reason Francis had no interest in a Church council as a body representing all Christendom but looked upon it as a device that Charles might use to increase his own power. Francis was the most influential opponent of the calling of a general Church council.

Although Clement had as a cardinal been a consistent supporter of Charles, he chose to lean toward Francis after his election to the papacy. Believing that the French king, who had appeared in Italy with a large army, would easily defeat the imperialist forces and march in triumph to Naples as Charles VIII had, Clement signed a treaty with him, giving him permission to march through the papal lands. But the imperial victory at Pavia in February, 1525, and the Peace of Madrid of January, 1526, greatly changed the situation and resulted in the formation of the League of Cognac against the emperor. The struggle that followed led, as we have seen, to the sack of Rome.

A universal Church council could not be held in such disturbing circumstances. Because Clement sensed that Charles would now demand such a council, he attempted to checkmate him by calling a papal reform conventicle. When this move failed, Clement expressed his willingness to call a council but placed all kinds of obstacles in its way. Cardinal Wolsey came to his aid by getting England and France to agree that they would oppose a council called by Charles as long as the pope was at his mercy.

After the release of the pope from his imprisonment, relations between him and Charles improved sufficiently so that the latter could finally proceed to Italy to receive the imperial crown at the hands of the pope. The two lived in the same building in Bologna for four months in the winter of 1529–1530, during which time Charles did his best to induce Clement to call a council. The upshot of these attempts was that Clement agreed to do so, but only after peace had been restored between Charles and Francis. After the coronation on February 24, 1530, the birthday of Charles and the anniversary of his victory at Pavia, the emperor set out for Augsburg to attend the diet that assembled in that city.

During the absence of Charles from Germany since 1521, the German Reformation had become a strong political movement, supported by powerful estates, although few people believed that a permanent split had occurred in the Church. The majority of the estates still demanded, as at Speyer in 1526, that Charles urge the pope to call a "free general council on German soil," but if that were impossible, they insisted that he call a national council. Because Charles did not seem to comprehend the seriousness of the doctrinal differences, he still believed that the Protestants could be brought back into the Catholic Church. When his efforts failed at Augsburg in 1530, he decided to use force. But because he had brought no army into Germany, he gave the Protestants until April 15, 1531, to reconsider their refusal. When they remained adamant and formed the Schmalkaldic League to defend their position, it appeared as though the emperor and the pope would now use the methods followed fifteen years later. But the clearer it became that Charles did not have the military power to enforce his decision, the more the demand for a Church council increased.

After another meeting at Bologna between Charles and Clement in the winter of 1532–1533, the pope announced that he would call a council, but secretly he had no intention of doing so. When the papal nuncio made known Clement's promise to Charles, the Protestant princes for the first time openly declared that they would not participate in a council led by the pope, for it would not be "a free Christian council." At a meeting between the pope and Francis I at Marseilles in the fall of 1533, the latter openly expressed his opposition to the calling of the council, stating that it could not be convened so long as the conflict continued between him and Charles. The papal friendship with the French king was shown by the pope's appointment soon after of four new French cardinals and the marriage of Catherine de' Medici to Duke Henry of Orléans. In Germany, general bitterness followed the failure of the last attempts of Charles to compel Clement to act. To have surmounted all the complicated issues involved in the calling of a council would have required a strong will, which was lacking in Clement VII.

## Paul III

Clement nevertheless showed his interest in the cause of reform by recommending, shortly before his death, that the highly gifted and earnest Alessandro Farnese (b. 1468), who as a cardinal had demonstrated his desire for a reform council, be made his successor. He was elected pope as Paul III (1534–1549). Although the new pope had demonstrated his moral laxity by having fathered four illegitimate children before taking priest's orders, he regretted his earlier indiscretions. He appointed sincere reformers to the cardinal college, created a reform commission to study the abuses in the Church, centralized the Inquisition in Rome, and called a Church council that finally met in Trent in 1545.

Paul III's failure to accomplish more during the fifteen years of his pontificate was not a consequence of his lack of energy or insight into the seriousness of the many dangers confronting Catholicism. Yet he at first believed that he could accomplish his tasks with a few simple, bold strokes. When it became clear that he himself would be compelled to bear the consequences of his reforming activity, he tried to avoid them. In dealing with the great powers, he tried to steer a neutral course; but he would not desert his dynastic politics. Instead, he enriched his children and nephews, especially his oldest son, Pier Luigi, and sought by marriages to provide political security for his Farnese family. It is for this reason that he could not become a vigorous leader of the Catholic Reformation.

Although Paul began his pontificate inauspiciously by naming two of his nephews to the cardinal college, he gradually strengthened this body by adding worthy men from time to time. Among these were Gasparo Contarini, Bishop Jean du Bellay, Caraffa, Reginald Pole, Jacopo Sadoleto, and Pietro Bembo. By the inclusion of English, French, and Spanish prelates he hoped to give the cardinal college a more neutral and international character. By appointing younger men with a sincere interest in reforms, he hoped to offset the influence of those older cardinals who were still permeated with the Renaissance attitude toward Christianity and had little understanding of the new religious forces.

Realizing that he could not reform the Church at Rome without reforming the entire Church, that this could be done only by a general Church council, and that such a council could be held only if the rulers agreed to send representatives, Paul bent every effort toward obtaining their support. The nuncio Pietro Paolo Vergerio (1497–1564), who was convinced that a German national council would be called if the pope did not act, was sent to Germany to win support there for the papal program. In November, 1535, Vergerio discussed the matter with Luther in Wittenberg. Luther declared at that time that he would attend the council. But the outbreak of the third Hapsburg-Valois war (1536–1538) made his attendance impossible.

The attitude of the rulers made the pope's task of gaining widespread support for the council insuperable. Henry VIII was the chief opponent of the council, and Charles V and Francis I alternated in courting the favor of the English king. Charles, who had gone to Rome in April, 1536, sought to induce the pope to give up his policy of political neutrality and to support him against France. When Charles failed, he tried to gain a stronger control over the religious forces in Germany by attempting to conciliate the Protestants. His opposition to the papal program continued until shortly before the meeting of the Council of Trent. In 1544 he went so far as to recall his ambassadors from the papal court. The Catholic princes of Germany, determined to preserve their "liberties," were reluctant to follow either the pope or the emperor. As late as 1539 they seemed to prefer coming to an agreement with the Protestant princes. Ferdinand of Austria alone consistently favored the calling of a general Church council.

This complication of political and religious issues on the part of the pope as well as the princes and the inability of the pope to direct the bellicose interests of the western rulers against their common enemies—the heretics and the Turks—became apparent when, in June, 1536, it was agreed in the consistory to call a general Church council. Pope Paul issued a bull convoking such a council in Mantua for the next spring. But it was twice adjourned because of local and international disturbances, and in 1538 it convened at Vicenza. Yet, when the legates made their formal appearance, they found no representatives. Three further adjournments followed, the last and final one in the spring of 1539. Paul III must share the blame for the failure of this council, for he refused to submit a thoroughgoing reform program consonant with the demands of the day and continued to play a political game that he could not win.

## The Papal Reform Commission

Opposing the view of most of the cardinals that nothing could be done until a complete catastrophe had overwhelmed the Church, the pope appointed a reform commission of nine prelates, headed by Contarini, to begin reforms in Rome and to make preparations for a general council. Consisting of such enthusiastic proponents of reform as Contarini, Caraffa, Giberti, Pole, and Sadoleto, this commission made a comprehensive study of the conditions of the Church, especially in the papal *Curia*, and embodied the results in a report called *Advice . . . Concerning the Reform of the Church,* which it submitted to the pope in February, 1537.

The preface to the *Advice* stated that all the abuses in the papacy stemmed from the secularization of a spiritual office; that the popes, like other rulers, had permitted flatterers to convince them that their power was absolute, especially with respect to the granting of benefices, which the canonists had encouraged them to sell to their financial profit; and that the venality of the popes and the cardinals had been the chief cause of the defections from the Church.

In the twenty-six sections that followed, the *Advice* listed the various evils that demanded immediate attention: the venality of worldly cardinals who took advantage of their important offices to amass wealth; the absence of the cardinals from the papal court; the evasion of the canon law by criminals, including clergymen, by means of dispensations obtained for cash; the laxity among the monastic orders; the cheapening of sacred things by the free granting of confessionals and portable altars; the hawking of indulgences without regard for their spiritual significance; the condoning of prostitution, particularly in Rome; and the permeation of the schools by the pagan spirit of the Renaissance. It is no wonder that when the *Advice* was published, the Protestants used it to substantiate their attacks upon Catholicism.

Despite the opposition of a number of cardinals, Contarini induced Paul III to take steps toward correcting some of the abuses, particularly those concerned with the government of the Church. Accordingly a congregation of four cardinals, including Contarini and Caraffa, was chosen in the consistory of April, 1537, for the purpose of reforming the bureaucratic offices. This congregation began its attack upon the *dataria*, or datary, which had charge of dating and authenticating documents that granted spiritual favors such as the bestowing of benefices. It is estimated that the income from compositions and the sale of offices alone reached as high as 100,000 ducats annually under Clement VII, that is, about one fourth of the entire papal income. It is easy to see why the curials objected to the changes advocated by this and other reform commissions.

By following some of the suggestions incorporated in the *Advice*, Paul III was able to correct a number of the most glaring abuses in the *Curia*, such as the almost promiscuous granting of dispensations for monetary considerations. Although much remained to be done, his bold action gained for him many friends among the Catholics in other countries, so that he could now proceed with his plans for reforming the entire Church at a general council. At the same time he made it clear that he would in no way appease the Protestants, for he recognized the Society of Jesus and centralized the Roman Inquisition in a commission of cardinals, soon called the Holy Office (1542).

# The Council of Trent (1545–1563)

Paul III, having gained considerable prestige by initiating a reform of the papacy and marshaling new forces within Catholicism to its service, felt strong enough in 1542 to summon another general Church council. This time he selected Trent, in Austrian Tirol. The choice fell upon this city for it technically met the requirement of Charles V that the council be held in Germany. On the other hand, it lay on the Italian side of the Alps, where the sessions would be relatively safe from outside interference and could be dominated by the papacy. But with the outbreak of the fourth and last war between Francis I and Charles V (1542–1544), the attendance was so insignificant that the council was prorogued until after the Treaty of Crépy in 1544.

The Council of Trent did not officially convene until December 13, 1545, more than a quarter of a century after Luther had demanded that he be given a hearing at a general council of the Church. But by this time the Protestants and the Catholics had drifted so far apart that there was little chance for reconciliation. The Lutherans now refused to attend the council, and Luther wrote one of his most violent treatises against the papacy, *Against Roman Popery Founded by the Devil.*

The many sessions of the Council of Trent fall into three periods, or assemblies (1545–1547, 1551–1552, 1562–1563). Because of the opposition between Charles V, who wanted a thorough reformation of the Church, and Paul III, who was primarily interested in a definitive statement of Church doctrines, few prelates appeared at the first sessions. The deliberations did not begin until twenty-five had arrived. By the end of the first period only about seventy were present, most of whom were Italians. In addition to these voting members, there were legates of Ferdinand of Austria, about fifty theologians, and about fifty canonists who served as consultants.

The first three sessions were devoted to determining the organization of the council and the conduct of its business. Three cardinal legates— Giovanni del Monte, Marcello Cervini, and Reginald Pole—represented the pope. They not only presided over the sessions but assumed the initiative in preparing the agenda and appointing and guiding the activities of the congregations, or commissions. These consisted of prelates and consultants who discussed questions of doctrine and reform and submitted them to the plenary sessions for ultimate approval.

Only the prelates, that is, the more politically minded archbishops, bishops, generals of religious orders, and influential abbots, were given the right to vote. The universities and the middle and lower clergy, whose representatives had been a thorn in the flesh of the papacy at the Council of Basel, were not invited to Trent, and the role of the theologians and canonists was restricted to advising the prelates. Moreover, voting was by individuals—not by nations as at Constance and Basel—and voting by proxy was not permitted, with but few exceptions. Thus the preponderance of the Italian prelates and papal control of the papacy were assured from the outset.

One of the first questions to be decided was whether doctrinal matters or the reform of abuses should have precedence. After much argument over this question, it was agreed that both should be discussed simultaneously. The decisions of the council on doctrinal matters were made to refute the new heresies and clearly state the orthodox faith of the Church with respect to the doctrines that had been called into question. The disciplinary decrees dealt with abuses within the Church and provided for a unified control of the hierarchy by the papacy.

The sessions were frequently marked by heated debates. Among the leaders in the first sessions who favored far-reaching reforms and conciliation of the Protestants were the Christian humanist cardinals Reginald Pole and Girolamo Seripando. Seripando, the general of the Augustinians, had been trained as a humanist and had leaned toward the acceptance of the doctrine of justification by faith. Opposed to these was Caraffa, who, as we have seen, was a proponent of the vigorous extirpation of all heresies. He was supported by Ambrogio Catarino (d. 1553), a Dominican, who had written polemical tracts against the Protestants, and by two papal theologians, the Jesuits Salmerón and Lainez, whose task it was to prevent any doctrinal changes. Salmerón and Lainez exerted a strong influence upon the delegates not only as advisers in scholastic doctrine but as preachers.

Sessions four through eight of the first period were concerned with a number of important doctrinal and a few minor disciplinary problems. The first decision concerned the relative importance of Scripture and tradition. It was agreed that they were equally authoritative as standards of divine revelation. The Vulgate translation of Jerome was declared the authentic text, although textual emendations were not excluded. No decision was reached with respect to translations of the Vulgate into the vernacular. The Church, in which the Holy Ghost was believed to dwell, was declared to have the sole right to interpret Scripture, therefore the tradition of the Church with respect to doctrinal matters was not considered open to question.

Next the council considered the doctrine of original sin, which raised the much-disputed questions of freedom of the will and justification. Although Charles V wanted to have these questions deferred so as not to preclude a subsequent understanding with the Protestants, the papal legates and Lainez and Salmerón carried the day. Every attempt of Seripando and others to have a formula accepted that would permit a Protestant interpretation met with failure. Contrary to the Protestant position that human nature was "wholly depraved" after the fall of man, the council maintained that only the consequence of sin, not sin itself, was retained by all men. By declaring that Christ's merits, imparted to many by faith, produced man's merits, Lainez implied the importance of good works. Even though Thomistic theology was somewhat modified, it emerged stronger than ever.

The decree on justification, with its thirty-three canons condemning Protestant views, was promulgated in January, 1547. It is a masterful summary that steers a course between Pelagianism on the one hand and

Protestantism on the other. Man can reach a state of grace and become a child of God only by baptism and by the merits of the sufferings of Christ, in which he must believe. God calls the adult through prevenient grace, without man's merit, but man can exercise his free will in rejecting or cooperating with this grace. Grace enables him to cooperate. Justification implies not only forgiveness of sins but sanctification of the soul. Faith alone is not enough, for hope and love must also be present. When man has faith, hope, and love and follows the commandments of God and the Church, he does virtuous deeds. But he can never be certain of his election, for this remains a divine secret.

The next decision was to the effect that all seven sacraments, themselves considered good works, were indispensable to salvation, although men were cautioned not to rely exclusively upon them. Because all the sacraments—excepting baptism in cases of necessity—were to be administered solely by the clergy, a powerful blow was struck against the Protestant doctrine of the universal priesthood of believers. The dogmatic decree of March, 1547, contained canons on the sacraments in general and on baptism and confirmation. The other sacraments were dealt with during the second period of the council sessions.

The reform decrees and canons of the first period were promulgated simultaneously with those concerning dogmas. The first disciplinary decree dealt with the regulation of the teaching of theology, preaching, and the collection of alms. Another decree had to do with the residence of the bishops and incumbents of ecclesiastical benefices and still another with pluralities, exemptions, and the legal affairs of the clergy. Because the council refused to state that episcopal residence was a divine obligation and permitted the pope to give dispensations with respect to pluralities and absenteeism, these abuses continued, particularly among the cardinals.

During the seventh and eighth sessions of the council the relations between the pope and the emperor became increasingly strained. Charles, seeing that his demands for thoroughgoing reforms were being ignored and that the reconciliation of Catholics and Protestants was becoming highly improbable, began to bring strong pressure upon the prelates. Paul III, fearing that the emperor would appear at the council in person after his military victory over the Schmalkaldic League, took advantage of the fact that a few cases of the plague had broken out at Trent and induced the majority of the prelates to vote to move the council to Bologna in March, 1547.

Charles succeeded in having fourteen of the prelates remain at Trent and made it clear that he considered the proceedings at Bologna illegal. And at the Diet of Augsburg he tried to settle the religious affairs of Germany by means of the Interim of May 15, 1548, which was to be in force until the return of the council to Trent. Consequently the ninth and tenth sessions at Bologna accomplished virtually nothing. In September, 1549, Paul III suspended the Council of Bologna. His plan to carry out further reforms through a commission of cardinals came to naught with his death in November, 1549.

## The Second Assembly (1551–1552)

Cardinal Giovanni del Monte, one of the three papal legates during the first period of the Council of Trent, ascended the papal chair as Julius III (1550–1555). Desirous of keeping the papal power undiminished, Julius agreed to recall the council, to consider it an open question whether the decrees of the previous sessions were binding, and even to permit the Lutherans to attend. But before the council could convene, he got into difficulties with Henry II of France, who refused to recognize the council because the pope would not join him in his struggle with the emperor. Because not enough prelates were present when the council assembled in its eleventh session in May, 1551, no business was concluded except that of setting September 1 as the date for the next session.

Although Julius had apparently made concessions to Charles V, he counteracted these by appointing as papal legate and president of the council Marcello Cardinal Crescenzio, a strong proponent of papal authority and the old theology. When the twelfth session met, only a few German and Spanish prelates were present. Because of the decision that the work of the council should resume where it had been discontinued, the previous decrees were considered binding. Thus the presence of the Protestant delegates from January to March, 1552, did little more than show how great a theological chasm separated them from the Catholic Church. This was particularly apparent in the discussions concerning the sacrament of the Eucharist, for there was little disposition even to grant the request of the German prelates that Communion in both kinds be permitted. The conservative influence of Salmerón and Lainez was apparent in the dogmatic decrees of the thirteenth and fourteenth sessions concerning the Eucharist, penance, and extreme unction. The disciplinary decrees of these sessions prohibited abuses in episcopal jurisdiction and in the administration of ecclesiastical benefices. At the fifteenth session, decisions concerning the subjects under discussion were postponed while the fathers deliberated with the Protestant delegates.

After the Protestant delegates had left the council, Maurice of Saxony, who had turned against his former ally Charles V, led the victorious Protestants south, causing Charles to flee from Innsbruck and leading the delegates at Trent to believe that Maurice would try to overpower the council. Accordingly a decree was promulgated at the sixteenth session, in April, 1552, suspending the council. It did not meet again until nearly a decade later.

## Paul IV

After the brief pontificate of Marcellus II (1555), Caraffa became Pope Paul IV (1555–1559), in the same year in which the Peace of Augsburg recognized the disruption of the unity of Western Christendom. Although he was already seventy-nine years of age when he became pope, he carried out his program of reform with considerable vigor and success. Yet even he was hindered to some extent by his concern for the political power of the papacy and his hatred for the Spaniards, now ruled by Philip II (1556–1598). For political reasons he also felt impelled to resort to nepotism, leaving these matters to nephews whom he advanced in the papal service and who for a while undid previous reforms. It was their intention to destroy the Spanish hegemony in Italy and set themselves up as princely rulers with the aid of France. Again there was the typically Renaissance spectacle of a reforming pope using German and Swiss mercenaries—many of whom were Protestants —to fight the Catholic king of Spain.

When the powerful army of the duke of Alva appeared before Rome in 1557, however, Paul believed that he saw in this a warning of God that he should place reform above political considerations. Accordingly he concluded a treaty with the Spaniards, put an end to nepotism, and on his deathbed urged that Philip II be considered the bulwark of Catholicism.

Although Paul IV never seriously considered reopening the Council of Trent, he not only issued many reform regulations for the Roman *Curia* and the Church in the Papal States but rigidly enforced them. He took stern measures against simony in all its manifestations, ordered the datary to dispense the religious graces without pay, and made up for the loss of this income by greatly reducing his own expenditures and those of the cardinals and having the people contribute directly to the upkeep of the papacy by the payment of tithes. Strong action was taken to improve morals at Rome. Prostitutes, questionable entertainers, and usurers were driven out of the city, and even hunting and dancing were forbidden— though not without serious opposition. Fully in accord with the Jesuit spirit, he suppressed liberal Catholicism as well as Protestantism.

The year in which Paul IV died, 1559, marks a turning point in the history of religion as well as in politics. Not only had the great political figures of the first half of the sixteenth century—Charles V, Francis I, and Henry VIII—passed from the scene, but the long rivalry between France and Spain had been brought to an end in the Treaty of Cateau-Cambrésis (April, 1559). The new rulers of Europe, whose lands had been exhausted by wars, were disposed to maintain the peace and to devote their attention to internal affairs.

As far as religion was concerned, Protestantism had become so firmly established in much of northern Europe and the theology of its several manifestations had become so thoroughly defined that few of its leaders were inclined to hope any longer for a reconciliation with Catholicism. The Catholic Church itself, now well on the road to Reformation and more closely united in doctrines than previously, was preparing to reconquer what it had lost and to counteract Protestantism by the weapons that the latter had forged—reforms, preaching, and education.

Following the death of Paul IV, the popes were no longer selected from the great noble families of Italy but from the lower classes. Gian Angelo de' Medici, who became Pope Pius IV (1559–1565)—not related to the Medici of Florence—was the son of a Milanese notary. Although he, like many of his predecessors, was greatly influenced by the spirit of the Renaissance, he devoted his energies to his religious responsibilities. He not only brought to a successful conclusion the Council of Trent but continued the work of reform in Rome without becoming involved in politics. His able assistant in carrying out his reforms was his nephew Charles Borromeo (1538–1584), the cardinal archbishop of Milan.

## The Third Assembly (1562–1563)

By a papal bull of November, 1560, the council was ordered to assemble at Trent at Easter, 1561. This third assembly (sessions seventeen to twenty-five) finally began its deliberations on January 18, 1562, and lasted to December 4, 1563. It was characterized by much inner strife, frequently violent and unedifying, primarily between the curial party, made up largely of the Italian fathers, and the ultramontane party. The latter party consisted of three groups: the Spaniards, the imperialists, and the French. Although all three represented decentralizing tendencies within the Church, differences arose among them that enabled the pope to gain complete control of the council.

The most resolute of these three groups were the Spaniards, who exerted an influence far out of proportion to their numbers. Supported by Philip II (1556–1598), these austere fathers insisted upon a thorough renovation of the papacy and a diminution of its powers, but they were adamant in their insistence that no changes be made in doctrine or ritual. Emperor Ferdinand and the French and Bavarian prelates, on the other hand, demanded that the council make doctrinal concessions for the purpose of winning over the moderate Protestants and quieting the dissatisfied Catholics in their lands. The reforms that they requested included the performing of the Mass in the vernacular, Communion in both kinds, the reform of the papal *Curia*, the enforcement of ecclesiastical residence, the limitation of the use of excommunication, and the abolition of dispensations.

Because of the differences among the political powers with respect to doctrines and ritual, the pope succeeded by skillful diplomacy in winning over one after the other of the rulers and causing them to look to him rather than to their representatives in the council for leadership in carrying out reforms. By thus breaking with the tactics of his predecessors, who had opposed the temporal powers, Pius IV finally succeeded in closing the council in complete control of both doctrines and reforms.

The first of the problems that confronted the fathers was concerned with the "continuation," that is, the question whether the council should be considered a continuation of the previous assemblies. The imperialists and the French wished to have the council take up the doctrinal and disciplinary reforms anew, whereas Philip II, who had already enforced the earlier decrees in Spain, insisted that the council resume where it had left off. The issue was solved by the avoidance of the word *continuation* and the taking for granted of the earlier decrees of Trent.

Further difficulties were encountered when it appeared that the cardinal legates had changed the wording of the decree opening the council by adding a phrase that would deprive the council of its initiative. Led by Guerrero, the Spanish prelates fought vigorously to have the added phrase deleted, but to no avail. Feelings were thus tense when the seventeenth session opened. There were present at that time four cardinal legates, one additional cardinal, three patriarchs, eleven archbishops, forty bishops, four abbots, four generals of orders, and thirty-four theologians. This session was concerned largely with the order in which the dogmatic and disciplinary questions should be considered and with the revision of the Roman Index of Prohibited Books, published by Paul IV in 1559.

At the eighteenth session the fathers decided to revise the Index. A commission of eighteen was appointed for the purpose of drawing up a list of forbidden books and of preparing procedures for carrying out its purposes. At the same time a safe-conduct was granted the Protestants so that they could send representatives to Trent to defend their positions. Although no one expected Protestant representatives to appear, the discussion of the problem was significant, for it involved the fathers in questions concerning the relation of church and state. Philip II and the Spanish prelates opposed the safe-conduct because of the effect that it might have upon the Inquisition in Spain, whereas Ferdinand wished to have the Protestants attend.

The most bitter conflict centered around the articles of reform concerned with the previously discussed question of episcopal residence. Not only the fathers but the papal legates were divided on this issue. The debates centered around the question of whether episcopal residence was obligatory by divine right or merely by ecclesiastical law, thus involving the whole issue of papal authority over the bishops. When the question was submitted for debate, all the prelates agreed that residence was obligatory, but a large number, supported by the governments of Spain, France, and the Empire, argued that residence was by divine right and could therefore not be dispensed with by the pope. When the matter finally came to a vote, the ultramontanes were barely defeated, even though there was a preponderance of Italian prelates. Consequently the complaint over the "captive council" was heard in many parts of Europe. The reform decrees concerning episcopal residence were not passed until the twenty-first session, July 16, 1562. The only important reform of the eighteenth session was the one that abolished the office of the indulgence seller.

Meanwhile the council considered the question of Communion, particularly the demand of the emperor that the cup be given to the laity in Germany, Bohemia, and Hungary. Although Pius IV was willing to grant this concession, the Italians and the Spaniards, led by Lainez, vigorously opposed it. Despite the pressure exerted by the emperor, the legates, fearing the hostility of Spain, shelved the matter, thus leaving Ferdinand no recourse but to take his request to the pope, to whom the council finally referred the question. Four canons and decrees of the twenty-first session affirmed that the Church had the right to regulate the administration of the sacraments and denied that Communion in both kinds was obligatory.

Although there was considerable dispute over certain articles concerning the Mass, Salmerón and Lainez succeeded in bringing about unanimity in the acceptance of the strictly orthodox position. It was agreed that Christ offered himself as a sacrifice in the Last Supper as well as on the cross, but as a propitiation for our sins only on the cross; that the Mass as a sacrifice was available for the dead as well as the living; that the Mass could be said without communicants; and that it should be read in Latin. The nine canons and decrees concerning these doctrines were accepted in the twenty-second session.

The debates over the sacrament of orders once more involved the fathers in the question of episcopal residence and papal authority. Although many bishops argued that the keys were given to all the apostles, Lainez argued the papal case, but so poorly that emotions over the question ran high. At this juncture, on November 13, 1562, Cardinal Charles of Lorraine arrived and further stirred up ill feelings by demanding thoroughgoing reforms and stating his view that bishops exercised their authority by divine right.

It was during the hectic months preceding the opening of the stormy twenty-third session that Pius IV won over the secular princes to his program of reform under papal leadership. His first step was to gain the reluctant support of Ferdinand, who had gone to nearby Innsbruck to attempt to save the council from complete collapse. Although the cardinal of Lorraine, who visited him there in February, 1563, tried to persuade him to go to Trent to enforce reforms, Ferdinand was beginning to despair of the ability of the council to accomplish anything worthwhile. Largely responsible for his change of attitude was the Jesuit Peter Canisius, who was at this time in the emperor's entourage and impressed him with the advisability of coming to terms with the pope.

Cardinal Morone, who had been made a papal legate at Trent to replace one of the two legates who had died, was chiefly responsible for carrying out the pope's plan of dividing the rulers before they could plan concerted action against him. At the suggestion of Canisius, Morone went to Innsbruck. By promising that the pope would grant the cup to the laity after the termination of the council, he finally gained the emperor's support for the continuation of the council under papal leadership, despite the fact that few of his original demands for reform had been realized. Not unimportant was the fact that Ferdinand wished to and finally did obtain the pope's consent to the election of his son Maximilian as king of the Romans.

The cardinal of Lorraine was just as cleverly drawn into the papal camp. When, after the murder of the cardinal's brother, the duke of Guise, and after the Peace of Amboise, which had made concessions to the Huguenots, the pope saw that the cardinal's position in France was being greatly weakened, he followed the tactics of denouncing him in public but courting his favor in private. When the pope finally offered the cardinal the position of apostolic legate in France, he capitulated, gave up the reform program of the French clergy, and eventually won over Catherine de' Medici, who had begun to regret having made concessions to the Huguenots. Thus when the long-awaited twenty-third session met on July 15, 1563, the Spanish party stood virtually alone in its opposition to papal control of the council.

The chief doctrinal accomplishment of the twenty-third session was the promulgation of the decrees on the sacrament of orders. Although the controverted points were dropped or deferred, two decrees of great importance were included, one enforcing episcopal residence and the other demanding the establishment of seminaries in all the dioceses. By substituting a systematic training of the clergy under the direct supervision of the bishops for the haphazard and inadequate methods that had prevailed in much of Europe during the first half of the century, the Catholic Church was provided with a trained and devoted clergy who deserve much credit for the subsequent gains of Catholicism.

Strife was by no means absent during the preparations for the last two sessions of the council, for the Spanish bishops continued to press for reforms. Yet most of the fathers began to weary of the conflicts and became amenable to the papal proposal to bring the council to a speedy close. At the twenty-fourth session, which met on November 11, 1563, a dogmatic canon and a corresponding disciplinary decree on the sacrament of marriage were passed in which clerical celibacy was reasserted, clandestine marriages were invalidated, and civil marriage was recognized as valid.

The preparation of the general decree on reforms published at this session brought the fathers into conflict not only with the secular princes, whom they would deprive of such ancient rights as interference in ecclesiastical courts, taxation of clergy, and participation in the publication of papal bulls, but with the cardinals at Rome, who resented the reforms aimed at them. Only the firmness of the Spanish bishops prevented the fathers from rendering the reforms of the clergy meaningless. However, the proposed "reform of the princes," which would have deprived the governments of their ancient rights, was not included and was finally dropped by order of the pope during the preparation of the decrees for the last session.

As early as October, Pius IV gave the legates the authority to bring the council to a close, for the various issues under discussion tended to alienate the rulers whom he had won over to his program. Although the Spanish bishops continued resolute, the large majority of the prelates were growing weary of the arguments. The question of whether or not the council was to continue came to a head on November 30, when news arrived in Trent that the pope was seriously ill. Because most of the prelates feared the confusion that would follow if the council had to experience the uncertainties of a papal election, it was decided to hold the last public session as soon as possible and to bring the council to a speedy close.

Prior to the twenty-fifth and last session, held on December 3 and 4, 1563, the pope had ordered the legates to withdraw the articles that infringed upon the rights of the states. The decrees submitted were passed almost unanimously. With respect to doctrines, the existence of purgatory was affirmed, as well as the efficacy of prayers for those who were detained there; the invocation of saints was pronounced "good and useful"; and indulgences were declared beneficial. Although a clause forbidding the payment of money for indulgences was withdrawn, the evils connected with the selling of indulgences were condemned. A decree was passed referring to the pope the preparation of the list of forbidden books as well as new editions of the catechism, the missal, and the breviary. A reform decree of twenty-two chapters dealt with abuses among the monks and the nuns, another of twenty-one chapters with the life of the clergy in general. Finally, it was proclaimed that all the decrees passed by the council in its twenty-five sessions were binding, that the secular rulers accept them, and that the pope confirm them. This done, Morone declared the council closed.

On January 26, 1564, the pope issued the bull *Benedictus Deus*, confirming the canons and decrees of the Council of Trent, which had been signed by the 215 prelates present and by proxies for the 39 who were absent. The bull stated that the pope alone had the right to interpret the canons and decrees. On August 2 of the same year he appointed a congregation of cardinals to supervise their enforcement. The next month he summarized the doctrines accepted at Trent in *The Creed of Pope Pius IV*.

### Significance of the Council of Trent

Although the Council of Trent did not succeed in restoring the unity of Christendom, it no longer left in doubt the position of the Church with respect to doctrinal matters. Furthermore, unity within the Church was affected with respect to discipline. No decree described the power and functions of the papacy, yet the council assured the primacy of the pope by ordering that its decrees be accepted at provincial synods and that incumbents of ecclesiastical offices promise obedience to the pope, and also when it submitted the decrees to him for his confirmation. Not until the meeting of the Vatican Council of 1870, however, were papal infallibility and supremacy clearly defined.

The doctrinal decrees were accepted by all the Catholic governments of Europe. But that was not true with respect to the disciplinary decrees. Ferdinand accepted them as a whole for his hereditary possessions, as did the kings of Poland and Portugal. But the Empire and France never accepted them, and Spain did so with many reservations. Nevertheless, the unity of the Church was retained. It was the strict definition of dogma under papal leadership, accompanied by a resurgence of spiritual life, that made Catholicism a closely knit, dynamic movement after the Council of Trent.

## Papal Leadership

The reforms of the Council of Trent could not have constituted a powerful force in sixteenth-century Europe without the leadership of popes dedicated to the ideals of the council and in complete command of the resources of the Church. Abandoning the strong secular interests of their Renaissance predecessors, most of them made the revival of Catholicism their primary concern.

One of the most important accomplishments of Pius IV after he had brought the Council of Trent to a successful conclusion was the compilation of the Index of Prohibited Books, referred to him by the council. This new Index, designed to replace that of Pope Paul IV, was published in a papal brief in March, 1564. It consisted of two parts. The first contained the ten rules governing the condemnation of books, and the second comprised a list of condemned books. This list was to be enlarged by bishops and inquisitors from time to time. Less severe than its predecessor, it condemned heretical books but not scholarly books written by heretics on nonreligious subjects. The keeping and reading of heretical books was made punishable by excommunication.

A second achievement of Pius IV was the preparation of the Roman Catechism, although he did not live to see it published. The prelates at Trent had requested the preparation of a manual of Church doctrines to serve both the clergy and the laity. The catechisms of Canisius, which he had written at the request of Ferdinand I, proved so successful among the laity, however, that this new catechism, a classic with respect to both style and content, was designed primarily for the clergy. The Catholic Church does not yet have one official catechism for universal use in the education of its laity. But the Catholics now for the first time had available an authoritative statement of doctrines.

Pius IV also addressed himself to the revision of the breviary, or book of prayers and readings to be used daily by the members of the clergy in the major orders. This revision had been requested not only by the fathers at Trent but also by Charles V and Ferdinand I. The best known of the reformed breviaries to date had been that of Francisco Quiñones (1482–1540), general of the Franciscans, published in 1535. Greatly simplified and revised for the purpose of arousing personal devotion and study, it had gained wide acceptance and had even influenced the English *Book of Common Prayer*. The prelates at Trent, however, considered it too great a departure from tradition and accordingly delegated the revision of the breviary to the commission of the Index, to which two other persons were eventually added for this purpose. Although the new breviary was completed in 1566, it was not formally authorized by the pope until 1568.

The reform of the missal, the book that contains the prayers and rites used in the celebration of the Mass, was assigned to the same commission. Like the breviary, it was completed after the death of Pius IV, that is, in 1570. The papal bull of that year made the reformed and simplified missal the sole one to be used in the celebration of the Mass, with the exception of those rites that had been in constant use for two or more centuries.

Although the chief instruments of Catholic reform had been fashioned by the Council of Trent and by Pius IV, the actual work was carried out by Pius V (1566–1572), a former Dominican monk who had a great reputation for austerity and piety as inquisitor-general and as a reforming cardinal. He was canonized in 1712. Like Paul IV he was a zealous reformer and devoted his energies to suppressing heresy, reviving the crusading ardor of earlier centuries against the Turks, and reforming the clergy. He was assisted in these tasks by such able men as Philip Neri in Rome, Archbishop Borromeo of Milan in northern Italy and Switzerland, Peter Canisius in the Empire, the cardinal of Lorraine in France, and Juan d'Ávila in Spain.

Pius V ruthlessly rooted out heresy in Italy by giving the Inquisition there a free hand and increasing its powers. Autos-da-fé again became common, especially in Rome and those cities where Protestantism had gained a foothold, and many heretics were condemned and burned at the stake. Heresy in other countries was attacked by the publication of the revised bull *In coena domini*, a papal excommunication of heretics that was read annually on Maundy Thursday. Although it was resented by many secular rulers because it implied the pope's supremacy over them, it was not discontinued until 1773. The pope even sent troops to be used against the Huguenots in France, aided the Catholics who were plotting against Queen Elizabeth—whom he had declared deposed—and congratulated the duke of Alva on the severity of his Council of Blood in the Low Countries.

The pope's crusading zeal against the Ottoman Turks coincided with the hatred of the Venetians aroused by the Turkish capture of Cyprus. The pope was instrumental in creating the Holy Alliance with Venice and Spain that supplied the large fleet with which Don Juan of Austria defeated the Turks at the Battle of Lepanto in 1571.

Pius V was as relentless in opposing immorality and corruption as in persecuting heretics and unbelievers. He himself remained impeccably honest and carried on a vigorous attack upon simony. By forbidding the alienation of Church property by a papal bull of 1567, he put an end to that method whereby the Renaissance popes had enriched their relatives. He also insisted upon episcopal residence, discouraging the flocking of worldly minded prelates to Rome by practicing strict monastic austerity in his own papal household.

Although Gregory XIII (1572–1585), the successor of Pius, had been lax with respect to morals before becoming pope, he could not now withstand the reforming spirit in the *Curia,* and he himself became a model of propriety. Formerly a professor of law, he pursued the reform of the Church primarily from a legal point of view. He was responsible for the new edition of the *Corpus iuris canonici* and for reorganizing the system of nuncios.

The best-known achievement of Gregory XIII was the reform of the calendar. Because the Julian calendar, adopted by Julius Caesar, exceeded the astronomical year by an error amounting to a day every 128 years, the Church could not easily follow the decrees of the Church councils with respect to certain festivals of the Church year. A special commission was appointed to revise the calendar. The final result, known as the Gregorian calendar, was proclaimed in a papal bull in 1582. The year of this calendar exceeds the astronomical year by but one day in 3,323 years. It was almost immediately accepted by most of the Roman Catholic countries. The Protestant countries, viewing its promulgation as a papal deceit, did not follow until much later. It was accepted in Germany in 1700 and in England and her colonies in 1752. The Greek Orthodox countries, including Russia, used the Julian calendar into the twentieth century.

Gregory XIII gave unstinting support to the Jesuit order, especially to its educational institutions. He handsomely endowed the Roman (1572), German (1573), Greek (1577), and English (1579) Jesuit colleges in Rome and gave liberally to those in other countries, particularly in Germany. He also supported the erection by the Jesuits of pontifical seminaries for the training of priests. Many bishops were neglecting this duty, despite the decrees of the Council of Trent. By the time of Gregory's death, the Society of Jesus numbered about five thousand members.

The militant character of Gregory's leadership is demonstrated by his enthusiastic response to the news concerning the massacre of St. Bartholomew and his celebration of the event with a *Te Deum* in the Church of St. Mark and with a Mass in the Church of St. Louis; his incitement of revolts in Ireland against Queen Elizabeth; his sending of the Jesuits Robert Parsons and Edmund Campion to England to arouse the English Catholics to resistance against Elizabeth; his encouragement of Philip II of Spain and the Guises in France in their military plans against the Protestants; and his assistance to the German emperor in his struggle with the Protestant estates. Wherever possible, he stiffened Catholic resistance to antipapal forces by liberal grants of money and interference in the internal affairs of the various countries.

Even more vigorous in pursuing the work of Catholic reform was Sixtus V (1585–1590), a person of lowly birth who had become the vicar-general of the Franciscans and a cardinal. He was a great lover of books and works of art, but he also displayed remarkable administrative abilities. Conscious of the fact that the power and prestige of the papacy still rested to a large degree upon its possession of the Papal States, he set himself to the task of establishing law and order there, ensuring economic prosperity, and providing an efficient administrative system. He also improved the papal administration of the Church by fixing the number of "congregations," or committees of cardinals entrusted with Church business, at fifteen and by systematically distributing the administrative functions among them. By another papal bull he fixed the number of cardinals at seventy and divided them into three orders consisting of six bishops, fifty priests, and fourteen deacons. In his greed to raise and hoard money, however, he revived the sale of offices, created new offices to be sold, and increased taxes.

Although Sixtus V was frugal with respect to the expenditures of his own papal household and hoarded a large amount of silver in the Castle of Sant' Angelo, he spent money lavishly in satisfying his passion for architecture. Rome was beautified by the erection of many architectural monuments in the popular new baroque style, which was well-suited to express the power and the splendor of the revived papacy and the Catholic Church.

Like his predecessor, Sixtus entertained almost fantastic ambitions for the Church. He hoped to carry on a grand crusade against the Turks, which would restore the Holy Land to Catholicism; he promised Philip II aid in launching an armada against England; he urged the duke of Savoy to attack Geneva; he played an independent role with respect to Spain by throwing his influence to the side of Henry IV, whom he had encouraged to become a Catholic; and he aided Sigismund III of Poland in the latter's struggle with Protestantism in both Poland and Sweden. By maintaining a balance of power among the European states, he once more involved the papacy in politics, but in the interest of Catholicism at large, not of his family or the Papal States.

The brief pontificates of Urban VII, Gregory XIV, and Innocent IX were followed by that of Clement VIII (1592–1605), who continued the policies laid down by his predecessors. Even though he was elected with the help of the Spaniards, he was anti-Spanish in his foreign policy. He finally came to the support of Henry IV of France, despite the fact that the latter had granted the Huguenots toleration in the Edict of Nantes. By the Treaty of Vervins the papacy gained the duchy of Ferrara, thereby indicating the revived political interests of the popes. Clement, however, continued to carry out the reforms requested by the Council of Trent. He was particularly successful in bringing about liturgical reforms and in providing a scholarly revision of the Vulgate translation of the Bible.

The moving spirit behind the revision of the Vulgate was the great Jesuit scholar, St. Robert Bellarmine (1542–1621), a Tuscan by birth. He early distinguished himself as a professor of rhetoric and later as a professor of theology. For twelve years he taught theology at the Roman College, where he demonstrated his skill as a controversialist. His systematic work, the *Controversies,* became one of the chief references for Catholic theologians in their defense of Catholicism. Because it suggested putting limitations upon the temporal power of the papacy, Sixtus V ordered it put on the Index until corrected. But the cardinals appointed to try the case postponed the decision until after the death of the pope. Pius XI canonized Bellarmine in 1923 and proclaimed him a Doctor of the Church in 1931.

Bellarmine pointed out a number of errors in the Sistine edition (1590) of the Vulgate, which Sixtus V had helped prepare and which had been officially declared the "true, legitimate, authentic, and certain" text. This Vatican edition has remained the standard edition of the Roman Catholic Church to this day. Pope Clement VIII was so much impressed with Bellarmine's scholarship, piety, and service to the Church that he made him a cardinal.

Another cardinal, outstanding scholar, and leader of the Catholic Reformation was Caesar Baronius (1538–1607), an Oratorian. His greatest service was the publication of his *Annales ecclesiastici* (1588–1607), which carried the history of the Church from the birth of Christ to 1198 in many folios. It was written primarily to refute the *Magdeburg Centuries* (1559–1574) of Flacius and other Lutherans. Convinced that the historical documents would support the authority and claims of the Catholic Church, Baronius developed with great industry an account based upon the wealth of source materials in the Vatican Library. For this reason, and despite the author's strong bias, parts of this work are still used today.

By the end of the sixteenth century the authority of the papacy was so firmly established that it could once more play a leading and more or less independent role in European affairs. What is more important, it had corrected the worst abuses within Catholicism and had marshaled powerful religious and cultural forces in the service of the Catholic Church. It had also gained a greater control over the administration of the Church and the spiritual life of its people than had the popes of the Middle Ages.

# Part Four

## Religious Conflicts and Consequences

# 9 Militant Catholicism and Calvinism

By the middle of the sixteenth century the main lines of religious development had been established. Roman Catholicism had finally come to grips with the doctrinal issues raised by the rise of Protestantism and had settled them by reviving a conservative, scholastic theology adapted to the needs of the sixteenth century. It had, moreover, guaranteed the preservation of orthodoxy by placing the right to interpret the Bible and tradition firmly in the hands of the papacy, at the same time providing the means for the enforcement of theological uniformity—the Inquisition and the Index of Prohibited Books. A basis had also been laid for a universal reform of the personnel and the institutions of the Church, likewise under papal leadership. However, because these reforms touched upon the rights of the political powers, uniformity could not be achieved with respect to them.

Greek Orthodox Christianity remained virtually untouched by the forces unleashed by the Reformation, despite the fact that Lutherans and Calvinists as well as Roman Catholics occasionally made overtures to its religious and political leaders. Of much greater significance to eastern European Christianity than the Reformation was the establishment of the independence of the Russian Church by the creation of the patriarchy of Moscow in 1589 and the subsequent shifting of the center of gravity of Greek Orthodoxy from Constantinople to Moscow. Doctrinally the Greek Orthodox Church tended to restate its basic tenets in the light of the controversies caused by the rise of Protestanism.

Lutheranism became involved in internal doctrinal

controversies and suffered the consequences of German particularistic politics. Peace reigned in Germany for more than half a century; yet it was an ominous peace during which little of a constructive nature was accomplished in religion in particular or culture in general. Calvinism, on the other hand, became associated with dynamic economic and political forces that made it appear as the most active religious force of the latter half of the century. Thus the most acute struggles between Catholicism and Protestantism occurred in those countries of western Europe where Calvinism had made the most progress.

But in Calvinism, as in Lutheranism and Catholicism, one finds virtually no religious changes. The most significant ones are those induced by political exigencies, and the stakes over which men fought become primarily political stakes. Even in France, where hundreds of thousands of sincere Protestants desired nothing more than the right to worship as their consciences dictated, religion became so thoroughly involved in political matters that it is difficult to disentangle them.

When Charles V died, in 1558, the ideal of a medieval empire working in harmony with a universal Christian Church died with him. The rulers who dominated the European scene after his death thought first in terms of their dynastic control of the rising national states, and religious matters were increasingly used to further this end. That is to say, religion became more than ever involved in political conflicts. As a consequence, Europe was plunged into a series of wars in which religion was eventually relegated to a sphere all its own, and politics, like society in general, became increasingly secularized. Europe entered a period of international rivalries that have grown in intensity and destructiveness to our day.

## Spanish Catholicism Under Philip II

Most of the political and religious history of Europe during the latter half of the sixteenth century was determined by the ambitions of Philip II (1556–1598) of Spain, whom the dying Pope Paul IV had recognized as the strongest pillar of Catholicism. Born in Valladolid, Spain, in 1527, Philip considered himself first of all a Spaniard. He was married to a Portuguese princess who died after the birth of Don Carlos, when Philip was only eighteen. He left Spain for an extended stay for the first time when he accompanied his father to the Diet of Augsburg of 1548 and to the Low Countries, which Charles was planning to attach to Spain. Philip returned to Spain in 1551, but three years later he was again in the Low Countries. In 1554 he was married to Queen Mary of England, for Charles hoped through this marriage to bring England into an alliance with Spain and against France.

King Philip II of Spain

*by Titian*

# Part Four: Religious Conflicts and Consequences

Made king of Spain in 1556, after his father's abdication, released from his childless union with Mary Tudor by her death in 1558, and having concluded his struggle with France with the Treaty of Cateau-Cambrésis in 1559, Philip returned to his native land for the remaining years of his life, determined to carry out the admonition of his father, whom he idolized, not to conquer new lands but to consolidate those that he had inherited. To offset the danger to Spain inherent in the fact that Mary Stuart, queen of the Scots and the wife of a French prince, might reign over both England and France, Philip married by proxy Elizabeth of Valois, who was still a child.

Philip II was by character, education, and experience well suited to the role of a monarch of Spain and a champion of Catholicism. He was personally devout, ascetically inclined, impressed by the traditions of his dynasty and Catholicism, and as fully determined to enforce his will as his father had been. Discarding the feudal display still loved by his father, he preferred to spend many hours on his knees before the images and relics of saints or before the altar. He was also highly appreciative of the culture that the Church was using to regain the allegiance of the people. He played no small part in promoting the brilliance of Spain's "golden age," which set the standards for much of Europe. He spoke and wrote French, Italian, and Latin, in addition to Spanish. He showed his love for literature by gathering a library of more than four thousand volumes. He also collected precious works of art and loved music, in which he himself was proficient. Despite his strong convictions, intolerance, and outward austerity, he was a devoted husband and father and showed sympathy with all those about him, including his servants. No more suitable monument could have been erected to him than the Escorial, the palace that he constructed near the then almost barren Madrid—a massive, austere structure, a combination of palace, museum, monastery, and mausoleum.

From the relative seclusion of the Escorial, Philip ruled his widely extended dynastic inheritance, which included not only the kingdoms of Castile and Aragon but the Burgundian possessions, the Low Countries, and Franche-Comté (Free County of Burgundy); the Aragonese lands of northern Italy, Naples, Sicily, Sardinia, and the Balearic Islands; Milan, which Charles had detached from the Empire; and the widespread colonial possessions in America, northern Africa, and the Far East. After 1580 he even ruled Portugal and its colonial possessions.

## Bureaucratic Government

Highly conscientious and faithful to what he considered his duty, Philip labored long and hard in caring for the most minute governmental details and completed the development of that absolutism that had been begun by his predecessors. Not only administrative, but military, matters were conducted by him through his cabinet secretaries, who often became more influential than his royal councilors. But even his secretaries were informed only on matters that concerned their restricted fields of activity. To maintain his independence, he frequently had two councilors with differing points of view, and he occasionally commissioned a third to supervise these two, while all were watched by spies and feared the wrath of the king. Thus he avoided the danger of having powerful court favorites; but he also found it difficult to come to quick decisions, much to the consternation of his governors, diplomats, and generals. He became lost in details, unable to differentiate between what was trivial and what important.

At the top of Philip's bureaucratic system was the *Consejo de Estado,* or council of state, which was completely dependent upon the king for its authority and served primarily in an advisory capacity with respect to foreign affairs. The other royal councils, twelve in number by the time of his death, administered either certain territories or departments of government. He usually communicated with these councils through his secretaries of state, almost invariably men of low birth. This bureaucratic system worked relatively well. Especially successful was the administration of the colonial empire and its expanding trade. Not only was the ruthless spirit of the conquistadors curbed, but trade was regulated for the good of the state, and the Indian natives were protected from selfish exploitation. Moreover, the comparatively successful regulation of the colonies enabled the missionaries of a number of Catholic orders to enjoy a period of exceptional success.

Recognizing the potential danger to his royal authority of the grandees, or upper nobility, who had large estates and many armed retainers, he continued the policy of his father of reducing them to the status of a court nobility. With but few exceptions, he refrained from using them as military leaders and courtiers. The lesser nobility, the hidalgos, who were used in both the army and the bureaucracy and who came to represent the Castilian cities in the Cortes, were encouraged to look to him for personal advancement. In this they showed greater concern than in the economic prosperity of their constituents. Thus the Castilian Cortes became to all intents the willing instrument of royal absolutism by means of which the king obtained money and kept in touch with public opinion. The Cortes of Aragon, on the other hand, remained stubborn in the preservation of inherited "liberties" until a revolt, which had followed the king's interference in Aragonese justice, gave him the excuse to overpower the Cortes with a Castilian army in 1592. But Aragon was not completely deprived of its special position within the kingdom until after the accession of the Bourbon rulers in 1700. For this reason the king relied most heavily upon Castile for financial and moral support in carrying out his ambitious plans.

## Philip and Catholicism

Philip II was a true Spaniard in his consistent support of Catholicism while strengthening his royal authority. His defense of the faith and the Church against unbelievers and heretics endeared him to his people. The union of the Escorial and the Vatican, moreover, strengthened his position as the dominant political figure of Europe. The Treaty of Cateau-Cambrésis of 1559 had given him a free hand in Italy, where the papacy was dependent upon his good will for the maintenance of its authority in the Papal States. Because France became deeply involved in its religious wars, the popes could not, as previously, play off the French king against the Spanish. Philip used his favorable position cautiously in influencing both the elections of popes and papal politics.

As far as the internal Spanish policies were concerned, Philip, like the other rulers of his day, used the Church to strengthen the state and insisted upon maintaining religious uniformity. Accordingly, he upheld the doctrinal position affirmed at the Council of Trent but set limits to the interference of the papacy in the Spanish Church. He made his will felt in the appointment of Spanish prelates, permitted no legal cases to be tried outside the country, used clerical income for political purposes, and allowed no papal bulls to be published in Spain without his prior approval.

Philip pursued a policy of maintaining strict religious uniformity not only because of his strict Catholicism but because of his fear that Protestantism, particularly Calvinism, might be used by the Spanish nobles to defy his royal authority. Therefore he gave considerable power to the Spanish Inquisition with its autos-da-fé.

The Spanish Inquisition, or Holy Office, as it was called, had been established by Ferdinand and Isabella with papal authority in 1480 for the purpose of converting or eliminating all Jews and Moors. By the beginning of Philip II's reign it had become an instrument of papal as well as royal authority for the purpose of rooting out all forms of heresy. When fully developed, it was headed by a grand inquisitor who was nominated by the king and confirmed by the pope. He presided over a high council, the *Consejo Supremo,* consisting of five members and a number of advisers, all appointed by the grand inquisitor with the approval of the king. Most of the members were Dominicans. It served as a court of first instance in all important cases, but it also heard appeals from other Spanish courts. Under it were a number of local courts—nineteen in 1538—to which people were encouraged to bring their accusations.

Ordinary legal rights were not given the accused in the court of the Inquisition, although they were given a "term of grace" of about a month, were defended by trained lawyers, and were imprisoned only upon the unanimous consent of the court. However, they were tried in secret, were not confronted by their accusers, and were tortured for the purpose of getting them to confess their heresies. Both ecclesiastical and civil in its organization and functions, the institution was used by the Spanish monarch to further political as well as religious ends. So harsh were its measures that Pope Pius V protested to Philip and on one occasion rescued the archbishop of Toledo from its jurisdiction. Even Ignatius Loyola and St. Teresa were pursued by it. Within a decade virtually all Protestantism was stamped out, and heretical ideas were kept from spreading by the publication of a Spanish Index of Prohibited Books.

Both religious and political motives were apparent also in the Spanish attack upon the Moriscos, or converted Moors, of southeastern Spain, many of whom still retained Mohammedan doctrines and practices. The popular hatred of them was intensified by the fact that they occasionally supported the Barbary pirates in their attacks upon the Spanish coast. They were also despised because they labored for relatively low wages as artisans, farmers, and horticulturists.

Goaded to action by attempts to deprive them of their language and customs, the Moriscos of Granada resorted to revolt in 1568. This revolt, which lasted two years and in which barbarous acts of cruelty were frequently perpetrated by both sides, was finally suppressed by Don Juan, Philip's half brother and an illegitimate son of Charles V. An edict of 1570 ordered the Moriscos to be settled among the Christians of Castile and Leon. In 1609 Philip III issued an edict that provided for their expulsion from the rest of Spain.

The revolt of the Moriscos coincided with the attempt of the Turks, under Selim II (1566–1574), to take the Island of Malta, held by the Knights of St. John, and to add other territory at the expense of Venice. Having succeeded in suppressing the Moriscos, Philip II joined Venice and the pope in the Holy League of 1571, aimed against the Turks and the corsairs of Tunisia, Tripolitania, and Algeria. Don Juan was placed in command of a great crusading fleet of more than two hundred vessels manned by fifty thousand seamen and twenty-eight thousand soldiers. Supported by the crusading spirit and national enthusiasm of the Spaniards, this great fleet met virtually the entire Turkish navy, comprising about three hundred vessels and one hundred thousand men, in the Bay of Lepanto. The battle that followed, on October 7, 1571, ended in a glorious victory for Don Juan. Although Philip, bogged down by details and hampered by the divisions between him and his allies, did not follow up the virtual annihilation of the Turkish fleet by an attack upon Constantinople, the Battle of Lepanto marks the beginning of the end of the Turkish naval domination of the Mediterranean.

Success also attended Philip in his brief war to annex Portugal. When King Sebastian was killed in a crusade in Morocco in 1578 and left no heir, he was followed by his aged great-uncle, Cardinal Henry (1578–1580). Philip, one of several claimants to the throne, sent to Portugal Ferdinand Alvarez de Toledo, the duke of Alva (1508–1582). This brilliant general seized Lisbon and proclaimed his sovereign king of that country. Although Philip permitted Portugal to remain an independent kingdom and respected the rights and customs of the people, the Spanish rule was never popular and lasted only until 1640. But for the rest of his life, Philip added the cares of this kingdom and its far-flung colonies to his own. The additional income, however, was not enough to offset the increasing responsibilities of the king.

## Philip as the Leader of Catholicism

After little more than a decade of his rule in Spain, Philip II could view an international situation made to order for his basic policies of maintaining a status quo with respect to his dominions and re-establishing Catholicism throughout Europe. France, long Spain's chief rival, was involved in bitter religious wars; England, in a position to block the sea route to the Low Countries, was threatened by religious dissension and by Mary Stuart's claim to the throne; Turkey and the Barbary corsairs, threats to Spain's communications with her dominions in the Mediterranean, had been weakened to the point that they never again attacked southwestern Europe; the Spanish possessions in Italy enabled Philip to maintain overland communications with the Low Countries through Franche-Comté; and the Empire, ruled by a branch of the Hapsburg family, was helpless not only because of the old particularism of the territorial princes but because of a serious religious division. Despite this favorable position, however, Philip's plans were thwarted by one unforeseen event after another.

Philip's most persistent difficulty was the stubborn resistance of the Low Countries to his attempts to use them for the furtherance of his own policies. Their revolt greatly taxed his resources and involved him in other costly struggles.

How difficult it was to maintain the status quo in the complicated European situation of his day Philip learned when, in 1583, the duke of Anjou, brother of King Henry III of France, died and Protestant Henry of Navarre became the next person of royal blood in the line of succession. Moreover, when it appeared that Henry III might be offered the sovereignty of the Low Countries, and that they too might eventually fall to Henry of Navarre, Philip felt compelled to intervene in French affairs. In January, 1585 he concluded the Treaty of Joinville with the Guises by the terms of which heresy was to be eradicated in France, a Catholic uncle of Henry of Navarre was to be made the next king, and Navarre and Béarn were to be given to Spain.

For a number of years it appeared as though Philip would attain his goal with respect to France with little expense to himself. But in 1588 the duke of Guise was assassinated, Henry III joined Henry of Navarre to save himself from the enraged French Catholics, and in 1589 Henry III himself was murdered. Thus Philip became involved in a war with Henry of Navarre, who became King Henry IV, the first Bourbon ruler of France. This war proved too much for Philip's ability and resources, especially after Henry IV became Catholic in 1593. Finally, while Philip lay dying, he and Henry concluded the first of the Hapsburg-Bourbon struggles with the Treaty of Vervins, in May, 1598, which provided for a mutual restitution of territories, with the exception of Cambrai, retained by Philip. Although Philip had played a predominant role in maintaining Catholicism in France, it was apparent that Spain's hegemony in European affairs was nearing a close.

Even more indicative of the shape of things to come were the relations between Spain and England. Elizabeth, whose devotion to Protestantism did not equal Philip's devotion to Catholicism, was shrewd enough to see that England needed a long period of peace to enable her to meet any future attacks from the Continent. While her subjects developed a strong hatred for the Spanish Catholics and her sea dogs plundered Spanish commerce and even Spanish towns, she took advantage of the rivalry between Philip and the Guises, for she realized that Philip would not support Catholic Mary Stuart's claim to the English throne so long as there was a likelihood that Mary and her descendants might rule England, Scotland, and France. Therefore Elizabeth secretly supported the enemies of Spain while publicly listening to a proposal of marriage from Philip and, when that did not materialize, engaged in other diplomatic maneuvers too intricate to enumerate here.

When, after Philip's treaty with the Guises had been made in 1585, he was ready to strike at England, Elizabeth was prepared; and when she learned of the plot to place the imprisoned Mary Stuart on the throne of England, she had Mary executed. The next year, 1588, Philip launched the Spanish Armada of about one hundred and thirty ships and twenty-four thousand men against England. This magnificent fiasco, however, left Philip undaunted, for he soon planned another armada. But he and his country had spent themselves. That Spain had lost command of the sea was apparent when the English sacked the principal Spanish port of Cadiz in 1596.

Philip died in September, 1598, completely worn out and tortured by disease. Although he had been considered the most powerful ruler in Europe and had made of Spain a strongly centralized power, he had failed to restore Catholicism in Europe. Moreover, his failure to grasp the nature and significance of the important economic changes of his day led to the rapid decline of his country and its empire.

It is true, as recent scholars have shown, that Philip II, like his father, made many positive contributions to the economic life of Spain and Europe, for he helped provide security for international trade, improved the postal system and the roads, organized and regulated a lucrative colonial trade, and protected Spanish commerce by a policy of monopoly and restriction. On the other hand, there is no evidence of a systematic economic policy. The flow of precious metals into Spain from the colonies temporarily inflated prices and stimulated the country's economic life. But Philip's basic policies encouraged the traditional tendencies of the Spaniards to seek outlets for their energies in war, romantic adventure, or the Church. Because industry was not encouraged—the persecution of the Moriscos deprived Spain of capable artisans—foreigners flooded the country with their wares. The rigid regulation of commerce and the tardiness in making the changes necessary to meet new conditions made it almost inevitable that hostile powers, particularly the Low Countries and England, should become dangerous competitors. The encouragement of sheep raising tended to decrease agricultural production. The sources of capital from foreign loans were almost dried up by a disastrous fiscal policy. Philip increased taxation to a point where it discouraged Spanish economic initiative. The *alcabala,* or sales tax of 10 per cent, for example, increased the value of commodities by that much every time they changed hands. Three times Philip declared the country bankrupt, thereby ruining his German and Genoese bankers and weakening his credit to the point where it became next to impossible to obtain money except at usurious rates. Toward the end of his reign as much as two-thirds of his income was needed to meet interest payments.

Conscientious as Philip II was about money matters, Spain did not have the resources to support his ambitious policies. The brilliance of Spanish culture and learning continued for a while after his death; but during the reigns of the last Hapsburgs—Philip III (1598–1621), Philip IV (1621–1665), and Charles II (1665–1700), who seemed to deteriorate in ability in geometric progression—Spain gradually sank to the position of a third-rate European power.

## The Revolt of the Low Countries

Philip II's plan of re-establishing Catholicism in Europe received its most serious setback in the Low Countries. There political and religious motives combined in opposition to his policies, especially after 1559, when he left his Burgundian lands for Spain. Catholics as well as Protestants resented his encroachments upon their ancient "liberties," his attempts to centralize the government, the presence of Spanish troops in their lands, his heavy taxation designed to support his European plans, and his policies that would inevitably make the Low Countries the battleground in his wars with France. What they wanted above all was the

100 MILES

THE
**LOW
COUNTRIES**
DURING THE
REFORMATION

UNITED
NETHERLANDS

SPANISH
NETHERLANDS

GRONINGEN
Groningen
FRIESLAND
OVERYSSEL
BISHOPRIC
ZUIDER
ZEE
Zwolle
Amsterdam
Haarlem
Deventer
Zutphen
The Hague
Leyden UTRECHT
GELDERLAND
HOLLAND Gouda
Utrecht Arnheim
Brill
Rotterdam
OF
MÜNSTER
Dort
Nijmegen
CLEVES
ZEELAND
Hertogen-
Breda bosch
Middelburg
UPPER
Vlissingen
GELDER-
LAND
BERG
Ostend
Sluis
Antwerp
Bruges
BRABANT
Ghent
JULICH
FLANDERS
Louvain
Calais
Dunkirk
Brussels
Maestricht
Lille
LIÈGE
Liège
LIMBURG
ARTOIS
Douai
Mons
NAMUR
Valenciennes
Arras
HAINAUT
Catequ-
Cambresis
LUXEMBURG
ARCHB.
Amiens
BISHOPRIC
OF CAMBRAY
Trier
OF
TRIER
Luxemburg
Metz
F R A N C E
Reims
Verdun
LORRAINE

353

retention of their traditional rights as provinces, which Philip had sworn to observe, and peace, which would enable them to make the most of their rising importance as a commercial people.

Added to the particularistic interests of the provinces and the economic interests of the townsmen was the aggressive spirit of Calvinism, which had been embraced not only by large numbers of the bourgeoisie but by a number of influential nobles. The religious solidarity of the Calvinists had been secured by the adoption of the Belgic Confession as early as 1566.

### Margaret of Parma and Granvelle

That Philip intended to make the Low Countries serve his Spanish and Catholic interests became apparent in the arrangements that he made to rule them from Spain. He made his half sister Margaret, duchess of Parma, his regent. Despite the fact that she was an illegitimate daughter of Charles V and a woman of Ghent, she was fairly well liked by the people, for they considered her a Fleming; and the nobles respected her for her intelligence and good horsemanship. Even the fact that she was married to a nephew of Clement VII and, after this husband's early death, to a nephew of Paul III, and had gained an Italian outlook during her many years in that country did not seem to detract from her prestige. What harmed her in the long run was that Philip made her a mere tool, giving her no final authority in important matters. Upon making her regent he compelled her to agree to continue the policy of centralizing the government of the provinces and enforcing the detested edicts (placards) of Charles V against the Protestants, which had made heresy a civil as well as a religious offense. He also made her accept the advice of his faithful favorite, Antoine Perronet de Granvelle (1517–1586), bishop of Arras and, after 1561, archbishop of Malines and a cardinal.

Opposition to Granvelle arose as a consequence of his attempt to centralize the government along the lines developed in Spain. This involved both administrative and religious uniformity. Despite the efforts made in this direction by Charles V, the seventeen provinces were loosely bound together in a personal union, united only in their determination to be disunited. There was, to be sure, the estates-general of the thirteen older provinces; but it was little more than a conference of representatives of the provincial estates from whom they obtained their instructions. Since the time of the great dukes of Burgundy, there had been an embryonic bureaucracy, but it could accomplish little in the face of the particularism of the provinces, the selfish interests of the townsmen, and the ambitions of the great nobles—the proudest and most venerable of Europe, who controlled the offices of stadholders, or viceroys, in the various provinces, played important roles at the court, and looked upon their monarch as the *primus inter pares,* or first among equals.

# 9. Militant Catholicism and Calvinism

The chief instruments that Margaret had agreed to use in carrying out the policies of Philip II were the three councils previously established: the council of state, the privy council, and the council of finance. The council of state, which considered questions concerning foreign affairs, relations among the provinces, and all other important matters, overshadowed the other councils. At first it consisted of five councilors, the chief of whom was Granvelle. Two of the other councilors supported Granvelle in his policy of centralization and, together with him, constituted a *consulta,* or secret cabinet. The remaining two, the count of Egmont and the prince of Orange, became the leaders of all those who resented Philip's attempts to govern through his favorites. These two, members of the venerable Knights of the Golden Fleece, were men of wealth, prestige, and ability, who epitomized the strong reaction of their countrymen against the centralization of the government and their determination not to have their country used in the interests of the Spanish king.

Lamorel, count of Egmont and prince of Gavre (1522–1568), was a member of an ancient noble family, a brother-in-law of Elector Frederick III of the Palatinate, and the owner of large estates. He had gained fame as a soldier and was eventually made stadholder of the important provinces of Brabant and Artois. Though not always stable, he was a man of action.

William of Nassau, prince of Orange (1533–1584), though younger, was much more able than Egmont. He was later known as William the Silent because of his diplomatic shrewdness and discretion. But he was also an experienced and capable military leader. Furthermore, he exerted a great influence because of his vast possessions in Germany and France as well as in the Low Countries, and through his position of stadholder of Holland, Zeeland, and Utrecht. Although born of Lutheran parents, he was sent to Brussels, where he was educated as a Catholic in the court of Regent Mary. He later became a Lutheran again, then a Calvinist; but he always subordinated religion to his political interests and consistently supported freedom of conscience in religious matters. He had become a favorite of Charles V, but he almost immediately got into difficulties with Philip II. When he learned that Philip was preparing to root out heresy with fire, he became his chief opponent and, as early as 1559, urged the estates-general to demand the withdrawal of the detested Spanish troops.

The Spanish troops were withdrawn after about a year, but the oppressive taxation and the religious persecution continued. Matters were made worse by the fact that Granvelle was compelled to carry out the plan of reorganizing the bishoprics of the Low Countries, begun by Charles V. The purpose of this reorganization was to make the ecclesiastical divisions conform more nearly to the political. The four original bishoprics were accordingly separated from the archbishoprics of Rheims and

William the Silent

Cologne and increased to thirteen in number. These were placed under three newly created archbishoprics, those of Cambrai, Utrecht, and Malines, to the last of which was attached the primacy of the Low Countries. The selection of the bishops and the archbishops was placed in the hands of the king. Thus the church became a territorial church, as it were, patterned after that of Spain.

Granvelle, made archbishop of Malines, thus became the primate of the church of the Low Countries. There followed a more rigid enforcement of the decrees against heresy. Whereas the previous bishops had frequently been lax in the enforcement of these decrees, Granvelle, despite his dislike for the use of force in religious matters, was compelled to carry out the will of his king, who now could follow every move of the bishops. The Inquisition, which had been revived in 1559, began to function with brutal precision.

William of Orange and the other stadholders, wherever possible, declined to execute the sentences of the Inquisition. He and Egmont had in 1560 resigned their joint command of the Spanish regiments in the Low Countries and had requested the king to relieve them of their duties in the council of state because their advice was not being sought. Relations were further strained when, in 1561, William took as his second wife the Lutheran Anne, the only child of Elector Maurice of Saxony and the granddaughter of Philip of Hesse. Because Anne was ill in both mind and body, she made William's life miserable. However, among the children whom she gave him was Maurice, who completed the liberation of the Low Countries.

Intent upon enforcing their policy of providing peace and religious toleration for the Low Countries, William and Egmont joined another noble, Philip of Montmorency (1520–1568)—who was count of Hoorn, admiral of Flanders, and stadholder of Gelderland and Zutphen—in forming a league against Granvelle. Having won several influential nobles to their cause, these three wrote the king in 1563, requesting that he save their country from ruin by removing Granvelle. When matters grew worse, even Margaret, either because of her decreasing confidence in Granvelle or her jealousy of him, sent her own secretary to Philip, requesting the cardinal's removal. After much deliberation the king gave in, and in 1564 the Netherlanders were rid of the detested "red dragon" and "pope's dung."

That Granvelle had been but the reluctant tool of the king, not the instigator of the policy of repression, became apparent when, late in 1564, an order was received from Philip II demanding that the decrees of the Council of Trent be enforced in the Low Countries. The next year he demanded that the decrees against heretics be strictly enforced. The nobles in the council of state protested that the Tridentine decrees contained provisions that ran counter to the ancient privileges of the provinces and demanded that their publication should be suspended and the persecution be relaxed. But Philip remained inflexible. The result was widespread opposition and even lawlessness. Many of the stadholders and magistrates simply refused to enforce the edicts against their Protestant countrymen, who probably numbered fifty thousand at that time.

Meanwhile, the lesser nobility—led by Louis of Nassau, a younger brother of William and a tolerant Lutheran, and Philip of Marnîx, lord of Sainte-Aldegonde, a strict Calvinist—took the first step toward revolt by meeting in secret and obtaining hundreds of signatures to a document called the Compromise, which denounced the royal edicts. This group, called the *noble compagnie,* consisted largely of lesser nobles, landed gentry, and townsmen, men who had embraced Calvinism or were Catholics with Erasmian leanings. They pledged themselves to protect the persecuted and resist the Inquisition, although professing to be loyal to the king.

### Protest of the Beggars

To attain their ends, the militant young nobles drew up a moderate petition requesting the regent to abolish the Inquisition, modify the decrees against the heretics, refrain from enforcing the Tridentine decrees, and call the estates-general. When, in April, 1566, about two hundred and fifty excited young men appeared at the palace in Brussels to present the petition, Margaret sought the advice of her councilors on what action to take. One of them urged her not to fear "these beggars" (*ces gueux*), which term of derision was soon proudly adopted by all the opponents of the king.

Margaret answered the petition by promising to refer the matter to Philip. Its presentation, however, became the signal for a general popular tumult in which approximately a tenth of the population of the Low Countries participated. While the king, characteristically, did not act with promptness, mobs of people, among them hungry, unemployed workers of the large cities, were stirred to action by enthusiastic preachers, both Calvinists trained in Geneva and Anabaptists. An iconoclastic fury broke loose in 1566 and spread throughout the country. Joined by many returning refugees and carrying the beggar's symbols—the wallet and bowl—on their hats or girdles, they smashed images, church windows, and pictures and destroyed books and manuscripts. At the same time Louis of Nassau began negotiating with Huguenot leaders in France and Protestant leaders in Germany for military assistance. The upper nobility, including the stadholders, seemed helpless and left the regent to fend for herself. The Catholic and Lutheran nobles would have nothing to do with the Calvinist "church robbers." William of Orange sold all his movable possessions and left for his ancestral home in Germany. There he laid plans for gaining support among the enemies of Spain for an invasion of the Low Countries.

### Alva's Reign of Terror

Although Philip had hoped to postpone the issue, he was compelled to act by the spread of the iconoclastic outrages and the open worship of the Calvinist congregations. His solution was to send to the Low Countries his able but brutal general, the duke of Alva, at the head of ten thousand veteran troops (1567) and to attempt to suppress the revolt by a bloody reign of terror. It is possible that Philip could have won the upper nobility and well-to-do merchants to his side by attacking only the leaders of the revolt and granting pardon to others, as Pope Pius V wished him to do. But the king, who would not compromise in such matters, was determined to break the backbone of resistance once and for all. Alva, who had been given full civil and military authority, carried out his orders with utmost brutality. Margaret, seeing that she had lost complete control of the situation, resigned.

In the terror that followed, Egmont and Hoorn, despite their loyalty to Philip and refusal to join William, were publicly executed, thereby becoming martyrs in the eyes of their countrymen. Between six and eight thousand people suspected of heresy were tried by the newly created tribunal, the "Council of Troubles," called the "Council of Blood" by the Netherlanders, and were executed. Hundreds of thousands of others fled, among them wealthy merchants and able artisans who carried their capital and skills to neighboring lands. The possessions that the refugees could not take with them, as well as those of the executed, were confiscated by the state. Although Alva boasted of this new source of income, he soon learned that it would not suffice for his purposes and that the economic life of the Low Countries was temporarily ruined.

To help defray the great costs involved in the military subjection of the Low Countries, Alva increased the taxes. He compelled the estates-general to levy a tax of 1 per cent on all personal and real property, to be levied only once; a tax of 5 per cent on the sale of real estate; and a tax of 10 per cent on the sale of movable goods. Almost complete economic paralysis followed—and also a renewed determination, particularly in the north, to resist the Spaniards.

Meanwhile William of Orange, whose own property in the Low Countries had been confiscated, emerged as a redoubtable hero in the ensuing struggle for independence. Not heroic by nature, generally indifferent with respect to religious matters, and not a brilliant soldier, he nonetheless deserves the honor given him because of his strong will and diplomatic skill. He soon learned that he could not succeed against the religious fanaticism of Philip II unless he had the support of the equally

*359*

fanatical Calvinists. This support he obtained with the aid of his faithful friend and companion Philip Marnîx, a great statesman, soldier, theologian, and author.

William had great difficulty in obtaining money and military support for his attack upon Alva. The Huguenots, who were willing to help as long as Coligny was in favor at the French court, were helpless after the massacre of St. Bartholomew in 1572. The Protestant princes of Germany, most of whom detested Calvinism or did not wish to endanger the peace signed at Augsburg in 1555, rendered little or no aid. Although Queen Elizabeth sympathized with the Low Countries and opened her ports to Calvinist refugees, she did not wish to intervene until she was sure on which side victory lay. Therefore the small number of troops that William could muster were no match for the many veterans commanded by Alva, and his expedition into the Low Countries from Germany ended in failure.

It was then that William learned that the most reliable support was to be found in those northern provinces of which he was stadholder— Holland, Zeeland, and Utrecht—in which Calvinism was making great gains. There his brother Louis, in imitation of the French Huguenots whom he had visited at La Rochelle, granted letters of reprisal to daring sailors, the "wild beggars of the sea," who daily increased in numbers and obtained ships with which to prey upon Spanish commerce. They seized one coastal city after another and finally even defeated the Spanish fleet in the Zuiderzee. When much of the north was in William's hands, representatives of the cities that had revolted met in Dordrecht (July, 1572) and elected him the commander-in-chief of the army in Holland, Zeeland, Utrecht, and West Friesland. Later the estates-general elected him royal stadholder, in which capacity he carried on the struggle against Spain.

## Requesens and the Siege of Leyden

Although Alva regained most of the towns seized by "the beggars of the sea," the people of the northern provinces fought back with such heroic vigor and determination—even opening up the dikes against the Spanish soldiers—that he was compelled to admit the failure of his efforts. Faced by ruin, even the Catholic provinces in the south were becoming bitterly anti-Spanish, a sentiment that Alva failed to understand. Furthermore, he could get no more financial support from Philip, who realized that the religious struggles in France and the ominous threat of England required many more resources than he had at his disposal. Therefore Philip was now willing to make halting, though insincere, concessions. He removed Alva at the latter's own request in December, 1573, and replaced him with Don Luis de Requesens, one of his dependable favorites, who was loathed by the proud nobles of the Low Countries.

# 9. Militant Catholicism and Calvinism

The attempt of Philip II to bring an end to the bloody struggle by offering to negotiate was doomed to failure, to a large degree because this had become a religious struggle, especially in the northern provinces. William now demanded through the estates-general not only the ancient privileges and the removal of Spanish troops but religious freedom. This the king could not grant. The Calvinists went much further by demanding the establishment of their church as the only true one. Calvinism and Dutch patriotism thus merged. This merger was illustrated by the fact that the University of Leyden, founded in 1575, that is, a year after the heroic rescue of that city following a seige of nine months, became an important center of Calvinism.

When Requesens died of typhus in 1576, he was not replaced for an entire year, during which time the council of state at Brussels attempted to exercise royal authority. It sought in vain, however, for specific directions from Philip for bringing hostilities to a close. Meanwhile the Spanish troops at Antwerp, who had long not received their pay—Philip had declared bankruptcy a second time in 1575—mutinied, seized everything of value, set fire to public buildings, raped the women, and murdered about six or seven thousand of the citizens.

## The Pacification of Ghent

The "Spanish Fury" of November, 1576, as the mutiny at Antwerp was called, finally electrified all the provinces to united action. Holland and Zeeland succeeded, under the leadership of William, in bringing the southern provinces into a federation by means of a treaty called the Pacification of Ghent (November, 1576). The thirteen signatory provinces gave William virtually sovereign authority for the duration of the war and agreed to turn over the solution of the religious problems to the estates-general that was to meet later. In January, 1577, the rest of the provinces joined the thirteen in what was called the Union of Brussels, a confirmation of the Pacification of Ghent by the estates-general.

When Don Juan of Austria, the hero of Lepanto and the new governor-general of the Low Countries, arrived in Brussels in May, 1577, with instructions to negotiate with the provinces, it was too late, for the signatories of the Union were determined to drive out the Spaniards. Even before his appearance, Don Juan had been compelled to sign the Perpetual Edict, promising to respect the ancient privileges of the provinces, free the political prisoners, and withdraw the Spanish troops in return for money for their back pay. He actually withdrew some of the troops. Too hotheaded, however, to stand the endless negotiations with the estates of the provinces, he left Brussels in utter disgust for the fortress Namur and called upon Philip to send the troops back to the Low Countries to suppress the traitors by force.

William took full advantage of Don Juan's failure at reconciliation.

# Part Four: Religious Conflicts and Consequences

In September, 1577, when William appeared in Brussels, he was received by the largely Catholic population with enthusiastic acclaim and was made stadholder of Brabant by the estates-general, a position tantamount to that of governor of the Low Countries. He had reached the height of his career, with the prospect in sight of uniting all the provinces into a national state. But appearances were deceptive, for underneath the enthusiasm over the temporary success against the Spanish lay the age-old particularism of the provinces; the strong racial differences among the Dutch, the Flemings, and the Walloons; the distrust of the nobles and the upper bourgeoisie of the popular movement behind William; and, more important still, the great cleavage between the Catholics in the southern and the Calvinists in the northern provinces. These tensions reached the breaking point in the spring of 1578, when the masses, who disliked the Catholic clergy as much as the nobility and upper bourgeoisie, again broke out in an iconoclastic fury.

In the meantime Philip sent Alessandro Farnese of Parma, son of Margaret of Parma, to the Low Countries with twenty thousand troops. Probably the most brilliant soldier of his day, he and Don Juan utterly routed the federal army at Gembloux in January, 1578. To gain outside support in the face of Parma's military success, the estates-general induced the young Archduke Matthias of Austria to become the stadholder and the ambitious Duke Francis of Anjou, for eleven years the hapless suitor of Queen Elizabeth, to be the "Defender of Liberty of the Low Countries." William willingly took a position subordinate to the future emperor because this action might split the Hapsburgs, thereby weakening Philip. William also hoped that the selection of these two Catholic rulers might keep the Catholics loyal to the cause. Finally, he continued scrupulously to maintain the constitutional principles of the provinces and never succumbed to the temptation of setting up a dictatorship or a new dynasty for himself.

## The Emergence of the United Provinces

After the sudden death of Don Juan in October, 1578, Parma was given his place. The equal of William as a diplomat, he succeeded within a year in drawing the estates of the Walloon provinces and even some of the cities of Flanders and Brabant, consisting predominantly of Catholics, into a union for the purpose of helping him maintain order and good government. In the Union of Arras of January, 1579, the signatories promised to seek reconciliation with the king in return for the promise that their ancient privileges and Catholic worship would be safeguarded.

The Union of Arras was followed a few weeks later by the Union of Utrecht, negotiated by William's brother John, stadholder of Gelderland, and signed by the representatives of Holland, Zeeland, Utrecht, Gelderland, Friesland, Overyssel, and Groningen. The signatories expressed the same general objectives as those of Arras, but they emphasized their intention of maintaining religious freedom in their lands. Although each union hoped ultimately to bring in all the provinces, the complicated sequence of events made each the beginning of a new national state. The chief issue that divided them was religious, despite the fact that William struggled valiantly to make it secondary to the issue of political unity.

Outright revolutionary action was invited by Philip II, who believed that resistance would collapse if he were rid of William. Accordingly, in the summer of 1580, he declared William an outlaw and offered a handsome reward to anyone who would hand him over dead or alive. This personal attack upon William endeared him still further to the people. Using this swell of devotion to political advantage, he presented to the estates-general, which opened at Delft in December, 1580, his famous *Apology,* in which he vindicated his honor against the attack of Philip and for the first time publicly renounced the overlordship of the Spanish king, giving as his reason that Philip had failed in his duty to the Low Countries. This was the first practical application of the theory expressed by the anonymous Huguenot author of the *Vindicae contra tyrannos* (1579), namely, that the people have not only the right but the moral obligation to remove a sovereign who does not carry out his royal duties.

## Declaration of Independence

The presentation of the *Apology* was followed by the declaration of independence of the estates-general, meeting at The Hague in July, 1581. There the representatives of the provinces of Holland, Zeeland, Utrecht, Gelderland, Friesland, Groningen, Overyssel, Malines, Flanders, and Brabant chose William head of the government until a new sovereign could be selected, and then declared Philip II deposed. After these preliminaries the young Matthias, the nominal governor-general under Philip, was dismissed and the duke of Anjou was made Philip's successor as duke of Brabant. But the people did not want Anjou. By supporting him during the following three years, William himself made impossible the unity for which he had toiled with so many sacrifices. Nonetheless, at the moment Anjou's rule seemed the only possible means of keeping France and England—Anjou's courtship was still being favorably received by Elizabeth—from aiding Spain.

Unfortunately, Anjou had neither the personality nor the military ability to save the Low Countries, hold the provinces together, or draw France into an alliance with them. William's control over the people, however, was strengthened by the fact that a Portuguese merchant, eager to recoup his dissipated fortunes, had one of his clerks attempt to assassinate William. Miraculously the shot through his cheeks and jaw did not kill him. While William was recovering at Antwerp, Anjou attempted a *coup d'état* to get complete control by unleashing the "French Fury" in that city. Despite this stupid treachery, William persisted in his support of Anjou, for he still believed that only a French alliance would save the country.

Meanwhile Parma took one large city after the other by long sieges, regained much of the country for his king, and reduced William's support largely to the northern provinces. Yet William continued the unequal struggle until a second assassin, a Burgundian supporter of Philip, gained access to his home in July, 1584, and in the presence of his family shot and killed him. But the work of the "father of his country," as he was called, had been accomplished. Despite the desperate appearance of his cause, expressed in his last words, "God have pity on this poor people," it was now inextricably involved in the broader European struggles in which Philip lost and the Dutch republic emerged. Even more important, the faithful followers of William, now reduced to a small but more homogeneous part of the Low Countries, had the heroism, tenacity, and religious motivation that enabled them to take advantage of the increasingly favorable European situation.

Because Anjou died shortly after the assassination of William, it was necessary for the estates-general to select another ruler. Maurice of Nassau, William's seventeen-year-old son, was made captain-general and admiral of the United Provinces, as the provinces in revolt were now called, while the council of state of eighteen members was entrusted with administrative affairs. Owing to the predominant role that Holland and Zeeland had played, their wishes were followed in most respects. This was particularly true after Parma had overrun Brabant and Flanders and taken the important city of Antwerp. Incidentally, when Antwerp was lost to Spain, the Dutch blocked its access to the sea, and Amsterdam became the great entrepôt of continental commerce. Under the leadership of Holland and Zeeland, the estates-general continued William's policy of seeking foreign aid against Spain. When Henry III of France refused to become the protector of Holland and Zeeland and sovereign over the other provinces, they turned to Elizabeth (1585).

The queen of England, still not willing to become embroiled in war with Philip, agreed only to send to the Low Countries, for a monetary consideration, a force of about six thousand men under the command of her favorite, Robert Dudley, earl of Leicester. Again the policy of seeking foreign aid ended in failure. Without Elizabeth's prior consent, Leicester permitted himself to be made governor-general with almost absolute control. This position he greatly abused. He interfered with the lucrative carrying trade of the Dutch with Spain, failed to pursue the war with vigor, ignored the ancient privileges of the provinces, and alienated the Catholics with his radical Protestantism. Although his intentions were good, he was not equal to all the problems facing him. Consequently he left the country in August, 1587, never to return.

After the departure of Leicester, the estates-general was finally compelled to rely upon its own leadership and resources. Administrative and diplomatic matters gravitated into the hands of the legally trained Johan van Oldenbarnevelt (1547—1619), friend and supporter of William, who became the advocate, or syndic, of Holland in 1586 and played the dominant role in the estates-general. Holland, which had two thirds of the population of the United Provinces and paid three fourths of the expenses, remained the leading province and even gave its name, in popular parlance, to the new state. From the outset Oldenbarnevelt defended the principle that, upon the abjuration of Philip, sovereign powers had reverted to the several provinces.

Military matters, as we have seen, were placed in the hands of Maurice of Nassau (1567–1625), captain-general and admiral of the union, who was ably assisted by his cousin William Louis of Nassau, a thorough student of military science. Devoting much of his time to the reform and the equipment of his army, Maurice created a fighting machine that enabled him to assume the offensive and, by 1593, drive the Spaniards out of virtually all the lands and cities of the northern provinces. Important to his success was the fact that Parma was handicapped by Philip's attempted invasion of England in 1588 and his involvement in French politics, which compelled Parma to shift most of his troops to France. Furthermore, when Parma died in 1592, he was replaced by Archduke Ernest of Austria and, about a year after the latter's death, by Archduke Albert, neither of whom pursued the war with great vigor. In 1598 Philip married his eldest daughter, Isabella, to Archduke Albert and gave him the southern provinces as a separate state, to revert to Spain if there were no heirs. Finally, soon after Henry of Navarre became Henry IV of France, that country joined England in forming an alliance with the United Provinces (1596), whose independence both France and England recognized. Although France made peace with Spain in 1598, the war, in which the Dutch were even more successful on sea than on land, dragged on until 1609, when the Twelve Years' Truce gave the United Provinces virtual independence.

## The United Provinces

The new state north of the Scheldt River comprised seven provinces: Holland, Zeeland, Utrecht, Friesland, Gelderland, Overyssel, and Groningen. It was bound together racially and linguistically, with respect to economic interests, and by the long struggle with the Spaniards. But whenever the danger of war abated, especially after 1609, the particularism of the provinces and the weaknesses of the central institutions became obvious. The United Provinces consisted of a conglomeration of provinces and town corporations in which long-entrenched oligarchies jealously guarded their traditional rights. The majority of the people still had no voice in their local governments, much less in the estates-general, which merely reflected the wishes of the provincial estates.

It is inconceivable that such a state could have carried on the struggle with Spain and emerged independent without a strong economic basis. The northern provinces—especially Holland and Zeeland, which had gained much of the northern European trade after the decline of the Hanseatic League—were able to stand the staggering expenses connected with the war. As a matter of fact, the war itself greatly increased their trade and industry. Not only had many prosperous and skilled townsmen fled to the north during the bloody campaigns in the south, bringing with them their capital and industries, but centuries of seafaring life had given them seamen who could take advantage of the weaknesses apparent in the Spanish and Portuguese colonial empires. The trade with Spain alone covered most of the cost of the war. Lucrative, also, were the piratical attacks upon Spanish shipping and coastal towns, as well as the invasions of the Spanish and Portuguese colonial trading posts. To organize the highly profitable trade with the Orient, the adventurous merchants organized their small commercial companies into the Dutch East India Company, granted a charter by the estates-general in 1601. In rivalry with the English East India Company, founded about the same time, it laid the basis for the emergence of the United Provinces as a great colonial power.

Although the rise and spread of Calvinism to the northern provinces, the last to be influenced by Protestantism, served as a powerful motivation in the struggle with Spain, Calvinism also served as a dividing force. Embraced largely by influential townsmen who dominated their respective estates, it made impossible the carrying-out of William's policy of unity with political freedom. At the same time Calvinism helped accentuate the political differences that became apparent when internal issues were at stake. In the long run, however, Calvinism was purged of its dissenting elements and became a unifying force in the new state.

The religious life of the provinces south of the Scheldt, where Protestantism had found its first adherents, was part of the story of the Catholic Reformation, which was introduced after the signing of the Twelve Years' Truce. Flanders and Brabant, once the most prosperous lands in Europe, suffered most from the war and lost heavily in population. They soon came completely under the influence of the Walloon provinces, and French became the language of the nobles and the educated burghers. With the coming of the Jesuits and other religious orders, Catholicism was revived, the remnants of Protestantism were vigorously suppressed, and the entire cultural life was dominated and utilized by the Church.

Not only the schools but the fine arts served the interests of a revived Catholicism. These southern provinces, called the Spanish Netherlands and today known as Belgium, became the battleground of the Hapsburgs and the Bourbons in subsequent wars.

## The Religious Wars in France

Although Calvin had consistently objected to the use of other than constitutional means by the Huguenots in their attempts to obtain freedom of worship, the religious movement in France became involved in the national political struggles to such an extent that it was almost completely submerged by them. By becoming identified with the centrifugal forces within the country, which opposed the monarchical state-church policy of "one king, one law, one faith," Calvinism became a strong political force. The Huguenots, brought together into a national organization in 1559, eventually constituted a virtual state within a state that not only commanded large military forces and negotiated with foreign powers but frequently bargained with the monarchy itself.

After the death of the last strong Valois ruler, Henry II, Calvinism was joined by many of the lesser nobles who had long sought redress against royal enroachments upon their ancient privileges and the autonomy of the provinces. Thus the Protestant movement was supported not only by an ambitious middle class but by a strong feudal opposition to the king, his court favorites, and his growing bureaucracy. Furthermore, there was widespread resentment against the royal evasion of ancient legal rights; a jealousy of the higher Catholic clergy, who usually belonged to the upper nobility; and an increasing demand for provincial autonomy. Although the Huguenots were to be found throughout France, they constituted a majority of the population only in Dauphiné and eastern Languedoc. The Catholic side consisted primarily of the upper nobility, government officials, most of the peasants, and the masses in most of the large urban centers.

The outbreak of hostilities in 1562 coincided with the beginnings of the Counter Reformation throughout Europe, so that fanatical religious emotions were inflamed to white heat and put to use by political leaders for the attainment of their political ends. Moreover, the internal religio-political struggle of France also became a matter of concern for all Europe. Consequently all the great powers came to have a stake in the outcome.

### Outbreak of Hostilities

When Duke Francis of Guise sought to gain the support of Philip II; massacred members of Huguenot congregations at Vassy, Toulouse, and Orléans; gained control over Catherine de' Medici and the boy king

Catherine de' Medici

Charles IX; and declared his intention of having the January Edict of Toleration revoked, the first of the religious wars broke out that kept France in a state of turmoil for more than thirty years (1562–1598). The Huguenots, no longer satisfied with the right of toleration, were determined to wipe out the "papists and idolaters" and appealed to foreign powers for aid. They were particularly hopeful of English support, which, however, never amounted to much. While the Catholic forces under the duke of Guise included Spanish, Savoyard, and papal troops, the Huguenot forces under Coligny and Condé included German soldiers from Hesse and the Palatinate and, at first, a number of English troops. The battle cry of the Huguenots at this time was to free Catherine and Charles from the Guises.

During the first eight years of desultory fighting, characterized to a large degree by assassinations, massacres, incendiarism, and destruction of property on the part of both Catholics and Huguenots, no decisive action took place. Leadership in both camps changed hands, however, when Duke Francis of Guise was murdered by a fanatical Huguenot, leaving Duke Henry as the new head of the house of Guise, and when King Anthony of Navarre, who had joined the Catholic side, and Prince Louis Condé were killed in battle, leaving young Henry of Navarre and Henry of Condé to serve under the older Gaspard de Coligny, admiral of France. Despite the fact that the Catholics were in a majority, Catherine's negotiations with Philip II of Spain and Alva's attacks upon the leaders of the revolt in the Low Countries aroused such a strong anti-Spanish sentiment that Catherine found it wise to bring hostilities to a close.

The Peace of Saint-Germain-en-Laye (1570) granted the Huguenots complete amnesty, freedom of conscience, the right to hold public office, and the right to worship in the homes of the nobility in the cities where they had previously worshiped and in two cities in each of the provinces. For their security the Huguenots were allowed to have four fortified cities: La Rochelle, Montauban, La Charité, and Cognac. On the other hand, they agreed to the restoration of Catholicism in those places where they had suppressed it. Although the Huguenots were generally pleased with the treaty, the Catholics, under the leadership of the duke of Guise, were resolved to regain their influence in the court and undo this formal recognition of the Protestants.

Catherine and her son Charles IX, who had been declared of age, were at this time developing a strong anti-Spanish policy that was designed to bring peace at home, assure the permanence of the Valois dynasty, and regain certain portions of the Burgundian lands that had once been French. They accordingly made Coligny a member of the royal council and showered him with other favors. They hoped to seal reconciliation with the Huguenots by the marriage of Catherine's youngest daughter, Margaret, to Henry of Bourbon, who became King Henry of Navarre upon the death of his mother soon after her arrival in Paris for the wedding ceremony. At the same time, Catherine proposed the marriage of the duke of Alençon, later the duke of Anjou, her favorite son, to Queen Elizabeth of England. Only a defensive alliance could be made with Elizabeth, however, for it was her consistent policy to permit neither France nor Spain to dominate the Low Countries. Charles IX was betrothed to Elizabeth, daughter of Emperor Maximilian II.

The wedding of Henry of Navarre and Margaret took place in Paris outside the cathedral of Notre Dame, August 18, 1572. Many French Huguenots were present at the ceremony. Their presence served to increase the tensions in Paris, especially because the Huguenots were becoming impatient over the delay in sending troops to the Low Countries and because Duke Henry of Guise was growing increasingly resentful of Coligny's influence over the king. Duke Henry soon won Catherine to his side, for she was beginning to feel that her policy of mediating between the two religious groups and maintaining a balance between them was weakening rather than strengthening the throne. She further came to the conclusion that the Huguenots would not be satisfied until they had converted all Frenchmen to Protestantism and had gained control of the government. She may also have seen the difficulties involved in opposing the wishes of the pope, the Spanish king, and the majority of the French people. It has even been suggested that she now turned to the Guises for reasons of faith.

Whatever the reasons for her *volte-face*, Catherine plotted with Duke Henry to get rid of Coligny, whose influence over her son had aroused her jealousy. The thug hired to assassinate Coligny, however, failed to kill the victim, for he only shot off one finger and broke an arm. The Huguenots threatened to take appropriate action, and the king was so incensed at the deed that he vowed to run down the culprit and sent his own physician, Ambrose Paré, to care for Coligny. Catherine, fearing the consequences of such a search and subsequent trial, apparently decided, in a state of panic, to liquidate all the Huguenot leaders as though they were of no greater importance than the small cliques so frequently murdered in the turbulent political life of the Italian city-states. To give the plot the semblance of legality, she convinced the king that the Huguenots were plotting to murder him, Catherine, and the duke of Anjou.

### The Massacre of St. Bartholomew

Before dawn on August 24—St. Bartholomew's Day—1572, at a prearranged signal, the conspirators fell upon the unsuspecting Huguenots. Duke Henry of Guise himself supervised the murder of Coligny, whose body was thrown out onto the street and mutilated beyond recognition. The frenzied mobs of Paris, whose bestial instincts had been aroused in the name of religion, joined the melee, slaying suspected heretics until the Seine was filled with corpses. From two to three thousand persons were killed in Paris alone, about twenty thousand in all France. That there was a well-organized plot seems indicated by the fact that the assassinations occurred simultaneously in many scattered cities.

Whether or not the massacre was deliberately planned in all its gruesome details, Catherine let it be known that she intended to maintain strong control in France and to make no significant changes in her domestic or foreign policies. Despite the brutality of the massacre, foreign reactions to it were not on the whole unfavorable. Pope Gregory XIII, although at first dismayed, attended a special thanksgiving service and prescribed an annual *Te Deum* that was observed for many years. Philip II, who is said to have laughed publicly for the first time in his life, also had a *Te Deum* sung and ordered his bishops to celebrate the event with appropriate ceremonies. Maximilian II was greatly disturbed by the massacre, but he took no more vigorous action than to warn the Poles of the designs of France when they were considering making the duke of Anjou their king.

The Protestants, on the other hand, were struck with horror. Queen Elizabeth wore mourning to show her grief; yet a few months later she agreed to serve as godmother to the daughter of the French king. William of Orange, as we have seen, had the duke of Anjou proclaimed the "Defender of the Liberty of the Low Countries." The Poles likewise ignored the massacre and elected Duke Henry of Anjou their king. King Charles IX, however, seems never to have overcome his grief and sense of guilt because of his part in the brutal action. He died less than two years later and was succeeded by the duke of Anjou and king of Poland as King Henry III (1574–1589).

Although the Massacre of St. Bartholomew did not adversely affect Catherine's foreign policy, it made it impossible for her to carry out her domestic policy. All the old animosities were revived and intensified. The new king, though chivalrous, brave, and not without intellectual ability, was exceptionally effeminate, inclined to vice, and without a strong will; and his obviously zealous Catholicism at times made it difficult for Catherine to follow a primarily political policy.

Because of the massacre and the inconspicuous role of Henry III, the prestige of the crown and the conception of divine-right monarchy, built up over the centuries by the Capetian and Valois dynasties and their supporters, suffered irreparable damage. The attacks upon the discredited monarchy began almost immediately after the massacre. Huguenot publicists who had fled to Geneva wrote highly inflammatory pamphlets, calling upon the French people to revolt against the illegal tyranny in France and justifying their revolutionary demands by references to the age-old rights and privileges of the French estates.

# Part Four: Religious Conflicts and Consequences

## Revival of the Struggle

The Huguenots soon regained their morale, despite the loss of so many leaders on St. Bartholomew's day. After all, they still retained two fortified places, La Rochelle and Montauban, had the allegiance of many of the lesser nobles, and could look for eventual aid from Henry of Navarre and Prince Henry of Condé, who had not suffered the fate of Coligny because they had abjured their Protestant faith. Meanwhile, the entire nature of the Huguenot struggle changed. The Huguenots were now no longer content with arguing that they were merely wishing to free the king from the control of the Guises and to have the Bourbon member of the royal family share the government with him. Now the struggle was avowedly one against the king as a tyrant, against the murderers, and for the rights of Frenchmen as described by the publicists. The families of the lesser nobility, who had lost so many of their sons on the eve of St. Bartholomew, now thirsted for revenge. The war for religious freedom had become a war for political freedom, which was joined by all disaffected elements.

More important still, the Huguenots of southern and western France now created a powerful political organization of Protestant estates. It had its own army, its legislative, executive, and judicial institutions, and administrative control of the royal taxes in these lands. The effectiveness and unity of this organization stood in strong contrast to the confusion that reigned at the royal court. Catherine's negotiations with Protestant as well as Catholic rulers, as though no massacre had occurred, lessened her prestige, and Henry III pursued his costly pleasures at Paris and permitted his questionable court favorites to exert a strong political influence over him.

## The Politiques

The mismanagement of governmental affairs and the exclusion of the members of great Catholic families from the court aroused the opposition of a third party, the *Politiques,* or Politicians. These were Catholics and Huguenots who placed the common good and the unity of France above matters of religion. When they joined the Huguenots early in 1575 and the ambitious Duke Francis of Alençon appeared as the leader of this opposition to his brother Henry III, it seemed as though royal absolutism and Catholic unity of faith would finally come to an end in France. In May, 1576, the king agreed to the Peace of Beaulieu, which gave the Huguenots complete religious freedom in France—except in Paris—and six additional fortified places. At the same time, the duke of Alençon was made duke of Anjou, and Condé was made governor of Languedoc. Henry of Navarre, alarmed at the threats against his life, left Paris, publicly announced that he was a Calvinist, and assumed the leadership of the Huguenots.

## The Catholic League

When the Catholic nobles realized that the king could not be relied upon to defend Catholicism, they formed the Catholic League (1576), another state within the state, for the purpose of re-establishing royal authority and Catholicism. Its purpose was well expressed by its motto, "One faith, one law, one king." The League spread rapidly. The young Duke Henry of Guise emerged as its leader. Although the king, placed between two fires, at first tried to oppose the League, he finally joined it because he realized that it represented the will of the majority of the people.

So successful was the League that the meeting of the estates-general at Blois, which had been promised in the Peace of Beaulieu, proved to be overwhelmingly Catholic and voted for the re-establishment of Catholicism as the sole religion of France. In the renewed struggles that followed, the *Politiques* broke their alliance with the Huguenots. The king, however, fearing the growing strength of the Guises, issued the Peace of Bergerac (1577), giving the Huguenots liberty of conscience; but freedom of worship was granted only in places where the local authorities would permit it.

During the seven years of nominal peace that followed, Henry of Navarre alienated the strict Calvinists by setting up a brilliant and gay court at Nérac, where he was joined by his wife. It seemed as though this peace might continue for a long time. In 1584, however, Duke Francis of Anjou, who had returned from his unsuccessful adventure in the Low Countries, died. Because he had been the king's sole surviving brother and because Henry III remained childless, Henry of Navarre became the legal successor to the throne of France. According to the Catholic Church, however, he was a lapsed heretic who should be punished with the death penalty. The Catholic League took vigorous measures to prevent him from becoming king. It not only planned to call the estates-general to change the order of succession but obtained a papal dispensation that enabled it to conclude an alliance—the Treaty of Joinville of January, 1585—with Philip II against the French king.

Instead of taking advantage of this situation and enlisting the loyal nobles in a struggle with Spain, Henry III long remained undecided, refused to bring pressure to bear upon Henry of Navarre to return to Catholicism, and finally, when most of France appeared to sympathize with the League, made a treaty with it, the Treaty of Nemours of July, 1585. The king then agreed to publish an edict making Catholicism the only recognized religion of France and compelling the people to conform or leave the country. Later in the same year Pope Sixtus V issued a bull excommunicating both Henry of Navarre and the prince of Condé as heretics and excluding them from the succession to the throne.

## The War of the Three Henries

Without the money to raise an army, Henry III was at the mercy of the League in the War of the Three Henries, which now broke out. Henry of Navarre, who refused to return to Catholicism, was compelled to assume the defensive against both Henry III and the League. Henry of Guise, on the other hand, seemed to possess unlimited power, supported as he was by the pope and the masses of the French people who were being aroused to action by the Jesuits and the Capuchins. Hailed as a second Moses, Duke Henry made plans to have himself made king of France in place of the unpopular king and in May, 1588, entered Paris despite the fact that the king had forbidden him to do so. The excited populace even threw up barricades to prevent the royal troops, whom the king had engaged to protect him, from going to the palace. Seeing that his situation in Paris was hopeless, the king fled to Chartres, leaving Guise in control of Paris.

Henry III, humiliated and with no visible means out of his difficulty except treating with the League, agreed to convoke the estates-general at Blois, the meeting of which marked the nadir of royal authority. The king was reduced to such extremities that he had Duke Henry of Guise and his brother Louis, cardinal of Guise, murdered in the castle of Blois during a meeting of the council. But this liquidation of his chief enemies did not restore his authority, for all Catholic France was stupefied by this act of tyranny and no longer considered him king. The final stroke came from Pope Sixtus V, who issued a bull demanding that "Henry of Valois" appear in Rome within ten days to be tried for the murder of the cardinal of Guise or be excommunicated.

In these circumstances Henry III called to his side those nobles who had been alarmed by the excesses of the adherents of the League in Paris and had joined Henry of Navarre, who had issued a declaration to the effect that he wished reconciliation with the king and peace for France. In the spring of 1589 the two Henries joined forces and marched on Paris. As Henry of Navarre prepared to take the city by storm, Henry III was assassinated by a demented Dominican monk. Before he died, the king commanded the officers to recognize Henry of Navarre as his successor and warned the new king that he would have many difficulties unless he again embraced Catholicism. He had been preceded in death by only a few months by his mother, Catherine de' Medici. With the death of the last of the Valois kings, the crown went to the Bourbon Huguenot, who was detested by the great majority of the French people.

# The Reconstruction of France

When Henry of Navarre and Bourbon became king of France as Henry IV (1589–1610) at the age of thirty-five, he came to the realization that he could not continue the internal wars and at the same time prevent Philip II of Spain from seizing the French throne. Philip claimed this throne through his deceased wife, Elizabeth of Valois, sister of Henry III, and on behalf of their daughter, Isabella. Henry IV accordingly tried to end the civil wars by vigorously pursuing his opponents, supported by money from England and troops from Germany. The sight of a determined king, fighting at the head of his troops against overwhelming odds, won increasing numbers of supporters to his side.

When, however, Philip II sent Parma with his well-disciplined army into France, Henry came to the conclusion that he could not win a decisive victory over the Catholic League. He therefore reluctantly decided to return to Catholicism and to treat with the League.

Henry now appeared as the savior of France and was welcomed in Paris in 1594 by the formerly hostile masses. The Parlement of Paris declared the claims of Philip II to the French throne through Elizabeth of Valois contrary to French law. In 1595 Pope Clement VIII, who feared that the French bishops, who had crowned Henry king at Chartres, might set up a national church similar to that of England under Henry VIII, removed the ban of excommunication from Henry. The Catholic League, which had become unpopular because of its connections with Philip II, collapsed. The Jesuits were exiled as teachers of tyrannicide. Soon one after another of Henry's former enemies flocked to him to vie for royal favors. The few nobles who refused to make peace with him were ruthlessly punished.

Henry's victory over the Catholic League coincided with a gradual change in Europe as a whole that enabled France to play a significant role in international affairs. France became the continental hub of a growing opposition to Spain at the same time that the English and the Dutch were bringing their conflicts with Spain to a successful conclusion and were challenging Spanish supremacy as a maritime and colonial power. That the "golden age" of Spain was drawing to a close was evident in the changing diplomacy of the popes, who became more interested again in maintaining a balance of power between France and Spain than in rooting out Protestantism. In other words, the Catholic Counter Reformation was no longer the key to international diplomacy.

Henry IV continued his conflict with Spain with the support of nearly all France and brought it to a successful conclusion in the Treaty of Vervins (1598), mediated by the pope. Although the *status quo* was reestablished by this treaty, Spain had exhausted her resources, and France emerged as the dominant continental power.

# Part Four: Religious Conflicts and Consequences

## The Edict of Nantes

When Clement VIII had made peace with Henry IV, he had not insisted that the latter enforce the Tridentine decrees in France. Thus Henry was at liberty to solve the religious problem in his country in his own way. The Edict of Nantes (1598), largely the work of the Huguenot statesman Duplessis-Mornay, made the Catholic Church the official state church and restored to it its former rights, possessions, and income. On the other hand, the Edict made far-reaching concessions to the approximately 1.25 million Huguenots, consisting largely of nobles and prosperous townsmen. It granted them (1) religious rights, such as freedom of conscience and permission to worship in those places where they had worshiped prior to 1597; (2) civic rights, such as legal protection and eligibility to hold public offices; and (3) many political rights, including the permission to hold public assemblies and maintain two hundred fortified places supplied with garrisons and supported in part by the king. Although the Edict did not satisfy the extremists in either of the religious camps, it brought an end to the religious wars and was strictly enforced by Henry until his death in 1610.

## Beginnings of Absolutism

Henry IV, having brought both the internal and the foreign wars to a close, turned his complete attention to laying the bases for the divine-right absolutism that reached its height in the reign of Louis XIV. He was supported in this by the majority of the French people, for they realized that peace and prosperity could be maintained only under a firm rule. He refused to call the estates-general, which had been hostile to him in the past, and greatly restricted the rights of those provincial estates that had not been abolished. He still permitted the Parlement of Paris to register and criticize royal decrees, but he tolerated no political opposition from this body. Whenever possible, he placed royal officials in control of towns, and he made the central government more efficient by reducing the size of the royal council to twelve in number, adding experts in law and finance to special sessions of the council when the occasion demanded and presiding over it in person.

Although Henry could not deprive the nobles of their ancient privileges, he decreased their political influence by using middle-class officials in his government, making their positions in the Parlement of Paris hereditary—thus creating the nobility of the robe—and using capable ministers instead of royal favorites to assist him. Best known of these ministers was Maximilien de Béthune, the duke of Sully, a Huguenot and a personal friend of Henry. Under Sully's capable management, agriculture, commerce, and industry were stimulated to such an extent that the financial situation of the country was greatly improved. Henry even laid the foundations of a French colonial empire in America by sending to its shores Champlain, who established settlements at Port Royal and Quebec in 1608.

No sooner had peace and prosperity been restored, however, than Henry IV began to make his influence felt in European affairs. He supported the United Provinces against Spain, revived French interests in Italy by marrying Marie de' Medici, and, in 1609, planned to support the German Protestants in an attack upon the Hapsburgs. But before he could carry out his grandiose plans, he was assassinated by an insane Catholic fanatic in a narrow Parisian street on May 14, 1610.

The development of French absolutism was temporarily halted when Marie de' Medici became regent for her young son, Louis XIII. The nobles once more sought to regain their political influence, the Huguenot leaders revived the religious struggle with attacks upon the Catholics, and the nobility of the robe sought to enhance their own position. These forces of opposition to the crown cooperated in compelling the regent to call the estates-general in 1614, but they could not agree on a common program. The complete disintegration of royal authority was prevented when, in 1617, Louis declared himself of age and, in 1624, made Richelieu his chief minister. Richelieu continued the policies of Henry IV and was notably successful in making the king supreme in France and France predominant in Europe.

## French Calvinism and Catholicism

The long struggle of the Huguenots with the Valois rulers and their ultimate legal recognition by the Edict of Nantes had a great influence not only upon the development of their political as well as religious ideas but also upon the development of Calvinism throughout Europe and later in North America. Building upon Calvin's views concerning the Christian community, in which all members are free and equal before God and which is responsible for the conduct of its members, Huguenot writers came to emphasize the ideas of popular sovereignty current in late antiquity and the Middle Ages. Because the religious conflicts of the Huguenots, like those of Calvinists elsewhere, were involved in politics, the reign of law, political freedom, and the individual responsibility of the people were given religious justification and greatly influenced subsequent political revolutions. Moreover, Calvin's emphasis upon the Christian's duty to bear testimony to God's grace and divine election had important social and economic consequences. The exemplary character and remarkable achievements of the French Huguenots illustrate this fact. Finally, the representative character of their church organization, in which the laity participated alongside the clergy, had important consequences in the development of representative political institutions.

Roman Catholicism in France was also strongly influenced by the religious wars of the sixteenth century. On the one hand, Gallicanism was revived to such an extent that Pierre Pithou's *The Liberties of the Gallican Church* (1594), based upon old legal sources, was widely read and approved. On the other hand the necessity of finding a happy medium between the two religious extremes during the wars led to the expression of ideas of tolerance and even skepticism. Jean Bodin, with his humanist, Neoplatonic background, frequently expressed his belief that man was unable to acquire an absolute knowledge of the divine truth, and Michel Montaigne (1533–1592), in his essays, became the spokesman of a morality of natural reason that was placed above the fallible acquisition of truth by one's senses and reason. This kind of skepticism led directly to the deism of the Enlightenment.

Catholicism, however, was also imbued with the spirit of the Catholic Reformation. Schools, colleges, convents, and societies were established for the education of the young, congregations and diocesan seminaries for the training of the clergy, hospitals and homes for the care of the unfortunates, and missions for the conversion of lost souls. So strong was the Church that it weathered the criticisms of the Enlightenment and has continued as a powerful force in French life and culture to our own day.

# 10 Protestantism and Catholicism in England, Germany, and Eastern Europe

## Temporary Restoration of Catholicism in England

In England, where the supremacy of the ruler over the affairs of the Church had been established, it looked as though the accession of Queen Mary (1553–1558) heralded the return of the kingdom to Catholicism. Charles V, realizing his opportunity to intervene, sought to accelerate this transformation by trying to bring the country into his dynastic imperial system. The prospects for this appeared to be excellent, for Mary had long depended upon the advice of her cousin Charles, and at first all went well. Charles detached the Low Countries from the Empire and gave them to his son Philip, who was then married to the English queen in 1554, despite the opposition of the great majority of the English people and in the face of the attempts of Parliament to prevent the match.

The queen's marriage, like most of her undertakings, ended in failure. Philip tried in vain to ingratiate himself with the barons, among whom rebellions had broken out, and he made the most of his marriage to a sickly woman who was his senior by twelve years. In 1555, however, when it became obvious that the royal couple would have no heir, Philip left England and the queen. Yet opposition to Mary continued and reached a climax when she joined the Hapsburgs in an attack upon France and lost Calais (1558), England's last foothold on the Continent. Patriotic Englishmen were further incensed when Mary Stuart, the heiress to the Scottish throne, was married to Francis, the heir to the French throne—another union that boded ill for England.

# Part Four: Religious Conflicts and Consequences

Meanwhile, Mary, sincere in her desire to restore England to Catholicism by moderate means, in 1553 induced Parliament to repeal the ecclesiastical legislation of Edward VI and in 1554 that of Henry VII. By virtue of her position as "supreme head" of the church, she appointed ten Catholic bishops to replace the Protestant bishops who had been sent to the Tower, had been deprived of their offices, or had fled to the Continent. Cardinal Pole, the moderate papal legate, granted papal absolution to Parliament for its earlier schismatic legislation. When it came to carrying out the details of the restoration of Catholicism, however, Mary ran into many difficulties. In order to appease those barons who were strongly opposed to royal supremacy, she permitted them to retain part of the secularized Church lands. Despite her intentions to proceed tactfully in this matter, most of the people who had obtained such lands feared that she would restore them all to the Church. Furthermore, when Parliament was compelled to give up the annates and tithes appropriated by Henry VIII and to find new sources of income to meet the expenses incurred by the attack upon France, wealthy Englishmen feared still more the adverse economic effects of the restoration of Catholicism.

Mary's difficulties were greatly intensified when Pope Julius III, who had approved her moderate policy, was replaced, after the brief pontificate of Marcellus II, by Pope Paul IV (1555–1559), whose politics were strongly anti-Spanish. Paul demanded that Mary, whom he detested, restore all the confiscated Church lands. As an ally of France he declared war on England and deprived Reginald Pole, who had been made archbishop of Canterbury in 1556, of his office as papal legate and cited him to Rome, even insinuating that he was suspected of heresy. Englishmen needed little more to convince them that Mary's Catholic regime was proving hostile to their interests.

The subsequent lack of moderation and tact with respect to enforcing religious changes also alienated many influential Englishmen who had welcomed Mary's accession to the throne. It was in 1555, the same year in which Philip left England and Mary's moderate chancellor, Stephen Gardiner, bishop of Winchester, died, that the queen began her vigorous attacks upon the Protestants. The persecutions began with the martyrdom of John Rogers, editor of Matthew's Bible, and five of the Protestant bishops who had been replaced by Catholics. Among these were Hooper, former bishop of Gloucester, who died with great courage; Hugh Latimer, former bishop of Worcester, a masterful preacher, now an octogenarian; and the "late archbishop of Canterbury," Thomas Cranmer, who recanted seven times but died heroically. In all, nearly three hundred persons suffered a martyr's death under Mary. But the burning of humble folk as well as the leaders of the Protestants tended to confirm the people in their Protestantism rather than terrorize them. Of the Protestants who remained alive, approximately eight hundred went to the

Continent, together with a large number of continental exiles who had previously sought refuge in England. Many of the Protestants who remained at home aided the Marian exiles and maintained contact with them.

Mary's treatment of the Protestants was not different from the treatment accorded nonconformists in other countries. She therefore does not deserve the names "Bloody Mary" and "Wicked Jezebel." Yet the relatively large number of Protestants executed caused a sullen discontent throughout England, intensified by her failure to bring prosperity to the country and to carry out a successful foreign policy. When this unhappy queen died in November, 1558, and was buried in a nun's habit, England breathed a sigh of relief, for the majority of the people were now inclined toward Protestantism; and the old order, which had given her the most support, was being replaced by a new order in which townsmen were playing an increasingly important role. Cardinal Pole, who, like Mary, seemed unaware of the changing social and intellectual structure of England, followed her in death only twelve hours later.

## The Marian Exiles

Of great importance in the subsequent development of Protestanism in England and later in the English colonies of North America were the Marian exiles. They comprised approximately eight hundred Englishmen, the majority of whom had left their country at the beginning of Mary's reign. Because Bishop Gardiner and the queen were at that time still pursuing a moderate course against the Protestants and were apparently eager to have the extremists among them leave the country, the exiles were relatively unmolested in their departure. Whole families of gentry (the largest group), clergy, theological students, merchants, artisans, and printers migrated, apparently after definite arrangements had been made for their residence on the Continent.

The largest number of the exiles went to Germany, where their activities obviously were directed by a group of Protestants who remained in England. One of their settlements, in the Lutheran town of Emden on the coast of the North Sea, seemed particularly active in disseminating printed propaganda in England. Another colony, the one in Lutheran Wesel, was compelled to leave that town in 1557 after the political activities of its leaders appeared dangerous to the town council. Most of the members of this congregation went as a body to Aarau in Switzerland, the only group permitted to be gainfully employed as artisans and the only stable English congregation on the Continent. Because of its experiences in exile as a congregation under the leadership of a pastor, without benefit of supervision by a bishop, it undoubtedly served as a model for later Puritan congregations.

There were other important settlements at Frankfurt, Strassburg, Geneva, and Zurich. The religious and political views of the Zwinglians and the Rhenish Protestants exerted the greatest influence upon these exiles, who later participated in the re-establishment of Protestantism in England under Elizabeth I.

The most radical of the many attacks made by the exiles upon Queen Mary came from the pen of John Ponet, formerly the bishop of Winchester, whose *A Shorte Treatise of Politike Power* was published in 1556, probably at Strassburg. Like Francis Hotman, who was also a resident at Strassburg at that time and who later published the *Franco-Gallia,* Ponet argued that the individual Christian must obey God rather than the inferior civil power. If necessary, he may go so far as to kill a tyrant if God gives him the command. Although such radical theories were set aside when the exiles returned to England after the accession of Elizabeth, they were revived by the Puritans when they revolted against the Stuarts. Ponet's treatise was published again in 1639 and in 1642. Although many of the ideas of religious and political freedom later developed by the Puritans were basically indigenous to England, there is no doubt that the experiences in exile of an important segment of Englishmen had much to do with their solidarity as a political party during the reign of Elizabeth and with the crystallization of opinion that had important consequences in England and America during the reign of the Stuarts.

## The Elizabethan Settlement

England became the leading Protestant country during the reign of Elizabeth I (1558–1603), whose claim to the throne had not been challenged, even by her half sister Mary. The circumstances of her birth and the harsh treatment suffered by her during Mary's reign—she was confined to the Tower for a while—help explain her preference for Protestantism. By accepting the offer of marriage made by Philip II at the beginning of her reign, the twenty-five-year-old queen could have paved the way for a reconciliation with Rome and the forces of Catholicism. True daughter of Henry VIII, however, she preferred to free England from dependence upon the papacy, the Hapsburgs, or any other European power. She clearly saw that, in order to do this, it would be necessary to unite the English people by solving the divisive religious problems and to develop the economic resources of the country.

Elizabeth was aided in carrying out her difficult policies by able men who understood her vanity and changeable temperament and knew how to use her many good qualities. For forty years her chief adviser was the astute Protestant William Cecil (1520–1598), whom she created Lord Burghley in 1571 and who served her faithfully, first as secretary of state and later as lord treasurer. His legal training, indefatigable energy, and cautious policy are evident in much that was accomplished during the

Queen Elizabeth I of England

queen's long reign. For many years he was supported in the royal council by his brother-in-law, Sir Nicholas Bacon, lord keeper of the great seal and father of Francis Bacon. Sir Francis Walsingham (1530–1590), secretary of state from 1573 to 1590, was a staunch Protestant who urged the support of the continental Protestants and became particularly active in unearthing Catholic plots against Elizabeth by an espionage system that extended throughout England and much of the Continent. Alongside these men, Robert Dudley, her chief favorite, whom she made earl of Leicester, appeared exceptionally incompetent, self-indulgent, and unreliable. In the last analysis, however, the queen made her own decisions, even when these were opposed by her advisers.

At the beginning of Elizabeth's reign, England's position in Europe seemed most precarious. Philip II had dragged Mary into a costly war with France and had marshaled the forces of a reviving Catholicism against the citadels of Protestantism. But his hope of keeping France occupied in war at that time proved stronger than his desire to crush Protestantism in England. France's position seemed especially propitious, for she had taken Calais from England. Mary, regent in Scotland, moreover, was a member of the powerful Guise family and her daughter, Mary, was the wife of Francis, the French dauphin. To prevent encirclement by Catholic powers, Elizabeth not only tried to keep out of continental entanglements by refusing to marry and by giving up all claims to Calais in the Treaty of Cateau-Cambrésis (1559), but soon demonstrated her own diplomatic ability by playing off against one another the conflicting groups in the lands of her rivals. Although Philip married Elizabeth, daughter of Henry II of France—his third matrimonial venture—he preferred for a decade to protect England as an effective check upon the growth of France.

## Religious Changes

Elizabeth took the first important step in restoring the unity of her people by making a religious settlement that, with but few modifications, has lasted to our day. Always discreet and evasive in her pronouncements on theological matters, she nonetheless showed her distaste for her Catholic subjects and for those radical Protestants who were led by the returned exiles and wished to place greater authority in the hands of the clergy. Accordingly she revived the Anglican Church established by her father, with its episcopal system and its conception of the unity of the Christian Church. The authority of "king and Parliament," with the consent of the Convocation of the clergy, remained final in matters of both doctrine and discipline.

The new queen made Matthew Parker, former chaplain of Anne Boleyn, archbishop of Canterbury. He was consecrated by three former bishops who had been expelled by Mary. Thus the apostolic succession was maintained in England. Parker, a scholar with moderate Protestant views, let it be known that he favored restoration rather than innovation.

The Elizabethan Settlement was affected by two acts of Parliament in the year 1559, the Act of Supremacy and the Act of Uniformity. By the Act of Supremacy the Catholic legislation of Mary's reign was repealed, foreign princes or prelates were refused the right to exercise authority in the land, and Elizabeth was designated the "only supreme governor of this realm, as well in all spiritual or ecclesiastical things or causes, as temporal." She preferred this title to that of "supreme head of the church," given to both Henry VIII and Edward VI and borne by Mary in the first year of her reign, for she did not wish to offend the Catholics, who looked upon the pope as their head, or the radical Protestants, who recognized only Christ as their head. Nor did she want to appear to claim the right of ministering "either of God's Word or of sacraments." Although she did not have the name, she exercised the functions of the head of the Church of England.

In the Anglican Church only those doctrines were considered heretical that were contrary to Scripture, the decrees of the general Church councils, or the acts of Parliament supported by Convocation. The administration of ecclesiastical matters was commonly delegated to commissioners who acted in the name of the sovereign and who came to constitute the Court of High Commission, a body not unlike the consistorial courts of the Lutheran princes. Enforcement of the Act of Uniformity was assured by the imposition of an oath, acknowledging the queen's dominant role in the church, upon all incumbents of religious and civil offices. Punishments for disobedience ranged from dismissal from office to loss of property and life.

The Act of Uniformity re-established the liturgy and some of the doctrines of Edward's reign by making a revised form of the second *Book of Common Prayer* of 1552 compulsory throughout England. Clerical vestments, pictures, crucifixes, and church music were retained, and the strong statement against the pope was deleted. All the clergy were required to adhere to this common form of worship and all persons were compelled to attend church.

A new confession of faith, the Thirty-nine Articles, a moderate, revised version of Cranmer's Forty-two Articles, was accepted by a convocation of the clergy of Canterbury and given royal assent in 1563, the same year in which the Council of Trent concluded its work of redefining Catholic doctrine. The divines who framed this confession were eager not to intensify the continental conflict between the Lutherans and the Calvinists, which centered chiefly in the Lord's Supper. Therefore they included a statement on that sacrament that could be accepted by both sides. In general, the Thirty-nine Articles occupied a theological position midway between Lutheranism and Calvinism, a position held by Martin

Bucer, the Strassburg divine who had come to England and had exerted a strong influence upon the development of English Protestantism. Despite the compromises embodied in the new confession, no deviations in doctrine were to be permitted.

The great majority of the English people accepted the Elizabethan Settlement. Staunch Catholics and radical Protestants, however, were dissatisfied with it and soon caused trouble. All but two of the remaining seventeen Marian bishops refused to take the new oath of supremacy and were deprived of their sees. Two fled to the Continent and the rest were for a short time confined to the Tower. But of the total of approximately nine thousand English clergy, only about two hundred refused to take the oath during the first six years of Elizabeth's reign. Royal commissioners were appointed to visit the dioceses and see to it that the settlement was being enforced. In practice, however, the queen and her commissioners frequently closed their eyes to private worship in the old faith in the hope that the old generation would soon die out. But their expectations were not realized. Some of the Catholic clergy fled to the Continent, where they established small colonies from which they hoped eventually to regain England for Catholicism. The radical Protestants, desirous of "purifying" the church of all extraneous matters, also received encouragement from the Continent and soon emerged as a strong religious party, well represented in the royal council and in Parliament.

## Elizabeth and Mary Stuart

Elizabeth's political as well as religious plans were greatly modified by what transpired in Scotland. Mary Stuart returned to Scotland in 1561, after the death of her husband, Francis II of France. This charming, well-educated young queen of eighteen years was not satisfied with ruling Scotland alone but hoped to wrest the throne of England from Elizabeth. To achieve her ends she identified herself with the forces of Catholicism. Her uncles, the Guises, suggested that she marry Don Carlos, son of Philip II of Spain; but when it appeared that this boy was becoming insane, the match was dropped. Elizabeth then proposed her favorite, Leicester. Mary, however, feeling more secure because of the growing rift between the clergy and the nobles at home, ignored the plans of the matchmakers and took as her husband her cousin Lord Darnley, a Catholic, whose claim to the English throne was almost as good as her own.

Mary's Catholic plans soon became apparent, especially after her half brother, the earl of Moray, and other Protestant lords failed to gain support for a revolt and fled to England. Mary then made herself leader of the Catholics in both Scotland and England, confiscated the lands of the Protestant lords, attempted to obtain aid from Philip II and Pope Pius V, and laid her plans with the aid of her secretary David Rizzio, a Piedmontese agent of the aggressive Catholic forces in Spain and Italy. Darnley, almost insane with jealousy over the role being played by Rizzio, had him murdered in March, 1566. He was aided in his plot by the exiled Protestant nobles, whom he had only recently fought.

Although Mary pretended to forgive her weak, dissipated husband and permitted those Protestant nobles to return who had not been involved in the crime, she planned her revenge, even after the birth of a son in June, 1566, who was destined to become King James VI of Scotland and King James I of England. Her contempt for Darnley increased when she fell passionately in love with a dashing young Protestant nobleman, the earl of Bothwell. The internal situation became highly complicated by struggles among the Catholics, the Protestants, and various groups of lords and ended in outright violence and civil war when the house in which Darnley was recovering from an illness was blown up and he was killed. Bothwell was widely suspected of having committed the murder. Although he was legally acquitted, emotions were further aroused when, having obtained a divorce from his wife, he was married to the queen in May, 1567.

Outrage over this perfidy led to an open revolt supported by most of the Scots. Mary was confined in a prison and compelled to abdicate in favor of her infant son and to name Moray his regent. She escaped prison; but when her resort to arms failed to regain her her throne, she fled in despair to Queen Elizabeth in May, 1568. Because the English queen could not restore her to her throne without alienating the Scottish Protestants or imprison her without arousing the English Catholics and the Catholic powers, she pursued a tactful policy of procrastination, granting a trial to the queen but prolonging its hearings and finally announcing an ambiguous outcome. The forcible detention of Mary in England lasted for nineteen years and ended in Mary's execution in 1587.

Mary's presence led to a gradual change in Elizabeth's policy with respect to the Catholics at home and the continental powers. In both cases these changes were dictated by political expediency, which nonetheless placed her irrevocably on the side of the Protestants. During a decade of tactful handling of the opposition, she postponed the solution of the grave issues confronting her until she had secured her rule at home and had furthered the economic prosperity of her subjects. Under the direction of Sir Thomas Gresham, for example, English commercial activity was greatly expanded at the expense of Venetian and German merchants. The Hanseatic Steelyard was closed in 1593. When, finally, Elizabeth was seriously threatened by revolts at home and plots engineered from abroad, she was in a position to carry out a vigorous policy.

The first serious revolt broke out in northern England in the autumn of 1569, when Thomas Howard, the Protestant duke of Norfolk, planned to marry Mary Stuart and seize both the Scottish and the English thrones. After Elizabeth had thrown him into the Tower, the earls of Westmoreland and Northumberland staged a rebellion supported by the Catholics, who wished to have their religion restored, and by those nobles who resented the loss of their ancient privileges to the Tudor rulers. The earl of Sussex, at the head of Elizabeth's army, quickly defeated the divided rebels. Westmoreland fled to the Continent. Northumberland and about eight hundred common folk were executed. Yet many of the rebels remained to conspire with Spain and the papacy for the restoration of Catholicism.

Meanwhile Pope Pius V, unduly encouraged by the news concerning the opposition of the Catholics in northern England, issued a bull excommunicating and deposing Elizabeth in February, 1570, significantly without first having informed Philip II or Maximilian II of his intentions. This was the last attempt on the part of the papacy to arrest the progress of Protestantism by medieval means. Pius tried to put an end to the dual obedience of the English Catholics to their queen and the Church of Rome and to compel them to choose between them. Actually this attempt strengthened the queen's position at home and abroad and was followed by further acts against the English Catholics. Parliament, in 1571, made it high treason to state that Elizabeth was a heretic and should be deposed or to publish papal bulls in England. At the same time Elizabeth's commissioners became more active in examining the religious faith of the clergy.

Sterner measures followed the Ridolfi Plot of 1571. The leader of this plot was an Italian financier who hoped to free Mary with the assistance of the pope, Philip II, and Alva and marry her to Norfolk. When the plot was discovered, Norfolk was tried for treason and later executed, and a number of his associates were thrown into prison. These events not only thoroughly broke the reactionary resistance of the nobles but greatly damaged Mary's cause. On the other hand, Elizabeth's refusal to exact the last pound of flesh from her opposition won her the respect of large numbers of Englishmen who had previously opposed her.

The English Catholics in exile, meanwhile, prepared for the day when they could return to their homeland and restore it to Catholicism. William Allen (1532–1594), a Catholic refugee, had established an English college, or seminary, at Douai in 1568 for the purpose of rallying Catholic exiles from England and educating youths from fourteen to twenty-five years of age by Jesuit methods. The college was moved to Rheims in 1578. So successful was it in attracting devoted young Englishmen who were willing to suffer martyrdom if necessary to win their countrymen back to Catholicism, that similar colleges were established at Rome (1579), Valladolid (1589), and Seville (1592). Although there is no evidence to show that Allen's missionaries planned to use force, their activities in England were considered conspiratorial because their cause was supported by the papacy and Spain. Nevertheless, their number increased until there were about a hundred in England in 1580. They did much to foster recusancy, or the refusal of Catholics to attend Anglican services.

Elizabeth's severity against Catholicism was further increased by the activities of Pope Gregory XIII (1572–1585), who now led the attacks upon the "wicked Jezebel" of England. His impulsiveness and ignorance of the complicated internal situation of England, however, led him to acts of rashness that were construed by the English as support of treason. For example, in 1579 he gave his sanction to those English exiles who plotted to stage revolts in Ireland, Scotland, and Wales. A revolt in Ireland, in which Italian and Spanish soldiers were involved, was put down with great brutality. The Guises sent Esmé Stuart, a cousin of Darnley, to Scotland with the purpose of converting the young king James VI to Catholicism and reviving the Franco-Scottish alliance. Stuart gained the boy's good will and was made the duke of Lennox by him. When he planned to call in Spanish troops to help him with his plans, however, the nobles forcibly spirited the king away and sent Lennox out of the country.

In 1581, during the Catholic attack in Ireland, Edmund Campion and Robert Parsons, two Jesuits, headed a mission to England that circulated Catholic literature and converted many people. Because it was believed that their mission was the advance guard of an attack upon England, Parliament passed an act that made it high treason to convert Englishmen to Catholicism, and recusancy was made punishable by heavy fines. Following a plot (1583) to kill Elizabeth and make Mary queen, Parliament passed an act that demanded that all Jesuits leave England within forty days. Those who remained were to be executed for high treason. English students residing abroad were declared traitors.

Thus when, in the eyes of Lord Burghley, Catholicism and high treason came to be considered identical, a policy of suppression of Catholicism was launched under Sir Francis Walsingham and strongly supported by public opinion. Despite Elizabeth's attempt to pursue a moderate course, probably half of England's approximately one hundred sixty Catholic priests and sixty Catholic laymen died a martyr's death. The total number of martyrs during her reign was about two hundred fifty, as compared with the approximately three hundred during Mary's short reign.

In her religious, as in her other, policies, Elizabeth had the support of the great majority of her people, for it was generally conceded that she had the right to rule the church through Convocation as she had the right to rule society through Parliament. Whereas Catholicism was retained by only a small number of Englishmen, living largely in the northern part of the country, Protestantism became identified with loyalty to the queen and her government with a patriotic dislike of Catholic interference in English affairs, with a desire for profit from the commercial opportunities now opening up to English merchants, and with a national enthusiasm over the exploits of the "Elizabethan sea dogs." The sea dogs were privateers who boldly challenged Spain's commercial and colonial monopoly in the New World. Because Philip II was determined to put an end to their depredations and punish Elizabeth for sending substantial aid to the Low Countries in 1585, he laid plans for an attack upon England. Parma was to land an army in England, dethrone Elizabeth, and make Mary the queen.

Philip's plans were spoiled by the Babington Plot of 1586. Walsingham, who learned of this plot almost at the outset, permitted Mary to become so deeply involved in it that when it was exposed, she was promptly tried and sentenced to death. Although Parliament petitioned that the execution be carried out immediately, Elizabeth hesitated. When, after two months, she signed the death warrant, the council ordered Mary to be beheaded. The execution took place in February, 1587.

### The Spanish Armada

The death of Mary was the signal for Philip's Armada against England. But it was now too late. The English Catholics no longer trusted him but felt that he wished the throne for himself. Moreover, he now had to act virtually alone, for the papacy, which had often urged him to take this step, now only promised papal anathemas and money payable after the Spaniards had landed on English soil. Sixtus V had no desire to have Philip rule England.

Because of Philip's tardiness in completing his preparations and Drake's plundering expedition to Cadiz, Lisbon Bay, and Cape St. Vincent, the great Armada of about one hundred and thirty ships, seven thousand sailors, and seventeen thousand soldiers did not get under way until July, 1588. The destruction of this imposing military undertaking by the intrepid Englishmen, aided finally by storms, was an indication that Spain's power had passed its zenith. The war between England and Spain dragged on until 1604, but it was already clear that Spain no longer mastered the seas. Even though her military power on the Continent continued to be an important factor for a number of decades, the Protestants there, as well as those in England, no longer needed to fear that Catholic Spain would compel them by force to return to Rome.

### Differences Among English Protestants

After the Spanish Armada of 1588, the English Catholics ceased to look for help from the outside, and Protestantism was by then firmly established under a queen who retained state control of religious affairs. But as time went on, differences among the Protestants manifested themselves. In Elizabeth's court and among the nobility, the religious settlement was accepted without a great change in religious outlook. As previously, the noble families sought livings in the church for their younger sons, pluralism and simony continued, and the bishops became staunch supporters of royal authority. The Elizabethan aristocracy, moreover, stimulated by the achievements of the Italian Renaissance, produced a brilliant but secularized culture that reflected an increasing indifference toward religion.

It is not surprising that the middle and lower classes became critical of the established church and that those who had followed the fortunes of their Protestant brethren on the Continent during the religious wars caused Elizabeth considerable trouble. A strong minority of earnest Protestants arose who were determined to carry the reformation of the church in England to its logical conclusions. Because they wished to purify it of all vestiges of Roman Catholicism, they came to be called Puritans. Supported by indigenous religious movements reaching back into the Middle Ages and by Protestant doctrines and practices developed at Zurich, Strassburg, and Geneva, Puritanism went back to Apostolic times for its standards of church polity, doctrine, and conduct, seeking to ascertain the will of God in the Bible alone. In other words, the Puritans refused to accept the church of Rome as the true church. To them the pope was the Antichrist of which the Bible spoke. Because the Anglicans still stressed the continuity of the Church of England with the Catholic Church, the Puritans refused to accept the Elizabethan Settlement as final.

Because of the various origins of English Protestantism, it is natural that it should manifest itself in different forms. Those who wished to cleanse the church of its Roman ceremonies and forms while remaining in the church were designated as Puritans in a narrower sense. Those who challenged the episcopal church polity and wished to substitute a system that recognized the equality of all clergymen were called Presbyterians. Those who were opposed to every form of state church and wished to place all authority in the hands of congregations consisting only of individuals who had covenanted to walk in the ways of Christ were called Congregationalists, Separatists, or Independents.

That the Puritans, or "Precisians," were well organized at the beginning of the reign of Elizabeth was demonstrated by their first attack upon the established order, the Vestiarian Controversy. As early as 1563 they introduced in Convocation a proposal to eliminate "Romish" forms and ceremonies. This proposal failed to pass in the lower house by only two votes. Elizabeth did not wish to persecute these Puritans, for she did not recognize dissent. She felt compelled to act, however, when they began meeting in conventicles, or "prophesyings," that is, unauthorized religious services, at which they used their own simple orders of worship rather than those of the *Book of Common Prayer*. To stop these deviations from the established service, she had Archbishop Parker issue official "advertisements" that explained the official ceremonies prescribed by law.

The controversy that followed was called *vestiarian* because the Puritans, desirous of following the authority of Scripture and restoring the purity of the primitive Church, objected particularly to vestments, although they objected also to virtually all forms and ceremonies, including the sign of the cross, the use of music, and the observance of saints' days. The chief centers of the conflict were London and Cambridge. The leaders of the movement maintained a heavy correspondence with the Swiss divines, particularly those at Zurich, who urged that they refrain from breaking with the Anglican Church and postpone the question until it could be settled at a free religious synod.

Because Elizabeth's position was being threatened by Catholic support of Mary Stuart, Archbishop Parker proceeded vigorously against all nonconformity. Among those active ministers who were forbidden to preach was the aged Miles Coverdale, who was deprived of this right in June, 1567. Because the more determined Puritans continued to meet in private conventicles, Separatism may be said to have orginated at this time.

It is natural that the attack upon the ceremonies and forms should be accompanied by an attack upon the episcopal system. The most outspoken leader of the group that wished to replace the episcopal by a Presbyterian system was Thomas Cartwright (d. 1603), a fellow of Trinity College, Cambridge. In 1571 and 1572 he and his supporters presented two Admonitions to Parliament that demanded in vigorous language the establishment of the Presbyterian system. Cartwright was relieved of both his professorship and his fellowship. Summoned to appear before the ecclesiastical commissioners in 1574, he fled to the Continent.

Edmund Grindal, who followed Parker as archibishop of Canterbury in 1576, was dismissed the next year because he proceeded too leniently against the holding of conventicles. He was later restored. In 1583 he was followed by John Whitgift (1583–1604), who did not consider the episcopal system necessary for salvation, but who nonetheless made it his duty to root out Puritanism. Although he was greatly aided by the reconstitution of the Court of High Commission as a Protestant court of inquisition in 1583, he was hampered by strong opposition in Parliament, where Puritanism steadily gained more adherents.

The continued growth of nonconformity was evinced by the acceptance at a synod held in Cambridge in 1588 of the Holy Discipline by five hundred clergymen. This discipline, drawn up by Cartwright and William Travers, was designed to regulate more closely the spiritual life of the people, especially with respect to honoring the Sabbath.

Although opposition to the episcopal system increased, a large number of Puritans tended to be less demanding of the aging queen, whom they respected for what she had done for Protestantism even though they disliked her settlement. Many of these moderately inclined Puritans were opposed to the activities of those radicals who branded the archbishop as Antichrist, the bishops as petty popes, and the clergy as drunken dogs. When the queen demanded a more vigorous prosecution of these zealots, Parliament passed an act aimed to suppress the "sectaries" who attended conventicles and were disloyal to the queen (1593). Attendance at conventicles was to be punished by imprisonment, nonconformity with banishment. That same year John Greenwood and Henry Barrow, who had led conventicles in London and had demanded complete separation from the Anglican Church, were executed, but ostensibly for attempting to provoke rebellion.

An attempt on the part of the Puritans to have the doctrinal position of the Thirty-nine Articles clarified, particularly Article Seventeen concerning predestination, led to the formulation of the Lambeth Articles by Archbishop Whitgift and others, including a Calvinist professor at Cambridge. Elizabeth refused to accept these articles, and differences among the Anglican divines continued, which in turn accentuated differences over church organization.

The danger of the division among the Protestants was recognized by Francis Bacon, a member of Parliament. Yet he did not feel that uniformity should be achieved by Whitgift's policy of forceful suppression. On the contrary, he argued that the Puritans, whose nonconformity he did not like, should be won over to a unified attack upon Catholicism.

A much more forceful plea for unity was made by a student of divinity and a holder of a minor office, Richard Hooker (d. 1600). In his widely read *Ecclesiastical Laws of Church Polity* he maintained that the constitution of the Church of England was a product of an implied social contract from which no group could withdraw at will. He based his arguments upon reason as well as upon the authority of Scripture. In this he went much further than John Jewel (d. 1571), bishop of Salisbury, who in his *Apology for the Anglican Church* of 1562 had based his arguments in the main upon Scripture, the decrees of the Church councils, and the writings of the Church fathers.

Despite the attempts of the majority of the Puritan leaders to steer a moderate course, their attitude toward the established church, the persistence of conventicles, and the contacts of English Protestants with the continental reformers led to the formation of a number of different radical groups. Opposed both to the all-inclusiveness of Anglicanism and the rigidity of Calvinism as being unscriptural, they proposed a church without ritual and a learned ministry.

Among the radical leaders was Robert Browne, a graduate of Cambridge who founded a nonconformist conventicle at Norwich in 1580 and another at Middelburg, in Zeeland, a little later. He did not wish to create isolated congregations, separated from the established church, but he did want to limit the state to the administration of church property and have a church in which the people in congregations determined their own doctrines and selected their own religious servants. This limitation of the activities of the state church got him into difficulties not only with Archbishop Whitgift but with the Presbyterians. Although Browne himself submitted to the authority of the state church by 1588, many of his followers developed still further his earlier ideas. One of the Brownists who fled to Holland was Francis Johnson, who became the leader of the English Separatists in that country. He and his followers exerted a considerable influence upon the development of sects in England.

The appearance of a large number of critics of the Elizabethan Settlement must not blind us to its greatness and the almost universal acceptance of it. One can find but a few who wished to destroy the Anglican Church. The radicals as a rule sought merely to develop it in their own respective ways. And the Catholics who openly defied the Anglican Church and confessed their adherence to Rome numbered only about two hundred thousand at the end of Elizabeth's reign.

## The Kirk of Scotland

The activities of the leaders of the Kirk of Scotland during the latter half of the sixteenth century were determined to a large extent by the almost anarchic conditions that prevailed during the minority of James VI —three of the original four regents met violent deaths—and by the rapacity of many of the nobles who had supported the Reformation and were now obtaining their reward by appropriating church property. The preachers were more concerned with extirpating vice than with eradicating heresy and used their influence in having the state punish offenders.

News of the Massacre of St. Bartholomew (1572) gave the new clergy greater popularity than ever. When John Knox died, in the same year as this tragic event, he was succeeded as leader of the Scottish Kirk by Andrew Melville (1545–1622), who infused not only the church but the universities of Glascow and St. Andrews with a strict Calvinist spirit.

The *Second Book of Discipline* of 1581, which more clearly defined the relations between church and state, demanded for the church the sole right to inflict ecclesiastical penalties and it demanded of the state that it carry out the punishments. It maintained that Christ exercised discipline only through his servants in the church. The seizure by the nobles of the ecclesiastical revenues, church properties, and various ecclesiastical privileges was branded as simony.

Serious difficulties with the government followed. In 1584 the young king had Parliament pass an act that affirmed the state's supremacy in ecclesiastical affairs and re-established the authority of the bishops. But the

Protestant party, supported by England, soon regained control. After the execution of Mary in 1587 and England's successful defense against the Spanish Armada in 1588, Calvinism was firmly established in Scotland by an act of Parliament (1592). The disciplinary excesses of Melville and others, however, made it unpopular among the people as well as at court.

# Lutheranism and Calvinism in Germany

Although the religious conflicts that grew out of the Reformation were being resolved by powerful rulers along national lines in western Europe, they became accentuated in central and eastern Europe because of the lack of political centralization. Whereas the Protestants in these lands were sharply divided into mutually hostile groups, Catholicism, reformed and united after the Council of Trent, made phenomenal gains for about half a century.

In Germany approximately nine tenths of the people and nearly all the secular rulers had become Protestant by 1555. Protestantism and Catholicism were more evenly matched than this would seem to indicate, however, because of the presence in the diet of the ecclesiastical princes —three in the college of electors and thirty-eight of the fifty-six in the house of princes—and because the emperors remained Catholic. The Peace of Augsburg of 1555 legalized the precarious balance between the two religious forces, neither of which had been able to suppress the other. By so doing, it provided the Germans with a peace that lasted for more than sixty years. But it was not one of the creative periods of German history. Exhausted by years of intensive, emotional conflict, most of the rulers and ruled alike seemed content with maintaining the status quo.

The first two emperors to rule Germany after the Peace of Augsburg were no exceptions to this rule. Ferdinand I (1558–64), although sincere in his Catholicism, remained conciliatory toward the Protestant princes and continued to respect his "Declaration" to the effect that the Protestant subjects of the Catholic ecclesiastical princes would be granted protection. Moreover, the personal enmity between him and Pope Paul IV, who had considered refusing to recognize him as the successor of Charles V, led him to decide not to go to Italy for the papal coronation. In religious matters he showed that he was more concerned with a reformation of the Church than with a counterreformation. Consequently the Jesuit Canisius did not have so great an influence upon Ferdinand as the Erasmian reformers.

While Philip II, his nephew, followed aggressive political and religious policies, Ferdinand tended to become the virtual ally of the German princes and devoted most of his energies to securing his control over the Hapsburg inheritance. He had Maximilian, his eldest son, elected king of Bohemia in 1549, Roman king in 1562, and king of Hungary in

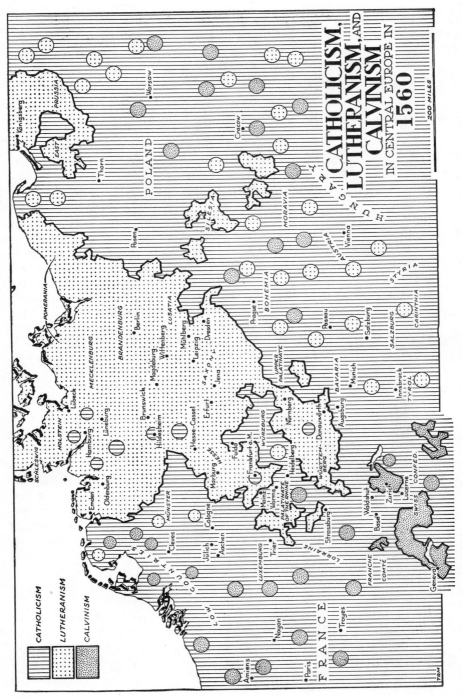

CATHOLICISM, LUTHERANISM, AND CALVINISM IN CENTRAL EUROPE IN 1560

200 MILES

CATHOLICISM
LUTHERANISM
CALVINISM

1563. He gave the administration of the Hapsburg lands to his three sons. Maximilian got Upper and Lower Austria; Charles got Inner Austria, comprising Styria, Carinthia, Carniola, Gorizia, Internal Istria, and Trieste; Ferdinand got the Tyrol and Anterior Austria. These lands were not again brought together under one ruler until 1665.

Maximilian II (1564–76) was likewise concerned primarily with the Hapsburg dynasty and its possessions. Even though he had been won over to Lutheranism as a young man and retained his interest in it to his death—he refused to receive the sacrament of extreme unction on his deathbed—he bowed to the wishes of his father by remaining formally a Catholic. When he had asked the Protestant princes whether they would support him with military force if he were driven from Austria for religious reasons, only Frederick III of the Palatinate had appeared willing to do so.

Maximilian's prior dynastic concern was further evinced by the fact that he sent two of his sons—including Rudolf, who became his successor —to be educated at the Spanish court of their mother, the sister of Philip II. In 1570 he gave his eldest daughter, Anne, in marriage to Philip II as the latter's fourth wife. This marriage illustrates the extent to which the policy of intermarriage was carried among the Hapsburgs, for Maximilian, the cousin and brother-in-law of Philip II, now became also his father-in-law. But he refused to follow Philip in the use of force in religious matters and permitted Lutheran worship in his lands. Like his father, he was not crowned emperor by the pope and therefore did not consider himself the protector of Catholicism. But he attempted to mediate between Catholicism and Protestantism. Not until the reign of Rudolph II (1576–1612) were the Jesuits given a virtually free hand in carrying out the Counter Reformation in Austrian lands.

The failure of the emperors to solve political and religious matters on broad, national bases was paralleled by the particularism of the imperial cities, whose golden age as great economic, political, and cultural centers was drawing to a close. Satisfied with resting upon the gains that they had made during the first stages of the commercial revolution, they continued their late-medieval practices and, as a whole, failed to adjust themselves to the gradual shift of the center of commercial activity from the Mediterranean and Baltic seas to the Atlantic Ocean.

While the merchants of the western European countries were cooperating with their rulers in pursuing new economic practices along national lines and extending their interests to colonial activities, the German patricians maintained their short-sighted mercantilistic policies, tried to retain the guild system, and clung to the remnants of a barter economy—officials still received much of their income in kind. Although many of the merchants of northern Germany remained active in trade, those in other areas tended to invest their capital in land and luxurious homes and to withdraw from trade. Commercial activity in the Baltic area and in such centers as Hamburg, Bremen, Frankfurt am Main, Leipzig, and Augsburg increased somewhat, but it did not keep pace with that of the cities of western Europe. Without the protection of a strongly centralized state, German merchants could not compete with their neighbors. Not only the emperors and the cities were responsible for this state of affairs, but primarily the princes were.

## The Particularism of the German Princes

The particularism of the territorial princes, which had triumphed over the centralizing attempts of the German kings and emperors, was now made more pronounced by religious differences that touched the deepest interests of the people. Thus there developed in Germany the many, relatively small territorial states, whose princes, Catholic and Protestant alike, ruled their people as religious as well as political and economic leaders. These small Christian welfare states of sixteenth-century Germany were unique insofar as their rulers took their obligations to their people so seriously that they showed little concern for the outside world, either for territorial expansion or economic aggrandizement. Paternalistically concerned with their obligations to God and their subjects, they did their utmost to provide economic prosperity, police protection, fair justice, and well-organized churches.

Because the Peace of Augsburg had recognized the abolition of episcopal authority in the Protestant territories without stipulating who should exercise it, the Lutheran princes in general appropriated it. They could thus legally assume greater authority in religious matters than the Catholic princes. They made the administration of the church an integral part of their territorial governments.

By means of consistories, comprising both clergy and laity, the princes maintained their control over church doctrines, confirmed the appointment of the clergy and teachers, and, in some territories, administered church properties. Superintendents appointed by the princes supervised the clergy and presided over their synods. The tendency of the princes to regulate doctrines by legal means led to the formulation of separate confessions in virtually all the territories.

## Theological Disputes

The chief opposition to this princely encroachment upon the spiritual sphere of action came from the theologians at their respective universities. But during this struggle and the many theological controversies that accompanied it, there developed a Protestant scholastic orthodoxy that tended to stifle the dynamic, evangelical movement begun by Luther. Although the princes had originally accepted the clergymen who had been trained and ordained at Wittenberg, they now tended to employ only those who had been educated at their own universities. These, as well as the territorial schools (*Fürstenschulen*) and city schools, were under the authority of the consistories. In all the institutions of higher learning, the humanist interests of an earlier day tended to give way to the theological.

At the same time, many theologians sought to arrive at an understanding with the theologians of other territories who purported to adhere to the Augsburg Confession. But before this could be achieved, the sharp differences, the *"rabies theologorum,"* or the "madness of the theologians," as Melanchthon called it, had to be cured.

When Luther died, a year after the opening of the Council of Trent, his followers felt the absence of his strong personality. The various tendencies to deviate from his theological teachings found expression in the formation of distinct parties that frequently lost sight of the basic principles of the Lutheran Reformation in their zeal to be correct.

Philip Melanchthon, the logical successor to Luther, had forfeited the leadership of Protestantism by his lack of firmness with respect to carrying out the Augsburg Interim of 1548. This weakness elicited the bitter criticism of such good friends as John Calvin and the Lutheran reformer of Swabia, Johannes Brenz (1499–1570). Consequently Melanchthon's role was reduced to that of the leader of a Lutheran faction called Philippists. These were opposed by another party called the Gnesiolutherans, or conservative Lutherans, led by the fiery Slav Matthäus Vlacich, or Flacius, also called Illyricus (1520–1575). A former humanist who had studied at Venice, Basel, and Tübingen, he came to Wittenberg in 1541, where he found religious satisfaction in Luther's doctrine of justification by faith alone. He remained there as a professor of Hebrew from 1544 to 1549. Having fought in vain against the Augsburg and Leipzig interims, which provided for important concessions to Catholicism, he went to Magdeburg. He helped to make this city the center of the Gnesiolutheran party.

The major conflict between these two groups was known as the Adiaphoristic Controversy, for Melanchthon and his followers were willing to bow to the wishes of the elector of Saxony, that is, to accept the Augsburg Interim and thus make concessions with respect to such *adiaphora,* or nonessentials, as the retention of the episcopal system. The Gnesiolutherans insisted that there were no *adiaphora.* Although Melanchthon later privately modified his position, the controversy was not resolved because Flacius demanded of him a public statement of repentance.

The two groups were driven further apart by the Majoristic Controversy when the Gnesiolutheran Amsdorf attacked the Wittenberg professor Georg Major (d. 1574) for maintaining that good works were necessary for salvation. During the conflict over this question, the Antinomian Controversy was revived (1556) and, in connection with this, the

# Part Four: Religious Conflicts and Consequences

Synergistic Controversy, in which Flacius and Amsdorf emphasized the complete inability of man to do anything toward earning salvation.

Meanwhile the Sacramentarian Controversy broke out anew, provoked when Calvin came to an agreement with the Zwinglians over the interpretation of the Lord's Supper and when this compromise gained adherents in Germany. When Calvin was attacked by a Gnesiolutheran for threatening the independence of Lutheranism and appealed to Melanchthon for support, the latter remained discreetly silent and was in turn accused of Cryptocalvinism (secret Calvinism). This was followed in a number of German territories by serious disturbances over the questions of the real presence and the ubiquity of Christ.

Both parties joined in opposing a third headed by Andreas Osiander —a Nürnberg reformer who had become a professor at the new University of Königsberg in Prussia—over the doctrine of justification. This was known as the Osiandrian Controversy. Osiander's systematically developed doctrine not only approached that of the Catholics but tended to question the Protestant conception of the certainty of salvation. The controversy continued in East Prussia even after the death of Osiander in 1552 and did not end until the execution in 1566 of his loyal follower Johann Funck, the court preacher of the aged Duke Albert.

Such theological differences understandably were carried over into the rivalry between the universities of Wittenberg and Jena. Duke John Frederick of Ernestine Saxony, who had lost the city of Wittenberg to Maurice in the Schmalkaldic War, tried to move the entire university to Jena. When this failed, he established a school in the monastery of St. Paul in that city in 1548. This was made a full-fledged university ten years later and became an important center of orthodox Lutheranism.

Flacius, who taught at Jena a number of years, was compelled to leave during the Synergistic Controversy. Pursued by the elector of Saxony, the count palatine, and even the emperor, he went from pillar to post until his death in 1575. He is remembered not only for his polemical writings but especially for his *Key to Sacred Scripture* (1567) and the *Magdeburg Centuries,* or *Ecclesiastical History* (begun in 1559). The former is an exegetical work in the form of a biblical dictionary. The latter, written in collaboration with others, appeared in thirteen volumes and carried the history of the Church down to the year 1308. Although it was frankly antipapal, it was based upon sources from many different libraries.

The need for resolving the religious controversies within Protestantism became particularly obvious after the signing of the Peace of Augsburg in 1555, when the estates of the diet took seriously the task of creating harmony between Catholicism and Lutheranism. To this end a religious colloquy was called to meet at Worms in 1557. But when Melanchthon, at this meeting, stated that no real differences existed among

*400*

the adherents to the Augsburg Confession, Flacius accused him and his followers of a number of heresies. The orthodox, or Flacian, position was restated and, in 1559, published under the title, *Book of Confutation*. Canisius, who had only recently been made provincial of southern Germany, was present at the colloquy. The intransigence of the two parties reassured him in his belief that no settlement could be reached; and he began to formulate his plans for a Counter Reformation with a reasonable hope of success.

When the Protestant theologians demonstrated their inability to resolve their differences, the Protestant princes became interested in establishing doctrinal agreement, particularly because the Council of Trent was about to meet in its third and last assembly. One of the leaders of this movement was Elector Frederick III (1559–1576) of the Palatinate, who had become a Calvinist in 1559 and who wished to have Calvinism brought under the legal protection of the Augsburg Confession. At the Naumburg Diet of princes of 1561, in which theologians were not permitted to participate, an impasse was reached over which edition of the Augsburg Confession was to be used as a standard, the original edition of 1530 or that of 1540, called the *Variata*. The princes finally compromised on the edition of 1531. But the orthodox Lutheran Duke John Frederick of Saxony suddenly departed and the duke of Mecklenburg refused to sign the agreement, whereupon the meeting broke up. It is significant, however, that the *de facto* recognition of Calvinism by the princes led to its further spread in Germany. On the other hand, the conflict between Lutheranism and Calvinism now became an important consideration in imperial politics.

The controversies among the Lutheran theologians meanwhile continued unabated, even after the death of Melanchthon in 1560. The Gnesiolutherans, with their chief centers at Jena and Königsberg, were best represented by Cyriakus Spangenberg (1528–1604), a poet and author as well as a theologian, who carried on the work of Flacius. Although these orthodox Lutherans are often criticized by some church historians for their theological rigidity and bitter polemics, they are praised by others for preserving the distinguishing characteristics of German Lutheranism and taking a sincere interest in the religious welfare of their people.

On the other extreme were the Philippists at Wittenberg, led by Kaspar Peutzer (1525–1602), Melanchthon's son-in-law. Most of these theologians were humanistically inclined. Although some of them still hoped for a reconciliation with Roman Catholicism, others, like Peutzer, were Cryptocalvinists. In 1574 Elector Augustus of Saxony (1553–1586) put an end to both Philippism and Cryptocalvinism in his lands by imprisoning the outstanding leaders.

Between the Gnesiolutherans and the Philippists there developed a middle group of theologians whose chief centers were the universities of

# Part Four: Religious Conflicts and Consequences

Leipzig, Rostock, Marburg, and Tübingen. Like their foremost representative, Jakob Andreae (1528–1590), they were eager to preserve Lutheranism by avoiding extremes. Therefore they strongly supported the attempts of a number of princes to arrive at a doctrinal formula that would put an end to the bitter theological controversies.

## The Formula of Concord

An important step toward doctrinal unity among the Lutherans was taken when, in 1575, the churches of Swabia and Lower Saxony subscribed to a series of articles originally prepared by Jakob Andreae. This *Swabian-Saxon Formula of Concord,* as it was called, was followed the next year by the *Torgau Book,* subscribed to by the theologians of Saxony, Brunswick, Mecklenburg, and Württemberg. Elector Augustus of Saxony, with the approval of the rulers of the other principalities that had cooperated, thereupon selected a commission, including Jakob Andreae, which revised the *Torgau Book.* The final revision, called the Formula of Concord, was published together with the three ecumenical creeds and the previous Lutheran symbols, or creeds—the Augsburg Confession, the Apology of the Augsburg Confession, the Schmalkaldic Articles, and the Large and Small Catechisms—in the *Book of Concord* in June, 1580. This *Book of Concord* was subscribed to by eighty-six rulers, princes, and imperial cities and between eight and nine thousand theologians.

The Formula of Concord consists of two main parts, the *Epitome* and the *Solida declaratio,* both of which deal with the same doctrines, the former in a summary fashion, the latter in greater detail. All the questions raised in the doctrinal controversies are enumerated and refuted.

## The Reformed Church

Because of the clear distinction made in the Formula of Concord between the adherents of Luther and those of the other reformers, its acceptance marked the definite division of the German Protestants into Lutherans and Reformed. The term *Lutheran,* which had first been used by Eck as a term of derision, was in general use by the end of the sixteenth century. The term *Reformed* was used by the Calvinists in France, the Low Countries, and England from the beginnings of their struggles with Catholicism. In Germany they called themselves Reformed to distinguish themselves from the Lutherans and to show their desire to reform the church by purging it of the papal remnants still found in the Lutheran liturgy and ecclesiastical government.

Of great cultural significance for western Germany is the fact that the members of the German Reformed Church took an active interest in the struggles of the Calvinists in western Europe. They were thus brought into contact with those powerful political and cultural movements that greatly stimulated their own life and thought. However, the German Calvinists could not develop the same kind of popular churches as their brethren in western Europe, for, like the Lutherans, they found the tendency toward the territorial control of religion too powerful to oppose with any degree of success.

Although the Reformed theologians and rulers adhered to the Augsburg Confession in order to remain under the protection of the Peace of Augsburg, they developed their own distinct doctrines. An unsuccessful attempt was made at Frankfurt am Main in 1577 to bring all the German Reformed Protestants together under a Reformed formula of concord. In place of such a theological statement, the Heidelberg Catechism of 1563 served to hold their churches together.

The first important German territory to become Reformed was, as we have seen, the electoral Palatinate of the Rhine. Its Elector Frederick III (1559–1576) had become Calvinist in the year of his accession. He made the University of Heidelberg the strong intellectual center of the Reformed faith and was personally responsible for the writing of the Heidelberg Catechism. Although his son Louis VI (1576–1583) reintroduced Lutheranism, Calvinism was once more made the state religion by John Casimir (d. 1592), uncle of and regent for Frederick IV (1583–1610) during the latter's minority.

The Reformed faith was soon recognized in other territories and cities, such as Nassau, which had strong connections with the Low Countries through the house of Orange; Bremen, which was represented at the Synod of Dordrecht in Holland in 1619; Anhalt, where the church was organized according to the example set by the Palatinate of the Rhine; Hesse-Kassel, where the University of Marburg became a strong theological center; and Cleves, Jülich, and Berg, where the Calvinist refugees from the Low Countries had maintained active congregations.

Of great significance to the subsequent growth of Protestantism in Germany was the fact that Elector John Sigismund (1608–1619) of Brandenburg ended his adherence to the Formula of Concord and embraced the Reformed faith. His father had sent him to Heidelberg to study, an evidence of his intention to forsake the political alliance of the Hohenzollerns with Saxony and the Hapsburgs for one with the elector of the Palatinate. John Sigismund was won over to Calvinism at that time. He defended his theological views in his *Confessio Sigismundi,* in which he gave evidence of his adherence to the Augsburg Confession, yet reflected a modified Calvinist conception of the Lord's Supper. When even this moderate statement aroused a storm of protest among his people, he did not use force to bring them into the Reformed Church, but permitted Lutheranism to continue, thereby furthering the idea of equality between the two confessions and adumbrating the emergence of the Evangelical Church in the nineteenth century.

The German Protestant princes were thus drawn into two opposing camps: the Reformed, led by the ambitious elector of the Palatinate, whose objectives drew him to the side of the Calvinists of western Europe; and the Lutherans, led by the elector of Saxony, who wished to support the status quo in the Empire. The duke of Ernestine Saxony even sent troops to fight on the side of the Spanish king against the Huguenots. Consequently the Protestant princes and the emperor played a pathetic role both within the Empire and in European affairs. At the crucial meeting of the electors at Regensburg in 1575 for the purpose of choosing a successor to the ailing Maximilian II, Elector Augustus of Saxony would not support the elector of the Palatinate, who wished to exact a charter of religious liberties from the new emperor. In October of that year the electors unanimously made Rudolph king of the Romans, leaving the religious questions to be settled at the next diet. But the opportunity for the Protestant princes to secure their religious rights was lost, for opposition to them increased at subsequent diets. And when Rudolph II became emperor in 1576, the Counter Reformation began in earnest.

## The Revival of Catholicism

It is significant that the Catholic Counter Reformation began in the secular, not the ecclesiastical, German territories. Unlike Protestantism, this movement did not originate among the people. Directed from one center, the papacy at Rome; motivated by one desire, the enforcement of the decrees of the Council of Trent; led by the loyal shock troops of Catholicism, the Jesuits; and supported by territorial, then ecclesiastical, princes, the movement had a great advantage over divided Protestantism.

### Catholicism in Bavaria

The Counter Reformation experienced its first successes in Bavaria. Duke Albert V (1550–1579) had been compelled to grant his nobles and townsmen, represented in the Bavarian diet, such concessions as Communion in both kinds, marriage of the clergy, abolition of fast days, and even some doctrinal reforms. After the conclusion of the Council of Trent, however, he considered himself strong enough to oppose both Lutheranism and the decentralizing political tendencies in his duchy. Supported by the pope, who freed him from financial worries by giving him one tenth of the ecclesiastical lands; by the Jesuits, who had gained almost complete control of the spiritual and cultural life of Bavaria; and by his Chancellor Simon Thaddeus Eck (d. 1574), who showed him how to use the Counter Reformation to increase his political power, Albert proceeded to crush the political rights of his nobles and towns, represented in the Bavarian diet, and to stamp out Protestantism.

The methods used by Albert and Chancellor Eck became the models for Counter Reformation procedure in other parts of Germany. The nobles and the townsmen were forced to accept the Tridentine decrees, visitations were used to ferret out heresies, the school system was reorganized under the Jesuits, a strict censorship of books was maintained, young men were forbidden to attend schools and universities in other lands, Protestant preachers and teachers were exiled, and all state officials and teachers were compelled to take an oath to support the decrees of the Council of Trent.

Albert V also assumed a position of leadership in imperial and foreign affairs. His marriage to a daughter of Ferdinand I led to his cooperation with the Austrian Hapsburgs, the traditional rivals of his Wittelsbach dynasty. In 1569 he attempted to create a league of Catholic princes and bishops to support both Spain and Rome. This league, however, failed because of the opposition of Emperor Maximilian II. By ignoring the provisions of the Council of Trent with respect to pluralism, Albert heaped upon his secular-minded son, Ernest, a number of bishoprics (Freising, Hildesheim, Liége, and Münster) and even the archbishopric of Cologne and the abbacies of Stablo and Malmédy. Other relatives were similarly provided for.

## Catholicism in the Austrian Lands

Although attempts were made to imitate Albert in the territories of the Austrian Hapsburgs, religious and political conditions there were so complicated that no unified action was possible. In Tyrol, where most of the nobles had remained Catholic, Archduke Ferdinand (1564–1595) had little difficulty in maintaining unity of faith. In Styria, Carinthia, and Carniola, on the other hand, Archduke Charles II (1564–1590), son-in-law of Duke Albert V of Bavaria, was compelled, because of fear of the Turks and lack of money, to grant the Lutheran nobles the right to retain their churches and schools. But he created the University of Graz (1586) and put it into the hands of the Jesuits to counteract the work of the excellent Protestant schools. Eventually, however, under the rule of Archduke Ernest and, after 1596, under the rule of Archduke Ferdinand II (son of Archduke Charles and trained by the Jesuits at Ingolstadt), the Protestants were deprived of their privileges. By 1602 the Counter Reformation was thoroughly established in these lands, although the nobles were still permitted to retain their Protestant faith. In 1628 Ferdinand, then emperor, deprived the nobles of even this right, and eight hundred of them are said to have migrated, together with many craftsmen and peasants.

Whereas Maximilian II had granted religious freedom to those of his subjects in Upper and Lower Austria who adhered to the Augsburg Confession, a different spirit prevailed under Emperor Rudolph II (1576–1612), his son and successor. Rudolph, who had been educated at the Spanish court, was a retiring bachelor who, although impressed with the dignity of his position, preferred to devote the most of his time and energy to astrology and alchemy at the Hradčany, the palace in Prague. Both Johannes Kepler and Tycho Brahe enjoyed his patronage. Mental illness finally overcame him in 1600, and five years later he was relieved of most of his administrative responsibilities. These, however, had never been great, for he had from the outset given the government of Upper and Lower Austria to Archduke Ernest and had turned over his other responsibilities to his Jesuit counselors. Chief among these was the able and versatile convert Melchior Khlesl (d. 1630), who became bishop of Vienna in 1598. In 1578 all Protestant preachers were driven out of Vienna. Soon after that, only Catholics were appointed to the city councils, and the nobles were gradually deprived of privileges granted them by Maximilian II. After the suppression of a bitter revolt of the peasants in Upper Austria (1595–1597), the authority of the Catholic Church was completely restored there.

In Bohemia the Brethren, the Lutherans, and the Calvinists, who had united in 1542, were recognized by Maximilian II in 1562. In 1575 they presented to him their *Confessio bohemica*. Rudolph II, however, withdrew their religious privileges in 1581 and attempted to exile the Bohemian Brethren. This failed because of the strenuous objection of the nobles and the cities. A second, more vigorous attempt, made by Rudolph in 1602, eventually led the Bohemian diet to wrest from him the *Letter of Majesty* of 1609, which guaranteed freedom of conscience to all Bohemians adhering to the *Confessio bohemica* and freedom of worship in their own churches to the approximately fourteen hundred nobles and forty-two towns. During the Thirty Years' War, however, the Counter Reformation was carried out with great severity in Bohemia, so that virtually the entire country was restored to Catholicism.

It was much more difficult to restore Hungary to Catholicism, primarily because of the Turks, who supported the anti-Hapsburg princes in those parts that they did not rule directly. When Rudolph II used force to compel a number of towns to accept Catholicism, he was deposed as king of Hungary (1604). Two years later his brother Matthias was made the king, but not until he had promised to grant freedom of worship to Lutherans and Calvinists. There as in Bohemia the cause of Protestantism suffered reverses during the Thirty Years' War. By the end of the seventeenth century the Jesuits completely dominated the religion and culture of the Hapsburg lands through their six universities, fifty-five colleges, and twenty-eight seminaries.

## Protestantism in the Ecclesiastical Principalities

It was in the ecclesiastical principalities of North Germany that the Protestants continued to make gains after the Peace of Augsburg. Because the eventual conquest of these would have given the Protestant princes a majority in the college of electors and the diet, which would more nearly reflect the preponderance of Protestants in Germany, it is no wonder that they did not adhere strictly to the provisions of the peace. In Saxony, the cathedral chapters of Merseburg and Naumburg, under pressure from Elector Augustus, agreed to elect only Saxon princes as their administrators. Meissen was completely absorbed into the Saxon possessions. A similar procedure was followed in Brandenburg. The great archbishopric of Magdeburg regularly elected only princes of electoral Brandenburg and was completely Protestant by 1566. Halberstadt, Bremen, Lübeck, Verden, and Minden all received Protestant administrators, chosen from the ruling houses of Saxony, Brandenburg, Brunswick, and Holstein. Because these administrators were elected and no conflict existed between the administrator and his chapter, the Protestants maintained that the ecclesiastical reservation of the Peace of Augsburg did not apply to these lands. Although the pope would not give his approval, the emperor gave the administrators the permission to carry out their duties and even to sit in the imperial diet.

In all the other important ecclesiastical states, however, in which Protestantism had made great inroads, Catholicism eventually triumphed, and almost invariably because the divided Protestants could not provide political support. In Salzburg, for example, where Protestantism had gained many adherents and where one of the archbishops had been compelled to grant Communion in both kinds, a mandate was issued in 1588 by his successor, who had been trained in the Jesuit College in Rome, demanding that all Protestants leave the archbishopric. Yet many remained.

In the monastic territory of Fulda, which had become almost entirely Protestant, the attempts of the abbot to carry out a Counter Reformation with the aid of the Jesuits in 1572 led to a revolt of the nobles, who expelled him. He was not reinstated until 1602, and then only because of the aid given him by the emperor. Thereupon he carried out his program with great force and considerable success.

The bishop of Würzburg declared himself on the side of the Counter Reformation only after he saw how weak Protestantism had shown itself politically in the case of Fulda, which he had hoped to obtain with the help of the Protestant nobles. When he saw which way the wind was blowing, he proceeded vigorously in his efforts to win his people back to Catholicism. In this he was aided by the Jesuits, whom he placed in control of the faculties of theology and philosophy at the University of Würzburg, which he had founded in 1582.

Of the three great archbishoprics whose rulers were also imperial electors, Trier most easily suppressed Protestantism. One of its archbishops drove out the Protestants as early as 1560, and another carried out the Tridentine decrees and deprived the city of Trier of its autonomy. Because Protestant nobles were excluded from the court, one after the other returned to Catholicism.

In Mainz the Protestants were so strong that the chapter, in 1555, chose a reliable Catholic archbishop by a majority of only one. Because of the proximity of Mainz to the Palatinate, the archbishop proceeded slowly against the Protestants. He and his successors also used Jesuits in the gradual restoration of Catholicism throughout the archbishopric.

The most acrimonious struggle occurred over the electorate of Cologne, for the success of the Protestants there would have given them a majority in the college of electors and enabled them to elect a Protestant emperor. Their hopes for success in this strategic area were aroused as early as 1535, when Archbishop Hermann von Wied began to think of reforming the electorate and when, seven years later, he invited Melanchthon and Bucer to establish a new church order there. Although the archbishop did not embrace Protestantism, it continued to spread under him and his successors. In 1577 the dissolute Gebhard II of Waldburg, a Swabian noble supported by the elector Palatine, was elected by a small majority, was confirmed by both the pope and the emperor, and ruled without important incidents until 1582. At that time Gebhard announced his intention to marry his mistress, Agnes, sister of the counts of Mansfeld; become Protestant and Protestantize his lands, but retain his archbishopric; and declare Protestantism legal alongside Catholicism. All this was in defiance of the ecclesiastical reservation.

Although Gebhard had been led to believe that he would have the military support of the Protestant princes for his venture, only John Casimir of the Palatinate came to his aid with a small army. Gebhard withdrew to his dominions in Protestant Westphalia and in February, 1583, married Agnes. Two months later the pope deprived him of his see, and in May, Ernest of Bavaria was elected archbishop in his place.

## Conflicts Between Lutherans and Catholics

The desultory military events that followed in the so-called Cologne War demonstrated the lack of harmony among the Protestant princes and the increasing effectiveness of Bavarian leadership. The hoped-for cooperation of John Casimir, Henry of Navarre, William of Orange, and Elizabeth of England did not materialize. After William of Orange was assassinated in 1585 and Dutch aid could no longer be expected, Ernest was accepted as one of the seven electors and Gebhard fled to Strassburg.

# 10. Protestantism and Catholicism

In Strassburg, Gebhard joined the Protestant faction of the cathedral chapter that in 1592 elected a Hohenzollern prince as bishop and sought the aid of Henry of Navarre. The other faction elected Cardinal Charles of Lorraine, son of the duke of Guise, and sought the support of the Catholic League in France. If it had not been for the lack of money, this conflict would have become a part of the religious wars of western Europe. In 1598 the emperor bought off the claims of the Hohenzollern prince and secured the election of the eleven-year-old Archduke Leopold of Austria as coadjutor for the Cardinal of Lorraine. Gebhard died in 1601, and in 1604 the Protestant faction had to give up the struggle because of the lack of support from the Protestant princes, who feared a widespread religious war. Elector Ernest of Cologne, although a man of questionable morals, did much to help re-establish Catholicism in the bishoprics of Paderborn, Osnabrück, Münster, and Hildesheim.

Another serious conflict developed over the status of the imperial city of Aachen and its lands. In 1580 the Lutherans and the Calvinists, supported by a large number of Protestant refugees from the Low Countries, demanded from the Catholic city council freedom of worship. When this was denied, they revolted and seized control of the government. Under pressure from the emperor, who was supported by Spanish troops under the duke of Parma, the Protestants agreed to turn the matter over to the diet. The diet, however, failed to resolve the issue at stake. Again the Protestant princes did not present a united front. Accordingly, in 1593, the emperor accepted the conclusions of the *Reichshofrat,* or aulic council, the emperor's own court consisting of Catholic judges, to the effect that the old Catholic city council be restored and Protestantism be wiped out. In 1598 the city was placed under the imperial ban and the emperor's orders carried out with the aid of Spanish troops.

During the many conflicts between the Protestants and the Catholics, only a few of which could be enumerated here, the following important questions were raised: (1) Could the ecclesiastical reservation of the Peace of Augsburg be enforced? (2) Could the Protestant administrators exercise all the rights of the Catholic bishops and archbishops whom they had replaced? (3) Did the imperial cities have the right to determine their religion according to the principle of *cuius regio, eius religio?* In the various attempts to solve these problems, the entire system of imperial justice collapsed. The imperial court could not give unequivocal decisions, and the Protestants would not accept the conclusions of the Catholic aulic council. Moreover, the emperor was no longer a mediator between the two groups but an avowed partisan. Finally, in the controversy over the imperial city of Donauwörth, the authority of the diet itself broke down and the Peace of Augsburg was sabotaged, despite the fact that both sides still earnestly wished to preserve peace.

Donauwörth was an imperial city in the Swabian Circle that had become almost entirely Lutheran. There, however, the abbot of the Benedictine monastery of the Holy Cross and the monks, many of whom had been educated at the Jesuit college of Dillingen, were determined to win the city back to Catholicism. A conflict between them and the Lutheran city council arose when the former, contrary to previous custom, aroused the populace by waving banners during their religious processions. Despite the prohibition of such demonstrations, a particularly provocative procession was staged in 1606, supported by the bishop of Augsburg and a mandate from the aulic council. When this procession ended in a riot, Emperor Rudolph gave Duke Maximilian I of Bavaria (1598–1651) the authority to investigate the causes of the friction and protect the Catholic minority.

Maximilian, who had been educated by the Jesuits at Ingolstadt, continued the policies begun by Albert V, his grandfather, with utmost severity. When the city council refused to promise freedom of worship to the small Catholic minority, he obtained an imperial ban against the city, forcibly brought it back into the Catholic fold, and incorporated it in his highly centralized territorial state (1607), despite the objections of the Swabian Circle and in defiance of the Peace of Augsburg.

### The Diet of Regensburg of 1608

The diet that met at Regensburg in January, 1608, reflected the sharp divisions between the Protestant and the Catholic estates and among the Protestants. When Archduke Ferdinand II, representing the emperor, asked for a grant of money to enable him to carry on the war against the Turks, the Protestant estates made such a grant conditional upon the confirmation of the Peace of Augsburg. The Catholic estates countered with the proposal that all ecclesiastical property that had changed hands since 1555 be restored. When Ferdinand suggested that both sides agree upon a simple confirmation of the Peace of Augsburg, the Protestants, led by the Calvinist Elector Frederick IV of the Palatinate, insisted that the Catholic proposal be expressly rejected by the diet and then withdrew with a majority of the Protestant estates. The important exception was the elector of Saxony.

When the diet broke up, Elector Frederick IV was prevailed upon to take vigorous steps against what appeared to be a concerted Catholic attempt to deprive the Protestants of their religious and political gains. Therefore there was created, in May, 1608, the Protestant Union, consisting of most of the Reformed and Lutheran princes and cities. Saxony consistently refused to cooperate. Determined to retain its defensive character, however, the Union came to no definite military agreements with the other Protestant rulers of Europe.

Although Maximilian of Bavaria continued to hold Donauwörth, the Catholic cause suffered reverses elsewhere, particularly in the Hapsburg lands and in Hungary and Bohemia. In the confusion accompanying the last years of Emperor Rudolph II's reign, the Protestant nobles and townsmen constantly pressed for a return of their religious privileges. They were most successful in Bohemia, where an overwhelming majority of the population had become Protestant, and where the ailing emperor had to contend with the conniving of his brother Matthias as well as with the demands of the Bohemian diet, which had hopes of electing a Protestant prince as Bohemian king upon his death. In July, 1609, Rudolph was compelled to sign the *Letter of Majesty,* which gave the Bohemians the right to choose between Catholicism and the Bohemian Confession of 1575 and permitted the estates to erect churches where they were needed. Rudolph made similar concessions to the Silesians.

Meanwhile the Catholic cause was threatened in the northwest, where, in April, 1609, Spain had signed the Twelve Years' Truce with the United Provinces and the latter had concluded a treaty of alliance with England and France. To strengthen Catholicism within Germany, Duke Maximilian of Bavaria formed a defensive Catholic Union—later called the Catholic League—in July, 1609. Although it at first consisted only of a few bishops and abbots with the duke of Bavaria as the director, it was soon joined by the ecclesiastical electors of Cologne, Mainz, and Trier. It had an army commanded by Count Johann von Tilly, announced its determination to protect Catholicism, and made overtures to both Spain and the papacy for support. Nevertheless, like the Protestant Union, its aims remained defensive.

Despite the desires of both sides to maintain peace, a major war almost broke out between them over the question of the succession to Jülich, Berg, Cleves, Mark, and Ravensburg. With the death, in 1609, of the childless Duke John William, ruler of these lands, the complicated question of inheritance, in which the religious controversy was involved, demanded an immediate solution. The persons most interested were Elector John Sigismund of Brandenburg, who claimed the lands through his wife; Philip Louis of the Palatine Neuburg, who claimed them for his son Wolfgang William; the elector of Saxony, who based his claim upon previous promises made to him by the emperor; and the emperor himself, who could add the lands to his own by escheat in the event that the claims of the others were disavowed by the electors.

Emperor Rudolph, immediately upon the death of John William, had his nephew Archduke Leopold, bishop of Passau and Strassburg, occupy the fortress of Jülich and summoned the claimants to appear before his aulic council. But the rulers of Brandenburg and Neuburg had meanwhile agreed to divide the lands between themselves without prejudice to their ultimate claims to the entire inheritance. Thereupon Wolfgang William and a brother of John Sigismund entered the city of Düsseldorf and refused to submit their claims to the aulic council.

Although neither side had many troops in the region, their controversy immediately involved the major European powers. Henry IV of France, who had from the outset supported the claims of the Protestant princes, made an agreement with the Protestant Union whereby the latter promised to join him if the French and Dutch troops attacked the Spanish Netherlands and took Jülich. James I of England likewise promised to send troops. In the face of such preparations, Archduke Leopold and Emperor Rudolph made plans to resist the attack. But just as a general war threatened to break out, Henry IV was struck down by an assassin (May, 1610). The French troops, already on the way, joined the Dutch and English forces under Maurice of Nassau and the German troops under the two claimants in taking the fortress of Jülich. Thereafter the troops of both sides disbanded, with the exception of the few commanded by the rival claimants.

John Sigismund and Wolfgang William now engaged in a bitter dispute during which each changed his religion for the purpose of obtaining outside support. Wolfgang William became Catholic and married the sister of Duke Maximilian of Bavaria, who, together with Philip III of Spain, supported his claims. John Sigismund became Calvinist and appealed to Maurice of Nassau for aid. When it again looked as though war would break out, the two princes, by the Treaty of Xanten (1614), once more agreed to a partition of the duchies without prejudice to the ultimate claims of either. John Sigismund took over the administration of Cleves, Mark, and Ravensburg, and Wolfgang William that of Jülich and Berg, a division that lasted for two hundred years.

The long struggle between Rudolph II and Matthias, which had made effective leadership impossible in either the Empire or the Austrian lands, came to an end with the death of the former and the election of the latter as emperor. Matthias (1612–1619), however, could not subdue those forces of opposition that he himself had aroused during his conflict with Rudolph. Although the Catholics in the Empire clamored for a restoration of all their lands, the Protestants in the Austrian lands and in Bohemia and Hungary caused the emperor and his adviser Khlesl to employ tact and patience to maintain peace and order. But finally Matthias himself joined the Catholic League and assured Archduke Ferdinand II that he would become his successor.

Ferdinand, educated by the Jesuits at Ingolstadt, laid plans for a vigorous program of action against the Protestants. Elected king of Bohemia in 1617 and of Hungary in 1618, he promised to maintain the religious privileges of his Protestant subjects. At the same time he prepared to break his promises. By the defenestration at the Hradčany—throwing the royal councilors out of the window—in May, 1618, the Bohemian estates showed that they were willing to defend their rights with force.

Ferdinand's conflict with the Bohemian estates served as the prelude to the Thirty Years' War, a conflict that was wanted by neither the Catholics nor the Protestants but that came in spite of the desire for peace on the part of virtually all the rulers of Europe and certainly all the people. During this war, Catholic and Protestant goals were obscured and everyone lost except those territorial rulers who had taken advantage of the religious beliefs of the great majority of the German people to strengthen their own authority.

## The Counter Reformation in Poland

Neighboring Poland was not drawn into this devastating war. Lacking a strongly centralized government, like Germany, its religious problems were nevertheless solved before Germany was plunged into war. Although the Protestants there had secured religious freedom as a constitutional right at the Diet of Warsaw in 1573, they had already reached the height of their successes in that country and now began their decline. Responsible for their declining influence were (1) the disputes among the Lutherans, the Calvinists, the Bohemian Brethren, and the anti-Trinitarians; (2) the strong loyalty of the peasants to Catholicism; (3) the shrewd planning of Stanislav Hosius (d. 1579), bishop of Ermland and a cardinal; and (4) the devoted labors of the Jesuits.

Canisius had visited Poland as early as 1558. Soon Polish youths began to attend the Jesuit schools at Vienna. Among these was Stanislav Kostka (d. 1568), who became the patron saint of Poland. By 1565 the Jesuits had been established in the country and the king had agreed to accept the decrees of the Council of Trent. Although King Stephen Báthory (1576–1586) of Transylvania, a Protestant who had become Catholic to gain this crown, continued to permit religious freedom to all groups, he greatly favored the Jesuits. At the end of his reign they numbered more than three hundred and fifty and had twelve colleges in the country.

Sigismund III (1587–1632), nicknamed the "king of the Jesuits," completed the task of converting Poland to Catholicism. Because he refused to grant royal honors to non-Catholics, most of the nobles found it expedient to give up their Protestant beliefs and drive the Protestant peasants from their estates. Administrators and judges, trained in Jesuit schools, found ways and means of recovering churches and other ecclesiastical property for Catholicism, despite the constitutional provision of freedom for the Protestants. In the predominantly German cities of Cracow, Danzig, and Thorn, Protestantism was attacked as a treasonable offense. Even a number of bishops of the Orthodox Church were won over to Catholicism.

When Sigismund III became also the king of Sweden (1592–1599) upon the death of his father John III (1568–1592), he renewed the latter's attempts to reintroduce Catholicism in that country. But because he was looked upon as a foreigner, as an apostate, and as the ruler of the great rival of Sweden for the control of the Baltic, the Swedes made him agree that only the teachings of the Augsburg Confession should be permitted. All vestiges of Catholicism were wiped out by the end of his reign.

When, in 1598, Sigismund attempted to reduce Sweden by military force, Charles Vasa defeated him decisively in the province of East Gothland. Thereupon Sigismund was deposed and Charles was made regent. In 1604 the latter was crowned king as Charles IX (1604–1611). Charles was in turn succeeded by the great champion of Protestantism in the Thirty Years' War, Gustavus Adolphus (1611–1632).

Upon his return to Poland, Sigismund attempted to compensate for his failure in Sweden by making a determined effort to win Russia for himself and Catholicism. The struggle that followed led to the internal strengthening of Russia by the emergence of the Romanov dynasty in 1613 and to the further weakening of royal authority in Poland. But an insurrection, led by disgruntled nobles and Protestants, was easily suppressed in 1608. Thereafter the Protestants comprised but a small minority and the Jesuits were in complete control.

# 11 The Secularization of the European States

By the beginning of the seventeenth century, Protestantism and Catholicism in Germany were again poised for war, despite the universal desire for peace. Catholicism had made such astounding progress in consolidating its power in western Europe and in regaining lost lands and peoples in central and eastern Europe that Protestantism was clearly on the defensive. To retain their authority in their respective lands, the Protestant rulers of Germany were reluctantly compelled to unite and forestall further Catholic gains with armed resistance.

The devastating Thirty Years' War that followed began primarily as a religious war, for religion and politics were still inseparable and the most intense problems of the day were still religious ones. But it degenerated into a barbarous power-political struggle between Catholic France and the Catholic Hapsburgs. When the German phase of this conflict was brought to a close by the Peace of Westphalia in 1648, the overwhelming importance of the secularized power-political state received general recognition. This marked the end of the Reformation Era, in which man had been concerned with remaking society to conform with his religious convictions, and the beginning of the Age of the Enlightenment, in which man merged the humanist emphasis upon the dignity of man with the optimistic belief in man's ability to construct a perfect world on the basis of reason and according to the laws of nature.

Although individual rulers had occasionally acted according to the Machiavellian principle of *raison d'état,* or state necessity, during the sixteenth century, their domestic and foreign policies usually were in harmony with their re-

*415*

ligious convictions. By the middle of the seventeenth century, however, state necessity began to supersede every other consideration and practical expediency to replace religious and moral objectives. Absolute monarchies, supported primarily by the middle classes, alone seemed able to weaken the centrifugal forces of feudalism and provide peace, security, and economic well-being on a national scale.

In England, where Parliament had maintained its parity with the monarchy, this same tendency toward secularization made its appearance. Puritanism, a dynamic religious force, became identified with parliamentarianism and the interests of the rising merchant classes and provided much of the theoretical ammunition for the struggle against Stuart pretensions. But the constitutional ideas there also were soon divorced from medieval or Calvinist ideas and became totally secular. By the end of the Puritan Revolution and the Interregnum, it was generally recognized that king and Parliament constituted an all-powerful secular state, operating according to natural laws and clearly understandable contracts.

# The Thirty Years' War

## The Bohemian Period (1618–1620)

The Thirty Years' War, which eventually involved most of the European states, broke out in Bohemia. There, in 1617, the predominantly Protestant estates had recognized Archduke Ferdinand of Styria, leader of the opposition to Khlesl's policy of compromising with the Protestants, as king of Bohemia, while Matthias was still emperor. But these estates soon realized that their surrender of the ancient right to elect their own king would lead to their loss of other, especially religious, rights. Accordingly they met again in a Protestant assembly and sent the emperor a petition of protest against the violation of their constitution. Matthias answered by defending the previous action and declaring the present assembly illegal. On May 23, 1618, after a number of incidents had aroused strong feelings on both sides, Count Heinrich von Thurn, the dashing but conceited leader of the radical Protestant nobles, entered with an armed force the Hradčany at Prague, where two regents of Matthias were meeting. After an acrimonious exchange of words, in which the Protestants demanded a strict adherence to Rudolph II's *Letter of Majesty* of 1609, they threw the two regents and their secretary out of the window into the palace moat about fifty feet below. This defenestration became an important symbol of Bohemian resistance to the Hapsburgs.

The Protestant assembly immediately set up an insurrectionary government. It placed Thurn at the head of the Bohemian forces, and banished the Jesuits from the kingdom. While the weak Protestant Union could not make up its mind whether or not to remain on the defensive

# 11. The Secularization of the European States

and Archduke Ferdinand was beset by many difficulties at home and on the borders of the Austrian lands, Thurn, with an army of about ten thousand men, advanced toward Vienna, hoping to gain the support of the Protestant estates in the Austrian lands and of the dissatisfied Hungarians.

In March, 1619, Emperor Matthias died and Archduke Ferdinand was faced with the task of gaining support for his election as emperor. Although he had been trained by the Jesuits and believed it a sin to permit political matters to interfere with the Counter Reformation, he did not act vigorously and was, like most other rulers, eager to prevent a general European war. Yet his policy remained unchanged and succeeded in the long run. Even though the Protestant estates arose against him in Bohemia and its crown lands of Moravia, Lusatia, and Silesia, and also in Upper and Lower Austria, he gathered his faithful supporters about him, gained the aid of Spain in return for important concessions in Italy, and carried on the struggle without any decisive battles. When Thurn saw that he did not have a large enough army to besiege Vienna and learned that his forces in Bohemia had been routed, he returned home.

Ferdinand next went to Frankfurt to obtain the imperial election. If the Protestants could have united at this time, they could have prevented his election. But neither the elector of Saxony nor the elector of Brandenburg was inclined to follow a purely Protestant course, and the elector of the Palatinate stood alone in his opposition. Archduke Ferdinand was elected as Emperor Ferdinand II (1619–1637).

Shortly before the election, two events had occurred that resulted in continued opposition to the new emperor. One was the uprising of the Calvinist Prince Bethlen Gabor of Transylvania, in which most of Hungary became involved; the other was the election by the Protestant Bohemian estates of Elector Frederick V of the Palatinate as their king. Frederick, son-in-law of James I of England and leader of the Protestant Union, however, was not the man to lead the attack against the Hapsburgs, for he had few political virtues outside a determined will and a charming personality. He finally accepted the Bohemian throne, urged to do so by the radical Calvinist leader of the Protestants, Prince Christian von Anhalt. But he was unaware of all the implications of such an act. His decision made the Bohemian uprising a matter of international concern.

Frederick was crowned king of Bohemia in Prague in November, 1619. He was recognized only by the Protestant Union, Venice, the United Provinces, and Sweden, but he could not depend upon their military support. Bethlen Gabor alone continued the struggle as an ally of Bohemia until early in 1620, when he was compelled to sign a truce. The emperor was then free to concentrate upon Bohemia. He was supported not only by ample funds from the pope, Genoa, and Spain but by the

*417*

military strength of the Catholic League, whose leader was Duke Maximilian of Bavaria. In return for the support of the League, Ferdinand promised Maximilian the electoral title if it should be taken from Frederick V and control of those lands that Maximilian might obtain while executing the ban against Frederick. Even the Lutheran Elector John George of Saxony gave Ferdinand his support in return for a promise of additional territory. In April, 1620 the emperor issued a mandate demanding that Frederick leave Bohemia and threatened him with the imperial ban. In July Count Tilly appeared in Upper Austria with a large armed force.

It now became apparent how foolhardy it had been for Frederick V to accept the Bohemian crown without having prepared the way by diplomatic and military agreements. Not even England's James I, his father-in-law, would intervene. When Marie de' Medici of France offered to mediate between Frederick and Ferdinand, the Protestant Union was neutralized and then disbanded. Thus Frederick was virtually isolated. Even at Prague this "Winter King" and his English queen could not command unified support, partly because of their indifferent leadership but primarily because of the cost of their government, which was arousing much discontent.

Frederick's army, commanded by Anhalt and Thurn, was decisively defeated at the battle of White Hill near Prague on November 8, 1620, by the imperial forces under Count Tilly. The surprised Protestants succumbed in about an hour to the fierce determination of the Catholics, who went into battle with the cry, "For the Virgin Mary." With this defeat Frederick's rule in Bohemia collapsed, and Maximilian of Bavaria entered the city of Prague. By the spring of the next year the insurrection had been suppressed throughout Bohemia, and the elector of Saxony had subdued the Silesian estates and occupied the Lusatian lands, which had been assigned to him to hold until he had been repaid for his expenditures.

The collapse of Protestant resistance in Bohemia was followed by a ruthless conversion, expatriation, and confiscation of property. A special tribunal was set up for trying the insurrectionists. Many of the leaders were tried and executed, and their possessions were confiscated. More than a half of the landed property of Bohemia was seized for the emperor. This he in turn gave to his supporters or sold at ridiculously low prices to replenish his treasury. His political officials and military commanders profited tremendously from these transactions. Chief of these beneficiaries was Albert von Waldstein, or Wallenstein (1583–1634), a member of a Bohemian noble family who earlier had given up the faith of the Bohemian Brethren and by marriage had obtained large estates in Moravia. He had supported the emperor by loans and military service since 1617.

The reconversion of Bohemia was enforced by soldiers billeted in the homes of the Protestants and supported by the Jesuits. The university at Prague was given over to the Jesuits. By 1624 all the Protestant clergy had been driven out of Bohemia and all Protestants had been deprived of civil and religious rights. Finally, in 1627, a special "Reformation Tribunal" was instituted that forced more than thirty thousand Protestant families of all classes to leave the country, many of them carrying their wealth and skills to nearby Saxony. One of the best-known intellectuals among these refugees was the great educator Comenius. The royal towns were deprived of self-government and their lands—probably a third of the country—were seized. The class most severely affected were the Czech landed nobles. Their places were taken by a new landowning class of Germans, Frenchmen, and Italians who had little interest in the country and owed their allegiance primarily to the emperor. A new constitution (1627) made Bohemia a hereditary kingdom and gave the king control over the diet, thereby destroying the autonomy of this once proud and prosperous land and merging its interests with those of the Austrian Hapsburgs, who ruled the country from Vienna.

Moravia was treated the same as Bohemia. Upper and Lower Lusatia, retained by the Lutheran elector of Saxony, were granted religious liberty. In Hungary, where Bethlen Gabor could no longer carry on the struggle alone, Catholicism was restored by vigorous ecclesiastics supported by the crown. A revolt against stern Catholic measures in Upper Austria was followed by the execution of terrible vengeance that led to the emigration of thousands of nobles, townsmen, and peasants in 1626. In Lower Austria, the nobles retained their personal freedom of worship. But this meant little, for all Protestant clergy and teachers were expelled, and the University of Vienna was placed under the control of the Jesuits.

## The Palatinate Period (1621–1623)

The defeat of Frederick V's army on White Hill did not lead to a general pacification, for while the Catholic forces moved against Frederick in the east, the Spanish troops under Spinola entered the Palatinate. Frederick, instead of going to the Palatinate to prepare it for its defense, began his futile wandering from court to court in search of support for his claim to Bohemia. The ultimate disposition of the electoral title attached to the Palatinate was a matter of great concern to all the Protestant rulers of Europe. Giving this title to a Catholic would deprive the Protestants of another vote in the electoral college. James I therefore intervened, though half-heartedly, in behalf of his son-in-law. Sweden under Gustavus Adolphus could not bring her growing power to bear at this time because of her involvement in a conflict with Poland. And Denmark's policy of expansion in Lower Saxony aroused the apprehensions of the Protestant princes in northern Germany.

Spain, on the Catholic side, having resumed the war with the United

# Part Four: Religious Conflicts and Consequences

Provinces after the termination of the Twelve Years' Truce in 1621, did not want England to intervene there and consequently supported the restoration of Frederick V in the Palatinate. The emperor, however, could not play a pacifying role because he was bound by his promises to Maximilian of Bavaria. But Maximilian was in no position to carry out alone the imperial ban against Frederick. Further bloodshed might thus have been averted if it had not been for the methods being used at that time for maintaining mercenary armies. The *condottieri,* or captains, paid their troops by permitting them to live off the land, that of friend or foe, without depending upon the voting of funds by assemblies. These *condottieri,* for whom war was an end in itself, thus profited from international friction and therefore encouraged it.

Although the Catholic Spinola had introduced this system into the Palatinate, three Protestant military leaders, the best known of whom was Count Ernest von Mansfeld, gathered armies to be supported similarly and for Frederick's cause. But Count Tilly, at the head of the army of the Catholic League, defeated each of these Protestant armies separately in 1622. Lutheranism was promptly suppressed in the Upper Palatinate by the Bavarian officials and the Jesuits. The Calvinist ministers, and then the Lutheran, were driven out of their churches in the Lower Palatinate. The University of Heidelberg, the intellectual center and seminary of German Calvinism, received especially harsh treatment. In 1623 its great treasure of books and manuscripts was carried off to Rome and deposited in the Vatican Library, where it still lies, with the exception of the manuscripts returned in 1816.

Despite the fact that Spain joined England and the Protestant princes of Germany in protesting against the increase of the power of the duke of Bavaria, Ferdinand, supported by the papacy, secretly gave Maximilian the electoral title and the electorate in 1621. At the diet of the princes in 1623, he obtained their recognition of the title, but only for Maximilian's lifetime. Maximilian, however, kept the title for his successors. As reimbursement for his expenditures in the two wars, he was permitted to retain the Upper Palatinate and also, for the time being, the Lower Palatinate east of the Rhine and Upper Austria. Spain continued to hold the Palatinate west of the Rhine.

All these arrangements accentuated rather than solved the conflicts between the Protestants and the Catholics. Furthermore, once the Catholics had defeated the Protestants, differences began to appear among the former. The interests of Spain and Bavaria, for example, clashed in the Palatinate, and while Spain continued to lean toward England, Bavaria began a *rapprochement* with France. Those Catholic powers that were developing their strongly centralized monarchies with the aid of the Counter Reformation soon became bitter rivals. Meanwhile Tilly and the Protestant captains kept their armies in the field, awaiting new opportu-

# 11. The Secularization of the European States

nities to fight, especially as they developed in the Lower Saxon Circle of the Empire, to which Tilly moved at the head of the forces of the League in pursuit of the Protestant troops.

## The Danish Period (1625–1629)

The aging James I of England had finally come to the realization that he could not marry Charles, the Prince of Wales, to a Spanish infanta and thereby consummate an alliance with Spain. His failure in this project made Parliament more patriotic and more Protestant than ever. Consequently he began negotiations toward an alliance that would enable him to regain the Palatinate for his son-in-law. Gustavus Adolphus could not be induced to join, for he was still involved in his struggle with Poland. But Christian IV of Denmark, desirous of fame as a leader of Protestantism and eager to annex land in the Lower Saxon Circle, of which he as the ruler of Holstein was a member, agreed to enter the war against the emperor and the Catholic League. Accordingly he was made head of the Lower Saxon Circle and placed in command of its military forces.

Charles I, who had meanwhile succeeded James I as king of England, agreed to send an English fleet to attack the Spanish coast and to provide Christian of Denmark with a monthly subsidy of £30,000. These provisions were incorporated in a treaty concluded in May, 1625. Cardinal Richelieu, the chief minister of Louis XIII of France from 1624 to 1642, reversed the policy of Marie de' Medici and returned to that of Henry IV by joining England and Denmark against the Hapsburgs.

Christian's war, however, was doomed at the outset. The British fleet failed to take Cadiz; Richelieu, fearing the consequences of a march across part of France by Mansfeld's poorly disciplined army, found an excuse for not carrying out his part of the bargain; and the English Parliament, already at odds with Charles I, made impossible the payment of the subsidies to Christian. The Danish king could not even obtain allies among the Protestant rulers of northern Germany, for they feared him almost as much as they did the Catholic princes. More important still, Christian was no match for Tilly and Wallenstein.

Wallenstein, the most daring and ambitious adventurer of his age, had been created duke of Friedland in 1623 in recognition of his services as soldier, statesman, and administrator. He was not a great soldier but an ambitious politician who appeared as a brilliant meteor for about a decade. Inwardly undecided and hesitating, he gained certainty with respect to his ambitious plans from astrology, believing that the stars had destined him to a brilliant career.

While Tilly was devastating the regions of Lower Saxony, Mansfeld began to negotiate with Richelieu; and Maximilian, fearing that a new coalition was being formed against him, asked the emperor to create a new army to assist him. Accordingly Ferdinand, who had hesitated because of lack of funds, accepted the offer of Wallenstein to provide an army largely at his own cost and made him commander-in-chief of all the imperial troops.

With this new army of more than twenty thousand, officered largely by Italians, Spaniards, and Frenchmen, Wallenstein marched westward, paying little attention to orders from the emperor. Instead of supporting his troops by plundering the lands through which he marched, he made cities and territories of friend or foe pay large contributions that he and his officers distributed among the men. He entered Lower Saxony in October, 1625, where he spent the autumn and winter, fortifying his position at the Dessau Bridge on the Elbe River.

While Christian was pursuing Tilly, Mansfeld attacked Wallenstein at the Dessau Bridge in April, 1626. Although Mansfeld was routed, he got away with most of his army, thereby preventing Wallenstein from joining Tilly. Christian finally met Tilly at Lutter am Barenberge in the Harz Mountains in August and suffered a complete rout. This calamity was followed by imperialist and Bavarian gains everywhere. While Tilly occupied Brunswick and sent soldiers into Brandenburg, Wallenstein occupied Silesia. Then the two joined forces and marched into Schleswig, Holstein, and Jutland. Early in 1628 the dukes of Mecklenburg-Schwerin and Mecklenburg-Strelitz were put under the imperial ban for having aided Christian, and Wallenstein was ordered to occupy their lands.

The imperialists now held the Baltic shore from Lübeck to Danzig; but they had no navy to pursue Christian, who had fled to one of his islands. The consequence of this impasse was the Peace of Lübeck of 1629. Christian retained devastated Denmark, Schleswig, and Holstein but renounced all his claims to the bishoprics of Lower Saxony, promised to interfere no more in imperial affairs, and accepted the Edict of Restitution.

Ferdinand reached the apex of his career in 1629. Both Mansfeld and Bethlen Gabor were now dead, and in Wallenstein he had a leader who apparently agreed with the Hapsburg policies and could free him from the restraining influence of Maximilian and other particularistic German princes.

The high point of the Counter Reformation was reached in the Edict of Restitution of 1629, issued by Ferdinand before the Peace of Lübeck and without the consent of the imperial diet. Interpreting the Peace of Augsburg solely from a Catholic point of view, he demanded that all ecclesiastical lands alienated since 1552 be returned, that the administration of ecclesiastical lands by Protestants be forbidden, that Catholic prelates be reinstated in such Church lands, and that the Calvinists be excluded from the privileges of the peace. The strict enforcement of this edict would have crushed Protestantism, for the two remaining Protestant electors had absorbed many ecclesiastical lands and one of these, the elec-

# 11. The Secularization of the European States

tor of Brandenburg, was a Calvinist. The other, the elector of Saxony, contented himself with uttering feeble protests.

But the Catholic powers were unable to take full advantage of prostrate Protestantism because political considerations now almost completely dominated the religious ones. Bavaria disputed with Austria the possession of such bishoprics as Minden and Verden. Even the old Catholic religious orders fell into bitter disputes with the Jesuits over reclaimed Church property. Ferdinand's dynastic and political interests, moreover, aroused the apprehensions of all German princes. At the same time, the victories of the Catholic forces to 1629 were accompanied by a Hapsburg predominance throughout Europe that elicited powerful opposition among other Catholic powers. Thus, while Maximilian and the German princes were planning to prevent further strengthening of the emperor's position, France prepared to check Spain, and Pope Urban VIII looked for ways in which to check Spanish aggrandizement in Italy.

## International Conflict in the Valtellina

In no area was the confusion of religious and political motives more clearly demonstrated than in the Valtellina. This valley, stretching from Lake Como northwest into the Rhaetian Alps, had been in the possession of Grisons since 1386. The Valtellina was solidly Catholic, Grisons Protestant. Because of the important Alpine passes of the Valtellina, a rivalry developed as early as 1601 between Spain and Austria on the one hand, and France, Grisons, and Venice on the other. Encouraged by the Spanish viceroy of Milan and Archbishop Borromeo, the inhabitants revolted against their masters and massacred many Protestants. The valley then came under Spanish and Austrian protection and assumed international importance. When Richelieu joined Venice and Savoy in pledging the restoration of the status quo so that France, Venice, and Savoy would all have free access to the passes, the pope urged that the valley be given to him to administer and sent his troops there. But Cardinal Richelieu made it clear that he would risk war against the pope if the troops were not withdrawn.

Richelieu, however, could not carry out his plans at this time, for he was now concerned primarily with a revolt on the part of the Huguenots, who were being supported by Spanish money. Consequently France and Spain agreed to the Treaty of Monzon (1626). By its terms, the Valtellina was returned to Grisons with certain autonomous rights, and Catholicism alone was permitted there. Thousands of Spanish troops passed through its passes during the Thirty Years' War.

With the defeat of the Huguenots and the seizure of their last stronghold, La Rochelle, in 1628, Richelieu could begin the second part of his program, to break the Hapsburg encirclement of France. His first step was to conclude hostilities with England at Susa in 1629. He then took advantage of a disputed succession in the duchies of Mantua and Mont-ferrat in Italy and, at the invitation of Pope Urban VIII, marched an army into the area to gain a foothold there for France. The struggle be-tween him and the Spaniards and the Austrians dragged on until 1631, when a French subject was given the two duchies and the French re-mained in possession of Pinerol, from which they could threaten Haps-burg control of Italy. North of the Alps the future also seemed propitious because of the appearance of a military genius and opponent of the Hapsburgs who was the equal of the Catholic generals—King Gustavus Adolphus of Sweden.

There is no doubt that Gustavus was motivated by strong religious convictions and that he aspired to become the leader of Protestantism. But his prior concern for the welfare of his country is illustrated by the fact that he did not enter the struggle with Catholicism until he had se-cured Sweden's hegemony in the Baltic Sea region, had defeated Chris-tian IV, and had made an armistice with Poland with the aid of Riche-lieu. A war with Ferdinand, however, seemed inevitable, for the latter now had control of the southern shores of the Baltic. It would be advan-tageous for Gustavus to assume the offensive and fight the war on Ger-man soil, thereby opening up the possibility of obtaining the coastal lands and thus making the Baltic a Swedish lake.

Gustavus was in a much better position than Christian IV to carry on a war against Ferdinand. Not only was he a better warrior, diplomat, and leader of his people, but he and his officers and men had had many years of experience of fighting Poles, Danes, and Russians. Furthermore, he had developed a highly centralized administrative system of government and had promoted Sweden's economic prosperity, even to the point of estab-lishing Swedish settlements in North America. More important still, he did not have to oppose Wallenstein, who had been relieved of his com-mand of the imperial forces because of his inordinate ambition to create out of Germany an absolute national state under the rule of the Haps-burgs. To achieve his purpose Wallenstein had opposed the strict Catho-lic position reflected in the Edict of Restitution and had favored, instead, the establishment of an equilibrium between Catholicism and Protestant-ism. For this reason, among others, Maximilian and the Catholic League had violently opposed him, and the conservative Ferdinand had dis-missed him soon after the Swedes had landed in Germany.

### The Swedish Period (1630–1635)

The Swedish king landed in Pomerania with a small but well-disci-plined army of thirteen thousand men in June, 1630. Few Protestants joined him, however, largely because of their distrust of him but also be-cause of the apparent hopelessness of his cause. The elector of Saxony re-fused outright to aid him, and the elector of Brandenburg, whose sister

Die Bayerischen Staatsgemäldesammlungen

Gustavus Adolphus

*by Van Dyck*

425

Gustavus had married, urged him to return home and immediately began to mediate between him and the emperor. But Gustavus could not be stopped, for he believed himself divinely called to crush the Hapsburg power and the papacy.

Because of the dismissal of Wallenstein and the reorganization of the imperial troops under Tilly, the Catholic League general, Gustavus met no opposition for half a year. He devoted his time to securing his ports of entry on the Baltic and preparing his army for action. In January, 1631, Richelieu made a treaty with him, promising to pay him four hundred thousand thalers over a period of six years in return for maintaining an army of at least thirty-six thousand men against Ferdinand. But Gustavus had to promise not to stamp out Catholicism in conquered lands or to change the imperial constitution in any way.

Magdeburg, the first Protestant city of considerable size to come to the support of Gustavus, was the first to feel the impact of this new phase of the war. It was besieged by General Pappenheim and then Tilly and finally captured (May, 1631), sacked, and burned. Gustavus lost prestige because of his failure to save the city, but he gained in other ways. Tilly could not use the city defensively, the Protestants became thoroughly aroused, and many princes, including the elector of Brandenburg, now came to the support of Gustavus. Ferdinand, certain of ultimate victory, demanded that the Elector John George of Saxony disband his forces and, when the latter did not comply, seized Leipzig and began to plunder Saxony. John George then made a treaty with Gustavus that placed the Saxon troops on the side of the Swedish king. When, on September 17, 1631, this combined army met the imperial army under Tilly at Breitenfeld, north of Leipzig, Gustavus won a decisive victory that made this "Lion of the North" the hero of Protestant Germany. Virtually all the Protestant princes now accepted his leadership.

Breitenfeld was but the beginning of a series of victories that culminated in the Swedish king's entry into Munich in May, 1632, and the subsequent plundering of Bavaria. Even Prague fell into the hands of the Protestant forces led by Elector John George. When Tilly was mortally wounded near Munich early in 1632, the fortunes of the emperor and the Catholic League were at a low ebb. Ferdinand consequently turned again to Wallenstein, who had toyed with the idea of joining Gustavus. Wallenstein agreed to aid the emperor, but only on the condition that he have sole control over all the imperial forces and that the Edict of Restitution be revoked.

Wallenstein drove the Saxons out of Bohemia, joined the forces of Maximilian, and, after several encounters with the Protestants, went into winter quarters in Saxony. But on November 16, 1632, Gustavus compelled him to fight at Lützen, southwest of Leipzig. The Swedish army was victorious, but it paid for its victory with the death of its king. De-

# 11. The Secularization of the European States

spite the able leadership of the Swedish chancellor, Oxenstierna, the Protestant cause began to suffer reverses. The dismissal and assassination of Wallenstein for alleged treason in 1634 relieved the emperor of his fears concerning this ambitious general who had been negotiating on his own with Saxony, Sweden, and France for a peace settlement. In September of that same year, the imperial forces defeated the Protestants at Nördlingen. By that time the ultimate outcome of the struggle was clear. The battles of Breitenfeld and Lützen had shown that the Catholic forces could not subdue the Protestant north of Germany, and the battle of Nördlingen had shown the futility of the Protestant attempt to control the Catholic south.

The Swedish period of the war was finally brought to a conclusion by the Peace of Prague, signed on May 30, 1635. The basic problem of the ownership of ecclesiastical lands was solved by an agreement that these should revert to those who had held them in 1627 and remain in their possession for forty years. During that period their ultimate ownership was to be decided amicably or by the process of law. The *Reichskammergericht* was given superior judicial authority again and was to consist of an equal number of Catholic and Protestant judges. Saxony was given Lusatia, which it had occupied since the Bohemian War. All territories lost by the emperor and his allies were to be returned. All leagues and armies were to be disbanded and replaced by one imperial army that alone should be used in maintaining peace.

This settlement reflected in the main the wishes of the great majority of Germans, for they were tired of war. But the Swedes and the French, deprived of their territorial gains by the peace, continued the struggle. And Spain, after the Battle of Nördlingen, prepared a full-scale attack upon France. In a pact with the Heilbronn Alliance of 1633, comprising Sweden, Baden, Hesse-Kassel, and Württemberg, in November, 1634, Richelieu agreed to attack the Spanish Netherlands. He subsequently made an alliance with Savoy, Mantua, and Parma for the purpose of obtaining Milan. Finally, in May, 1635, he declared war on Spain. In September, 1636, the emperor declared war on France.

## The Franco-Swedish Period (1635–1648)

The Franco-Swedish period of the war was no longer a religious war by the wildest stretch of the imagination. Everyone knew that France, the ally of Sweden and the German Protestants, was Catholic and that Catholic cardinals directed French affairs; and Pope Urban VIII did nothing to interfere with Richelieu's plans. The age of the *condottieri* was now past. From that time on, the great powers engaged in a huge power-political struggle that ended with the establishment of a precarious balance of power. Germany, no longer a leading figure in the international scene, became the battleground of these great powers, although the war was carried to many other parts of Europe.

Almost from the beginning of this period, attempts were made by the anti-Hapsburg powers to negotiate a peace. Not until the fundamental weaknesses of Spain became apparent in 1640, when revolts occurred in Catalonia and Portugal, were both sides willing to conclude hostilities. Despite a large number of victories on the part of France and Sweden, these countries could not attain their ultimate objectives. And the German princes, who had been denied the fruits of the Peace of Prague, made renewed efforts to close the war.

### The Peace of Westphalia (1648)

The negotiations among the contending powers, begun at Regensburg and Hamburg in 1640–1641, dragged on until Sweden concluded its part of the fighting at a gathering of representatives at Osnabrück in Westphalia, August 8, 1648, and France did likewise at Münster, also in Westphalia, September 17, 1648. In March of that year, the United Provinces had concluded hostilities with Spain. Despite the intransigence of the radical Catholic group and the bitter war of pamphlets, the spirit of compromise prevailed, and on October 24 1648, the Peace of Westphalia was signed.

This peace settled the major religious conflicts among the Germans once and for all. The Peace of Augsburg of 1555 was reaffirmed and its provisions extended to the adherents of the Reformed faith. The problem of the possession of ecclesiastical lands was solved by the use of January 1, 1624, as the test date. All ecclesiastical lands in the hands of the Protestants at that time, such as the secularized bishoprics of Magdeburg, Halberstadt, Bremen, Minden, and Verden, were to remain Protestant, and the Catholic bishoprics of southern Germany remained Catholic. An exception was made in the hereditary dominions of the Austrian Hapsburgs, where the fruits of the Catholic Reformation were retained. In judicial matters, equality was to be maintained. The *Reichskammergericht* was to consist of equal numbers of Catholic and Protestant judges. The right to the change of religion was permitted; but in the event of such a change, the minorities of the other faith that had existed before 1624 were to be tolerated. A prince who changed his religion could permit Protestantism and Catholicism to exist side by side. He could not, however, confiscate the property of those whom he exiled for religious reasons.

The most important territorial changes of the Peace of Westphalia were the following: (1) Sweden obtained Western Pomerania, including Stettin on the mouth of the Oder River, and the secularized bishoprics of Bremen and Verden. (2) As compensation to electoral Brandenburg for her loss of Western Pomerania, she was confirmed in the possession of

Eastern Pomerania and received in addition the bishoprics of Camin, Minden, Halberstadt, and most of Magdeburg. (3) Saxony kept Lusatia and part of Magdeburg. (4) The duke of Bavaria retained the Upper Palatinate and the electoral title. (5) The Lower Palatinate was restored to the legitimate ruler, who was given a new (eighth) electoral title. (6) France received confirmation of her possession of the bishoprics of Metz, Toul, and Verdun, Pinerol, and imperial lands in Alsace (excluding Strassburg). (7) The signatories of the peace also recognized the independence of the United Provinces and Switzerland.

The Peace of Westphalia marked the end of the medieval papacy with strong political influence as well as of the medieval Empire with strong religious interests. Although Pope Innocent X (1644–1655) refused to recognize the peace, both Catholics and Protestants ignored his protests. Emperor Ferdinand III (1637–1657) had to recognize loss of authority and lands in the Empire. The more than three hundred small entities of the Empire retained their autonomy, with complete freedom to carry on diplomatic negotiations with the great powers. These states and France, but not the emperor, became the guarantors of the peace.

The continued economic decline of the German lands, accentuated by the great devastation everywhere, explains why the German merchants and capitalists could not compete with those of western Europe during the seventeenth century. Only slowly did rulers like Frederick William, the Great Elector (1640–1688) of Brandenburg, revive economic prosperity and play significant roles in European affairs.

The destruction and confusion during the many years of war also adversely affected the religion and culture of Germany. Many churches and schools remained leaderless for decades, and the universities lost their previous significance. On the other hand, the Germans now took for granted that members of the Catholic, the Lutheran, and the Reformed faiths could live side by side. Religion became disentangled from political interests and became increasingly a matter of individual conscience, despite the fact that the churches remained under state control.

The continuation of the war outside Germany need not concern us here. Suffice it to state that the rivalry between France and Spain was concluded with the Peace of the Pyrenees in 1659, which marked the beginning of French hegemony in Europe, and the war among Sweden, Poland, and Brandenburg was concluded by the Treaty of Oliva in 1660, which recognized the sovereignty of Brandenburg-Prussia.

## Absolute Monarchies and State Churches

The first half of the seventeenth century witnessed the consolidation of the control of the European states over religious affairs, for rulers with absolutist tendencies found it difficult to envisage a society in which the people did not follow the religion of the sovereign; and they found it to their political advantage to be clothed with divine-right authority. At the same time, the impetus given by the rise of Protestantism to the search for truth in the Bible alone was continued among individuals and groups in defiance of state churches. Where the state control was the strongest, there these dissenters were forced underground or were compelled to seek an asylum elsewhere. In either case, dissent became a powerful religious force, especially in those countries in which it combined with political, social, and economic forces.

## The Monarchies and the Popes

The frequent clashes between the Catholic sovereigns and the popes were a consequence of the desire of the former to develop national state churches and of the latter to maintain ecclesiastical autonomy in all the countries. Despite their growing prestige in religious matters, demonstrated by the fact that three million pilgrims attended the jubilee of the year 1600, the popes played a declining role within the European states and in international affairs.

Pope Paul V (1605–1621), for example, a member of the Borghese family, was compelled to recognize the limitation of his authority in his conflict with the Republic of Venice, whose clergy were subject to state law. Considering himself divinely appointed to free the Church from the authority of the secular states and having successfully carried out such a program in Spain, Naples, Savoy, Genoa, and Lucca, he decided to bring Venice to her knees. He accordingly demanded that the senate of that republic free two clergymen who had been arrested for infractions of the Venetian laws and annul a statute of 1604 that refused the Church the right to establish religious orders or erect religious buildings without permission of the state and another law of 1605 that opposed the alienation of property in mortmain. When the senate refused to comply, Paul V placed it under the ban and the entire republic under the interdict. The senate responded by compelling the clergy to perform their religious functions and expelled the Jesuits from Venetian territory.

Henry IV of France mediated the quarrel, which ended in a compromise in 1607. The senate gave up the two priests, but it refused to readmit the Jesuits and retained in force the laws denounced by Paul V. The pope was compelled to annul the ban and the interdict without having pronounced absolution.

The most vocal defender of the Venetian position during this conflict was Fra Paolo Sarpi (1552–1623), general of the order of the Servites. He denied the secular authority of the papacy and criticized the attempt to exempt the clergy from the laws of the state. So great was the hostility of the papal supporters toward Sarpi that Paul V's nephew, Scipio Cardinal Borghese, sent assassins to liquidate him. He escaped with his life, however, and gave vent to his hatred of the papal *Curia* by writing his *History of the Council of Trent,* published in England in 1619.

The conflict between the papacy and Venice gave a temporary stimulus to the revival of Gallicanism in France. In 1605 Edmond Richer (1560–1631), a professor of theology at the University of Paris, was prevented from publishing the works of Gerson by the papal nuncio. Thereupon he wrote an apology of the great French conciliarist and, in 1607, published his works in three volumes with the protection of the Parlement of Paris. In a subsequent book, *On Ecclesiastical and Political Power,* he maintained that the authority of the Church councils was higher than that of the popes and that the state was independent of the Church in purely temporal matters.

The unfortunate experience of Paul V in the Venetian affair led him to proceed with much more caution. He refused to give his support to the Spanish proposal that the Valtelline Protestants be massacred; and when, later, several hundred were put to death, he gave no sign of approval. Maintaining a position of neutrality in this struggle, he devoted his energies to increasing his family's wealth, beautifying Rome, and enforcing such reforms as episcopal residence. In addition to completing St. Peter's, he erected numerous buildings, including the Palazzo Borghese.

Paul V's successor, the aged Gregory XV (1621–1623), permitted his nephew, Ludovico Cardinal Ludovisio, to control papal affairs. The latter devoted himself assiduously to furthering the interests of his family but also to the support of the Catholic reaction in all Europe. Motivated by a Jesuit spirit, he played a leading role in all the courts of Europe and maintained troops in Germany and in the Valtelline. For the purpose of carrying out a well-organized missionary program, he established, in 1622, the important Congregation for the Propaganda of the Faith. A new law concerning papal elections (1621) bound the members of the conclave to a secret vote. In recognition of the achievements of the Catholic Reformation, Gregory canonized its outstanding leaders: St. Ignatius, St. Francis Xavier, St. Philip Neri, and St. Teresa. Pope Paul V had already canonized St. Charles Borromeo.

Urban VIII (1623–1644), the pope during much of the Thirty Years' War, continued the work of the Catholic Reformation. The breviary, which had been revised by Clement VIII, was put into its present form by Urban. But he also, like Clement, adhered rigidly to the belief in the theocratic sovereignty of the pope, expressed in the Maundy Thursday Bull, which condemned all interference with papal prerogatives on the part of princes, bishops, and councils. Although he maintained a strict formal neutrality among the warring powers, it was no secret that Urban supported France and Sweden in their conflict with Spain and the Empire and that he hoped thereby to break the hold of the Hapsburgs in northern and southern Italy. By engaging in a dangerous political game

—gambling on the ultimate success of France—he was able to add Urbino to the Papal States. To further his interests and those of his nephews, the Barberini, he built up a large military force. This, however, made a miserable showing in a war provoked with the duke of Parma in 1643–1644 by his nephews. Humiliated by this defeat, and seeing the Papal States in want and misery, Urban died a broken man.

Papal influence over international affairs came to an end under Innocent X (1644–1655). Lacking moral strength, this pope was dominated by his ambitious sister-in-law, Donna Olimpia Maldachini, who conducted papal affairs in the interest of Innocent's nephews. Not only did the representatives of the European powers at Münster and Osnabrück refuse to listen to the pope's demand that no peace be made with the Protestants, but Spain and Portugal permitted no more papal interference in their internal affairs. Indicative of the victory of political over religious forces was the general reaction to Innocent's bull, *Zelo domus Dei,* published after the Peace of Westphalia. It declared the treaty null and void and stated that no one who had given an oath to uphold it was bound by the oath. The states of Europe simply disregarded the papal pretension to the right of freeing men from their oaths. Although Innocent, during the jubilee of 1650, voiced his prayers for a reunited Christendom, the Peace of Westphalia had brought the period of the Reformation to a close.

## The Monarchies and the Jesuits

Although the reforming zeal of the papacy seems to have spent itself and Rome again became a brilliant cultural center during the first half of the seventeenth century, other institutions continued to work in the interests of Catholicism. This was particularly true of the Society of Jesus, which stirred the Catholic rulers to action against the Protestants during the Thirty Years' War. In their devotion and zeal, however, the Jesuits aroused considerable opposition among Catholics as well as Protestants, in the first place, because they developed a political philosophy which opposed the growth of absolute monarchies, and, in the second place, because they developed a highly systematized moral casuistry.

Jesuit political thought was based largely upon late-medieval theories concerning natural rights. These they advanced in order to show that the state had derived its authority from the people, whereas the papacy had obtained its authority directly from God. Political opposition to such political thought was strongest among the Catholic supporters of Henry IV of France after the French religious wars and in England during the reign of Elizabeth I. The Jesuits continued to exert a strong influence upon political developments in the seventeenth century, even though they had been instructed by their general in 1602 not to become involved in politics. Later generals not only permitted them this right, but urged them to obtain political advantages for the Society of Jesus and the papacy as court confessors, preachers, tutors of princes, and governmental officials.

## Jesuit Casuistry

Opposition to the Jesuits tended to increase also because they espoused and helped develop a systematic moral theology called casuistry, which was much more considerate of man's weaknesses than the moral theology of the Protestants and the Catholic Jansenists. This casuistry did not originate with the Jesuits; but their scholars, especially in Spain, systematized it with great legal and scholarly skill. It is therefore wrong to state that there developed a distinctly Jesuit moral theology and ethics. To be sure, a few Jesuits, like the compiler Antonio Escobar (d. 1669)— from his name came a new French word, *escobarder,* meaning to "equivocate"—made statements that made the Jesuits vulnerable to serious criticism.

The chief casuist principles developed by the moral theologians since medieval times were the following: probabilism, according to which a confessor might, in questions of lawfulness of action, follow a probable opinion in favor of liberty, even though the opposing view was more probable; laxism, which involved restricting the number of mortal sins to those involving only the infraction of great divine or ecclesiastical laws and committed deliberately; intentionalism, which emphasized the duty of the confessor to inquire concerning the intent of the penitent who had committed a sin; mental reservation, which permitted one to give a promise or an oath an interpretation not of itself obvious; and attrition, a development of the late-medieval doctrine that the fear of punishment and anguish resulting from having committed a sin may be considered a satisfactory penance.

It was in the confessional that the Jesuits employed these principles with astounding results. It is not surprising that they made the hearing of confessions one of the chief functions of the priest and that in their enthusiasm many carried the principles of laxity too far.

The deleterious effects of the lax moral principles became apparent to many Catholics by the middle of the seventeenth century, especially after the bitter attacks of the enemies of the Jesuits. Consequently Pope Alexander VII (1655–1667) condemned probabilism in 1656 and induced the Dominicans and other orders to discontinue the doctrine. Innocent XI (1676–1689) urged the Jesuits to abandon the doctrine and influenced the election of a general who agreed with him. But the society refused to follow either its general or the pope in this matter. Many Jesuits now espoused the most extreme form of the doctrine, called lax probabilism, which obligated the confessor to accept a probable view demanded by a penitent, even if this was contrary to the confessor's conscience.

Most of the bitter attacks upon the Jesuits grew out of envy, fear, or hatred and were pure figments of the imagination. The most notorious collection of such lies is the forgery known as *The Secret Counsels of the Jesuits,* first published in 1612. The most widely used phrase to appear in the anti-Jesuit literature after the beginning of the nineteenth century, that "the end justifies the means," is not found in any of their writings.

## Church and State in France

The best example of the triumph of the absolute state over the church is found in France. The work of Henry IV was systematically continued by Jean Armand du Plessis, duke of Richelieu, bishop of Luçon, and a cardinal, who was the chief minister of Louis XIII (1610–1643) from 1624 to 1642. He was one of the few statesmen of his day who forbade the Jesuits to interfere in governmental affairs.

Because the Huguenots, given political as well as civil and religious rights by the Edict of Nantes, constituted an armed corporation, or state within a state, they were joined by those internal forces that were opposed to the growth of royal absolutism. Richelieu, whose main purpose it was to strengthen the monarchy, waged a bitter conflict with the Huguenots and, in 1628, finally took their last fortified place, La Rochelle. The Peace of Alais of 1629, which concluded the last of the religious wars in France, deprived the Huguenots of all their political and military rights but reaffirmed the civil and religious rights granted by the Edict of Nantes. Thereafter the Huguenots, purged of political opportunists, became strong supporters of the monarchy. By their industry and skill they contributed greatly to the economic progress of France.

The growth of royal absolutism was continued under Cardinal Mazarin, regent of Louis XIV (1643–1715) from 1643 to 1661. When the upper nobility made a final attempt to stem this tide in the revolts of the Fronde (1648–1652), the Huguenots refused to participate and were praised for their loyalty by a royal proclamation at the close of the struggle. They retained their special religious status and for a number of years made notable contributions to Protestant theology and the spiritual life of France in general. Their chief intellectual centers were their schools at Saumer, Montauban, and Sedan. At their national synods, the last of which was held in 1659, attempts were made to establish uniformity of doctrine and practice.

With the conclusion of the war between France and Spain by the Peace of the Pyrenees in 1659 and the death of Mazarin in 1661, Louis XIV assumed complete control of France. Thoroughly imbued with the spirit of "one God, one king, one faith," he followed the advice of the Jesuits and began to persecute the Huguenots by various means. Finally, by the revocation of the Edict of Nantes in 1685, he forced them to become Catholic or leave the country.

French Catholicism, which had felt the impact of the Catholic Reformation almost from its beginnings, continued to show evidences of renewed spiritual life. But it also reflected a strong antipapal strain in its revived Gallicanism, which reached a climax in the conflict between Louis XIV and the papacy. It found its most outspoken expression in an edict of 1682, called Four Articles on the Liberties of the Gallican Church, drawn up by Bossuet, approved by the national assembly of the French clergy, accepted by the Sorbonne, and registered by the French parlements. According to these articles: (1) The pope's authority is restricted to purely spiritual matters. (2) The ultimate authority in spiritual matters is the general Church council. (3) The pope must respect the customs and treaties of the Gallican Church. (4) Papal decisions in matters of faith are binding only with the approval of the Church—probably meaning the general Church council.

Louis XIV may have had in mind the creation of a strictly national church in France, similar to that of Henry VIII in England; yet he found it to his advantage not to break with the papacy. He finally agreed not to enforce the articles, although they remained the law of the land, and seemed satisfied with extending to all France the *régale,* that is, the right to administer vacant bishoprics and appoint the lower clergy to their benefices during such vacancies. It was this demand that had originally started the struggle.

### Jansenism

Gallican principles were also strong in Jansenism, a puritanical movement within Catholicism that had originated in the Spanish Netherlands and had taken its name from Cornelius Jansen (1585–1638). It reflected the strong reaction of a number of pious representatives of the bourgeois class against the prevalent secularism and religious indifference in seventeenth-century French Catholicism.

Jansen was a professor of the Bible at the University of Louvain, where a strong anti-Jesuit spirit had long prevailed. He was particularly influenced by the works of Augustine, from which he developed his doctrine of two kinds of grace: the common grace, which is given to all men and enables them to do good; and the higher kind of grace, which is given only to the elect and is virtually irresistible. God thus freely and arbitrarily predestines some men to eternal salvation, others to eternal damnation. Like the Puritans of his day, he demanded that Christians lead strict, exemplary lives. He opposed not only all kinds of sensuality but even scientific curiosity and worldly ambition. These doctrines were given forceful expression in his many writings, published posthumously under the title *Augustinus* (1640), and exerted a strong influence upon his followers, particularly after the Jesuits had purported to find a number of heresies in it. Jansen himself died in good repute as the bishop of Ypres.

435

# Part Four: Religious Conflicts and Consequences

The emergence of Jansenism was to a large extent the work of Jansen's close friend, Jean du Vergier de Hauranne (1581–1643), a native of Bayonne and abbot of St. Cyran. Vergier first aroused the hostility of the Jesuits by publishing a work written by a nephew with the title *The Ecclesiastical Hierarchy*, published in Paris in 1631. In it the episcopal organization was defended on the basis of the Bible and the Church fathers in opposition to the highly centralized papal authority supported by the Jesuits.

In 1632 Vergier went to Paris, but he remained in constant contact with Jansen, with whom he had vowed to reform the Church. A few years later he became the spiritual adviser of the nuns of the Cistercian convent of Port Royal des Champs near Versailles. The abbess of this convent was the daughter of Antoine Arnauld, an advocate who had delivered a strong address against the Jesuits in the Parlement of Paris in 1594. During the decade in which these nuns resided in new quarters in Paris (1626–1636), the abbess's brothers, including the young Antoine Arnauld (1612–1694) and several other earnest men of high social position, lay as well as clerical, established a society in the old monastic buildings of the nuns. There these *solitaires,* as they called themselves, sought refuge from the immorality and corruption of Paris. They engaged in meditation, studied the lives of the hermits whom they imitated, read and discussed the Bible and the works of Augustine, cultivated gardens, and taught young boys in schools that soon rivaled those of the Jesuits. The nuns who returned to Port Royal in 1636 added a strongly emotional element to the movement and remained its most loyal proponents in times of persecution.

Vergier became the guiding spirit of this group of *solitaires* and imbued them with the doctrines and puritanical ideas of Jansen. When he was imprisoned by Richelieu, whose personal displeasure he had incurred, his mantle fell upon the shoulders of Antoine Arnauld. In 1543 Arnauld published his *On the Frequency of Communion,* in which he criticized the Jesuit emphasis upon frequent confessions and attendance at Communion, and especially the Jesuit principle of attritionism. The Jesuits countered by calling all *solitaires* Jansenists, or heretics. In the ensuing controversy the *solitaires* admitted that they were Jansenists but denied that they were heretics.

In 1653 Innocent X, seeing his opportunity to divide the French Gallicans, formally condemned as heretical five propositions of the *Augustinus:* (1) that not even good men can carry out certain commands of God; (2) that man cannot resist divine grace; (3) that freedom from compulsion, but not freedom from necessity, is required for meriting reward of punishment in man's fallen state; (4) that it is semi-Pelagian heresy to hold that man can freely accept or resist grace; and (5) that it is semi-Pelagian heresy to state that Christ died for all, not for only the elect.

# 11. The Secularization of the European States

Arnauld answered that the pope, infallible in matters of doctrine, had the right to condemn such propositions as heretical but that the pope could and did err in matters of fact; that in this case he had erred in declaring that Jansen had taught the enumerated propositions. The Jansenists accepted this solution. But in 1656 both the Sorbonne, to which the question of fact had been referred, and Pope Alexander VII declared that these propositions had been held by Jansen.

Jansenism might have died out at this time if it had not been for the fact that Blaise Pascal (1623–1662), the eminent mathematician and physicist, now took up the cause and presented it forcibly to the people. In his *Letters to a Provincial* (1656–1657), a series of essays famous for their lucidity of thought, clever wit, and beauty of expression, he submitted the moral principles and doctrine of heresy of the Jesuits to a withering attack that was enjoyed by a large reading public.

So effective were the attacks of Pascal, although based upon a misunderstanding and misinterpretation of his sources, that the Jesuits appealed to Louis for help. This he was glad to give, for he considered the Jansenists treasonous for having supported some of the leaders of the Fronde. The Jansenists were given the alternative of adhering to the papal decree of 1653 or being dealt with as heretics. The persecution continued for eight years. In 1668 the Jansenist bishops agreed in ambiguous phraseology to accept the decree, and the next year Louis established peace in the church by proclaiming the *Pax Clementina*.

Thereafter the Jansenists used their "golden pens" primarily against Protestants and freethinkers, until 1679, when they aroused the anger of the king by supporting the independence of the bishops in the conflict over the *régale*. The crisis came in 1701, when Pasquier Quesnel, now the leader of the Jansenists, declared that "the five articles" were not to be found in the *Augustinus* of Jansen. With the support of a papal bull, the government expelled the nuns from Port Royal, destroyed the buildings of the Jansenists, and imprisoned or drove into exile their leaders. In 1713 the papal bull *Unigenitus* condemned as heretical 101 propositions held by Quesnel and his followers. Jansenism, however, did not disappear entirely. It was partially responsible for the state of public opinion that in 1762 helped force the expulsion of the Jesuits from France.

In the final analysis, both the Jesuits and the Jansenists lost ground in their struggle with each other. The victors were the king, who succeeded in establishing a divine-right absolute state that permitted no interference in political affairs, and the rationalists, who were inclined to accept the accusations and question the claims of both sides. The secularization of culture accompanied the growth of absolute monarchies. Nowhere was this more evident than in France, whose bureaucratically administered absolute monarchy became the ideal of monarchs throughout Europe.

*437*

# Protestant State Churches and Dissenters

It was difficult for the governments of the Protestant countries to contain dissenters. Reasons for this are to be found primarily in the nature of Protestantism itself. Although neither Luther nor Calvin treated religion as a subjective matter or taught religious individualism, their basic doctrines of justification by faith alone, the Bible as sole authority, and the universal priesthood of believers encouraged the development of a personal approach to religion and led to basic differences among their respective followers. Eventually, however, political and economic matters gradually took precedence over the religious in the thought and action of the rulers, and growing antipathy to religious controversy encouraged skepticism.

## The Lutheran Churches

In the Lutheran lands of Germany the princes retained their control over their state churches with relatively little opposition from dissenting groups. Lutheranism continued to develop along the orthodox lines apparent after the acceptance of the Formula of Concord in 1580; but interpretive studies of this doctrinal statement appeared in large numbers and resulted in bitter polemics.

Although great emphasis was placed upon the importance of the Lutheran confessions, the theologians of the first half of the seventeenth century did not lose sight of the prior importance of the Bible as the Word of God and accordingly devoted considerable attention to defining the doctrine of biblical inspiration. On the other hand, they did not ignore the practical religious problems of their day. Using Melanchthon's doctrine concerning natural law as a starting point, they developed the dogma of satisfaction, their most important contribution to the study of theology. Even though they used Aristotelian methods—metaphysical rather than rhetorical—their neoscholasticism was not yet stultified by logical formalism and artificiality, as was the case in the "high orthodoxy" of the latter half of the century.

The influences of Erasmian and Melanchthonian humanism were active at only a few Lutheran universities, notably at Helmstedt in Brunswick. There Georg Calixtus (1586–1656) taught a kind of syncretism that minimized the importance of Reformation confessions by distinguishing between fundamentals and nonfundamentals, and he emphasized the importance of a eudaemonistic morality that would lead man to eternal happiness. His doctrines touched off the bitter Syncretistic Controversy, which did not end with his death but continued to divide Lutheran theologians for about three decades.

The Lutheran princes supported the clergy in the development of a religious education not only in doctrine but in ethics, for certainty of salvation and Christian comfort were greatly needed during the period of the Counter Reformation and the Thirty Years' War. Thus the theologians combined dogmatics and practical piety with many commendable results. The attempt to make the certainty of salvation demonstrable, however, led to a rationalization that tended to relegate to the background Luther's dynamic doctrine of justification by faith alone. In other words, people were taught both doctrines and ethics, but their teachers, servants of states that were becoming secularized, failed to awaken in them the originally strong evangelical piety of the early Lutherans.

This weakness in Lutheran education led to the infiltration of many elements of late-medieval mysticism and natural philosophy, as seen in the many fine hymns and books of devotion of that time. There are also evidences of the influence of Jesuit meditation and self-examination. Good examples of the new mystical tendencies are found in the works of Jakob Böhme (d. 1624), the philosopher-shoemaker of Görlitz in Silesia, and Johann Arndt (d. 1621), the general superintendent of Celle.

Böhme added to his basically Lutheran doctrines thoughts gleaned from Paracelsus and Schwenkfeld and especially subjective ideas derived from his own practical, mystical speculations. He probably developed the doctrine of the inner light of the mystics further than any of his contemporaries. One of the first of his accounts of his mystical experiences was the *Aurora,* published in 1612. In this he pictured God as the great creative being who sends up into the world from the *Ungrund,* or original abyss, forces such as love that enable it to survive. Man cannot comprehend God unless he has experienced a rebirth. The world in which he lives will pass through several stages, in the last of which good will triumph over evil. Böhme's many followers in England later merged with the Quakers.

The works of Arndt, who had studied medicine as well as theology, show an even greater religious eclecticism than those of Böhme. In his widely read and influential *Four Books Concerning True Christianity* and in his other writings are found extracts from the works of the Renaissance Neoplatonists, the *Natural Theology* of the scholastic Raymond of Sabunde, *A German Theology* of an unknown German mystic, the *Imitation of Christ* of the Brethren of the Common Life, and *The Love of God* of Staupitz. The works of these men and others of similar leanings helped prepare the way for the strong German reaction to Lutheran orthodoxy as expressed in both the Enlightenment and Pietism.

Because of the sharp criticisms of Lutheran orthodoxy by the liberal theologians of a later day, it is easy to overlook the deep spirituality and piety of many of its proponents. Even though they were inclined to place the confessions on a par with the Bible, they rendered a great service to Protestantism by calling attention to the basic, dynamic Lutheran doctrine of salvation by faith alone and defending it against both syncretism and rationalism. One of the staunchest defenders of orthodoxy, Paul Gerhardt (1607–1676), put his doctrines into hymns that are still considered among the choicest gems of Protestantism. Men like Johann Valentin Andreae (1586–1654), a widely traveled court preacher, urged the adoption of the successful practices of non-Lutheran church bodies, stressed the fundamental unity of all Christians, anticipated some of the pedagogical principles of Comenius by opposing formal dialectics and stressing the importance of the religious views of individuals, recognized the spiritual value of ascetic contemplation, and took an interest in sports, court life, and other affairs of this world. Orthodoxy was not necessarily synonymous with sterility.

## The Reformed Churches

The Reformed churches, most of which looked to the United Provinces for leadership, experienced tendencies similar to those of the Lutheran churches. In the United Provinces, however, political circumstances were such that a greater divergence of religious views could develop, despite the state recognition of a strictly orthodox Calvinism.

Although Maurice of Nassau (1567–1625) and Johan van Oldenbarnevelt (1547–1619) continued for a number of years to cooperate in the management of the affairs of state, they soon began to reflect fundamentally contrary views in both politics and religion. Maurice had been granted certain duties connected with the previous monarchical rule, such as appointing important state officials and supervising justice. Because he also maintained a court at The Hague, though at his own expense, he satisfied the desire of the nobility and the majority of the people for certain monarchical trappings.

Oldenbarnevelt, on the other hand, the representative of the patricians of Holland, ultimately reflected the interests of the patricians throughout the republic. During the war, he interfered constantly in the military affairs of Maurice and, in concluding the truce with Spain, acted contrary to the wishes of Maurice and those nobles who did not want to stop fighting until Spain had been thoroughly beaten and all the provinces had been brought into the republic.

The division of the two leaders over religious matters is more difficult to understand. Under Oldenbarnevelt's leadership the patricians had, by 1591, virtually all been induced to adhere to the Calvinist confession of faith, especially because Catholicism was identified with pro-Spanish sentiments. Thenceforth Calvinism was the only recognized religion, despite the fact that nearly half of the population had remained Catholic during the wars of liberation. By a policy of neglect on the part of the Catholic Church, most of the people were eventually brought into the Reformed Church.

Within Dutch Calvinism, however, a sharp division eventually became apparent. Under the leadership of Jacobus Arminius (1560–1609), who had become a professor at Leyden through the influence of Oldenbarnevelt, there developed a liberal Calvinism that contained much of Erasmian piety and Netherlandish mysticism and was greatly influenced by the humanist theology of the Italians Acontius and Castellio. The humanistically trained patricians, who had adapted themselves to Calvinism, supported this trend.

After the death of Arminius, Johan Wtenbogaert (1577–1644), theological adviser of Oldenbarnevelt and once the court preacher of Maurice, assumed the leadership of the Arminians. He was responsible for presenting to the Estates of West Friesland and Holland the Remonstrance (1610) of this group, in which they expressed their objection, among other things, to the rigid Calvinist doctrine of predestination. This Remonstrance gave the party its name—the Remonstrants.

The strictly orthodox Calvinists, comprising the broad masses of townsmen, were led by another professor at Leyden, Franciscus Gomarus (1563–1641). The orthodoxy of Gomarus went so far as to include the most extreme form of predestination, known as supralapsarianism, or the doctrine that even the fall of man was foreordained by God. The reply of the Gomarists to the Remonstrants was given in a Counter Remonstrance. It was this party of Counter Remonstrants, representing the majority of the clergy, that insisted upon the calling of a national synod to solve the doctrinal problems dividing the Calvinists.

This religious conflict took on a political complexion when Oldenbarnevelt and the patricians publicly came to the support of the Remonstrants, who had no strong objections to the state control of the church and were not inclined to apply the rigid discipline of Calvin's Geneva to the United Provinces. Although Maurice, like his father, was indifferent to theological matters, he finally, about 1616, became involved on the side of the Counter Remonstrants. All those joined him who opposed the oligarchical control of the patricians. This was particularly true of the lower classes, who were strict Calvinists. The political problem, then, reduced itself to the question whether the patricians should retain control of the state through their provincial estates or whether a more centralized monarchical form should take its place. The political-religious problem reduced itself to the question whether or not a national synod should be held.

Meanwhile the Twelve Years' Truce was running out and preparations were being made for a religious war in Germany. Not only religious enthusiasm but a desire for the increased trade that accompanies war led to an enthusiasm for war in the United Provinces, supported by Maurice. Opposition to this enthusiasm further isolated Oldenbarnevelt. By urging Holland, where he had the strongest support, to raise troops against the Counter Remonstrants and Prince Maurice, he took the fatal step that gave Maurice an opportunity to attack him. After a lengthy trial by a court consisting of his enemies, Oldenbarnevelt was unjustly accused of disloyalty and was beheaded (May, 1619). One of his supporters, Hugo Grotius, was sentenced to life imprisonment, but he escaped with the aid of his wife two years later. Maurice of Nassau now ruled with undisputed authority.

During the trial of Oldenbarnevelt and his followers, the national synod, which they had opposed, assembled at Dort (Dordrecht) on November 13, 1618. Its many sessions lasted until May 29, 1619. Of the more than one hundred representatives, twenty-seven came from Calvinist churches in other countries, including Germany, Switzerland, the Palatinate, England, and Scotland. The Remonstrants were condemned as heretics and the respective provincial synods and local presbyteries were ordered to remove them from offices. The Heidelberg Catechism was declared the authoritative Reformed statement of doctrine. Provision was made for a new translation of the Bible. Teachers were compelled to teach religion in the lower schools. The clergy were to receive systematic theological training. The doctrine of predestination was reaffirmed, although not in its supralapsarian form. In the last session, in which only the representatives of the United Provinces took a part, no agreement was reached with respect to a constitution or a uniform order of service. The estates-general retained the right to approve the calling of future synods and to supervise them by means of its own commission. The estates of most of the provinces, however, retained control of their own churches, and no second national synod was ever called.

The doctrines agreed upon at the Synod of Dort were rigidly adhered to by the official church and interpreted by scholastic methods by its chief theologians. Yet, as in German orthodoxy, there was a growth of a strong popular piety and an increasing interest in Christian ethics.

Religious groups outside the state church continued to develop their doctrines and practices. The Remonstrants, for example, condemned as heretics at the Synod of Dort, met at Antwerp in the fall of 1619, and laid the basis for a "Remonstrance-Reformed Brotherhood," for which Simon Episcopius (d. 1643) wrote a confession. They first settled in Brabant, France, and Silesia; but many of them returned to the United Provinces when Maurice died and was succeeded by his brother Frederick Henry of Orange (1625–1647). The latter realized that a rigid orthodoxy was just as impossible in his country as a highly centralized monarchy. The representatives of too many faiths and philosophies, including those of Portuguese and Spanish Jews, had found refuge there. The upshot of the bitter struggle over Calvinism was in the long run an official tolerance, the first in a European state.

Under the leadership of Episcopius and his successors, a seminary was established at Amsterdam where the basic tenets of Arminianism were developed. The Arminians held that reason and faith should not contradict each other; the doctrine of the Trinity was not of great importance; Christ's death was not a satisfaction for the sins of others but an example of God's punishment of sin; and the sacraments were merely signs of a communion of believers to be used in strengthening faith. These views later exerted a strong influence upon the development of both deism and Pietism.

At Rhynsburg a group of returning Remonstrants was induced by Gÿsbert van der Codde, a layman, to establish a congregation without pastors and without a confession, in which the members spoke freely about the "apostolic truth" as the spirit moved them. These Collegiants, as they were called, baptized their members by immersion into "the universal church." Although this congregation remained small, it influenced both Rhenish Pietism and English Baptism.

Arminianism also influenced an English religious movement called Latitudinarianism, a position midway between strict Calvinism and Anglicanism, in which there was little emphasis upon doctrines. The best-known Latitudinarians were William Chillingsworth (d. 1644) and Jeremy Taylor (d. 1667), who wished to reduce Christianity to a few basic doctrines. They even defended the Socinians, who were then being driven from Poland.

Arminian and Socinian doctrines also influenced some of the Mennonite congregations, which were revived and reunited during the period of toleration following the Synod of Dort. Confessional writings appeared that were intended not to provide doctrinal uniformity but to affect mutual understanding. There appeared, especially among the more liberal groups, a fine spiritual literature and hymnology in which personal piety and ascetic mysticism found beautiful expression. The Mennonites exerted their strongest influence upon the development of English Baptism through John Smyth (d. 1612), whose congregation in the United Provinces became the mother congregation of one founded in London.

The Reformed churches of Germany felt the impact not only of the orthodoxy but of the pietistic tendencies of the United Provinces, stimulated by outstanding scholars. Furthermore, they maintained contacts with the Lutheran churches of Germany, and a number of their theologians and princes furthered an interest in the union of the two Protestant groups. This movement was particularly strong at the University of Heidelberg, where Lutheran professors now taught alongside the Calvinist.

Pietistic and union tendencies were reflected in the writing of Reformed hymns, which, like the Lutheran hymns, reached a high point at this time. In 1653 there appeared in Berlin the Runge collection of hymns, the publication of which was sponsored by the Dutch-born Luise Henriette (1627–1667) of Brandenburg, the first wife of the Great Elector. She was the writer of the well-known hymn "Jesus, My Redeemer,

Lives." One of the most successful Reformed composers of hymns was Joachim Neander (1650–1680), whose "Praise Thou the Lord, the Omnipotent Monarch of Glory," "Jesus, Brightness of the Father," and "Open Thou Thy Gates of Beauty" are still found in many Protestant hymnals.

## The Anglican Church Under James I

Protestantism in England, as in the United Provinces, became deeply involved in the political and economic struggles of the seventeenth century. However, whereas Dutch dissent was allayed after the Synod of Dort, English dissent, in the form of Puritanism, became closely allied with the growth of a revolutionary parliamentarianism. But by so doing it lost much of its original vigor and international solidarity and split up into many segments; yet it continued to make valuable contributions to western civilization, particularly in the British colonies in North America.

Opposition to the moderate Elizabethan Settlement continued to grow during the life of the queen, became intensified under the rule of James I (1603–1625), and was one of the most important forces leading to the decapitation of Charles I (1625–1649). Although Elizabeth I, in true Tudor fashion, had understood how to manage the vigorous forces of Puritanism, parliamentarianism, and commercialism and thus retained control over the religious, political, and economic affairs of England, her Stuart successors seemed to ignore these forces in their attempts to govern by divine-right authority.

Apparently oblivious to the fact that the English people considered their rulers bound to respect the common law and the rights of Parliament, the first two Stuarts provoked a civil war that ended by curtailing the authority of the monarch both in theory and in fact. In religious affairs this meant the desertion of the moderate policy of Elizabeth I, which permitted religious heterogeneity as long as there was outward conformity, and the development of a conservative Episcopalianism, called High-Church Anglicanism after 1662, that sought to maintain absolute uniformity of discipline under a theocratically inclined monarch.

James I, son of Queen Mary of Scotland and king of that country as James VI (1567–1625) since his infancy, had given expression to his theocratic views and divine-right pretensions in his *Trew Law of Free Monarchies,* published in 1598. The "free monarchy," he maintained, was created by God through lawful descent, free from all control, and responsible only to God. James considered himself not only God's lieutenant but "an image of God on earth, a god sitting upon God's throne, and called a god by God himself." Defiance of a king, even of a tyrant, was both sacrilege and blasphemy.

Because James was well educated in humanist and patristic literature and in Calvinist theology and because he had sworn to uphold the Presbyterian Church in Scotland, the Puritans had reason to believe that he might be sympathetic to their desire to simplify the Anglican services. Accordingly a number of the Puritan clergy drew up the so-called Millenary Petition, requesting the abolition of such practices as making the sign of the cross and giving the ring in marriage, and making optional others, such as wearing the cap and surplice. This moderate petition was submitted to the king on his way to London.

James, who enjoyed religious discussion, called a conference of the heads of the church and four Puritans to meet under his presidency at Hampton Court in January, 1604. Although he was in agreement with most of the English clergy with respect to theology, he had had such humiliating experiences at the hands of the Presbyterian divines in Scotland that he was determined to uphold the episcopal system of the Anglican Church. Instead of the Presbyterian system and the tendency of the Calvinist clergy to interfere in the affairs of the state, James preferred the English custom of having the king appoint the bishops and rule the church through them. Therefore, when one of the Puritan divines suggested changes in church government, James gave a lengthy discourse on the subject in which he uttered the famous phrase "No bishop, no king," and made the threat that he would make the Puritans conform or "harry them out of the land."

Although the Hampton Court Conference resulted in a number of minor changes in liturgy and in the appointment of a commission to make a new translation of the Bible, it proved highly disappointing to the Puritans and increased the cleavage between them and the supporters of the Anglican system. The translation of the Bible, made by a committee of more than fifty scholars, was completed in 1611 and came to be known as the Authorized (King James) Version. Convocation in 1604 adopted 161 new canons, confirmed by the king, which codified existing practices, incorporated some additions, and threatened with excommunication those who questioned the apostolic character of the church, the office of the bishop, the Thirty-nine Articles, or the liturgy.

Whereas the Puritans stressed strict conformity to Calvinist doctrines and minimized the importance of ceremonies, their opponents, the High-Church royalists, looked upon the episcopal system as a divine institution (*jure divino*) and tended to become indifferent toward doctrine. Most of them rejected the Calvinist doctrine of predestination for, in their eyes, it tended to weaken the authority of the church as an instrument of grace. For this reason they were erroneously called Arminians. Among the most influential Anglicans was William Laud (1573–1645). From the beginning opposed to the Puritan conception of church government, Laud developed extreme views concerning the necessity of uniformity in the observance of the episcopal system. But he became so enamored with traditional observances that only his reluctance to accept the pope as the ultimate religious authority prevented him from becoming a Catholic.

It was Laud who advised James in the reintroduction of the episcopal system in Scotland, a task that he had begun in 1599 and did not complete until 1612. Bishops replaced the moderators at the head of the provincial synods, with the right to ordain the clergy and administer the affairs of the synods and the presbyteries. Although James proceeded with caution, Scottish Calvinism was vigorously opposed to his policies and became more than ever identified with Scottish nationalism.

## The Puritans

The disappointment of the Puritans with the announced opposition of James had a number of important consequences. In the first place, it tended to increase the number of extremists, or Separatists, some of whom began to migrate from England. One such congregation at Scrooby in Nottinghamshire first fled to Leyden in the United Provinces in 1607–1608. Feeling ill at ease in their new home, especially after the Synod of Dort, this congregation obtained from the Virginia Company a grant of land in Virginia. The *Mayflower,* on which these "Pilgrim Fathers" sailed in 1620, ran out of her course and landed on the shores of Cape Cod Bay, where, on the basis of the Mayflower Compact, they set up a government by the right of squatter sovereignty, for the land was beyond the jurisdiction of the Virginia Company. The Plymouth colony, which they established, was based upon the democracy of their congregational form of church government and played an important part in the development of political democracy in the New World.

In the second place, the Puritan zeal in maintaining a high degree of moral conduct was greatly accentuated by the worldliness of many Anglican divines. In 1618, for example, the king published the *Book of Sports,* which the clergy were asked to read to their people. It recommended the continuation of such Sunday amusements as dancing, attending harlequinades, and participating in sports. As a consequence, the Puritans stressed more than ever the importance of "keeping the Sabbath holy."

In the third place, many Puritans began to make cause with the political opponents of divine-right absolutism and provided them with political theories that gave the revolutionary movement under Charles I much of its dynamic character. The ideas concerning popular sovereignty, the social contract, and the right to resist a tyrant, developed by the Calvinists after the St. Bartholomew Massacre, were revived and adapted to the English scene.

## English Catholicism

The English Catholics were, like the Puritans, destined to disappointment. They had expected much from the son of Mary Stuart, especially because he, immediately upon his accession, sought Pope Clement VIII's support in England and negotiated with Catholic Spain in the interest of peace. He had demonstrated his good will toward the English Catholics by relaxing the penal laws against them and concluding peace with Spain in 1604.

James, however, soon learned that he could obtain no support from the pope without submitting to his religious authority. James also became alarmed over the fact that the number of recusants greatly increased after the relaxation of the penal laws. For these reasons, and because he wanted the support of the Parliament that was soon to meet, James, in February, 1604, ordered Catholic priests banished. Later, Parliament reinforced the laws against the Catholics, and the justices soon began to put them into effect. Several Catholics were executed.

These actions led to the attempt of a number of Catholic hotheads to blow up Parliament while both houses, the king, his eldest son, and the royal council assembled on November 5, 1605. This Gunpowder Plot had been so long in the making, and its secret had been shared by so many persons, that the government learned of it in time, discovered the vast amount of gunpowder placed in the basement of the Parliament buildings, and ferreted out the leaders. They were promptly tried and executed. The celebration of Guy Fawkes' Day—named after one of the plotters—as a national holiday annually for more than two hundred years served to intensify the hatred of Catholicism in England.

The Gunpowder Plot gave the opponents of Catholicism an opportunity to punish all Catholics for the crime of a few. In 1606 Parliament passed a severe law against the recusants and another imposing upon all Catholics a new oath of allegiance that declared that the pope did not have the right to depose the English king or authorize English subjects to take up arms against him. Although these severe laws were not enforced, the Catholics deeply resented their existence, whereas the Protestants, particularly the Puritans, criticized the king for his leniency.

In foreign affairs, James I hoped to keep a foot in both the Catholic and the Protestant camps and thereby maintain peace. After making peace with Spain in 1604, he tried to make an alliance with that country by marrying his eldest son, Henry, to the Spanish infanta. When that scheme was nullified by Henry's death in 1612, James continued the negotiations, now for a marriage between his remaining son, Charles, and another daughter of the Spanish king. When this failed, Charles was married to Henrietta Maria, sister of Louis XIII of France (1624). The clever Richelieu included in the treaty of alliance a secret article pledging James to relax the penal laws against the recusants, even though the king had promised Parliament that he would not do so.

The French marriage treaty, like the earlier marriage of James' daughter, the Princess Elizabeth, to Elector Frederick of the Palatinate (1613), helped involve England in the Thirty Years' War on the Protestant side. Although a majority of the members of Parliament approved of this step, they took advantage of the king's need for money by demanding his recognition of basic constitutional rights.

In the many struggles between James and Parliament over foreign affairs, the recusancy laws, constitutional rights, the king's use of "benevolences," or forced loans, to supplement his inadequate income, and the granting of royal monopolies to favorites, the tensions mounted until, at the time of the king's death in 1625, the majority of the people were in a rebellious mood. He bequeathed this legacy, together with an empty treasury, to his son, Charles.

## The Puritan Revolution

Charles I did not have the ability to solve the many problems inherited from his father. Although he was regal in his bearing, frugal in his expenditures, sincere in his religious convictions, and cultured in his tastes, he lacked those qualities of statesmanship necessary to harness the dynamic forces of the England of his day. Like James, he failed to gauge the strength of Puritanism, offended the majority of the members of Parliament with his conception of divine-right monarchy, and alienated the merchant classes by the granting of monopolies. He went much further than his father in ignoring widely accepted principles of common law, defying the growing importance of the House of Commons, and raising money by irregular means. To make matters worse, he ruled through unpopular court favorites, such as the vain and ambitious duke of Buckingham.

Although the Puritans had not been actively persecuted during the reign of James, their demands for religious concessions had not been met, and the many conflicts with the High-Church party had helped to consolidate them. Moreover, their zealous observance of Bible reading and private services led to a spread of their religious views. During the first years of the reign of Charles, their opposition to the king was intensified by a number of tendencies and incidents. For one thing, Charles openly supported the High-Church party, and his queen insisted upon the right to worship freely in her Catholic religion and berated the king for not making the concessions to the recusants that had been promised in the marriage alliance. Furthermore, the attempt of Charles and Buckingham to induce Richelieu to join in a grand Protestant alliance had failed, and the affairs of the continental Protestants went from bad to worse, reaching nadir in the Edict of Restitution of 1629. Six poorly conceived and poorly executed military expeditions to the Continent ended in failure, arousing the resentment of the Puritans, and also the national feeling of most Englishmen.

In these circumstances Charles found it difficult to obtain from Par-

# King Charles I of England

*by  Van  Dyck*

200 MILES

# THE
# BRITISH ISLES
## DURING THE
# CIVIL WAR
# 1642-1649

DEE R.

• Aberdeen

Scone •
Perth •

Glasgow • Edinburgh
×
Dunbar
×

Philiphaugh
×

TYNE R.

Carlisle •

TEES R.

Londonderry •

Marston
Moor ×
York

Manchester •

HUMBER R.

Drogheda •

Gainsborough •

Dublin •

Chester •

Nottingham •

SEVERN R.

× Naseby

Edge
Hill
×

Cambridge •

Wexford •

Worcester •
×

× Cropredy Bridge

Gloucester •

Oxford
×

Chalgrove
×

LONDON •

THAMES R.

Bristol •
Roundway
Down
×

× Newbury
Basing

Canterbury •

• Dover

Exeter •
Plymouth •

DISTRICTS HELD BY PARLIAMENT

AT THE OPENING
OF THE CIVIL WAR

DISTRICTS HELD BY CHARLES I

TRM

450

liament the funds needed for meeting the expenses of governing a growing country and carrying on his costly ventures abroad. The House of Commons of this first Parliament, which was dominated by enemies of the king, showed its distrust of him by granting him an utterly inadequate sum of money and devoting most of the time to discussing grievances and criticizing Buckingham. To prevent further discussions, the king dissolved the first Parliament. The second, which met in 1626, went even further than the first by drawing up articles of impeachment against Buckingham. To prevent the impeachment, Charles dissolved this Parliament also, without having obtained the grant of money that had been resolved upon by the House of Commons.

Desperate because of his lack of funds, Charles sought to supplement his income by resorting to extensive borrowing, levying tonnage and poundage without parliamentary authority, securing "free gifts" of the amounts that the parliamentary grant would have allowed him, and exacting a forced loan. He also attempted to provide for his troops by quartering them in English homes. Such high-handed acts intensified opposition. A large number of gentlemen, including Puritan leaders in the House of Commons, refused to make the loan or give money to the king and were imprisoned.

## The Petition of Right

Because Charles could not obtain sufficient income by such means, he decided to free all these prisoners and call his third Parliament, which met in March, 1628. The members of the House of Commons, however, made the granting of subsidies conditional upon the king's acceptance of a petition, called the Petition of Right. To this the king finally acceded, although he looked upon it as granting no new liberties. It stipulated (1) that no man be compelled to make any "gift, loan, benevolence, tax, or such like charge" without the consent of Parliament; (2) that no free man be imprisoned or detained without cause shown; (3) that the billeting of soldiers and sailors in private homes in time of peace cease; and (4) that commissions to execute martial law be revoked. As an important step in the development of political and religious liberty, this document— although its immediate effects were negligible—deserves to be placed alongside the Magna Carta and the Bill of Rights, for it implied an important constitutional change, a limitation upon the monarchy of revolutionary significance.

The Petition of Right left for later decision two important questions: the right of the king to levy tonnage and poundage without consent of Parliament and the ultimate authority in religious matters. No sooner had the petition been granted than the House of Commons made the requested grants; but it then turned to other grievances. In a sharp remonstrance it insisted upon the enforcement of the penal laws, attacked the High-Church party, and demanded the removal of Buckingham. When it then began to draw up a remonstrance stating that tonnage and poundage could not be levied without parliamentary consent, Charles prorogued Parliament.

The murder of Buckingham removed one great grievance of the House of Commons, but Sir Thomas Wentworth, a more able opponent of Puritanism and parliamentary supremacy, took his place as the chief adviser to the king. The religious issue reached a climax when Charles sought to protect his High-Church supporters by his Declaration of 1628. In it he forbade the discussion of church questions and stated that all religious changes should be made solely in Convocation with royal approval. When Parliament met again in January, 1629, the House of Commons passed three important resolutions to the effect that those persons should be considered capital enemies of the country who (1) introduced religious innovations that would bring in "popery or Arminianism," (2) advised the levying of tonnage and poundage without the consent of Parliament, or (3) paid tonnage and poundage not granted by Parliament. The passage of these bills was followed by the king's adjournment of Parliament and eleven years of personal government (1629–1640).

## Personal Government of Charles I

The gentry and the merchants, among whom the Puritans had found the most supporters, now had no opportunity to express their opposition by legal means. Consequently their pent-up grievances accumulated until an emotional desire for revenge began to outweigh attempts to right wrongs by traditional methods. Charles, on his part, failed to head off the catastrophe. Instead of providing his people with an efficient government, he alienated them by using doubtful means for raising money, by continuing a vacillating foreign policy, and by permitting Laud, made archbishop of Canterbury in 1633, to carry out a vigorous High-Church policy.

Charles continued to levy tonnage and poundage and resorted to obsolete as well as new sources of income, thereby alienating many nobles as well as merchants and gentry. In 1630, for example, he revived a law that required freeholders with an annual income of £40 or more to assume knighthood and pay the heavy obligations involved, or pay a heavy fine for refusing to do so. In 1634 he put into effect ancient forestry laws and imposed huge fines upon great landowners who owned forests that had once belonged to the royal domain. New monopolies were granted to corporations, now that granting them to individuals was illegal. Old statutes against enclosures were also enforced and heavy fines imposed. Most vexatious and provocative of all was the ship money, which had previously been levied upon the port towns in time of war in order to furnish funds for the building of ships and the maintenance of a navy. This ship money Charles doubled and extended to inland towns and counties.

When it appeared as though Charles would make the ship money into a permanent direct tax, antiroyal feeling ran high. Men of all classes began to feel that the laws that had been designed to protect them were being used to despoil them. This was made clear in the Hampden Ship Money case of 1637. John Hampden, a country squire, was one of those who refused to pay the money, small as the amount was, and his opposition was made a test case. At the trial his counsel argued that the king could not levy taxes without the consent of Parliament and that he could not collect ship money unless the danger of invasion was so immediate that he did not have time to call Parliament. The attorney general and the judges, siding with the king, maintained that the ship money was not a tax and that the king could levy money upon all England in time of danger and could himself determine what constituted danger. One supporter even claimed that the king was the law.

Although Hampden lost his case, he became the hero of the increasing number of people who realized that their liberties could no longer be protected by Parliament, the laws, or the judges. Whether or not Charles acted by legal means is still a moot question. But it is obvious that he acted without tact and underestimated the Puritan temper.

Meanwhile Charles was offending Englishmen by his vacillating and ineffective foreign policy. Although he ended the war with France in 1629 and with Spain in 1630, thereby greatly increasing English trade, he aroused general dissatisfaction because the treaties implied the abandonment of aid to the Protestant powers.

It was in religious affairs that Charles made his greatest blunders, again while having the law on his side for the most part. The agent for carrying out his theocratic conceptions was Archbishop Laud, who, as the leading figure in the Privy Council, obtained control of the legal and administrative machinery, secular as well as ecclesiastical, needed for the enforcement of his policy of rigid uniformity. Able administrator that he was, he did much to establish order in the church and vigorously attacked indifference and corruption. But, like his master, he lacked tact and patience and rode roughshod over the consciences of the Puritans.

Laud, supported by the crown, rigidly enforced his system. The Puritans, unable to voice their opinions in Parliament or Convocation after 1629, were also denied the right to use the chief organs of public expression of opinion: the pulpit and the press. An order of 1622, compelling preachers to adhere to their prescribed texts, was strictly enforced. In 1637 a decree of the Star Chamber forbade the publication of any book or pamphlet not licensed.

The courts were also used in the interests of the Laudian system. Although most cases of ecclesiastical discipline were tried by the archidiaconal, diocesan, and provincial courts, with the right of appeal to a court of delegates, the most important ecclesiastical tribunal was the Court of High Commission. This court, which in 1611 had been given the right to inquiry concerning matters of heresy and recusancy, was intensely hated by the English, primarily because its procedure, like that of the Star Chamber, was contrary to common law. The Puritans detested it particularly because the bishops, their accusers, sat in it as parties to suits.

Although Laud had no one put to death for opposition to his system, he sanctioned cruel punishments. One of the celebrated cases, long remembered by the populace, was that of a learned, though narrow-minded, barrister by the name of William Prynne, who had written against the theater and the episcopacy. In 1637 he and two other writers were sentenced by the Star Chamber to pay heavy fines, lose their ears, and be imprisoned. During their mutilation they appealed to their onlookers to defend their religious and political liberties or suffer slavery. Although the populace had previously enjoyed such a spectacle, it now showed its strong disapproval.

By 1637 the Puritans had been completely alienated from the Anglican Church and were in a revolutionary mood, eager to do away with not only "indifferent" ceremonies, as in the reign of Elizabeth, but the entire episcopal system. Highly suspicious that Laud and the king were about to suppress all their liberties and bring England back into the Catholic fold, they developed an opposition that was charged with emotion. It was particularly dangerous because it could find no outlet in the usual channels of expression. Although about twenty thousand fled to North America in what was called the Puritan Migration, the rest conformed to the regulations in sullen discontent.

### Charles and Scotland

The Puritans saw the first rays of hope for a change in religious affairs come from Scotland. There opposition to the episcopacy was well organized, had long been associated with nationalism, and had the means of crystallizing and giving expression to its views. There, as in England, Charles underestimated the forces of opposition. Unlike his father, moreover, he did not even attempt to hold the nobles to his side in his determination to enforce the Laudian system in his native land.

Charles aroused resistance in Scotland by creating a new, more powerful High Commission for that country in 1634. The next year a new *Book of Canons,* declaring the king the absolute head of the kirk, was published and then put into effect without the consent of the General Assembly or Parliament. In the critical year 1637 he authorized a new *Service Book,* which closely followed the Anglican service and which Milton called "the skeleton of a Mass-book."

The reading of the new service provoked widespread opposition, even riots. Charles' refusal to heed the requests of representatives of all classes led to the signing, in 1638, of the National Covenant, in which the subscribers swore to oppose all the "errors and innovations of the Church of Rome," which tended toward "tyranny and popery." Although they promised to defend the crown, they would do so only in behalf of true religion, the laws, and the liberties of their land. It was soon to be seen that the Scots, who enthusiastically signed the Covenant in great numbers, placed Presbyterianism before the king.

Despite the fact that the Covenant had the support of all the Scottish classes, Charles made no concessions. To gain time, however, he permitted the meeting of a General Assembly and a free Parliament. But even the election of representatives to the former involved a fundamental issue. According to Presbyterian practice, lay leaders not only represented the presbyteries but participated in the election of the clerical representatives. Whereas Charles and Laud demanded that the laymen be excluded and the bishops included in the Assembly, the Scots insisted upon the inclusion of the laymen and the exclusion of the bishops. The Assembly, elected according to the Presbyterian plan, met in Glasgow in November, 1638. Although the royal commissioner ordered its dissolution, it remained in session, deposed the bishops, abolished the canons and the *Service Book,* and re-established the Presbyterian form of church government.

These acts of defiance were accompanied by preparations for war on both sides. But Charles could muster only a small army of about ten thousand undisciplined, poorly led men, whereas the Scots, eager to defend their liberties, flocked to their banner, were well trained, and were led by Alexander Leslie, who had fought under Gustavus Adolphus. Both armies, however, remained at the border, for Charles knew that he would suffer defeat, and the Scots feared that a successful attack would unite Englishmen behind their king. Thus the First Bishops' War of 1639 ended without a military engagement. By the Treaty of Berwick, the Scots agreed to disband, and Charles agreed to leave Scottish ecclesiastical matters to the General Assembly and civil matters to the Scottish Parliament.

The new Scottish Assembly, which met in Edinburgh in August, 1639, abolished the episcopal system and compelled all Scots to subscribe to the Covenant. The Scottish Parliament, meeting later in the same year, not only confirmed these measures, but took steps to free itself from all royal authority by selecting its own powerful Committee of the Lords of the Articles. Thereupon the royal commissioner ordered the dissolution of the Parliament. Charles, however, recalled his chief adviser, Thomas Wentworth, from Ireland, where he had been lord deputy, made him earl of Strafford, and gave him the task of preparing for a war with Scotland.

# Part Four: Religious Conflicts and Consequences

Strafford, who had been successful in his domination of the Irish Parliament by a policy of "thorough," suggested that Scotland could be subdued only by means of a strong army. If the English Parliament should refuse to make the necessary grants in the face of the present danger, then, he advised, the king would be justified in using "extraordinary means."

The Parliament that assembled on April 13, 1640, refused to make any grants without first discussing grievances against the crown. John Pym (1584–1643), who had been in every Parliament since 1614, well summarized the royal abuses under the following headings: attacks upon parliamentary privileges, religious innovations, and disregard for the right of private property. This speech, noisily acclaimed in the House of Commons, was printed and widely circulated. Charles, seeing that he could not obtain the grants without making many concessions, dissolved this Short Parliament, as it was called, on May 5.

Contrary to the usual custom, Charles did not dissolve Convocation at this time. This body aroused further hostility against the Laudian system by granting a large contribution to the king and promulgating seventeen new canons. One of these demanded that the clergy include in their morning prayers once every three months a definition of the divine-right authority of the king. Another made provision for the hated "Etcetera Oath," which demanded that all teachers and clerics swear not to advocate the change of government of the church by "archbishops, bishops, deans, and archdeacons, etc." Still another directed that the communion table be placed at the east end of the chancel and railed off and that people bow toward the east upon both entering and leaving the church. Not only Puritans but other Protestants resented this ostensible "drift to Rome." The obvious interweaving of episcopacy with divine-right monarchy led the opponents of the one to make common cause with the opponents of the other.

Meanwhile Strafford, arguing that the king was now "absolved from all rules of government" because Parliament had made no grants of money, urged Charles to use all possible means for raising the funds necessary for resuming the war with Scotland. In this he was firmly supported by Laud. But all these attempts met with stubborn resistance and failure. The few troops that were gathered frequently mutinied or deserted and even burned altar rails in demonstration against the Laudian system. Thus, when a Scottish army crossed the border into England, it was unopposed.

The Scots were assured of the good will of most Englishmen by issuing a manifesto in which they stated that they were in complete sympathy with them, that they fought only to preserve their common liberties, and that they would not plunder the counties in which they fought. Charles, compelled to relinquish Northumberland and Durham to the

Scots at the outset of this Second Bishops' War and to pay a huge indemnity, found it necessary to call another Parliament.

## The Long Parliament

The Parliament that met in November, 1640 is called the Long Parliament, for it was not formally dissolved until March, 1660. Considerable excitement and some evidences of modern electioneering attended the election. The great majority of the members were now determined to punish those ministers responsible for misgovernment, put an end to arbitrary government, and purify the church of the Laudian additions.

The temper of the Long Parliament was shown by the initiation of impeachment proceedings against Strafford for treason to the nation—a new offense. But because the leaders of the House of Commons feared that they might not be able to convict him of treason to the satisfaction of the House of Lords, they substituted for the impeachment a bill of attainder, which would carry the death penalty without trial. The House of Commons passed the bill of attainder in April, 1641. Soon after, when Pym disclosed evidence to the effect that Strafford and the queen were planning to use military force to overawe Parliament, the House of Lords likewise voted the attainder, and Charles was induced to add his signature. Strafford was executed on Tower Hill soon after. Laud was imprisoned but not sent to the block until four years later.

Meanwhile Parliament had begun its task of re-establishing constitutional government. The Triennial Act stipulated that Parliament should meet no later than three years after the dissolution of the previous one. A second measure provided that Parliament could not be dissolved except by its own consent. The king accepted this revolutionary bill without a protest. Another act granted tonnage and poundage for two months but stated that previous exactions made without parliamentary consent had been illegal. Other measures declared illegal such arbitrary exactions as ship money and fines for refusing knighthood. Finally, Parliament abolished such special courts as the Star Chamber and the Council of the North, as well as the Court of High Commission. Charles signed all these acts, but not without the determination to regain his absolute authority.

With the passage of this remedial legislation the remarkable unanimity of Parliament ceased. Serious dissensions developed over religious issues not only in the House of Commons but between it and the House of Lords. Although the popular party was united in its determination to establish parliamentary control over the church as well as the government, differences arose over the ways and means. Whereas one group preferred to reform the episcopal system, others wished to destroy it. Among the latter, three distinct groups became discernible: (1) the majority, led by Pym, who desired a Puritan state church controlled by a parliamentary committee of laymen; (2) a smaller group, supported by the Scots, who wanted a Presbyterian form of church government; and (3) the Independents, who demanded congregational control of both theology and worship.

These differences became apparent during the discussion of the "root and branch" petition, submitted to the House of Commons, requesting the abolition of the episcopacy "with all its roots and branches." A bill was passed by the House of Commons that would prohibit the clergy from participation in temporal affairs and exclude the bishops from the House of Lords. The House of Lords, resenting such interference in its own affairs, rejected the bill.

Because of these differences and the extremes to which some of the Independents went in attacking the church, Charles had an opportunity to win over a strong minority to his cause. Instead he engaged in dubious adventures that alienated the moderates. For example, he went to Scotland to gain support. Parliament, having opposed this visit, sent commissioners along to watch him. The bill to provide for this group of accompanying commissioners passed both houses without the concurrence of the king.

Meanwhile, events in Ireland tended to confirm the suspicion that the king was planning to restore Catholicism, the one fear that tended to bind all Protestants together and that the radicals constantly exploited to gain their ends. After the departure of Wentworth, the Irish believed the time ripe for an attack upon their predominantly Protestant Parliament. Filled with hatred of English rule, they massacred about five thousand people. But rumors exaggerated the numbers and connected the rebellion with a revival of Catholicism. Parliament was eager to put down the rebellion, but it was reluctant to place an army at the disposal of the king. Pym therefore suggested that in order to put down the rebellion and secure the parliamentary gains thus far made, it would be necessary to force upon the king councilors of its own choice or to raise an army under its own control. This radical suggestion tended to drive those who wished to retain the episcopal system into the royal camp, for they were reluctant to give Parliament that much power.

Striking while the iron was hot, Pym and his supporters made a bid for popular support by forcing the passage of the Grand Remonstrance in the House of Commons in November, 1641. Addressed to the king, but intended for the people, it listed the grievances of the popular party against the crown, explained past remedies, defended the present actions of the popular party, and outlined a program for future reforms that must be accepted by the king before Parliament would support him in suppressing the Irish rebellion. The passage of the Remonstrance by the small majority of 159 to 148 indicates the approximate division of the English people on the major issues of that time.

Charles, deceived by the fact that a party of constitutional royalists had come into being during the arguments over the Remonstrance, returned from Scotland, avoided the issues raised, and then committed the folly of illegally ordering his attorney general to impeach as traitors Pym, Hampden, and three other members of the House of Commons. When the House of Lords refused to arrest them, the king appeared in person in the House of Commons with an armed force, prepared to seize them. But he found that "the birds are flown."

Five days after the failure of his *coup d'état*, Charles left London with his family, and both he and Parliament vied for control of the militia, the fortresses, and military supplies. Meanwhile Parliament, convinced that Charles would try other means to deprive its members of their privileges, prepared a list of Nineteen Propositions for his acceptance. These demanded that the important officers of the state should henceforth be appointed only with the consent of Parliament; that Parliament have control of the army; that the king's children be married to persons acceptable to Parliament; that the church be reformed by Parliament; and that the laws against the Catholics be strictly enforced. Charles answered that to accept these propositions would be tantamount to the destruction of his royal authority. Although supported by no substantial force, he set up his standard at Nottingham in August, 1642. Parliament retaliated by voting funds for the creation of its own army. These acts marked the beginning of the civil war.

## The Civil War and the Interregnum (1642–1660)

Economic and social motives were not absent in the struggle that ended in the decapitation of Charles I and the establishment of a short-lived republic, for the supporters of the king consisted mainly of nobles and gentry, called Cavaliers, whereas his opponents were predominantly townsmen and yeomen, called Roundheads because they had their hair cropped close to their heads. The main issues, however, were political and religious. But the driving force behind the whole movement was Puritanism, and therefore the civil war can be called a religious war.

Puritanism had undergone important changes during the struggle between Parliament and the crown. Not only had the great majority of the people who went by that name grown to hate the Anglican establishment as such, together with the monarchy that supported it, but, influenced by revolutionary theories of government, they had become reconciled to the use of force to obtain their ends. As in many such movements, the more belligerent minority gained control. In this case it was the Independents, representing the masses of artisans and workers, who seized the initiative. Their ultimate aim was the separation of church and state. Their chief spokesman was Oliver Cromwell (1599–1658), a member of the gentry, and their chief instrument was his army.

To the surprise of the popular party in Parliament, many people who came to feel that the king stood for the preservation of their inherited rights and the preservation of the Elizabethan Settlement flocked to his standard. During the first two years of the war, before Parliament could marshal its superior resources, Charles had the advantage of a definite plan of attack and well-trained men well led. During this period Parliament found it necessary to make an alliance with the Scots, called the Solemn League and Covenant (1643). Its purpose was to preserve the Presbyterianism of Scotland, reform the church in England and Ireland, extirpate Catholicism, preserve the political liberties of the countries, and "defend" the king against his evil advisers.

Before the alliance was signed, the Westminster Assembly (1643–1649) was called for the purpose of reforming the English Church along Presbyterian lines, that is, setting up a Calvinist state church. Although this attempt failed and precipitated a bitter conflict between the majority in Parliament and the Independents, its Confession of Faith and Larger and Shorter Cathechisms were so well formulated that they were used by all Presbyterian churches.

The chief opponent of the Presbyterians in Parliament was Oliver Cromwell, who as an Independent opposed all creeds and ceremonies and preached complete religious toleration for Protestants. He gained his great influence by means of his newly organized, well-equipped, thoroughly disciplined New Model Army, which consisted of zealous soldiers of various shades of Protestant belief. He infused this army with his own biblical faith, puritanical simplicity, and strong sense of a divine mission to serve the welfare of the English people. Although this army never constituted more than a third of the parliamentary forces, it was responsible for most of the victories that ended in the surrender of Charles to the Scots. The Scots turned him over to Parliament in 1647.

While Parliament punished the vanquished royalists with intolerance and cruelty, it also turned against the army that had made possible its victories. It believed that it could now dismiss the army, make terms with the king, establish a Presbyterian form of discipline, and suppress the many sects whose growth had been encouraged by Cromwell. The army, however, refused to comply, seized the king, marched to London, and demanded that Parliament dissolve itself. While the army chiefs began negotiations with the king for the establishment of a liberal monarchy and tolerant Anglicanism, Charles fled to the Isle of Wight and subsequently made an "Engagement" with the Scots that resulted in the "Second Civil War." This was speedily put down.

Because of this turn of events, the army came to the conclusion that the king would not be bound by any agreements and that it was now

Oliver Cromwell

*by Sir Peter Lely*

461

necessary to execute him as a traitor. Because the House of Commons was more fearful of the radical elements in the army than of the king, the army decided to purge it of its Presbyterian members. By means of Pride's Purge in December, 1648, only the ninety-six members who were known to favor the army were permitted to sit; the rest were arrested. This Rump Parliament became a tool in the hands of the army, and particularly of Cromwell, who had just returned from northern England.

The victory of the radicals was apparent in the subsequent resolutions of the Rump. It declared that the king was a traitor for having warred against Parliament and the people and that the supreme power rested in the House of Commons. In January, 1649, it created a high court of justice of 135 members to try the king. Of the 68 who attended the trial, 58 voted for his impeachment and execution. Charles was beheaded on a scaffold placed before Whitehall on January 30, 1649. His courage and dignity were not lost upon the people, who eleven years later welcomed the restoration of the monarchy under his son Charles II.

The attempt of Cromwell to rule England by democratic methods and by granting religious toleration to all Protestants during the Interregnum (1649–1660) failed, not because of his lack of ability or want of achievements at home or abroad but because he and his followers represented only a small minority of the English people. The enthusiastic restoration of the Stuart monarchy in 1660 showed that the English people were not ready or willing to rule themselves through Parliament. They still preferred the rule of king and Parliament and the re-establishment of the Anglican Church. But the Puritan Revolution had had a powerful impact upon the outcome of the Protestant Reformation.

## The Independents

Cromwell's toleration in his army and during the period of the Commonwealth and the Protectorate proved a great boon to the many small religious groups that went by the name of Independents. The older groups, such as the Congregationalists and the Baptists, now increased in great numbers. Among the newer sects were the followers of John Everard (1575?–1650?), whose spiritualistic mysticism was the product of the study of most of the great mystics of the past, and of John Saltmarsh, who based his teaching of freedom of conscience upon his conception of continued revelation.

Antinomianism was represented by John Eaton (1575?–1641), who vigorously opposed Calvinist legalism, and William Dell (1607?–1664), who stressed the importance of having Christ build his church within man. Apocalyptic tendencies were found among the Ranters, who frequently disturbed church services, and the Fifth Monarchy Men, who took up arms against Cromwell because he did not establish the kind of government described in the Revelation of St. John and in Daniel. Because the end of the world did not appear as expected, apocalyptic speculations gave way to a pietistic quietism that found its best expression in the *Pilgrim's Progress* of John Bunyan (1628–1688) and among the Seekers, or Family of Love, who furthered inner spirituality as opposed to formal Christianity. Their silent meetings with occasional utterances and prayers, prompted, as they believed, by the Holy Spirit, were the direct antithesis of High-Church worship.

Of considerable influence in political and social, as well as religious, matters, were the Levellers, whose prophet was John Lilburne (1614–1657). Their teaching that all men are born equal in liberty and freedom gained many adherents during the Puritan Revolution. Even more radical views were expressed by Gerard Winstanley, founder of the Diggers, whose communism was demonstrated by the ploughing-up of common and waste lands.

Although most of these new religious groups disappeared after the Restoration, one of them, the Society of Friends, or Quakers, continued to grow in numbers and influence and constituted one of the finest fruits of the Puritan Revolution. Its founder, George Fox (1624–1691), was a weaver's son and shoemaker's apprentice who found little spiritual satisfaction in the Protestant creeds of his day. After four years of wandering in search of religious peace, he found it in a personal contact with God and in the inner light, that is, the working of the Holy Spirit in his heart.

In 1647 Fox began preaching his message with a fervor that attracted many followers. Christ, he maintained, cannot be found in "steeple houses," or even in Scripture, but must live in the hearts of men. Because he and his followers refused to accept many of the social customs of their day and frequently ignored the authority of magistrates and ministers, they were despised by the ruling classes and often persecuted. Because of their fundamental pacifism, they were opposed by the leaders of the army, although Cromwell himself respected them.

There were occasional excesses among the followers of Fox. One of them, Jacob Naylor, rode into Bristol in 1656 as Christ had ridden into Jerusalem and was hailed by some enthusiastic women as the Son of God. But Fox had the ability to give his followers a definite organization that assured the continuation of the society. It was characterized by its silent meetings, its notable care of the poor and sick, and its widespread missionary activity.

## Growing Toleration

It is natural that the great proliferation of Protestantism into many sects should be accompanied by a growing toleration. The Anglican

Church itself was satisfied with a formal adherence to the Thirty-nine Articles, which contained enough ambiguities to permit a considerable latitude of belief. Moreover, because England in the seventeenth century was politically consolidated and no longer faced the danger of an attack from the outside, Englishmen felt little need for absolute uniformity of religious belief. The chief concern of the Anglicans was for uniformity of worship for the maintenance of order. Calvinism, itself fundamentally intolerant, was the faith of the Presbyterians, the Independents, and many Baptists. It could not persecute without destroying itself.

The great spokesman of the growing toleration, and at the same time the epitome of the religious ferment that accompanied the Puritan Revolution, was John Milton (1608–1674). Many of his views were Calvinist, especially his conception of God and God's relation to man. But he frequently gave expression to shades of Puritanism and also Renaissance conceptions of natural law. His was a continuous search for truth and beauty of expression.

Milton deserted his study of mathematics and literature in Italy to return to England in 1639 to participate in the religious struggles there. He soon became involved in the attack upon the episcopacy, but he offended the Presbyterians by arguing in behalf of the toleration of sects, which were to him necessary in the search for truth. An unfortunate marriage led him to a defense of divorce for reasons other than adultery. The difficulties that he encountered with the censors because of his pamphlets on divorce led him to write the *Areopagitica* (1644), his noble plea for the freedom of the press. In his *Defense of the English People* (1651), written in Latin, he defended the execution of Charles I. After the failure of the Commonwealth and the Protectorate, of which he had been a secretary of the Council of State, he retired, blind and disheartened. It was then that he wrote his sublime *Paradise Lost* (1663–1667), in which he attempted to portray the divine plan and order of the universe.

Milton, like Cromwell and others of his day, carried the torch of toleration, but not yet of religious liberty. His toleration of the sects was based upon a differentiation between what he considered the essentials and the nonessentials of Christian faith. According to his interpretation of essentials, toleration could not be granted to Catholics and Unitarians.

Milton's contemporary Roger Williams (1603–1683), who worked in both England and the American Colonies, carried toleration a step further by coming to the conclusion that the government had no right to enforce a religious creed and also that each individual should be permitted to act in religious matters according to his own conscience. Freedom was for him absolutely essential for the spread of the gospel and the mysterious working of divine grace. At Providence, in 1635, he established an asylum for all who had been persecuted for the sake of their consciences, whether he considered them to be in error or not. Because he drew a sharp distinction between the church and the state, maintaining that only the few regenerate belonged to the former, he advocated complete separation of church and state.

# 12 The Legacy of the Reformation

## Impact of the Reformation on Western Thought

The Reformation Era, the period between 1500 and 1650, was above all else an age of religious faith, when what people believed had a significant bearing upon political, economic, and social theories and upon literary and artistic expression. That is not to say that other than religious motives were not at times decisive, for secular interests were present throughout the period, as in earlier centuries. It was not until the end of the era, however, that these secular interests began to take precedence over the religious.

Much has been written concerning the question whether the Reformation was medieval or modern. The fact that it contained so many elements of both, that it was a period in which the domination of society by the Church and feudalism gave way to a secularization of society and the triumph of the territorial state, bespeaks its significance in the development of our western civilization. This secularization of society, which had its largest roots in the medieval urban centers, attained its first widely accepted cultural expression in the Italian Renaissance. Although its leaders did not question the authority of the medieval Church, they criticized medieval scholastic methods, laid greater emphasis upon the development of personality, and paid greater attention to man and nature and the sensual enjoyment of the things of this world.

Although the early Protestant reformers stressed man's corruption through Adam's fall and were essentially inimical to the humanist belief in man's ability to solve his own problems, they continued to emphasize man's individuality, his personal relation to God, and his responsibility to his neighbor. Luther's bold statement at Worms, to the effect that he would retract his religious views only if he were proved to be in error, did much to further individuality, even though such a thought was furthest from his mind. His *The Freedom of the Christian Man* was not a manifesto in behalf of religious freedom from authority but of the freedom of his conscience, for both Protestants and Catholics still believed that there was only one truth. By the end of the era, however, there was considerable toleration of the religious views of dissenters and some outright skepticism. The rulers of the secularized European states were now more concerned with the maintenance of law and order and the outward conformity to their state churches than with the theological views of their subjects. Religious dissenters were accordingly frequently discriminated against and exiled, but they were no longer executed for their religious beliefs.

## Political Thought of the Reformers

Nonetheless, the teachings of the Reformers and their followers had a considerable influence upon the development of modern political, economic, and social thought. It is a historical axiom that opposition to the state develops among the minorities whose interests are not furthered by the established order. Throughout the Reformation Era, from the Peasants' Revolt to the Puritan Revolution, the most radical political theories did not evolve from the necessity of logic but grew out of the demands of dissatisfied minorities. In most cases, their religious and political views coincided. Therefore they drew their political, economic, and social theories from religious sources, particularly the Bible.

Although Luther and Calvin both dared to challenge the authority of Catholicism, they did so with the assistance of their respective states and taught allegiance to those states by reference to the Pauline injunctions to obey established governments as divinely established institutions. Nevertheless, their revolutionary religious views were often accompanied by revolutionary political conceptions.

Although Luther's political, economic, and social views remained medieval in many respects, he made a number of important positive contributions to the development of modern political and social thought. He taught that the state, like the church, was divinely established and therefore not necessarily subservient to the church; that the church was an invisible communion of the faithful, not a "perfect society" that should dominate the state; that the state did not have the right to determine spiritual matters but only to carry out the decisions of the church with respect to them; and that the state was the only recognized social institution, the smallest unit of which was the family. But the ruler, like any

468

other individual, was obligated to serve both God and man in his calling, the same as a miller or a maid. This service included the maintenance of peace and provision for the general welfare of all classes, as commanded by God in the Bible.

According to Luther, the individual Christian had gained religious freedom through faith; yet his love of God bound him to serve his neighbor. Moreover, if his conscience, which was free, conflicted with the commands of the state, he must suffer punishment rather than obey the state. This theory of passive disobedience did not imply either complete obedience, on the one hand, or the right of the individual to resist the government, on the other. Yet Luther demonstrated by his own bold actions and words that the citizen had the right to criticize the government and finally admitted that the imperial estates had the right to resist the emperor by force if he acted contrary to the laws of the land.

Calvin's political views were not unlike those of Luther with respect to the origin and nature of the state. Differences appeared, however, because of Calvin's emphasis upon predestination, the majesty of God as the only true king, and church and state as a new Israel. Moreover, his doctrines were put into practice in different circumstances from those that prevailed in Lutheran lands. Because his state of Geneva was a republic, he, for example, laid greater emphasis upon man's political duties. He himself actively participated in the affairs of his community.

According to Calvin the state should be Christian. Therefore it should further Christianity by supporting the church in carrying out its administrative, disciplinary, and doctrinal functions; maintain correct doctrine and worship; suppress heresy by force; and regulate society according to the Word of God as interpreted by the clergy. But like Luther, he maintained that the Christian owed obedience to all rulers, even to tyrants, and that there was no defense against the tyrant except in prayer and flight. Both reformers agreed, however, that one should obey God rather than man. In the event that a ruler demanded what was contrary to the Word of God, passive disobedience was obligatory. Yet Calvin went further than Luther in clarifying the right of resistance. Like Bucer before him, he believed that a ruler who violated the laws of God, nature, and man could be resisted by duly constituted "inferior magistrates," such as the plebeian tribunals of ancient Rome.

The form of government, as we have seen, did not greatly concern Calvin, although he felt that a monarchy detracted from the glory of God and a democracy tended toward anarchy. He believed that an aristocracy of the godly would be inclined to permit God to be the real sovereign of the state. He was so certain that the meaning of the Word of God was unequivocal and demonstrable that he believed that every honest ruler could readily comprehend it and apply it to political exigencies.

## Antimonarchic Tracts

Although the Calvinists in Germany supported paternalistic rulers as the Lutherans did, those of France, the Low Countries, Scotland, and England, who consituted minorities and became involved in political revolutions against their states, developed radical political philosophies that were later used to justify purely political and social revolutions. The first devastating attacks upon the French monarchy were written by Huguenots who had fled from France after the Massacre of St. Bartholomew. One of these was the *Franco-Gallia* (1573), a political pamphlet published by François Hotman (1524–1590), an eminent jurist. Following the argument then being revived from feudalism, that the French monarchy was limited by law and custom, the author went so far as to state that the king should be elected and his power limited by the estates-general.

The most influential of all these political pamphlets was the *Vindiciae contra tyrannos,* or *Defense Against Tyrants,* published in 1579. The author, who is not known, revived the medieval doctrines concerning constitutional growth, natural law and the law of the land, and the sovereignty of the people as the source of the law of the land. Upon the basis of these doctrines he developed the conception of a double contract, one between God on the one hand and the king and the people on the other, by which the community became a church; a second between the king and the people, by which the community became a state. The people, not as individuals but acting through their public leaders and institutions, thus had the right to oppose a heretical king—who was still believed to rule by divine right—and to resist by force the king who abused his power. A manifest tyrant could be executed, but only after having been deposed by the proper "public magistrates and deputies."

Such revolutionary theories were not exclusively Protestant in origin, for antiroyalist Catholic writers, especially Jesuits, developed similar views. One of their best spokesmen was Robert Cardinal Bellarmine (1542–1621). On the basis of the political philosophy of Thomas Aquinas, he argued that the pope was the spiritual head of the universal, divinely instituted Church and as such had the right to influence secular matters indirectly; but secular rulers derived their authority solely from the community by contract, which could be revoked in the event that the king abused his power. In certain circumstances, therefore, the pope would be justified in deposing a heretical king and absolving his subjects from allegiance to him.

The Spanish Jesuit Juan de Mariana (1536–1624), a theologian who had taught at Rome and Paris and had returned to Spain to devote himself to the writing of political and historical works, went so far as to maintain that the development of a government was a purely natural process, growing out of the needs of, and directed by the will of, the community. Like the Huguenot Hotman, he showed his appreciation for medieval representative institutions such as the Cortes of Aragon. In his work *On the Authority of the King*, published in 1598, he argued that the king derived his authority from the people through a social contract and that the people retained the right to depose him if he violated the fundamental law of the kingdom. De Mariana also stated that if a king's tyranny became unbearable, he could be removed by tyrannicide, but only after a representative assembly had declared him a public enemy.

Whereas de Mariana based most of his arguments on nontheological reasoning, the Jesuit Francisco Suárez (1548–1617), a Spanish philosopher and jurist, developed his theories in harmony with his conception of scholastic philosophy. His tract, *On Laws and God the Legislator* (1612), advanced the thesis that the pope, as head of a universal and divine institution, had the authority to regulate secular rulers in spiritual matters, for these were the heads of particular, secular states and derived their authority from the social group by natural law. Because, according to natural law, it was the purpose of the government to serve the general welfare of the community, that government that failed to do so could be changed. Although it was the purpose of Suárez to prove the divine-right authority of the papacy, his systematic development of the doctrine of natural law did much to separate political theory from theology and to pave the way for a scientific approach to problems of constitutional and international law.

## Ideas Concerning Sovereignty

As an antidote to the impassioned political pamphlets of the Huguenots, there appeared in France, in 1576, the *Six Books on the Republic*, written by Jean Bodin (1530–1596). Reflecting in general the views of the French *politiques*, the author sought to re-establish peace and order by strengthening the authority of the king and minimizing religious differences. Although he still believed that the stars influenced the history of states, he laid considerable stress on the importance of environment and showed an exceptional understanding of economic processes. He thus advocated the historical and comparative approach, a combination of history and philosophy, rather than the customary reference to texts. He had explained this new approach in his *Method for the Easy Understanding of History*, published in 1566. Deeply religious as well as scholarly, he criticized Machiavelli for visualizing a state without morality or religion.

Although Bodin did not succeed in his aim to build up a well-organized system of principles similar and superior to that of Aristotle and despite the fact that his works contain many contradictions and confusions, he made valuable contributions to the history of political thought, particularly in his development of the doctrine of sovereignty. The state, he maintained, is made up of the heads of families who, because of the need of protection, recognize a common sovereign. The chief end of the state is the preservation of peace, justice, and private property, that is, the unlimited good. Whereas, according to the law of nature, private property belongs to the family, sovereignty belongs to the prince and his officials. This sovereignty is perpetual, indivisible, undelegated, inalienable, and limited only by natural and divine law and "the fundamental laws of the land," for sovereignty is the authority to make the law. Bodin was the first to differentiate between the state and the government, for he held that the former had absolute sovereignty and that the latter, consisting of machinery for exercising sovereignty, was subordinate to the state. The best state, according to Bodin, is that one in which the sovereignty is not divided, that is, a monarchy.

Bodin's doctrine of sovereignty was practically applied in France after the accession of Henry IV and the cessation of the religious wars. The Huguenots, having been granted religious, political, and civil rights by the Edict of Nantes, gave up their radical political philosophy and loyally supported the monarchy. In the Low Countries, where the religious and political revolt proved successful, the Calvinists embodied their theories in their constitution of 1580 and in the document of 1581 that announced the deposition of Philip. In both there was a recognition of the sovereignty of the people and their elected representatives, based upon customary as well as natural and divine law. But with the establishment of peace, and in harmony with the general process of secularization, less emphasis was placed upon religious, and more upon natural and rational, arguments. This separation of political philosophy from theology was discernible especially in the works of Johannes Althusius (1557–1638) and Hugo Grotius (1583–1645), both Calvinists.

Although Althusius followed the French Huguenots in identifying natural law with the law of Moses, his political thought was developed logically from his conception of the social contract. According to this contract he explained not only the relation between the ruler and his people but the social interrelation of all groups. Like Bodin, he held that the state was sovereign, but only as a corporate body to which the other groups had delegated sovereignty by contract. Sovereignty ultimately resides in the people and cannot be alienated but only delegated to their administrators. Therefore it reverts to them if the administrators do not live up to their contract. Tyranny can be resisted but only through the communities or corporate bodies that originally made the contract with the state.

The final step in divorcing political thought from theology was taken by Grotius. Realizing that the greatest cause of human misery in his day was the conflict among the rising territorial monarchies, he devoted his attention to the presentation of rules governing the relations among the states. In his *The Law of War and Peace,* first published in 1625, he appealed primarily to the validity of the generally accepted law of nature. But he re-examined it in the light of the needs of his day and explained it in a rational manner, developing its principles with a lucidity that he hoped would make them apparent to all men.

This methodology of Grotius, so common among the precursors of the Enlightenment, had little in common with the Reformation appeal to scriptural authority, for he insisted that theology was not essential to the comprehension of reason. Yet he was a deeply religious man and suffered persecution for his religious views. Aware of the fact that religious faith itself had left a legacy of war, he applied his new methodology to religion. As an exegete he treated the books of the Bible purely as literary sources. As an apologist he laid the bases for the interpretation of Christianity as a "natural religion." As an irenicist he sought to bring all Christians together into one Church.

## Political Thought in Scotland and England

Calvinism in Scotland became at the outset identified with popular and national opposition to the Catholic regent, the queen, the court, and the ecclesiastical hierarchy, all allied with France. Because John Knox was for a long time in exile and his followers were in the minority, he saw that he could not reform his country without offering strong resistance. Therefore he rejected Calvin's doctrine of passive disobedience, maintaining that it was the duty of Christians to repress "such crimes as idolatry, blasphemy, and others that touch the majesty of God," but only through their leaders. Furthermore, the Scottish General Assembly, with its presbyteries and provincial synods, became truly representative, unlike the consistory of Geneva. The Scottish humanist George Buchanan (1506–1582), in his *The Right of Royalty Among the Scots,* argued that royal power was derived from the people, that the monarch must obey the laws of the community that are made by the people, and that punishment of a blasphemous tyrant, even tyrannicide, was justified if demanded by a majority of the people.

In England, where the Henrician Reformation had placed the king and Parliament in control of the church, there was relatively little serious opposition during the reign of the Tudors. Few tracts were written against the Elizabethan Settlement during her reign. Nevertheless, the Anglican Church could not be accepted by either the Catholics or the Calvinists, both of whom held to the doctrine of the autonomy of the church. The Catholics understandably could accept no head of the Church but the pope, and the Calvinists taught both the autonomy of the church and the obligation of the state to carry out the decisions of the church.

# Part Four: Religious Conflicts and Consequences

Among the Puritans, the Independents carried the idea of the separation of church and state to such lengths that both became completely independent entities. The principle of a voluntary association of believers who have no spiritual lord save Christ eventually led to the principle of free assent in religious matters and, finally, in Cromwell's army, to active resistance to both the king and the majority in Parliament. It was this fact of revolution of the left-wing Protestants that, in the voluminous pamphlet literature of the time, led to the formulation of theories of toleration and individual rights that were embodied in later revolutionary liberalism. It was in these circumstances that the Levellers, small as they were in number, could propagate their radical democratic theories and the Diggers their communistic philosophy.

Virtually no religious writers of the time of the Puritan Revolution advocated a republic as opposed to a monarchy. The Commonwealth was established not on the basis of republican theories but because Cromwell and his followers did not believe they could come to a satisfactory agreement with the king. It is significant that the most important republican ideas, those outlined by James Harrington (1611–1677) in his *Commonwealth of Oceana* (1656), were based not upon religious doctrines but upon observations of the political, economic, and social realities of his day. The most effective answer to the Puritan Revolution, given expression in the masterful analysis of Thomas Hobbes (1588–1679), especially in his *Leviathan* of 1651, also owed little or nothing to the religious thought of the Reformation. His works, like those of Grotius, were the product of keen, rational analysis, inspired by the scientific achievements of the era between Galileo and Newton.

## Economic and Social Theories

Although little attention was given to the principles regulating economic and social activities, the reformers exerted considerable influence also in these fields. Luther's views concerning society were in the main still medieval and conservative. Yet the economic and social implications of his *The Freedom of the Christian Man,* his doctrine of the universal priesthood of believers, and his glorification of labor through his conception of man's calling made themselves felt, often in ways that he had not anticipated. Far from preaching rugged individualism, he demanded that the state provide for the general welfare of its citizens, urged an efficient and systematic care of the poor, and sought public education for all. By precept and example he increased the sanctity of family life and by regular visitations generally improved the moral conditions in Lutheran lands.

Despite the fact that Luther's environment was predominantly agricultural, he had a good grasp of the principles of economics as a whole and particularly of the ills that grew out of the greed and avarice of the businessmen of his day. Far from condoning these evils by various forms of casuistry, as many late-medieval scholastics were doing, he made an honest effort to eradicate them by insisting upon the application of Christian ethics and the principle of equity—the law of Christian love and the law of nature—to business transactions. Although he and the other reformers no longer retained the medieval authorities with respect to economic practices, Deuteronomy and Aristotle, they retained the medieval ethical system and infused it with new meaning.

Luther detested avarice in business as much as he did blasphemy in spiritual matters, especially as it was displayed in the taking of interest. He did not refer to the present-day "rate of interest," but to the canonically acceptable buying of interest that involved a *damnum emergens,* or damage resulting from a tardy return of the capital borrowed, and a *lucrum cessans,* or profit lost because the creditor could not himself use the money that he had loaned. He believed that this kind of transaction, if continued, would eventually encumber most property in Germany with debts and eventually ruin the country.

Luther made the following suggestions for reforming the credit system of his day: (1) that the buying of interest be permitted only if there was security in the form of productive property, so that the debtor could make the money with which to repay the loan; (2) that both the creditor and the debtor share the risk; (3) that the debtor, rather than the creditor, determine the date for the repayment of the loan; and (4) that, if the above conditions were met, interest of from 5 to 7 per cent might be charged. He would permit the buying of interest without security only to the aged who had no other means of livelihood.

Luther also attacked those monopolistic merchants who took advantage of the people in times of scarcity. He stated that the government should have the right to curtail such profits by enforcing a just price for the necessities of life based upon the daily wages of a laborer. He did not, however, condemn wealth as such or support those evangelical radicals who would abolish private property and repudiate all debts.

The chief contribution of Calvin to modern social and economic theory was his interpretation of man's calling in an activist sense. That is to say, he emphasized man's duty to serve society in harmony with God's will and to the honor of God. This vocational activism proved to be a powerful dynamic in western civilization.

Calvin devoted much less attention to the question of usury than Luther, despite the fact that he developed his ideas in a thriving commercial community. Like Luther, whose economic views he probably learned through Bucer, he stressed the importance of obeying the laws of equity and Christian love, and he bitterly opposed the buying of interest without security, avaricious speculation, and the accumulation of wealth at the expense of one's neighbors. Far from encouraging capitalism, his

*475*

teaching concerning economic matters served as a brake upon it for many years after his death.

Calvin went further than Luther, however, in his refutation of the Aristotelian dictum that money is sterile; in his interpretation of the Mosaic law, which forbade exacting interest on loans to one's brother (Deuteronomy XXIII: 19–20); and in his more systematic treatment of equity. He accepted the principle that money could make money. Like Luther and Bucer, however, he favored strict government control of usury. He believed that the Mosaic injunction was applicable to all persons, for all people are brothers. But he interpreted it in the light of the individual conscience and the public welfare. Usury is not wrong if it is exacted according to the principle of equity contained in the Golden Rule and is not injurious to one's fellow man. One must not forget, however, that he would permit usury only on a very limited scale, for both parties must gain in the transaction and must abide by the law. In answer to a clergyman's query whether it would be right for him to loan some of his money on interest, Calvin advised him to play safe by not doing so.

Market opportunities ultimately had more to do with the rise of the capitalist spirit than theological pronouncements. Despite the fact that the followers of Luther and Calvin long sought to infuse economic life with the Christian spirit, the secularization of society prevailed. Hugo Grotius was among the first persons to justify the taking of interest on rational grounds, without reference to religious authorities. Claudius Salmasius (1588–1653), in his work *On Usury*, published in 1638, went even further than Grotius in destroying the economic theories of the reformers and spreading the theory that economic activity was a law unto itself. He argued that the taking of interest was indispensable for modern life and culture and that low interest rates would follow if the bankers were permitted to engage in free competition.

One must not, however, overlook the economic and social importance of such minority groups as the continental Anabaptists and the English Quakers, who, as refugees and pilgrims in various parts of Europe and America, combined active service and advanced agricultural and industrial techniques with the higher service to God. The recognition of individual responsibility among these and other Protestant groups did much to further the liberal conception of both individualism and social responsibility.

## The New Scientific Outlook

In science as in other areas of thought, the Reformation Era witnessed a questioning and ultimate repudiation of inherited systems and ideas. This marked the beginnings of a scientific revolution that became one of

# 12. The Legacy of the Reformation

the most distinctive contributions of western civilization to our contemporary world. Just as men ventured into new geographical areas, they dared to compare and question basic assumptions about the universe, to experiment and accumulate new data, to formulate general laws of natural phenomena, and to express these laws in mathematical terms.

Although men laid the bases for the beginning of the modern scientific revolution at a time when religion lay at the center of their concerns, one cannot maintain that Catholicism or any one form of Protestantism provided the most congenial climate for such studies. And opposition to new scientific systems and ideas can be found among representatives of all religious groups. On the other hand, the scientific thinkers of the period were not skeptics who saw no place for God in their new systems. On the contrary, they considered God's role in them to be the one unifying element in the universe and their desire to discover and understand God's handiwork provided much of the motivation for scientific advance.

The remarkable advances in science were based on the following: (1) the preparatory work of the scholastics who trained men in logical thinking and looked upon the world as an orderly creation of God, operating according to natural and divine laws; (2) the revival by the humanists of the classical knowledge concerning the sciences; (3) the scientific observations of such late-medieval scholars as Nicholas of Cusa, Regiomontanus, and Toscanelli; and (4) the expansion of Europe, which enlarged man's horizons and provided new, practical incentives for desiring to master the forces of nature.

The new scientific systems of the sixteenth and seventeenth centuries were made possible by great advances in mathematics. Making use of what their predecessors had learned about classical geometry and Arabic and Hindu algebra, men of various countries combined these two and developed a scientific language by means of which they could quantify thought about the universe. Nicholas Copernicus (1473–1543), son of a Polish father and a German mother, discovered the principles of spherical trigonometry; Girolamo Cardano (1501–1576), an Italian, speculated with a theory of numbers and produced a valuable algebraic synthesis; John Napier (1550–1617), a Scot, advanced the study of trigonometry by helping devise logarithms; Simon Stevin (1548–1620), a Dutchman, helped develop a decimal system; and René Descartes (1596–1650), a Frenchman, laid the groundwork for the development of a practicable system of analytical geometry.

## The Copernican Revolution

It was the attempts of Copernicus to calculate the orbits of the planets, including the earth, that led him to question the geocentric system of Ptolemy with its series of transparent spheres in which the planets were supposed to move. After much observation of the skies from a room in

477

# Part Four: Religious Conflicts and Consequences

the castle of an uncle, he concluded that he could calculate the movements of the planets mathematically if he assumed that they revolved about the sun. His *On the Revolutions of the Heavenly Bodies,* containing his simplified heliocentric theory, was published in Nürnberg in 1543 and was given to him shortly before his death. It had a dedication to Pope Paul III and a preface written by the Lutheran pastor of St. Lorenz in Nürnberg, Andreas Osiander, who had come into possession of the manuscript and who explained that the work was merely a mathematical hypothesis. Even if many of Copernicus' observations were inaccurate and inadequate, his work eventually precipitated what has been called the Copernican Revolution.

As the significance of Copernicus' new cosmology became apparent toward the end of the sixteenth century, a bitter religious and intellectual controversy developed that lasted well into the seventeenth century. This was intensified by the suggestion of numerous followers of Copernicus that the planets moved in unlimited space and not in spheres. Among these was Giordano Bruno (1548–1600), an Italian who was burned at the stake by the Inquisition for announcing his theory of the infinite universe and the possibility of worlds other than our own.

Meanwhile men of science developed instruments by means of which they could accumulate new data and test the validity of the Copernican cosmology. Their faith in the traditional theories was shaken by two events of great importance. In 1572 a new star appeared that grew in brightness and then disappeared within sixteen months, showing that heavenly bodies were not incorruptible, as previously supposed; and in 1577 there appeared a comet that apparently traveled across the supposedly impervious heavenly spheres, confirming the opinions of those who believed in the unlimited universe.

Among the scientists who observed and measured these two events was Tycho Brahe (1546–1601), a Dane who sought to harmonize the differences between the Copernican and Ptolemaic systems. He made many amazingly accurate observations of the heavenly bodies and gathered a veritable chaos of data to be used by successors with a better command of mathematics. He worked first at the advanced astronomical laboratory of Uraniborg under the patronage of the king of Denmark and later at the Hradčany at Prague under the patronage of the emperor and with the assistance of the young German mathematician Johannes Kepler (1571–1630). Kepler defended the Copernican cosmology and made use of Brahe's data in formulating his famous three laws of planetary motion, which he published in 1609.

Galileo Galilei (1564–1642), a versatile Italian scientist, scholar, and musician, provided further proof of the validity of the Copernican assumptions by the perfection of the telescope. He used this to demonstrate that the moon and other planets were not perfect orbs and that four satellites moved around Jupiter. He was encouraged in this work by Kepler, with whom he corresponded, but discouraged by the Church and conservative scholars who compelled him to retract the Copernican hypothesis. He also furthered the study of physics by his experiments with the laws of the pendulum and falling bodies, thereby laying the foundation of our modern principles of dynamics.

Other noteworthy discoveries of physical laws and their practical application soon followed. William Gilbert (1540–1603), an English physician, laid the foundations for the study of magnetism and electricity by the publication of his observations. Christian Huygens (1629–1695) of Amsterdam applied the law of the pendulum in his invention of the pendulum clock; a German physicist, Otto von Guericke (1602–1686), made an air pump that he used in studying the properties of air; and an Italian, Evangelista Torricelli (1608–1647), invented the barometer.

## Changes in Chemistry, Biology, and Cartography

Notable discoveries were likewise made in chemistry. A Flemish physician, Jean Baptiste van Helmont (1577–1644), described the behavior of some gases, recognized carbon dioxide, and suggested the use of alkalies for the correction of acidity. Robert Boyle (1627–1691), in his *The Skeptical Chymist,* disproved the Aristotelian assumption that there were four basic elements (earth, air, fire, and water), suggested the modern theory of elements, and formulated the law concerning the effect of pressure upon gases that still bears his name.

As early as the first half of the sixteenth century, Georg Bauer, a German better known as Agricola (1494–1555), laid the basis for the scientific study of metals. In his work, *On Metals,* he showed how to estimate the amount of metal in ore and explained the puddling process of making steel.

In the field of anatomy the almost slavish use of the works of old Greek physicians gradually gave way to independent anatomical and physiological studies. Leonardo da Vinci (1452–1519) dissected more than thirty human bodies and made exceptionally accurate anatomical sketches. Andreas Vesalius (1514–1564), a Fleming, published the first modern book on anatomy, *The Structure of the Human Body,* in which he included his own observations. A revolutionary advance in the study of physiology was made when William Harvey (1578–1657), an English physician, published his discovery that the blood was forced by the beating of the heart through the arteries and back through the veins to the heart and that the functioning of the other organs of the body was dependent upon the circulation of the blood.

The study of medicine was advanced by the Swiss physician, Theophrastus Bombastus von Hohenheim, better known by the name of Paracelsus (1493–1541), who pioneered in the use of various chemicals and drugs in the treatment of his patients. The well-known treatment of wounded soldiers by Ambroise Paré (1517–1590) would not have been possible without such experiments as those of Paracelsus. An Italian, Girolamo Fracastoro (1483–1553), published a book in 1546 in which he suggested that contagious diseases were transmuted by minute organisms that propagated themselves.

Probably the first biologist worthy of the name was the Swiss Konrad Gesner (1515–1565), whose *Catalogue of Plants* and *History of Animals* contained the results of much careful observation. Leonard Fuchs (1501–1566), one of several German botanists of note of that century, published a remarkable collection of woodcuts illustrating the structure and the habitat of plants and the first modern glossary of botanical terms. The development of the simple and compound microscopes at the beginning of the seventeenth century greatly facilitated the study of plant and animal tissues and led to a complete change in man's conception of life.

The science of cartography was greatly stimulated by the important geographical discoveries of the fifteenth and sixteenth centuries, which for the first time brought all the great land masses of the world to the attention of the Europeans and made the old maps of classical Greece and Rome out of date. The demands of the early modern mariners were met by many cartographers. The best known of these was the Fleming Gerhard Kramer, or Mercator (1512–1594), who devised the projection that bears his name and has remained a model for the making of maps and charts to our own day.

It is not surprising that the educated world became less enthusiastic over the attainment of knowledge by deduction and placed much greater emphasis upon induction. The methods used by the scientists of this period were best described and propagandized by Francis Bacon (1561–1626) in his *Advancement of Learning* and *Novum Organum,* works in which he opposed the scholastic method and urged men to acquire knowledge by observation and experimentation. Accordingly he advocated that men discard all inherited errors, traditions, and prejudices, which he called "idols," and rely upon clear thinking. Ironically enough, he retained one of his own "idols" by refusing to accept a number of important scientific discoveries, including the heliocentric system of Copernicus.

## Changes in Philosophy

The amazing accumulation of scientific data during the Reformation Era was accompanied by a revolutionary change in philosophy. Whereas its chief interest had long been religious, it now gradually became physical and mathematical. Long the handmaid of theology, it now tended to become independent of it. Protestantism did much to make possible this change, for Luther and the early reformers were bitter in their attacks upon scholasticism and the influence of Aristotle, "the damned heathen," although later Protestants were not averse to explaining their theology by scholastic methods.

Much more important in the development of a new philosophy, however, was the growth of skepticism, never wholly absent during the late Middle Ages. It became widespread after France and other countries had become embroiled in religious wars. Michel de Montaigne (1533–1592), who remained aloof from the bitter religious struggles of his day, sought consolation in the study of the classics and the observation of man's behavior, customs, and beliefs. In his widely read *Essays* he expressed his interest in enjoying this world as much as possible, cast mild doubts upon all inherited institutions and beliefs, and opposed all attempts to establish religious uniformity. The multiplicity of the religious divisions of his day led him to conclude that religious faith owed more to chance of birth than reason, that God was in the last analysis not knowable. The ultimate aim of philosophy was for him to teach man to be happy and despise death. Yet he did not break with Catholicism.

The impact of the new scientific spirit upon the development of philosophy is best seen in the life and work of Giordano Bruno. His attempt to comprehend God as at once the infinite Being, immanent in the entire universe, and the ultimate Cause outside the universe, provided a powerful stimulus to the development of modern thought. It was his reference to God as the soul of the universe, the "monad of all monads," that especially aroused the animosity of his contemporaries, including Kepler, and led to his death at the stake. Sir Francis Bacon also did much to further the scientific approach to philosophy by advocating inductive and experimental methods.

The most influential rational system of this period was developed by Descartes. In his "Discourse on Method," published in 1637 with three other essays under the title *Philosophical Essays,* he explained the essentials of his philosophical thought. Like Montaigne, he believed that inherited customs and beliefs depended upon things other than reason and that, therefore, all other philosophers had failed to disclose ultimate reality. He would avoid the errors of the past by discarding all authorities and beginning with only that which he himself knew. The one truth, or axiom, that he could not deny was his own existence, expressed in his famous maxim, *cogito ergo sum* ("I think, therefore I am").

Beginning with this axiom, Descartes constructed his system by applying the principles of his analytical geometry. Accordingly he sought to reduce all problems to their simplest terms, to accept only what was logically self-evident, and to proceed from the simple to the complex. By this process he proved to his own satisfaction the existence of God as the embodiment of perfection and proof of the reality of science, the laws of nature, and the material world, for God had to give us the ability to comprehend the creation. In distinguishing between bodies of matter as mathematically extended things and souls as thinking things, he presented a dualism that occupied philosophers for several centuries.

Although the Cartesian system was based upon Descartes' a priori deduction of his principles from his conception of a perfect God, its laws nonetheless greatly influenced scientists as well as theologians and philosophers. But it also aroused strong opposition, not only from Catholicism —his writings were placed on the Index in 1663—but from Protestantism, for it encouraged people to believe only what they could understand and explained the phenomena of nature as mere matter and motion. But that did not prevent his works from being widely read by the representatives of all classes during his day and from marking out the chief metaphysical problems that have occupied philosophers down to our own time.

# The Spirit of the Age

Despite the fact that important steps had been taken in the development of a rational, scientific attitude toward the phenomena of nature, the great majority of western Europeans were still influenced by magic and superstition. People of all classes still believed in ghosts, evil spirits, and fairies, and alchemy and astrology still occupied the serious attention of scholars. Both Cardan and Kepler cast horoscopes for rulers, merchants, and mariners.

### Demonology

But whereas superstitions gradually declined, the belief in demonology increased. Systematic demonology had been made a part of the imposing theological structure of the late Middle Ages. The devil was depicted as the leader of all the evil spirits, which distorted church rites in obscene rituals and made pacts with human beings, mostly women, for the purpose of blaspheming God and propagating evil.

The witchcraft mania of the sixteenth century appeared after a series of attempts, beginning with a papal bull of 1484, to stop what was purported to be a growing intercourse of persons with evil spirits. It spread like fire during the bitter religious conflicts connected with the rise of Protestantism and was encouraged by the Protestant reference to the biblical story of the Witch of Endor and the injunction that a witch should not be permitted to live. Fanned by such books as Bodin's *The Demonology of Sorcerers* and Richard Baxter's *Certainty of a World of Spirits,* alleged witches were tortured and burned or hanged by the hundreds, especially in war-torn Germany and France, but also in England, New England, and the Spanish colonies. At its height, the papal *Curia* considered witchcraft a delusion, and the Roman Inquisition, like the Spanish, greatly relaxed the persecutions by insisting upon a careful examination of evidence. The most thorough and effective Protestant condemnation of witchcraft was *The Discovery of Witchcraft,* published by Reginald Scot, a Kentish squire, in 1584. But the mania persisted for more than a century after that date.

## Religious Toleration

The Reformation, as an age of faith, was also an age of religious persecution in general. The rise of Protestantism did not of itself assure the end of trials and punishment for heresy, for Protestants, like Catholics, believed that they were in possession of the sole, objective truth; that heresy would lead to the damnation of the individual and the corruption of society as a whole; and that the persecution of heretics was pleasing to God and beneficial to society. Although Luther maintained that force should not be used in matters of faith, he later permitted religious persecution in effect by making heresy virtually identical with blasphemy. Calvin, by stressing the majesty of God, made heresy an insult to God and one of the greatest of crimes. He went further than the Catholics by making heresy itself, not a relapse into heresy, punishable by death.

One of the most important differences between Catholics and Protestants with respect to persecution lay in the fact that the latter discarded canon law and substituted for it the Bible and Roman law. In time, however, it became evident that the Bible was too uncertain a guide to persecution, and the Justinian Code of the Roman law, which provided the death penalty for the denial of the Trinity and a repetition of baptism, gradually lost its popularity. Because the Protestants relied primarily upon the Roman law, it is easy to see why the chief heresies punished by them in the sixteenth century were anti-Trinitarianism and Anabaptism and why the Anabaptists insisted that they did not believe in rebaptizing but only in adult baptism.

Although the Protestants held theories concerning persecution that were in the main similar to those of the Catholics, they contributed more to the theory of religious liberty. In the first place, the presence of a large number of creeds tended to raise among Protestants the question whether any one was absolutely right in every respect, especially when ethics came to be considered a test for the validity of the creeds. In the second place, there was a growing tendency among Protestants to reduce the essentials of Christianity to a common denominator, to a few basic doctrines common to all the Christian creeds. In the third place, many Protestants began to feel that, because men were predestined to salvation, persecution could not produce the desired results.

The growth of religious toleration was furthered largely by (1) the sectarian theory of the church, (2) favorable political conditions, and (3) the growing number of liberal and rational thinkers. The sectarians from the outset maintained that a church existed only where believers covenanted to walk in the ways of Christ. Therefore they could not accept the theory of a state church.

The territorial particularism of Germany was responsible for the inclusion of the principle of *cuius regio, eius religio* in the Peace of Augsburg of 1555 and the Peace of Westphalia of 1648. The bitterness of the religious wars in France led the *politiques* to favor a policy of including both Catholics and Protestants in one state, a policy embodied in the Edict of Nantes. In the Compact of Warsaw of 1573, the Protestants of Poland agreed to live together in peace. In England, also, there was an attempt to retain all Protestant groups in the Anglican Church, although the dissenters refused to be included in it.

Protestantism, greatly divided yet firm in its religious convictions, was gradually influenced by the arguments of the liberal and rational religious thinkers but did not sacrifice the fundamentals of Christianity. The broad tolerance of Erasmus found a few courageous defenders in the age of persecution. Probably the greatest plea for religious toleration was made by Sebastian Castellio, the Erasmian who joined Calvin in Geneva, only to break with him over the question of the divine inspiration of the Song of Songs in the Old Testament. In his *Concerning Heretics* and subsequent writings, prompted by the execution of Servetus, Castellio drew a distinction between essentials and nonessentials in Christianity, including among the latter the doctrines of the Trinity, predestination, and the location of Christ's body. He argued that only a belief in the clear scriptural statements concerning the way of salvation should be made mandatory. Reason, through which God continued to reveal the plan of salvation, must correct what we learn by sensual perception and revelation. Reason and ethical considerations show how wrong it is for Christians to persecute their fellow believers.

A mystical approach to religious tolerance was demonstrated in the life and work of David Joris (1501–1556), an eccentric Anabaptist from the Low Countries. Long the leader of a persecuted underground movement, he readily became an advocate of religious liberty. God, he maintained, impartially gives grace to all nations and sects, to all people who personally experience Christ's incarnation and passion. Because faith was for Joris an experience of the eternal Word of God in the heart, not an affirmation of the Bible and creeds, no rulers were competent to judge whether or not a person was a heretic. Persecution was thus contrary to this faith and also to the nature of the true church, which was always a suffering, persecuted church.

Bernardino Ochino, the general of the Capuchins who became Protestant after he had reached the age of fifty and who was compelled to wander from place to place during five exiles, derived his ideas concerning religious liberty not only from his experiences among Protestants of different faiths but from his conception of the operation of the Holy Spirit, who continued to guide the hearts and minds of man. His influence was great because of his brilliant sermons, which won him the support of high and low alike in Italy, Geneva, Basel, England, Zurich, Poland, and finally Moravia. Like Castellio, Ochino distinguished between essentials and nonessentials, stating that the bitter disputes among the Protestants were an evidence of lack of faith, for Paul had urged Christians to love one another. Heretics should therefore be treated with love and patience, and enemies should not be met with armed resistance.

Equally significant in the development of religious toleration was the work of Giacomo Aconcio, better known as Jacobus Acontius (1492–1566?), who published his *The Stratagem of Satan* in Basel in 1565. He was a jurist and humanist of Trent who embraced Protestantism, visited a number of Protestant centers on the Continent, and ended his days in the service of Queen Elizabeth I of England. He became particularly disturbed over the brutality connected with the wars of religion in France and the evil consequences of attempting to enforce religious uniformity. In *The Stratagem* he argued that it is Satan who induces men to kill one another over religion. To counter the work of Satan, he stressed the spiritual content of the Bible, demanded that the secular powers refrain from interference in religious matters, and urged complete freedom of conscience within the framework of what he considered the few essential Christian doctrines. The truth, he maintained, could be arrived at only by free discussion and inquiry.

Dirck Volkertzoon Coornheert (1522–1590), a Dutch merchant and statesman who never renounced his Catholicism but was nonetheless strongly influenced by mysticism, Erasmian humanism, Lutheranism, Calvinism, and Anabaptism, consistently opposed the persecution of heretics. His views on spiritual Christianity and religious toleration contributed much to the development of Arminianism and Pietism.

So far had religious toleration progressed by the end of the sixteenth century that punishment of heresy with death gradually disappeared. In England only two persons were compelled to die for their faith in the seventeenth century, and on the Continent the usual punishment was banishment or imprisonment. The struggle for religious liberty was thereafter furthered mostly by Englishmen who were simultaneously carrying the torch for greater personal freedom in the political and economic as well as the religious spheres. In these circumstances Milton could eloquently defend the toleration of the sects as long as they did not deny what he considered the essentials of Christianity, and Roger Williams could advance his belief that each individual should be allowed to believe and act according to the dictates of his own conscience. But Williams believed that only the select few could belong to the true Christian

Church. It remained for John Locke to formulate the most potent theories for religious toleration and liberty, and for men of later centuries to carry them into practice.

## Education and the Writing of History

The Reformation, both Protestant and Catholic, also greatly influenced education. Inherited scholastic methods and content were retained; but they were gradually modified by the humanism of the Renaissance, the theology and pedagogy of the reformers, and, eventually, the development of rational, scientific thought.

Probably the most significant influence of Protestantism was its extension of education to a much larger segment of the population. Luther insisted that all the cities, towns, and villages of Germany should establish schools supported by public funds and compel the children to attend. He thus gave the first great impetus to free, compulsory education for all children, for he wished to provide them all not only with religious instruction but also with an appreciation of culture. Melanchthon, called the *praeceptor Germaniae,* or teacher of Germany, helped the civil authorities of Saxony establish schools, suggested the division of the children into classes, and wrote a number of widely used textbooks. The schools of Wittenberg, Strassburg, and Geneva served as models for the many Protestant educators who came into contact with them.

In England the dissolution of the monasteries and the suppression of chantries and chantry schools led Henry VIII to order the clergy to instruct the young; but the king did little to support schools. Edward VI, however, endowed about thirty grammar schools. By the end of the seventeenth century, nearly five hundred new schools had been founded in England. The so-called public schools of Eton, Winchester, and Westminster were supported by private or royal endowments and were attended only by the sons of the nobles, the gentry, and the wealthy townsmen. Scotland, by a law of 1641, provided free elementary education for all children. But education was first made compulsory as well as universal and free in the American colonies. Two laws of the General Court of Massachusetts, passed in 1642 and 1647, finally incorporated those provisions that had been recommended by many educators since the days of Luther and served as models for the other colonies.

In the Catholic countries, education remained in the hands of the Church and by the end of the sixteenth century was advanced most rapidly by the Jesuits. In their schools, less emphasis was placed upon flogging than upon the stimulation of ambition and love of learning and discipline. They were usually subsidized by the state as well as the Church and private endowments and were soon opened to outsiders.

The fact that Protestant governments began to take over the responsibility of educating children did not at first notably alter the contents and purposes of education, for the chief subjects remained religion and the classics. The main changes made by the educators of the sixteenth century were concerned with method, that is, improving the teaching of the old subjects—religion, reading, writing, Latin, Greek, and, in some schools, Hebrew. The entire approach remained literary. History and science were studied only as by-products, the former of the study of Livy, the latter of Pliny. Yet a few bold spirits demanded the enlargement of the scope of education. Rabelais wanted schools to teach morals, physical well-being, and science; Montaigne advocated the study of modern languages; Bacon complained of the lack of laboratories for the study of science; Milton suggested such practical subjects as geography, navigation, engineering, law, politics, music, and the natural sciences; and the Jesuits demanded a more thorough study of history and scholastic philosophy.

## The Universities

The Reformation Era also witnessed the modification of university instruction, but only to a slight degree. The most significant changes were connected with the introduction of humanism. This involved an increased emphasis on the classics and the development of a literary, rather than a philosophical, approach to culture. As important as the universities were, however—one out of every thirty-six hundred Englishmen was attending Oxford or Cambridge in 1630—they failed to measure up to their great opportunities because of their conservatism, outside control, and religious controversies.

Nearly all the universities were centers of conservatism, clinging to inherited curricula, methods, and organization with a tenacity that proved deadening. Therefore most of the advances in mathematics, science, and even philosophy were made by persons not connected with the universities, by men like Copernicus, Kepler, Boyle, Bacon, Guericke, Napier, and Descartes, to mention only a few. Instead of stimulating the minds of young people with the great mass of new knowledge being made available, the majority of professors were preoccupied with filling the minds of their students with old philosophies and classical authorities. And it must be admitted that this was done with considerable success.

The universities were also prevented from making the best possible contributions by their lack of freedom of thought. Virtually everywhere professors were compelled to swear oaths of allegiance and to subscribe to certain creeds. Territorial rulers made them serve the interests of the state, either by maintaining and propagating the accepted doctrinal position of the state or by training clergymen and lawyers to become obedient servants of the state. Coercion of public opinion by the state through education was widely accepted. Only a few raised their voices in behalf of academic freedom. Protestant and Catholic universities alike thus became involved in all the bitter political and religious struggles in which their rulers participated.

The University of Wittenberg, for example, which had promised to become one of the most progressive centers of learning, where humanist reforms had been introduced at an early date, which was attended by such well-known foreigners as Tyndale, Tycho Brahe, and Giordano Bruno, and where the Copernican system was openly taught, became so involved in the confessional controversies of Germany that it lost its fine reputation. And it became so much an instrument in the hands of its ruler that it did little more than prepare clergymen and servants of the state by the end of the Reformation Era.

The professors at the University of Leyden, founded during the revolt of the Low Countries, were practical enough to teach politics, economics, cosmography, chronology, and physics alongside the older courses. Yet they were compelled to subscribe to the Calvinist confession and forbidden to discuss the issues raised by the Arminian controversy. The professors at Oxford and Cambridge were forced to subscribe to the Anglican faith and the Act of Supremacy. During the Puritan Revolution they were compelled to recognize by oath the divine right of kings and during the dictatorship of Cromwell to swear allegiance to the Commonwealth and the Protectorate. Even the new university founded in Massachusetts in 1636, later called Harvard, was placed under the strict supervision of six magistrates and six ministers appointed by the General Court.

The Catholic universities fared no better, with the possible exceptions of Padua, which was under Venetian rule, and Pisa. At the latter, courses were given in engineering and applied mathematics, the first anatomical theater was constructed, and Galileo presented his theories. But at Bologna and all the other Italian universities, the professors were invariably compelled by oath to uphold Catholicism. Salamanca, the most famous of the many universities in Spain, flourished for a while but declined rapidly when the Inquisition and the censorship of books began to take their toll. The once-proud University of Paris exhausted itself in its conflicts with the Huguenots and the Jesuits and succumbed to the conservatism demanded by the state. When Cartesianism found a few proponents among its faculty, the Parlement forbade any attacks upon the ancient philosophers.

Nevertheless, by the end of the Reformation Era, new, more practical subjects began to find their way into the schools and universities and the new pedagogical theories began to bear fruit. It is difficult to assess the influence of such a work as Erasmus' *Colloquies* in making education more attractive and available to more people, of Ludovico Vives' *De disciplinis* in pointing out the value of observation and experiment and advocating education for women, or of Roger Ascham's *The Scholemaster* (1570) in its appreciation of the psychology of boys.

## Comenius

The greatest pedagogue of the Reformation Era was Johannes Amos Comenius (1592–1670), a Moravian churchman. Suffering greatly from the ravages of the Thirty Years' War and driven from place to place until he finally found a home in the United Provinces, he, like many of his illustrious contemporaries, sought a way to bring peace to the world. Whereas Grotius relied upon international law to achieve this end, Comenius relied upon education. In his most important pedagogical work, *The Great Didactic,* published in Czech in 1632 and in English in 1642, he presented his plan for a complete system of education for every province or country, from the home through the elementary public and Latin schools to the university. In all he would have people educated by simultaneously learning facts, doing things, and expressing thoughts. In other words, he believed that, from the beginning, observation of one's physical environment (physics), his own body (physiology), the skies (astronomy), the features of one's own country (geography), as well as a practical application and understanding should accompany the acquisition of linguistic ability. Like Vives, he desired the education of girls as well as boys.

## Advancement of Learning

Despite the tardiness of the educators of the period in accepting new pedagogical theories and adapting themselves to new scientific discoveries and the practical needs of their day, they did much to arouse an interest in learning and to prepare the way for the great achievements of later centuries. When the religious controversies receded and the lines dividing the various bodies of Christendom were well defined, the secularization of education followed rapidly and greater attention was given to secular interests.

Not the least of the consequences of the rise of Protestantism was the stimulus given to the publishing of books and the accumulation of manuscripts and books by libraries. Throughout the sixteenth century, Germany was the greatest producer of books, and the fair at Frankfurt was the greatest center for their distribution. These books reflected the predominant religious interests of the age.

The search for truth and power, characteristic of the age, was also evinced by the building up of great libraries, not only by the clergy and humanists, as in the past, but by secular rulers and the universities. The great Vatican Library was housed in a beautiful new building, constructed in 1558. Francis I and Marie de' Medici added many books and manuscripts to the Royal Library of France, which has become one of the most complete in the world. In 1672 it contained approximately thirty thousand books and ten thousand manuscripts. The most famous among the many university libraries was the one founded at Oxford University by Sir Thomas Bodley in 1602. By 1620 there were six thousand books in this collection. In 1610 the Stationer's Company gave the library a copy of every book published by its members. Because this practice was later made a law, the Bodleian Library today has a copy of virtually every book published in England since 1610.

## Historiography

The religious controversies associated with the rise of Protestantism also gave a great impetus to the study and writing of history. The Protestants, by comparing the status of the church in their time with that in the time of Christ and the apostles, by challenging the foundations upon which the Catholic Church rested, became historically minded and soon forced their opponents to examine these foundations for their counterattacks. Moreover, the identification of the larger Protestant groups with territorial and national states helped stimulate an interest in national histories. Although much of the historical writing of the period was polemical and subjective, the historians brought to light many neglected sources, dispelled many erroneous views, and established many new historical data.

Whereas the humanists considered history a form of literature in which they imitated the style of the ancients and concerned themselves primarily with political and aristocratic topics, the writers of church history, which was born in the Reformation Era, generally dispensed with literary qualities and concentrated upon the long-neglected topics of religion and ecclesiastical institutions. Whereas the chief purpose of most humanist historians was to provide examples of good and bad conduct for moral guidance, that of the church historians was to make history the handmaiden of their respective theologies.

The first comprehensive history of the Church was published by Matthäus Flacius (1520–1575) and six collaborators between the years 1559 and 1574. This monumental work of thirteen volumes, covering the history of the Church to the year 1300, was called *Magdeburg Centuries,* for it was written a century to a volume. It was frankly biased, viewing all history as a struggle between God and the devil in which the pope was Antichrist and the Catholic Church his empire. Although the authors amassed a great number of sources, these were selected and used to serve polemical ends. Miracles were also accepted if they proved the authors' contentions, and so absurd a legend as that of the female Pope Joan was taken at face value. Yet this bitter attack upon Catholicism, poorly arranged and exceptionally dull, provided a strong impetus to the study of history and served the cause of historical criticism by exposing the forgeries known as the Pseudo-Isidorian Decretals.

The Catholic answer to the *Magdeburg Centuries* was the equally biased, poorly arranged, and dull *Ecclesiastical Annals* of Caesar Baronius (1538–1607), published in many folios between the years 1588 and 1607. Baronius had a great advantage over the centuriators in that he had access to the Vatican and other excellent libraries in Italy, although he lacked a command of Greek and Hebrew and a broad knowledge of the past. Yet his imposing history was long accepted as authoritative and provided historians with much material otherwise inaccessible.

Much more bitter was the polemical historiography concerned with contemporary events. The first important Protestant history of the Reformation, however, the *Commentaries on the Religious and Political History of Charles V,* written by the Lutheran Johann Sleidan (1506–1556) and published in 1555, was remarkably free of bias. Because the author was a humanist and a diplomat, he recorded the events of the stirring period from 1517 to 1555 in a lively style and included all the documents available to him. Even though he gave no interpretation of the events leading to the Reformation, his work long remained the best single source for the period.

Probably the most brilliant and provocative historical writing of the period came from the pen of the Venetian friar Pietro Paolo Sarpi (1552–1623), whose role in the conflict between Venice and the papacy made him a controversial figure. Exceptionally proficient in Latin, Greek, and Hebrew; thoroughly familiar with classical scholarship, history, and law; widely informed with respect to mathematics and the natural sciences, he was without a doubt one of the most educated men of his day. He wrote a number of works in which he reflected the Venetian views concerning the separation of church and state. Although he remained a Catholic, he hurled his sharpest shafts at the political pretensions of the popes and the intrigues of the Jesuits and criticized the lack of scholarship displayed in the *Annals* of Baronius.

The best-known polemical history by Sarpi was his *History of the Council of Trent,* published first in Italian in London in 1619 and subsequently in Latin, French, German, and English translations. It was his purpose to show that the Council of Trent, called to re-establish the unity of the Church, made the schism permanent and irreconcilable. Although the book is tendentious and bitter, it is based on information obtained directly from important men who participated in the council and from the secret archives of Venice. For data not covered by such sources, he relied heavily upon Sleidan, whom he considered an accurate writer.

Naturally papal supporters, particularly the Jesuits, bitterly assailed Sarpi's account of the Council of Trent. Terentio Alciati, a Jesuit teacher at the Roman College, was selected to write a refutation of it, but he died before he could make use of the many sources that he had gathered. His place was then taken by the Jesuit Sforza Pallavicino (1607–1667). His *History of the Council of Trent,* published 1656–1657, embodied the results of a tremendous amount of labor in the archives and libraries of Italy and contained much material inaccessible to Sarpi. Yet it suffers from the same tendentious spirit as Sarpi's work and is so obviously intended to prove Sarpi wrong in point after point that it is exceedingly uninspiring.

One of the best political histories of the Reformation is the *History of His Times,* written by Jacques Auguste de Thou, or Thaunus (1553–1617). The author was a member of a well-known French family, was well trained in law, and had valuable experience as a councilor of Henry III and Henry IV and as president of the Parlement of Paris. His work, finally published in five volumes in 1620, was primarily a history of France from 1546 to 1607. It shows the author's love for Henry IV, his hatred of the Guises, and his advocacy of religious tolerance. Although he was a Catholic, he defended Gallicanism, for which reason his book was placed on the Index.

Among the many good histories written by Netherlanders, those from the pen of Pieter Cornelissen Hooft (1581–1647), "the Dutch Tacitus," deserve mention here. Determined to make Dutch a literary vehicle, he wrote a number of dramas and histories in that language. His *Nederlandsche Historien,* covering the period from 1555 to 1587, shows exceptional ability and vast learning.

Juan de Mariana (1536–1624), who is best known for his works on political thought, was the outstanding Spanish historian of the Catholic Reformation. He wrote his widely read *History of Spain* in Latin, primarily to acquaint non-Spaniards with the history of his country.

The well-known *History of the World,* written by Sir Walter Raleigh (1552?–1618) while in prison, was carried down to about 130 B.C. Although limited in his sources and by his desire to make history teach moral lessons, he presented a large mass of material in a beautiful style and showed the importance of the study of geography for history. The best English historian of the period was William Camden (1551–1623), whose *Britannia,* published in 1586, won him immediate recognition as an outstanding scholar. His later works, though equally thorough and critical of sources, never reached the popularity of the *Britannia.* Despite his patriotism and loyalty to the Anglican Church, his work was unusually free of prejudice and bitterness. He was one of the first historians to show the interrelation between religious and political history and to point to the importance of geography and institutional and social history. The Camden Society, founded in 1838, was named for him.

The *History of Scotland* by George Buchanan (1506–1582), a Scottish historian and publicist, was written in an excellent Latin style. It is still valuable as a source for the history of Scotland during the author's life.

## Critical Historiography

The first successful application of the critical method to the study of historical sources was made by the Bollandist Fathers, a society of Jesuit scholars. They took upon themselves the task of purging the lives of the saints of spurious materials for the purpose of discovering their true importance in the history of Christianity and of making use of these lives in the work of the Catholic Reformation. They took their name from Jean Bollandus (1596–1665), a Belgian Jesuit who organized the group and prepared the first volumes of the work, called *Acta sanctorum,* or *Lives of the Saints.* The first two volumes appeared in 1643. It is still in the process of publication. The preface, written by Bollandus for the first volume, constitutes the first comprehensive statement concerning historical method.

Great contributions to historical scholarship were also made by the Benedictine scholars of the Congrégation de St. Maur, another product of the Catholic Reformation. These Maurists were eager to restore the high degree of scholarship that had been achieved by the Benedictines of the Middle Ages. They made excellent use of the vast collections of sources found in their houses throughout France. Their particular contributions to the development of historical method consisted of developing the auxiliary sciences of paleography, or the study of the handwriting of the medieval sources, and diplomatics, or the study of the circumstances surrounding the origins of official documents.

With the aid of these newly developed sciences, one of the first famous scholars of St. Maur, Dom Luc D'Archery (1609–1685), edited and published thirteen volumes of original medieval documents. He was followed by a large number of able scholars whose major contributions to the study of medieval history fall outside the period of the Reformation.

# Literature, Art, and Music

A brief glance at the literature, art, and music of the Reformation Era will show that both the form and the content were influenced by the powerful religious forces unleashed by the Protestant and Catholic reformers. The impact of the Italian Renaissance, with its aristocratic urbanity, half-hearted skepticism, and classical restraint, was long felt in northern Europe; but it soon gave way to a spirit reflecting the more elemental religious, social, and political concerns of the people as a whole, particularly as evinced in the national rivalries so closely associated with the religious conflicts. The element of youthful daring, virility, and imagination, not far removed from the Gothic spirit of the high Middle Ages, flowered toward the end of the period in what has come to be called the baroque spirit with its youthful exuberance, religious fervor, and unbounded drive for power.

# Part Four: Religious Conflicts and Consequences

## Literature

Attention has already been called to the vitality and majesty of the religious literature of the great reformers. Its influence upon the development of the national literatures of our day is suggested by the mere mention of Luther's translation of the Bible, Calvin's *Institutes,* Tyndale's Bible, Cranmer's *Book of Common Prayer,* Foxe's *Book of Martyrs,* the Authorized Version of the Bible, Loyola's *Spiritual Exercises,* and St. Teresa's *Way to Perfection.*

The Catholic Reformation immediately influenced the literature of Italy, as seen in the beautiful poetry of Michelangelo and his friend Vittoria Colonna (1490–1547). Interest in the medieval romances and religious ideals was revived by the epics of Ludovico Ariosto (1474–1533) and Torquato Tasso (1544–1595). The *Orlando Furioso* of Ariosto utilized the legends connected with Charlemagne and King Arthur, and the *Gierusalemme Liberata* of Tasso told the story of the First Crusade with sincere Catholic devotion. The revulsion against the sensualism and paganism of the Italian Renaissance is found in the many poems of remorse, probably best represented by the *Tears of St. Peter* of Luigi Tansillo (1510–1565), imitated by Catholics in many countries.

Medieval romances had exerted their greatest influence in Spain; but they received their death blow by the ridicule of Miguel de Cervantes (1547–1616), a typically baroque personality. His *Don Quixote* (1605, 1615) unquestionably ranks among the best novels ever written. The exploits of the romantic hero and Sancho Panza, the simple but practical peasant squire, laughed chivalry out of existence and reflected the new national interests of Cervantes' country and Europe.

It is difficult to explain the brilliant literary creativity of Spain during her period of political and economic decline. One is amazed at the lyrical versatility of Lope de Vega (1562–1635), the creator of many novels, sonnets, odes, epics, ballads, and hundreds of comedies and sacred plays; the great productivity of the priest Tirso de Molina (1571–1648), who wrote rollicking comedies and devout sacred dramas; and the brilliance of Pedro Calderon (1600–1681), trained by the Jesuits, who brought Spanish drama to its height. All showed with consummate skill the great conflict between the patriotic duties to their king and the higher duties to God, between reality and illusion, between the spirit of the conquistador and that of the saint. In the true baroque spirit, the transcendence of God triumphed over the materialism of the world, which is depicted as the great illusion and vanity.

Both Protestants and Catholics made use of the drama in bringing religious ideas and ideals to the people. These plays were usually presented by students. One is reminded of Theodore Beza's *Sacrifice of Abraham,* performed by students in Geneva and Lausanne in 1552, and the *Holy*

*Tragedies,* written by Desmazures about the same time. It was the Jesuits, however, who made the best use of the drama in their colleges, playing to numerous houses throughout Catholic lands. Montaigne, in 1554, as a lad of eleven, acted a part in a play by George Buchanan while attending the Jesuit college at Guyenne. There is no doubt that these plays had a considerable influence upon French drama through Pierre Corneille (1606–1684), the greatest French playwright of this period, who had studied at the Jesuit college at Rouen for seven years.

Corneille's first great drama was *Le Cid,* first performed in 1636. It shows the influence of classical and Spanish models, but it was so completely adapted to the tastes and interests of his day that the new *Académie Française* raised serious questions about its form. Although Corneille subsequently adhered more closely to the rules of dramatic art as laid down by Aristotle, that is, to the spirit of *les précieux,* the characters of his plays now show the baroque tendencies of the Jesuit dramas. This was particularly true of his *Polyeucte* (1643), in which an Armenian nobleman is won over to Christianity, earns the crown of martyrdom, brings others to the Lord, and induces the Roman emperor to relax the persecution.

The tremendous creative activity of the United Provinces after the successful revolt against Spain found expression in the rise of Dutch literature, first encouraged by the dramatist and historian Pieter Cornelissen Hooft. In this he was aided by his contemporary Joost van den Vondel (1587–1679), the greatest Dutch poet and dramatist. His tragedy, *Lucifer,* in which he combined classical and Christian elements in baroque fashion, exerted a strong influence upon Milton. Vondel, like Milton and Grotius, had a strong aversion for strict Calvinism, especially predestination, and he eventually joined the Catholic Church.

Vondel also greatly influenced the German baroque dramatists, the best known of whom was Andreas Gryphius (1616–1664), the poet of the Thirty Years' War. Gryphius carried the pathos of the baroque to greater extremes than any other well-known contemporary literary figure. The realistic and sensual characteristics of the baroque spirit were best portrayed in the *Simplicius Simplicissimus* of Hans Jakob Christoph von Grimmelshausen (1620–1676), a picaresque novel concerned with the adventures of an ordinary rascal during the Thirty Years' War.

Influences of the Italian Renaissance were long felt in England, but they were so modified by the patriotism, the adventurous spirit, and the new religious enthusiasm of the Elizabethans that historians of English literature scarcely use the word *Renaissance* in reference to sixteenth-century England. The first of the great Elizabethan poets was Edmund Spenser (1552?–1599), a devout Puritan and a patriotic Englishman. Although he still used medieval allegory and the romance of King Arthur in his great epic, the *Faerie Queen,* he wrote with a definite moral purpose, "to fashion a gentleman or noble person in a virtuous or noble discipline." Yet he shared the typically Elizabethan love for sensuous delight and splendor.

It was in the drama that the youthful vigor and joy of living of the rapidly rising national state of England found its best expression. The names of the many excellent dramatists of Elizabethan England have been obscured by the brilliance of the greatest of them all, William Shakespeare (1564–1616), who had the ability to present graphically to all classes all the elemental passions and drives of human nature. When he retired to Stratford on Avon, his birthplace, at the age of forty-five, his place in London was taken by Ben Jonson (1573–1637), a close scholar of the classical drama.

Before Jonson's death, however, the youthful, sensual, and romantic enthusiasm of Elizabethan England had given way to the mature, ascetic, and somber forces of Puritan England. Sobered by the bitter internal political and religious conflicts with the Stuart kings and the practical application of Calvinism to the actualities of life, people could appreciate the moral earnestness of the poetry of John Milton (1608–1674) and the prose of John Bunyan (1628–1688).

*Paradise Lost,* one of the greatest epics of all time, was a synthesis of Protestant thought as the *Divine Comedy* of Dante was of medieval thought. In unexcelled blank verse Milton portrayed the horrors of hell and the glories of heaven with an imagination and a beauty appreciated by people of our own day as well as by his contemporaries.

Bunyan epitomized in his life the depths of despair and the fear of damnation that came to the poor, uneducated people of his day. Driven by his personal religious experiences and the Puritan ideas that he had assimilated without a formal education, he preached to the masses without the authority of the church. During many years of imprisonment he gleaned from a study of the Bible and Foxe's *Book of Martyrs* the thoughts that he finally presented in his *Pilgrim's Progress,* one of the best allegories in the history of literature. Countless numbers of people have suffered with the humble Christian as he traveled from the City of Destruction to the Celestial City.

## The Fine Arts

The fine arts reflected even more clearly than literature the various spiritual and intellectual forces unleashed by the Reformation. Whereas Luther affirmed the good and beautiful things of this world, especially music, which he considered the greatest gift of God next to the Bible, Zwingli, Calvin, the Anabaptists, and the Jansenists were inclined to minimize the importance of the fine arts in their strict biblicism, if they did not condemn them outright. Catholicism, especially under the leadership of the Jesuits, made full use of the products of the Italian Renaissance, now brought into a new synthesis with the Gothic, to proclaim to the world its unity, majesty, and power.

The form that art assumed during the latter half of the Reformation has been called *baroque,* at first a term of derision. Expressing both the mystical unity with God and the dynamic drive for power, the supersensuous ideals of the Gothic and the sensuous elements of the Renaissance, medieval transcendentalism and Renaissance naturalism, ecstatic piety and mathematical clarity, it readily reflected the chief characteristics of both the Catholic Reformation and royal absolutism.

## Architecture

As the medieval unity of Christendom had been reflected in the synthesis of the arts in the Gothic cathedral, so the new conception of unity was reflected in a new architectural synthesis, not only of the church but especially of the palace. Although the purer conceptions of classical architecture were furthered by the widely imitated work of Andrea Palladio (1518–1580), the classical conceptions of the Renaissance had already been greatly modified by Michelangelo (1475–1564) in his changes of Bramante's plans for the church of St. Peter's at Rome. The massive colonnade and much of the interior decoration of St. Peter's were the work of the greatest baroque artist of Italy, Giovanni Lorenzo Bernini (1598–1680). But the purest example of early baroque architecture was Il Gesù, the church built in Rome by the Jesuits between 1568 and 1575, a basilica with a square front and centering in a small dome.

Among the chief characteristics of baroque architecture, as seen in Il Gesù, are the following: (1) emphasis upon spatial unity and grandeur, with the subordination of all lesser parts; (2) an agitated rhythmic character, connecting all the various parts with the main space in great, sweeping waves and curves; (3) a synthesis with architecture of painting, sculpture, even music, and, in the case of the palaces, of landscape architecture, conceived mathematically; and (4) profuse ornamentation consisting of twisted columns, brilliant colors, skillful lighting, agitated sculpture, and paintings of animated cherubs, angels, and religious figures. So many baroque structures were erected in Rome in the seventeenth century that the city took on a distinctly baroque character, which it has not lost to our day.

In Spain the unity of conception characteristic of the baroque found expression in the Escorial, built for Philip II between 1563 and 1584. A combination of palace, museum, and mausoleum, it was impressive but lacked the beauty of the French palace, the Louvre. This was enlarged by Claude Perrault (1613–1688), who combined certain baroque features with the simpler classical features more congenial to the French. Baroque elements were introduced into England by Inigo Jones (1573–1652), who built the banqueting house of Whitehall. But in England, as in France, the interest in pure classical forms prevailed over the baroque. Baroque architecture probably reached its finest expression in Vienna.

## Baroque Sculpture

The most representative and powerful of the baroque sculptors was Bernini. His most striking and most discussed work was his "St. Teresa in Ecstasy" (1646), an altar figure made for the Santa Maria della Vittoria in Rome. Teresa, overcome by the ecstasy and resting on a billowy cloud, is faced by a smiling angel, both illuminated by a mystic, golden light from colored windows. Bernini's dramatic, emotional, yet natural sculpture was imitated by artists throughout Europe, particularly in France. His influence is apparent, for example, in the well-known "Tomb of Mazarin" by Antoine Coysevox (1640–1720).

## Baroque Painting

Baroque painting had its inception in the combination of the form of Michelangelo with the coloring of Titian. Its most characteristic features were the use of chiaroscuro (distribution of light and shade), the merging of central figures with their background, the gradual softening of the sharp outlines of the figures, the profuse use of pigments, and imaginative and spiritual portrayal.

Among the first of the Italian masters to display these baroque characteristics in painting was the Venetian Jacopo Robusti, better known as Tintoretto (1518–1594). Although he consciously imitated Michelangelo and Titian, his treatment of Christian and classical themes illustrated his unusual imagination, originality, power, and technical skill. His "Presentation of the Virgin in the Temple" is a worthy product of the Catholic Reformation.

Tintoretto was followed by a large number of artists who imitated the manner of one or another of the masters and thus came to be called mannerists. Another group of painters, the eclectics, sought to copy the best features of all the great artists. Although these eclectics lacked originality, they contributed many well-known paintings illustrative of the spirit of militant Catholicism. The reaction to this imitative painting was led by Michelangelo da Caravaggio (1573–1610), who excelled in portraying martyrs, miracles, and visions with a new vitality and a naturalism that did not omit the ugly and the brutal in man.

The dualism of the Spaniard, his Catholicism and nationalism, mysticism and realism, asceticism and gaiety, found expression in the masterpieces of El Greco (1547?–1614), Velasquez (1599–1660), and Murillo (1618–1682). It is strange that a Greek, Domenico Theotocopuli, called El Greco, was the first to portray on canvas the spirit of the militant Catholicism and nationalism of the Spaniards. Having absorbed the baroque spirit in Venice, he protrayed deep spiritual emotions in his elongated, almost Gothic, figures and by the use of unusual coloring, producing an expressionism that was widely imitated in the twentieth century. Probably the best examples of his unique style are his "Christ on the Cross" and the "Resurrection."

Whereas El Greco used his talents primarily in the service of the Church, Diego Velasquez served almost exclusively the court, that is, Philip IV and his royal family. Although he had been greatly influenced by Titian and Tintoretto, he preferred to retain the sharper classical lines of their predecessors and to paint what he actually saw. He devotedly sought to flatter and please his royal patron, yet he faithfully portrayed the degeneracy of the Spanish Hapsburgs, their unhealthy faces, and their weak characters, as in his well-known "Maids of Honor" and his many portraits of Philip IV. He showed his mastery in depicting the might and glory of Spanish arms in his "Capture of Breda," commemorating the Spanish victory over the Dutch at Breda in 1625.

Bartolomé Esteban Murillo was at his best in portraying both mysticism and naturalism. He won universal acclaim by his devout treatment of the Catholic devotion to the Church and the love of Mary. He painted at least fifteen pictures of the "Immaculate Conception of Mary," in which he elevated her to the skies and brought the angels down to earth. Because of his beautiful madonnas he was called "The Raphael of Seville." His realistic genre paintings, such as the fascinating "Flower Girl" and "Dice Players," are among the best of that country.

All the vigor of the ten southern provinces of the Low Countries, which had finally chosen to break with the northern provinces in their struggle for independence, seemed to find expression in the glorification of Catholicism and the monarchy. Baroque painting flourished in those circumstances. Imitative not only of the realism and the religious sincerity of the Flemish followers of the van Eycks but also of the imagination and the sensuous qualities of the Italian and Spanish masters, it adapted all these to the romantic longings of the people.

The great master of the Flemish baroque was Peter Paul Rubens (1577–1640), who had learned his art in Antwerp, Italy, and Spain. In his attempts to glorify the princes whom he adored and the Catholic Church, he painted what he thought his subjects should be, not what they actually were. In his religious as well as secular pictures he combined pathos and sensuality to present a grand, cosmic unity in which all the highly animated figures were drawn together by an almost overwhelming unity of movement. In his "Elevation of the Cross" (1610–1611), for example, one notices the powerful movement of all the main figures, brought out boldly by the use of bright light against a dark background. But in both his religious and his secular themes there is the same strong pagan sensuousness that sometimes makes one wonder whether he was sincere in his avowed intention to teach virtue.

Rubens painted many excellent, well-known portraits, such as his "Anne of Austria." In this form of painting, however, he was excelled by his pupil Anthony Van Dyck (1599–1641), who became the court painter of Charles I of England. Although it was his purpose to portray the splendor of the English aristocracy, he did so with restraint and delicate taste.

Unlike the Flemish, the inhabitants of the United Provinces were Protestant and antiroyal in sentiment. Frowning upon the aristocratic and the ornate, they preferred a simple, unpretentious expression of religion in their art and delighted in the portrayal of Dutch landscapes and simple Dutch life. Yet the Dutch painting of this period also contained such baroque features as deep religious emotion and powerful realism.

Virtually all the main interests of Protestant Europe were reflected in the masterpieces of Rembrandt van Rijn (1606–1669), a native of Leyden and a well-educated Mennonite. Unlike Rubens, he did not flatter the aristocracy or even the wealthy burghers of the great commercial city of Amsterdam, where he did most of his work. On the contrary, he remained true to his conception of his task as an artist, despite the many misfortunes and even dire poverty that plagued him during the last decades of his life.

Although Rembrandt portrayed human nature with all its shortcomings and simple charms, he invested his subjects with an inner spirituality and life. This is apparent in "The Sortie of the Civic Guard" (1642), erroneously called "The Night Watch," one of the greatest of all baroque paintings; "The Syndics of the Cloth Guild" (1662); and "Dr. Tulp's Anatomy Lesson" (1632). In all these the figures, realistically portrayed as individuals, are skillfully merged into one unified whole. But it is in his religious paintings that he best demonstrates his consummate skill. In these Protestant biblicism, popular Christianity, and inner spirituality find their loftiest expression. Jesus appears not as a mighty potentate or deeply moved being but as a humble laborer and preacher, ministering to the needs of the common people. In his "Supper at Emmaus" of 1648, for example, Rembrandt pictures the two disciples seated at a simple table in an unprepossessing room, served by an ordinary waiter. None of the three is outwardly aware of the presence of Christ. Yet the disciples are completely transformed by Christ's presence and are filled with a profound spiritual power.

The baroque painting of France, like its architecture and literature, was much more strongly influenced by classicism than that of Spain and the Spanish Netherlands. The outstanding French painter of this period, Nicholas Poussin (1594–1665), had spent many years in Italy, where he had come into contact with both classicism and the baroque. His paintings resemble Corneille's dramas in many respects. For example, he delighted in producing classical stage effects, similar to those of Raphael;

but the undercurrent of passion and tension, the heroic and the ideal, are distinctly baroque, as is evident in his "Triumph of David" and "Rape of the Sabine Women." His landscapes, like those of other baroque painters, were attempts to improve upon nature, which many of his contemporaries considered lacking in order and symmetry.

Painting flourished in Germany during the first decades of the Reformation; but this country, like England, produced no great painters during the baroque period. The masterful portrayal of religious themes and personalities by Albrecht Dürer (1471–1528), in both paintings and woodcuts; the almost completely Renaissance portraits of Holbein the Younger (1497–1543); and the devout paintings and illustrations of Lucas Cranach the Elder (1472–1553), the painter of the Lutheran Reformation, had a number of imitators in the second half of the sixteenth century; but no painters of genius gave Germany a place alongside the other major continental countries of Europe with respect to art.

## Music

Music, the most abstract of all the arts, usually responds more slowly than the others to prevailing modes of expression. During much of this period counterpoint and polyphony were developed to a high degree, particularly in the Low Countries; but harmony, which had merely been incidental to polyphony, now received particular attention, alongside melody and rhythm. Furthermore, vocal music and instrumental music were gradually developed separately, especially because the latter better expressed the rising secular spirit. Among the most popular forms of secular music were the madrigal, a polyphonic setting for a poem, and the chanson, or descriptive song.

Probably the most important Protestant influence on the development of music was Luther's love for it, for he considered it the most glorious gift of God, next to the gospel. For this reason he appreciated it to the fullest, regardless of the confessional allegiance of the composer. One of his favorite composers was the Swiss Catholic Ludwig Senfl (c. 1492–1555), a musician at the Bavarian court in Munich, to whom he wrote a well-known letter. Following Senfl as Bavarian court musician was the Flemming Orlandus de Lassus (c. 1532–1594), one of the ablest and most prolific composers of his day, who produced many well known chansons, madrigals, Masses, and motets.

Considering music an important means of worshiping God, Luther and his co-workers developed to a high degree the chorale, or congregational hymn. Through it and by means of exceptionally good musical instruction in the schools, they brought music to all the people. Luther wrote not only such well-known hymns as "A Mighty Fortress Is Our God" and "Out of the Depths I Cry to Thee," but, according to his musician friend Johann Walther (1496–1570), the first part of the German

Mass. Undoubtedly one of the greatest composers of Lutheran hymns during the latter part of the Reformation Era was Paul Gerhardt (1607–1676), many of whose hymns still are sung by Protestants. Lutheran music reached its noblest expression in the work of Johann Sebastian Bach (1685–1750), who considered it his chief purpose to praise God in the spirit of Luther's theology.

Zwingli was, like Luther, an accomplished musician. His determination to retain nothing in the church service not derived from the Bible, however, led him to whitewash churches and remove pictures and organs from them. Under his successors music gradually reappeared in Zwinglian churches and the Swiss love for singing found an outlet in congregational song.

Calvin influenced the development of Protestant music by supporting the versification of Psalms and having them set to music. The first Calvinist Psalter, published in 1539, contained 18 Psalms, 5 of them versified by Calvin and 12 by the French poet Clément Marot, a protégé of Margaret of Navarre. The Calvinist Psalter of 1562 contained 150 versified Psalms, most of them versified by Marot and set to popular French chansons. Elizabethan England excelled in secular music, although considerable church music was written by such composers as William Byrd (1543–1623).

In musical forms other than the chorale, Italy provided the leadership after the middle of the sixteenth century. The Catholic Church preferred the singing of highly trained choirs to the popular singing of hymns and therefore obtained the best possible musicians to train and direct the choirs. Best known of the sixteenth-century Italian composers was Giovanni Pierluigi da Palestrina (1524–1594), papal organist and director of the papal choir. His compositions were written in the tradition of Flemish counterpoint, but they were purged of all secular elements and were adapted to the spirit and needs of the Catholic Reformation.

During the period of Italian hegemony in music, two new musical forms were produced, the oratorio and the opera, both expressions of the baroque spirit. The oratorio grew out of the desire to provide religious drama with a musical setting. The opera, its secular counterpart, expressed the baroque spirit better than any other art form. In this *dramma di musica,* vocal and instrumental music, the ballet, the drama, painting, sculpture, and architecture were brought together into one grand synthesis. The best of the early operatic composers was Claudio Monteverdi (1567–1643), whose well-known *Orfeo* was produced in Mantua in 1607 and whose *The Combat of Tancred and Clarinda* was successfully revived by the Metropolitan Opera Company in New York in 1929.

The Italian passion for music, and especially the opera, was so great that more than three thousand people were attracted to a single performance at the Barberini palace in 1639. Regardless of the bitter religious controversies of the day, northern Europeans were also attracted by Italian music and came to study in Italy. The strict Calvinist Duke Maurice of Hesse sent Heinrich Schütz (1585–1672), a law student, to study music under Italian musicians. Schütz became one of the great Protestant baroque musicians of Germany, the composer of such noble spiritual concerts as "When My Eyelids Close in Sleep." He composed several volumes of sacred symphonies, two stories of the resurrection, and three passions. In all he displayed exceptional dramatic power and sincere religious devotion.

From this brief summary of the heritage of the Reformation it is apparent that the search for truth, predominant at its beginning, was being superseded by a search for power at its close. Although the search for truth took place in every area of thought, it was primarily concerned with religion and found its noblest manifestations in the various forms of the Protestant and Catholic Reformations. The religious teachings of the reformers, which proved to be dynamic forces in society during the Reformation Era, have been frequently revived in subsequent centuries, particularly in times of storm and stress.

The search for power, arising out of the secular interests of the Reformation Era and stimulated by the astounding discoveries about man and the world in which he lives, found its best expression in the development of the national state. By 1660, this institution had become a highly organized unit with an interest in directing all the activities of its citizens. The ultimate consequences of giving to the secularized state complete control of society have not yet been made clear in the twentieth century.

# Appendix: The Popes of the Reformation Era

| | |
|---|---|
| 1503–1513 | Julius II (della Rovere) |
| 1513–1521 | Leo X (Medici) |
| 1522–1523 | Adrian VI (Dedel, Utrecht) |
| 1523–1534 | Clement VII (Medici) |
| 1534–1549 | Paul III (Farnese) |
| 1550–1555 | Julius III (del Monte) |
| 1555 | Marcellus II (Cervini) |
| 1555–1559 | Paul IV (Caraffa) |
| 1559–1565 | Pius IV (Medici, Milan) |
| 1566–1572 | St. Pius V (Ghislieri) |
| 1572–1585 | Gregory XIII (Buoncompagni) |
| 1585–1590 | Sixtus V (Peretti) |
| 1590 | Urban VII (Castagna) |
| 1590–1591 | Gregory XIV (Sfondrati) |
| 1591 | Innocent IX (Facchinetti) |
| 1592–1605 | Clement VIII (Aldobrandini) |
| 1605 | Leo XI (Medici) |
| 1605–1621 | Paul V (Borghese) |
| 1621–1623 | Gregory XV (Ludovisi) |
| 1623–1644 | Urban VIII (Barberini) |
| 1644–1655 | Innocent X (Pamphili) |

# Appendix: Rulers of the Chief Countries During the Reformation Era

## Holy Roman Empire

| | |
|---|---|
| 1493–1519 | Maximilian I |
| 1519–1556 | Charles V |
| 1558–1564 | Ferdinand I |
| 1564–1576 | Maximilian II |
| 1576–1612 | Rudolph II |
| 1612–1619 | Matthias |
| 1619–1637 | Ferdinand II |
| 1637–1657 | Ferdinand III |

## France

| | |
|---|---|
| | *Valois* |
| 1498–1515 | Louis XII |
| 1515–1547 | Francis I |
| 1547–1559 | Henry II |
| 1559–1560 | Francis II |
| 1560–1574 | Charles IX |
| 1574–1589 | Henry III |
| | *Bourbon* |
| 1589–1610 | Henry IV |
| 1610–1643 | Louis XIII |
| 1643–1715 | Louis XIV |

## England

| | |
|---|---|
| | *Tudor* |
| 1485–1509 | Henry VII |
| 1509–1547 | Henry VIII |
| 1547–1553 | Edward VI |
| 1553–1558 | Mary |
| 1558–1603 | Elizabeth I |
| | *Stuart* |
| 1603–1625 | James I |
| 1625–1649 | Charles I |

## Spain

| | |
|---|---|
| 1479–1504 | Ferdinand and Isabella |
| 1504–1506 | Ferdinand and Philip I |
| 1506–1516 | Ferdinand and Charles I |
| 1516–1556 | Charles I (also emperor) |
| 1556–1598 | Philip II |
| 1598–1621 | Philip III |
| 1621–1665 | Philip IV |

## Poland

| | |
|---|---|
| 1506–1548 | Sigismund I (Jagiello) |
| 1548–1572 | Sigismund II (Jagiello) |
| 1573–1574 | Henry (Valois) |
| 1575–1586 | Stephen Báthory (of Transylvania) |
| 1587–1632 | Sigismund III (Vasa) |
| 1632–1648 | Vladislav IV (Vasa) |
| 1648–1668 | John Casimir (Vasa) |

## Bohemia

| | |
|---|---|
| 1516–1526 | Louis II (Jagiello) |
| 1526–1564 | Ferdinand I (Hapsburg) |
| 1564–1576 | Maximilian I (Hapsburg, Maximilian II of Empire) |
| 1576–1612 | Rudolph II (Hapsburg) |
| 1612–1619 | Matthias (Hapsburg) |
| 1619–1620 | Frederick (of Palatinate) |
| 1619–1637 | Ferdinand II (Hapsburg) |
| 1637–1657 | Ferdinand III (Hapsburg) |

## Hungary

| | |
|---|---|
| 1516–1526 | Louis II (Jagiello) |
| 1526–1564 | Ferdinand I (Hapsburg) |
| 1526–1540 | John Zapolya |
| 1564–1576 | Maximilian (Hapsburg) |
| 1576–1608 | Rudolph (Hapsburg) |
| 1608–1619 | Matthias II (Hapsburg) |
| 1619–1637 | Ferdinand II (Hapsburg) |
| 1637–1657 | Ferdinand III (Hapsburg) |

## Ottoman Empire

| | |
|---|---|
| 1451–1481 | Mohammed II |
| 1481–1512 | Bayazid II |
| 1512–1520 | Selim I |
| 1520–1566 | Suleiman I |
| 1566–1574 | Selim II |
| 1574–1595 | Murad III |
| 1595–1603 | Mohammed III |
| 1603–1617 | Ahmed I |
| 1617–1618 | Mustapha I |
| 1622–1623 | |
| 1618–1622 | Osman II |
| 1623–1640 | Murad IV |
| 1640–1648 | Ibrahim I |

# Bibliography

## Bibliographical Aids and Works of Reference

The **basic sources** for reference works in all fields of historical research are Constance M. Winchell, *Guide to Reference Books,* 8th ed. (Chicago, 1967); Theodore Bestermann, *A World Bibliography of Bibliographies,* 5 vols. (Lausanne, 1965–1966); Louise Noëlle Malclès, *Les Sources du travail bibliographique,* Vol. 2, Parts 1 and 2: *Bibliographies spécialisées, sciences humaines* (Geneva, 1952); Edith M. Coulter and Melanie Gerstenfeld, *Historical Bibliographies* (Berkeley, Calif., 1935; New York, 1965); and George M. Dutcher and others, *A Guide to Historical Literature* (New York, 1931, 1949). Especially helpful for the Reformation Era are the seven fascicles published by the Comité International des Sciences Historiques in the *Bibliographie de la Réforme 1450–1648* (Leiden, 1958–1970), listing works on the Reformation published in Europe and the United States from 1940 to 1955.

For the history of the Reformation in **Germany,** the most comprehensive bibliography is Karl Schottenloher, *Bibliographie zur deutschen Geschichte im Zeitalter der Glaubensspaltung, 1517–1585,* 6 vols. (Leipzig, 1933–1939). Volume 7, *Das Schrifttum von 1938–1960* (Stuttgart, 1962), is an important supplement. There is a brilliant discussion of the sources in Franz Schnabel, *Deutschlands geschichtliche Quellen und Darstellungen in der Neuzeit,* Vol. 1 (Leipzig and Berlin, 1931). Gustaf Wolf, *Quellenkunde der deutschen Reformationsgeschichte,* 3 vols. (Gotha, 1915–1923), is still valuable. Also helpful is the extensive bibliography of German history by F. C. Dahlmann-G. Waitz, *Quellenkunde der deutschen Geschichte,* 9th ed. (Leipzig, 1931). Among helpful manuals containing detailed bibliographies are *Handbuch der Kirchengeschichte,* ed. by G. Krueger, Part 3: *Reformation und Gegenreformation,* 2nd ed., revised by Heinrich Hermelink and Wilhelm Maurer (Tübingen, 1931);

and *Handbuch der Kirchengeschichte,* ed. by Hubert Jedin, Vol. 4: *Reformation, Katholische Reform und Gegenreformation,* ed. by Erwin Iserloh, Joseph Glazick, Hubert Jedin (Freiburg i. Br., Basel, and Vienna, 1967).

The standard bibliographical aids for **English** history during the Reformation Era are the two volumes of the *Bibliography of British History:* the *Tudor Period, 1485–1603,* ed. by Conyers Read, 2nd ed. (Oxford, 1959), and the *Stuart Period, 1603–1714,* ed. by Godfrey Davies and Mary F. Keeler (Oxford, 1970). See also Alfred W. Pollard and G. R. Redgrave, *A Short Title Catalogue of Books Printed in England, Scotland and Ireland and of English Books Printed Abroad 1475–1640* (London, 1963). There also is the continuing bibliography, *Writings on British History,* containing titles of books and articles published since 1934, compiled by Alexander T. Milne (London, 1937–    ). See also Louis B. Frewer, *Bibliography of Historical Writings Published in Great Britain and the Empire, 1940–1945* (Oxford, 1947), and Joan C. Lancaster, *A Bibliography of Historical Works Issued in the United Kingdom, 1946–56* (London, 1957, 1964).

For **France** the most important bibliographies are Henri Hauser, *Les Sources de l'histoire de France. Le XVIᵉ siècle (1494–1610),* 4 vols. (Paris, 1906–1915), and Émile Bourgeois and Louis André, *Le XVIIᵉ Siècle (1610–1715),* 8 vols. (Paris 1913–1938); Pierre Caron and Henri Stein, *Répertoire bibliographique de l'histoire de France,* 6 vols. (Paris, 1923–1938); and A. Cioranesco, *Bibliographie de la littérature française du siezième siècle,* in collaboration with V. L. Saulnier (Paris, 1959).

The standard bibliographical reference for **Switzerland** is the *Bibliographie der Schweizer Geschichte,* published annually in the *Zeitschrift für Schweizer Geschichte,* called *Schweizer Zeitschrift für Geschichte* since 1951. For **Belgium** consult Henri Pirenne, *Bibliographie de l'histoire de Belgique,* 3rd ed. (Brussels, 1931), and the monthly *Bibliographie de Belgique* (Brussels, 1876–    ); for **The Netherlands,** C. L. Brinkman, *Catalogus van Boeken* (Leiden, 1833–    ), and *Bibliographie Neerlandica* (The Hague, 1962); for **Sweden,** S. E. Bring, *Bibliografisk Handbok till Sveriges Historia* (Stockholm, 1934); for **Denmark,** B. Erichsen and A. Krarup, *Dansk Historisk Bibliografi,* 3 vols. (Copenhagen, 1928–1929); for **Finland,** J. Vallinkoski, *Suomen historiallinen bibliografia, 1544–1900* (Helsinki, 1961); for **Poland,** *The Cambridge History of Poland,* ed. by W. F. Reddaway and others, Vol. 1: *From the Origins to Sobieski (to 1696)* (Cambridge, 1950); for **Russia,** Charles Morley, *Guide to Research in Russian History* (Syracuse, N.Y., 1951); for **Spain,** Raphael Ballester y Castell, *Bibliografía de la historia de España* (Gerona and Barcelona, 1921), Benito Sánchez-Alonso, *Fuentes de la historia española e hispano-americana,* 3rd ed., 3 vols. (Madrid, 1952), and, since

1954, the periodical *Bibliografía histórica de España e Hispanoamérica.*
**Journals** devoted exclusively to the Reformation era are the *Archiv für Reformationsgeschichte,* revived as an international journal in 1951 by the German Verein für Reformationsgeschichte and the American Society for Reformation Research; the *Luther Mitteilungen* and the *Luther Jahrbuch* of the Luther-Gesellschaft; and the *Zwingliana* of the Swiss Zwingli Verein. The following journals contain many articles and book reviews concerned with the Reformation: *Church History,* published by the American Society of Church History; the *Catholic Historical Review,* published by the Catholic Historical Association; *The Renaissance News* and *Studies in the Renaissance,* published by the Renaissance Society of America; *The Journal of Ecclesiastical History,* published in England; the *Records* of the Scottish Church History Society; the German *Zeitschrift für Kirchengeschichte;* the French *Revue de l'histoire de l'Eglise de France;* the *Bulletin historique et littéraire écclésiastique* and the *Ephemerides theologicae Lovaniensis* of Louvain, Belgium; the *Nouvelle revue théologique* of Lovain and Paris; the *Nederlands Archief voor Kerkgeschiedenis* of the Netherlands; the *Kyrkohistorisk Arsskrift* of Sweden; the *Zeitschrift für Schweizerische Kirchengeschichte* and the *Bibliothèque d'Humanisme et Renaissance* of Switzerland; the Italian *Il Rinascimento;* the *Jahrbuch für die Geschichte des Protestantismus in Österreich* of Austria; and the Polish *Reformacja w Polsce.*

Useful **works of reference** are *The New Catholic Encyclopaedia,* 15 vols. (New York, 1967); the *New Schaff-Herzog Encyclopedia of Religious Knowledge,* 13 vols. (Grand Rapids, Mich., 1949–1950), with two supplemental volumes prepared by American scholars (Grand Rapids, Mich., 1955); *Die Religion in Geschichte und Gegenwart,* 3rd ed., 6 vols. (Tübingen, 1957–1962); the *Lexikon für Theologie und Kirche,* 2nd ed., *10 vols.* (Freiburg i. Br., 1957–1965); and the *Dictionnaire de théologie catholique,* 15 vols. (Paris, 1925–1950). See also Karl Heussi, *Kompendium der Kirchengeschichte,* 11th ed. (Tübingen, 1957).

Numerous **sets of historical works** contain useful volumes on the Reformation. The detailed accounts in *The Cambridge Modern History,* Vols. 2–4 (New York and London, 1904–1906), have been replaced by two volumes in the *New Cambridge Modern History,* Vol. 2: *The Reformation, 1520–1559,* ed. by G. R. Elton (Cambridge, 1958); and Vol. 3: *Counter-Reformation and Price Revolution, 1559–1610,* ed. by R. B. Wernham (Cambridge, 1968). The *Rise of Modern Europe* series, ed. by W. L. Langer, includes Myron P. Gilmore, *The World of Humanism* (New York, 1952), and Carl J. Friedrich, *The Baroque Age* (New York, 1952). The *Geschichte der Neuzeit,* ed. by Gerhard Ritter, includes Erich Hassinger, *Das Werden des neuzeitlichen Europa, 1300–1600* (Braunschweig, 1959). The *Historia Mundi* has as Vol. 7 *Übergang zur Moderne* (Bern, 1957). *Peuples et civilisations,* ed. by L. Halphen and P. Sagnac, includes Vol. 8: H. Hauser and A. Renaudet, *Les Débuts de l'âge moderne,* 4th ed. (Paris, 1956), and Vol. 9: H. Hauser, *La Prépondérance espagnole* (Paris, 1933). The universal history, *Histoire générale des civilisations,* contains as Vol. 4 R. Mousnier's *Les XVIᵉ et XVIIᵉ Siècles* (Paris, 1954). C. Barbagallo's Vol. 4 of his *Storia universale* is *L'età della Rinassenza e della Riforma, 1454–1556* (Turin, 1936). The Foundation for Reformation Research is publishing *The Sixteenth Century Journal,* ed. by Carl S. Meyer (St. Louis, 1970–    ).

Among widely used **single volumes** are Roland H. Bainton's *The Reformation of the Sixteenth Century* (Boston, 1952) and *Women of the Reformation,* Vol. 1 (Minneapolis, Minn., 1971); *Reformation Studies: Essays in Honor of Roland Bainton* (Richmond, Va., 1962); Heinrich Bornkamm, *Das Jahrhundert der Reformation* (Göttingen, 1960); Owen Chadwick, *The Reformation* (Baltimore, Md., 1964); A. G. Dickens, *Reformation and Society in Sixteenth-Century Europe* (New York, 1966); G. R. Elton, *Reformation Europe, 1520–1559* (Cleveland, Ohio, 1963); Lucien Febvre, *Au Coeur religieux du XVIᵉ siècle* (Paris, 1957); Fritz Hartung, *Deutsche Geschichte im Zeitalter der Reformation, der Gegenreformation und des 30 Jährigen Krieges,* 2nd ed. (Berlin, 1963); Hajo Holborn, *A History of Modern Germany: The Reformation* (New York, 1959); Albert Hyma, *Renaissance to Reformation* (Grand Rapids, Mich., 1951); Paul Joachimsen, *Die Reformation als Epoche der deutschen Geschichte* (Munich, 1951); H. G. Koenigsberger and G. L. Mosse, *Europe in the Sixteenth Century* (New York, 1968); Franz Lau and Ernst Bizer, *A History of the Reformation in Germany,* trans. by B. A. Hardy (London, 1968); Harold H. Lentz, *Reformation Crossroads* (Minneapolis, Minn., 1948); Émile G. Leonard, *A History of Protestantism,* Vol. 1: *The Reformation,* ed. by H. H. Rowley, trans. by Joyce M. H. Reid (London and Camden, N.J., 1965); J. Russell Major, *The Age of the Renaissance and Reformation* (Philadelphia, Pa., 1970); Wilhelm Pauck, *The Heritage of the Reformation,* 2nd ed. (Glencoe, Ill., 1961); Preserved Smith, *The Age of the Reformation* (New York, 1920); Lewis W. Spitz, *The Renaissance and Reformation Movements* (Chicago, 1971); and *Illustrated History of the Reformation,* ed. by Oscar Thulin (St. Louis, Mo., 1967).

**Catholic,** like Protestant, historiography since World War II reflects the spirit of cooperation evinced in the ecumenical movements of our day as well as a determination to write the history of the Reformation dispassionately. One of the best-known irenic Catholic historians is the German scholar Joseph Lortz. See his *The Reformation in Germany,* 2 vols., trans. by R. Walls (New York, 1968). Other examples of the new conciliatory spirit are Ernst Walter Zeeden, *Die Entstehung der Konfessionen* (Munich, 1965); Henri Daniel-Rops, *The Catholic Reformation,* trans. by John Warrington (London and New York, 1962); Philip Hughes, *A Popular History of the Reformation* (New York, 1957); John P. Dolan, *History of the Reformation* (New York, Tournai, Paris, and Rome, 1965); and George H. Tavard, *Holy Writ or Holy Church: The Crisis of the Protestant Reformation* (New York, 1959).

Following are some of the important **collections of sources** for the Reformation: *The Library of Christian Classics,* ed. by John Baillie, John T. McNeill, and Henry P. Van Dusen (Philadelphia, 1953–    ), of which Vols. 13 to 26 are devoted to the Reformation; *Corpus Reformatorum* (Halle, Braunschweig, Berlin, Leipzig, 1834–    ); *Corpus Catholicorum* (Münster, Westphalia, 1919–    ); *Deutsche Reichstagsakten, Jüngere Reihe,* from 1519, reprint (Göttingen, 1962–    ); *Nuntiaturberichte aus Deutschland nebst ergänzenden Aktenstücken, Section I, 1533–59,* 12 vols. (Gotha, 1892–1912; Tübingen, 1959–    ); *Quellen und Forschungen zur Reformationsgeschichte* (Leipzig, Gütersloh, 1911–    ); and *Reformationsgeschichtliche Studien und Texte* (Münster, Westphalia, 1906–    ). Among the most helpful single-volume collections in English are *Portable Renaissance Reader,* ed. by J. B. Bruce and M. M. McLaughlin (New York, 1953); Roland H. Bainton, *The Age of the Reformation* (New York, Princeton, Toronto, and London, 1956); G. R. Elton, *Renaissance and Reformation: 1300–1648* (New York, 1963); Hans J. Hillerbrand, *The Reformation in Its Own Words* (London, 1964); and *Documents Illustrative of the Continental Reformation,* ed. by B. J. Kidd (Oxford, 1911).

# Chapter 1: Changing Social Structure About 1500

Excellent recent surveys of **economic conditions** in Europe at the beginning of the Reformation are *The Cambridge Economic History of Europe,* ed. by M. M. Postan and H. J. Habakkuk, Vol. 4: *The Economy of Expanding Europe in the Sixteenth and Seventeenth Centuries,* ed. by E. E. Rich and C. H. Wilson (Cambridge, 1967); Hans Haussherr, *Wirtschaftsgeschichte der Neuzeit,* 2nd ed. (Weimar, 1955); Herbert Heaton, *Economic History of Europe,* rev. ed. (New York, 1948); J. Kulischer, *Allgemeine Wirtschaftsgeschichte des Mittelalters und der Neuzeit,* Vols. 1 and 2 (Munich and Berlin, 1928–1929); Gino Luzzatto, *Storia economica dell' età moderna e contemporanea,* 3rd ed., Part 1 (Padua, 1950); and Frederick L. Nussbaum, *A History of Economic Institutions of Western Europe* (New York, 1953).

# Bibliography

For discussions of broad **economic developments in various countries** see Heinrich Bechtel, *Wirtschaftsgeschichte Deutschlands,* Vols. 1 and 2 (Munich, 1951); L. Dechesne, *Histoire économique et sociale de la Belgique* (Paris, 1932); Philippe Dollinger, *The German Hansa,* trans. by D. S. Ault and S. H. Steinberg (Stanford, Calif., 1970); Alfred Doren, *Italienische Wirtschaftsgeschichte,* Vol. 1 (Jena, 1934); E. Lipson, *The Economic History of England,* Vol. 1: *The Middle Ages,* 9th ed. (London, 1947); P. L. Ljascenko, *History of the National Economy of Russia* (New York, 1949); Fritz Rörig, *Vom Werden und Wesen der Hanse,* 3rd ed. (Leipzig, 1943); Jan Rutkowski, *Histoire économique de la Pologne* (Paris, 1927); Henri Sée, *Histoire économique de la France* (Paris, 1939); and *Tudor Economic Documents,* ed. by R. H. Tawney and Eileen Power, 3 vols. (London, 1924).

The standard reference for **commercial history** is Clive Day, *A History of Commerce,* 4th ed. (New York, 1938). See also Fernand Braudel, *La Méditeranée et le monde-mediterranéen à l'époque de Philippe II* (Paris, 1949); David Hannay, *The Great Chartered Companies* (New York, 1926); *Histoire du commerce,* ed. by J. Lacour-Gayet, Vols. 3, 4, and 6 (Paris, 1953–1955); Walter F. Oakeshott, *Commerce and Society* (Oxford, 1936); and L. B. Packard, *The Commercial Revolution* (New York, 1927).

The most useful account of the **industry** of the period is George Unwin, *Industrial Organization in the Sixteenth and Seventeenth Centuries,* 2nd ed. (London, 1957). This book should be supplemented by the brilliant study by John E. Hef, "Industrial Europe at the Time of the Reformation," *Journal of Political Economy,* **49** (1941).

The story of the **expansion of Europe** is told by W. C. Abbott, *The Expansion of Europe,* 2nd ed. (New York, 1938); J. N. L. Baker, *A History of Geographical Discovery and Exploration* (London, 1937); E. E. Gillespie, *A History of Geographical Discovery* (New York, 1933); and H. Plischke, *Die Völker Europas und das Zeitalter der Entdeckungen,* 2nd ed. (Göttingen, 1943). Excellent for studies of the **geographical basis** of the Reformation are Hugo Hassinger, *Geographische Grundlagen der Geschichte,* 2nd ed. (Freiburg, i. Br., 1953), and Gerald Strauss, *Sixteenth Century Germany: Its Topography and Topographers* (Madison, Wis., 1959). Kenneth S. Latourette, in his *A History of the Expansion of Christianity,* 7 vols. (London, New York, 1937–1945), discusses missionary activity in the age of discovery.

The most satisfactory general accounts of **agricultural production** are those by N. S. B. Gras, *A History of Agriculture in Europe and America,* 2nd ed. (New York, 1940); R. Grand and R. Delatouche, *L'Agriculture au moyen âge de la fin de l'empire au XVI<sup>e</sup> siècle* (Paris, 1950); and B. H. Slicher van Bath, *Agrarian History of Western Europe,* trans.

by O. Ordish (London, 1963). The agricultural problems of England are related in R. H. Tawney, *The Agrarian Problem in the Sixteenth Century* (London, 1912), and in *The Agrarian History of England and Wales,* ed. by J. Thirsk, Vol. 4: *1500–1640* (Cambridge, 1967); of Germany, by Friedrich Lütge, *Deutsche Sozial- und Wirtschaftsgeschichte* (Berlin, Göttingen, Heidelberg, 1952); of France, by Marc Bloch, *Les Caractères originaux de l'histoire rurale française* (Paris, 1952).

For special accounts concerning **finance and capitalism,** see R. Ehrenberg, *Capital and Finance in the Age of the Renaissance* (New York, 1928); Clemens Bauer, *Unternehmung und Unternehmungsformen im Spätmittelalter und in der beginnenden Neuzeit* (Jena, 1936); N. S. B. Gras, *Business and Capitalism* (New York, 1939); Earl J. Hamilton, *American Treasure and the Price Revolution in Spain, 1501–1650* (Cambridge, Mass., 1934); Götz von Pölnitz, *Jakob Fugger,* 2 vols. (Tübingen, 1949–1951), and *Anton Fugger,* 2 vols. (Tübingen, 1958–1963); Raymond de Roover, *The Medici Bank* (New York, 1949), and *The Rise and Decline of the Medici Bank* (Cambridge, Mass., 1963); Henri Sée, *Modern Capitalism* (New York, 1928); Werner Sombart, *The Quintessence of Capitalism,* trans. and ed. by M. Epstein (New York, 1967); Jakob Strieder, *Jacob Fugger the Rich,* trans. by M. L. Hartsough (New York, 1931); and *The Fugger News-Letters,* ed. by V. von Klarwill, trans. by P. de Chary (London and New York, 1924), and a second series, trans. by L. S. R. Byrne (London, 1926).

**Social conditions** are described in T. A. Lacey, *The Reformation and the People* (London and New York, 1929); A. von Martin, *Sociology of the Renaissance,* trans. by W. L. Luetkens (New York, 1944); Bernd Moeller, *Reichsstadt und Reformation,* "Schriften des Vereins für Reformationsgeschichte," No. 180 (Gütersloh, 1962); H. Richard Niebuhr, *The Social Sources of Denominationalism* (Hamden, Conn., 1954); R. Pascal, *The Social Basis of the German Reformation* (London, 1933); *The Social History of the Reformation: Essays in Honor of Harold J. Grimm,* ed. by Lawrence P. Buck and Jonathan W. Zophy (Columbus, Ohio, 1972); Heinrich Schmidt, *Die deutschen Städtechroniken als Spiegel des bürgerlichen Selbstverständnisses im Spätmittelalter* (Göttingen, 1958); L. Stone, *The Crisis of Aristocracy, 1558–1641* (Oxford, 1965); *Manifestations of Discontent in Germany on the Eve of the Reformation,* trans. and ed. by Gerald Strauss (Bloomington, Ind., 1971); Guy E. Swanson, *Religion and Regime: A Sociological Account of the Reformation* (Ann Arbor, Mich., 1967); G. M. Trevelyan, *English Social History* (London and New York, 1947); and Ernst Troeltsch, *The Social Teaching of the Christian Churches,* 2 vols., trans. by Olive Wyon (New York, 1950).

Among the many excellent accounts of the **political history,** the

# Bibliography

following are particularly helpful: Hajo Holborn, *A History of Modern Germany: The Reformation* (New York, 1959); A. J. Grant, *A History of Europe from 1494 to 1610,* 5th ed. (New York, 1951); Heinrich Lutz, *Ragione di stato und christliche Staatsethik im 16. Jahrhundert* (Münster, 1961); C. Oman, *The Sixteenth Century* (New York, 1937), and *History of the Art of War in the Sixteenth Century* (New York, 1937); W. F. Reddaway, *A History of Europe, 1610–1715* (London, 1948); Robert Schwoebel, *The Shadow of the Crescent: The Renaissance Image of the Turk (1453–1517)* (New York, 1967); and Stephen A. Fischer-Galati, *Ottoman Imperialism and German Protestantism, 1521–1555* (Cambridge, Mass., 1959).

The **diplomatic history** of Europe is covered by D. J. Hill, *History of Diplomacy in the International Development of Europe,* 3 vols. (New York, 1904–1914); Garrett Mattingly, *Renaissance Diplomacy* (London, 1955); R. B. Mowat, *A History of European Diplomacy, 1451–1789* (New York, 1928); and C. Petrie, *Earlier Diplomatic History, 1492–1713* (New York, 1949).

# Chapter 2: Religious and Intellectual Life

The church and religious life during the **late Middle Ages** are described in *Handbuch der Kirchengeschichte,* ed. by Gerhard Ficker and others, Vol. 2: *Das Mittelalter,* ed. by Gerhard Ficker and Heinrich Hermelink (Tübingen, 1929), and Vol. 3: *Reformation und Gegenreformation,* 2nd ed., ed. by Heinrich Hermelink and Wilhelm Maurer (Tübingen, 1931); Karl H. Dannenfeldt, *The Church of the Renaissance and Reformation* (St. Louis, Mo., 1970); F. Flick, *Decline of the Medieval Church,* 2 vols. (New York, 1930); Philip Hughes, *History of the Church,* Vol. 3 (London, 1947); H. C. Lea, *Historical Sketch of Sacerdotal Celibacy,* 3rd ed., 2 vols. (New York, 1907), *History of Auricular Confession and Indulgences,* 3 vols. (Philadelphia, 1896), and *History of the Inquisition of the Middle Ages,* 3 vols. (New York, 1888); Heiko A. Oberman, *The Harvest of Medieval Theology: Gabriel Biel and Late Medieval Nominalism* (Cambridge, Mass., 1963), and *Forerunners of the Reformation: The Shape of Late Medieval Thought* (New York, 1966); B. Smalley, *The Study of the Bible in the Middle Ages,* 2nd ed. (Oxford, 1951); and A. S. Turberville, *Medieval Heresy and the Inquisition* (London, 1920).

**Christian mysticism** is discussed by James M. Clark, *The Great German Mystics* (Oxford, 1949); Albert Hyma, *The Christian Renaissance* (Grand Rapids, Mich., 1924), and *The Brethren of the Common Life* (Grand Rapids, Mich., 1950); Ray C. Petry, *Late Medieval Mys-*

*ticism,* "Library of Christian Classics," Vol. 8 (Philadelphia, Pa., 1957); and Regnerus R. Post, *The Modern Devotion* (Leiden, 1968). See also J. Blau, *The Christian Interpretation of Cabala in the Renaissance* (New York, 1944).

**Popular Piety** is covered by Willy Andreas, *Deutschland vor der Reformation,* 6th ed. (Stuttgart, 1959); Georges de Lagarde, *La Naissance de l'esprit laique au déclin du Moyen Age,* 6 vols. (Paris, 1934–1946); Will-Erich Peuckert, *Deutscher Volksglaube des Spätmittelalters* (Stuttgart, 1942); and Rainer Rudolf, *Ars Moriendi: Von der Kunst des Heilsamen Lebens und Sterbens* (Cologne, 1957).

Some **important figures** of the late Middle Ages are discussed in *Marsilius of Padua,* ed. by Alan Gewirth, 2 vols. (New York, 1951–1956); R. F. Bennett and H. S. Offler, *William of Ockham: Opera politica* (Manchester, 1940–   ); *William of Ockham: Opera non politica,* ed. by E. Buytaert, I. Daam, G. Mohan, and E. Moody, Vol. 1 (Paderborn, 1958); Richard Scholz, *Wilhelm von Ockam als politischer Denker* (Leipzig, 1944; Stuttgart, 1952); Léon Baudry, *Guillaume d'Occam, sa vie, ses oeuvres, ses idées sociales et politiques,* Vol. 1: *L'Homme et les oeuvres* (Paris, 1950); Erwin Iserloh, *Gnade und Eucharistie in der philosophischen Theologie des Wilhelm von Ockham: Ihre Bedeutung für die Ursachen der Reformation* (Wiesbaden, 1956); K. B. MacFarlane, *John Wycliffe and the Beginnings of English Non-Conformity* (New York, 1953); G. M. Trevelyan, *England in the Age of Wycliffe* (London, 1899; New York, 1963); H. B. Workman, *John Wyclif,* 2 vols. (Oxford, 1926); Matthew Spinka, *Advocates of Reform, from Wycliff to Erasmus,* "Library of Christian Classics," Vol. 14 (Philadelphia, Pa., 1953), *John Hus' Concept of the Church* (Princeton, N.J., 1966), and *Jan Hus and the Czech Reform* (Chicago, 1941); J. Loserth, *Huss und Wiclif,* 2nd ed. (Munich and Berlin, 1925); Howard Kaminsky, *A History of the Hussite Revolution* (Berkeley and Los Angeles, Calif., 1967); Frederick G. Heymann, *John Žižka and the Hussite Revolution* (Princeton, N.J., 1955), and *George of Bohemia, King of Heretics* (Princeton, N.J., 1965); Ferdinand Seibt, *Hussitica: Zur Struktur einer Revolution* (Cologne and Graz, 1965); M. Ferrara, *Savonarola: Prediche e scritti commentati e collegati da un racconto biografico,* 2 vols. (Florence, 1952); Roberto Ridolfi, *The Life of Girolamo Savonarola,* trans. by Cecil Grayson (New York, 1959); Donald Weinstein, *Savonarola and Florence: Prophecy and Patriotism in the Renaissance* (Princeton, N.J., 1970); R. Merton, *Cardinal Ximenes and the Making of Spain* (London, 1934); and Jane Dempsey Douglas, *Justification in Late Medieval Preaching: A Study of John Geiler of Keisersberg* (Leiden, 1966).

Among studies devoted to **the papacy** there are Ludwig Pastor, *History of the Popes from the Close of the Middle Ages,* trans. from the

# Bibliography

German, 40 vols. (London, 1891–1953); F. X. Seppelt, *Geschichte des Papsttums*, Vol. 4: *Das Papsttum im Spätmittelalter und in der Zeit der Renaissance* (Leipzig, 1941); and Walter Ullmann, *The Growth of Papal Government in the Middle Ages*, 3rd ed. (London, 1970). The most important generally available collection of sources is that by Carl Mirbt, *Quellen zur Geschichte des Papsttums und des Römischen Katholizismus*, 4th ed. (Tübingen, 1924).

Excellent surveys of **learning** are Frederick B. Artz, *The Mind of the Middle Ages* (New York, 1953); Wilhelm Dilthey, *Auffassung und Analyse des Menschen im 15. und 16. Jahrhundert*, Vol. 2 of *Gesammelte Schriften* (Leipzig and Berlin, 1921); Wallace K. Ferguson, *Europe in Transition* (Boston, 1962); Myron P. Gilmore, *The World of Humanism* (New York, 1952); L. Oelschke, *Vom Geist des ausgehenden Mittelalters* (Halle, 1929); Will-Erich Peuckert, *Die Grosse Wende; das apokalyptische Saeculum und Luther* (Hamburg, 1948); and H. O. Taylor, *The Medieval Mind*, 4th ed., 2 vols. (New York, 1930), and *Thought and Expression in the Sixteenth Century* (New York, 1920). The history of the interpretation of the Renaissance to the present day is covered by Wallace K. Ferguson, *The Renaissance in Historical Thought* (Boston, 1948).

Helpful in the study of late medieval **philosophy** are Ernst Cassirer, *The Individual and the Cosmos in Renaissance Philosophy,* trans. by Mario Domandi (New York, 1963); Etienne H. Gilson, *History of Christian Philosophy in the Middle Ages* (New York, 1955), and *Elements of Christian Philosophy* (Garden City, N.Y., 1960); *The Renaissance Philosophy of Man,* ed. by E. Cassirer, P. O. Kristeller, and J. H. Randall, Jr. (Chicago, 1948); P. O. Kristeller, *Eight Philosophers of the Italian Renaissance* (Stanford, Calif., 1964), and *The Philosophy of Marsilio Ficino* (New York, 1943); Gerhard Ritter, *Studien zur Spätscholastik,* Vols. 1 and 2 (Heidelberg, 1921–1922); and N. A. Robb, *Neoplatonism of the Italian Renaissance* (London, 1935).

Useful as references for the **literature** of the period are *The Cambridge History of English Literature,* ed. by A. W. Ward and A. R. Waller, Vols. 1 and 2 (Cambridge, 1908); Douglas Bush, *The Renaissance and English Humanism* (Toronto, 1939); J. B. Fletcher, *Literature of the Italian Renaissance,* 2 vols. (New York, 1934); F. de Sanctis, *History of Italian Literature,* 2 vols. (New York, 1931); G. Highet, *The Classical Tradition* (Oxford, 1949); J. Huizinga, *The Waning of the Middle Ages* (London, 1934); Raymond Lebègue, *La Tragédie religieuse en France: Les Débuts (1514–1573)* (Paris, 1929); C. S. Lewis, *English Literature in the Sixteenth Century* (Oxford, 1954); G. T. Northup, *An Introduction to Spanish Literature,* 3rd ed. (Chicago, 1960); J. G. Robertson, *History of German Literature* (New York, 1931); and A. A.

Tilley, *The Literature of the French Renaissance,* 2 vols. (Cambridge, 1904).

Among discussions of **humanism,** the following are particularly helpful: Hans Baron, *The Crisis of the Early Italian Renaissance,* rev. ed. 2 vols. (Princeton, N.J., 1966), and *From Petrarch to Leonardo Bruni: Studies in Humanistic and Political Literature* (Chicago, 1968); William S. Bouwsma, *Venice and the Defense of Republican Liberty* (Berkeley, Calif., 1968); Eugenio Garin, *Italian Humanism, Philosophy, and Civic Life in the Renaissance,* trans. by Peter Munz (New York, 1965); Herman Arend Enno van Gelder, *The Two Reformations in the 16th Century: A Study of the Religious Aspects and Consequences of Renaissance and Humanism* (The Hague, 1961); Giovanni Gentile, *Il pensiero italieno del Rinascimento,* 3rd ed. (Florence, 1940); Myron P. Gilmore, *The World of Humanism, 1453–1517* (New York, 1952); L. Halkin, *Courants religieux et humanisme à la fin du xvᵉ et au début du xviᵉ siècle* (Paris, 1959); John W. O'Malley, S.J., *Giles of Viterbo on Church and Reform: A Study in Renaissance Thought* (Leiden, 1968); W. J. Ong, S.J., *Ramus, Method and the Decay of Dialogue* (Cambridge, Mass., 1958); Augustin Renaudet, *Humanisme et Renaissance* (Geneva, 1958); Charles Trinkaus, *In Our Image and Likeness: Humanity and Divinity in Italian Humanist Thought,* 2 vols. (Chicago, 1970); B. L. Ullmann, *Studies in the Italian Renaissance* (Rome, 1955); and Ernst Walser, *Gesammelte Aufsätze zur Geistesgeschichte der Renaissance* (Basel, 1932).

For the correspondence of a number of **German humanists** see *Die Amerbach-Korrespondenz,* ed. by Alfred Hartmann, 6 vols. (Basel, 1943–1967); Conrad Peutinger, *Briefwechsel,* ed. by Erich König (Munich, 1923); *Joannes Cuspinianus Briefwechsel,* ed. by H. Ankwitz v. Kleehoven (Munich, 1933); *Der Briefwechsel des Konrad Celtis,* ed. by Hans Rupprich (Munich, 1934); *Johann Reuchlins Briefwechsel,* ed. by Ludwig Geiger (Tübingen, 1875); *Der Briefwechsel des Mutianus Rufus,* ed. by Carl Krause (Kassel, 1885); and *Willibald Pirckheimers Briefwechsel,* ed. by Emil Reicke, 2 vols. (Munich, 1940–1956).

The best recent treatments of the German humanists are E. H. Harbison, *The Christian Scholar of the Reformation* (New York, 1956); Lewis W. Spitz, *The Religious Renaissance of the German Humanists* (Cambridge, Mass., 1963), and *Conrad Celtis, the German Arch-Humanist* (Cambridge, Mass., 1957); Karl Hagen, *Deutschlands literarische und religiöse Verhältnisse im Reformationszeitalter. Mit besonderer Rücksicht auf Wilibald Pirckheimer,* 3 vols., reprint of 1868 ed. (Aalen, 1966); F. Halbauer, *Mutianus Rufus* (Leipzig, 1929); H. Ankwitz von Kleehoven, *Der Wiener Humanist Joh. Cuspinian* (Graz, 1959); Heinrich Lutz, *Conrad Peutinger* (Augsburg, 1958); Werner Naef, *Vadian und*

# Bibliography

*seine Stadt St. Gallen,* 2 vols. (St. Gall, 1944–1945); Charles G. Nauert, *Agrippa and the Crisis of Renaissance Thought* (Urbana, 1965); Gerald Strauss, *Historian in an Age of Crisis: The Life and Work of Johannes Aventinus, 1477–1534* (Cambridge, Mass., 1963); Hajo Holborn, *Ulrich von Hutten and the German Reformation,* trans. by Roland H. Bainton (New Haven, Conn., 1937); and Joseph Benzing, *Ulrich von Hutten und seine Drucker* (Wiesbaden, 1956).

**Erasmus** studies were greatly furthered by P. S. Allen and his wife, who prepared the important collection of the humanist's letters, the *Opus epistolarum Des. Erasmi Roteradami,* 12 vols. (Oxford, 1906–1958). Among the many editions of his other writings there is the still indispensable *Desiderii Erasmi opera omnia,* 12 vols. (Oxford, 1906–1958; reprint, London, 1961–1962). On the occasion of the five hundredth anniversary of his birth, there appeared the first volume of a new edition of his complete works, *Opera omnia Desiderii Erasmi Roterodami recognita et adnotatione critica instructa notisque illustrata,* Vol. 1 (Amsterdam, 1969). Among the many English translations of his works are *Erasmus and His Age: Selected Letters of Desiderius Erasmus,* trans. by Marcus A. Haworth, S.J., ed. by Hans J. Hillerbrand (New York, 1970); *Essential Works of Erasmus,* ed. by W. T. H. Jackson (New York, Toronto, and London, 1965); *The Adages of Erasmus,* trans. and ed. by Margaret Mann Phillips (Cambridge, 1964); *The Praise of Folly,* trans. and ed. by Hoyt Hudson (Princeton, N.J., 1941); *Discourse on the Freedom of the Will,* trans. and ed. by Ernest F. Winter (New York, 1961); *The Education of a Christian Prince,* trans. and ed. by Lester K. Born (New York, 1936); *Our Struggle for Peace,* trans. and ed. by J. Kelley Sowards (Bloomington, Ind., 1968); and Craig Thompson, *Colloquies of Erasmus* (Chicago, 1965).

P.S. Allen wrote two important **studies of Erasmus,** *The Age of Erasmus* (Oxford, 1924), and *Erasmus: Lectures and Wayfaring Sketches* (New York, 1934). See also Roland H. Bainton, *Erasmus of Christendom* (New York, 1969); Marcel Bataillon, *Erasme et l'Espagne* (Paris, 1937); Léon-E. Halkin, *Érasmus et l'humanisme chrétien* (Paris, 1969); Albert Hyma, *The Youth of Erasmus* (Ann Arbor, Mich., 1930); Johan Huizinga, *Erasmus of Rotterdam,* trans. by F. Hopman (New York, 1952); Ernst-Wilhelm Kohls, *Die Theologie des Erasmus,* 2 vols. (Basel, 1966); K. A. Meissinger, *Erasmus von Rotterdam,* 2nd ed. (Berlin, 1948); K. H. Oelrich, *Der spätere Erasmus und die Reformation* (Münster, 1961); John B. Payne, *Erasmus, His Theology of the Sacraments* (Richmond, Va., 1970); Margaret Mann Phillips, *Erasmus and the Northern Renaissance* (London, 1949); Augustin Renaudet, *Erasme et l'Italie* (Geneva, 1954); Gerhard Ritter, *Erasmus und der deutsche Humanistenkreis am Oberrhein* (Freiburg i. Br., 1937); Karl Schätti, *Erasmus von Rotterdam und* *die römische Kurie* (Basel and Stuttgart, 1954); and D. F. S. Thomson and H. C. Porter, *Erasmus and Cambridge* (Toronto, 1963). For a survey of recent writings on Erasmus see Jean-Claude Margolin, *Quatorze Années de bibliographie érasmienne (1936–1949)* (Paris, 1969).

**Humanism in England** is discussed in the following: Douglas Bush, *The Renaissance and English Humanism* (Toronto, 1939); Fritz Caspari, *Humanism and the Social Order in Tudor England* (Chicago, 1954); W. T. Constello, S.J., *The Scholastic Curriculum at Early Seventeenth Century Cambridge* (Cambridge, Mass., 1958); Hardin Craig, *English Religious Drama of the Middle Ages* (Oxford, 1955); John R. Hale, *England and the Italian Renaissance* (London, 1954); W. S. Howell, *Logic and Rhetoric in England, 1500–1700* (Princeton, N.J., 1956); Ernest W. Hunt, *Dean Colet and His Theology* (London, 1956); Sears Jayne, *John Colet and Marsilio Ficino* (New York, 1963); Stanford E. Lehmberg, *Sir Thomas Elyot, Tudor Humanist* (Austin, Tex., 1960); J. K. McConica, *English Humanists and the English Reformation* (London, 1959); and Paul Meissner, *England im Zeitalter von Humanismus, Renaissance und Reformation* (Heidelberg, 1952).

*The English Works of Sir Thomas More* is a critical edition of More's works, ed. by W. E. Campbell, 7 vols. to date (London, 1927–    ). There also is the Yale Edition of the *Complete Works of St. Thomas More* (New Haven, Conn., 1961–    ). See also *The Correspondence of Sir Thomas More,* ed. by Elizabeth F. Rogers (Princeton, N.J., 1947). There are numerous editions of the *Utopia.* The best, well-balanced biography is that by R. W. Chambers, *Thomas More* (London, 1935). Russel Ames, *Citizen Thomas More and His Utopia* (Princeton, N.J., 1949), follows Karl Kautsky, *Thomas More and His Utopia* (New York, 1927), in his socialist interpretation. W. E. Campbell, *Erasmus, Tyndale and More* (London and Milwaukee, Wis., 1949), emphasizes More's Catholicism. J. H. Hexter, *More's Utopia: The Biography of an Idea* (Princeton, N.J., 1952), explains the purpose behind the writing of *Utopia.*

**French humanism** is discussed by Jos. Bohatec, *Budé und Calvin: Studien zur Gedankenwelt des französischen Frühhumanismus* (Graz, 1950); Augustin Renaudet, *Préréforme et humanisme à Paris pendant les premières guerres d'Italie* (Paris, 1953); and Pierre Imbart de la Tour, *Les Origines de la réforme,* Vol. 2: *L'Eglise catholique, la crise et la Renaissance,* 2nd ed. (Melun, 1944), and Vol. 3: *L' Évangélisme* (Paris, 1914).

For **Spanish and Portuguese humanism** see Marcel Bataillon, *Érasme et l'Espagne: Recherches sur l'histoire spirituelle du XVIᵉ siècle* (Paris, 1937); Otis Green, *Spain and the Western Tradition,* 4 vols. (Madison, Wis., 1963–1966); Elizabeth Hirsch, *Damiâgo de Gois: The Life and*

*Thought of a Portuguese Humanist, 1502–1574* (The Hague, 1967); John E. Longhurst, *Erasmus and the Spanish Inquisition: The Case of Juan de Valdés* (Albuquerque, N.M., 1950); J. N. Bakhuizen van den Brink, *Juan Valdés, Reformator in Spanje en Italie, 1529–1541* (Amsterdam, 1962); Jose C. Nieto, *Juan de Valdés and the Origins of the Spanish and Italian Reformation* (Geneva, 1969); and *Vives' Introduction to Wisdom,* ed. by Sister Marian Tobriner (New York, 1968).

## Chapter 3: Luther's Break with Rome

Among the many **bibliographical aids** to the study of Luther, the following deserve special notice: *Luther-Jahrbuch,* an annual publication of the Luther-Gesellschaft (1925–1929; 1957–    ), which contains current lists of publications; *Luther-Forschung Heute,* ed. by Vilmos Vajta (Berlin, 1958), containing summaries of research in various countries, presented at the first International Congress for Luther Research at Aarhus, Denmark, 1956; Wilhelm Pauck, "The Historiography of the German Reformation in the Past Twenty Years," *Church History,* **9** (1940); John Dillenberger, "Literature in Luther Studies, 1950–55," *Church History,* **25** (1956), and "Major Volumes and Selected Periodical Literature in Luther Studies, 1956–1959," *Church History,* **30** (1961); Harold J. Grimm, "Luther Research Since 1920," *Journal of Modern History,* **32** (1960); W. von Loewenich, "Die Lutherforschung in Deutschland seit dem 2. Weltkrieg," *Theologische Literaturzeitung,* **81** (1956); and V. Vinay, "Lutero e il Luterenesimo nel giudizio della cultura italiana negli ultimi quarant' anni," *Rivista Protestantesimo,* **7**, (1952).

Changes in the **interpretation of Luther** and his work are discussed by Heinrich Bornkamm, *Luther's World of Thought,* trans. by M. H. Bertram (St. Louis, 1958); Edgar M. Carlson, *The Reinterpretation of Luther* (Philadelphia, Pa., 1948); Adolf Herte, *Das katholische Lutherbild im Bann der Lutherkommentare des Cochlaeus,* 3 vols. (Münster, 1943); Johannes Hessen, *Luther in katholischer Sicht,* 2nd ed. (Bonn, 1949); and Ernst W. Zeeden, *Martin Luther and the Reformation in the Estimation of the German Lutherans,* trans. by Ruth M. Bethell (London, 1954).

Indispensable **research aids** are Georg Buchwald, *Luther-Kalendarium,* "Schriften des Vereins für Reformationsgeschichte," No. 147 (Leipzig, 1929, 1935), and Kurt Aland, *Hilfsbuch zum Lutherstudium,* assisted by E. O. Reichert and G. Jordan (Berlin, 1957), which contains an alphabetical list of Luther's works as well as their location in the most widely used collections of sources.

The standard critical edition of **Luther's works,** *D. Martin Luthers Werke* (Weimar, 1883–    ), the "Weimar Edition," is divided into four parts, the *Werke,* now comprising 58 vols.; the *Briefwechsel,* consisting of 14 vols.; the *Tischreden,* complete in 6 vols.; and the *Deutsche Bibel,* complete in 12 vols. Because the old Walch edition in German translation, *D. Martin Luthers sämtliche Schriften,* 24 vols. (Halle, 1740–1753), contains sources other than those written by Luther, the second edition of 24 vols. in 23 vols. (St. Louis, Mo., 1880–1910) is still frequently used. The most complete publication of Luther's writings in English translation is the "American Edition," *Luther's Works,* ed. by Jaroslav Pelikan and Helmut T. Lehmann (St. Louis, Mo., 1955–   ; Philadelphia, Pa., 1957–   ), which eventually will comprise 55 vols.

Of the numerous scholarly editions of **selections of Luther's works,** mention should be made of the following: the "Munich Edition," *Martin Luther: Ausgewählte Werke,* ed. by H. H. Borchert and Georg Mertz, 3rd ed. (Munich, 1948–   ); *Luthers Werke in Auswahl,* ed. by O. Clemen, 2nd ed., 8 vols. (Berlin, 1950–1956); *Luther Deutsch,* ed. by Kurt Aland (Berlin, 1948–   ); the "Philadelphia Edition," *Works of Martin Luther,* ed. by H. E. Jacobs, 6 vols. (Philadelphia, Pa., 1915–1943); *Reformation Writings of Martin Luther,* 2 vols., trans. and ed. by B. L. Woolf (New York, 1953–1956); *Luther's Correspondence and Other Contemporary Letters,* 2 vols., trans. and ed. by Preserved Smith, the second volume in collaboration with C. M. Jacobs (Philadelphia, Pa., 1913–1918); *Luther: Early Theological Works,* trans. and ed. by James Atkinson, "Library of Christian Classics," Vol. 18 (Philadelphia, Pa., 1955); and *Martin Luther: Selections from His Writings,* ed. by John Dillenberger (Chicago, 1961). Ewald Plass, *What Luther Says,* 3 vols. (St. Louis, Mo., 1959), is a useful anthology.

Because most recent **biographies** are concerned primarily with the young Luther, the older work by Julius Köstlin and Gustav Kawerau, *Martin Luther: Sein Leben und seine Schriften,* 5th ed., 2 vols. (Berlin, 1903), is still useful. The reformer's role in world history is ably presented by Gerhard Ritter, *Luther: His Life and Work* (New York and Evanston, Ill., 1963), trans. by John Riches of the 6th German edition. Roland H. Bainton, *Here I Stand: The Life of Martin Luther* (New York and Nashville, Tenn., 1950), is a brilliant analysis of Luther's religious development. E. G. Schwiebert, *Luther and His Times* (St. Louis, Mo., 1950), is a masterful survey of various aspects of the reformer's life. A more detailed treatment is that by James Mackinnon, *Luther and the Reformation,* 4 vols. (London, 1925–1930). Karl Holl, *Gesammelte Aufsätze zur Kirchengeschichte,* Vol. 1: *Luther,* 5th ed. (Tübingen, 1927), marks a break with the liberal interpretations. Heinrich Bornkamm, *Luther's World of Thought,* trans. by M. H. Bertram (St. Louis, Mo., 1958), is an outstanding study of the reformer in his cultural environment.

# Bibliography

Among other recent biographies, the following deserve mention: A. G. Dickens, *Luther and the Reformation* (London, 1967); Heinrich Dittmar, *Martinus Luther: Sein Leben in Bildern* (Stuttgart, 1957); Ricardo V. Feliu, *Lutero en España y America Española* (New York, 1956); Richard Friedenthal, *Luther: His Life and Times*, trans. by J. Nowell (New York, 1970); V. H. H. Green, *Luther and the Reformation* (London, 1964); Jan Willem Kooiman, *By Faith Alone*, trans. by John Schmidt (Philadelphia, Pa., 1961); Franz Lau, *Luther*, trans. by Robert H. Fischer (Philadelphia, Pa., 1963); Henri Strohl, *Luther: Sa Vie et sa pensée*, 2nd ed. (Strassburg, 1953); Oskar Thulin, *Martin Luther: Sein Leben in Bildern und Zeit-Dokumenten* (Berlin, 1958); and Walter J. Tillmanns, *The World and Men Around Luther* (Minneapolis, Minn., 1959). There are excellent essays on Luther in the reports of the International Congress for Luther Research, *Lutherforschung Heute*, ed. by V. Vajta (Berlin, 1958), and *Luther und Melanchthon* (Göttingen and Philadelphia, Pa., 1961); and in the 5 vols. of *Martin Luther Lectures*, published by Luther College, Decorah, Iowa: *Luther Today* (1957), *More about Luther* (1958), *The Mature Luther* (1959), *Luther and Culture* (1960), and *Luther in the 20th Century* (1961).

Luther's **impact on western civilization** is evaluated by Andrew Drummond, *German Protestantism Since Luther* (London, 1951); Werner Elert, *The Structure of Lutheranism*, trans. by W. A. Hansen, Vol. 1 (St. Louis, Mo., 1962); Hanns Lilje, *Luther Now*, trans. by C. J. Schindler (Philadelphia, Pa., 1952); *Luther, Erasmus and the Reformation, A Catholic-Protestant Appraisal*, ed. by John C. Olin (New York, 1969); Gerhard Ritter, *Die Weltwirkung der Reformation*, 2nd ed. (Munich, 1959); Herbert Schöffler, *Wirkungen der Reformation* (Frankfurt, 1960); and Georg Wünsch, *Luther und die Gegenwart* (Stuttgart, 1961).

Luther's **early development** is discussed by Otto Scheel, *Martin Luther: Vom Katholizismus zur Reformation*, 3rd ed., 2 vols. (Tübingen, 1921–1930), a detailed study that dispels many legends but overemphasizes the point that there was nothing unusual in Luther's youth. See also James Atkinson, *The Trial of Luther* (New York, 1971); Ernst Bizer, *Fides et auditu: Eine Untersuchung über die Entdeckung der Gerechtigkeit Gottes durch Martin Luther* (Neukirchen, 1958); Heinrich Boehmer, *Road to Reformation*, trans. by J. W. Doberstein and T. G. Tappert (Philadelphia, Pa., 1946); W. Borth, *Die Luthersache (causa Lutheri) 1517–1524: Die Anfänge der Reformation als Frage von Politik und Recht* (Lübeck, 1970); R. H. Fife, *The Revolt of Martin Luther* (New York, 1957); Leif Grane, *Protest of konsekvens. Faser i Martin Luthers taenkning indtil 1525* (Copenhagen, 1968); Gerhard Hennig, *Cajetan und Luther. Ein historischer Beitrag zur Begegnung von Thomismus und Reformation* (Stuttgart, 1966); Helmar Junghans, *Ockham im Licht der* *neueren Forschung* (Berlin and Hamburg, 1968); Steven E. Ozment, *Homo Spiritualis: A Comparative Study of the Anthropology of Johannes Tauler, Jean Gerson and Martin Luther (1509–1516) in the Context of Their Theological Thought* (Leiden, 1969); Jaroslav Pelikan, *Spirit Versus Structure: Luther and the Institutions of the Church* (New York, Evanston, Ill., and London, 1968), and *Obedient Rebels: Catholic Substance and Protestant Principle in Luther's Reformation* (New York, 1964); James S. Preus, *From Shadow to Promise: Old Testament Interpretation from Augustine to the Young Luther* (Cambridge, Mass., 1969); *Der Reichstag zu Worms: Reichspolitik und Luthersache,* ed. by Fritz Reuter (Worms, 1971); E. G. Rupp, *Luther's Progress to the Diet of Worms* (London, 1951); Reinhard Schwarz, *Fides, Spes und Caritas beim jungen Luther unter besonderer Berücksichtigung der mittelalterlichen Tradition* (Berlin, 1962); Carl Stange, *Die Anfänge der Theologie Luthers* (Berlin, 1957); and Gerhard Zschäbitz, *Luther, Grösse und Grenze,* Vol. 1: *1483–1526* (Berlin, 1967), a Marxist account that portrays Luther's work as leading to the early phase of the bourgeois revolution. Indispensable for the study of the indulgence controversy is Walther Köhler, *Dokumente zum Ablasstreit von 1517,* 2nd ed. (Leipzig, 1934).

A recent scholarly debate concerning the **Ninety-five Theses** involved numerous persons. Hans Volz, in his *Martin Luthers Thesenanschlag und dessen Vorgeschichte* (Weimar, 1959), argued that the posting of the Theses took place November 1, 1517, not October 31. Erwin Iserloh, a Catholic ecumenist, in his *The Theses Were Not Posted: Luther Between Reform and Reformation,* trans. by Jared Wicks (Boston, 1968), maintains that Luther did not post the Theses but only sent them to Archbishop Albert of Mainz and Bishop Jerome Schulz of Brandenburg, the appropriate representatives of the Church, for their approval. Among those who challenged these views are Heinrich Bornkamm, in *Thesen und Thesenanschlag Luthers* (Berlin, 1967), and *Martin Luther's Theses,* ed. by Kurt Aland, trans. by P. J. Schroeder and others (St. Louis, Mo., and London, 1967).

The best-known **Catholic biographies** of Luther are those by Heinrich Denifle, *Luther and Lutherdom,* trans. by Raymond Volz (Somerset, Ohio, 1917), scholarly but bitter; Hartmann Grisar, S.J., *Martin Luther: His Life and Work,* adapted from the German (Westminster, Md., 1950), and *Luther,* trans. by E. M. Lamond, 6 vols. (St. Louis, Mo., 1914–1917). See also Ernesto Buonaiuti, *Lutero e la Riforma in Germania,* 2nd ed. (Rome, 1945); Thomas M. McDonough, O.P., *The Law and the Gospel in Luther* (New York, 1963); Harry J. McSorley, *Luther: Right or Wrong?* (New York and Minneapolis, Minn., 1969); O. H. Pesch, *Theologie der Rechtfertigung bei Martin Luther und Thomas von Aquin* (Mainz, 1967); and Jared Wicks, S.J., *Man Yearning for Grace* (Washing-

# Bibliography

ton, D.C., and Cleveland, Ohio, 1968). For bibliograhpical summaries see Werner Beyna, *Das moderne katholische Lutherbild* (Essen, 1968), and Richard Stauffer, *Luther as Seen by Catholics* (Richmond, Va., 1967).

**Psychological and psychoanalytical methods** of interpreting Luther were revived by Paul J. Reiter, a Danish psychiatrist, with the publication of his *Martin Luthers Umwelt, Charakter und Psychose*, 2 vols. (Copenhagen, 1937–1941), a doctrinaire account in which he tries to show that Luther was a manic depressive. He was challenged by the theologian and physician Eberhard Grossmann in his *Beiträge zur psychologischen Analyse der Reformatoren, Luther und Calvin* (Basel, 1958). Widely read is the book by the American psychiatrist Erik H. Erikson, *Young Man Luther: A Study in Psychoanalysis and History* (New York, 1958).

The dynastic and imperial policies of **Charles V** are discussed by Rafael Altamira y Crevea, *A History of Spain from the Beginnings to the Present Day*, trans. by Muna Lee (New York, 1958); R. B. Merriman, *The Rise of the Spanish Empire*, 4 vols. (New York, 1918–1934); Jean Babelon, *Charles-Quint* (Paris, 1947); Karl Brandi, *The Emperor Charles V*, trans. by C. V. Wedgwood (New York, 1939); B. Chudoba, *Spain and the Empire* (Chicago, 1952); R. T. Davies, *The Golden Century of Spain* (London and New York, 1937); J. H. Elliott, *Imperial Spain, 1469–1716* (New York, 1964); M. A. S. Hume, *Spain, Its Greatness and Decay* (Cambridge, 1925); Helmut G. Koenigsberger, *The Habsburgs and Europe, 1516–1660* (Ithaca, N.Y., 1971); John Lynch, *Spain Under the Hapsburgs*, Vol. 1: *Empire and Absolutism, 1516–1598* (New York, 1964); J. H. Parry, *The Spanish Theory of Empire in the Sixteenth Century* (Cambridge, 1940); Ramon Ménéndez Pidal, *Idea imperial de Carlos V* (Madrid, 1941); Peter Rassow, *Die politische Welt Karls V*, 2nd ed. (Munich, 1945), and *Karl V: Der Kaiser und seine Zeit* (Cologne, 1960); and John B. Trend, *The Civilization of Spain* (New York, 1944). A challenging biography of Maximilian I is that by G. E. Waas, *The Legendary Character of Kaiser Maximilian* (New York, 1941).

The position of **Germany** in the Hapsburg system is discussed by Hans Baron, "Imperial Reform and the Hapsburgs, 1486–1504," *American Historical Review*, 44 (1938–1939); G. Barraclough, *The Origins of Modern Germany* (Oxford, 1947); Fritz Hartung, *Deutsche Verfassungsgeschichte vom 15. Jahrhundert bis zur Gegenwart*, 6th ed. (Stuttgart, 1954); and Hajo Holborn, *A History of Modern Germany*, Vol. 1: *The Reformation* (New York, 1959).

On the role of **cities** in the Reformation see Hans Baron, "Religion and Politics in the German Imperial Cities during the Reformation," *English Historical Review*, 52 (1937); Miriam Chrisman, *Strasbourg and the Reform* (New Haven, Conn., 1967); Klaus Friedland, *Der Kampf der*

*526*

*Stadt Lüneburg mit ihren Landesherren* (Stuttgart, 1953); Wilhelm Jannasch, *Reformationsgeschichte Lübecks* (Lübeck, 1958); H. Mauersberg, *Wirtschafts- und Sozialgeschichte zentraleuropäischer Städte in neuerer Zeit* (Göttingen, 1960); Bernd Moeller, *Reichsstadt und Reformation* (Gütersloh, 1962); William Monter, *Calvin's Geneva* (New York, 1967); C. Petit-Dutaillis, *Les Communes françaises* (Paris, 1947); *Nürnberg—Geschichte einer europäischen Stadt,* ed. by Gerhard Pfeiffer (Munich, 1971); Ruth Prange, *Die bremische Kaufmannschaft des 16. und 17. Jahrhunderts in sozialgeschichtlicher Betrachtung* (Bremen, 1963); Johannes Schildhauer, *Soziale, politische und religiöse Auseinandersetzungen in den Hansestädten Stralsund, Rostock und Wismar im ersten Drittel des 16. Jahrhunderts* (Weimar, 1959); and Gerald Strauss, *Nuremberg in the Sixteenth Century* (New York, London, and Sydney, 1966).

For studies of the **Ottoman Empire** see Stephan A. Fischer-Galati, *Ottoman Imperialism and German Protestantism, 1521–1555* (Cambridge, Mass., 1959); A. H. Lybyer, *The Government of the Ottoman Empire in the Time of Suleiman the Magnificent* (Cambridge, Mass., 1913); R. B. Merriman, *Suleiman the Magnificent, 1520–66* (Cambridge, Mass., 1944); and P. Wittek, *The Rise of the Ottoman Empire* (London, 1938). There is an excellent survey of the involvement of the Turks in European affairs immediately preceding the Reformation in Sydney N. Fisher, *The Foreign Relations of Turkey 1481–1512* (Urbana, Ill., 1948).

**Melanchthon's works** have been published in the *Corpus Reformatorum,* 28 vols. (Halle, 1834–1860), the *Supplementa Melanchthonia,* 4 vols. (Leipzig, 1910–1929), and the edition of selections by Robert Stupperich, *Melanchthons Werke in Auswahl* (Gütersloh, 1951–     ). In English we have *The Loci Communes of Philip Melanchthon,* trans. and ed. by Charles L. Hill (Boston, 1944); *Melanchthon on Christian Doctrine: Loci Communes 1555,* trans. and ed. by Clyde L. Manschreck (New York, 1965); and *Melanchthon: Selected Writings,* trans. by Charles L. Hill, ed. by E. E. Flack and L. J. Satre (Minneapolis, Minn., 1962). For bibliography concerning Melanchthon see Wilhelm Hammer, *Die Melanchthonforschung im Wandel der Jahrhunderte,* Vol. 1: *1519 bis 1799,* "Quellen und Forschungen zur Reformationsgeschichte," Vol. 35 (Gütersloh, 1967). Outstanding studies are those by Ernst Bizer, *Theologie der Verheissung. Studien zur theologischen Entwicklung des jungen Melanchthon 1519–1524* (Neukirchen, 1964); Jean Boisset, *Melanchthon: Educateur de l'Allemagne* (Paris, 1967); Peter Fraenkel, *Testimonia Patrum: The Function of the Patristic Argument in the Theology of Philip Melanchthon* (Geneva, 1961); Peter Fraenkel and Martin Greschat, *Zwanzig Jahre Melanchthonstudium, 1945–1965* (Geneva, 1967); Klaus Haendler, *Wort und Glaube bei Melanchthon,* "Quellen und Forschungen zur

527

# Bibliography

Reformationsgeschichte," Vol. 37 (Gütersloh, 1968); K. Hartfelder, *Melanchthon als Praecaptor Germaniae* (Berlin, 1899); F. Hildebrandt, *Melanchthon: Alien or Ally?* (New York, 1946); Guido Kisch, *Melanchthons Rechts- und Soziallehre* (Berlin, 1967); Clyde L. Manschreck, *Melanchthon: The Quiet Reformer* (New York, 1958), and *Melanchthon on Christian Doctrine* (New York, 1965); Wilhelm Maurer, *Melanchthon-Studien,* "Schriften des Vereins für Reformationsgeschichte," No. 181 (Gütersloh, 1964), and *Der junge Melanchthon zwischen Humanismus und Reformation,* 2 vols. (Göttingen, 1967–1969); Wilhelm Neuser, *Der Ansatz der Theologie Ph. Melanchthons* (Neukirchen, 1957); Michael Rogness, *Philip Melanchthon, Reformer Without Honor* (Minneapolis, Minn., 1969); Hansjörg Sick, *Melanchthon als Ausleger des alten Testaments* (Tübingen, 1959); Adolf Sperl, *Melanchthon zwischen Humanismus und Reformation* (Munich, 1959); and Robert Stupperich, *Melanchthon,* trans. by Robert Fischer (Philadelphia, Pa., 1965).

For recent bibliographies on **Martin Bucer** see Bard Thompson, "Bucer Study Since 1918," *Church History,* **25** (1956), and Robert Stupperich, "Forschungsberichte," *Archiv für Reformationsgeschichte,* **42** (1951). Interest in Bucer was stimulated by the beginning of the publication of a critical edition of his works, *Martini Buceri Opera Latina,* Vol. 15: *De regno Christi,* and Vol. 15, *bis: Du royaume de Jesus-Christ,* a French translation of 1558, both ed. by François Wendel (Paris and Gütersloh, 1954–1955); and *Martin Bucers deutsche Schriften,* ed. by Robert Stupperich (Gütersloh, 1960–     ), of which 4 vols. had been published by 1972. J. V. Pollett, O.P., has made an important beginning in the publication of Bucer's correspondence with his *Martin Bucer: Études sur la correspondance avec de nombreux textes inédits,* 2 vols. (Paris, 1958–1963). The 1880–1891 edition of M. Lenz, *Briefwechsel Landgraf Philipps des Grossmütigen von Hessen mit Bucer* was reprinted in 3 vols. (Amsterdam, 1966). Heinrich Bornkamm, *Martin Bucers Bedeutung für die europäische Reformationsgeschichte,* "Schriften des Vereins für Reformationsgeschichte," No. 169 (Gütersloh, 1952), contains a list of Bucer's works as well as a good bibliography. See also Johann Wilhelm Baum, *Capito und Butzer, Strassburgs Reformatoren,* reprint of 1860 edition (Nieuwkoop, 1967); Willem F. Dankbaar, *Martin Bucers Beziehungen zu den Niederlanden* (s'Gravenhage, 1961); Hastings Eells, *Martin Bucer* (New Haven, Conn., 1931); C. Hopf, *Martin Bucer and the English Reformation* (New York, 1946); Karl Koch, *Studium Pietatis: Martin Bucer als Ethiker* (Neukirchen, 1962); Ernst-Wilhelm Kohls, *Die Schule bei Martin Bucer in ihrem Verhältnis zu Kirche und Obrigkeit* (Heidelberg, 1963); Friedhelm Krüger, *Bucer und Erasmus: Eine Untersuchung zum Einfluss des Erasmus auf die Theologie Martin Bucers*

(Wiesbaden, 1970); Johannes Müller, *Martin Bucers Hermeneutik* (Gütersloh, 1965); Wilhelm Pauck, *Das Reich Gottes auf Erden, Utopie und Wirklichkeit* (Berlin, 1928); Gerrit Jan van der Poll, *Martin Bucer's Liturgical Ideas* (Assen, 1954); W. P. Stephens, *The Holy Spirit in the Theology of Martin Bucer* (Cambridge, Mass., 1970); and François Wendel, *L'Eglise de Strasbourg: Sa constitution et son organisation, 1532–35* (Paris, 1942).

Among studies of other **early contemporaries of Luther** are Hermann Barge, *Andreas Bodenstein von Karlstadt*, 2 vols. (Leipzig, 1905); *Karlstadts Schriften aus den Jahren 1523–25*, ed. by Erich Hertzsch, 2 vols. (Halle, 1956); Erich Hertzsch, *Karlstadt und seine Bedeutung für das Luthertum* (Gotha, 1932); Karl Müller, *Luther und Karlstadt* (Tübingen, 1907); E. Gordon Rupp, *Patterns of the Reformation* (Philadelphia, Pa., 1969), containing accounts of Carlstadt and others; Irmgard Höss, *Georg Spalatin: Ein Leben in der Zeit des Humanismus und Reformation* (Weimar, 1956); E. Iserloh, *Die Eucharistie in der Darstellung des Johannes Eck* (Münster, 1950); Hans von Schubert, *Lazarus Spengler und die Reformation*, ed. by Hajo Holborn (Leipzig, 1934); Gottfried Seebass, *Bibliographia Osiandrica: Bibliographie der gedruckten Schriften Andreas Osianders d. Ä.* (Nieuwkoop, 1971), and *Das reformatorische Werk des Andreas Osiander* (Neustadt, 1967); Walter Delius, *Justus Jonas: Lehre und Leben* (Gütersloh, 1952); Gustav Kawerau, *Der Briefwechsel des Justus Jonas*, 2 vols. (Halle, 1884–1885), reprinted 1963; Martin Lehmann, *Justus Jonas, Loyal Reformer* (Minneapolis, Minn., 1963); Ludwig Keller, *Johann von Staupitz und die Anfänge der Reformation*, reprint of 1888 ed. (Nieuwkoop, 1967); Ernst Wolf, *Staupitz und Luther* (Leipzig, 1939); David C. Steinmetz, *Misericordia Dei: The Theology of Johannes von Staupitz in Its Late Medieval Setting* (Leiden, 1968); Bernhard Klaus, *Veit Dietrich: Leben und Werk* (Nürnberg, 1958); Eberhard Ruhmer, *Cranach*, trans. by Joan Spencer (London, 1963); W. Mejer, *Der Buchdrucker Hans Lufft zu Wittenberg*, reprint of 1923 ed. (Nieuwkoop, 1965); Martin Brecht, *Johannes Brenz: Neugestalter von Kirche, Staat und Gesellschaft* (Stuttgart, 1971); Martin Spahn, *Johannes Cochläus: Ein Lebensbild aus der Zeit der Kirchenspaltung,* reprint of 1898 ed. (Nieuwkoop, 1964); Peter Brunner, *Nikolaus von Amsdorf als Bischof von Naumburg*, "Schriften des Vereins für Reformationsgeschichte," No. 179 (Gütersloh, 1961); Gerhard Hennig, *Cajetan und Luther: Ein historischer Beitrag zur Begegnung von Thomismus und Reformation* (Stuttgart, 1966); Paul Kirn, *Friedrich der Weise und die Kirche* (Leipzig, 1926); Georg Mentz, *Johann Friedrich der Grossmütige, 1503–1554*, 3 vols. (Jena, 1903); and Iselin Gundermann, *Herzogin Dorothea von Preussen, 1504–1547* (Cologne and Berlin, 1965).

*529*

# Bibliography

## Chapter 4: The Growth of Lutheranism

For discussions of Luther's relations with **the radicals at Wittenberg** see Karl G. Steck, *Luther und die Schwärmer* (Zollikon and Zurich, 1955), and *Aktenstücke zur Wittenberger Bewegung*, ed. by H. Barge (Leipzig, 1912). For the writings of **Thomas Müntzer** see *Thomas Müntzer: Schriften und Briefe*, ed. by Günther Franz and Paul Kirn, "Quellen und Forschungen zur Reformationsgeschichte," Vol. 33 (Gütersloh, 1968), which contains everything he wrote. The following discussions of Müntzer deserve mention: Manfred Bensing, *Thomas Müntzer* (Leipzig, 1965), a Marxist interpretation; Ernst Bloch, *Thomas Müntzer als Theologe der Revolution* (Berlin, 1960); Hans-Jürgen Goertz, *Innere und äussere Ordnung in der Theologie Thomas Müntzers* (Leiden, 1967); Eric W. Gritsch, *Reformer Without a Church: The Life and Thought of Thomas Muentzer, 1488?–1525* (Philadelphia, Pa., 1967); Carl Hinrichs, *Luther und Müntzer: Ihre Auseinandersetzung über das Widerstandsrecht* (Berlin, 1952); M. M. Smirin, *Die Volksreformation des Thomas Müntzer und der grosse Bauernkrieg*, trans. by Hans Nichtweiss, 2nd ed. (Berlin, 1956); M. Steinmetz, *Das Müntzerbild von Martin Luther bis Friedrich Engels* (Berlin, 1971), and *Deutschland von 1476 bis 1648: Von der frühbürgerlichen Revolution bis zum Westfälischen Frieden* (Berlin, 1965), Neo-Marxist interpretations, as is Gerhard Zschäbitz, *Zur mittelalterlichen Wiedertäuferbewegung nach dem Grossen Bauernkrieg* (Berlin, 1958), which shows that Müntzer's doctrines were kept alive after the Peasants' Revolt.

Luther's conception of **church and state** is discussed by Franz Lau, *Luthers Lehre von den beiden Reichen* (Berlin, 1953), which surveys the research to 1953; F. Edward Cranz, *An Essay on the Development of Luther's Thought on Justice, Law, and Society* (Cambridge, Mass., 1959); Ulrich Duchrow, *Christenheit und Weltverantwortung: Traditionsgeschichte und systematische Struktur der Zweireichelehre* (Stuttgart, 1970); John M. Headley, *Luther's View of Church History* (New Haven, Conn., and London, 1963); William A. Mueller, *Church and State in Luther and Calvin* (Nashville, Tenn., 1954); Hermann A. Preus, *The Communion of Saints* (Minneapolis, Minn., 1948); Ernst Rietschl, *Das Problem der unsichtbaren-sichtbaren Kirche bei Luther*, "Schriften des Vereins für Reformationsgeschichte," No. 154 (Leipzig, 1932); Otto Scheel, *Evangelium, Kirche und Volk bei Luther*, "Schriften des Vereins für Reformationsgeschichte," 156 (Leipzig, 1934); Karl G. Steck, *Lehre und Kirche bei Luther* (Munich, 1963); H. Storck, *Das allgemeine Priestertum bei Luther* (Munich, 1953); Vilmos Vajta, *Luther on Worship*, trans. by U. S. Leupold (Philadelphia, Pa., 1958); and Gustaf Wingren, *Luther on Vocation,* trans. by C. C. Rasmussen (Philadelphia, Pa., 1957).

Luther's **liturgical writings** are contained in *Martin Luther: Liturgische Schriften,* 2nd ed. (Munich, 1950). For general accounts see Leonhard Fendt, *Der lutherische Gottesdienst des 16. Jahrhunderts* (Munich, 1923), and L. D. Reed, *The Lutheran Liturgy* (Philadelphia, Pa., 1947).

The most important critical edition of **Protestant church orders** is *Die evangelischen Kirchenordnungen des 16. Jahrhunderts,* ed. by Emil Sehling, 5 vols. (Leipzig, 1902–1913), publication of which was resumed after the Second World War with Vols. 6 and 7 (Tübingen, 1955–1961). The beginnings of the Saxon church order are covered by C. A. H. Burkhardt, *Geschichte der sächsischen Kirchen- und Schulvisitation, 1524–45* (Leipzig, 1879). The developments in Hesse are covered by R. L. Winters, *Francis Lambert of Avignon* (Philadelphia, Pa., 1938). See the excellent discussion by Wilhelm Maurer, *Gemeindezucht, Gemeindeamt, Konfirmation* (Kassell, 1940).

For **Luther's contribution to music** and use of the hymn in spreading the Reformation see Klaus Burba, *Die Christologie in Luthers Liedern,* "Schriften des Vereins für Reformationsgeschichte," No. 175 (Gütersloh, 1956); Walter E. Buszin, "Luther on Music," *The Musical Quarterly,* **32** (1946); Theodore Hoelty-Nickel, *The Musical Heritage of the Church* (St. Louis, Mo., 1954); Edwin Liemohn, *The Chorale Through Four Hundred Years* (Philadelphia, Pa., 1953); Paul Nettl, *Luther and Music* (Philadelphia, Pa., 1948); L. D. Reed, *Luther and Congregational Song* (Philadelphia, Pa., 1947); Charles Schneider, *Luther, poete et musicien et les Enchiridien de 1524* (Geneva, 1942); Wilhelm Stapel, *Luther Lieder und Gedichte* (Stuttgart, 1950); and the general accounts listed in the bibliography for Chapter 12.

On Luther's development of the **evangelical sermon** see Paul Althaus, *Luther auf der Kanzel* (Rostock, 1921); Elmer C. Kiessling, *The Early Sermons of Luther and Their Relation to the Pre-Reformation Sermon* (Grand Rapids, Mich., 1935); Harold J. Grimm, *Luther as a Preacher* (Columbus, Ohio, 1929); Hans Preuss, *Martin Luther: Seele und Sendung* (Gütersloh, 1927); and Hermann Werdermann, *Luthers Wittenberger Gemeinde wiederhergestellt aus seinen Predigten* (Gütersloh, 1929). *Luther: Letters of Spiritual Counsel,* ed. and trans. by Theodore G. Tappert, "Library of Christian Classics," Vol. 18 (Philadelphia, 1955), contains important information on the reformer's cure of souls.

**Printing and the use of pamphlets** in the spread of the Reformation are discussed in Arnold E. Berger, *Die Sturmtruppen der Reformation: Ausgewählte Flugschriften der Jahre 1520–25* (Leipzig, 1931); W. T. Berry and H. E. Poole, *Annals of Printing: A Chronological Encyclopedia*

# Bibliography

*from Earliest Times to 1950* (London, 1966); Peter G. Bietenholz, *Basle and France in the Sixteenth Century: The Basle Humanists and Printers* (Toronto, 1971); *Flugschriften aus den ersten Jahren der Reformation,* ed. by O. Clemen, 4 vols., reprint of 1907–1911 ed. (Nieuwkoop, 1967); H. Dannenbauer, *Luther als religiöser Volksschriftsteller, 1517–1520* (Tübingen, 1930); M. Gravier, *Luther et l'opinion publique* (Paris, 1942); Louise W. Holborn, "Printing and the Growth of a Protestant Movement in Germany," *Church History,* 11 (1942); and Hans Volz, *Hundert Jahre Wittenberger Bibeldruck* (Göttingen, 1954).

For special treatments of the relation between **Luther and Erasmus** see Heinrich Bornkamm, "Erasmus und Luther," *Luther Jahrbuch,* Vol. 25 (1958); *Erasmus-Luther: Discourse on Free Will,* ed. by Ernst F. Winter (New York, 1961); *Luther and Erasmus: Free Will and Salvation,* trans. and ed. by E. G. Rupp, Philip S. Watson, and others, "Library of Christian Classics," Vol. 17 (Philadelphia, 1969); H. J. McSorley, *Luther: Right or Wrong? An Ecumenical-Theological Study of Luther's Major Work, the Bondage of the Will* (New York and Minneapolis, Minn., 1969); and Robert H. Murray, *Erasmus and Luther* (New York, 1920).

On the **Knights' Revolt** see Karl Schottenloher, *Flugschriften zur Ritterschaftsbewegung des Jahres 1523* (Münster, 1929); O. Brunner, *Adeliges Landleben und europäischer Geist* (Salzburg, 1949); R. Fellner, *Die fränkische Ritterschaft von 1495–1524* (Berlin, 1905); and William R. Hitchcock, *The Background of the Knights' Revolt* (Berkeley and Los Angeles, Calif., 1958).

The standard work on the **Peasants' Revolt** is that by Günther Franz, *Der deutsche Bauernkrieg,* 7th ed. (Darmstadt, 1965), and its companion volume of sources, *Quellen zur Geschichte des Bauernkriegs* (Munich, 1963). See also *Reformation and Authority,* ed. by Kyle C. Sessions, "Problems in European Civilization" (Lexington, Mass., 1968), and the Marxist accounts, E. B. Bax, *The Peasants' War in Germany* (London, 1903); Friedrich Engels, *The German Revolutions: The Peasant War in Germany,* trans. by M. J. Olgin, ed. by Leonard Krieger (Chicago, 1967); and M. M. Smirin, *Deutschland vor der Reformation* (Berlin, 1955). On Luther's attitude toward the peasants see Paul Althaus, *Luthers Haltung im Bauernkrieg* (Basel, 1953), and Hubert Kirschner, *Luther and the Peasant's War* (Philadelphia, Pa., 1972).

A reliable and brief setting for the **Reformation in Switzerland** is provided by W. Oechsli, *History of Switzerland,* trans. by E. and C. Paul (Cambridge, 1922). The publication of Zwingli's works, the *Sämtliche Werke,* in the *Corpus Reformatorum* (Leipzig, 1905– ), is nearing completion. *H. Zwingli, Hauptschriften,* ed. by F. Blanke, O. Farner, and R. Pfister (Zurich, 1940– ), is a good edition of selections. There is an excellent translation of some of Zwingli's works in G. W. Bromily, *Zwingli and Bullinger*, "Library of Christian Classics," Vol. 24 (Philadelphia, Pa., 1953).

For discussions of recent **Zwingli research** see *Zwingliana*, 10 (1958); Bard Thompson, "Zwingli Study Since 1918," *Church History*, 19 (1950); Georg Finsler, *Zwingli-Bibliographie* (Nieuwkoop, 1962), a reprint of the Zurich edition of 1897; Rudolf Pfister, "Die Zwingli-Forschung seit 1945," *Archiv für Reformationsgeschichte*, 48 (1957); J. V. Pollet, O.P., "Zwinglianisme, Bibliographie," *Dictionnaire de théologie catholique*, Vol. 15, (1950), and *Huldrych Zwingli et la réforme en Suisse d'après les recherches récentes* (Paris, 1963); and Gottfried W. Locher, "The Change in the Understanding of Zwingli in Recent Research," *Church History*, 34 (1965).

S. M. Jackson, *Huldreich Zwingli* (New York, 1901), is still the best biography in English. Oskar Farner, *Zwingli the Reformer*, trans. by D. G. Sear (New York, 1952), is a brief popular account by a distinguished Swiss scholar. See also his *Huldrych Zwingli*, 4 vols. (Zurich, 1943–1960). Among special studies of Zwingli, the following deserve mention: Fritz Büsser, *Das katholische Zwinglibild* (Zurich, 1968); Jacques Courvoisier, *Zwingli: A Reformed Theologian* (Richmond, Va., 1963); Charles Garside, *Zwingli and the Fine Arts* (New Haven, Conn., 1966); Martin Haas, *Zwingli und der erste Kappelkrieg* (Zurich, 1965), and *Huldrych Zwingli und seine Zeit* (Zurich, 1969); Roger Ley, *Kirchenzucht bei Zwingli* (Zurich, 1948); Gottfried W. Locher, *Die Theologie Huldrych Zwinglis*, Part 1: *Die Gotteslehre* (1952); C. C. Richardson, *Zwingli and Cranmer on the Eucharist* (Evanston, Ill., 1949); Jean Rilliet, *Zwingli: Third Man of the Reformation*, trans. by Harold Knight (Philadelphia, Pa., 1960); Siegfried Rother, *Die religiösen und geistigen Grundlagen der Politik Zwinglis* (Erlangen, 1956); H. Schmid, *Zwinglis Lehre von der göttlichen und menschlichen Gerechtigkeit* (Zurich, 1959); Kurt Spillmann, *Zwingli und die zürcherische Politik gegenüber der Abtei St. Gallen* (St. Gall, 1965); and Robert C. Walton, *Zwingli's Theocracy* (Toronto, 1968).

The standard study of Zwingli and Luther with respect to the **Lord's Supper** is Walther Köhler, *Zwingli und Luther: Ihr Streit über das Abendmahl*, 2 vols. (Leipzig and Gütersloh, 1924–1953). See also Köhler's *Das Marburger Religionsgespräch*, "Schriften des Vereins für Reformationsgeschichte," No. 148 (Leipzig, 1929); Hans von Schubert, *Bündnis und Bekenntnis, 1529–30*, ibid., 98 (Leipzig, 1908); and Hermann Sasse, *This Is My Body: Luther's Contention for the Real Presence in the Sacrament of the Altar* (Minneapolis, Minn., 1959).

For works of **Heinrich Bullinger**, Zwingli's successor, see *The De-*

*cades of Henry Bullinger,* ed. by T. Harding for the Parker Society, 4 vols. (Cambridge, 1849–1852), and *Heinrich Bullinger, Korrespondenz mit den Graubündnern, 1533–75,* ed. by T. Schiess 3 vols., (Basel, 1904–1906). For secondary accounts see Fritz Blanke, *Der junge Bullinger* (Zurich, 1942); Andre Bouvier, *Henri Bullinger: réformateur et conseilleur oecuménique* (Zurich and Neuchâtel, 1940); Heinold Fast, *Heinrich Bullinger und die Täufer* (Weierhof, 1959); Joachim Staedtke, *Die Theologie des jungen Bullinger* (Zurich, 1962); and P. Walser, *Die Prädestination bei Heinrich Bullinger im Zusammenhang mit seiner Gotteslehre* (Zurich, 1957). Leo Weiss, *Leo Jud, Ulrich Zwinglis Kampfgenosse* (Zurich, 1942), discusses one of Zwingli's co-workers.

Sources for the political developments in the **Holy Roman Empire** from 1521 to 1531 are *Deutsche Reichstagsakten unter Karl V, Jüngere Reihe,* ed. by A. Kluckhohn and A. Wrede, 2nd ed., Vols. 1–4, 7 (Munich, 1893–1905; 1929), now being reprinted (Göttingen, 1962– ); Hans von der Planitz, *Berichte aus dem Reichsregiment in Nürnberg 1521–23,* assembled by E. Wulcher, ed. by H. Virck (Leipzig, 1899); *Die Korrespondenz Ferdinands I.,* Part 1: *Familienkorrespondenz,* ed. by Wilhelm Bauer and R. Lacroix, 2 vols. (Vienna, 1912 and 1930), covering the period to 1530; *Correspondenz Kaisers Karl V.,* 3 vols. (Leipzig, 1844–1846), reprinted 1965; *Die Reichsbücher Karls V., 1519–1556,* ed. by Lothar Gross (Vienna and Leipzig, 1930); *Die Politische Korrespondenz der Stadt Strassburg im Zeitalter der Reformation,* 5 vols. (Strassburg and Heidelberg, 1882–1933); and Valentin von Tetleben, *Protokoll des Augsburger Reichstages 1530,* ed. by H. Grundmann, "Schriften des Vereins für Reformationsgeschichte," No. 177 (Gütersloh, 1958).

In addition to the studies of **Charles V** listed in Chapter 3, the following should be noted: Martti Salomies, *Die Pläne Kaiser Karls V. für eine Reichsreform* (Helsinki, 1953); Kurt Forstreuter, *Vom Ordensstaat zum Fürstentum* (Kitzingen, 1951), on the secularization of Prussia; Johannes Kühn, *Die Geschichte des Speyrer Reichstages 1929,* "Schriften des Vereins für Reformationsgeschichte," No. 146 (Leipzig, 1929); Hans von Schubert, *Der Reichstag zu Augsburg im Zusammenhang der Reformationsgeschichte,* "Schriften des Vereins für Reformationsgeschichte," No. 150 (Leipzig, 1930); and Ekkehart Fabian, *Die Entstehung des Schmalkaldischen Bundes und seiner Verfassung,* 2nd ed. (Tübingen, 1962).

The best critical edition of the **Augsburg Confession** is that in *Die Bekenntnisschriften der evangelisch-Lutherischen Kirche,* 5th ed. (Göttingen, 1963). See also *The Book of Concord,* ed. by H. E. Jacobs, 2 vols. (Philadelphia, 1882–1893); J. M. Reu, *The Augsburg Confession* (Chicago, 1930); and Edmund Schlink, *Theologie der lutherischen Bekenntnisschriften* (Berlin, 1954).

# Chapter 5: Consolidation of Lutheranism (1530–1555)

Sources for Protestant and imperial **politics from 1530 to 1555** are the *Nuntiaturberichte aus Deutschland nebst ergänzenden Aktenstücken,* Section I: *1533–1559,* 13 vols. (Gotha, 1892–1912; Tübingen, 1959); *Venetianische Depeschen vom Kaiserhof. Dispacci di Germania,* ed. by E. Turba, 3 vols. (Vienna, 1889–1896); *Politische Korrespondenz des Herzogs und Kurfürsten Moritz,* ed. by E. Brandenburg, 2 vols. (Leipzig, 1900–1904); *Quellen zur Geschichte der Reformationsbündnisse und der Konstanzer Reformationsprozesse 1529–1548,* ed. by Ekkehart Fabian, "Schriften zur Kirchen- und Rechtsgeschichte," Vol. 34 (Tübingen and Basel, 1967); and *Briefwechsel Landgraf Philipps des Grossmütigen von Hessen und Bucer,* Parts 1–3, ed. by Max Lenz (Leipzig, 1880–1891). For special accounts see C. Augustin, *De Godsdienstgesprekken tussen Rooms-Katholieken en Protestanten van 1538 tot 1541* (Haarlem, 1967); Karlheinz Blaschke, *Sachsen im Zeitalter der Reformation,* "Schriften des Vereins für Reformationsgeschichte," No. 185 (Gütersloh, 1970); Karl Brandi, *Der Augsburger Religionsfriede . . . 1555,* 2nd ed. (Göttingen, 1927); Hermann Buck, *Die Anfänge der Konstanzer Reformationsprozesse: Österreich, Eidgenossenschaft und Schmalkaldischer Bund* (Tübingen, 1964); Ekkehart Fabian, *Die Entstehung des Schmalkaldischen Bundes und seiner Verfassung,* 2nd ed. (Tübingen, 1962); Fritz Hartung, *Karl V. und die deutschen Reichsstände 1546–55* (Halle, 1910); Hildegard Jung, *Kurfürst Moritz von Sachsen* (Hagen, 1966); Hans-Walter Krumwiede, *Zur Entstehung des landesherrlichen Kirchenregiments in Kursachsen und Braunschweig-Wolfenbüttel* (Göttingen, 1967); G. Mentz, *Johann Friedrich,* 3 vols. (Jena, 1903–1908); Klaus Rischar, *Johann Eck auf dem Reichstag zu Augsburg 1530,* "Reformationsgeschichtliche Studien und Texte," No. 197 (Münster, 1968); William W. Rockwell, *Die Doppelehe des Landgrafen Philipp von Hessen* (Marburg, 1904); C. D. Rouillard, *The Turk in French History, Thought and Literature, 1500–1660* (Paris, 1939); and Karl Schornbaum, *Zur Politik des Markgrafen Georg von Brandenburg* (Munich, 1906).

Among the general discussions of **Luther's theology,** the following are particularly helpful: Gerhard Ebeling, *Luther: An Introduction to His Thought,* trans. by R. A. Wilson (Philadelphia, Pa., 1970), a penetrating study; Adolf von Harnack, *History of Dogma,* 7 vols. in 4, tr. from 3rd German ed. by Neil Buchanan (New York, 1961), a liberal interpretation; Reinhold Seeberg, *Text-book of the History of Doctrines,* trans. by Charles E. Hay, 2 vols. (Philadelphia, Pa., 1905); Karl Holl, *Gesammelte Aufsätze,* Vol. 1: *Luther,* 4th and 5th eds. (Tübingen, 1927); Erich Seeberg, *Luthers Theologie: Motive und Ideen,* Vol. 1: *Die Gottes-*

# Bibliography

*anschauung* (Göttingen, 1929), and Vol. 2: *Christus, Wirklichkeit und Urbild* (Stuttgart, 1940), which stresses the influence of Ockham; Paul Althaus, *Die Theologie Martin Luthers* (Gütersloh, 1962); Ulrich Asendorf, *Eschatologie bei Luther* (Göttingen, 1967); James Atkinson, *Martin Luther and the Birth of Protestantism* (Baltimore, Md., 1968); Heinrich Bornkamm, *Luther's World of Thought,* trans. by Martin H. Bertram (St. Louis, Mo., 1958); John Dillenberger, *God Hidden and Revealed* (Philadelphia, Pa., 1953); Brian Gerrish, *Grace and Reason: A Study in the Theology of Martin Luther* (New York, 1962); Walther von Loewenich, *Luther und das Johanneische Christentum* (Munich, 1935), and *Luthers Theologia Crucis,* 4th ed. (Munich, 1954); Thomas M. McDonough, *The Law and the Gospel in Luther* (New York, 1963); Anders Nygren, *Agape and Eros,* trans. by Philip S. Watson, 2 vols. (London, 1953); Jaroslav Pelikan, *From Luther to Kierkegaard* (St. Louis, Mo., 1950); Regin Prenter, *Spiritus Creator,* trans. by John M. Jensen (Philadelphia, Pa., 1953); Valdo Vinay, *Martin Lutero, la teologia della croce e la crisi spirituale del nostro tempo* (Rome, 1947); P. S. Watson, *Let God Be God* (London, 1947); and Carl F. Wislöff, *Abendmahl und Messe: Die Kritik Luthers am Messopfer* (Darmstadt, 1969).

For studies concerning **Luther's Bible translation and interpretation** see *The Cambridge History of the Bible,* ed. by S. L. Greenslade, 3 vols., Vol. 3: *The West from the Reformation to the Present Day* (Cambridge, 1963); Heinz Bluhm, *Martin Luther: Creative Translator* (St. Louis, Mo., 1965); Heinrich Bornkamm, *Luther and the Old Testament* (Philadelphia, Pa., 1969); Karin Bornkamm, *Luthers Auslegung des Galaterbriefs von 1519 und 1531: Ein Vergleich* (Berlin, 1963); Gerhard Ebeling, *Evangelische Evangelienauslegung* (Munich, 1942); Walter Grundmann, *Der Römerbrief des Apostels Paulus und seine Auslegung durch Martin Luther* (Weimar, 1964); Willem J. Kooiman, *Luther and the Bible,* trans. by John Schmidt (Philadelphia, Pa., 1961); Erwin Mühlhaupt and Eduard Ellwein, *D. Martin Luthers Evangelienauslegung,* 3rd ed., 5 vols. (Göttingen, 1960–1961); and Jaroslav Pelikan, *Luther the Expositor: Introduction to the Reformer's Exegetical Writings* (St. Louis, Mo., 1959).

Following are excellent discussions of **Luther's social ethics:** Walter Dress, *Versuchung und Sendung* (Gütersloh, 1951); George W. Forell, *Faith Active in Love* (New York, 1954); Armas K. Holmio, *The Lutheran Reformation and the Jews* (Hancock, Mich., 1949); Olavi Lähteenmäki, *Sexus und Ehe bei Luther* (Turku, 1955); and Gustav Wingren, *Luther on Vocation,* trans. by Carl C. Rasmussen (Philadelphia, Pa., 1957).

**Luther's role in education** is treated in G. M. Bruce, *Luther as an Educator* (Minneapolis, Minn., 1928); Frederick Eby, *Early Protestant Educators* (New York, 1931); Harold J. Grimm, "Luther's Impact on the Schools," and "Luther's Catechisms as Textbooks," *Luther and Culture*

(Decorah, Iowa, 1960); F. V. N. Painter, *Luther on Education* (Philadelphia, Pa., 1889, and St. Louis, Mo., 1928); J. M. Reu, *Dr. Martin Luther's Small Catechism* (Chicago, 1929); and Theodore G. Tappert, "Luther in His Academic Role," *The Mature Luther* (Decorah, Iowa, 1959). On the training and ordination of clergy, see Helmut Lieberg, *Amt und Ordination bei Luther und Melanchthon* (Göttingen, 1962).

The Reformation in the **Scandinavian countries** is discussed by S. M. Toyne, *The Scandinavians in History* (New York, 1949), and Georg Schwaiger, *Die Reformation in den nordischen Ländern* (Munich, 1962), a scholarly Catholic account. Bibliography for the Reformation in **Denmark** is discussed by B. Kornerup, "Reformationsgeschichtliche Forschung in Dänemark," *Archiv für Reformationsgeschichte,* **37** (1940). General accounts of the Reformation are J. Danstrup, *A History of Denmark* (Copenhagen, 1948); E. H. Dunckley, *The Reformation in Denmark* (London, 1948); and J. O. Anderson, *Die Reform des Katholizismus und die dänische Reformation* (Gütersloh, 1934).

Bibliography for the Reformation in **Sweden** is discussed by Hjalmar Holmquist, "Forschungen zur Kirchengeschichte Schwedens in der Wasazeit 1523–1654," *Archiv für Reformationsgeschichte,* **36** (1939). Among general accounts are Ingvar Andersson, *History of Sweden,* trans. by Carolyn Hannay (New York, 1956); A. A. Stomberg, *A History of Sweden* (New York, 1931); H. M. Waddams, *The Swedish Church* (London, 1946); Conrad Bergendoff, *Olavus Petri and the Ecclesiastical Transformation of Sweden* (New York, 1928); Hjalmar Holmquist, *Reformationstidevarvet, 1521–1611* (Stockholm, 1933), Vol. 3 of *Svenska Kyrkans Historia;* J. G. Hoffmann, *La Réform en Suède 1523–72 et la succession apostolique* (Neuchâtel and Paris, 1945); and E. E. Yelverton, *The Manual of Olavus Petri* (London, 1953). Two helpful studies on Gustavus Vasa are Sven Lundkvist, *Gustav Vasa och Europa: Svensk Handels- och Utrikespolitik, 1534–1557* (Uppsala, 1960), and Herman Schück, *Ecclesia Lincopensis: Studies om Linkopingskyrkan under Medeltiden och Gustav Vasa* (Stockholm, 1959). See also Michal Roberts, *The Early Vasas: A History of Sweden, 1523–1611* (Cambridge, 1968).

The Reformation in **Norway** is discussed in K. Larsen, *A History of Norway* (Princeton, N.J., 1948); T. B. Willson, *History of Church and State in Norway from the Tenth to the Sixteenth Century* (Philadelphia, Pa., 1903); and Halvdan Koht, *Krisear i Norsk Historie. Vincens Lunge kontra Henrik Krummedige, 1523–25* (Oslo, 1950), and *Olav Engelbriktsson og Sjolstandetapet* (Oslo, 1951).

The history of the Reformation in the **Baltic countries** is covered by *Baltische Kirchengeschichte,* ed. by R. Wittram (Munich, 1956); Leonid Arbusow, *Die Einführung der Reformation in Liv-, Est- und Kurland* (Leipzig, 1921); Wilhelm Kahle, *Die Begegnung des baltischen Protestan-*

# Bibliography

*tismus mit der Russisch-orthodoxen Kirche* (Leiden, 1959); Otto Pohit, *Reformationsgeschichte Livlands* (Leipzig, 1928); and O. Greifenhagen, *Luthers persönliche Beziehungen zur Revaler Reformation* (Reval, 1933).

The best recent survey of literature concerned with the Reformation in **Poland** is that by Bernhard Stasiewski, *Reformation und Gegenreformation in Polen: Neue Forschungsergebnisse,* "Katholisches Leben und Kämpfen im Zeitalter der Glaubensspaltung," Vol. 18 (Münster, 1960). See also Teador Wierzbowski, *Bibliographia polonica XV ac XVI ss.* (Nieuwkoop, 1961). For a scholarly general account, see O. Halecki, *A History of Poland* (Chicago, 1966). There are good essays in *The Cambridge History of Poland,* Vol. 1: *To 1669,* ed. by W. F. Reddaway and others (New York, 1950), and in *Gestalten und Wege der Kirche im Osten,* ed. by H. Kruska (Ulm, 1958). Recent articles by Polish scholars are contained in the journal *Reformacja w Polsce* (Warsaw), revived in 1953, which reflects their present tendency to treat the Renaissance and the Reformation as one movement with particular emphasis on the political, economic, and social conflicts and on the role of the Antitrinitarians as the representatives of progress. For accounts of the growth of humanism, see H. Barycz, *Historja Uniwersytetu Jagiellonskiego w epoce Humanizmu* (History of the Jagiellon University in the Epoch of Humanism) (Cracow, 1935), and O. Halecki, "The Renaissance in Poland: Cultural Life and Literature," *The Cambridge History of Poland,* Vol. I. For a general account of the Reformation, see Paul Fox, *The Reformation in Poland* (Baltimore, 1924). K. E. J. Jorgensen discusses the attempts of Polish Protestants to cooperate with one another in his *Ökumenische Bestrebungen unter den polnischen Protestanten bis zum Jahr 1645* (Copenhagen, 1942). See also Gottfried Schramm, *Der polnische Adel und die Reformation 1548–1607* (Wiesbaden, 1965). The history of the Anti-Trinitarians is provided by E. M. Wilbur, *A History of Unitarianism,* 2 vols. (Cambridge, Mass., 1945–1952); Stanislaw Kot, *Socinianism in Poland,* trans. from the Polish ed. of 1932 (Boston, 1957); and *Studia nad Arianizmen,* ed. by Ludwik Chmaj (Warsaw, 1959). Hermann Dalton's *John à Lasco* (London, 1886) now is superseded by Ockar Bartel, *Jan Laski,* Vol. I: *1499–1556* (Warsaw, 1955), which contains an excellent bibliography. Important for religious ideas is *Fausto Soccino, Listy* (Letters), ed. by Ludwik Chmaj (Warsaw, 1959). For a general survey of Slavic history, see Francis Dvornik, *The Slavs in European History and Civilization* (New Brunswick, N.J., 1962), and W. H. McNeill, *Europe's Steppe Frontier, 1500–1800* (Chicago, 1964).

The background of the Reformation in **Bohemia and Moravia** is ably presented by S. Harrison Thomson, *Czechoslovakia in European History* (Princeton, N.J., 1943); Matthew Spinka, *John Hus and the Czech Reform* (Chicago, 1941); Paul De Vooght, *L'Hérésie de Jean Huss* (Louvain,

1960), and *Hussiana* (Louvain, 1960); Frederick G. Heymann, *John Žižka and the Hussite Revolution* (Princeton, N.J., 1955); Peter de Beauvoir Brock, *The Political and Social Doctrines of the Unity of Czech Brethren in the Fifteenth and Early Sixteenth Centuries* (The Hague, 1957); Josef Macek, *The Hussite Movement in Bohemia* (Prague, 1958); and the critical edition of *Magistri Johannis Hus tractatus de ecclesia,* ed. by S. Harrison Thomson (Cambridge and Boulder, Colo., 1956). On the Reformation itself, see S. Harrison Thomson, "Luther and Bohemia," *Archiv für Reformationsgeschichte,* **44** (1953), and Gerhard J. Neumann, "Nach und von Mähren," ibid., **48** (1957).

The history of the Reformation in **Austria** is discussed by Grete Mecenseffy, *Geschichte des Protestantismus in Oesterreich* (Graz, 1956), and E. Tomek, *Kirchengeschichte Oesterreichs,* Vol. 2: *Die Zeit des Humanismus, der Reformation und Gegenreformation* (Stuttgart, 1949).

The following works deal with the Reformation in **Hungary:** Mihaly Bucsay, *Geschichte des Protestantismus in Ungarn* (Stuttgart, 1959); T. Mende, *Hungary* (London, 1944); J. Eppstein, *Hungary* (Cambridge, 1945); William Toth, "Highlights of the Hungarian Reformation," *Church History,* **9** (1940), and "Stephan Kis of Szeged," *Archiv für Reformationsgeschichte,* **44** (1953); and Imre Revesz, *History of the Hungarian Reformed Church,* trans. by G. A. F. Knight (Washington, D.C., 1956). For the Reformation in Transylvania see Karl Reinerth, *Die Reformation der siebenbürgisch-sächsischen Kirche* (Gütersloh, 1956), and Erich Roth, *Geschichte des Gottesdienstes der Siebenbürger Sachsen* (Göttingen, 1954) and *Die Reformation in Siebenbürgen. Ihr Verhältnis zu Wittenberg und der Schweiz,* 2 parts (Cologne, 1962 and 1964). Contacts of Lutheranism in Byzantium are covered by Ernst Benz, *Wittenberg und Byzanz* (Marburg, 1949).

## Chapter 6: New Forms of Protestantism

The first general account of the entire **Left Wing of the Reformation** is that by George H. Williams, *The Radical Reformation* (Philadelphia, Pa., 1962), a scholarly analysis of the many movements formerly grouped together as "Anabaptists" or completely ignored. See also his "Studies in the Radical Reformation: A Bibliographical Survey," *Church History,* **27** (1958), and Roland H. Bainton's "The Left Wing of the Reformation," *Journal of Religion,* **21** (1941).

The first of two **bibliographies** designed to cover in detail the entire Anabaptist-Mennonite movement to the present is *A Bibliography of Anabaptism, 1520–1630,* compiled by Hans J. Hillerbrand under the general editorship of Harold S. Bender (Elkhart, Ind., 1962). There are excellent bibliographies in the *Mennonite Quarterly Review* (1926– ),

# Bibliography

*The Mennonite Encyclopedia* (1955– ), and the *Mennonitisches Lexikon* (1913– ). For Menno Simons see Irvin B. Horst, *A Bibliography of Menno Simons, ca. 1496–1561, Dutch Reformer* (Nieuwkoop, 1962), and Cornelius Krahn, "Menno Simons Research (1910–1960), "*Church History*, 30 (1961). Robert Friedmann, with the assistance of Adolf Mais, has compiled a complete bibliography on the Hutterian Brethren: *Die Schriften der Huterischen Täufergemeinschaften . . . 1529–1667* (Vienna, 1965).

The growing interest in the Left Wing of the Reformation is shown by the large number of **Anabaptist sources** published in the *Quellen und Forschungen zur Reformationsgeschichte* under the title, *Quellen zur Geschichte der Wiedertäufer* (or *Täufer*), Vol. 1: *Württemberg* (Leipzig, 1930); Vol. 2: *Bayern I* (Leipzig, 1934); Vol. 3: *Glaubenszeugnisse oberdeutscher Taufgesinnter I* (Leipzig, 1938); Vol. 4: *Baden-Pfalz* (Gütersloh, 1951); Vol. 5: *Bayern II* (Gütersloh, 1951); Vol. 6: *Hans Dencks Schriften*, 3 parts (Gütersloh, 1955–1960); Vol. 7: *Elsass I: Stadt Strassburg 1522–1532* (Gütersloh, 1959); Vol. 8: *Elsass II: Stadt Strassburg 1533–1535* (Gütersloh, 1960); Vol. 9: *Schriften, von Balthasar Hubmaier* (Gütersloh, 1962); Vol. 10: *Bibliographie des Täufertums*, ed. by Hans J. Hillerbrand (Gütersloh, 1962); Vol. 11: *Oesterreich* (Gütersloh, 1964). In addition to these, there are the *Quellen zur Geschichte der Täufer in der Schweiz*, Vol. 1: *Zürich*, ed. by L. V. Muralt and W. Schmid (Zurich, 1952), and *Urkundliche Quellen zur hessischen Reformationsgeschichte*, Vol. 4: *Wiedertäuferakten 1527–1626*, ed. by Günther Franz (Marburg, 1951). Selections are provided by *Der Linke Flügel der Reformation: Glaubenszeugnisse der Täufer, Spiritualisten, Schwärmer und Antitrinitarier*, ed. by Heinold Fast (Bremen, 1962). There are available in English translation *Spiritual and Anabaptist Writers*, ed. by George H. Williams and Angel M. Mergal, "Library of Christian Classics," Vol. 25 (Philadelphia, Pa., 1957), and *The Complete Writings of Menno Simons (c. 1496–1561)*, trans. by Leonard Verduin, ed. by John C. Wenger, with a biography by Harold S. Bender (Scottdale, Pa., 1956). See also Menno Simons, *Dat Fundament des Christlycken Leers*, ed. by H. W. Meihuisen (The Hague, 1967); *Die älteste Chronik der Hutterischen Brüder*, ed. by A. J. F. Zieglschmid (Philadelphia, Pa., 1943); *Conrad Grebel's Programmatic Letters of 1524*, trans. by J. C. Wenger (Scottdale, Pa., 1970); and Caspar Schwenckfeld, *Corpus Schwenckfeldianorum*, 15 vols. (Leipzig, 1907–1939).

Useful studies of **Anabaptism** are Rollin S. Armour, *Anabaptist Baptism* (Scottdale, Pa., 1966); Günther Bauer, *Anfänge täuferischer Gemeindebildung in Franken* (Nürnberg, 1966); Elsa Bernhofer-Pippert, *Täuferische Denkweisen und Lebensformen im Spiegel oberdeutscher Täuferverhöre*, "Reformationsgeschichtliche Studien und Texte," No. 96

(Münster, 1967); Claus-Peter Clasen, *Die Wiedertäufer im Herzogtum Württemberg und in benachbarten Herrschaften* (Stuttgart, 1965); Norman Cohn, *The Pursuit of the Millenium* (New York, 1961); Robert Friedmann, *Mennonite Piety Through the Centuries* (Goshen, Ind., 1949); Delbert Gratz, *Bernese Anabaptists* (Goshen, Ind., 1953); *The Recovery of the Anabaptist Vision,* ed. by Guy F. Hershberger (Scottdale, Pa., 1957); Hans J. Hillerbrand, *A Fellowship of Discontent* (New York, 1967), and *Die politische Ethik des oberdeutschen Täufertums* (Leiden and Cologne, 1962); Rufus M. Jones, *Spiritual Reformers in the 16th and 17th Centuries* (London, 1914); W. E. Keeney, *Dutch Anabaptist Thought and Practice* (Nieuwkoop, 1968); Peter James Klassen, *The Economics of Anabaptism* (The Hague, 1964); Cornelius Krahn, *Dutch Anabaptism: Origin, Spread, Life, and Thought, 1450–1600* (The Hague, 1968); Franklin H. Littell, *The Anabaptist View of the Church* (Chicago, 1952), and *The Origins of Sectarian Protestantism* (New York, 1964); John S. Oyer, *Lutheran Reformers Against Anabaptists* (The Hague, 1964); Paul Peachey, *Die soziale Herkunft der Schweizer Täufer in der Reformationszeit* (Karlsruhe, 1954); C. H. Smith, *The Story of the Mennonites,* 3rd ed., rev. by C. Krahn (Newton, Kans., 1950); R. J. Smithson, *The Anabaptists* (London, 1953); A. L. E. Verheyden, *Anabaptism in Flanders, 1530–1650,* trans. by Kuitse, J. Matthiissen, and J. H. Yoder (Scottdale, Pa., 1961); Wilhelm Wiswedel, *Bilder und Führergestalten aus dem Täufertum,* 3 vols. (Kassel, 1928–1952); John Yoder, *Täufertum und Reformation in der Schweiz,* Vol. 1: *Die Gespräche zwischen Täufern und Reformatoren in der Schweiz, 1523–1538* (Karlsruhe, 1962); and Z. K. Zeman, *The Anabaptists and the Czech Brethren in Moravia, 1526–1628* (The Hague, 1969).

**Individual Anabaptists** are discussed in Harold S. Bender, *The Life and Letters of Conrad Grebel,* Vol. 1 (Goshen, Ind., 1950); Ekkehard Krajewski, *Leben und Sterben des Zürcher Täuferführers Felix Mantz* (Kassel, 1957); Torsten Bergsten, *Balthasar Hubmaier, Seine Stellung zu Reformation und Täufertum* (Kassel, 1961); H. C. Vedder, *Balthasar Hübmaier* (New York, 1905); Hans Fischer, *Jakob Huter: Leben, Frömmigkeit, Briefe* (Newton, Kans., 1956); Robert Friedmann, *Hutterite Studies* (Goshen, Ind., 1961); J. A. Brandsma, *Menno Simons von Witmarsum,* trans. by B. Loets (Kassel, 1962); H. W. Meihuzen, *Menno Simons* (Haarlem, 1961); J. ten Doornkaat Koolman, *Dirk Philips, Vriend en Medewerker van Menno Simons, 1504–1568* (Haarlem, 1964); and Bernd Moeller, *Johannes Zwick und die Reformation in Konstanz,* "Quellen und Forschungen zur Reformationsgeschichte," Vol. 28 (Gütersloh, 1961).

Following are special studies of **other left-wing reformers**: Roland H. Bainton, *The Travail of Religious Liberty* (Philadelphia, Pa., 1951), and

# Bibliography

*Hunted Heretic: The Life and Death of Servetus* (Boston, 1953); *Autour de Michel Servet et de Sébastien Castellion,* ed. by B. Becker (Haarlem, 1954); Roland H. Bainton, B. Becker, and others, *Castellioniana: Quatre Études sur Sébastien Castellion et l'idée de la tolerance* (Leiden, 1951); Austin P. Evans, *An Episode in the Struggle of Religious Freedom* (New York, 1924), on the Nürnberg sectaries; Stanislaw Kot, *Socinianism in Poland: The Social and Political Ideas of Polish Antitrinitarians in the 16th and 17th Centuries,* trans. by Ernst Morse Wilbur (Boston, 1957); Ernst Morse Wilbur, *A History of Unitarianism. Socinianism and Its Antecedents* (Cambridge, Mass., 1947); A. Coutts, *Hans Denck* (Edinburgh, 1927); F. L. Weiss, *Johann Denck* (Strassburg, 1924); J. F. Gerhard Goeters, *Ludwig Hätzer (ca. 1500 bis 1529): Spiritualist und Antitrinitarier,* "Quellen und Forschungen zur Reformationsgeschichte," Vol. 25 (Gütersloh, 1957); Paul L. Maier, *Caspar Schwenckfeld on the Person and Work of Christ* (Assen, 1959); Gottfried Maron, *Individualismus und Gemeinschaft bei Caspar von Schwenckfeld* (Stuttgart, 1961); Selina G. Schultz, *Caspar Schwenckfeld von Ossig* (Stuttgart, 1946); Joachim H. Seyppel, *Schwenckfeld, Knight of Faith* (Pennsburg, Pa., 1961); Mainulf Barbers, *Toleranz bei Sebastian Franck* (Bonn, 1964); K. Klemm, *Das Paradoxon als Ausdrucksform der spekulativen Mystik Sebastian Francks* (Leipzig, 1937); Hermann Korner, *Studien zur geistesgeschichtlichen Stellung Sebastian Francks* (Breslau, 1935); and Kuno Räber, *Studien zur Geschichtsbibel Sebastian Francks* (Basel, 1952).

Accounts of the evangelical movements in the **Romance countries** are given in the following: for **Spain,** C. A. Wilkens, *Spanish Protestants in the Sixteenth Century* (London, 1897), an older, but still valuable account; M. Bataillon, *Erasme et l'Espagne* (Paris, 1937); E. Schäfer, *Beiträge zur Geschichte des spanischen Protestantismus und der Inquisition,* 3 vols. (Gütersloh, 1902); E. Cione, *Juan de Valdes* (Bari, 1938); J. Heep, *Juan de Valdes: Seine Religion, sein Werden und seine Bedeutung* (Leipzig, 1909); John E. Longhurst, ed., *Erasmus and the Spanish Inquisition: The Case of Juan de Valdes* (Albuquerque, N.M., 1950), and *Luther and the Spanish Inquisition: The Case of Diego de Uceda* (Albuquerque, N.M., 1953).

For evangelical movements and reformers in **Italy,** see *Opuscoli e lettere di reformatori italiana del Cinquecento,* ed. by Giuseppe Paladino, 2 vols. (Bari, 1913–1927); P. Brezzi, *Le origini del Protestantesimo* (Rome, 1961); George K. Brown, *Italy and the Reformation to 1550* (Oxford, 1933); Delio Cantimori, *Eretici italiani del Cinquecento* (Florence, 1939); Frederick C. Church, *The Italian Reformers* (New York, 1932); Francesco Lemmi, *La riforma in Italia* (Milan, ca. 1938); Joseph C. McLelland, *The Visible Words of God: An Exposition of the Sacramental Theology of Peter Martyr Vermigli* (Grand Rapids, Mich., 1957);

E. P. Rodocanachi, *La Réforme en Italie,* 2 vols. (Paris, 1920–1921); Francesco Ruffini, *Studi sui rèformatori italiani* (Turin, 1955); Delio Cantimori, *Bernardino Ochino: Uomo del Rinascimento e Riformatore* (Pisa, 1929); D. M. Cory, *Faustus Socinus* (Boston, 1932); Erich Hassinger, *Studien zu Jacobus Acontius* (Berlin, 1934); and Paolo Rossi, *Giacomo Aconcio* (Milan, 1952).

For **France** before the rise of Calvinism, see Augustin Renaudet, *Préréform et humanisme à Paris pendant les premières guerres d'Italie, 1494–1517,* 2nd ed. (Paris, 1953); H. M. Bower, *The Fourteen of Meaux* (London, 1894); and René-Jacques Lovy, *Les Origines de la réforme française: Meaux, 1518–1546* (Paris, 1959). For the influence of Erasmian Basle and its printers on the French, see Peter G. Bietenholz, *Basle and France in the Sixteenth Century: The Basle Humanists and Printers in Their Contacts with Francophone Culture* (Toronto, 1971).

The chief collections of sources for the Reformation in **England** are H. Gee and W. J. Hardy, *Documents Illustrative of English Church History* (London, 1914); The Parker Society Publications, 55 vols. (Cambridge, 1843–1855); the works of John Strype, 23 vols. (Oxford, 1821–1840); *State Papers During the Reign of Henry VIII,* 15 vols. (London, 1830–1835), containing documents from the Public Record Office; *Letters and Papers, Foreign and Domestic, of the Reign of Henry VIII,* 21 vols. (London, 1862–1910), containing also material from private archives; *Calendars of State Papers,* comprising papers preserved in Rome, 1 vol.; Spain, 15 vols.; Venice, 22 vols.; Ireland, 10 vols.; Foreign papers of Edward VI, 1 vol.; Mary, 1 vol.; Elizabeth I, 19 vols.; and Milan, 1 vol.; *Tudor Royal Proclamations,* Vol. 1: *The Early Tudors 1485–1553,* ed. by Paul L. Hughes and James F. Larkin (New Haven, Conn., and London, 1964). Among recent publications of miscellaneous sources are C. C. Butterworth, *The English Primers* (Philadelphia, Pa., 1953); G. R. Elton, *The Tudor Constitution, Documents and Commentary* (Cambridge, 1960), indispensable; various editions of J. Foxe, *Book of Martyrs;* G. B. Harrison, *The Elizabethan Journals* (1939), and *A Jacobean Journal* (New York, 1941); Millar MacLure, *The Paul's Cross Sermons, 1534–1642* (Toronto, 1958); S. Morison, *English Prayer Books* (Cambridge, 1949); *British Pamphleteers,* ed. by George Orwell, Vol. 1 (London, 1948); Helen C. White, *The Tudor Books of Private Devotion* (Madison, Wis., 1951); M. Stanley, *English Prayer Books* (Cambridge, 1945); *Select Statutes and Other Constitutional Documents Illustrative of the Reigns of Elizabeth and James I,* ed. by G. W. Prothero, 4th ed. (Oxford, 1913); and R. H. Tawney and Eileen Power, eds., *Tudor Economic Documents,* 3 vols. (London, 1951).

The **background of the English Reformation** is discussed in James Gairdner, *Lollardy and the Reformation in England,* 4 vols. (London,

# Bibliography

1908–1913); A. G. Dickens, *Lollards and Protestants in the Diocese of York* (London, 1959); F. A. Gasquet, *The Eve of the Reformation* (London, 1905); J. Mackinnon, *The Origins of the Reformation* (London and New York, 1939); O. A. Marti, *Economic Causes of the Reformation in England* (New York, 1929); E. G. Rupp, *Studies in the Making of the English Protestant Tradition* (New York, 1938); and A. H. Hamilton, *The English Clergy and Their Organization in the Later Middle Ages* (Oxford, 1947).

For general accounts of the **Reformation in England,** see Robert Walcott, *The Tudor-Stuart Period of English History: A Review of Changing Interpretations,* "Service Center for Teachers of History," No. 58 (New York, 1964); Sidney R. Brett, *The Tudor Century, 1485–1603* (London, 1962); William A. Clebsch, *England's Earliest Protestants, 1520–1535* (New Haven, Conn., 1964); A. G. Dickens, *The English Reformation* (New York, 1964); G. R. Elton, *England Under the Tudors* (London, 1955), and *The Tudor Revolution in Government: Administrative Changes in the Reign of Henry VIII* (Cambridge, 1962); James Gairdner, *The English Church in the Sixteenth Century* (London and New York, 1902); Cyril Garbett, *Church and State in England* (London, 1950); Philip Hughes, *The Reformation in England,* 3 vols. (London, 1950–1954); Stanford E. Lehmberg *The Reformation Parliament 1529–1536* (Cambridge, 1970); James K. McConica, *English Humanists and Reformation Politics Under Henry VIII and Edward VI* (Oxford, 1965); *English Reformers,* ed. by T. H. L. Parker, "Library of Christian Classics," Vol. 26 (Philadelphia, Pa., 1966); Thomas M. Parker, *The English Reformation* (New York, 1950); Frederick M. Powicke, *The Reformation in England* (New York, 1941); Edward C. Rich, *Spiritual Authority in the Church of England* (New York, 1953); and George W. O. Woodward, *Reformation and Resurgence, 1485–1603: England in the Sixteenth Century* (London, 1963). See also Frederick F. Bruce, *The English Bible: A History of Translations,* new ed. (New York, 1970), and Clifford W. Dugmore, *The Mass and the English Reformers* (New York, 1958), a defense of the "continuity" of the Church of England. The standard references on the religious orders and the dissolution of the monasteries are David Knowles, *The Religious Orders in England,* 3 vols. (Cambridge, 1948–1959); Geoffrey Baskerville, *English Monks and the Suppression of the Monasteries* (New Haven, Conn., 1937), and Francis A. Gasquet, *Henry VIII and the English Monasteries,* 6th ed. (London, 1902). For Lutheran influences see Henry E. Jacobs, *The Lutheran Movement in England During the Reigns of Henry VIII and Edward VI* (Philadelphia, Pa., 1916). Political thought is discussed in Christopher Morris, *Political Thought in England, Tyndale to Hooker* (London, 1953).

**Economic and social conditions in England** are described in William Cunningham, *The Growth of English Industry and Commerce,* 5th ed., 3 vols., (Cambridge, 1903–1921); George N. Clark, *The Wealth of England from 1496 to 1760* (New York, 1946); Frederick C. Dietz, *English Government and Finance, 1485–1558* (Urbana, Ill., 1921); John U. Nef, *Industry and Government in France and England, 1540–1640* (Philadelphia, Pa., 1940); Thomas A. Lacey, *The Reformation and the People* (London, 1929); Roger L. Palmer, *English Social History in the Making* (London, 1934); Conyers Read, *Social and Political Forces in the English Reformation* (Houston, Tex., 1953); R. B. Smith, *Land and Politics in the England of Henry VIII: The West Riding of Yorkshire: 1530–46* (New York, 1970), excellent on the rise of the gentry; G. M. Trevelyan, *Illustrated English Social History,* Vol. 1 (London and New York, 1949); Helen C. White, *Social Criticism in Popular Literature of the Sixteenth Century* (New York, 1944); and I. D. Colvin, *The Germans in England, 1066–1598* (London, 1915).

The following describe **intellectual conditions:** H. S. Bennett, *English Books and Readers, 1475–1577,* 2nd ed. (Cambridge, 1969); J. W. Blench, *Preaching in England in the Late Fifteenth and Sixteenth Centuries* (New York, 1964); G. T. Buckley, *Rationalism in Sixteenth Century English Literature* (Chicago, 1933); Lily B. Campbell, *Divine Poetry and Drama in Sixteenth-Century England* (Cambridge and Berkeley, Calif., 1959); William E. Campbell, *Erasmus, Tyndale and More* (London, 1949); Fritz Caspari, *Humanism and the Social Order in Tudor England* (Chicago, 1954); Mark H. Curtis, *Oxford and Cambridge in Transition, 1558–1642* (Oxford, 1959); L. E. Elliott-Binns, *England and the New Learning* (London, 1937); Germain Marc'hadour, *L'Universe de Thomas More, chronologie critique de More, Erasme, et leur époque (1477–1536)* (Paris, 1963); Charles H. George, *The Protestant Mind of the English Reformation* (Princeton, N.J., 1961); H. C. Porter, *Reformation and Reaction in Tudor Cambridge* (New York, 1959); and N. Wood, *The Reformation and English Education* (London, 1931).

Among useful studies of the **early Tudor rulers** are F. L. Baumer, *Early Tudor Theory of Kingship* (New Haven, Conn., and London, 1940); A. D. Innes, *England Under the Tudors,* 10th ed. (London, 1953); J. D. Mackie, *The Earlier Tudors, 1485–1558* (Oxford, 1952); K. Pickthorn, *Early Tudor Government* (Cambridge and New York, 1934); Conyers Read, *The Tudors* (New York, 1936); L. B. Smith, *Tudor Prelates and Politics* (Princeton, N. J., 1953); and W. G. Zeeveld, *Foundations of Tudor Policy* (Cambridge, Mass., 1948). The standard biography of Henry VIII is A. F. Pollard, *Henry VIII* (London, 1913). The best biography since that of Pollard is that by J. J. Scarisbrick, *Henry VIII* (Berkeley, Calif., 1968). Herbert M. Smith, *Henry VIII and the Reforma-

*tion* (London and New York, 1948), provides information concerning personalities and institutions. See also Erwin Doernberg, *Henry VIII and Luther* (Stanford, Calif., 1961); Neelak Tjernagel, *Henry VIII and the Lutherans* (St. Louis, Mo., 1966); and Garrett Mattingly, *Catherine of Aragon* (New York, 1960). On Henry's separation proceedings, see *Römische Dokumente zur Geschichte der Ehescheidung Heinrichs VIII. von England, 1527–34,* ed. by S. Ehses (Paderborn, 1893), and Hans Thieme, *Die Ehescheidung Heinrichs VIII. und die europäischen Universitäten* (Karlsruhe, 1957).

There are the following published works of **Thomas Cranmer:** J. Strype, *Memorials of Archbishop Cranmer,* 2 vols. (Oxford, 1812); *The Works of Thomas Cranmer,* ed. by J. E. Cox for the Parker Society, 2 vols. (Oxford, 1844–1846); *The Work of Thomas Cranmer,* ed. by E. E. Duffield (Philadelphia, Pa., 1965); *Cranmer's First Litany,* ed. by J. E. Hunt (New York, 1939); *The English Liturgies of 1549 and 1661* (London, 1920); *Cranmer's Selected Writings,* ed. by Carl S. Meyer (London, 1961); and H. R. Willoughby, *The First Authorized English Bible and the Cranmer Preface* (Chicago, 1942). Among biographies are Hillaire Belloc, *Cranmer* (Philadelphia, Pa., and London, 1931); G. W. Bromily, *Thomas Cranmer Theologian* (New York, 1956); Peter Brooks, *Thomas Cranmer's Doctrine of the Eucharist* (London, 1965); A. C. Deane, *Life of Thomas Cranmer* (London, 1927), a hostile account; F. E. Hutchinson, *Cranmer and the English Reformation* (New York, 1951); Albert F. Pollard, *Thomas Cranmer and the English Reformation* (London and New York, 1904), still valuable; Cyril C. Richardson, *Zwingli and Cranmer on the Eucharist* (Evanston, Ill., 1949); and Jasper Ridley, *Thomas Cranmer* (Oxford, 1962).

For studies on **Thomas More,** see bibliography for Chapter 2.

For biographies of **other persons of this period** see E. G. Rupp, *Six Makers of English Religion, 1500–1700* (New York, 1957); A. F. Pollard, *Wolsey* (London, New York, etc., 1929); Charles W. Ferguson, *Naked to Mine Enemies: The Life of Cardinal Wolsey* (Boston, 1958); Allan G. Chester, *Hugh Latimer, Apostle to the English* (Philadelphia, Pa., 1954); Winthrop S. Hudson, *John Ponet,* 2 vols. (Chicago, 1942); Harold S. Darby, *Hugh Latimer* (London, 1953); Stanford E. Lehmberg, *Sir Thomas Elyot, Tudor Humanist* (Austin, Tex., 1960), and *Sir Walter Mildway and Tudor Government* (Austin, Tex., 1964); Michael Macklem, *God Have Mercy, The Life of John Fisher of Rochester* (Ottowa, 1967); Edward Surtz, S.J., *The Works and Days of John Fisher . . . Bishop of Rochester* (Cambridge, Mass., 1967); J. F. Mozley, *William Tyndale* (London, 1937); and E. W. Perry, *Under Four Tudors* (London, 1940), a life of Matthew Parker.

For the reign of **Edward VI,** see Hester W. Chapman, *Last Tudor*

*King: A Study of Edward VI* (New York and Toronto, 1959); W. K. Jordan, *Edward VI: The Young King. The Protectorship of the Duke of Somerset* (Cambridge, Mass., 1968), and *Edward VI, The Threshold of Power: The Dominance of the Duke of Northumberland, 1549–1553* (Cambridge, Mass., 1970); C. Hopf, *Martin Bucer and the English Reformation* (Oxford, 1946); and Wilhelm Pauck, *Das Reich Gottes auf Erden. . . . Eine Untersuchung zu Butzers De regno Christi und zur englischen Staatskirche des 16. Jahrhunderts* (Berlin, 1928).

The historical background for the **Reformation in Scotland** is given in Peter H. Brown, *History of Scotland,* Vols. 1 and 2 (Cambridge, 1902); I. F. Grant, *The Social and Economic Development of Scotland Before 1603* (Edinburgh, 1930); Andrew Lang, *A History of Scotland,* Vols. 1–3 (New York, Edinburgh, and London, 1907); A. M. MacKenzie, *The Scotland of Queen Mary and the Religious Wars* (London, 1936); James MacKinnon, *The Constitutional History of Scotland . . . to the Reformation* (London, 1924); R. S. Rait, *The Parliaments of Scotland* (Glasgow, 1924); and Duncan Shaw, *The General Assemblies of the Church of Scotland, 1560–1600* (Edinburgh, 1964). See also M. Lee, Jr., *James Stewart, Earl of Moray* (New York, 1953), a biography of Mary Stuart's bastard brother.

On the history of the Reformation in Scotland there are Gordon Donaldson, *The Scottish Reformation* (Cambridge, 1960), which stresses the institutional development; J. K. Hewison, *The Covenanters,* 2 vols. (Glasgow, 1908); Andrew Lang, *John Knox and the Reformation* (London, 1905); W. McMillan, *The Worship of the Scottish Reformed Church, 1550–1638* (Edinburgh, 1902); W. L. Mathieson, *Politics and Religion,* Vol. 1 (Glasgow, 1902); A. F. Mitchell, *The Scottish Reformation* (Edinburgh, 1900); John H. Burleigh, *A Church History of Scotland* (New York, 1960); S. A. Hurlbut, *The Liturgy and the Church of Scotland,* 4 vols. (Charleston, S.C., 1944–1952); W. Perry, *The Scottish Prayer Book* (Cambridge, 1929); and William D. Maxwell, *John Knox's Genevan Service Book* (Glasgow, 1931), which has a good discussion of the development of the Calvinist liturgy from its beginnings in Strassburg.

For the writings of **John Knox,** see his *Works,* ed. by D. Laing, 6 vols. (Edinburgh, 1895), the first two volumes of which comprise his *History of the Reformation in Scotland.* There is an excellent recent edition of this history, ed. by W. C. Dickinson, 2 vols. (New York, 1950). The best biography of Knox is still that by Peter H. Brown, *John Knox* (New York and London, 1905). See also H. Cowan, *John Knox* (New York and London, 1905); E. Muir, *John Knox* (London, 1929); E. Percy, *John Knox* (London, 1937); Jasper Ridley, *John Knox* (New York and London, 1968); and H. Watt, *John Knox in Controversy* (New York, 1950).

# Bibliography

There is a concise bibliography of **Mary Stuart** by S. A. and D. R. Tannenbaum in *Marie Stuart, Queen of Scots,* 3 vols. (New York, 1944–1946). Of the many biographies of the queen, the following are particularly useful: Antonia Fraser, *Mary, Queen of Scots* (New York, 1969); R. Gore-Browne, *Lord Bothwell and Mary Queen of Scots* (New York, 1937); T. F. Henderson, *Mary Queen of Scots,* 2 vols. (New York, 1905); M. A. S. Hume, *The Love Affairs of Mary Queen of Scots* (London, 1943); A. Lang, *The Mystery of Mary Stuart* (London, 1904); E. Linklater, *Mary Queen of Scots* (London, 1952); R. H. Mahon, *Mary, Queen of Scots* (Cambridge, 1924); F. A. Mumby, *The Fall of Mary Stuart* (London, 1921); and J. H. Pollen, *Mary Queen of Scots and the Babington Plot* (Edinburg, 1922).

For accounts of **Ireland** during the Reformation Era, see R. D. Edward, *Church and State in Tudor Ireland* (London, 1935); R. H. Murray, *Ireland, 1494–1603* (London and New York, 1920); and M. V. Ronan, *The Reformation in Ireland under Elizabeth 1558–1580* (London, 1930).

# Chapter 7: The Emergence of Calvinism

For **bibliographies** concerned with John Calvin and Calvinism see John T. McNeill, "Thirty Years of Calvin Study," *Church History,* **17** (1948); Edward A. Dowey, Jr., "Survey, Continental Reformation: Works of General Interest. Studies in Calvin and Calvinism since 1948," *Church History,* **24** (1955) and **29** (1960); Alfred Erichson, *Bibliographia Calviniana* (Nieuwkoop, 1960), reprint of Braunschweig edition 1863–1900; and Wilhelm Niesel, *Calvin-Bibliographie* (Munich, 1961).

The complete collection of **Calvin's works** is the *Calvini opera quae supersunt omnia,* 58 vols., in the *Corpus reformatorum,* Vols. 29–87 (1863–1900). Scholarly and reliable is the collection, *J. Calvini opera selecta,* ed. by Peter Barth and Wilhelm Niesel, 6 vols. (Munich, 1926–1952). The best English translation and critical edition of the *Institutes* is *John Calvin. Institutes of the Christian Religion,* ed. by John T. McNeill, trans. by Ford L. Battles, 2 vols., in the "Library of Christian Classics," Vols. 20 and 21 (Philadelphia, Pa., 1960). Much of Calvin's correspondence is contained in an older work, *The Letters of John Calvin,* compiled by J. Bonnet, trans. by D. Constable, 2 vols. (Edinburgh, 1855–1857). More recent is the collection of a hundred letters by W. de Zwart, *Calvijn in het Licht zijner Brieven* (Dampen, 1938). Reprints of the *Commentaries of John Calvin,* 46 vols. (Edinburgh, 1843–1855), are being published in the United States (Grand Rapids, Mich., 1947–    ). Deliberations and decisions of the Venerable Company of Pastors at Geneva are presented in *Registres de la Compagnie des Pasteurs de Genève au temps de Calvin,* Vol. 1: *1546–1553,* ed. by Jean-François Bergier (Geneva, 1964); Vol. 2: *1553–1564*, ed. by Robert M. Kingdon (Geneva, 1962); and Vol. 3: *1565–1574*, ed. by Olivier Fatio and Olivier Labarthe (Geneva, 1969). Philip E. Hughes has translated an abridged form as *The Registers of the Pastors of Geneva in the Time of Calvin* (Grand Rapids, Mich., 1966).

**Calvin's preaching** is the subject of renewed scholarly interest, following the discovery of a large number of his sermons and the beginning of the publication of a selection of these by Erwin Mülhaupt in *Johann Calvin, Diener am Wort Gottes, eine Auswahl seiner Predigten* (Göttingen, 1934). For excellent studies concerning his preaching, see Erwin Mülhaupt, *Die Predigt Calvins* (Berlin and Leipzig, 1931), and T. H. L. Parker, *The Oracles of God* (London, 1947).

The best study of the **life and work of Calvin** is that by E. Doumergue, *Jean Calvin*, 7 vols. (Lausanne, 1899–1927), a detailed work which is very favorable to Calvin. See also *The Life of John Calvin*, written by Theodore Beza, Calvin's successor at Geneva, trans. by H. Beveridge (Philadelphia, Pa., 1909); Jean D. Benoit, *J. Calvin: La Vie, l'homme, la pensée*, 2nd ed. (Paris, 1948); Quirinus Breen, *John Calvin: A Study in French Humanism* (Grand Rapids, Mich., 1931); Fritz Büsser, *Calvins Urteil über Sich Selbst* (Zurich, 1950); R. Freschi, *Giovanni Calvino* (Milan, 1935); Francis M. Higman, *The Style of John Calvin in his French Polemical Treatises* (New York, 1967); R. N. Carew Hunt, *Calvin* (London, 1933); Pierre Imbart de la Tour, *Les Origines de la réforme*, Vol. 4: *Jean Calvin* (Paris, 1935), which pictures Calvin as able but lacking in human feeling; James McKinnon, *Calvin and the Reformation* (London, 1936), unsympathetic; Henri Naef, *Les Origines de la Réforme à Genève*, 2 vols. (Geneva, 1968); and W. Walker, *John Calvin* (New York and London, 1906), still valuable.

**Calvin's doctrines** are discussed by Lorraine Boettner, *The Reformed Doctrine of Predestination* (Grand Rapids, Mich., 1932); Arthur Dakin, *Calvinism* (Philadelphia, Pa., 1946); E. A. Dowey, *The Knowledge of God in Calvin's Theology* (New York, 1952); P. T. Fuhrmann, *God-Centered Religion* (Grand Rapids, Mich., 1942); Alexandre Ganoczy, *Calvin: Théologien de l'église et du ministère* (Paris, 1964); Charles A. M. Hall, *With the Spirit's Sword: The Drama of Spiritual Warfare in the Theology of John Calvin* (Richmond, Va., 1968); A. M. Hunter, *The Teaching of Calvin*, rev. ed. (London, 1950); Werner Krusche, *Das Wirken des Heiligen Geistes nach Calvin* (Göttingen, 1957); H. Kuiper, *Calvin on Common Grace* (Grand Rapids, Mich., 1930); Kilian McDonnell, O.S.B., *John Calvin: The Church and the Eucharist* (Princeton, N.J., 1968); Benjamin C. Milner, Jr., *Calvin's Doctrine of the Church* (Leiden, 1970); John T. McNeill, *The History and Character of Calvinism* (New York, 1954); Wilhelm Niesel, *The Theology of Calvin*,

# Bibliography

trans. by H. Knight (Philadelphia, Pa., 1956); Karl Reuter, *Das Grundverständnis der Theologie Calvins,* Part 1 (Neukirchen, 1963); Luchesius Smits, *Saint Augustin dans l'oeuvre de Jean Calvin* (Assen, 1957); Henri Strohl, *La Pensée de la réforme* (Paris, 1951), which compares Calvin with other reformers; Ronald S. Wallace, *Calvin's Doctrine of the Christian Life* (Grand Rapids, Mich., 1959); and François Wendel, *Calvin: The Origins and Development of His Religious Thought,* trans. by P. Mairet (New York, 1963), an outstanding survey.

**Calvin's views on the sacraments** are discussed in Alexander Barclay, *The Protestant Doctrine of the Lord's Supper: A Study of the Eucharistic Teaching of Luther, Zwingli, and Calvin* (Glasgow, 1927); Joachim Beckmann, *Vom Sakrament bei Calvin* (Tübingen, 1926); and W. F. Dankbaar, *De Sakramentsleer van Calvijn* (Amsterdam, 1941).

Among studies concerned with **Calvin's views on the Bible** are J. A. Cramer, *Die Heilige Schrift bei Calvin* (Utrecht, 1926), which maintains that Calvin distinguished between Word and Scripture; R. E. Davies, *The Problem of Authority in the Continental Reformers* (London, 1946); D. J. DeGroot, *Calvijns Opvatting over de Inspiratie der Heilige Schrift* (Amsterdam, 1931), which opposes the contention of Cramer; H. Jackson Forstmann, *Word and Spirit: Calvin's Doctrine of Biblical Authority* (Stanford, Calif., 1962); and Hans H. Wolf, *Die Einheit des Bundes, das Verhältnis von Altem und Neuem Testament bei Calvin* (Neukirchen, 1958). On the use of the catechism, see Thomas F. Torrance, *The School of Faith: The Catechisms of the Reformed Church* (New York, 1959).

Calvin's views concerning **the church and ecumenism** are covered in John T. McNeill, *Unitive Protestantism* (New York, 1930). See also Karlfried Frölich, *Gottesreich, Welt und Kirche bei Calvin* (Munich, 1930); W. Kolfhaus, *Christusgemeinschaft bei Calvin* (Neukirchen, 1939); Geddes MacGregor, *Corpus Christi, The Nature of the Church According to the Reformed Tradition* (Philadelphia, Pa., 1959); W. D. Maxwell, *John Knox's Genevan Service Book* (Glasgow, 1931), which traces the development of Calvin's views on the liturgy; and Pieter J. Richel, *Het Kerkbegrip van Calvijn* (Utrecht, 1942). Calvin's pastoral work is discussed by Jean D. Benoit, *Calvin, directeur d'âmes* (Strasbourg, 1947).

The views of the Genevan Reformer on **art** are discussed in M. P. Ramsay, *Calvin and Art* (Edinburgh, 1938), and Léon Wencelius, *L'Esthétique de Calvin* (Paris, 1937), and *Calvin et Rembrandt* (Paris, 1937). His views on church music are covered by W. S. Pratt, *The Music of the French Psalter of 1562* (New York, 1939); P. A. Scholes, *The Puritans and Music in England and New England* (London, 1934); Charles Schneider and Louis Piachaud, *La Restauration du Psaltier Huguenot* (Neuchâtel and Paris, 1930); and P. Jourda, *Marot, l'homme* *et l'oeuvre* (Paris, 1950), a biography of the man with whom Calvin collaborated in the versification of the psalms.

For the **political and social ideas** of Calvin, see Hans Baron, *Calvins Staatsanschauung und das konfessionelle Zeitalter* (Berlin, 1924), and "Calvinist Republicanism and Its Historical Roots," *Church History,* **8** (1939); André Biéler, *L'Homme et la femme dans la morale calviniste* (Geneva, 1963), and *The Social Humanism of Calvin,* trans. by P. T. Fuhrmann (Richmond, Va., 1964); Josef Bohatec, *Calvin und das Recht* (Feudingen, 1934); Marc E. Chenevière, *La Pensée politique de Calvin* (Geneva, 1937); W. Fred Graham, *The Constructive Revolutionary: John Calvin and His Socio-Economic Impact* (Richmond, Va., 1971); Georgia Harkness, *John Calvin: The Man and His Ethics* (New York, 1931); *Calvin and Calvinism: Sources of Democracy?* ed. by Robert M. Kingdon and Robert D. Linder (Lexington, Mass., 1970); John T. McNeill, *John Calvin on God and Political Duty* (New York, 1950); Pierre Mesnard, *L'Essor de la philosophie politique au XVIᵉ siècle en France* (Paris, 1936); William A. Mueller, *Church and State in Luther and Calvin* (Nashville, Tenn., 1954); and Ronald S. Wallace, *Calvin's Doctrine of the Christian Life* (Grand Rapids, Mich., 1959).

The **influence of Bucer and Strassburg** is discussed in the works on Bucer listed for Chapter 3 and in the following: Gustav Anrich, *Strassburg und die calvinische Kirchenverfassung* (Tübingen, 1928); Jacques Courvoisier, *La Notion d'église chez Bucer* (Paris, 1933); Jacques Pannier, *Calvin à Strasbourg* (Strassburg, 1925); Wilhelm Pauck, "Calvin and Butzer," *Journal of Religion,* **9** (1929); and François Wendel, *L'Église de Strasbourg. Sa Constitution et son organisation, 1532–35* (Paris, 1942).

For accounts of **Calvin's labors at Geneva** and the diffusion of Calvinism, see *Livre des habitants de Genève,* Vol. 1: *1549–1560,* ed. by Paul-F. Geisendorf (Geneva, 1957), a study of the registered refugees in Geneva; *Le Livre du recteur de l'Académie de Genève* (1559–1878), Vol. 1: *Le Texte* (Geneva, 1959), which contains the register of the students who came to Geneva; *Ginevra e l'Italia,* "Biblioteca Storica Sansoni," N.S., Vol. 34, ed. by Delio Cantimori and others (Florence, 1959); G. Berthoud and others, *Aspects de la propagande religieuse* (Geneva, 1957); Charles Borgeaud, *Histoire de l'Université de Genève,* Vol. 1: *L'Académie de Calvin* (Geneva, 1900); Alexander Ganoczy, *La Bibliothèque de l'Académie du Calvin* (Geneva, 1969); Robert M. Kingdon, *Geneva and the Coming of the Wars of Religion in France, 1555–1563* (Geneva, 1956), and *Geneva and the Consolidation of the French Protestant Movement, 1564–1572* (Madison, Wis., 1967); Walther Köhler, *Zürcher Ehegericht und Genfer Konsistorium,* Vol. 2 (Leipzig, 1942); John T. McNeill, *The History and Character of Calvinism* (New York,

# Bibliography

1954); E. William Monter, *Studies in Genevan Government (1536–1605)* (Geneva, 1964), and *Calvin's Geneva* (New York, 1967); Henri Naef, *Les Origines de la Réforme à Genève,* 2 vols. (Geneva, 1936–1968); and A. A. van Schelven, *Het Calvinisme gedurende zijn Bloeitijd in de 16e en de 17e Eeuw,* Vol. 1: *Genève, Frankrijk;* Vol. 2: *Schotland, Engeland, Noord-Amerika* (Amsterdam, 1943–1951).

On the life and work of **Theodore Beza,** see Frederic Gardy, *Bibliographie des oeuvres théologiques, littéraires, historiques et juridiques de Théodore de Bèze,* with the collaboration of Alain Dufour (Geneva, 1960); *Correspondance de Théodore de Bèze,* ed. by F. Aubert and H. Meylan (Geneva, 1960–      ); H. M. Baird, *Theodore Beza* (New York and London, 1899); *Du Droit des magistrats: Theodore Beza,* ed. by Robert M. Kingdon (Geneva, 1971); and Paul-F. Geisendorf, *Théodore de Bèze* (Geneva, 1949).

On **Calvin's relations with other reformers,** see Roland H. Bainton, *Bernardino Ochino* (Florence, 1940), which covers Ochino's stay in Geneva; Josef Bohatec, *Budé und Calvin* (Graz, 1950); Andre Bouvier, *Henri Bullinger* (Paris, 1940), which discusses Calvin's cooperation with Bullinger; H. R. Guggisberg, *Sebastian Castellio im Urteil seiner Nachwelt* (Basel, 1956); P. Jourda, *Marot* (Paris, 1950); and Robert D. Linder, *The Political Ideas of Pierre Viret* (Geneva, 1964).

# Chapter 8: The Catholic Reformation

**Recent research** in the history of the Catholic Church during the Reformation Era is discussed by George H. Tavard, "The Catholic Reform in the Sixteenth Century," *Church History,* **26** (1957), and J. Dagens, *Bibliographie chronologique de la littérature de spiritualité et de ses sources* (Paris, 1952).

The most important **published sources** are the dispatches of the papal nuncios: *Nuntiaturberichte aus Deutschland nebst ergänzenden Aktenstücken,* published by the Prussian and the Austrian Historical Institute in Rome, Part 1: *1533–59,* 12 vols. (Gotha, 1892–1912); Part 2: *1560–72,* 7 vols. (Vienna and Graz, 1897–1953); Part 3: *1572–85,* 5 vols. (Gotha, 1892–1909); and Part 4, still in the process of publication. The Görresgesellschaft published the following *Nuntiaturberichte* for the years 1585–1590: Part 1: *Die Kölner Nuntiatur,* 2 vols. (Paderborn, 1895); Part 2: *Die Nuntiatur am Kaiserhofe,* 3 vols. (Paderborn, 1905–1919); and the supplementary volume, *Nuntiaturkorrespondenz Kaspar Groppers, 1573–76* (Paderborn, 1898). For Switzerland and France there are the *Nuntiaturberichte aus der Schweiz,* 4 vols. for the years 1579–1581 (Freiburg and Solothurn, 1906–1929), and *Nonciatures de France, Non-*

*ciatures de Paul IV,* Vol. 1: *Nonciatures de Sebastiano Gualterio et de Cesare Brancatio* (1554–1557), 2 parts (Paris, 1909–1911); for Spain, *Correspondencia diplomática entre España y la Santa Sede durante el pontificado de Pio V,* ed. by L. Serrano, 4 vols. (Madrid, 1914).

Other important sources are *Acta reformationis catholicae ecclesiam Germaniae concernentia saeculi 16. Die Reformverhandlungen des deutschen Episkopats von 1520 bis 1570,* 3 vols. to date, ed. by Georg Pfeilschifter (Regensburg, 1959–1968); *Acten und Correspondenzen zur Geschichte der Gegenreformation in Innerösterreich unter Erzherzog Karl II (1578–1637),* 3 vols. of the *Fontes rerum Austriacarum* (Vienna, 1898–1907); *Corpus catholicorum* (Münster, 1919–    ), containing works of Catholic writers during the Reformation; *Ecclesia et status,* ed. by J. B. Grasso, S.J. (Rome, 1939), containing important papal bulls of the period; *Quellen zur Geschichte des Papsttums,* ed. by K. Mirbt, 4th ed. (Tübingen, 1924); *Sacrorum conciliorum,* 53 vols. in 58, ed. by G. D. Mansi (Paris, 1901–1927); *Concilium tridentinum,* ed. by S. Ehses, G. Bushbell, V. Schweitzer, and H. Jedin, 12 vols. to date (Freiburg i. Br. and Rome, 1901–    ), containing diaries, official acts, letters, and other sources of the Council of Trent; *Monumenta historica societatis Jesu,* 63 vols. (Madrid, 1894–1936); Ignatius Loyola, *Spiritual Exercises,* in many editions; *Acta sanctorum* of the Bollandists, 68 vols. (Paris, 1863–1940); and *Lives of the Saints,* compiled by A. Butler and revised by F. Thurston and O. Attwater, 12 vols. (London, 1939).

Among **recent accounts of the Catholic Reformation** as a whole are Edward M. Burns, *The Counter Reformation* (Princeton, N.J., 1964); L Cristiani, *L'Église à l'époque du Concile de Trente* (Turin, 1948); H. Daniel-Rops, *The Catholic Reformation,* trans. by J. Warrington (London and New York, 1961); Jean Delumeau, *Naissance et affirmation de la Réform* (Paris, 1965); A. G. Dickens, *The Counter Reformation* (New York, 1969); H. Outram Evennett, *The Spirit of the Counter-Reformation,* ed. by John Bossy (Cambridge, 1968); Philip Hughes, *Rome and the Counter-Reformation* (London, 1942); Pierre Janelle, *The Catholic Reformation* (Milwaukee, Wis., 1949); Hubert Jedin, *Kirche des Glaubens, Kirche der Geschichte* (Freiburg i.Br., 1966); B. J. Kidd, *The Counter-Reformation* (London, 1933); Fernand Mourret, *A History of the Catholic Church,* trans. by Newton Thompson, 8 vols., Vol. 5 (St. Louis, Mo., 1930–1957); *The Catholic Reformation: Savonarola to Ignatius Loyola,* ed. by John C. Olin (New York, 1969); Gustav Schnürer, *Katholische Kirche und Kultur in der Barockzeit* (Paderborn, Vienna, and Zurich, 1937); Hermann Tüchle, C. A. Bouman, and Jacques le Brun, *Réforme et Contre-Réforme* (Paris, 1968), Vol. 3 of *Nouvelle Histoire de l'église;* Léopold Willaert, S.J., *Après le Concile de Trente.*

# Bibliography

*La Restauration catholique 1563–1648* (Tournai, 1960), Vol. 18 of *Histoire de l'Église;* and E. W. Zeeden, *Das Zeitalter der Gegenreformation* (Freiburg i.Br., 1967).

For the beginnings of the Catholic Reformation in **Germany**, see James Brodrick, *Saint Peter Canisius* (London, 1935); J. Greven, *Die Kölner Kartause und die Anfänge der Gegenreformation in Deutschland* (Müster, 1935); W. Lipgens, *Kardinal Johannes Gropper (1503–59) und die Anfänge der katholischen Reform in Deutschland* (Münster, 1951); Joseph Lortz, *Die Reformation in Deutschland*, 3rd ed., Vol. 2 (Freiburg i.Br., 1949); Maria E. Nolte, *Georgius Cassander* (Nijmegen, 1951); Ernst Reiter, *Martin von Schaumberg, Fürstbischof von Eichstätt (1560–1590), und die Trienter Reform* (Münster, 1965); F. Siebert, *Zwischen Kaiser und Papst: Kardinal Truchsess von Waldburg und die Anfänge der Gegenreformation in Deutschland* (Berlin, 1943); and Winfried Trusen, *Um die Reform und Einheit der Kirche: Zum Leben und Werk Georg Witzels* (Münster, 1957). See also Oskar Garstein, *Rome and the Counter-Reformation in Scandinavia* (Oslo, 1963).

For **France**, see P. Broutin, *Le Réforme pastorale en France au XVIIᵉ siècle*, 2 vols. (Paris, 1956); Jean Dagens, *Bérulle et les origins de la restauration catholique, 1571–1611* (Bruges, 1952); and Ruth Kleinman, *Saint François de Sales and the Protestants* (Geneva, 1962).

For **Spain**, see A. Martín Melquícedes, *Historia de la teología en España (1470–1570)*, Vol. 1 (Rome, 1962); H. Kamen, *The Spanish Inquisition* (London, 1965); P. Sainz Rodriques, *Introducción a la historia de la literatura mistica en España* (Madrid, 1927); E. A. Peers, *Studies of the Spanish Mystics*, 4 vols. (New York, 1927–1935); Eugene Marcotte, *La Nature de la théologies d'après Melchior Cano* (Ottawa, 1949); *The Complete Works of Saint Teresa of Jesus*, trans. and ed. by E. A. Peers, 3 vols. (London, 1946); *The Letters of Saint Teresa of Jesus*, trans. and ed. by E. A. Peers (Westminster, Md., 1950); *The Life of St. Teresa of Jesus . . . Written by Herself*, ed. by David Lewis, 5th ed. (London, 1932); Marcelle Auclair, *Saint Teresa of Avila*, trans. by Kathleen Pond (London, 1953); E. W. T. Dicken, *The Crucible of Love* (London, 1963); Elizabeth Hamilton, *Saint Teresa* (New York, 1959); M. Lepee, *Sainte Thérèse d'Avila, le réalisme chrétien* (Paris, 1947); *The Complete Works of St. John of the Cross*, trans. and ed. by E. A. Peers, 3 vols. (Westminster, Md., 1949); J. Baruzi, *Saint Jean de la Croix et le problème de l'expérience mystique*, 2nd ed. (Paris, 1931); and E. A. Peers, *St. John of the Cross* (London, 1946).

For **Italy**, see the *Corpus reformatorum italicorum*, directed by L. Firpo and G. Spini with the collaboration of A. Rotondo and J. A. Tedeschi, Vol. 1: *The Opera of Camillo Renato (c.1500–1575)* (Florence and Chicago, 1968). This series will replace the *Opuscoli e lettere di* *riformatori italiani del Cinquecento,* ed. by G. Paladino, 2 vols. (Bari, 1913, 1927). For secondary accounts see M. Andrews, *Men and Women of the Italian Reformation* (New York, 1914); William J. Bouwsma, *Venice and the Defense of Republican Liberty: Renaissance Values in the Age of the Counter Reformation* (Berkeley and Los Angeles, Calif., 1968); G. K. Brown, *Italy and the Reformation to 1550* (London, 1933); Domenico Caccamo, *Eretici italiani in Moravia, Polonia, Transilvania (1558–1611)* (Florence and Chicago, 1970); F. C. Church, *Italian Reformers* (New York, 1932); Jean Delumeau, *Vie économique et sociale de Rome dans la seconde moitié du XVI<sup>e</sup> siècle,* 2 vols. (Rome, 1957–1959); Richard M. Douglas, *Jacopo Sadoleto (1477–1547): Humanist and Reformer* (Cambridge, Mass., 1959); Hubert Jedin, *Contarini and Camaldoli* (Rome, 1953); Philip McNair, *Peter Martyr in Italy, an Anatomy of Apostasy* (Oxford, 1967); Pietro Misciatelli, *The Mystics in Italy* (New York, 1949); Gerhard Müller, *Die römische Kurie und die Reformation 1523–1534. Kirche und Politik während des Pontifikates Clemens VII* (Gütersloh, 1969); John W. O'Malley, S.J., *Giles of Viterbo on Church and Reform* (Leiden, 1968); C. Orsenigo, *Vita di Carlo Borromeo,* 3rd ed., 2 vols. (Milan, 1929); L. Ponelle and L. Bordet, *St. Philip Neri and the Roman Society of His Times,* trans. by Ralph Francis Kerr (London, 1932); Marcel Jouhandeau, *St. Philip Neri,* trans. by George Lamb (New York, 1960); Paolo Prodi, *Il Cardinale Gabriele Paleotti (1522–1597)* (Rome, 1967); Adriano Prosperi, *Tra evangelismo e controriforma: G. M. Giberti, 1495–1543* (Rome, 1969); Giovanna R. Solari and Frederic Tuten, *The House of Farnese* (New York, 1968); *Italian Reformation Studies in Honor of Laelius Socinus,* ed. by John A. Tedeschi (Florence, 1965); Orestes Ferrara, *Gasparo Contarini et ses missions* (Paris, 1956); Hubert Jedin, *Kardinal Contarini als Kontroverstheologe* (Münster, 1949); and Hanns Rückert, *Die theologische Entwicklung Gasparo Contarinis* (Bonn, 1926).

Accounts of the **religious orders** of the Catholic Church are G. G. Coulton, *Five Centuries of Religion,* 3 vols. (Cambridge, 1923–1927); M. Heimbucher, *Die Orden und Kongregationen der katholischen Kirche,* 3rd ed., 2 vols. (Paderborn, 1933–1934); O. L. Kapsner, *Catholic Religious Orders* (Collegeville, Minn., 1948); Pio Paschini, *La beneficenza in Italia e le Compagnie del Divino Amore nei primi decenni del Cinquecento* (Rome, 1925); P. A. Kunkel, *The Theatines in the History of the Catholic Reform Before the Establishment of Lutheranism* (Washington, D.C., 1941); Fr. Cuthbert Hess, *The Capuchins* (New York, 1929); Fr. Anscar Zawart, *The Capuchins* (Washington, D.C., 1928); and Sr. M. Monica, *Angele Merici and Her Teaching Idea* (London, 1927), which discusses the founder of the Ursulines.

The standard Protestant account of the **Society of Jesus** is Heinrich

# Bibliography

Boehmer, *The Jesuits,* trans. from 4th ed. by P. Strodach (Philadelphia, Pa., 1928). Other excellent accounts are James Brodrick, *The Origins of the Jesuits* (London and New York, 1940), *The Progress of the Jesuits* (London and New York, 1947), and *The Economic Morals of the Jesuits* (London, 1934); T. J. Campbell, *The Jesuits,* 2 vols. (New York, 1921), with a good bibliography; A. P. Farrell, *The Jesuit Code of Liberal Education* (Milwaukee, Wis., 1938); R. Garcia-Villoslada, *Manual de historia de la Compañía de Jesús,* 2nd ed. (Madrid, 1954); Joseph de Guibert, S.J., *The Jesuits: Their Spiritual Doctrine and Practice,* trans. by W. J. Young, S.J. (Chicago, 1964); M. P. Harney, *The Jesuits in History* (New York, 1941); F. de Dainville, *La Naissance de l'humanisme moderne* (Paris, 1940); J. Schröteler, *Die Erziehung in den Jesuiteninternaten des 16. Jahrhunderts* (Freiburg i. Br., 1940); and *Jesuit Thinkers of the Renaissance,* ed. by G. Smith (Milwaukee, Wis., 1939).

Following are some English translations of the **writings of Ignatius Loyola:** *The Autobiography of St. Ignatius,* ed. by J. F. X. O'Conor (New York and Cincinnati, 1900); *Letters and Instructions of St. Ignatius Loyola,* trans. by D. F. O'Leary, ed. by A. Goodier (St. Louis, Mo., 1914); E. A. Fitzpatrick, *S. Ignatius and the Ratio Studiorum* (New York and London, 1933); and *The Spiritual Exercises of St. Ignatius,* trans. by J. Rickaby, 2nd ed. (London, 1923). Excellent recent **biographies** are James Brodrick, *St. Ignatius Loyola: The Pilgrim Years* (New York, 1956); Heinrich Boehmer, *Ignatius von Loyola,* new ed. (Stuttgart, 1950); Fr. P. Dudon, *St. Ignatius of Loyola,* trans. by W. J. Young, S.J. (Milwaukee, Wis., 1950); P. Leturia, *El gentilhombre Iñigo Lopez de Loyola en su siglo,* 2nd ed. (Barcelona, 1949); Hugo Rahner, *Ignatius von Loyola* (Freiburg i. Br., 1956); and H. D. Sedgwick, *St. Ignatius Loyola* (New York, 1923).

The following are biographies of **other important Jesuits** of the Reformation Era: James Brodrick, *Saint Peter Canisius* (London, 1935), *Saint Francis Xavier* (London, 1952), and *The Life and Work of Blessed Robert Francis Cardinal Bellarmine,* 2 vols. (London, 1928); Georg Schurhammer, *Franz Xaver: Sein Leben und seine Zeit,* Vol. 1 (Freiburg i. Br., 1963); and E. A. Ryan, *The Historical Scholarship of Saint Bellarmine* (Louvain, 1936).

For the **activities of the Jesuits** in various countries, see M. P. Harney, *The Jesuits in History* (London, 1902); Antonio Astrain, *Historia de la Compañía de Jesús en la Asistencia de España (1540–1758)* (Madrid, 1902–1925); Francisco Rodrigues, *Historia da Companhia de Jesu na Assistência de Portugal,* 2 vols. in 7 (Oporto, 1931–1950); Pietro Tacchi Venturi, *Storia della Compagnia di Gesù in Italia,* 2nd ed., Vols. 1 and 2 (Rome, 1922–1950), Vol. 3 by Mario Scaduto (Rome, 1964); Henri Fouqueray, *Histoire de la Compagnie de Jésus en France (1528–1762),*

5 vols. (Paris, 1910–1925); Bernhard Duhr, *Geschichte der Jesuiten in den Ländern deutscher Zunge,* 4 vols. (Freiburg i. Br., 1907–1928); A. Poncelet, *Histoire de la Compagnie de Jésus dans les anciens Pays-Bas,* 2 vols. (Brussels, 1927–1928); S. Zaleski, *Jesuite w Polsce,* 5 vols. (Lemberg, 1907–1911); and L. Velics, *Geschichte der Jesuiten in Ungarn,* 2 vols. (Budapest, 1912–1914).

The most helpful history of **the popes** is the monumental work begun by Ludwig von Pastor, one of the first German scholars given access to the Vatican archives. The English translation, *The History of the Popes from the Close of the Middle Ages* (St. Louis, Mo., 1891–    ), will eventually comprise 40 vols. Helpful for differing points of view are Leopold von Ranke, *History of the Popes,* 3 vols., trans. by E. Foster (London, 1873); J. A. Corbett, *The Papacy: A Brief History* (Princeton, N.J., 1956); M. Creighton, *A History of the Papacy,* new ed., 3 vols. (London and New York, 1897–1903); Paul Herre, *Papsttum und Papstwahl im Zeitalter Philipps II.* (Leipzig, 1907); C. Hirschauer, *Pius V.* (Freiburg i. Br., 1920); and Konrad Repgen, *Papst, Kaiser und Reich, 1521–1644* (Tübingen, 1961).

The historiography for the **Council of Trent** is discussed by Hubert Jedin, *Das Konzil von Trient. Ein Überblick über die Erforschung seiner Geschichte* (Rome, 1948). The first complete history of the council was written by Paolo Sarpi in 1609, trans. into English by Nathanael Brent under the title, *History of the Council of Trent* (London, 1676), a hostile account that was answered by the Jesuit Sforza Pallavicino in his *Istoria del Concilio di Trento,* 2 vols. (Rome, 1656–1657). A modern history is that by C. J. Hefele and H. Leclercq, *Histoire des concils,* Vols. 8–10 (Paris, 1917–1938). See also the outstanding account by Hubert Jedin, *History of the Council of Trent,* trans. by Ernest Graf, 2 vols. (London, 1957–1961), his *Papal Legate at the Council of Trent, Cardinal Seripando* (St. Louis, Mo., 1947), and *Tommaso Campeggio. Tridentinische Reform und Kuriale Tradition* (Münster, 1958). Italian influence is discussed by G. Alberigo, *I vescovi italiani al Concilio di Trento (1545–47)* (Florence, 1959). The role of the Dominicans is covered by Angelus Maria Walz, *I Domenicani al Concilio di Trento* (Rome, 1961). On the reforms concerning the education of priests, see James A. O'Donohoe, *Tridentine Seminary Legislation: Its Sources and Its Formation* (Louvain, 1957). A leading figure is discussed by H. O. Evenett, *The Cardinal of Lorraine and the Council of Trent* (Cambridge, 1930). For the canons and decrees of the council, see H. J. Schroeder, *Canons and Decrees of the Council of Trent* (London, 1941). George H. Tavard, *Holy Writ or Holy Church: The Crisis of the Protestant Reformation* (New York, 1959), discusses one of the main issues of the council.

Among works dealing with the **Catholic liturgy** are J. Baudot, *The*

# Bibliography

*Roman Breviary* (London, 1909); A. Fortescue, *The Roman Missal* (New York, 1951); R. Guardini, *The Spirit of the Liturgy,* trans. by A. Lane (London, 1930); J. A. Jungmann, *The Mass of the Roman Rite,* Vol. 1, trans. by F. A. Brunner (New York, 1951); E. C. Messinger, *The Reformation, the Mass and the Priesthood,* 2 vols. (New York, 1936–1937); Cardinal Schuster, *The Sacramentary,* trans. by A. Levelis-Marke, 5 vols. (London, 1924–1930); and R. R. Terry, *The Music of the Roman Rite* (London, 1931). On the Bible in Catholicism, see V. Baroni, *La Bible dans la vie catholique après la Réforme* (Lausanne, 1955).

On the **Index of Prohibited Books,** see F. S. Betten, *The Roman Index of Forbidden Books* (Chicago, 1935), a brief discussion; R. Burke, *What Is the Index?* (Milwaukee, Wis., 1952), which gives the position of the Catholic Church on reading; G. H. Putnam, *Censorship of the Church of Rome,* 2 vols. (New York and London, 1906–1907); *Die Indices Librorum Prohibitorum des 16. Jahrhunderts,* ed. by Fr. H. Reusch, reprint of 1886 ed. (Nieuwkoop, 1961).

**The Inquisition** is discussed in G. G. Coulton, *Inquisition and Liberty* (New York, 1938), and W. T. Walsh, *Characters of the Inquisition* (New York, 1940). On the Spanish Inquisition, see H. C. Lea, *History of the Inquisition in Spain,* 4 vols. (New York, 1922); Jean Plaidy, *The Spanish Inquisition, Its Rise, Growth, and End* (New York, 1967); C. Roth, *The Spanish Inquisition* (New York, 1938); and A. S. Turberville, *The Spanish Inquisition* (New York, 1932).

## Chapter 9: Militant Catholicism and Calvinism

For **general accounts** of the latter half of the sixteenth century, see *The Counter-Reformation and Price Revolution, 1559–1610,* ed. by R. B. Wernham (Cambridge, 1968), vol. 3 of *The New Cambridge Modern History,* and J. H. Elliott, *Europe Divided, 1559–1598* (New York, 1968). Social and economic conflicts are discussed in *Crisis in Europe, 1560–1660,* ed. by Trevor Aston (London, 1965).

The role of **Philip I** of Spain is covered in Fernand Braudel, *La Méditerranée et le monde méditerranéen à l'époque de Philippe II,* new ed., 2 vols. (Paris, 1967); C. J. Cadoux, *Philip of Spain and the Netherlands* (London, 1947); R. Trevor Davies, *The Golden Century of Spain, 1501–1621* (London, 1937); J. H. Elliott, *Imperial Spain, 1469–1716* (New York, 1964); M. A. S. Hulme, *Philip II* (London, 1911); Arthur Erwin Imhof, *Der Friede von Vervins 1598* (Aarau, 1966); Juan A. Llorente, *A Critical History of the Inquisition of Spain* (Williamstown, Mass., 1967); John Lynch, *Spain Under the Habsburgs,* Vol. 1: *1516–1598* (Oxford, 1964); E. Maass, *The Dream of Philip II,* trans. by E. Garside and N. Guterman (Indianapolis, Ind., and New York, 1944);

Gregorio Marañon, *Antonio Pérez: El hombre, el drama, la época,* 2 vols. (Madrid, 1948); J. H. Mariéjol, *Philip II,* trans. by W. B. Wells (New York, 1933); Sir Charles Petrie, *Philip II of Spain* (New York, 1963); L. Pfandl, *Philip II: Gemälde eines Lebens und einer Zeit,* 3rd ed. (Munich, 1951); W. H. Prescott, *History of the Reign of Philip II,* 3 vols. (Philadelphia, Pa., 1874); and *The Character of Philip II: The Problem of Moral Judgments in History,* ed. by John C. Rule and John J. TePaske, "Problems in European Civilization" (Boston, 1963).

The Revolt of the **Low Countries** is discussed by J. L. Motley, *The Rise of the Dutch Republic,* 3 vols. (New York, 1874), a classic, though long out of date; P. J. Blok, *A History of the People of the Netherlands,* 5 vols. (New York and London, 1898–1912), Vol. 3, trans. by R. Putnam, a standard work; Pieter Geyl, *The Revolt of the Netherlands, 1555–1609* (London, 1937), a brilliant interpretation that maintains that religion was not the main reason for the revolt, and *The Netherlands in the Seventeenth Century,* 2 vols. (London, 1961–1964); and Henri Pirenne, *Histoire de Belgique,* Vols. 3 and 4 (Brussels, 1950–1952).

For **religious developments** in the Low Countries, see J. Etienne, *Spiritualisme érasmien et théologiens louvanistes* (Louvain, 1956); H. A. Enno van Gelder, *Vrijheid en Onvrijheid in de Republik. Geschiedenis der Vrijheid van Drukpers en Godsdienst von 1572 tot 1798,* Vol. 1: *1572–1619* (Haarlem, 1947); Leon-E. Halkin, *La Réforme en Belgique sous Charles-Quint* (Brussels, 1957); W. J. Kühler, *Geschiedenis der Nederlandische Doopsgezinden in de Zestiende Eeuw* (Haarlem, 1932); J. Lindeboom, *De confessioneele Ontwikkeling der Reformatie in de Nederlanden* (The Hague, 1947); R. R. Post, *Kerkelijke Verhoudingen in Nederland voor de Reformatie van ca. 1500 tot ca. 1580* (Utrecht, 1954); and J. Reitsma, *Geschiedenis van de Hervorming en de Hervormde Kerk der Nederlanden,* 4th ed. (The Hague, 1949). The influence of Arminianism on English thought is discussed by Rosalie L. Colie, *Light and Enlightenment: A Study of the Cambridge Platonists and the Dutch Arminians* (New York, 1957).

The best recent biography of **William of Orange** is that by Cecily V. Wedgwood, *William the Silent* (New Haven, Conn., 1944), although it is highly laudatory. See also R. Putnam, *William the Silent* (New York and London, 1911); *Wilhelmus van Nassouwe,* ed. by Pieter Geyl (Middelburg, 1933); Nesca A. Robb, *William of Orange: A Personal Portrait,* Vol. 1: *1650–1673* (London, 1962); and A. A. van Schelven, *Willem van Oranje,* 4th ed. (Amsterdam, 1948).

On **other leaders** in the Low Countries, see Frans van Kalken and Tobie Jonckheere, *Marnix de Sainte Aldegonde (1540–1598)* (Brussels, 1952), and for Maurice of Nassau, A. Hallema, *Prins Maurits* (Assen, 1949); C. J. Cadoux, *Philip of Spain and the Netherlands* (London,

# Bibliography

1947); M. van Durme, *Anton Perrenot, Bisschop van Utrecht, Kardinal van Granvelle, Minister van Karel V en van Filips II (1517–86)* (Brussels, 1953); Léon van der Essen, *Alexandre Farnèse, gouverneur général des Pays-Bas,* 5 vols. (Brussels, 1933–1940); Walther Kirchner, *Alba. Spaniens eiserner Herzog* (Göttingen, 1963); and Jan den Tex, *Oldenbarnevelt,* Vol. 1: *Opgang 1547–1588,* and Vol. 2: *Oorlog 1588–1609* (Haarlem, 1960–1962).

Among sources for the **wars of religion in France** are *Relations des ambassadeurs vénitiens sur les affaires de France au XVI$^e$ siècle,* ed. by N. Tommaseo, 2 vols. (Paris, 1938); *Négociations, lettres et pièces diverses relatives au règne de Francis II,* ed. by A. L. Paris (Paris, 1841); *The Letters and Documents of . . . Baron de Biron (1524–1592),* ed. by J. W. Thompson, 2 vols. (Berkeley, Calif., 1936); *Lettres de Catherine de Médicis,* 10 vols. (Paris, 1880–1909); and *A Huguenot Family in the XVI Century. The Memoires of Phillipe de Mornay,* trans. by L. Crump (New York, 1926). See also *French Political Pamphlets 1547–1648,* compiled by Robert O. Lindsay and John New (Madison, Wis., Milwaukee, Wis., London, 1969–    ), and the *Checklist of French Political Pamphlets 1560–1644* in *The Newberry Library,* compiled by D. V. Welsh (Chicago, 1950). The Huguenot Society of London has published its *Proceedings* since 1885 and The Huguenot Society of America its *Proceedings* and *Publications* since 1884.

Helpful works on the French religious wars are E. Armstrong, *The French Wars of Religion,* 2nd ed. (Oxford, 1904); H. M. Baird, *History of the Rise of the Huguenots,* 2 vols. (New York, 1900), and *The Huguenots and Henry of Navarre,* 2 vols. (New York, 1909); Louis Batiffol, *The Century of the Renaissance,* trans. by E. F. Buckley (New York, 1916); W. F. Church, *Constitutional Thought in Sixteenth Century France* (Cambridge, Mass., 1941); G. H. Dodge, *The Political Theory of the Huguenots of the Dispersion* (New York, 1947); R. Doucet, *Les Institutions de la France au 16$^e$ siècle,* 2 vols. (Paris, 1948); A. J. Grant, *The French Monarchy, 1483–1789* (Cambridge, 1905), and *The Huguenots* (London, 1934); De Lamar Jensen, *Diplomacy and Dogmatism: Bernardino de Mondoza and the French Catholic League* (Cambridge, Mass., 1964); Robert M. Kingdon, *Geneva and the Coming Wars of Religion in France* (Geneva, 1956), and *Geneva and the Consolidation of the French Protestant Movement, 1564–1572* (Madison, Wis., 1967); J. Russell Major, *Representative Institutions in Renaissance France, 1421–1559* (Madison, Wis., 1960); Sir John Neale, *The Age of Catherine de Medici* (New York, 1943); Richard Nürnberger, *Die Politisierung des französischen Protestantismus* (Tübingen, 1948); Franklin C. Palm, *Politics and Religion in Sixteenth Century France* (Boston, 1927); Lucien Romier, *Les Origines politiques des guerres de religion,* 2 vols.

(Paris, 1913–1914); *The French Wars of Religion,* ed. by J. H. M. Salmon, "Problems in European Civilization" (Boston, 1967); N. M. Sutherland, *Catherine de Medici and the Ancien Regime* (London, 1966); J. W. Thompson, *The Wars of Religion in France* (Chicago, 1909); A. Tilley, *The French Wars of Religion* (New York, 1919); Gaston Zeller, *Les Institutions de la France au 16ᵉ siècle* (Paris, 1948); and O. Zoff, *The Huguenots,* trans. by E. B. Ashton and J. Mayo (New York, 1942).

The **religious aspects** of sixteenth-century France are emphasized in H. Bremond, *A Literary History of Religious Thought in France,* trans. by K. L. Montgomery, 3 vols. (New York, 1929–1930); C. G. Kelley, *French Protestantism, 1559–62* (Baltimore, Md., 1918); and Raoul Stéphan, *Histoire du protestantisme française* (Paris, 1961). Miscellaneous subjects are discussed in Sylvia L. England, *The Massacre of Saint Bartholomew* (London, 1938); J. Russell Major, *The Estates General of 1560* (Princeton, N.J., 1951); J. H. Mitchell, *The Court of the Connétablie* (New Haven, Conn., 1947); and J. Faurey, *L'Édit de Nantes et la question de la tolérance* (Paris, 1929).

The following studies of **Henry IV** deserve attention: B. Dufournier, *Le Conseil de commerce d'Henri IV* (Louvain and Paris, 1934); Q. Hurst, *Henry of Navarre* (New York and London, 1938); C. Jackson, *Last of the Valois, and Accession of Henry of Navarre,* 2 vols. (London, 1898); J. E. M. Lajeunie, *Correspondance entre Henri IV et Béthune* (Geneva, 1953); M. Reinhard, *Henri IV* (Paris, 1943); H. D. Sedgwick, *Henry of Navarre* (Indianapolis, Ind., 1930); and Pierre de Vaissiere, *Henri IV* (Paris, 1925).

For biographies of **other leading personalities,** see David Buisseret, *Sully and the Growth of Centralized Government in France, 1598–1610* (London, 1968); E. C. Lodge, *Sully, Colbert et Turgot* (London, 1931); C. Rist, *L'Œuvre économique de Sully* (Paris, 1941); Jean Héretier, *Catherine de Médicis* (Paris, 1941); P. Van Dyke, *Catherine de Medici,* 2 vols. (New York, 1922); Erich Marcks, *Gaspard de Coligny: Sein Leben und das Frankreich seiner Zeit,* 2nd ed. (Leipzig, 1918); A. W. Whitehead, *Gaspard de Coligny* (London, 1904); William J. Bouwsma, *Concordia Mundi: The Career and Thought of Guillaume Postel (1510–1581)* (Cambridge, Mass., 1957); A. Buisson, *Michel de l'Hôpital* (Paris, 1950); F. de Crue, *Anne de Montmorency sous les rois Henri II, François II et Charles IX* (Paris, 1889), still indispensable; P. Erlanger, *Henri III* (Paris, 1948); Armand Garnier, *Agrippa d'Aubigné et le parti protestant,* 3 vols. (Paris, 1928); H. D. Sedgwick, *The House of Guise* (Indianapolis, Ind., and New York, 1938); Robert D. Linder, *The Political Ideas of Pierre Viret* (Geneva, 1964); and Nancy L. Roelker, *Queen of Navarre: Jeanne d'Albret, 1528–1572* (Cambridge, Mass., 1968).

Bibliography

## Chapter 10: Protestantism and Catholicism in England, Germany, and Eastern Europe

**Sources for the reigns of Mary and Elizabeth** not listed in the bibliography for Chapter 6 are the following: *Calendar of Letters and State Papers Relating to English Affairs of the Reign of Queen Elizabeth,* from the archives of Simancas, Vol. 1: *Elizabeth, 1558–67* (London, 1892); *Calendar of State Papers Relating to Scotland and Mary, Queen of the Scots, 1547–1603,* 11 vols. to date; *Calendar and State Papers Relating to Ireland, 1509–1603,* 12 vols. (London, 1860–1912); *Calendar of Manuscripts of the Marquess of Salisbury,* preserved at Hatfield House, 17 vols. (1888–    ); *Journals of the House of Commons,* Vol. 1: *1547–1628* (London, 1803); *Journals of the House of Lords,* Vols. 1 and 2 (no place, n.d.); *Queen Elizabeth: Correspondence with James VI,* "Camden Society Publications," Vol. 46 (1849); *The Trial of Mary, Queen of the Scots,* ed. by A. F. Steuart (Edinburgh, 1951); John Knox, *History of the Reformation in Scotland,* ed. by W. C. Dickinson, 2 vols. (Edinburgh, 1949).

For accounts dealing with the reign of **Mary Tudor,** see M. A. S. Hume, *Two English Queens and Philip* (New York, 1908); Hilda F. M. Prescott, *Mary Tudor* (London, 1952), a rev. ed. of her *Spanish Tudor,* an outstanding biography; J. M. Stone, *The History of Mary, Queen of England* (London, 1901); Beatrice White, *Mary Tudor* (London, 1936); and K. Woodward, *Queen Mary* (London, 1927). See also J. A. Muller, *Stephen Gardiner and the Tudor Reaction* (New York, 1926); C. M. Anthony, *Reginald Pole* (London, 1909); M. Haile, *Life of Reginald Pole* (Edinburgh, 1910); and W. Schenk, *Reginald Pole* (New York, 1950). E. Harris Harbison, *Rival Ambassadors at the Court of Queen Mary* (Princeton, N.J., 1940), gives an excellent account of international affairs during Mary's reign.

The **exiles** of Mary's reign are discussed by Christina H. Garrett, *The Marian Exiles* (Cambridge, 1938), who treats them as a political faction that returned to England as a political party and a nucleus for the growth of Puritanism. See also Frederick A. Norwood, *The Reformation Refugees as an Economic Force* (Chicago, 1942). Among the few biographies of the Protestant figures of Mary's reign is Charles Sturge, *Cuthbert Tunstall* (London, 1938).

Of the many studies of **Elizabeth I** and her reign, the following should be mentioned: J. B. Black, *The Reign of Elizabeth,* 2nd ed. (Oxford, 1959); F. Chamberlin, *Elizabeth and Leycester* (New York, 1939); J. Clapham, *Elizabeth of England* (Philadelphia, Pa., 1951); Joel Hurstfield, *Elizabeth I and the Unity of England* (London, 1960); Elizabeth Jenkins, *Elizabeth the Great, a Biography* (New York, 1959); Wallace

562

MacCaffrey, *The Shaping of the Elizabethan Regime* (Princeton, N.J., 1968); T. Maynard, *Queen Elizabeth* (Milwaukee, Wis., 1940); M. A. S. Hume, *The Courtships of Queen Elizabeth,* 4th ed. (New York, 1904); D. Muir, *Queen Elizabeth* (London, 1939); Sir John E. Neale, *Queen Elizabeth* (New York, 1934), *Elizabeth I and Her Parliaments,* 2 vols. (London, 1953–1957), and "The Elizabethan Acts of Supremacy and Uniformity," *English Historical Review,* **65** (1952); Conyers Read, *Mr. Secretary Walsingham and the Policy of Queen Elizabeth,* 3 vols. (Oxford, 1925), *Mr. Secretary Cecil and Queen Elizabeth* (New York, 1955), and *Lord Burghley and Queen Elizabeth* (New York, 1960); M. Waldman, *Queen Elizabeth* (London and New York, 1952), and *Elizabeth and Leicester* (Boston, 1945); and E. C. Wilson, *England's Elizabeth* (Cambridge, Mass., 1939), a compilation of laudatory contemporary pieces.

**Political and social conditions** in Elizabethan England are described in M. Byrne, *Elizabethan Life in Town and Country* (London, 1947); C. C. Camden, *The Elizabethan Woman* (New York, 1952); M. Campbell, *The English Yeoman under Elizabeth and the Early Stuarts* (New Haven, Conn., 1942); A. Cecil, *The Life of Robert Cecil* (London, 1915); L. Lemonnier, *La Vie quotidienne en Angleterre sous Elisabeth* (Paris, 1950); *Englishmen at Rest and Play, 1558–1714,* ed. by R. V. Lennard (Oxford, 1931); Garrett Mattingly, *The Defeat of the Spanish Armada* (London, 1959); Christopher Morris, *Political Thought in England: Tyndale to Hooker* (London, 1953); George L. Mosse, *The Holy Pretense: A Study in Christianity and Reason of State from William Perkins to John Winthrop* (Oxford, 1957), and *The Struggle for Sovereignty in England: From the Reign of Queen Elizabeth to the Petition of Right* (East Lansing, 1950); Sir John E. Neale, *The Elizabethan House of Commons* (London, 1949), *Elizabeth I and Her Parliaments,* 2 vols. (London, 1953–1957), and *Elizabethan Government and Society, Essays Presented to Sir John Neale,* ed. by S. T. Bindoff (London, 1961); Wallace Notestein, *English Folk* (New York, 1938); Michael B. Pulman, *The Elizabethan Privy Council in the Fifteen-seventies* (Berkeley and Los Angeles, Calif., 1971); Alfred L. Rowse, *The Elizabethan Age,* 2 vols. (New York, 1951–1955), *Sir Richard Grenville of the Revenge, An Elizabethan Hero* (New York and Boston, 1937), *Sir Walter Raleigh, His Family and Private Life* (New York, 1962), and *Ralegh and the Throckmortons* (London, 1962); John Shirley, *Elizabeth's First Archbishop* (London, 1948), and *Richard Hooker and Contemporary Political Ideas* (London, 1949); Lawrence Stone, *The Crisis of the Aristocracy, 1558–1641* (Oxford, 1967); H. R. Trevor-Roper, *The Gentry, 1540–1640* (Cambridge, 1953); and R. B. Wernham, *Before the Armada: The Growth of English Foreign Policy, 1485–1588* (London, 1966).

# Bibliography

Economic conditions are discussed by E. Lipson, *The Economic History of England*, 5th ed., Vols. 2 and 3 (London, 1948); J. U. Nef, *Industry and Government in France and England 1540–1640* (Philadelphia, Pa., 1940); A. A. Ruddock, *Italian Merchants and Shipping in Southampton, 1270–1600* (Southampton, 1951); and T. S. Willan, *The Early History of the Russia Company, 1553–1603* (Manchester, 1956). The classical source for English voyages of discovery is Richard Hakluyt, *The Principal Navigations, Voyages, Traffiques and Discoveries of the English Nation,* originally published in 3 vols. (1598–1600), in a recent reprint in 10 vols. (London, Toronto, and New York, 1927–1928). See also D. B. Quinn, *Raleigh and the British Empire* (London, 1947); E. G. R. Taylor, *Tudor Geography, 1485–1583* (London, 1930); J. A. Williamson, *The Age of Drake* (London, 1946); and Louis B. Wright, *Religion and Empire: The Alliance between Piety and Commerce in English Expansion, 1558–1625* (Chapel Hill, N.C., 1943).

Various religious topics concerned with the reign of Elizabeth I are discussed in H. N. Birt, *The Elizabethan Religious Settlement* (London, 1907); J. W. Blench, *Preaching in England in the Late Fifteenth and Sixteenth Centuries* (New York, 1964); V. J. K. Brook, *Whitgift and the English Church* (London, 1957), and *A Life of Archbishop Parker* (Oxford, 1962); S. C. Carter, *The English Church and the Reformation* (London, 1926); J. Clayton, *The Historical Basis of Anglicanism* (London, 1925); J. B. Collins, *Christian Mysticism in the Elizabethan Age* (Baltimore, Md., 1940); Charles Cremeans, *The Reception of Calvinistic Thought in England* (Urbana, Ill., 1949); Claire Cross, *The Royal Supremacy in the Elizabethan Church* (London, 1969); E. T. Davies, *Episcopacy and Royal Supremacy in the Church of England in the XVIth Century* (Oxford, 1950); Powel M. Dawley, *John Whitgift and the English Reformation* (New York, 1954); W. H. Frere, *The English Church in the Reigns of Elizabeth and James I* (London, 1904); H. Gee, *The Elizabethan Prayer Book and Ornaments* (London, 1902); A. F. Herr, *The Elizabethan Sermon* (Philadelphia, Pa., 1940); Arthur J. Klein, *Intolerance in the Reign of Elizabeth* (Boston, 1917); Helmut Kressner, *Schweizer Ursprünge des anglikanischen Staatskirchentums,* "Schriften des Vereins für Reformationsgeschichte," No. 170 (Gütersloh, 1953); David Little, *Religion, Order, and Law: A Study in Pre-Revolutionary England* (New York, 1969); Albert J. Loomie, S.J., *The Spanish Elizabethans: The English Exiles at the Court of Philip II* (New York, 1963); D. J. McGinn, *The Admonition Controversy* (New Brunswick, N.J., 1949); Carl S. Meyer, *Elizabeth I and the Religious Settlement of 1559* (St. Louis, Mo., 1960); David Novarr, *The Making of Walton's Lives* (Ithaca, N.Y., 1958), covering the lives of John Donne, Sir Henry Wot-

564

ton, Richard Hooker, George Herbert, and Bishop Sanderson; Marvin R. O'Connell, *Thomas Stapleton and the Counter Reformation* (New Haven, Conn., and London, 1964); Arthur Pollard, *Richard Hooker* (London, 1966); F. J. Smithen, *Continental Protestantism and the English Reformation* (London, 1927); W. M. Southgate, *John Jewel and the Problem of Doctrinal Authority* (Cambridge, Mass., 1962); William Trimble, *The Catholic Laity in Elizabethan England, 1558–1603* (Cambridge, Mass., 1964); R. G. Usher, *The Reconstruction of the English Church,* 2 vols. (New York and London, 1910); and Louis B. Wright, *Religion and Empire* (Chapel Hill, N.C., 1943).

The following studies of **the Puritans** are helpful: Ian Breward, *The Work of William Perkins* (Abingdon, Berkshire, 1970), containing arguments against Marxist interpretations; J. Brown, *English Puritans* (Cambridge, 1910); C. Burrage, *Early English Dissenters,* 2 vols. (Cambridge, 1912); Patrick Collinson, *The Elizabethan Puritan Movement* (London, 1967), an important recent survey; John S. Coolidge, *The Pauline Renaissance in England* (Oxford, 1970); H. Davies, *The Worship of the English Puritans* (London, 1948); Michael Fixler, *Milton and the Kingdoms of God* (Evanston, Ill., 1964); William Haller, *The Rise of Puritanism* (New York, 1939), and *Foxe's Book of Martyrs and the Elect Nation* (London, 1963); Christopher Hill, *Society and Puritanism in Pre-Revolutionary England* (London, 1964), a Marxist interpretation; W. K. Jordan, *Men of Substance* (Chicago, 1942); E. Kirby, *William Prynne, A Study in Puritanism* (Cambridge, Mass., 1931); M. M. Knappen, *Tudor Puritanism* (Chicago, 1939); Samuel J. Knox, *Walter Travers: Paragon of Elizabethan Puritanism* (London, 1962); Perry Miller, *The New England Mind* (New York, 1939), *The Puritans* (New York, 1938), and *Puritanism and Democracy* (New York, 1944); John F. H. New, *Anglican and Puritan: The Basis of Their Opposition 1558–1640* (Stanford, Calif., 1964); G. F. Nuttal, *The Holy Spirit in Puritan Faith and Experience* (Oxford, 1946); A. F. S. Pearson, *Thomas Cartwright and Elizabethan Puritanism* (Cambridge, 1925), and *Church and State: Political Aspects of Sixteenth Century Puritanism* (Cambridge, 1928); P. A. Scholes, *The Puritans and Music* (London, 1934); Paul S. Seaver, *The Puritan Lectureships: The Politics of Religious Dissent, 1560–1662* (Stanford, Calif., 1970); Alan Simpson, *Puritanism in Old and New England* (Chicago, 1956); Michael Walzer, *The Revolution of the Saints: A Study of the Origins of Radical Politics* (Cambridge, Mass., 1965); and A. S. P. Woodhouse, *Puritanism and Liberty, Being the Army Debates (1647–49),* 2nd ed. (Chicago, 1951).

Some **cultural topics** are discussed by F. S. Boas, *Queen Elizabeth in Drama and Related Studies* (London, 1950); Paul H. Koster, *Christopher*

*Marlowe* (Chapel Hill, N.C., 1946); C. S. Lewis, *English Literature in the Sixteenth Century* (Oxford, 1954); M. M. Reese, *Shakespeare: His World and His Work* (London, 1953); Alfred L. Rowse, *William Shakespeare, a Biography* (London, 1963); Lawrence A. Sasek, *The Literary Temper of the English Puritans* (Baton Rouge, La., 1961); and E. Walker, *A History of Music in England,* ed. by J. A. Westrup, 3rd ed. (Oxford, 1952).

For materials concerning religious developments in the **Holy Roman Empire** between the Peace of Augsburg and the Thirty Years' War, see *Die Bekenntnisschriften der evangelisch-lutherischen Kirche,* 5th ed. (Göttingen, 1963); *The Book of Concord,* trans. and ed. by H. E. Jacobs, 2 vols. (Philadelphia, Pa., 1882–1883); *Concordia Triglotta,* trans. and ed. by F. Bente and W. H. T. Dau (St. Louis, Mo., 1921); W. D. Allbeck, *Studies in the Lutheran Confessions* (Philadelphia, Pa., 1952); Eduard Schlink, *Theologie der lutherischen Bekenntnisschriften* (Berlin, 1954); Heinrich Schmid, *The Doctrinal Theology of the Evangelical Lutheran Church,* trans. by C. A. Hay and H. E. Jacobs (Minneapolis, Minn., 1961), with excerpts from the symbolical books and a number of sixteenth- and seventeenth-century writings of Lutheran dogmaticians; Wilhelm Preger, *Matthias Flacius Illyricus und seine Zeit,* 2 vols., reprint of 1859–1861 ed. (Hildesheim and Nieuwkoop, 1964); Robert D. Preus, *The Theology of Post-Reformation Lutheranism* (St. Louis, Mo., 1970), and *The Inspiration of Scripture: A Study of the Theology of the Seventeenth Century Lutheran Dogmaticians* (Mankato, Minn., 1955); Martin Chemnitz, *The Two Natures of Christ,* trans. by Jacob A. O. Preus (St. Louis, Mo., 1971); Carl Heinz Ratschow, *Lutherische Dogmatik zwischen Reformation und Aufklärung,* 2 vols. (Gütersloh, 1964–1966); Robert P. Scharlemann, *Thomas Aquinas and John Gerhard* (New Haven, Conn., 1964); Heinz Scheible, *Die Entstehung der Magdeburger Zenturien,* "Schriften des Vereins für Reformationsgeschichte," 183 (Gütersloh, 1966); Hermann Schüssler, *Georg Calixt: Theologie und Kirchenpolitik* (Wiesbaden, 1961), a discussion of Calixt's ecumenical theology; Hans Emil Weber, *Reformation, Orthodoxie und Rationalismus,* 2 vols. (Gütersloh, 1937–1951); *Der Protestantismus des 17. Jahrhunderts,* ed. by Winfried Zeller (Bremen, 1962); *Reformed Dogmatics,* ed. and trans. by John W. Beardslee III (New York, 1965); *Reformed Confessions of the 16th Century,* ed. by Arthur C. Cochrane (Philadelphia, Pa., 1966); J. Good, *The Reformed Reformation* (Philadelphia, Pa., 1916); H. Heppe, *Reformed Dogmatics* (London, 1950); Walter Hollweg, *Der Augsburger Reichstag von 1566 und seine Bedeutung für die Entstehung der Reformierten Kirche und ihres Bekenntnisses* (Neukirchen, 1964); *Die Bekenntnisschriften der reformierten Kirche,* ed. by E. F. K. Müller

(Leipzig, 1903); *Reformierte Bekenntnisschriften und Kirchenordnungen in deutscher Übersetzung,* ed. by Paul Jacobs (Neukirchen, 1949); R. Wesel-Roth, *Thomas Erastus: Ein Beitrag zur Geschichte der reformierten Kirche und zur Lehre von der Staatssouveränität* (Lahr, 1954); Grete Mecenseffy, *Geschichte des Protestantismus in Österreich* (Graz and Cologne, 1956); Paul Dedic, *Der Protestantismus in Steiermarck im Zeitalter der Reformation und Gegenreformation,* "Schriften des Vereins für Reformationsgeschichte," No. 149 (Leipzig, 1930); and V. Conzemius, *Jakob III von Eltz, Erzbischof von Trier: Ein Kurfürst im Zeitalter der Gegenreformation* (Wiesbaden, 1956). For the decline of the Hanseatic League during this period, see G. Frh. von Pölnitz, *Fugger und Hanse* (Tübingen, 1953), and Philippe Dollinger, *The German Hansa,* trans. and ed. by D. S. Ault and S. H. Steinberg (Stanford, Calif., 1970).

For bibliography on the revival of Catholicism see references in Chapter 8, and on Poland, references in Chapter 5.

# Chapter 11: The Secularization of the European States

For sources on the **Thirty Years' War,** see the reports of the papal nuncios listed for previous chapters and the following: *Briefe und Akten zur Geschichte des Dreissigjährigen Krieges in den Zeiten des vorwaltenden Einflusses der Wittelsbacher,* ed. by Moritz Ritter and Friedrich Stieve, 11 vols. (Munich, 1870–1905); *Die Politik Maximilians I. von Baiern und seiner Verbündeten,* 4 vols. (Munich, 1907–1948); *Memoires du Cardinal Richelieu,* ed. by Robert Lavolee, 10 vols. (Paris, 1907–1931).

Still valuable as **general accounts** are S. R. Gardiner, *The Thirty Years' War* (London, 1874, 1912), and Moritz Ritter, *Deutsche Geschichte im Zeitalter der Gegenreformation und des Dreissigjährigen Krieges,* 3 vols. (Stuttgart, 1889–1905). See also *The New Cambridge Modern History,* Vol. 4: *The Decline of Spain and the Thirty Years War, 1609–48/59,* ed. by J. P. Cooper (New York, 1970); I. Anderson, *Sveriges Historia* (Stockholm, 1943); E. A. Beller, *Propaganda in Germany During the Thirty Years' War* (Princeton, N.J., 1940); Robert R. Ergang, *The Myth of the All-destructive Fury of the Thirty Years' War* (Pocono Pines, Pa., 1956); G. Pages, *La Guerre de Trente Ans, 1618–1648* (Paris, 1949); *The Thirty Years' War,* ed. by Theodore K. Rabb, "Problems in European Civilization" (Boston, 1964); and Cecily V. Wedgwood, *The Thirty Years' War* (London, 1938). The Empire's part in the war is described by P. Frischauer, *The Imperial Crown* (London and Toronto, 1939), a fascinating, essentially biographical account, and H. F. Schwarz, *The*

# Bibliography

*Imperial Privy Council in the Seventeenth Century* (Cambridge and London, 1943), describing attempts of the Hapsburgs to unify the country. For Bohemia's part see S. Harrison Thomson, *Czechoslovakia in European History*, 2nd ed. (Princeton, N.J., 1953). France's role is discussed by Jacques Boulenger, *The Seventeenth Century in France* (London, 1920, and New York, 1963), and B. Baustaedt, *Richelieu und Deutschland* (Berlin, 1936). An excellent account of the history of Spain during the period is John H. Elliott, *Imperial Spain, 1469–1716* (New York, 1964). The Puritan attitude toward the war is discussed by Marvin A. Breslow, *A Mirror of England: English Puritan Views of Foreign Nations, 1618–1640* (Cambridge, Mass., 1970). The role of the Palatinate is discussed by Claus Peter Clasen, *The Palatinate in European History, 1559–1660* (Oxford, 1966).

Some **leading figures** of the Thirty Years' War are subjects of the following: H. Sturmberger, *Kaiser Ferdinand II. und das Problem des Absolutismus* (Vienna, 1957); Dieter Albrecht, *Richelieu, Gustav Adolf und das Reich* (Munich, 1959); Nils G. Ahnlund, *Gustav Adolf, the Great,* trans. by M. Roberts (Princeton, N.J., 1940); Charles R. L. Fletcher, *Gustavus Adolphus and the Struggle of Protestantism for Existence* (New York, 1928); G. F. McMunn, *Gustavus Adolphus* (London, 1930); Michael Roberts, *The Political Objectives of Gustavus Adolphus in Germany, 1630–1634* (London, 1957); *Briefe und Akten zur Geschichte Wallensteins (1630–1634),* ed. by Hermann Hallwich (Vienna, 1912); Max von Boehn, *Wallenstein* (Vienna and Leipzig, 1926); Walter Görlitz, *Wallenstein* (Frankfurt a. M., 1948); J. Pekař, *Wallenstein, 1630–1634,* 2 vols. (Berlin, 1937); F. Watson, *Wallenstein* (London, 1938); H. von Srbik, *Wallensteins Ende,* 2nd ed. (Vienna, 1952); *The Letters of Elizabeth, Queen of Bohemia,* ed. by L. M. Baker (London, 1953); M. A. E. Green, *Elizabeth, Electress Palatine and Queen of Bohemia,* rev. by S. C. Lomas (London, 1909); Dieter Albrecht, *Die Auswärtige Politik Maximilians von Bayern, 1618–1635* (Göttingen, 1962); Kurt Pfister, *Kurfürst Maximilian von Bayern und sein Jahrhundert* (Munich, 1948); A. Bailley, *The Cardinal Dictator: A Portrait of Richelieu* (London, 1936); C. Burckhardt, *Richelieu,* Vol. 1 (London, 1940); Cecily V. Wedgwood, *Richelieu and the French Monarchy* (London, 1949); and A. Hassall, *Mazarin* (London and New York, 1903).

Among sources for the **Peace of Westphalia** are the *Acta pacis Westphalicae,* ed. by Max Braubach and Konrad Repgen, 4 vols. to date (Münster, 1962–    ). Helpful accounts of the peace are Max Braubach, *Der Westfälische Frieden* (Münster, 1959); *Pax optima rerum: Beiträge zur Geschichte des Westfälischen Friedens 1648* (Münster, 1948); Fritz Dickmann, *Der Westfälische Frieden,* 2nd ed. (Münster, 1965); Jan Joseph Poelhekke, *De Vrede van Munster* (The Hague, 1948); and Konrad

Repgen, *Die römische Kurie und der Westfälische Friede,* Vol. 1, Part 1: *Papst, Kaiser und Reich, 1521–1644* (Tübingen, 1962).

Literature concerning the **Jesuits** is contained in the bibliography for Chapter 8. **Jansenism** is covered by *Les Lettres provinciales de Blaise Pascal,* ed. H. F. Stewart (Manchester, 1920); Jean Orcibal, *Les Origines du Jansénisme,* 5 vols. projected, Vol. 1: *Correspondance de Jansénius* (Louvain, 1947); L. Ceyssens, *La Fin de la première période du Jansénisme. Sources des années 1654–1660,* Vol. 1: *1654–1656,* with the collaboration of A. Lagrand (Brussels, 1963); Léon Brunschvicg, *Blaise Pascal* (Paris, 1953); F. T. H. Fletcher, *Pascal and the Mystical Tradition* (Oxford, 1954); Jean Mesnard, *Pascal,* trans. by G. S. Fraser (London, 1952); E. Romanes, *The Story of Port Royal* (London, 1907); F. Strowski, *Pascal et son temps,* 3 vols. (Paris, 1907–1913); and M. Tollemache, *The French Jansenists* (London, 1893).

The complete works of **Jakob Böhme** have been published under the title, *Sämtliche Schriften,* ed. by Will-Erich Peuckert, 11 vols. (Stuttgart, 1955–1961). The following works have been published in English: *Concerning the Three Principles of the Divine Essence* (London, 1910); *The Forty Questions of the Soul and the Clavis* (London, 1911); *An Exposition of Genesis* (London, 1924); *The Signature of All Things* (London and New York, 1912); and *The Way to Christ* (London, 1947). For studies of Böhme, see G. M. Alleman, *A Critique of Some Philosophical Aspects of the Mysticism of Jacob Boehme* (Philadelphia, Pa., 1932); M. L. Bailey, *Milton and Jakob Boehme* (New York, 1914); H. L. Martensen, *Jacob Boehme,* trans. by T. R. Evans (New York, 1949); C. A. Muses, *Illumination on Jacob Boehme* (New York, 1951); A. J. Penny, *Studies in Jacob Böhme* (London, 1912); and Alexandre Koyré, *La Philosophie de J. Boehme* (Paris, 1929), and *Mystiques, spirituels, alchimistes du XVI^e siècle allemand* (Paris, 1955).

**Arminianism** is discussed by Rosalie Littell Colie, *Light and Enlightenment: A Study of the Cambridge Platonists and the Dutch Arminians* (New York, 1957); Godfrey Davies, "Arminian Versus Puritan in England About 1620–1640," *Huntington Library Bulletin* (1934); A. W. Harrison, *The Beginnings of Arminianism* (London, 1926); and D. Nobbs, *Theocracy and Toleration* (Cambridge, 1938), covering disputes among Dutch Calvinists from 1600 to 1650. Protestantism of the seventeenth century is discussed by Winfred Zeller, *Der Protestantismus des 17. Jahrhunderts,* "Klassiker des Protestantismus," Vol. 5 (Bremen, 1962).

Standard works on the first two **Stuart rulers** are S. R. Gardiner, *History of England, 1603–1642,* 10 vols. (London, 1883–1884); Godfrey Davies, *The Early Stuarts, 1603–1660* (Oxford, 1937); Christopher Hill, *A Century of Revolution, 1603–1714* (Edinburgh, 1961); J. P. Kenyon,

# Bibliography

The Stuart Constitution, Documents and Commentary (Cambridge, 1966); and G. M. Trevelyan, England Under the Stuarts, first published 1904 (London, 1954). On James I, see C. H. McIlwain, The Political Works of James I (Cambridge, Mass., 1918); H. G. Stafford, James VI of Scotland and the Throne of England (New York, 1940); C. Williams, James I, new ed. (London, 1951); and David H. Willson, James VI and I (New York, 1956). On Charles I, see D. Mathew, The Age of Charles I (London, 1951), a Catholic account; Cecily V. Wedgwood, A Coffin for King Charles (New York, 1964); E. C. Wingfield-Stratford, Charles, King of England (London, 1949); and G. M. Young, Charles I and Cromwell (London, 1936).

Special studies concerned with the reigns of the first two Stuarts are G. E. Aylmer, The King's Servants: The Civil Service of Charles I, 1625–42 (London, 1961); R. Bagwell, Ireland Under the Stuarts, 3 vols. (London, 1909–1916); Thomas G. Barnes, Somerset, 1625–1640: A County's Government During the "Personal Rule" (Cambridge, Mass., 1961); Douglas Brunton and D. H. Pennington, Members of the Long Parliament (Cambridge, Mass., 1954); John D. Eusden, Puritans, Lawyers, and Politics in Early Seventeenth-Century England (New Haven, Conn., 1958), an excellent analysis of the political philosophy of the clergy and lawyers; Fr. J. Gerard, What Was the Gunpowder Plot? (London, 1897), a Catholic interpretation; G. P. Gooch, English Democratic Ideas in the Seventeenth Century, 2nd ed. (Cambridge, 1927); W. Holdsworth, A History of English Law, 10 vols. (London, 1931–1932), the standard authority; Margaret A. Judson, The Crisis of the Constitution . . . 1603–1645 (New Brunswick, N.J., 1949); Wallace Notestein, Winning of the Initiative by the House of Commons (London, 1925); John G. A. Pocock, The Ancient Constitution and the Feudal Law: A Study of English Historical Thought in the Seventeenth Century (Cambridge, 1957); J. R. Tanner, English Constitutional Conflicts, 1603–89 (Cambridge, 1928); Hugh Ross Williamson, The Gunpowder Plot (London, 1951); D. H. Willson, The Privy Councillors in the House of Commons, 1604–1629 (Minneapolis, Minn., 1940); F. D. Wormuth, The Royal Prerogative, 1603–49 (Ithaca, N.Y. and London, 1939), and The Origins of Modern Constitutionalism (New York, 1949).

For studies of the **Puritan Revolution,** see S. R. Gardiner, History of the Commonwealth and Protectorate, 3 vols. (London, 1894–1903); C. H. Firth, The Last Years of the Protectorate, 2 vols. (London, 1909), which completes Gardiner's work; Earl of Clarendon, History of the Rebellion, ed. by W. D. Macray, 6 vols. (Oxford, 1888), the most valuable of the contemporary histories; C. H. and K. George, The Protestant Mind of the English Reformation, 1570–1640 (Princeton, N.J., 1961), an attempt to show that religion played an insignificant role in the coming of the civil wars; Richard L. Greaves, *The Puritan Revolution and Educational Thought: Background for Reform* (New Brunswick, N.J., 1970); William Haller, *Liberty and Reformation in the Puritan Revolution* (New York, 1955), *Foxe's Book of Martyrs and the Elect Nation* (London, 1963), and *The Rise of Puritanism* (New York, 1938); Paul H. Hardacre, *The Royalists During the Puritan Revolution* (The Hague, 1956), an authoritative account of the followers of Charles I; Mary F. Keeler, *The Long Parliament, 1640–41: A Biographical Study of Its Members* (Philadelphia, Pa., 1954); William M. Lamont, *Godly Rule: Politics and Religion, 1603–1650* (New York, 1969); Valerie Pearl, *London and the Outbreak of the Puritan Revolution* (London, 1961); G. B. Tatham, *The Puritans in Power* (Cambridge, 1913); *The Origins of the English Civil War*, ed. by Philip A. M. Taylor, "Problems in European Civilization" (Boston, 1960); Hugh R. Trevor-Roper, *The Crisis of the Seventeenth Century: Religion, the Reformation, and Social Change* (New York, 1967, 1968); Cecily V. Wedgwood, *The Great Rebellion*, 2 vols. (London, 1955, 1958); John F. Wilson, *Pulpit in Parliament: Puritanism During the English Civil Wars, 1640–1648* (Princeton, N.J., 1969); George Yule, *The Independents in the English Civil War* (Cambridge, 1958), an analysis of their politics; and Perez Zagorin, *A History of Political Thought in the English Revolution* (London, 1954), and *The Court and the Country: The Beginning of the English Revolution* (New York, 1970).

On **Cromwell and the Protectorate,** see W. C. Abbott, *A Bibliography of Oliver Cromwell* (Cambridge, Mass., 1929); *The Writings and Speeches of Oliver Cromwell,* ed. by W. C. Abbott and C. D. Crane, 3 vols. (Cambridge, Mass., 1937–1945); C. H. Firth, *Oliver Cromwell* (New York, 1906), still the best biography, and *Cromwell's Army* (London, 1912), the standard work on the military and religious aspects of the revolt; Maurice P. Ashley, *Oliver Cromwell* (London, 1937), *The Greatness of Oliver Cromwell* (New York, 1958), and *Cromwell's Generals* (London, 1954); E. Barker, *Oliver Cromwell and the English People* (Cambridge, 1937); E. Bernstein, *Cromwell and Communism* (London, 1930), by a well-known Marxist; *Oliver Cromwell and the Puritan Revolt,* "Problems in European Civilization" (Boston, 1966); Charles H. Firth and Godfrey Davies, *The Regimental History of Cromwell's Army,* 2 vols. (Oxford, 1940); J. Morley, *Oliver Cromwell* (London, 1923); Leo F. Solt, *Saints in Arms: Puritanism and Democracy in Cromwell's Army* (Stanford, 1959), a study of the political and religious thought of a number of ministers in the army; Michael Walzer, *The Revolution of the Saints* (Cambridge, Mass., 1965); Cecily V. Wedgwood, *Oliver Cromwell* (London, 1939); and A. S. P. Woodhouse, *Puritanism and Liberty. Being the Army Debates (1647–9) from the Clarke Manuscripts with Supplementary Documents,* 2nd ed. (Chicago, 1951).

*571*

# Bibliography

On the **Levellers,** see *Leveller Manifestoes of the Puritan Revolution,* ed. by D. M. Wolfe (New York, 1944); *The Leveller Tracts,* ed. by W. Haller and G. Davies (New York, 1944); H. N. Brailsford, *The Levellers and the English Revolution,* ed. by C. Hill (Stanford, Calif., 1961), the fullest account; T. C. Pease, *The Leveller Movement* (Baltimore, Md., 1916); and D. B. Robertson, *The Religious Foundations of Leveller Democracy* (New York, 1951).

**General religious conditions** are discussed in C. C. Butterworth, *The Literary Lineage of the King James Bible 1304–1611* (Philadelphia, Pa., 1941); *The Cambridge History of the Bible,* ed. by S. L. Greenslade, Vol. 3 (Cambridge, 1963); Carl Bridenbaugh, *Vexed and Troubled Englishmen, 1590–1642* (New York, 1968); Alice Clare Carter, *The English Reformed Church in Amsterdam in the Seventeenth Century* (Amsterdam, 1964); Norman Cohn, *The Pursuit of the Millennium* (Fairlawn, N.J., 1957); G. D. Henderson, *Religious Life in Seventeenth-Century Scotland* (Cambridge, 1937); Wilbur K. Jordan, *The Development of Religious Toleration in England,* 4 vols. (Cambridge, Mass., 1932–1940); George L. Mosse, *The Holy Pretence: A Study in Christianity and Reason of State from William Perkins to John Winthrop* (Oxford, 1957); W. A. Shaw, *A History of the English Church, 1640–1660,* 2 vols. (London, 1900); Raymond P. Stearns, *Congregationalism in the Dutch Netherlands* (Chicago, 1940); and R. G. Usher, *Reconstruction of the English Church,* 2 vols. (New York, 1910).

For works on the **Quakers,** see George Fox, *The Book of Miracles,* ed. by H. C. Cadbury (Cambridge, 1948), and *The Journal of George Fox,* ed. by John L. Nickalls (Cambridge, 1952); Hugh Barbour, *The Quakers in Puritan England* (New Haven, Conn., and London, 1964); W. C. Braithwaite, *The Beginnings of Quakerism,* 2nd rev. ed. (Cambridge, 1955), the standard work; and R. M. Jones, *The Story of George Fox* (New York, 1919). On the **Presbyterians** there is L. H. Carlson, "A History of the Presbyterian Party from Pride's Purge to the Dissolution of the Long Parliament," *Church History,* 11 (1942). On the **Baptists** there are L. F. Brown, *The Political Activities of the Baptists and Fifth Monarchy Men in England during the Interregnum* (Washington, D.C., 1912), and W. T. Whitley, *A History of British Baptists* (London, 1923).

**Social and cultural** aspects of the Puritan Revolution are discussed in Maurice Ashley, *Life in Stuart England* (London, 1964); H. S. Bennett, *English Books and Readers, 1603–1640* (Cambridge, 1970); M. James, *Social Problems and Policy During the Puritan Revolution* (London, 1930), exhaustive and reliable; Wilbur K. Jordan, *The Charities of London, 1480–1660* (London, 1960), *The Charities of Rural England* (London, 1961), and *Philanthropy in England, 1480–1660* (London, 1959); J. B. Oldham, *A History of Shrewsbury School* (Oxford, 1952); W. Schenk,

*The Concern for Social Justice in the Puritan Revolution* (London, 1948); and Alan Simpson, *The Wealth of the Gentry, 1540–1660: East Anglian Studies* (Chicago, 1961).

Following are accounts of some **leading figures** during the reigns of the first two Stuarts not yet referred to: Sidney R. Brett, *John Pym* (London, 1940); Jack H. Hexter, *The Reign of King Pym* (Cambridge, Mass., 1941); C. E. Wade, *John Pym* (London, 1912); E. C. Wingfield-Stratford, *King Charles and King Pym* (London, 1949); W. H. Hutton, *William Laud* (London, 1895), written from an Anglican viewpoint; H. R. Trevor-Roper, *Archbishop Laud* (London, 1940), unsympathetic; Lady Burghclere, *Strafford*, 2 vols. (London, 1931); H. D. Trail, *Lord Strafford* (London, 1889); Cecily V. Wedgwood, *Strafford* (London, 1935), sympathetic; William R. Mueller, *John Donne, Preacher* (Princeton, N.J., 1962); Raymond P. Stearns, *The Strenuous Puritan, Hugh Peter, 1598–1660* (Urbana, Ill., 1954); *Richard Baxter and Puritan Politics*, ed. by Richard Schlatter (New Brunswick, N.J., 1957); Frederick J. Powicke, *A Life of the Reverend Richard Baxter, 1615–1691*, 2 vols. (Boston, 1924); Don M. Wolfe, *Milton and the Puritan Revolution* (New York, 1941); Arthur Barker, *Milton and the Puritan Dilemma, 1641–1660* (Toronto, 1942); and William R. Parker, *Milton: A Biography*, 2 vols. (Oxford, 1968).

## Chapter 12: The Legacy of the Reformation

For **general surveys** of the impact of the Reformation Era upon western civilization, see Preserved Smith, *History of Modern Culture*, Vol. I (New York, 1930); Carl J. Friedrich, *The Age of the Baroque, 1610–1660* (New York, 1952); Frederick B. Artz, *From the Renaissance to Romanticism* (Chicago, 1962), a discussion of intellectual history, including fine arts; Crane Brinton, *Ideas and Men: The Story of Western Thought*, 2nd ed. (Englewood Cliffs, N.J., 1963); J. Bronowski and Bruce Mazlish, *The Western Intellectual Tradition from Leonardo to Hegel* (New York, 1960), covering the relation between the history of science and the history of ideas.

**Religious influences** are emphasized by Gustaf Aulén, *Reformation and Catholicity*, trans. by E. H. Wahlstrom (Philadelphia, Pa., 1961); *The Role of Religion in Modern European History*, ed. by Sidney A. Burrell (New York, 1964); Herbert Butterfield, *Christianity and History* (London, 1957); C. H. Dawson, *Religion and the Rise of Western Culture* (London and New York, 1950), a Catholic account emphasizing the importance of the Christian tradition; Jules Delvaille, *Essai sur l'histoire de l'idée de progrès jusqu'à la fin du 18me siècle* (Paris, 1910), which traces the idea of progress back to the ancients; Werner Elert, *The Struc-*

# Bibliography

*ture of Lutheranism,* trans. by Walter A. Hansen, Vol. 1 (St. Louis, Mo., 1962); Manfred P. Fleischer, *Katholische und lutherische Ireniker* (Göttingen, 1968); Karl Holl, *The Cultural Significance of the Reformation,* trans. by K. and B. Hertz and J. H. Lichtblau (New York, 1959); Winthrop S. Hudson, *American Protestantism* (Chicago, 1961); F. W. Kantzenbach, *Das Ringen um die Einheit der Kirche im Zeitalter der Reformation* (Stuttgart, 1957); Bernhard Lohse, *Lutherdeutung heute* (Göttingen, 1968); A. C. McGiffert, *Protestant Thought Before Kant* (New York, 1913); John T. McNeill, *The History and Character of Calvinism* (New York, 1954); Peter Meinhold, *Luther heute: Wirken und Theologie Martin Luthers* (Berlin and Hamburg, 1967); *Wilhelm Pauck, The Heritage of the Reformation,* rev. ed. (Glencoe, Ill., 1961); Robert D. Preuss, *The Theology of Post-Reformation Lutheranism* (St. Louis, Mo., 1970); Sir Steven Runciman, *The Great Church in Captivity* (New York and London, 1968), which covers relations of the Greek church with the Protestant and Catholic churches during the sixteenth and seventeenth centuries; E. Gordon Rupp, *The Old Reformation and the New* (Philadelphia, Pa., 1967); Paul Tillich, *The Protestant Era* (Chicago, 1948); Ernst Troeltsch, *Protestantism and Progress,* trans. by W. Montgomery (New York, 1912); and Hans Emil Weber, *Reformation, Orthodoxie und Rationalismus,* 2 vols. Gütersloh, 1937–1951).

The best survey of the interpretations of the **political thought** of the Reformation Era is that by Felix Gilbert, "Political Thought of the Renaissance and Reformation," *The Huntington Library Quarterly,* 4 (1941). C. H. McIlwain, *The Growth of Political Thought in the West* (New York, 1932), and G. H. Sabine, *A History of Political Theory,* 2nd ed. (New York, 1950), are standard texts. For detailed treatments see J. W. Allen, *A History of Political Thought in the Sixteenth Century* (London and New York, 1928), and *English Political Thought 1603–1660,* Vol. 1 (London, 1938); J. Bowle, *Western Political Thought* (London, 1947); R. W. and A. J. Carlyle, *A History of Political Theory in the West,* Vol. 6 (Edinburgh, 1936); W. F. Church, *Constitutional Thought in Sixteenth-Century France* (London, 1941); G. Dodge, *The Political Theory of the Huguenots of the Dispersion* (New York, 1947); W. A. Dunning, *A History of Political Theories from Luther to Montesquieu* (New York and London, 1905); J. N. Figgis, *Studies of Political Thought from Gerson to Grotius,* 2nd ed. (Cambridge, 1923), and *The Divine Right of Kings* (Cambridge, 1914); J. S. Flynn, *The Influence of Puritanism on the Political and Religious Thought of the English* (London, 1920); Werner Goez, *Translatio imperii: Ein Beitrag zur Geschichte des Geschichtsdenkens und der politischen Theorien im Mittelalter und in der frühen Neuzeit* (Tübingen, 1958); G. P. Gooch, *English Democratic Ideas in the Seventeenth Century* (Cambridge, 1927);

Bernice Hamilton, *Political Thought in Sixteenth-Century Spain: A Study of the Political Ideas of Vitoria, De Soto, Suarez, and Molina* (New York, 1963); F. J. C. Hearnshaw, *The Social and Political Ideas of Some Great Thinkers of the Sixteenth and Seventeenth Centuries* (New York, 1949); Oscar Jaszi and John D. Lewis, *Against the Tyrant: The Tradition and Theory of Tyrannicide* (Glencoe, Ill., 1957); R. M. Jones, *Mysticism and Democracy in the English Commonwealth* (Cambridge, Mass., 1932); Paul Mesnard, *L'Essor de la philosophie politique au XVIᵉ siècle,* 2nd ed. (Paris, 1952); R. H. Murray, *The Political Consequences of the Reformation* (London, 1926); B. Reynolds, *Proponents of Limited Monarchy in Sixteenth Century France* (New York, 1931); and Erik Wolf, *Grosse Rechtsdenker der deutschen Geistesgeschichte,* 3rd ed. (Tübingen, 1951).

The **political theories of individuals** are discussed by L. H. Waring, *The Political Theories of Martin Luther* (New York, 1910); George W. Forell, "Luther and Politics," in Forell, Grimm, and Hoelty-Nickel, *Luther and Culture* (Decorah, Iowa, 1960); F. Edward Cranz, *An Essay on the Development of Luther's Thought on Justice, Law, and Society* (Cambridge, Mass., 1959); John T. McNeill, *John Calvin on God and Political Duty* (New York, 1950); Hans Baron, *Calvins Staatsanschauung und das konfessionelle Zeitalter* (Berlin, 1924); Josef Bohatec, *Calvin und das Recht* (Feudingen, 1934); Marc Edouard Cheneviere, *La Pensée politique de Calvin* (Geneva, 1937); Georges de Lagarde, *Recherches sur l'esprit politique de la Réforme* (Paris, 1926), a criticism of Calvin's views of church and state; H. Butterfield, *The Statecraft of Machiavelli* (London, 1940), which portrays him as strictly "Machiavellian"; Ernst Cassirer, *The Myth of the State,* ed. by C. W. Hendel (New Haven, Conn., 1946), which places Machiavelli in the general development of political thought; J. H. Whitfield, *Machiavelli* (Oxford, 1947), which emphasizes his Christian morality; J. H. Fichter, *Man of Spain: Francis Saurez* (New York, 1940); Winthrop S. Hudson, *John Ponet (1516–1556): Advocate of Limited Monarchy* (Chicago, 1942); W. S. M. Knight, *The Life and Works of Hugo Grotius* (London, 1925); J. Laures, *The Political Economy of Juan de Mariana* (New York, 1928); Ernst Reibstein, *Johann Althusius als Fortsetzer der Schule von Salamanca* (Karlsruhe, 1955); R. Chauviré, *J. Bodin, auteur de la Republique* (Paris, 1914); J. L. Franklin, *Jean Bodin and the Sixteenth-Century Revolution in the Methodology of Law and History* (New York, 1963); and R. Wesel-Roth, *Thomas Erastus, ein Beitrag zur Geschichte der reformierten Kirche und zur Lehre der Staatssouveränität* (Lahr, Baden, 1954).

There is a good survey of the controversy over the **Max Weber thesis** with excerpts from the writings of the chief participants in *Protestantism and Capitalism,* ed. by Robert W. Green, "Problems in European Civilization" (Boston, 1959). The controversy began with the provocative study by Max Weber, *The Protestant Ethic and the Spirit of Capitalism*, trans. by T. Parsons (London, 1930), which pointed to the strong connection between Protestantism and capitalism. This was followed by Ernst Troeltsch, *Protestantism and Progress* (London, 1912), and *The Social Teachings of the Christian Churches*, 2 vols. (New York, 1931, 1949), which stress the strong affinity of Calvinism and capitalism for each other and minimize the influence of Lutheranism. R. H. Tawney, in his *Religion and the Rise of Capitalism* (New York and London, 1926), develops the Weber thesis but stresses the various changes in the development of Calvinism. H. M. Robertson, in his *Aspects of the Rise of Economic Individualism* (Cambridge, 1933), opposes the Weber-Tawney thesis, asserting that capitalism was not influenced by the religious ethic but changed it. See also G. A. T. O'Brien, *An Essay on the Economic Effects of the Reformation* (London, 1923), a Catholic interpretation; M. Dobb, *Studies in the Development of Capitalism* (London, 1946), a Marxist interpretation; Amintore Fanfani, an Italian economist and statesman, *Catholicism, Protestantism and Capitalism,* trans. from the Italian (New York, 1955); and Henri Sée, *Modern Capitalism* (New York, 1928). The best summary on the taking of interest is that by Benjamin N. Nelson, *The Idea of Usury* (Princeton, N.J., 1949), which contains a detailed bibliography. See also Henri Hauser, *Les Débuts de capitalisme* (Paris, 1927); Hermann Barge, *Luther und der Frühkapitalismus*, "Schriften des Vereins für Reformationsgeschichte," No. 168 (Gütersloh, 1951); Clemens Bauer, "Conrad Peutingers Gutachten zur Monopolfrage," *Achiv für Reformationsgeschichte,* 45 (1954); Andre Bieler, *La Pensée économique et sociale de Calvin* (Geneva, 1959); Kurt Samuelsson, *Religion and Economic Action,* trans. by E. G. French (New York, 1961); and Jakob Strieder, *Studien zur Geschichte kapitalistischer Organisationsformen* (Munich, 1925).

The best brief survey of the development of **science** and the scientific spirit is that by Herbert Butterfield, *The Origins of Modern Science* (New York, 1952). More detailed is A. R. Hall, *The Scientific Revolution, 1300–1800* (Boston, 1954). Other helpful references are *The Rise of Modern Science*, ed. by George Basalla, "Problems in European Civilization" (Boston, 1968); Marie Boas, *The Scientific Renaissance, 1450–1630* (New York, 1962); J. Bronowski, *Science and Human Values* (New York, 1957), and *The Common Sense of Science* (London, 1951); Karl Heinz Burmeister, *Georg Joachim Rhetikus, 1514–1574,* 2 vols. (Wiesbaden, 1967–1968), an early supporter of the Copernican theory; Edwin A. Burtt, *The Metaphysical Foundations of Modern Science* (London, 1949); Max Caspar, *Johannes Kepler* (Stuttgart, 1948); Marshall Clagett, *The Science of Mechanics in the Middle Ages* (Madison, Wis., 1959);

Lane Cooper, *Aristotle, Galileo, and the Tower of Pisa* (Ithaca, N.Y., 1935); Alistair C. Crombie, *Medieval and Early Modern Science,* 2 vols. (New York, 1959); W. C. Dampier, *A History of Science,* 4th ed. (Cambridge, 1949); E. J. Dijksterhuis, *The Mechanization of the World Picture,* trans. by C. Dikshoorn (Oxford, 1961); John Dillenberger, *Protestant Thought and Natural Science* (New York, 1960); Herbert Dingle, *The Scientific Adventure: Essays in the History and Philosophy of Science* (New York, 1953); *Mechanics in Sixteenth-Century Italy,* trans. by Stillman Drake and I. E. Drabkin (Madison, Wis., 1969); J. L. E. Dreyer, *A History of the Planetary Systems from Thales to Kepler* (New York, 1953); P. Duhem, *Le Système du monde. Histoire des doctrines cosmologiques de Platon à Copernic,* to be published in 10 vols. (Paris, 1954–    ); Charles C. Gillispie, *The Edge of Objectivity: An Essay in the History of Scientific Ideas* (Princeton, N.J., 1960); Max Hartmann, *Die philosophischen Grundlagen der Naturwissenschaften* (Jena, 1948); Thomas P. Hughes, *The Development of Western Technology Since 1500* (New York, 1964); Thomas S. Kuhn, *The Copernican Revolution* (Cambridge, 1957); Walter Pagel, *Das medizinische Weltbild des Paracelsus: Seine Zusammenhänge mit Neuplatonismus und Gnosis* (Wiesbaden, 1962); Giorgio de Santillana, *The Crime of Galileo* (Chicago, 1955); George Sarton, *Introduction to the History of Science,* Vol. 2: *From Rabbi ben Ezra to Roger Bacon* (Washington, D. C., 1931), and *On the History of Science,* ed. by Dorothy Stimson (Cambridge, Mass., 1962); R. H. Shryock, *The Development of Modern Medicine* (Philadelphia, Pa., 1936); Charles Singer, *Studies in the History and Method of Science,* 2 vols. (Oxford, 1917–1921); Lynn Thorndike, *The History of Magic and Experimental Science,* 8 vols. (New York, 1923–1958); R. V. Tooley, *Maps and Map-Makers* (London and New York, 1949); William P. D. Wightman, *Science and the Renaissance,* 2 vols. (Edinburgh and London, 1962); A. Wolf, *A History of Science, Technology, and Philosophy in the 16th and 17th Centuries,* 2nd ed. (London, 1950); and L. Gallois, *Les Géographes allemands de la Renaissance,* reprint of 1890 ed. (Amsterdam, 1964).

**Demonology and witchcraft** are discussed in R. T. Davies, *Four Centuries of Witch-Beliefs* (London, 1947), and C. Hole, *Witchcraft in England* (New York, 1947), excellent summaries; G. L. Kittredge, *Witchcraft in Old and New England* (Cambridge, Mass., 1958), a standard reference; H. C. Lea, collector, *Materials Toward a History of Witchcraft,* ed. by A. C. Howland, 3 vols. (Philadelphia, Pa., 1939); W. Notestein, *A History of Witchcraft in England* (Washington, D.C., 1911); Keith Thomas, *Religion and the Decline of Magic* (New York, 1971); and G. Zilboorg, *The Medical Man and the Witch During the Renaissance* (Baltimore, Md., 1935).

# Bibliography

There are the following studies on the development of **religious liberty:** Roland H. Bainton, *The Travail of Religious Liberty* (Philadelphia, Pa., 1951), *Hunted Heretic: The Life and Death of Michael Servetus* (Boston, 1953), and *Sebastian Castellio Concerning Heretics* (New York, 1935); M. Searle Bates, *Religious Liberty* (New York, 1945); John B. Bury, *A History of the Freedom of Thought* (London and New York, 1913); W. M. Clyde, *The Struggle for the Freedom of the Press from Caxton to Cromwell* (London and New York, 1934); Hans R. Guggisberg, *Sebastian Castellio im Urteil seiner Nachwelt* (Basel, 1956); W. K. Jordan, *The Development of Religious Toleration in England*, 4 vols. (Cambridge, Mass., and London, 1932–1940); Henry Kamen, *The Rise of Toleration* (New York, 1967); J. Lecler, S.J., *Toleration and the Reformation*, trans. by T. L. Wilson, Vol. 1 (London, 1960); Perry Miller, *Roger Williams, His Contribution to the American Tradition* (Indianapolis, Ind., and New York, 1953); R. H. Murray, *Erasmus and Luther: Their Attitude to Toleration* (New York, 1920); Richard H. Popkin, *The History of Scepticism from Erasmus to Descartes* (Assen, The Netherlands, 1960); J. M. Robertson, *A Short History of Free Thought*, 4th ed., 2 vols. (London, 1936); E. L. Tuveson, *Millenium and Utopia* (Berkeley, Calif., 1949), on humanist biblical criticism; and A. S. P. Woodhouse, *Puritanism and Liberty* (Chicago, 1951).

Among useful surveys of **education** during the Reformation Era are Harry G. Good, *A History of Western Education* (New York, 1947); F. P. Graves, *A History of Education during the Middle Ages and the Transition to Modern Times* (New York, 1916); R. F. Butts, *A Cultural History of Education* (New York, 1947); F. Eby, *The Development of Modern Education* (New York, 1952), and *Early Protestant Educators* (New York, 1931); E. Garin, *L'educazione in Europa (1400–1600)* (Bari, 1957); Hubert Hettwer, *Herkunft und Zusammenhang der Schulordnungen* (Mainz, 1965); and William H. Woodward, *Studies in Education During the Age of the Renaissance, 1400–1600* (Cambridge, 1924).

On **Comenius,** see J. A. Comenius, *The Bequest of the Unity of Brethren* (Chicago, 1940), *The Labyrinth of the World and the Paradise of the Heart* (Chicago, 1942), both trans. and ed. by Matthew Spinka, and *Pampaedia,* ed. by D. Tschiżewskij, H. Geissler, and K. Schaller (Heidelberg, 1960); Anna Heyberger, *Jean Amos Comenius: Sa Vie et son oeuvre d'éducateur* (Paris, 1938); A. Molnár, *J. A. Comenius: A Perfect Reformation,* with preface by J. Hromadka (Prague, 1957); J. Piaget, *John Amos Comenius, 1592–1670* (Paris, 1957); and Matthew Spinka, *John Amos Comenius* (Chicago, 1943).

The best treatments of **the writing of history** during the Reformation Era are those in James W. Thompson, *History of Historical Writing,* 2 vols. (New York, 1942); *Church Historians,* ed. by P. K. Guilday (New

York, 1926); Harry E. Barnes, *History of Historical Writing* (Norman, Okla., 1937); Julian H. Franklin, *Jean Bodin and the Sixteenth-Century Revolution in the Methodology of Law and History* (New York and London, 1963); F. Smith Fussner, *The Historical Revolution: English Historical Writing and Thought, 1580–1640* (New York, 1962); Heinz Scheible, *Die Entstehung der Magdeburger Zenturien*, "Schriften des Vereins für Reformationsgeschichte," No. 183 (Göttingen, 1966); Preserved Smith, *A History of Modern Culture*, 2 vols. (New York, 1930–1934); and Gerald Strauss, *Historian in an Age of Crisis: The Life and Work of Johannes Aventinus, 1477–1534* (Cambridge, Mass., 1963).

General surveys of the **literature** of the Reformation Era are included in the bibliography for Chapter 2.

Good treatments of the **fine arts** of the Reformation Era are the following: W. Anderson, *The Architecture of the Renaissance in Italy* (New York, 1927); O. Benesch, *The Art of the Renaissance in Northern Europe* (Cambridge, Mass., 1947); B. Berenson, *The Italian Painters of the Renaissance* (Oxford, 1930); C. G. Blunt, *Gothic Painting* (London, 1947); Georg Dehio, *Geschichte der deutschen Kunst*, 4th ed., Vol. 2 (Berlin, 1930); W. R. Deutsche, *German Painting of the Sixteenth Century* (London, 1936); B. Fletcher, *A History of Architecture*, 17th ed. (London, 1961); J. Harvey, *The Gothic World, 1100–1600* (New York, London, and Toronto, 1950); A. Hauser, *The Social History of Art*, 2 vols. (New York, 1950); F. J. Mather, Jr., *A History of Italian Painting* (New York, 1923), and *Western European Painting of the Renaissance* (New York, 1950); Erwin Panofsky, *Gothic Architecture and Scholasticism* (Latrobe, Pa., 1951), *Dürer*, 4th ed. (Princeton, N.J., 1955), *Idea*, 2nd ed. (London, 1953), and *Studies in Iconology*, 2nd ed. (New York, 1962); N. Pevsner, *An Outline of European Architecture* (London, 1951); Wilhelm Pinder, *Vom Wesen und Werden deutscher Formen*, Vol. 3: *Die deutsche Kunst der Dürerzeit* (Leipzig, 1940); C. R. Post, *A History of Spanish Painting*, 12 vols. (Cambridge, Mass., 1930–1958); Heinrich A. Schmid, *Hans Holbein der Jüngere*, 3 vols. (Basel, 1945–1948); Rudolf Wittkower, *Architectural Principles in the Age of Humanism*, 3rd ed. (London, 1962); Heinrich Wölfflin, *The Art of Albrecht Dürer*, trans. by A. and H. Grieve (London, 1971), and *Classic Art*, trans. by P and L. Murray, 2nd ed. (London, 1953); and *Albrecht Dürers schriftlicher Nachlass*, ed. by H. Rupprich (Berlin, 1956). Pelican History of Art (London) has the following well-illustrated volumes: Anthony Blunt, *France, 1500–1700* (1953); H. K. Gerson and E. H. Kuile, *Belgium, 1600–1800* (1960); Eberhard Hempel, *Central Europe, 1600–1800* (1965); George Kubler and Martin Soria, *Spain and Portugal, 1500–1800* (1959); Jakob Rosenberg, *Dutch Art and Architecture, 1600–1800* (1966); J. H. Summerson, *Britain, 1530–1830* (1953); and Rudolf Wittkower, *Italy, 1600–1750* (1958).

# Bibliography

The standard reference works for the study of the **history of music** are *Grove's Dictionary of Music and Musicians,* 5th ed., 10 vols. (London, 1954–1961); *Harvard Dictionary of Music,* ed. by Willi Apel (Cambridge, Mass., 1944); *The New Oxford History of Music* (London, New York, and Oxford, 1954–        ), Vol. 3: *Ars Nova and the Renaissance, 1300–1540* (1960), and Vol. 4: *The Age of Humanism, 1540–1630* (1968); and *Die Musik in Geschichte und Gegenwart,* ed. by Friedrich Blume, 14 vols. (Kassel, 1949–1968). Special studies of value for the Reformation Era are P. Wackernagel, *Bibliographie zur Geschichte des deutschen Kirchenliedes im 16. Jahrhundert,* reprint of 1855 ed. (Frankfurt a. M., 1961); Willi Apel, *The Notation of Polyphonic Music, 900–1600,* 4th ed. (Cambridge, Mass., 1949); Morrison C. Boyd, *Elizabethan Music and Musical Criticism,* 2nd ed. (Philadelphia, Pa., 1962); Manfred F. Bukofzer, *Music in the Baroque Era, from Monteverdi to Bach* (London, 1948); Klaus Burba, *Die Christologie in Luthers Liedern,* "Schriften des Vereins für Reformationsgeschichte," No. 175 (Gütersloh, 1956); Walter E. Buszin, "Luther on Music," *The Musical Quarterly,* **32** (1946); Edward Dickinson, *Music in the History of the Western Church,* new ed. (New York, 1925); Maurice Frost, *English and Scottish Psalm and Hymn Tunes, c. 1543–1677* (London, New York, and Toronto, 1953); Theodore Hoelty-Nickel, "Luther and Music," *Luther and Culture* (Decorah, Iowa, 1960); Paul H. Lang, *Music in Western Civilization* (New York, 1941); E. Liemohn, *The Chorale* (Philadelphia, Pa., 1953); Paul Nettl, *Luther and Music,* reprint of 1948 ed. (New York, 1967); Gustave Reese, *Music in the Renaissance,* rev. ed. (New York, 1959); Johannes Riedel, *The Lutheran Chorale: Its Basic Traditions* (Minneapolis, Minn., 1967); and Ernest Walker, *A History of Music in England,* 3rd ed. (Oxford, 1952). German Swiss hymns of the sixteenth century are ably discussed by Markus Jenny, *Geschichte des deutsch-schweizerischen evangelischen Gesangbuches im 16. Jahrhundert* (Basel, 1962).

# Index

# Index

# Index

# Index

# Index

# Index

# Index

# Index

# T

# U

# Index

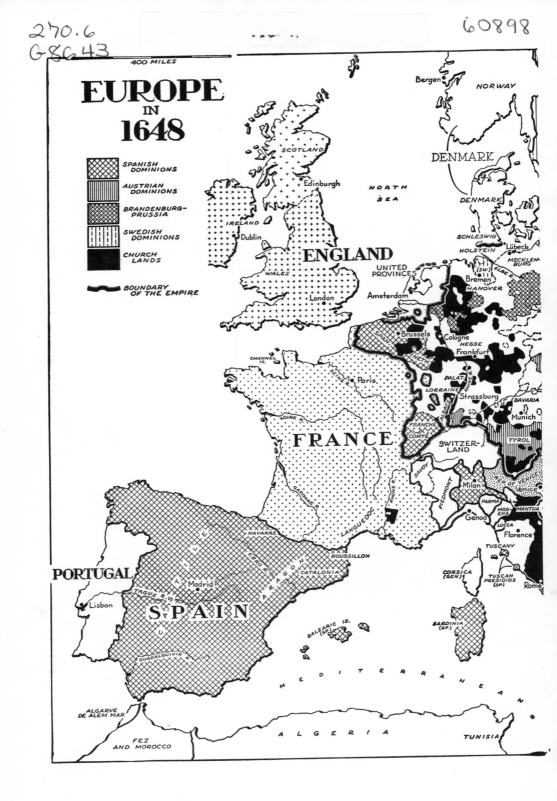

# EUROPE IN 1648

400 MILES

| | |
|---|---|
| SPANISH DOMINIONS | |
| AUSTRIAN DOMINIONS | |
| BRANDENBURG-PRUSSIA | |
| SWEDISH DOMINIONS | |
| CHURCH LANDS | |
| BOUNDARY OF THE EMPIRE | |

NORWAY

Bergen

DENMARK

DENMARK

SCOTLAND

Edinburgh

NORTH SEA

SCHLESWIG

HOLSTEIN

Lübeck

MECKLEN-BURG

IRELAND

Dublin

ENGLAND

WALES

London

UNITED PROVINCES

Amsterdam

(SW)
Bremen
HANOVER

ELBE R.

CHANNEL IS.

SPAN.
NETH.

Brussels

Cologne
HESSE
Frankfurt

PALAT.

LORRAINE

SEINE R.

Paris

Strassburg

BAVARIA

Munich

RHINE R.

SAAR

FRANCE

FRANCHE COMTE

SWITZER-LAND

TYROL

LOIRE R.

SAVOY

PIEDMONT

REP. OF VENICE

Venice

Milan

PARMA

MOD-ENA

MANTUA

GASCOGNE R.

RHONE R.

NAVARRE

EBRO R.

ARAGON

Genoa

LUCCA

Florence

TUSCANY

PORTUGAL

LANGUEDOC

ROUSSILLON

CATALONIA

CORSICA (GEN.)

TUSCAN PRESIDIOS (SP.)

Lisbon

Madrid

TAGUS R.

SPAIN

Rome

BALEARIC IS. (SP.)

SARDINIA (SP.)

GUADALQUIVIR

MEDITERRANEAN

ALGARVE DE ALEM MAR

FEZ AND MOROCCO

ALGERIA

TUNISIA